People, Society, and Mass Communications

PEOPLE, SOCIETY, AND MASS COMMUNICATIONS

Lewis Anthony Dexter

David Manning White

EDITORS

THE FREE PRESS, NEW YORK

COLLIER-MACMILLAN LIMITED, LONDON

For

HERMAN N. COHN

and

ADAM MACKENZIE DE SOLA POOL

Preface and Acknowledgments

This book is written with three different kinds of readers in view:

FIRST: *Professionals* in the mass media and in such related fields as advertising and public relations. It will, we believe, be of interest and value to them in presenting in organized form findings of contemporary social science which bear on their activities and roles.

SECOND: *Scholars.* By bringing together studies and analyses from several different disciplines which show how the "social process" approach to communications may be used, this book, we feel, will be useful as a review and as a stimulus to research.

THIRD, and most important: *students, both graduate and undergraduate, and those studying independently.* As a text for students, this book is organized around the conception of mass communication as profoundly and intrinsically *social.* By this, we mean to say: Mass communications take place *between* persons who are members of specific social groups. What is said, who hears it, how it is interpreted by those who hear it, and how, if at all, its message is transmitted by those who hear it to others, can best be understood in terms of the group memberships and institutional and interpersonal expectations of those originating, exposed to, or receiving messages from the mass media.

To some extent, this book is an anthology; but we would like to point out that it differs from most anthologies in several significant respects:

first, we have prefaced the set of readings with an extended interpretation of mass communications and the mass media in terms of the social history of the industrial revolution and the nature of modern society generally.

second, we include a bibliographic analysis of current research on mass communications, which reviews many hundred titles, a review of the literature, related to the theme of the text, of a sort not often found in anthologies, or texts for that matter.

third, in order to show the opportunities in the field, and of particular meaning to graduate students and younger scholars, we have described research needs and opportunities in the area of mass communications, suggesting a number of specific subjects for research, and showed how they relate to the social process approach. We believe that this chapter can be of particular value to the teacher in helping him make clear—something difficult to do with most texts—that there is a great deal of exploration and investigation yet to be done, and that the uncertainties outweigh the certainties, as is the case in any active and vigorous discipline.

fourth: each selection is (a) *preceded* by an analysis of its relationship to the major orientation of the book and/or of some particular issues it raises, and (b) *followed* by questions which will help students in reviewing and testing their understanding of the reading and of the way it is related to the other readings.

We wish to express our thanks to the contributors to this volume for permission to allow their separate contributions to be published in this attempt at a larger view of mass communications. We are particularly grateful to many of these authors for help and assistance beyond the mere permission to republish their essays. Over and beyond this, the influence of one contributor appears again and again in this book. Our approach to mass communications has been stimulated very significantly by our colleague, Professor Raymond Bauer. To a large extent, this book is what it is because we know him and his work, although he in no way is responsible for any of its shortcomings. We are additionally indebted to Dr. Bauer for administrative assistance. We are especially indebted to those colleagues who wrote articles, published initially in this book, to fill lacunae in the existing literature. Among these we want to thank particularly and especially George McCall also for editorial assistance under pressure.

Friends and students have helped us to fulfill our joint work as editors. Professor White's seminars in journalism research at Boston University, over the past three years, and his seminar in communications theory at Syracuse University in the summer of 1962, served the important function of providing critical and constructive reactions to most of the essays. Many of the questions and exercises which follow the essays were prepared as classroom exercises by students in a 1962 seminar at Boston University. We found these questions so apt and representative of how students perceive the essays that we decided to use them in the book. Students who helped us in this respect were Shibani Basu, Frank Mazzaglia, Zandy Slosson, Sydna Altschuler, Weston Kemp, David Cohen, Arthur Brodeur, Stephen Lighthill, George D. Kreutz, and Edward Allaire.

We want to express our appreciation for the competent and cheerful assistance of Mrs. Shirley Nourse Garand and Miss Joan Laws in preparing the manuscript. Martin Jezer, Mrs. Olivia Coolidge Dworkin, Catherine W. White, and Max A. White also assisted us at various stages of our work on the book. Dr. Robert Sokol of Dartmouth College contributed substantially to the idea of the book in its formative stages.

Finally, a private note of gratitude to Stanley K. Bigman of the United States Department of Health, Education and Welfare, who in a sense was the "godfather" of this book, since he purposefully introduced the editors to each other.

Lewis Anthony Dexter
David Manning White

Belmont, Massachusetts
December 18, 1963

Contents

Preface and Acknowledgments vii

Part I. **Introduction,** LEWIS ANTHONY DEXTER 3

Part II. **Sociological Perspectives on Mass Communications**

Sociological Perspectives on the Study of Mass
Communication, HAROLD MENDELSOHN 29

Human Communication, FRANKLIN FEARING 37

On the Effects of Communication, W. PHILLIPS DAVISON . . 69

Functional Analysis and Mass Communication,
CHARLES R. WRIGHT 91

Communication Research and the Image of Society:
Convergence of Two Traditions, ELIHU KATZ . . . 110

Part III. **The Communicator and His Audience**

The Communicator and the Audience, RAYMOND A. BAUER . 125

Newsmen's Fantasies, Audiences, and Newswriting,
ITHIEL DE SOLA POOL AND IRWIN SHULMAN 141

The "Gatekeeper": A Case Study in the Selection of News,
DAVID MANNING WHITE 160

News Is What Newspapermen Make It, WALTER GIEBER . 173

Mass Communication and Sociocultural Integration,
WARREN BREED 183

Part IV. **Looking at the Media**

Why Dailies Die, BEN H. BAGDIKIAN 205

The Leadership Role of the Weekly Newspaper as Seen by
Community Leaders: A Sociological Perspective,
ALEX S. EDELSTEIN AND J. BLAINE SCHULZ 221

Listening to Radio, HAROLD MENDELSOHN 239

From Mass Media to Class Media, THEODORE PETERSON . 250

Teen-agers, Satire, and *Mad,* CHARLES WINICK 261

Reality-Orientation and the Pleasure Principle: A Study of
American Mass-Periodical Fiction (1890–1955),
MARTIN U. MARTEL AND GEORGE J. MCCALL 283

Part V. **Social Institutions Studied in Terms of
Communications Theory: Some Examples**

The World of Biggy Muldoon: Transformation of a Political
Hero, W. LLOYD WARNER 337

Clues for Advertising Strategists, DONALD F. COX . . . 359

Communications—Pressure, Influence, or Education?
LEWIS ANTHONY DEXTER 395

Part VI. **Mass Communication, Conflict, and the
Strategy of Persuasion**

Word-of-Mouth Communication in the Soviet Union,
RAYMOND A. BAUER AND DAVID B. GLEICHER 413

The Mass Media and Their Interpersonal Social Functions in
the Process of Modernization, ITHIEL DE SOLA POOL . . 429

Media Research and Psychological Warfare,
ROBERT C. SORENSEN 444

Part VII. **The Frontiers of Communications Research**

Operation *BASIC:* The Retrieval of Wasted Knowledge,
BERTRAM M. GROSS 457

On Content Analysis and Critical Research in Mass
Communication, GEORGE GERBNER 476

The State of Communication Research, BERNARD BERELSON 501

Mass-Communications Research: A View in Perspective,
DAVID MANNING WHITE 521

Mass Communication and the Social Sciences:
Some Neglected Areas, MARTEN BROUWER 547

Opportunities for Further Research in Mass Communications,
LEWIS ANTHONY DEXTER 568

APPENDIX: **A Critique of Bibliographic Matter in Mass
Communications,** DAVID MANNING WHITE . . . 583

Index 589

PART I

INTRODUCTION

Lewis Anthony Dexter

Introduction

I. THE BASIS OF MASS COMMUNICATIONS IN SOCIETY

HOW MODERN SOCIETY DIFFERS FROM OTHER SOCIETIES

There are two particularly significant respects in which our modern society differs from all previous societies. One of these, of course, is the *power* of industrial technology—large-scale mass production, automation, speed of transportation.

Equally important, and related to the first-mentioned, is the existence of a system of mass communications, through the newspaper press, TV, radio, the paperback book, and similar media. In this volume we are concerned with the *social aspects* of these communications; that is to say, how they are related to people's opportunities and activities, to their hopes and attitudes about the world around them, and to their ideas about themselves.

The first and most vital way in which these communications affect people may seem obvious but is often overlooked or discussed in meaningless platitudes. Before mass communications, most people lived their entire lives in relatively small groups *in face-to-face relationships;* [1] now they do not.

1. An often-quoted saying of the Greeks is that true democracy is only possible within the sound of one man's voice. The assumption underlying this statement was that communication and understanding are only possible within a small area. Throughout the nineteenth century, political philosophers, accordingly, celebrated the Greek city-state, the New England town meeting, and the rural Swiss canton as particularly democratic because of the face-to-face communication which took place between all voting citizens. But the telegraph, the telephone, the radio, the TV set, and the public-opinion poll now make it possible for leaders to speak directly to their audiences and to learn quickly how most of the world is responding to their statements. An American President can now learn within a few days how people in New Delhi feel about a proposal of his, whereas 150 years ago it might have taken George Washington weeks to learn how Maine fishermen reacted to one of his suggestions.

The point is not simply that by means of the mass communications a *particular* speech or advertisement is heard by thousands or millions of people at a given moment. It is rather that these millions of people are *constantly* exposed to mass communications. Their area of attention and concern is created to a considerable degree by mass communications. What sociologists call *"consensus"* [2]—the common set of values and attitudes in terms of which life is lived—is set by *and with* people far away as well as by neighbors; and some people far away become closer and more meaningful than most neighbors. So, words like "neighbor" and "stranger" lose the distinctness and precision of meaning which they once had.

It is clear that the whole process is due not only to the revolution in communications technology (the book, the newspaper, the radio, the TV set) but also to the revolution in the technology of transportation (the highway,[3] the bus, the airplane). Any careful study of how communications affect people must start out with two truisms—two points that "everybody knows" but few people think through. Because people travel quickly and easily they not only learn to listen, read, and communicate widely but they yearn to do so; *and* because people heed mass media they learn and desire to travel, either physically or in imagination.

Mass communications affect nearly everybody. And technological change affects nearly everybody. Half a century ago, over much of the world, the immigrant was still a rather special sort of person. He had broken his ties with the tradition in which he had been brought up, and he could not quickly establish ties with another tradition. But now most of us—even those who remain in the same town where our ancestors have lived for generations—are constantly breaking with traditions and

2. Wherever in this text the student comes across a term which is used in a technical sense, he may wish to consult standard works of reference in the disciplines to which we refer—such as the *Encyclopedia of the Social Sciences* or several of the better-known textbooks. However, the best discussion of the way in which "consensus" is affected by and related to agencies of social change is to be found in the writings of the great sociologist Charles Horton Cooley—for example, in his *Social Organization: A Study of the Larger Mind* (Scribner, New York, 1909) Part II, "Communications," pp. 61–106. There he develops the argument that consensus depends on standard patterns of communications.

An exceptionally valuable discussion of consensus (limited chiefly to political consensus) is also provided by V. O. Key, *Public Opinion and American Democracy* (Knopf, New York, 1961), pp. 27–53.

3. "Specifically," said the late Speaker Sam Rayburn, "muddy roads result in isolation which tends to keep people away from the world, instead of [making them] part of it." (Quoted in Valton J. Young, *Speaker's Agent*, Vantage, New York, 1956), p. 55. Rayburn justified his life-long battle for good roads on this basis.

ways of life which we learned. *Change has become a way of life. Mass communication and easy transportation mean a new kind of world.*

America and Great Britain underwent the communications-technological revolution somewhat earlier than the rest of the world; accordingly, it is relatively difficult for those whose knowledge of history is largely based on American and British records and recollection to envision the kind of society in which communication was based largely on face-to-face relationships. Unfortunately, the authors of this book have not found any clear description of a village community with special attention to communications in that community which makes evident the difference between social groups where communication is largely within a small, face-to-face group, and the modern world.[4]

SECONDARY COMMUNICATIONS IN THE PAST

Historical contrasts always tend to be oversimplified. There have been, to be sure, people in the past who were dependent on secondary communications and had *some* of the characteristics of modern men living in a world of mass communications. Such people were one or the other of the following:

(*A*) *City People.* From earliest recorded history we see the contrast between city people, living in a world of change and variety, and the country folk, the peasants, the people to whom kin, clan, and neighborhood determined most of life. Today, for the first time in history, most people, *wherever they may live,* are affected by urbanization. There has been a disappearance of the sense of stability and solidity which certainly in Western Europe (and probably in most of the world) arose from the fact that most people belonged to a folk society [5] and from the fact that even the most citified people had ties to the more stable country.

4. Historians and anthropologists have prepared scores of studies of great value on everyday life in premodern villages and societies. Many of these studies of course describe the difference between our world and the premodern face-to-face social grouping brilliantly and competently. But we know of no study that analyzes as its central theme the difference between the face-to-face communications "system" and the mass communications "system" in the lives of people.

Among numerous available relevant accounts, two may be suggested which are of particular pertinence to our point; (1) the account of Lincoln's boyhood in Chap. II of Albert J. Beveridge, *Abraham Lincoln,* Vol. I (Houghton, Boston, 1928), pp. 38–99, describing his personal development in a society based on face-to-face relationships, and (2) the contrast shown by Margaret Mead in *New Lives for Old: Cultural Transformation—Manus, 1928–1951* (Mentor, New York, 1961).

5. In 1933 the writer preached in a small town in Indiana which, a year before, had for the most part been considered far from the county seat; because

(B) *Special Groups.* Members of some special trading or professional or governing class—Viking rulers or raiders, Jewish traders, Lombard merchants, Catholic priests, scholars, knights—who because of the particular demands of their occupation travelled, and found their "reference" group rather in occupation than in neighbors. Because most history has been written by members of such groups, historical records heavily emphasize their interests and concerns. Nevertheless, history shows, too, that, until very recently such people were generally a small minority.

Three generations ago, indeed, in much of the world a man's clothing could identify the very village from which he came. There still are specialists who can judge quite accurately (within a few miles) where a man was raised and where he has lived by his pronunciation and accent. Since World War II, however, such local differences in how the voice is used have become much less noticeable because of the influence of radio and TV. Such overt changes are correlated with changes in attitudes, values, and attention. This does not necessarily mean that we are moving toward universal conformity or a homogenized world. But it means that variation between people is increasingly on an individual or occupational basis rather than on a geographical one. And it means, too, that the political disagreements which take place between relatively wealthy and industrialized peoples—such as those between Russians and Americans—take place within a common framework of assumptions about science, change, progress, and technology. (This framework is not yet common to the Vietnamese peasant or the Congolese tribesman, and does not in general affect countries which are underdeveloped and on a subsistence economy.) [6]

---

of muddy and almost impassible roads, it usually took 60 hours, I was told, to haul up the groceries in the fall for the winter. But with the building of modern roads by the state, the county seat was only 15 minutes away. Thus, while in 1930 the people of this small town were still isolated "country cousins," rural as distinguished from urban, by 1943 this had begun to change and by 1962 these former country folk had become completely urbanized and characterized by secondary group relations. Of course, the creation of roads more or less coincided with the development of rural electrification and radios, the growth of rural telephone service and the building of more schools. Thus the town of English, Indiana is probably in many respects more different today from what it was in 1933 than it was then from the community life that Lincoln knew as a boy!

All this is said to suggest how much the focus of attention has changed from the neighborhood and the kin group to a larger world in a few short years.

6. There is a considerable body of sociological literature on the difference between *folk* society, society in which face-to-face contacts dominate life, and *urban* society. One of the outstanding studies of a folk society (a folk society in the process of change, particularly valuable because it shows the difference between different parts of the country, because of geographical factors) is Robert Red-

This increasing cultural homogeneity appears to move ahead even despite conscious efforts to slow it down. Just as the Briton who, in 1940, regarded American slang as intolerably vulgar, now finds himself using it as a matter of course, so the Puerto Rican grandmother who in 1940 bitterly resisted the adoption of continental dating patterns by her daughter now regards them as perfectly natural in her granddaughter.

II. SECONDARY VERSUS PRIMARY COMMUNICATIONS

If there were no mass communications, the whole complex pattern of relationships in our modern world could not work as it does. An Australian sheepherder on the outback can buy and sell shares of American Telephone and Telegraph or of some much obscurer company several times a week, about as readily (allowing for some extra cable costs, etc.) as a speculator in a boardroom on Wall Street itself. Italian workers can invest some extra money in a Japanese mutual fund. What is remarkable here is not simply the sheer physical fact. It is that men all over the world should have developed the set of attitudes, values, and expectations that make possible the *coordination* of such scattered interests and perceptions.

This similarity of attitudes and values, *the development of (world-wide) extended consensus,* is perhaps the most significant correlate of the mass media. Modern society, as we know it, depends [7] upon consensus, but, oddly enough, that phenomenon has been little studied. The most

---

field's classic, *The Folk Culture of Yucatan* (U. of Chicago, 1941). The student is especially recommended to Chapter V, "The Villager's View of Life."

In early German sociological literature the distinction is drawn between neighborhood-oriented society and business or occupation-oriented society. But since 1945 sociologists the world over have devoted little attention to these distinctions and increasingly ignore the neighborhood-oriented folk society. To the present writer, who spent a year in Puerto Rico in 1945, and also the summer of 1961 and spring of 1963, the greatest difference was simply this—while in 1945 the educated, literate minority still regarded themselves as special and different because they were oriented toward the outside world, in 1961 it was no longer remarkable at all to be so oriented!

7. "Depends upon" is not to say "caused by"; we are avoiding entirely the tangled issue of causation and merely say there is a *transactional* relationship between modern society and mass communications. See, for the discussion of "transaction," in J. Dewey and A. Bentley, *The Knowing and the Known* (Beacon, Boston, 1949), and A. Bentley, *An Inquiry Into Inquiries* (Beacon, Boston, 1954). For causation, see L. Dexter, "Causal Imputation and Purposes of Investigation," *Philosophy of Science,* vol. 6, 1939, pp. 404–411.

perceptive comments on it were made by pre-1925 writers,[8] when the large-scale organization of society and mass media had not yet developed to its present extent.

BASIS OF MASS COMMUNICATIONS RESEARCH

One explanation for the neglect of the vastly important questions we have been discussing is that historically the study of mass media and mass communications has developed in large measure in response to *immediate, practical,* needs or *immediate* curiosity. Someone wanted to know *and was willing to pay to learn* what the effectiveness of a given radio program was on increasing sales of a particular product; or someone else was curious to find out why newspapers seemed to have relatively little influence upon elections, at least under the secret ballot. Such questions as these appear practical and manageable. It is more difficult, however, to determine what the effect of mass communications *in general* upon a society [9] is.

CIVILIZATION VS. PRIMITIVISM; SECONDARY COMMUNICATIONS MAKE A SIGNIFICANT DIFFERENCE!

Secondary communications make the difference, between what is sometimes called "civilization" and what is sometimes miscalled "savagery" or "barbarism" but is better called *folk society.* The "savage" or "primitive" man can be just as sophisticated, ingenious, astute, wise, and virtuous as the urbanized man,[10] but the primitive is of necessity confined to a limited tradition and focus of attention. Most of the social stimuli which he receives, both directly and indirectly, come from those with whom he is personally acquainted; he may even find it difficult to envisage distant individuals as persons *like himself.*

Many primitives might find it difficult to leave their neighborhoods and kinfolk and still keep a sense of *personal identity,* because that sense depends upon a relationship to neighbors and kinfolk and the traditions associated with them.

---

8. Cooley, *op. cit.;* also R. Park and E. Burgess, *Introduction to the Science of Sociology,* U. of Chicago, 1921.

9. William F. Ogburn has of course written very extensively about social change; most students will probably have access to the lucid discussion of the effects of radio and of other social inventions in his introductory text (with M. Nimkoff), *Sociology* (Houghton Boston, any edition).

10. See on this point, P. Radin, *Primitive Man As Philosopher* (2nd ed., Dover, N.Y., 1957).

The fact that in the European High Middle Ages, for instance, or in Aztec Mexico, there were significant and influential classes of the population which did maintain *secondary* communications, is one reason why we think of the Aztecs or the French in the thirteenth century as far removed from barbarism; but the fact that in these periods there were not our modern mass communications separates them sharply from the present.[11] For, nowadays, the ruler or the priest knows that his subjects or his parishioners are *themselves* oriented towards secondary contacts and communications—something which probably has rarely or never been true before. That is, the ruler or priest might have been oriented towards secondary communications in Aztec Mexico or medieval France, but his people were not.

THE EFFECTS OF MASS COMMUNICATIONS IN GENERAL

We know a great deal about the effect of specific mass communications. But we know very much less about what it means to move from a world without mass communications to a world with them. It is as though some animal species, moving from land to sea, could expound learnedly and at length about either the currents at sea or the sands on the land but could say very little about what being in the sea meant as compared with being on dry land. Similarly, on the most important aspect of this historic change we have to rely far more on intuition than we do in regard to less important matters.

A NOTE ON OUR DEFINITION AND ITS LIMITATIONS

We have distinguished between "secondary" communications and "face-to-face" communications; we have in effect defined "mass" communications as secondary communications multiplied by some technological device to affect many people and indicated that it is significant that people exposed to mass communications realize that many others are also exposed to them.

In specific actual cases, the difference between secondary and face-to-

---

11. For some years I have been concerned with trying to determine what the difference is between the high-grade retarded (morons) and the rest of the population. They can earn a living, get along satisfactorily, and survive as well (sometimes better) under difficult natural conditions. One way of defining the difference adequately might be to say that the high-grade retarded are not well equipped for handling secondary communications. See Lewis A. Dexter, *The Tyrannies of Schooling; An Inquiry into the Problem of Stupidity* (Basic, New York, 1964).

face communications is hard to work out. Obviously, a grandmother *phoning* a beloved and loving grandchild is engaged in a "primary" (what we have called a face-to-face) communication; is a salesman's visit to the same grandmother, to try to sell her an encyclopedia, a primary or secondary communication? One has to know a good deal about the nature and context of the situation to classify it.

It is easy to puzzle ourselves with borderline cases. Sir Walter Scott's *Tales of a Grandfather* and Lewis Carroll's *Alice in Wonderland* were originally addressed to specific children—Scott's beloved grandson in one case, Alice herself in the other, but they became examples of mass communication (or mass culture) when printed and read by millions. Horace Walpole's *Letters* (notably those to Sir Horace Mann) were, to be sure, personal letters, but they were written with an eye cocked on distant posterity and, therefore, were, in part at least, secondary type communications. Indeed, it is perfectly arguable that one lecture presented in a university on a given morning is personal—it was planned for and delivered to *specific students as persons*—while another is a mass communication, an oral textbook, given by a teacher who does not notice students as persons, but is addressing them as members of the category, "students."

III. SOME DISTINGUISHING CHARACTER-ISTICS OF MASS COMMUNICATIONS

We are interested in how communications modify or are intended to modify significant behavior. We distinguish mass communications from mass culture in terms of effects on significant behavior.[12] The distinction between the study of mass culture and of mass communications as we deal with them lies in effect upon audiences rather than in the material substantively viewed. One man's "art" communicates significant political ideas to another; what may significantly influence one man's behavior will merely entertain another. Indeed, since the time of Plato,[13] analysts and commentators have explored the way in which works of imagination and entertainment reflect and influence political behavior. For example, the Gettysburg Address was both a work of art and a political speech.

To cite another example, recently two sociologists attacked the belief that the coronation of Elizabeth II as Queen of Great Britain was chiefly

12. See David Manning White and Bernard Rosenberg (eds.), *Mass Culture: The Popular Arts in America* (Free Press, New York, 1957).
13. *The Republic*, Book III (Jowett trans.).

a "mere" celebration but instead opined that these public ceremonies *per se* are a highly significant series of communications of the gravest political importance.[14] And, for another example, much popular and semipopular literature has *portrayed* foreigners in essentially derogatory stereotypes;[15] this has been read by some as "amusing," a kind of intellectual bear-baiting. But, cumulatively, the creation of such stereotypes reflects and to some extent reinforces the mass picture of foreigners, a picture which could and probably does at crucial points affect foreign policy and grave issues of war and peace. The fact that Stalin and the U.S.S.R. were seen by many in terms of such a simple caricature made it more difficult to bring home to the American people the seriousness of the Russian challenge to their military and scientific superiority in the early 1950s.

Similarly, a good many people listen to great orators, preachers and teachers—not to be instructed but to be entertained, "thrilled," amused, or comforted. Although a Billy Sunday,[16] a Jonathan Edwards, or some other evangelist may change a few people's behavior significantly, many others listen to such a man for the excitement with which he provides them. Conversely, however, much material which is actually or ostensibly designed to entertain does, in fact, directly or indirectly, affect behavior significantly. This is most obviously true of political satires. In the eighteenth century, for example, the great French writers, Montesquieu and Voltaire, put their most telling points in fictional form, and their works are sometimes said to have led to the French Revolution; so too, much of Jonathan Swift's *Gulliver's Travels* was originally designed to communicate *political* ideas. In our own period George Orwell's books *1984* and *Animal Farm* are regarded as among the great analyses of Communist doctrine and practice, but they are interesting as stories in and of themselves, to some uninterested in the message Orwell is conveying.

In the United States there is considerable concern about *censoring*

14. E. Shils and M. Young, "The Meaning of the Coronation," *Sociological Review,* vol. I, 1953, pp. 63–81, in S. M. Lipset and N. Smelser (eds.), *Sociology* (Prentice-Hall, N.Y., 1961), pp. 220–233.

15. A nineteenth-century example is Charles Dickens' novel *Martin Chuzzlewit,* which was of course a work of popular culture; but its picture of Americans, and its influence on British attitudes toward Americans, could have made it significant on Anglo-American international relations (e.g., at the time of the Civil War).

16. An excellent account of a branch of the mass media which we have not treated (nor has any other text on mass communications) is given by Wm. G. McLoughlin in *Billy Sunday Was His Real Name,* University of Chicago Press, 1955, especially the ingenious interpretation of Sunday's "effectiveness" on pp. 193ff.

comic books for juveniles, TV programs portraying violence, and the like, *because of the belief that these programs do affect behavior significantly* [17]—that they teach or at least instruct youth already predisposed to delinquency in techniques of antisocial behavior. It is not our purpose here to provide a detailed discussion of this controversial subject; suffice it to conclude here that *some* people under *some* circumstances are affected in *some* ways by such programs. (We should add that there is no reason to suppose that *only* youngsters are influenced by them; *some* adults also are probably influenced.) So we would study such programs as mass communications in addition to considering them from the standpoint of mass culture.

MASS MEDIA GENERALLY REINFORCE PREVAILING ATTITUDES

Partly because people generally treat the mass media as entertainment —and entertainment ceases for most people to be entertaining if it challenges what they already believe—the mass media most of the time reinforce whatever people are already inclined to believe.[18] That is to say, *most* efforts at mass communications most significantly influence behavior by confirming the beliefs which people already hold. Yet, much education, much psychological warfare, much scholarship, much political propaganda is designed to communicate or present the unfamiliar, the incomprehensible, and the unconventional; in these cases the communicators are confronted by a very real problem.

17. The best-known (and one of the most extreme) statements of this point of view is found in F. Wertham, *Seduction of the Innocent* (Holt, New York, 1953). Wertham, not a specialist in the field of communications, commits many sociological errors. An excellent and balanced statement of the arguments for and against "Censorship of Movies and TV" is given by Helen B. Shaffer in *Editorial Research Reports,* 1961, vol. 1, pp. 265–282. At the time of writing the text I had not seen Leonard Berkowitz' studies of "Film Violence and Subsequent Aggressive Tendencies," *Public Opinion Quarterly,* vol. 27, 1963, pp. 217–229 (see also his report in *Journal of Abnormal and Social Psychology,* vol. 66, 1963, pp. 405–412); Berkowitz concludes "film violence may well increase the probability that someone in the audience will behave aggressively (soon afterwards)."

18. The major finding of one of the classic works in modern communications research, a book sadly neglected by educators, and teachers, D. Waples, B. Berelson, and F. Bradshaw, *What Reading Does to People* (U. of Chicago, Chicago, 1940), was that most of the time for most people reading reinforces whatever they already do or believe. But no one yet knows very much about the kind and degree of reading that reinforces "antisocial tendencies" and *for whom* it may do so. Moreover, varied reading may reinforce one tendency and suppress contradictory tendencies (a boy might wish to be a Wild West bandit and also a detective; could reading strengthen the one desire and reduce the other?).

CEREMONIAL AND RITUAL

It appears likely that a good deal of speech, art, and expression, whether designed to communicate significant ideas or merely to entertain, is taken as a ritual or ceremonial. Even in the classroom this happens; ideas go from the textbook to the notebook of the student, in some instances only as part of a ritual of getting a good grade; in other cases, the textbook actually instructs; in still other (rare) cases, it may entertain. What happens depends upon the individual characteristics of teacher and student, the subject matter, the text, and the social subsystem within which teacher and student are operating. So, too, an evangelical message which alters some men's lives may be merely a ritual to others.

COMMUNICATIONS DO AFFECT PEOPLE EVEN WHEN THEY REINFORCE

It is important to stress the fact that communications do affect people even when they reinforce because so many of the findings of the studies in the field refer to the ineffectiveness of efforts at mass communication to alter beliefs and affect behavior. It may be said instead that mass communications often effectively reinforce and stabilize beliefs which might change otherwise. A case in point is a person inclined to vote Democratic and who may actually do so in spite of a promotion to a middle management post where most of his associates are Republican, only if he is *reinforced* in his initial intention by listening to radio or TV speeches by Democratic leaders. The devout member of a particular church group, because his allegiance to church doctrine is so frequently reinforced by religious books and pamphlets, may hardly admit to himself strong tendencies to violate its patterns of behavior. A girl who mourns the loss of a lover in war may be persuaded by the mass media's emphasis on patriotism and national danger to continue stressing the heroic aspects of the sacrifice he made for his country and to suppress the inclination to express resentment or bitterness at the war effort.

The fact is, however, that at present our knowledge on such matters as these is not as satisfactory as we might wish.[19] It seems reasonable to suppose that mass communications do stabilize beliefs, and in stabilizing beliefs stabilize social actions; it is probable, indeed, that in a society in which scientific technology leads to rapid change and movement, mass

19. Throughout our comments, we call attention frequently to matters as to which knowledge is very inadequate in order to emphasize the *needs* which are also *opportunities* for further study within the field of mass communications. See pages 568–579.

communications *in part* assume the functions of "tradition" in a slower-moving world. But no one yet knows how to analyze the "dynamics of social stability." [20]

Exceptions to the generalization that communications from the mass media tend to reinforce are obviously significant for understanding social change and development. It is worthwhile to consider cases where efforts at mass communication may lead to visible change.

Examples occur in every presidential election. There are people who are pushed in both directions, who are under what is sometimes called "cross-pressure," whose opinions are undecided or ambivalent and who, therefore, are particularly susceptible to influence from the mass media or other sources. For example, in 1940 some businessmen and capitalists were under cross-pressure when Franklin D. Roosevelt favored aiding the allies, because of their international business interests or because of their identification with and feeling for France, England, and Canada, even though as businessmen they opposed the New Deal. Similarly, some of the prairie farmers of German pacifist origin who were strongly anti-Roosevelt in 1944 because of the war, were by 1948 quite strongly attracted by the Democratic farm program and hostile towards the farm program endorsed (or believed to be endorsed) by the Republicans and Thomas E. Dewey; indeed, Truman's unexpected victory in 1948 is in large measure attributable to his capture of such farm support. Nevertheless, Truman and the Democrats were still to some extent identified as the party which conducted the war and in 1952, with the farm issue still vital, but with another war again being conducted during a Democratic administration—the Korean War—the cross-pressures upon these German farmers were even greater. The issue was further complicated for them by the fact that the Republican nominee was the supreme Allied Commander for Western Europe in World War II, Dwight D. Eisenhower. Accordingly one might expect that Midwest German pacifist farmers might be susceptible to influence from the mass media.

It is sometimes hard to distinguish whether or not people are under cross-pressure. Out of vanity and a belief that independence of thought is admirable a good many people will go through the motions of looking at several sides of an issue, with all the fine openmindedness of the man who said "in moments controversial, my position is quite fine. . . . I always see both viewpoints, the one that's wrong—and mine!" Others,

20. The phrase "dynamics of social stability" is based upon a parallel with the physical world. There we have learned that a state of equilibrium often is created not because everything is actually still, but because at a subvisible level the *net* effect of motions (e.g., of atoms) in different directions is to leave things at rest on the visible level.

out of "loyalty" and a desire to appear confident, who are actually under considerable cross-pressure, will conceal their hesitations and doubts.

CAN WE SEPARATE MASS COMMUNICATIONS FROM OTHER COMMUNICATIONS?

Katz (see pp. 112–120) and others suggest that the effect of mass communications in the U.S. occurs in two (or more) steps rather than directly. That is to say if an important government official endorses civil defense or if a particular movie star introduces a new hairdo, most people will not immediately declare themselves for or against civil defense or adopt the new hairdo, but they will wait until some one of prestige to or in their own group approves or adopts it. Probably the Katz hypothesis of the two-step flow of communication could be still further generalized, as follows: In reality most innovations and most efforts to influence behavior are adopted only after they have been *interpreted* and socially validated for particular groups and classes. In most cases, such as those described by Katz, interpretation and validation take place from within an individual's own immediate group. But actually we suggest as an elaboration on the Katz hypothesis that validation and interpretation do also take place from a respected national personage outside the group itself and by communication through the mass media from such an individual.

Mass communications may play a significant role in affecting (and sometimes even substituting for) very *personal* aspects of human behavior: sociability, child rearing, and love making. People watch TV programs, go to the movies, and read books as a *form* of sociability; people also learn through mass media how to make and treat friends, or how to make love, or how to raise children.

Indeed, for centuries there has been a wide market for books and magazines giving advice on child rearing, on etiquette and social behavior,[21] on how to get married, and on how to make oneself attractive to the opposite sex. It is likely that the media do have influence upon these types of behavior. It is also likely that material planned only to entertain influences behavior in many such areas of personal life. The saying "I care not who makes my country's laws so long as I can make its songs," has been often repeated, usually with the implication that in the long run songs have more influence on behavior than laws; for instance, almost unquestionably the cult of romantic love (a notion not known in most previous cultures) was spread by novels and poems.[22]

21. See, for instance, Arthur M. Schlesinger, Sr., *Learning How to Behave: A Historical Study of American Etiquette Books* (Macmillan, New York, 1946).

22. See R. Linton, *The Study of Man* (Appleton, New York, 1936), pp. 175–176.

IV. THE DIFFERENCES BETWEEN MASS COMMUNICATION AND SPECIALIZED COMMUNICATIONS

Another distinguishing feature of "mass communications" can best be stated in negative terms: mass communications are *not* designed for the expert, the specialist, the technologist *as such*. The important distinction is not whether material happens to be disseminated through mass media or not but whether it is directed to a specialized or mass (lay) audience; the garden page, for instance, of a good many newspapers, is in fact designed for people who have some expert knowledge of gardening and consequently will not be considered as a "mass communication." Some radio programs—for example, those which report vegetable prices —clearly are meant for specialists or experts, while other programs clearly are not. A textbook in high school civics or social studies may have some of the characteristics of mass communication; the present text probably lacks them. The greater part of some specialized medical journal is obviously designed for experts, but some of its editorials, especially those bearing on general issues of policy or ethics (and some of its advertisements too), may have the characteristics of what we call "mass communications."

Now this distinction is extremely important even though it cannot always be applied as rigorously as we would like, partly because there are always "borderline cases," and partly because it enables us to distinguish between (1) the approach toward communication which is employed in most more or less specialized education and (2) the approach towards communication most usefully applied to the mass media. Both approaches are valid; taken abstractly, out of context, neither is superior to the other; but it is misleading and intellectually dangerous to apply the former to situations where the latter is more pertinent. And because the former is such an important element in the whole process of schooling, it is natural to try to use it on all communications—particularly, perhaps, because this gives the intellectual a feeling of superiority over the masses!

In our society, education and specialized training consist in large part of conveying supposedly unambiguous statements and instructions which are to be interpreted and carried out literally the way in which they are intended. This is exemplified by a basic characteristic of "the industrial revolution," the generalization of the practice of interchangeable parts. In preindustrial society, most workmen developed an individual way of making parts and equipment and frequently were unwilling to repeat the same design a second time. But in the modern world, where mass production rather than individualized craftsmanship prevails, screws can be made with tolerances of one ten-thousandth of an inch, through the cooperation of an extensive team of technicians each precisely carrying out his part in a complex plan. For the same reason, men can plan to rendezvous vehicles in outer space.

Such enterprises are possible only if people can follow instructions with precision, which means of course that *they must interpret statements exactly in the way they are intended.*

In much the same way, modern society is also dependent upon a whole series of legal agreements and understandings which mean exactly the same thing to people who have never seen each other and have never discussed them in detail; the functioning of commodity and stock market exchanges is possible in consequence.

The scientific and legal training which underlies development of the sort just mentioned depends upon the ability to interpret statements just as they are intended by those who utter them.

Toward such ends, our educational system emphasizes the ability to interpret communications *accurately and exactly.* Becoming an expert in mathematics, science, history, sociology, law, automobile repairing, nursing, pharmacology, farming, athletic coaching, or many other activities requires the *precise* interpretation of what others have said or written— for example, the ability to apply and to adapt manuals of instructions. Anything which gets in the way of a precise understanding of what experts and specialists say is regarded as "interference" or "error"; it "distorts" the valid interpretation.

When thinking about the kind of communications which *typically* are transmitted through the mass media, many students and scholars tend to have the same expectations—namely, that a message has one "true" meaning and the failure to capture this meaning is a "distortion" or a "misconception."

But, as a matter of fact, the majority of listeners or viewers of mass communications do not strive for any such precision. Flowerman's [23] report that "good will" propaganda when heard by "prejudiced" people is interpreted to confirm what they already believe probably is representative of many responses to mass communications; they are interpreted as being compatible with preexistent viewpoints and fitted into what William James called "the apperceptive mass" of the reader or hearer. It is easy enough for Americans who believe that South African views about race relations are wrong to see how a strong supporter of the South African

23. See, for instance, S. Flowerman, "Mass Propaganda in the War Against Bigotry," *Journal of Abnormal and Social Psychology,* vol. 42, 1900, pp. 429–39, esp. pp. 435–37.

apartheid policy may "distort" what distinguished liberals, such as Alan Paton or Archbishop Blank, say on race relations; it is easy enough, too, for most Americans to see how "distorted" is the notion held by Leninist-Marxists that when we Americans advocate "capitalism" we are arguing for exploitation and imperialism. But, to put the shoe on the other foot, few Americans have enough knowledge of the precise ramifications of Leninist-Marxist doctrine to interpret correctly a statement made by a distinguished Russian on international relations—that is, to interpret it as the Russian intended it.

This is to say that to establish the intentions of a source demands a considerable knowledge of the circumstances under which the message is uttered, the purpose the speaker has in view, the assumptions about human behavior and the audience which he presupposes. But such knowledge and such precision can *not* be expected in or as a result of mass-media communications.

Accordingly, the effect of a statement or report may be quite different from what was intended. Upton Sinclair's intention in writing his famous novel *The Jungle* was definitely propagandistic; he wanted to indict the evils, as they appeared to him, of big-business control of manufacturing and to help spread countervailing socialist ideas. The novel, which dealt with the meat-packing industry, contained vivid and graphic descriptions stressing the filthiness of the meat-packing process at that time. There is a reference to a workman who fell into a vat and was turned into lard (lard is a by-product of meat-packing) through extreme carelessness. The book was an enormous success, one of the most talked-about books in American history; but insofar as anybody knows it had no particular effect in convincing people of the merits of socialism or the inequities of capitalism as the author intended. But it had, according to most historians, tremendous influence in encouraging people to support pure food and drug acts! People wanted to be sure the meat they ate was clean; they presumably wanted to be certain that the lard they used did not contain dissolved human beings.

Now, Sinclair in this instance communicated something which he had not intended to communicate (or at the very least which he had not intended to emphasize), and he failed to communicate the points that were central to him. What then is the "true meaning" of *The Jungle?*— that which the public found in it, or that which the author chiefly intended?

V. EXPECTATIONS, ROLES, AND MASS COMMUNICATIONS

The nature and significance of communications are determined in large part by expectations of communicator and of audience which tend to be reciprocally interrelated.

Writers, broadcasters, and political speakers all select what they are going to say and *decide* how they are going to say it in terms of their beliefs about the audience. One attitude common enough among candidates for office is expressed in the phrase "I've got to find myself an issue," meaning an issue that will appeal to the public. Similarly, college newspaper editors sometimes have been known to search for an issue. And likewise there is a tendency for some general newspapers to stress controversy, excitement, and conflict on the basis of the probably well-founded belief that the sensational does attract readers and sell newspapers. On the other hand, *some holders of public roles, such as those of ceremonial national leaders, or reassuring preachers* find that *their* conception of their audiences demands soothing statements stressing unity of purpose, minimizing controversial and conflicting elements in life and society.

ROLE AND EXPECTATION

But frequently those who stress harmony and those who report or stimulate controversy are addressing themselves to the same or at any rate to overlapping audiences. "Give 'em hell Harry" Truman got some of the same support given to much blander and less controversial Dwight David Eisenhower. This apparent contradiction can best be explained by the fact that people came to expect one kind of action and statement from Truman and another from Eisenhower. In other words, the type of *role* expected from Truman was different from that expected from Eisenhower. We are using *role* here in almost the literal sense in which the word describes the part an actor plays. An old-established buffoon is type-cast. He cannot suddenly play a tragic part; people will interpret it as humorous. And, vice versa—a romantic hero is type-cast, too.[24]

So it is that once a public figure has been identified with a given type of role, what he says will be interpreted in terms of that role. So too, a given mass medium may be identified with and its statements interpreted

24. A particularly succinct and clear discussion of type-casting is to be found in Dorothy Sayers, *Have His Carcase* (London, Gollancz, 1932), p. 309.

in terms of the role or image in which it has been cast. What Mendelsohn has to say (pp. 239–249) about the personalization of radio stations *by listeners* bears directly on this point.

SELECTION OF MATERIAL BY AUDIENCE MEMBERS IN TERMS OF THEIR PREFERENCES AND ROLES

The reverse of what has so far been said in this chapter is equally true. Readers, listeners, and viewers select what to read, listen to, and watch, in terms of their own preconceptions and points of view. Books, commentators, and programs generally find their audience among those who agree with their particular outlook, or at least by those who think better of themselves for having read them, listened to them, or watched them. Thus insofar as writers and speakers are aware of this fact, they tend—where their objective is attention, sales, and popularity—to shape what they say in terms of the audience to which they are writing. Several "sophisticated" authors—for instance, Nathaniel Hawthorne and William Dean Howells—have written campaign biographies of presidential candidates, but these biographies are, in fact, very much like other campaign biographies and not particularly like the novels that made authors like Hawthorne and Howells famous. The audience, or rather the notion of the audience which the writers (publishers and campaign advisors) had shaped the product far more than the writer's own "individuality."

Frequently where readers and listeners are exposed to a point of view or a fact which would, objectively, tend to cast doubt upon what they believe they overlook or disregard or *distort the report in order to confirm their pre-existent beliefs.*[25] They literally hear or read what they expect to hear or read, not what is said.

Frequently the fact that the writers know that the audience expects something different from what they wish to say—or that different groups within the audience have different expectations—leads to the use of vague, equivocal, and glittering generalities. Such generalities may have a very real social use; they permit different people to interpret the same message differently,[25] and thus conflict is avoided through misunderstandings.

25. See G. Myrdal, *American Dilemma* (Harper, New York, 1944), p. 462 on this point.

26. In other words, communications made on the mass media which are or strive to be explicit and are addressed to a genuinely mass audience of nonspecialists are likely to be "nonfunctional"; and in this sense the efforts of people of good will to avoid "glittering generalities" are (if we are right) sociologically ill-founded and inept.

ROLE, INTEREST, GROUP MEMBERSHIP, AND UNDERSTANDING

The fact is that people read, interpret and remember messages differentially in terms of their particular social role and function. Bauer and Pool have strongly suggested that the American businessman *abroad* actually tends to adopt a "more representative" middle-of-the-road position on American economic policy then he does at home, because when abroad he regards himself as a kind of unofficial ambassador.[27] There is every reason to suppose that a boy from a small South Carolina town in 1956 would have been less reluctant to read pro-integration material when North at college or in an integrated armed forces unit than when at home; and further, that he was more likely to *understand* the prointegration arguments as intended when away from home. For when at home he may focus on his role as a member of the white majority hostile to the Negro minority group; while when in the other circumstances, the demands of this role are not quite as immediate, and are to some extent offset by the desire to retain the respect of teachers or to recognize the realities of armed service integration and to feel comfortable with them.

In other words, the reader, listener, or viewer reads, interprets, and understands in terms of the particular role on which he is concentrating, in the social situation in which he is participating. For example, in 1941–43 there were many circles in the United States where negative statements of fact about the actions of Stalinist Russia were entirely discredited and disbelieved, because the U.S.S.R. was an ally, an ally was believed to be a friend, and people did not like discrediting friends; disbelief of the facts about the Katyn Forest Massacres (a massacre by Stalinists of Poles) is a case in point. A few years later, almost the reverse situation had occurred; any positive statement of fact about the U.S.S.R., any suggestion that the Russians were outstripping the United States in such matters as information retrieval (pp. 457–475) or in the use of women in science and medicine would have been regarded in many quarters in 1953 as downright unpatriotic, and so *many* citizens, Congressmen, and administrators did not believe such statements.

In most instances there was no actual coercion involved, either in 1942 or 1953, in the United States as to how "facts" were perceived and reported. No doubt some people deliberately protected themselves

27. Raymond Bauer, Ithiel de Sola Pool, and Suzanne Keller, "The Influence of Foreign Travel on Political Attitudes of American Businessmen," *Public Opinion Quarterly,* Spring 1956. See also R. Bauer, I. Pool, and L. Dexter, *American Business and Public Policy* (Atherton, New York, 1963), pp. 166ff.

from the risk of disapproval, ostracism, or loss of employment in both periods by refusing to think "dangerous thoughts," but the majority of Americans had enough leeway to notice and comment on the then heeded facts if they had chosen to do so. However, in both 1942 and 1953 it made many people feel uncomfortable—out on a limb, so to speak—to diverge far from widely held beliefs. Accordingly, most of those who heard about the Katyn Forest Massacre overlooked, minimized, forgot, or disbelieved the report; and so most Americans who were apprized of Russian advances in rocketry and nuclear energy in the early 1950s did not believe what they saw and heard.

Again in the early 1950s there were many Americans *in some groups* who believed and noticed everything that tended to support the absurd argument that the U.S. government was then riddled with traitors; but, on the other hand, there were many Americans in other groups, mostly "liberal intellectuals," who consistently denied the clear evidence that some prominent Americans, whom they had admired, had worked with Stalinists. In both groups, most would not listen, heed, or believe reports which might lead them to question these presuppositions, because they would not feel identified with their own groups, they would not feel like themselves, if they believed such unpleasantly unfashionable things.

VI. MASS MEDIA AND POLICY

MASS MEDIA MAKE POLICY PARTLY BECAUSE OF THE ROLES AND ROLE
CONCEPTIONS OF THE COMMUNICATORS—WRITERS AND EXECUTIVES

We have been speaking of the way in which listeners and readers select, interpret, and hear because of their own particular roles and social affiliations. The converse is also true. Despite the tendency of newspapermen, for example, to insist that they are dealing only in facts, and that the facts write the headlines, in reality individual newspapermen select and emphasize news items in terms of their conceptions of their own roles. Breed (pp. 183–200) and Pool and Shulman (pp. 141–159), and particularly White and Gieber on the "gatekeeper" role (pp. 160–182) make this abundantly clear.

No communicator can avoid selecting what to emphasize and what to minimize, and such selection is always made, in part, in terms of the publisher's, editor's, writer's view as to what is important, desirable, and fair. In part it is also made in terms of the tradition of the particular newspaper or station or medium; and in part in terms of the conception of truth value which Pool discusses in his essay on modernization (pp. 429–443).

Views about what is desirable, fair, and important, are, as Breed makes clear, related to the experience and background of the men who hold these views. If publishers are active in the Chamber of Commerce, if writers associate a good deal with "liberal intellectuals" (as some Washington correspondents, to our knowledge, do), if an editor is actively involved in local politics, such matters all play a.part in determining what is regarded as fair, and significant in news coverage.

IS PLAYING DOWN THE NEWS NECESSARILY "BAD"?

According to an admirable unpublished study by Stanley Bigman, confirmed by an analysis of relevant interviews by Stewart E. Perry [28] of the University of California, the major newspapers of a big city at a time of threatened riots over school desegregation well illustrated the points made in the foregoing paragraph. Many newspapers would have taken the attitude, "Here is a big, sensational story." Others would have said: "These are facts about which people are curious; our job is to publish the facts." Others might have regarded the events as occasion for affirmatively pushing a particular viewpoint for or against desegregation or about school administration.

The leaders of the press in the city in question clearly took the stand: "We are protectors of the public welfare—therefore we should 'play down' these stories." Although many high school students (and others) threatened to riot at the time of desegregation, the newspapers deliberately *failed* to report much of what was happening (to the reported great annoyance of many of the would-be rioters who felt they were being treated unfairly). The newspapers felt that giving normal news emphasis to these riots would stimulate the rioters, attract attention to them, and lead to more serious trouble.

Now, the decision of the press in this city to underplay the news of the riots out of a sense of "responsibility" was perhaps partly (1) because members of the press there come in contact with many foreigners of importance and feel themselves in a sense ambassadors to the world as well as just newsmen and (2) perhaps more because they are aware that such riots on a large scale would create great difficulty for community organizations and causes which they support. We may say that the playing down of the Katyn Forest Massacres and of many other unsavory aspects of Stalinism made the disillusionment of 1946–48 much more severe than it need have been in this country; we may say that there was a responsi-

28. Stewart E. Perry, "The Conflict for the News Editor in Desegregation Disturbances," *Psychiatry,* 26 (1963) pp. 352–367.

bility to alert the country to Russian scientific progress in the early 1950s; but can we say that the decision in the case in point was wrong?

The example just given suggests the way in which communicators' notions about their role and responsibilities determines what they notice, report, and emphasize. It also leads up to a question, not stressed in this book, but of great importance. What are the ethical responsibilities of communicators? The tradition of the U.S. press has been that everything significant ought to be made known to all citizens; recently, the U.S. Supreme Court (particularly Justice Black) has tended to say that freedom of expression and communication is an absolute value. But if, what is communicated and emphasized depends in fact upon the particular values of particular communicators, this tends to say: "People who happen to be in charge of newspapers or radio stations should be free to report whatever they regard as important." The question then becomes: Are their emphases, values, interpretations always those upon which public attention should be concentrated? It happens that we think the press of the city in question was right, because we think avoiding desegregation riots was more important than full reporting of the news, and we think that full reporting of the news might have provoked more serious desegregation riots; but we are reasonably certain many newspapermen of equal prominence in other cities would have done the reverse and we think they would have been wrong. In other words, the "right to know" and the right to communicate are very valuable, but, in our judgment, must be weighed against other values in specific situations to see which value ought to prevail.

We cannot, in concrete situations, separate the ethical from the social aspect of the problem. The judgment that full reporting of the news might have provoked further rioting is a sociological judgment. On the basis of that sociological judgment we reach the ethical judgment that it was wise to play down the news; but if we had a different sociological judgment, we would have not been concerned about the ethical issue because it would not have been relevant. In any question involving "the right to know" or "freedom of the press" ethical judgments and sociological judgments are likely to be interrelated in similar fashion.

QUESTIONS

1.   List all the subjects you recollect discussing during the last week. Indicate the part mass communications played in what you said about each subject.

2. Take that topic which seems to have the least element of mass communications in it which you discussed and spend twenty minutes trying to ascertain mass-communications aspects. If you cannot do so, submit it to your classmates.

3. It is often said that the agencies of mass communications nowadays make international democracy possible. List other requirements for international democracy without which such agencies could not function.

4. Do Republicans and Democrats—Communists and anti-Communists—share the same consensus? (Clue: The answer should be "Yes and No . . .")

5. "Some American may be far closer to some Indian in Calcutta or Russian in Vladivostok than to his next-door neighbor." How is this possible? In what sense is it likely to be true? False?

6. "The printing press is the single most important invention in the history of human thought. . . ." Criticize. Defend.

7. How would you try to investigate the truth of the statement: "Agencies of mass communications make international racial hostility more intense. . . ."?

PART II

SOCIOLOGICAL PERSPECTIVES ON MASS COMMUNICATIONS

Harold Mendelsohn

Sociological Perspectives on the Study of Mass Communication

DR. MENDELSOHN's major point may be restated as follows: Sociologists have looked at and interpreted mass communications in several different ways. But on the whole, they have until recently failed to interpret the influence of mass communications as taking place in terms of relationships between people occupying social roles and statuses. That is, Mendelsohn makes the point that in general sociologists have thought of the mass media as having a direct impact upon the hearer or listener, much as a baseball bat or billiard cue have when they hit something. Accordingly, most sociological interpretations and reports about the mass media have been unduly simple.

W. I. Thomas and G. H. Mead introduced, Mendelsohn points out, some modification of these simpler notions. Thomas stressed the idea that any social experience affects a given individual in terms of the latter's preexisting tendency to define situations in a given way. For example, to offer your left hand to some one in the United States is a minor deviation from custom, but in some Eastern countries it is a deadly insult. Mead helped to develop the awareness that people behave and react as they do in terms of the "generalized other," in terms, that is, of their image of what other people approve, or disapprove, like, or dislike, etc.

Following up the Mead-Thomas notion, a modern generation of sociologists is coming to see that communications operate within a social framework of "definitions of situations," conceptions of "generalized others," statuses, roles and traditions. Accordingly, they have started to study mass communications in terms of the complex social web within which any given instance of mass communications takes place. So, for the first time, we are ready to see mass communications as a societal phenomenon, rather than as a push or pull on an isolated individual. We no longer assume, therefore, that specific mass communications are necessarily influential or powerful, and we are beginning to realize that whereas interpersonal communications are basic to any kind of society, mass communications may range from very minor to very major in importance, depending on the basic set of social values and attitudes and habits of interpersonal communications in the society.

The limitations and oversimplifications which we find in sociological thought about mass communications have been even more common in popular and semipopular discussion of the same topic. Writers on advertising, publicity, political campaigns, propaganda, and similar topics are constantly attributing vastly exaggerated possibilities or powers to the fields they describe. We find credit given to mass communicators for changing the course of history and we find attacks on mass communicators for failing to use their "tremendous influence" as the critic would like, but very little effort to determine whether, taking into consideration the whole set of social circumstances, mass communications could be at most any more effective than the flea who sat on the elephant's back and chanted, "how powerful am I!" We are not saying mass communications are never important or significant or influential; we are saying "it is well to be cautious and to evaluate the whole social situation before attributing too much influence to one factor (mass communications) in a total social complex." Nowadays, a great many people do overemphasize this one factor because mass communications are more visible (easier to watch and study) than for instance, interpersonal communications or collective self-images.   L. A. D.

DR. MENDELSOHN is currently Professor in and Director of the Research Department of Radio-Television-Film, School of Communication Arts, University of Denver. Previously he did research for the Psychological Corp., and for an advertising agency in the field of Marketing Communications and Social Research. In 1951–52 he served as Senior Survey Analyst for the International Broadcasting Service of the U.S. State Department. He has also been Study Director for the Department of Scientific Research and Program Evaluation of the American Jewish Committee. Dr. Mendelsohn received his Ph.D. from the New School of Social Research in 1956.

PERSPECTIVE I

Society cannot exist without communication; communication cannot occur outside a social system.

Cooley (whose views on consensus Dexter discusses in the preceding essay) epitomized the thinking expressed in the first statement, while G. H. Mead reflected the latter most succinctly when he wrote:

The process of communication cannot be set up as something that exists by itself, or as a presupposition of the social process. On the contrary, the social process is presupposed in order to render communication possible.[1]

The orientation inherent in the Cooley point of view was a reflection of American sociological concern about the acculturation of different immigrant groups in the United States. Education *and communication* were regarded as being charged with the task of merging these groups into one democratic social organization of commonly shared ideals and values. Although early sociologists initially put great emphasis on the role of personal communications in this "binding together" process, their successors came to look forward eagerly to innovations in mass communications such as radio and motion pictures as means of facilitating the acculturation process. Some of us look back now in amusement at the utopian prospects for a better world that were naively foreseen as radio's mission by the sociologists and social philosophers of the 1920s.

The mass media's actual or imagined acculturating function influenced the way we perceive them even today, as exemplified by the current excitement about the prospects for binding together the peoples of the world through space-borne telecommunications satellites.

The stress that has been placed on the *cohesive* power of communications by sociologists has served to center both scholarly and public attention on the "social responsibilities" of the mass media. As a consequence, sociologists and other social scientists have engaged in critiques and polemics about the "proper" role of mass communications in society for the past forty years or so.

Our Social Heritage in 1921,[2] for instance, objected to the mass media's activities:

An accurate idea of the nation is essential if we are to have any reliable stimulus to large-scale cooperative emotion and cooperative action. The average citizen, however, has no systematic method for building up his idea of the nation. It is the unconscious and carelessly acquired product of his daily experiences. Much of it is due to conscious propaganda by the vested interests, for though the average citizen may be aimless, careless, and thoughtless, "the controllers of newspapers, especially of the sinister American or British journals whose writers are apparently encouraged to 'color the new' as well as their comments on the news, in accordance with the will of a multimillionaire proprietor, know pretty exactly what they are doing."

1. G. H. Mead, *Mind, Self and Society* (U. of Chicago, 1934), p. 260.
2. Quoted in H. E. Barnes, *An Introduction to the History of Sociology* (U. of Chicago, 1948), p. 711.

Along this line it should be borne in mind that the negative value-laden sociological concept of the *persuasible* mass society was popularized by theorists such as Simmel, Ortega y Gasset, and Le Bon. It was Le Bon who, drawing on Tarde's theories of imitation, among others, postulated in highly emotional terms the notion that through the control of the means of communication alone unscrupulous leaders could turn a nation into an unruly vicious mob rendered simultaneously incapable of rational behavior and capable of engaging in a wide range of odious excesses. This notion is still prevalent among us. Recent experiences with totalitarian control of the mass media have reinforced this notion, so that, for instance, pseudo-scientific writing on so-called "hidden persuasion" and the power of advertising have been sold to hundreds of thousands of readers in recent years.

Essentially two lines of perspective have emerged on the basic reciprocal relationship of society and communications. One focuses on the socially cohesive attributes of mass communications, while the other is concerned with their socially disintegrative potential. Currently, these conflicting points of view are often held simultaneously by the same person or agency with no awareness of the contradiction between them. Regard, if you will, one contemporary manifestation of this contradiction: the very same agency of the United States Government—the U.S. Department of Health, Education, and Welfare—is lending massive moral and financial support to fostering television as a particularly powerful instrument for educating the young, while at the same time it is giving support to efforts that will explore the influence of television upon juvenile delinquency.

PERSPECTIVE II

Mass communications affect the values and attitudes of those who use them and, in turn, the values and attitudes of these users influence mass communications.

Typical of one common attitude here is Simmel's observation decrying the negative influences of the mass upon the communicator: [3]

The difference between the individual and collective levels accounts for the fact that the necessity to oblige the masses, even habitually to expose oneself to them easily, corrupts the character. It pulls the individual away from his individuality and down to a level with all and sundry. To consider it a questionable virtue of the journalist, the actor, and the demagogue to "seek the favor of the masses" would not be altogether justified if these masses consisted

3. G. Simmel, "The Field of Sociology," K. Wolff (ed.), in *The Sociology of George Simmel* (Free Press, New York, 1950), p. 33.

of the sum of the total personal existences of their members. For there is no reason whatever to despise them. But actually, the mass is no such sum. It is a new phenomenon made up, not of the total individualities of its members, but only of those fragments of each of them in which he coincides with all others. These fragments, therefore, can be nothing but the lowest and most primitive. It is this mass, and the level that must always remain accessible to each of its members, that these intellectually and morally endangered persons serve—and not each of its members in its entirety.

American sociologists such as Cooley, G. H. Mead, and W. I. Thomas, however, rejected the European emphasis typified by Simmel's remark just quoted on what was considered the "lower" mass influences on social behavior and incorporated psychological insights into their own perspectives on the social roles of attitudes and values.

Some of them, in the spirit of democratic egalitarianism, stressed the two-way flow of communications *between* the people and their leaders in the reciprocal exchange of ideas, values, and beliefs. From such exchanges, it was declared, consensus regarding the common welfare emerges. Consequently, the effects of communications in either implementing or hindering the formulation of "socially responsible" public opinion became a primary focus of study in mass communications in this country.

In order to interpret the complex relationships between attitudes and social structure, W. I. Thomas developed an idea of considerable importance for the study of mass communication—the social "definition of the situation." [4] It was Thomas who taught us to view the interplay between the variables of personality, culture, and social structure as the real stuff of communications. Merton's *Mass Persuasion* [5] is an outstanding example of the modern application of this frame of reference to a particular problem in mass communication.

PERSPECTIVE III

Since mass communication is structured by and functions in relation to a social nexus, it must be viewed as only one of many factors bearing on individual and social behavior.

The "new look" in mass communications, as put forth by such contemporaries as Joseph T. Klapper, the Bauers of Harvard, and the Rileys of Rutgers, focuses on the *mediating* roles of other psychological and

4. W. I. Thomas and F. Znaniecki, *The Polish Peasant in Europe and America* (U. of Chicago, 1918–21).

5. Harper, New York, 1946.

sociological factors in influencing the impacts that the mass media can produce on individuals and groups.[6]

THE EFFECTS OF MASS COMMUNICATION

This new look emerges directly out of Thomas' conceptual framework as illustrated by this quotation from Klapper: [7]

The new orientation (to the study of the media's effects) . . . is in essence a shift away from the tendency to regard mass communication as a necessary and sufficient cause of audience effects, toward a view of the media as influences working *amid other influences* in a total situation. The old quest of specific effects stemming from the communications has given way to the observation of existing conditions or changes, followed by an inquiry into the factors, *including* mass communication, which produced those conditions and changes, and the roles which these factors played relative to each other. In short, attempts to assess a stimulus which was presumed to work alone have given way to an assessment of the role of that stimulus in a total observed phenomenon.

Essentially, this has been the keystone of the approach developed by Lazarsfeld, Berelson, Pool, Lasswell, etc., who have been interested for some years now in how primary group organization determines the way in which messages are transmitted from source to recipient.

In attempting an overview of the sociological impact on mass communication one point seems to me worth much emphasis. The analogy drawn by modern sociologists between mass communication and interpersonal communication has resulted in an undue stress on the sociopsychological importance of mass communication. That is to say, by equating the functions of the mass media with those of interpersonal communications in the socialization process, an undue stress on the overwhelming power of mass communication has resulted. In my view at least, the existence of society is based upon interpersonal communication—not upon mass communication. *Societies have existed and do so today without the benefit of any system of mass communication, as we know it, whatsoever.* Yet, the sociological stress on mass communications has resulted in the notion that it is either terrifyingly evil or capable of doing tremendous

6. Joseph T. Klapper, *The Effects of Mass Communication* (Free Press, New York, 1960); R. A. Bauer and A. H. Bauer, "America, Mass Society and Mass Media," *Journal of Social Issues,* vol. XVI, no. 3, 1960, pp. 3–66; J. W. Riley, Jr., and M. W. Riley, "Mass Communication and the Social System," in R. K. Merton, L. Broom, and L. S. Cottrell, Jr. (eds.), *Sociology Today* (Basic, New York, 1959).

7. J. T. Klapper, *ibid.,* p. 5.

good. There has been much anxiety and frustration, fruitless debate and polemic, and sterile, contradictory research and speculation by those who frame their orientations to mass communication within either the "good" or "evil" rubric. This is not to deny that mass communications are sociologically important. There is no doubt about this. However, the *unique* importance and social functions of mass communications must first be isolated and determined; they cannot be assumed. This calls for a reorientation of our past overconcern with the immediate *effects* of mass communication—e.g., on consumer or voting behavior—to a renewed concern with the broader societal functions of mass communications.

Such a reorientation necessitates incorporation of conceptual frames of reference from history, psychology, anthropology, and other branches of the social sciences in a statement defining what may be called the "communications situation."

SELECTED PUBLICATIONS BY DR. MENDELSOHN

"Toward Systematic Analyses of Community Research Data," *Sociology and Social Research,* vol. 36, no. 1, September–October 1951.

"The Effect of Autistic Pressure and Institutional Structure Preference in a Choice Situation," *Journal of Social Psychology,* vol. 36, 1952, with I. Crespi.

"Communist Broadcasts to Italy," *Public Opinion Quarterly,* vol. 16, no. 4, 1952–53, with W. J. Cahnman.

"How Effective is Our Student Exchange Program?" *Educational Research* Bulletin, vol. XXXIII, no. 2, 1954, with S. J. Niefeld.

"A Survey of American Fulbright Award Recipients," *Public Opinion Quarterly,* vol. 19, no. 4, 1955–56, with F. E. Orenstein.

"Measuring the Process of the Effect of Mass Communications," *Public Opinion Quarterly,* Fall 1962.

"A Plan for Investigating the Process of the Effect of Television in Inducing Action," to appear in Mark A. May and Leon Arons (eds.), *Television and Human Behavior: Tomorrow's Research in Mass Communications* (Appleton-Century-Crofts, New York, 1963).

QUESTIONS

1.   Mendelsohn is discussing different viewpoints held by sociologists towards mass communications. Do similar differences of viewpoint prevail among newspaper editors, and teachers of journalism? "A difference," it has been well said "to be a difference must make a difference." What difference in research and interpretation would the different perspectives which Mendelsohn discusses make?

2.   The following figures of speech are sometimes employed in regard to the mass media and mass communications. "Mass communications are the nervous system of societies, permitting feedback and corrective action. . . ." "Mass media are the cement which holds modern society together." What particular perspectives and assumptions about the effects of communications do such figures of speech involve?

3.   Collect advertisements for mass media and see if you can determine any perspective on mass communications implied in them. (e.g., one magazine has "an intimacy to share . . ."; another declares that it tells "two and a quarter million households" about significant business and political developments; and, finally, Radio Free Europe portrays itself as providing strength and support to those behind the Iron Curtain). There may well be other perspectives than those Mendelsohn discusses. Can you think of any?

4.   Describe, with examples, the difference between an *individualistic* interpretation of mass communications and a *sociological* one.

5.   The editors of this book have often received from well-meaning friends comments of this sort: "How wonderful that you are writing about mass communications! They are so powerful; it is so important that students should learn about them. . . ." In terms of Mendelsohn's article, can you guess why they may have found such comments irritating? Explain.

6.   What common presupposition relates the notion that mass communications have tremendous power to the one that all the world needs to achieve peace and virtue is education? Explain the relationship between these ideas and discuss them critically. (Some aspects of this issue are discussed in Lewis A. Dexter, *Tyrannies of Schooling; An Inquiry into the Problem of Stupidity* (Basic Books, New York, 1964).

Franklin Fearing

Human Communication *

IT WAS THE NIGHT of October 23, 1962. On television screens in millions of homes throughout the United States the evening schedule of escapist programs was interrupted. Thirty or forty million Americans saw the face of a man who had to make a decision that might affect every one of his viewers. In fact, he had made his decision and was now reporting it to the people who had elected him their President. By the technical virtuosity of Telstar, millions more would see and hear him in Europe. Whether Nikita Khrushchev was one of the millions who watched the deadly serious face of John F. Kennedy when he discussed his directives on Cuba, we do not know. For although the Telstar programs are not seen by the general public of Russian televiewers, it is technically feasible for select groups at the Kremlin to see what they wish. The complicated machinery of human communication had already been in operation prior to Mr. Kennedy's speech: there were many avenues by which Mr. Khrushchev could be aware of the address.

In the vastly complex process of verbal gamesmanship, which sometimes is called diplomacy, many of the notions about human communication that are so ably presented in Dr. Fearing's article may be discerned. In the particular event cited above, the one man (in all the hundreds of millions who would hear or read his words) with whom Mr. Kennedy had to communicate was Mr. Khrushchev. That, in this particular case, the communication was effective was evidenced by Khrushchev's subsequent actions. His first, immediate letter to Kennedy indicated that the Soviet Union would remove its missiles from Cuba and urged a quick meeting of Russian and American diplomats to engage in further human communication to avert a catastrophic nuclear conflict.

Central to Dr. Fearing's study is the notion formulated first by the noted social philosopher, George Mead, that if communication is to occur between human beings both parties must be implicated.

* Reprinted from *Audio-Visual Communication Review,* vol. 10, no. 3, 1962, pp. 78–108, by permission of the author's estate and the publisher. (Copyright 1962 by the *Audio-Visual Communication Review.*)

It is interesting to consider that when Khrushchev first met the President in Vienna, shortly after Kennedy's election, the Russian leader was ostensibly uncompromising about the Berlin problem. If Kennedy had taken Khrushchev at his then uttered word and had decided that the Russians were going to force the West out of Berlin, Khrushchev would have, indeed, scored a major victory without the firing of one shot. Yet, Mr. Kennedy (and his advisers) knew, as Fearing points out, that "responses to stimuli in communication situations are not automatic and mechanical, but rather are dependent on the totality of cultural and personality factors which each respondent brings to the situation."

It is this approach to the study of communications that makes Professor Fearing's essay a most valuable introduction to a variety of essential concepts in the field. That a theory of communication cannot be based on the notion that the communications process consists in the "simple transmission of 'ideas,' 'information' or some other unit of meaning from the communicator to the communicatee" is amply substantiated by Dr. Fearing. Elaborating his concept that there are communicators and interpreters (rather than communicatees,) Fearing examines in depth the dynamic interdependent relations between the two. He shows why a knowledge of the dynamics of behavior in the structuring of reality is a prerequisite for understanding how "communication situations" function in human relations. He then briefly reviews the part played in perception by the value system of the individual and its relevance to communications theory. But perhaps Fearing's most valuable contribution in this study is his analysis of how symbols function in the act of communicating. Drawing heavily upon the work of Kenneth Burke, Fearing wisely enjoins us not to get overinvolved in the problem of the reality behind symbols, but to remember that man uses symbols as a means of adapting himself to this world. As Burke succinctly puts it, "Symbols appear in the unending conversation that is going on at the point in history when we are born."

Professor Fearing's lucid approach to a "field" theory of communication [which perhaps should be considered only a tentative summary of his ideas,] makes his untimely death in March, 1962, a substantial loss for all who are concerned with communications theory.

D.M.W.

DR. FRANKLIN FEARING (1892–1962) was both a physiological and social psychologist. After moving from Northwestern University to the University of California, Los Angeles, in 1936, his interests in physiology began to be replaced by social psychology. This development was in part due to the impact of social changes on the national scene during the depression years and in part to the growing international tensions associated with the rise of German fascism. He published work on the mass media of communication, content analysis, propaganda and public opinion, and the social impact of motion pictures and radio. *The article included in this volume was on his desk, virtually complete except for references, at the time of his death.*

Traffic signal	Proverb
Religious ritual	News broadcast
Soap opera	A Bob Hope "gag"
Photograph	An etching
Trail marker in the forest	Conversation
Novel	Arm salute by a soldier
Symphony	Comic strip
Editorial	Map
Totem pole	Motion picture
Poem	Thumb to nose gesture
Constitution of the U.S.	Prayer
Advertisement	*Summa Theologica* by Thomas Aquinas
Cairn (of stones)	News broadcast

These are all communications, produced by human beings and reacted to by human beings. They are only a tiny, random sample of an inconceivably vast number of objects, sounds, and sights which enter into nearly every transaction with the environment. Human affairs and the business of living would be impossible without them. Without them, no society or culture would exist, no "progress" be achieved, no art be created, nor could the heavens be mapped, the atom be explored, people be amused, angered, or uplifted, and human wisdom or folly be shared or preserved.

How can a list of such diverse items be characterized? At first glance, it seems quite hopeless to find a common denominator. It is even difficult to find a name for them. They are not "things" or "objects" (although some of them are); they are not "acts" (although some of them are); they are not "language" (although most of them involve it).

An important distinction should be made at the outset. The words and phrases on the list all designate situations in which some form of human behavior possessing special characteristics occurs. This special kind of activity we shall provisionally call "communication," and the words and phrases on our list may be said to refer to communication situations. But these terms also characterize many other kinds of human activities. A traffic signal, or a motion picture film, or a painting appear in a variety of human situations. They may, for example, be commodities with monetary value, and, as such, are bought and sold. They may be objects with weight and size which must be taken into account in transporting or storing them. In each of these situations the objects acquire different meanings—a tricky word which we will have to deal with later—because they elicit different kinds of behavior. Not only is the observable behavior different, but we may infer that the human attitude towards these objects are different. It is essential that the communicative situation not be confused with any other.

By the term "situation" we mean that at a given time there exists a pattern of forces which has an overall meaning that can be designated by a term or phrase. Since these are human situations, these forces are manifested in behavior patterns, or patterns of interaction between persons, that appear to have a certain consistency and may be the basis for predictions. These predictions or expectations may be accurate or inaccurate, depending on the insights of the predictor. And even the most stable situation has within it the possibility of change. We indicate this when we say that we expect the situation to improve or to deteriorate, to become less tense or to reach a crisis. Further, when we speak of these human situations, we note that they are polarized with respect to particular factors, such as personalities, or issues, or physical conditions. Such polarization means that these factors play a central role in determining the character of all interacting behavior patterns, and especially the nature and course of social change.

THE COMMUNICATION SITUATION

In the case of the terms on our list, we have designated situations which have this unified character, and which are polarized around the thing, or act, or stimulus to which the term refers. Let us examine the list again and ask certain questions. What human purposes or ends are served in the situations designated by these terms? How are these purposes served? What is it that differentiates these from other situations in which social behavior occurs?

In the first place, the items, as stimuli, are produced by human beings *with the purpose of shaping or steering behavior* in a particular direction, or establishing some sort of relationship between the producers of the stimuli and those who respond. There is much variation as to precision of direction in each situation. The traffic signal is relatively unambiguous, but the Constitution of the United States requires a Supreme Court to interpret its directions, and a poem may be even more vague. In any event they all serve as means to ends, rather than ends in themselves.

Second, each item is responded to in terms of what it stands for. There are a number of confusing terms used to refer to stimuli that have this remarkable property. They are said, for example, to have meaning, to be symbols, signs, etc. Whatever the term used, it should be recognized that they elicit responses which imply significance beyond the object or the behavior itself, and that they are produced by a human agency.

Third, these items establish a particular relationship between the persons who produce them and the persons who respond, but it is not a mechanical pushbutton or steering relationship. If modification of human behavior is to occur there must be a *shared meaning* between the producer of the stimulus and the respondent. This is a transaction in which both parties must participate. George Mead, who laid the foundation for all subsequent work in this field, pointed out that if communication is to occur between human beings both parties must be implicated. This means that the person who produces the sign or symbol must be able to respond to it in the same manner as the other person is expected to respond. This Mead calls "taking the attitude of the other." For example, the person who puts up a trail marker in the forest is not engaging in random activity —he expects other persons to react in a certain way, and he must be able to react as he expects others to respond. This is something about which we shall have more to say. Now we merely point out that in communication the producer of the stimulus (sign-symbol) always makes certain assumptions regarding the capacities and potentialities of the other person. These assumptions may be general or specific; they may turn out to be essentially correct or wholly wrong; but in the communication situation the producer of the stimulus *must* make them. He even makes assumptions about the needs or motives of those whose behavior he is trying to steer. In this commonality of response lies its "meaning." Without this sharing process through mediation of the special kind of stimuli called signs or symbols there is *no communication and no socialized meaning*.

Finally, it should be noted that there is considerable variation in the responses which each stimulus is capable of eliciting. The response to a traffic signal will probably not show much variation, although a Navajo Indian who saw one for the first time would probably be puzzled. The responses to a symphony, a poem, or even a news broadcast may show enormous variability. The point of these observations is that responses to stimuli in communication situations are not automatic and mechanical, but are *dependent on the totality of cultural and personality factors* which each respondent brings to the situation.

This last point is significant for a theory of communication because it makes untenable the widely held notion that communication is merely a transmission system. That conception, which is stated in many forms, implies that the communication process consists in the simple transmission of "ideas," "information" or some other unit of meaning from the communicator to the communicatee, and that it is received intact. Or if it has not been received intact, it is said to have been affected by some sort of interference which resulted in distortion. In other words, the transmission-belt theory of communication in its simplest form assumes a simple linear, one-directional relationship between the communicator and the communicatee, subject only to interferences or disturbances analogous to those mechanical imperfections that would disturb or distort communication over a telephone system. There is an imposing array of research findings, mainly in the field of the psychology of perception, which makes such a mechanical conception of communication unacceptable. Rather, as will be shown later, the communicator and communicatee are interdependent. It is a two-way relationship which cannot be adequately understood in terms of simple engineering or mechanical analogies. It is a uniquely human relationship from which emerge all civilization and culture and without which man, as we know him, could not survive.

It might be said that communication and communicative situations involve the individual in *public* relationships. The sign-symbol stimulus material enables individuals to *share* experiences. In communicating, I make public something that has hitherto been private.

GENERALIZATIONS

Four generalizations regarding communication situations may now be made. (1) They are situations in which human beings enter into certain strategic relationships with each other or with their environment. (2) They are situations the central characteristic of which is the production and utilization of signs, symbols and symbolic acts. (3) They are situations which provide a maximal opportunity through the use of signs and symbols for the sharing of experience, achievement of goals, gaining of insight and, in general, mastering one's environment. (4) The sign or symbol material used in these situations is subject to the perceptual processes of the individuals involved.

Since the foregoing generalizations are condensed, they require some expansion. It is necessary, for example, to distinguish between those who produce symbolic material and those who react to it: *the communicators* and *the interpreters*. The symbolic material to which they both respond, though in different ways, is *communication content*. These terms will be more completely defined, and the dynamic interdependent relations between them will be more carefully examined. The terms *strategic, sign, symbol,* and *mastering the environment,* also require definition and elaboration. These are key concepts for the understanding of communication and what it does for human beings in their relations with each other and with their environments.

DYNAMICS OF BEHAVIOR; STRUCTURING REALITY

In order to understand how communication situations function in human relations, it is necessary to introduce certain psychological concepts, especially those that are concerned with the dynamics of behavior.

When we stand off and look at the larger aspects of our own or other people's behavior, the question most frequently raised is: What is the individual *trying* to do? Both the layman and psychologists can agree on a general answer. Human animals, and all other animals, are always striving for goals. The term "goal" can include such diverse things as a bit of cheese at the end of a rat maze, food in an icebox, making a good impression, getting an education, or understanding the structure of the atom. The pathways to these various goals are never wholly free from obstacles—delays, frustrations, and detours. As the individual confronts these obstructions, he must appraise them in the light of his previous experiences and readjust or remarshal his resources in order to surmount them. Or, of course, he may turn to other goals. In other words, he adopts strategies, especially symbolic strategies.

In perceiving obstacles and making adjustments in order to continue on the path to a goal, the individual is *coming to terms with reality*. In doing this, he utilizes whatever resources are available or that he believes are available, in order to overcome, or remove, or get around, or even escape from the obstacles which confront him. Psychologically, this involves his "seeing" his situation in a particular perspective. He identifies the forces which are friendly or unfriendly to his course of action—whether correctly or incorrectly is beside the point. When he does all this, he is said to cognitively *structure* the situation. We may assume the basic postulate that individuals need to cognitively structure their "worlds" in order to live in them. In a sense, every situation presents a problem to the individual. On the one hand, there are the external objective factors—objects, physical configurations of forces, "events," etc.—and on the other are the needs, values, beliefs, and attitudes of the individual himself, plus, of course, his perceptual apparatus (sense organs, neural mechanisms, etc.). This structuring may be simple or complex, adequate or inadequate, but it is always an action on the environment, and its function, broadly speaking, is to bring about a degree of order or coherence as a necessary condition of action.

There is another psychological concept that is useful for our purposes. This is the concept of *tension*. This refers to a characteristic of all human beings and, indeed, of all animals; namely that in their relations with the forces in the environment, they never achieve a state of absolute stability. A sort of temporary balance between all these forces may be reached, but, at best, it is precarious. There are always disturbances and unexpected changes in the environment, new needs to be served, and minor or major threats to one's course of action and goals. These and many other factors create a condition of mild or great disequilibrium. This instability produces tension.

The importance of this concept from the point of view of behavior dynamics is that the individual is always striving to reduce his tensions. The need for cognitive structuring, sometimes called "the need for meaning," is, in reality, the need to establish a more stable structure and hence reduce tension. Krech and Crutchfield who have discussed the concept in some detail make this point clearly:

. . . the history of the psychological field of the individual does not involve a series of excursions away from a stable state and return to the same state. It is, rather, a history of changing equilibriums, in which the psychological field re-structures continuously, never returning to a state in which it existed before. Thus, an individual who, by achieving a certain goal, reduces the tension that initiates his action toward that goal, does not thereby become satisfied. *His very achievement of the goal has so restructured his psychological field as to make possible all sorts of new instabilities and tensions, make desirable new kinds of goals, induce new aspirations, etc.* (Italics added.)

The structuring of a situation, then, serves not only to create a frame for some sort of action towards a goal; it also is tension-reductive. These tensional states may intrude themselves into consciousness in the form of feelings of restlessness, anxiety, or dissatisfaction. They may also, as Krech and Crutchfield point out, be reflected in a feeling that some particular aspect of the situation is especially important or desirable, or that the situation "demands" something—possibly action—from the individual.

The structuring process is not necessarily a highly organized intellectual activity to which the term "conscious plan" should be applied. It may be automatic and instantaneous. This is illustrated by the simple act of picking up an object from the floor. Before it is picked up, the object is perceived as having certain phenomenal properties. It is perceived as movable, as possessing a certain weight and size; there must be anticipatory muscular adjustment before it is lifted. At a more complex level, the skilled billiard player makes a shot which, as an act, contains within it the anticipation of a whole series of precisely planned and complicated outcomes. That these structurizations may, in fact, turn out to be inaccurate or "wrong" is, of course, beside the point.

When the structuring process is concerned with interactions between individuals, rather than between individuals and objects, it is more complicated and the assumptions are less certain, but its essential psychological character is not changed. Yet even here, in the rapid adjustments which we are constantly making in our relations with other persons, there need not be much in the way of conscious analysis or planning.

The most characteristic feature of our structurization of other individuals with whom we are in any way involved is the *imputation of motives*. We ascribe motives as a basis for our assumptions as to how the other person will respond *to us*. As a premise for our own behavior, it is necessary to perceive the other person as possessing certain motives, beliefs, attitudes, or interests.

This characteristic is the basis for all human relations and is central to certain situations. For example, the applicant who is being interviewed by a prospective employer is concerned with making a good impression. To do this he attempts to size up the potential employer's personality traits. He has to assume that he is a certain kind of person with certain likes and dislikes, and he adjusts his strategy in the light of these assumptions. This is a special case in which there is a particular premium on "reading" the motives behind the façade, but, in some degree, this occurs in all human social relations. Communication, even that which is brief and casual, could not occur without it. We sustain our position in the social fabric by making assumptions about what is going on in the mind of what George Mead has called "the other."

VALUE SYSTEM AND PERCEPTION

In these structuring activities it will be noted that the values, beliefs, and attitudes of the individual play an important role. Within certain limits we "see" what our interests, beliefs and values determine us to see. The part played in perception by the value system of the individual has recently received much attention from social psychologists.

For example, the investigation of Postman, Bruner and McGinnies showed that words which had a high value for a subject were more speedily recognized than those of low value. The investigators hypothesize that the value-orientation of the individual sensitizes him to certain external stimuli. When the stimulus is congruent with the value-orientation of the subject and his threshold is lowered for it, these investigators term the process *perceptual resonance*. When the value-orientation acts as a barrier and prevents the individual from perceiving certain aspects of his environment, the process is termed *perceptual defense*.

Such studies make it clear that perceiving is not merely photographic. Rather, the "world out there" is perceived in terms of the perceiver. This means that it is perceived as friendly or unfriendly, pleasant or unpleasant, and so on through the whole gamut of values and meanings. There is, however, a limit to the meanings which can be projected outward. The world out there has its own organization. It is filled with objects and people that have structure, shape, contour, size, solidarity and, unless we are hallucinated, these may not be evaded. They are the so-called structural factors in perception. The relative importance of these two sets of factors—the social or functional and the structural—and how they work together need not concern us here. The outcome of this combined operation is that we orient ourselves in the world so that we act in accordance with *our needs* as persons and *its character* as tangible reality.

In brief, we do not simply react to a world of things which are "there." Rather, we establish very complicated, interdependent relationships between the world out there and ourselves as organisms with needs, values, and attitudes. A meaningful behavioral environment is one so structured that it is congruent with "reality," on the one hand, and the needs and disposition of the organism, on the other. We create our environment as we go along. Tensions mount and are reduced; goals conscious or unconscious, are achieved, and new goals emerge. As organisms with needs and purposes operating in an environment which may be recalcitrant, or, at best, indifferent, we utilize whatever strategies of wit or insight we possess in coming to terms with it. We *must* assume that the environment in which we are acting or expect to act has certain characteristics. We must presuppose that other individuals have certain motives or characteristics, that events, expected or unexpected have certain "causes," that forces about us are friendly or hostile, that "things" can be utilized in certain ways, and that they possess specific physical characteristics.

It is clear that the individual's perceptual-cognitive transactions with the world "out there," the world of things, is not simple. A distinction made by some psychologists—notably Werner, Scheerer, Koffka, and Arnheim—may be useful. Werner, for example, distinguishes between "geometric-technical" and "physiognomic" perception. As distinct from the geometric-technical mode of perceiving, physiognomic perception is a mode of cognition in which the external world is directly apprehended as expressing its own inner form of life. It is, according to Werner, a "dynamization of things based on the fact that objects are predominantly

understood through the motor and affective attitude of the subject. . . .
A landscape may be seen suddenly as expressing a certain mood . . . it
may be gay or melancholy or pensive." Basically, in its pure form (if
such exists) it is a mode of perception in which the distinction between
the perceiver and the thing perceived is lost. The *me* and the *not-me* are
fused. There is evidence that this type of perceiving is especially characteristic of children and of people in the so-called primitive cultures.

At the other end of the perceptual continuum is the geometric-technical mode which sharply separates the perceiver from what is perceived.
This is the mode of "objective" science. It is based on the assumption
that the external world may be described by a neutral observer who is
able to exclude his own feelings, attitudes, and beliefs from his perception. This mode is highly sanctioned in our society, and the physiognomic mode is systematically discouraged.

SIGNIFICANCE OF METAPHOR

That the physiognomic mode is never eliminated is evidenced by the
omnipresent metaphor in our language behavior. The intimate relation
between language and perceptual-cognitive processes receives its most
powerful expression in verbal metaphor. The psychological basis of metaphorical reference is the cognition of one thing in terms of something
else. I. A. Richards characterizes metaphor in terms which are essentially
physiognomic:

I . . . include as metaphoric, those processes in which we perceive or think of
or feel about one thing in terms of another—as when looking at a building it
seems to have a face and to confront us with a peculiar expression. I want to
insist that this sort of thing is normal in full perception and that study of the
growth of our perceptions (the animistic world of the child and so on) shows
that it must be so.

Richards' assumptions regarding the development of perception are
supported by the studies of Murphy and Hochberg. They note that in
primitive stages, perception is "inextricably fused with the motion, position, and feeling state of the observer." Even in the laboratory where
every effort is made to rule out the "subjective" variable, it is impossible
to separate completely the affective-conative processes of the observer.

It is a reflection of the geometric-technical emphasis in our culture
that verbal metaphor (and not all metaphors are verbal) is commonly
regarded as merely poetic embroidery. But if physiognomic perception
and the related metaphoric expression are as fundamentally related to
the human way of apprehending the world as the studies of Piaget,

Werner, Murphy, and Hochberg, and others seem to indicate, the attempts at purely objective description may interfere with the basic creative nature of human cognition. That is, the capacity to become aware of the underlying relationships in the apparently confused flood of unrelated impressions which impinge on our sense organs from the outside world is a necessary part of creative thinking. This process is central to the human animal's transaction with his environment. This, plus the closely related capacity, the use of symbolic processes to share our awareness with others, lies at the basis of both art and science. Science has always used metaphorical description. The great scientific metaphors of science and philosophy have been extremely fruitful in generating hypotheses which may or may not have been empirically verified: for example, man is a *machine;* at birth, the mind is a *tabula rasa* on which experience writes; society and personality are *structured;* a *current* of electricity; *field* theory. We may underscore Arnheim's statement: "It is the function of the metaphor to make the reader penetrate the concrete shell of the world of things by combinations of objects that have little in common but the underlying pattern."

It is clear that the "reality" with which we grapple cannot be fully understood in terms of the external physical elements. Perceptual-cognitive processes always *organize and unify.* To this the organism makes a preponderant and inescapable contribution. The most common verbal expression of this is in the form of verbal metaphors, but the underlying dynamisms of experience are not limited to language. Non-linguistic metaphors are found in all visual art, in stage design, in photographs, motion pictures, and, in fact, in any representation or arrangement of objects, animate or inanimate, which has human significance. In the Olivier production of *Richard III* there is a scene in which the two princes meet at the end of a vast hall. The one boy runs across the hall to clasp his arms around his brother; they cower together on an immense throne. The size of the hall and the two boys alone at the end of it express a terrible isolation which is enhanced by the presence of the sinister Richard and his companions lurking in the background. By purely visual means without the aid of speech, the configuration of hostile forces closing in on the princes is expressed in essentially metaphorical terms.

It must be made clear as Arnheim points out, that a weeping willow tree does not look sad because it looks like a sad person. "It is more adequate to say that since the shape, direction, and flexibility of willow branches convey the expression of passive hanging, a comparison with the structurally similar state of mind and body that we call sadness imposes itself secondarily." It is not necessary to describe this process in terms of the "pathetic fallacy," anthropomorphism, or personification, nor is it based on similarities and analogies. The organism, as Arnheim points out, is primarily "interested in the forces that are active around it— their place, strength, direction. Hostility and friendliness are attributes of forces. And the perceived impact of forces makes for what we call expression." This is perception in depth.

WHAT IS THE REAL WORLD?

In Mark Twain's satirical story of a Connecticut Yankee who is transported to King Arthur's Court, there is a scene which amusingly depicts how differently two people may perceive the same objects. The matter-of-fact Yankee, Sir Boss, accompanied by the highly imaginative and talkative girl, Sandy, are approaching the end of a long quest for the castle in which, according to an accepted story, forty-five princesses were held prisoners by three giant ogres. But what do the twentieth-century Yankee and the girl of sixth century Britain see? The girl speaks:

'The castle! The castle! Lo, where it looms!'
What a welcome disappointment I experienced! I said:
'Castle? It is nothing but a pigsty; a pigsty with a wattled fence around it.'
She looked surprised and distressed. The animation faded out of her face; and during many moments she was lost in thought and silent. Then:
'It was not enchanted aforetime,' she said in a musing fashion, as if to herself. 'And how strange is this marvel, and how awful—that to the one perception it is enchanted, yet to the perception of the other it is not enchanted, hath suffered no change, but stands firm and stately still, girt with its moat and waving its banners in the blue air from its towers. And God shield us, how it pricks the heart to see again these gracious captives, and the sorrow deepened in their sweet faces!'
I saw my cue. The castle was enchanted to *me,* not to her. It would be wasted time to try to argue her out of her delusion, it couldn't be done; I must just humor it. So I said:
'This is a common case—the enchanting of a thing to one eye and leaving it in its proper form to another. You have heard of it before, Sandy, though you haven't happened to experience it. But no harm is done. In fact, it is lucky the way it is. If these ladies were hogs to everybody and to themselves, it would be necessary to break the enchantment, and that might be impossible if one failed to find the particular process of the enchantment. And hazardous, too; for in attempting a disenchantment without the true key, you are liable to err, and turn your hogs into dogs. . . . But here, by good luck, no one's eyes but mine are under the enchantment, and so it is of no consequence to dissolve it. These

ladies remain ladies to you, and to themselves, and to everybody else; and at the same time they will suffer in no way from my delusion, for when I know that an ostensible hog is a lady, that is enough for me, I know how to treat her.'

'Thanks, oh, sweet my lord, thou talkest like an angel. And I know that thou wilt deliver them. . . .

'I will not leave a princess in a sty, Sandy. Are those three yonder that to my distorted eyes are starveling swineherds—

'The ogres? Are *they* changed also? It is most wonderful. Now am I fearful; for how canst thou strike with sure aim when five of their nine cubits of stature are to thee invisible? Ah, go warily, fair sir, this is a mightier emprise than I wend.'

It is indeed!

A question that is almost certain to inject itself at this point is: To what extent does the "world" that is the result of structuring process differ from the "real" world? Or, in the case of Mark Twain's characters, which of the two perceptions of the "castle," the "ogres," and their high-born prisoners was the "true" one? They are clearly not the same. The answer need not be a metaphysical discourse on the nature of ultimate reality. In terms of the problems with which we are here concerned, the simplest answer is that there are not two worlds, one of illusion and one that is "real." There is one world—the world the individual lives in, bends to his needs, has relations with other persons in, loves in, and dies in. For our purposes it is sufficient to assume that both man and the world in which he lives are organizations of material energies. The striking thing, and that which furnishes the psychologist with most of his problems, is that the organization of material energies which we call man not only reacts *to* this world but, in the various ways we have described, *on* it. He manipulates it and constantly recreates it. Psychologically there is not just one world, but many worlds. The critical question is: How are they related?

It is at this point that the problem of "reality" becomes acute. The world or environment created by human activities is not only a world of things; it is a world of meanings and significations. The dog that is my pet is a much loved creature with a thousand engaging ways and a personality all his own. To me, my neighbor's dog is an unpleasant creature with annoying habits and a mean disposition. To a third person, the two animals are just dogs which he has difficulty in telling apart. Which of these are the real dogs? The answer is that the two dogs as stimulus objects are structured in different ways by different individuals, each with his special need-value-belief system. The resultant structurizations are real because they have real or objective effects on behavior.

STIMULUS FIELDS—BEHAVIORAL AND GEOGRAPHIC

It is possible, and indeed necessary, to distinguish between these "worlds" without assuming that one is real and the others imaginary. The scientific study of these different "worlds" may require different methodologies, different terminologies, and different conceptualizations, but we must not beg the question by assuming that some are real and some are not. A distinction that has proved useful to the psychologist is that between the *behavioral* stimulus field and the geographic stimulus field. This is a distinction roughly equivalent to that made earlier between the functional and structural factors in perception. The behavioral stimulus field is the field as the individual "sees" it; in its simplest form the "seeing" is physiogenic. An analysis of this field will probably employ such terms as "meaning," "needs," "values," "beliefs," "cognitive structuring," and the like. These are psychological terms. They characterize aspects of the internal dynamics of individuals. Although they present difficulties of observation and measurement, they are none the less real.

The geographic environment exists, presumably, independently of the structuring process. The description of this environment will employ the terminology of the physical sciences or the language of everyday life. The resulting descriptions give us another picture of reality without which modern man cannot survive, and paradoxically, with which he may destroy himself.

These various pictures of reality are illustrated in the example of the dog. He is my pet, but he is also a complex organization of energies—a physiochemical machine—which the physiologist, chemist, and many other scientific specialists may describe, each in his own jargon. He may be described also by the social psychologist in terms of the role of pets in western culture, or by the economist who is interested in the proportion of the American family income (or my income!) which goes to maintain pets. He is also my pet, and unlike any other dog in the world. "Behaviorally" speaking, he is a different dog for each of these specialists, including myself. "Geographically" speaking, he is the same dog. All these descriptions present significant aspects of the animal, and, geographically or behaviorally, he is certainly a "real" dog.

Let us consider another example. A town is a place where a number of people work and live. It is an environment which has been created by these people. Geographically, it is on a map, occupies a given terrain which has particular physical features, and has a certain configuration of streets on which are buildings of various shapes and sizes. Behaviorally, it is a different environment for each person who lives in it. In a real sense, each individual creates it. He sees it in terms of his personal interests, needs, and experience. Some have been residents since its beginnings— the old timers and pioneers; others are newcomers, and some are merely passing through. Some people live on the "right" side of the tracks, and some on the "wrong" side. To some it is perceived in romantic, sentimental or nostalgic terms. To others, the town is a place of struggle and failure. No two persons see it in quite the same way, and the divergencies may be very great.

It is apparent that the town as geographic environment—which seems so stable and "real"—is permissive of a variety of behavioral environments. In this sense, it is ambiguous—as, indeed, the geographic environment always is. To attempt to transcend these ambiguities by characterizing the geographic environment as the only real environment is both futile and naive, and will lead to serious social consequences. To do so, for example, implies that all the people in the town are suffering from delusions. It is extremely important to know more about these different environments, how they are created, how much they overlap, and under what conditions they change.

An example of a scientific approach to a problem of this sort is found in such studies as *Middletown* by the Lynds, *Plainville USA* by West, and *Elmtown's Youth* by Hollingshead. By using special techniques of observation and analysis, a town as a community of people carrying on widely diverse activities, pursuing a variety of goals, and having a variety of backgrounds and social attitudes, is described. Such a study, if conducted by competent persons, yields a picture of the community which is different from that of any nonscientific person who happens to live in it. Such studies are extremely useful since, among other things, they give us a set of reference points with which we can compare other more naive descriptions. Their "reality" depends on the extent to which objective reliable methods were used by the investigator. He must be careful not to think of the various behavioral environments as errors, mistakes, delusions, or distortions of some ultimate reality.

But the problem of discrepancies between these environments is practically and theoretically important. If these discrepancies are great, human relations will be seriously disturbed, and the social outcomes may be disastrous. This is true because structurization, as we have noted, is always the basis for action. The corrective lies in the fact that discrepant environments may always be cognitively re-structured so as to reduce the discrepancies, and hence, the tensions. Communicative techniques, because they demand at least a degree of sharing, play the dominant role in this process. When these techniques break down, or become seriously impaired, the result is that the "worlds" (behavioral environments) of individuals become isolated, the correctives which would normally reduce the discrepancies are not utilized, and the results, individually or globally, are likely to be catastrophic.

UNDERLYING ATTITUDES AND INTERPRETATION

An experiment reported by Eberhart and Bauer makes a significant contribution to these problems. These investigators were interested in discovering how beliefs and attitudes affect the interpretation or understanding of an event *after* it has occurred. They investigated the way in which a dramatic event with high emotional loading was recalled. In order to understand the relevance of this procedure to the present discussion, it should be stated that the need-value systems of individuals show themselves in how they *remember* events, as well as in the way they are structured at the time of occurrence. Forgetting (or remembering), like perceiving, is a dynamic process in which the individual retrospectively structures a situation in terms of his needs and values.

The event which Eberhart and Bauer utilized occurred in Chicago in 1937, and has since been referred to as the Memorial Day Massacre. On this day a clash occurred between police and strikers and strike sympathizers near the Republic Steel Plant. Ten strikers were killed, 90 others were injured—many by gunfire—and 35 police were injured. The incident received national attention, and the newspaper accounts of what occurred differed widely from each other, and from the report made later by the LaFollette investigating Committee of the U.S. Senate. The discrepancies between the accounts in the Chicago *Tribune* and the report of the Senate Committee were especially marked. These centered around three points: (1) what the crowd did, (2) what the police did, and (3) whether the crowd was armed. It was on these points that Eberhart and Bauer concentrated their study. They constructed a questionnaire in which the respondents were asked to indicate which version they believed most accurately described what happened.

Two and a half years after the event a group of 177 students at Northwestern University filled out the questionnaire and also indicated the newspaper from which they secured their information.

The alternatives that were presented to them, the response most frequently chosen, the version that had appeared in the Chicago *Tribune,* and the findings of the Senate Committee are given in Table 1.

Regarding the action of the crowd, 55 percent of the students selected response *b.* Regarding the action of the police, 71 percent selected choice *a.* Regarding the possession of arms, 87 percent of the students failed to select the Chicago *Tribune* version, but in this instance agreed with the

Senate Committee findings. The pattern of responses varied, but more than 40 percent reported, "The crowd intended to invade the plant and drive out the strikebreakers; the police acted in self-defense and to protect the rights of property; and the crowd carried objects which might be used for weapons, but were not armed for battle." This may be compared with the Senate Committee version—alternatives *a, c,* and *c.*

Table 1—Interpretation of an Event

	Student Selection	Chicago Tribune Version	Senate Committee Report
1. The crowd			
a. intended to establish a peaceful picket line outside the plant gate			X
b. intended to invade the plant and drive out the strikebreakers	X	X	
c. intended to attack the police			
2. The police			
a. acted in self defense and to protect the rights of property	X	X	
b. deliberately and brutally shot down peaceful citizens			
c. on slight but insufficient provocation attacked a group of defenseless men and women			X
3. The crowd			
a. was armed with pistols, baseball bats and meat hooks, and advanced in military formation		X	
b. was completely unarmed			
c. carried some objects which might be used for weapons but were not armed for battle	X		X

To test whether there was any relationship between the pattern of recall of such an event and underlying attitudes and usual sources of information, the students were given another questionnaire, the results of which were illuminating. Over 66 percent opposed the idea of workers as a potentially dominant group; they read only conservative magazines and newspapers, usually including the *Tribune.* There was a close relationship between the three variables, general attitude, sources of information, and the way a specific event was recalled.

To test these findings further, the investigators obtained results on the strike questionnaire from students in three Pacific Coast colleges and one New England college. In this questionnaire there was no mention of the Memorial Day incident as such. The subjects were merely told that it was a strike that occurred several years earlier, and were asked to indicate what they *thought* had probably occurred. In three of the four groups the same pattern of responses occurred. In one Pacific Coast college the results deviated sharply. Here 45 percent chose the *a, c,* and *c*-pattern— the Senate Committee findings. This deviation seemed to be explained by the fact that the students in this group were completing a course in social psychology in which there had been considerable emphasis on stereotyped thinking with respect to social phenomena. Otherwise, as Eberhart and Bauer note, it is significant that "student groups, one to three thousand miles apart . . . return almost identical group answers." Whether the incident was identified or not seemed to have little effect on the versions they are willing to accept regarding what happened in a situation involving violence between police and strikers.

We have considered this experiment in some detail because it throws light on several aspects of our problem.

In the first place, it throws into relief the relationships between "reality" and the perception of reality. The searcher for truth is bound to ask: "What *really* happened? What are the *facts?*" There were some brute facts: ten persons (strikers) were killed, 90 injured, and 35 police were injured. But much more is demanded: what were the intentions of the crowd? the police? who was armed? We move away from the relatively meaningless "facts" to the underlying dynamics of a *situation.* Who did what to whom? Why? What *made* people behave in this manner? Who is to *blame?*

At this point, structuring processes as determined by need-value system begin to operate, and the situation becomes ambiguous; that is, it permits different interpretations to be made. Can the "facts" be determined? In the case of the study we have been describing, a painstaking sifting of eyewitness stories resulted in an approximation of the "facts." Presumably, this was done by the U.S. Senate Committee investigation. The "facts" which they finally reported, however, are still only approximations. If careful comparisons between eyewitness accounts are made, if specific criteria of reliability and objectivity are established and applied, the result might be a description which may have a number of important uses, but it only approaches a description of the behavioral environment which is absolutely "objective."

STEREOTYPES AND PERCEPTION

In the second place, the study reveals that there are certain stable structurizations which are widely distributed and which function more or less independently of the actual situation. These are related to underlying attitudes, are relatively rigid, and operate in such a manner that certain situations or events, regardless of their objective characteristics, are structured alike.

In the study just described, it appears that individuals, whether the situation is specifically identified or not, have, so to speak, ready-made structurizations which "tell" them how certain situations will be patterned. These ready-made structurizations are sometimes called *stereotypes*. Stereotypes express the social appraisals and attitudes which the individual has acquired as a member of a particular class or group. They have two important psychological characteristics: (1) they serve to protect and support the existing status, privileges, or advantages of the individual or the group; and (2) they are highly resistant to modification. As regards the second characteristic, in extreme cases they may persist in the face of total contradiction from the geographic environment. In such a case, of course, they take on the character of delusions and become highly maladaptive. While stereotyping is potentially dangerous since it prevents the individual from freely structuring each situation he confronts, it may, within definite limits, serve a useful function in providing the individual with a kind of psychological shorthand for quick appraisals of situations. Stereotypes are, of course, only a special case of cognitive structuring.

CHARACTERISTICS OF STRUCTURING PROCESS

It will be useful to point out the more important implications of the structuring process from the point of view of the individual acting in an environment. We may first attempt a provisional definition. The term *structuring* refers to all the activities of an *individual* at a given moment in isolating, organizing, understanding, and *perceiving* his environment in order to come to terms with it so as *to pursue his goal* or goals in it. From the point of view of understanding human behavior in general, and communication situations in particular, the following are the more important characteristics of the process:

[1] The relationship between the individual and his environment is an interdependent one. He reacts to and on the environment which is "out there" in terms of his demands on it and its demands on him. This reaction to and on the environment is conceived to depend primarily on organizing tendencies within the individual to which the term structuring is applied. In structuring the environment the individual *isolates, selects,* and *interprets* those features which appear to be related to whatever needs at the moment he is trying to satisfy.

[2] In structuring the environment, the individual attributes to it a variety of characteristics and potentialities, and insofar as it contains other persons, he attributes to them motives and capacities. He himself adopts

attitudes towards the environment, based on his system of values and beliefs. These values, beliefs, and attitudes may be derived from his personal experience, his membership in a culture, his group memberships, his occupation, his position in the class structure, *etc.* Whatever their source, they have been interiorized in the individual. They are uniquely his.

[3] In structuring the environment, the individual makes use of a variety of devices among which symbols and symbolic acts are especially important. These will be discussed in more detail later. For the present discussion, their important characteristic is that they are *produced* and *manipulated* by the individual not as ends in themselves, but as a means of directing his own and other persons' behavior.

[4] The structuring process is essentially creative. In isolating, selecting, and interpreting aspects of the environment, the individual is, in effect, producing a new situation. He may bring aspects of the environment into relationships which have not previously existed. His capacity to use symbols, as we shall see later, is especially important in this connection. The relationships which appear in the structuring process may be regarded as emergent *gestalten,* not merely additive combinations of existing features. The individual may be said to perceive relationships which have not hitherto been perceived.

[5] A result of the selective aspect of the structurizations is that certain features or aspects of the external environment acquire a "demand" character. This means that they have acquired a stimulus value, have "insistence" for the organism which is not necessarily dependent on their physical intensity. These aspects may be perceived as attractive or repellent, but, in any case, they exert a control over behavior.

[6] These selective processes, based as they are on the need-value-belief system of the individual, make him susceptible to some features of the environment and not to others. The individual may be said to be vulnerable to those aspects of the situation which are, or appear to be, relevant to the needs and values that are dominant at the moment. This is sometimes called "interest." Kenneth Burke puts it this way: "It is not hard to imagine that if a grasshopper could speak he would indicate more interest in what you had to tell him about 'Birds That Eat Grasshoppers' than in a more scholarly talk on 'Mating Habits of the Australian Auk.'" This conception of "interest" is particularly important in understanding responses in communication situations which involve propaganda.

[7] The cognitive structures of the individual tend to maintain themselves even in the face of changes in the external situation. This persistence results in stability and consistency of the individual's behavior, but the structures may become so rigid that changes in the environment which are contradictory are not perceived at all. The term "stereotype" is applied

to those structurizations which determine the way in which individuals in one group perceive individuals in another. Stereotypes are highly resistant to change, and in general, serve to maintain the status, privileges, and powers of the members of the group against threats or presumed threats of other groups.

[8] The geographic situation in which the individual is reacting is always to some extent ambiguous, and therefore, as Luchins has suggested, may be susceptible to a number of structurizations, or to a few, or to only one. In other words, the external environment has degrees of permissiveness in regard to structurization. The Rorschach ink-blots are examples of stimuli which are in this sense highly ambiguous. Novel, unexpected, or threatening events are usually ambiguous.

At this point the reader might refer to the listing of situations with which this paper began. And, we may ask, where has this relatively long excursion into behavior dynamics brought us, and what contribution has it made to our understanding of those situations? A characteristic of all the situations was that in them individuals, through a variety of techniques, were engaged in "mastering" their environments. Most of the succeeding discussion has been concerned with the psychological mechanisms involved. In the broadest sense, this is a strategic operation that involves the establishment of a working relationship between the needs, goals, and values of individuals, on the one hand, and the objective environment, on the other. This is a creative process and the term "structuring" is applied to it.

SYMBOLIC STRATEGIES

Strategy is a military term. It is defined as the "science and art of military command, exercised to meet the enemy in combat under advantageous conditions." Metaphorically, we may apply the term to any organization of means to achieve ends. In this sense, strategy refers to all the forces which an organism utilizes in coming to terms with its environment. This includes the utilization not only of things and objects to achieve some goal, but much more importantly, the subtle organization of man's symbolic resources.

It is the symbol, as Leslie White points out,

which transformed our anthropoid ancestors into men and made them human. . . . It is the symbol which transforms an infant *homo sapiens* into a human being. . . . All behavior consists of, or is dependent upon, the use of symbols. Human behavior is symbolic behavior; symbolic behavior is human behavior.

In an illuminating paragraph in *Permanence and Change,* Kenneth Burke points out that all organisms are "critics" in the sense that they interpret the signs about them. They learn to discriminate between food and nonfood, or between the potentially dangerous and potentially friendly aspects of the environment. But, Burke says:

. . . the experimental, speculative technique made available by speech would seem to single out the human species as the only one possessing an equipment for going beyond the criticism of experience to a criticism of criticism. We not only interpret the characters of events (manifesting in our response all the gradations of fear, apprehension, misgiving, expectation, assurance for which there are rough behavioristic counterparts in animals) we may also interpret our interpretations.

The word "symbol," like most words, has acquired an aura of meanings, some of which make it a suspect term. Kenneth Burke rejects the word because it

usually implies the unreality of the world in which we live, as though nothing could be what it is, but always be something else, as though a house could never be a house, but must be, let us say, the concealed surrogate for a woman, or as though the woman one marries could never be the woman one marries, but must be a surrogate for one's mother, etc.

This identification of symbols with the unreal or fictitious is widespread and suggests to many that symbolic processes are not only unreal but even pathological. This interpretation is present, of course, in psychoanalysis. We are not here concerned with such special usage, except to point out that placing the symbolic process in the realm of the unreal introduces a distortion that is paradoxical. Rather than linking symbols with unreality "as though nothing could be what it is, but must always be something else," it would be a truer statement to say that nothing could be what it is *except* as it may be designated by symbols.

However, it is obvious—as Burke later points out—that there is an important difference between building a house and writing a poem about building a house. There is a difference between the architect's blueprints and the finished house. These distinctions are real, but they should not be made the basis of an unwarranted dichotomy between reality and unreality. The world of symbols is preeminently the world of man; it is not a world of illusion. Symbols are as real as bathtubs, and the behavior which makes use of them is as real as the behavior which does not.

Rather than being concerned with the pseudo-problem of the reality behind symbols, the important thing is to remember that man *uses* symbols as a means of getting along in the world. They are an inescapable part of all his transactions with his fellows and with his environment; they have no reality or meaning apart from these transactions. He didn't invent language as a game. Whenever or wherever a man is found in his present biological form, language and symbol systems of one kind or another already exist. They are being used as other tools are used, as a means of getting along in his world. In nearly all discussions of these problems a distinction is made between signs (sometimes called signals) and symbols (sometimes called signs). The sound of rain on the roof is said to be a sign of rain, and is interpreted as an indication that rain is falling. The flush on a person's face may be interpreted as an indication of anger. In each case the stimulus is interpreted as an indication of a state or condition beyond itself. However, a much more complicated process is involved when we *talk* about rain. Here a verbal sign is produced in place of another sign (the sound of rain or the sight of rain) and a science of meteorology becomes possible. The produced sign is a symbol which, following Morris, may be defined as a sign produced by its interpreter that acts as a substitute for another sign with which it is synonymous.

CHARACTERISTICS OF SYMBOLS

The distinction between signs and symbols is not always easy to make, and there are many borderline cases that are difficult to classify. Broadly speaking, signs occur naturally. For example, a person lost in a forest may interpret a column of smoke on the horizon as an indication of fire and possible human habitation. This is clearly a sign. If the fire has been built with the intent of producing smoke as a sign to another individual, it is a symbol. The symbolic character becomes clearer if we assume that *by prearrangement* the interpreter and producer of the fire have agreed that smoke of different qualities, shades, etc., have particular significations; they become a code which either party may utilize. The prearrangement may involve only two persons, or it may be implicit in the culture of a large number of individuals.

Symbols have three characteristics which have profound significance for their use in communication: (1) They are *produced* by human agents —there is no convincing evidence that subhuman animals produce and utilize symbols; (2) they have communicative significance only insofar as the communicators and communicatees have previously agreed on their meanings; (3) they are produced with intent to structure situations in which the parties have or are assumed to have a common interest.

It will be noted that these characteristics rule out many complex signs to which organisms react in nature. Bees, for example, as shown in the studies of von Frisch, on returning to a hive leave traces which serve as directions to other bees as to the location of pollen-bearing flowers. As Schneirla has shown, this process resembles symbol usage in human communication only superficially. Someone has shrewdly observed that the bees cannot lie. This points up the basic distinction between communication through the use of symbols and behavioral interchange among animals by means of signs. Symbols are manipulable (and therefore less reliable), are subject to intent, and may be used in a variety of contexts.

Symbols are central to the communicative process. In the context of communication, symbol meanings are public, not private, since their usage depends on a prearranged agreement between two or more persons. Those concerned may be said to constitute a communicative community. The whole question of precision is here involved. The degree of agreement as to the signification of symbols may be conceived as a continuum which extends from a theoretically perfect agreement to complete lack of agreement. In the second case, of course, there is no communication. Much time and ink is spent in our society in the endeavor to make symbol meanings completely unambiguous. In certain symbol communities—mathematics, for instance—a very high degree of precision may be achieved. Psychologically, however, a degree of ambiguity is implicit in all symbol usage. This is due to the fact that the cognitive-perceptual processes in two individuals are rarely, if ever, identical. Since the symbol content of communications is perceived, a degree of imprecision is practically inescapable. The signification of the storm warnings hoisted by the Coast Guard are relatively precise for the symbol community which is concerned, but even here they may be misperceived. Imprecision is not inherent in the symbolic material itself, but is a function of the degree to which the producer and the interpreter of the material share each others' perceptual-cognitive world.

This conception is basic to the formulations of George Mead. Communication by language or other significant symbols is part of a continuously changing social process. In using symbols each individual has to understand what he is saying; that is, he has to affect himself as he affects others. This contradicts the popular notion that meanings may be attached or detached from symbols at the will of the person who uses them. For Mead, there are no meanings or ideas that are not shared with other persons. The sharing is a behavior process that begins when individual A makes a gesture—for example, uses a word—to which he must incipiently react as he expects individual B to react. All meanings emerge from this social process and in no other way. Having acquired meanings and ideas—that is, significant symbols—through social interactions, the individual may use them "privately." That is, he may talk to himself or "think." But initially the significance of the symbols came through social intercourse.

All human thinking, imagining, persuading, moralizing—in fact, all activity involving symbols—is, from Mead's point of view, an unending conversation that men carry on with each other and with themselves. Burke makes an effective statement in regard to this when he discusses the origin of symbolic materials. Symbols, he says, appear in the

unending conversation that is going on at the point in history when we are born. Imagine you enter a room. You come late. Others have long preceded you, and they are engaged in a heated discussion, a discussion too heated for them to pause and tell you what it is about. . . . You listen for a while, until you decide you have caught the tenor of the argument, then you put in your oar. Some one answers; you answer him; another comes to your defense; another aligns himself against you . . . the discussion is interminable. The hour grows late, you must depart. And you do depart, with the discussion still vigorously in progress.

Some imaginary situations may clarify these relationships.

Situation I: A man and a little boy are walking on a road past an apple orchard. The boy sees the fruit, climbs over the fence, and attempts to pick an apple, but it is out of reach. He looks about, notices an empty box, drags it under a branch, climbs on it, and reaches the fruit which he picks and eats.

Situation II: A man and a little boy are walking on a road past an apple orchard. The boy points to the fruit and says he wants an apple. The man points to a sign on the fence which reads KEEP OUT. TRESPASSERS WILL BE PROSECUTED. The following conversation occurs:

BOY: What does the sign say?

MAN: It says to keep out or we may be arrested. Anyway, the apples don't belong to us.

BOY: But I'm hungry and I want one.

MAN: The farmer's house is up the road a bit; we'll stop and see if we can buy some.

They proceed up the road to the house and knock on the door. The farmer, accompanied by a barking dog on a leash, appears. The following conversation ensues:

MAN: I'd like to buy some of your apples.

FARMER: They're not for sale.

MAN: My little boy here is hungry, and I'd like to buy just a few.

FARMER: They're not for sale, or to give away. I haven't enough for my own use.

MAN: I don't want you to give them away; I only want one or two for the boy. Have a heart.

FARMER: I tell you they're not for sale, and I want you to get off the place. Boys have been stealing apples, and I've got a shotgun which I'm ready to use.

MAN: Now keep your shirt on, and don't get trigger-happy. You had better keep that vicious dog away from my boy.

As the farmer starts to close the door, the man sees a Masonic insignia on the farmer's coat.

MAN: I see you are a Mason. So am I.

FARMER: Why, yes, I am. I belong to the local lodge. (Ritualistic handclasp.)

MAN: Well, I must get along. Perhaps I can get something for my boy to eat in town. Nice looking dog you've got.

FARMER: Maybe I was a bit hasty. I always want to extend a helping hand to a brother Mason. Come around back to the house, and I'll see if I can't find some apples. That's a cute kid you've got. The dog's very friendly. His bark is worse than his bite.

MAN: Why, thanks. Jackie, you can pet the dog.

The most striking feature of Situation I is the direct and immediate character of the boy's response. He sees what he wants and how to get it with a minimum of delay. To be sure there are obstructions to be overcome—the fence has to be climbed, and the box must be utilized as a means of getting the fruit. These obstructions must be properly identified and appropriately reacted to. There is certainly "planning" of a sort, and there is utilization of past experience. The total situation is cognitively structured by the boy in such a manner that his experience is brought to bear, the obstacles overcome, and objects utilized as tools. In this, the boy may be said to have "mastered" the situation, and is prepared for action in it.

These are the strategies of direct action. The obstacles to achievement are physical rather than human. Nobody has to be persuaded, no permission has to be gained, no beliefs have to be modified, no loyalties won. Although there is planning, it is planning which requires no symbolic techniques. The techniques used are the techniques of direct aggression; in a sense, they are the techniques of violence.

In Situation II the boy confronts the same problem in the sense that there is fruit in sight and he wants it. But here the resemblance ends. The obstruction are of a different order, and their overcoming requires wholly different strategies. It is not simply a matter of seeing what one wants and getting it. Attitudes and motives must be assessed and changed, and loyalties explored and gained. Simple aggression will not solve the problem. Conflicting ideologies are involved, and the strategy of direct action will not suffice.

The first barrier is physical only in the sense that it is a painted piece of wood. It contains some odd black-on-white markings which have—from the point of view of a Man from Mars—an odd effect on the man and the boy. The man reads the sign and prevents the boy from responding to the apples in a direct manner. He interprets the sign for the boy in terms of assumed contingencies which are not objectively present and which bear no resemblance to the painted markings. The intents and purposes of persons not objectively present direct the behavior of those who are.

In the interchange between the man and the farmer, matters become even more complicated. Getting apples appears to involve "buying." It also involves threats and placation, the imputation of motives by each party to the other, and references to contingencies not visually present. All of this is accomplished by a complex interchange of vocal sounds and (probably) gestures, plus, of course, the actual presence of two people and the dog. Then, surprisingly (to the Man from Mars), the whole character of the situation suddenly changes. Wholly different motives are assumed to exist, the dog is no longer "vicious" but friendly, and the boy is no longer a potential thief, but is "cute." The nonpresent apples which could not be bought or obtained by cajolery, and access to which was barred by a nonpresent (and possibly nonexistent) shotgun, a "vicious" dog, and a threatening manner, suddenly become available. All of this occurs *without any change in the objective factors* in the situation, but because a hitherto unnoticed object (Masonic insignia) becomes central to the action. It is a truly remarkable effect which appears to emerge from an object which, considered as a physical stimulus, is extremely small.

Both Situation I and Situation II illustrate the structuring process. The man, the boy, and the farmer react to each other and to the objects in the environment selectively in terms of assumed meanings and potentialities. The assumptions made as the action progresses may or may not be correct. For example, the box which the boy utilized as a means of reaching the apple, might for some strange reason, have been anchored in a block of concrete, although the boy perceived it as a movable object possessing a certain weight. In this event, we may assume that he would have restructured the situation in some manner under the stress of need for the apple.

The striking difference between the two situations is the unique role played by symbolic techniques in Situation II. Here words, insignia, signs, and symbolic actions are utilized as devices in the structuring processes. They become, in fact, the central agency in organizing the relationships between individuals, and between the individual and his environment. Situation I was structured by the boy in a definite manner, but there was no use of symbols. This last statement may require some qualification, however. For the boy the use of symbols is "second nature," and he may have "talked to himself" in the process of mastering, that is, structuring, the situation. He could, perhaps, have "instructed" himself subvocally in solving the problem of getting at the apples by using the box. But we may assume that he could have solved the problem without the use of symbols since animals with no, or minimal, symbolic capacities solve similar problems in a similar manner.

In particular, it should be noted that the conversation between the man and the farmer employs words in combinations that would certainly puzzle the Man from Mars even if he understood the language. Such phrases as "keep your shirt on," "extend a helping hand," "his bark is worse than his bite" and "have a heart" signify something more than the literal meanings of the separate words. The essence of this more complex level of symbolic usage is, as Kenneth Burke points out (*Philosophy of Literary Form,* p. 503), the "seeing of something in terms of something else." Such a device is a metaphor. In perceiving that apparently unlike items—for example, keeping on one's shirt and keeping calm—have a psychological identity, we establish what Burke calls a new perspective. We thereby enlarge the meaning of some aspect of our surroundings.

HOW SYMBOLS FUNCTION

We may note that the symbols (words, insignia, etc.) as well as the symbolic act (symbolic handshake) in Situation II are used in a variety of ways. They are used in overcoming the obstructions which intervene between the boy and the apples and in structuring the shifting patterns of hostile-friendly relationships between the man and the farmer. These uses illustrate how symbols function in communication situations. These functions may be briefly summarized.

[1] They point to, or "place" in context by naming an object, person, act of attribute. The object or person is thus located; attention is directed towards it, and, in general, it becomes more easily manipulated. The boy is addressed as "Jackie," the dog is "vicious," etc. These symbols,

of course, may be used independently of and apart from their referents. Jackie not only may be spoken *to* (by name) but spoken *about*.

[2] They generalize the referent by placing it in a category of objects or acts towards which one has an attitude, and towards which one may be expected to adopt a course of action. In Situation II, the boy's intent to pick an apple is placed in the category of illegal actions by the words on the sign. The dog is successively referred to as "vicious" and "friendly," both of which categorize the animal and suggest appropriate actions.

[3] They have referents beyond themselves for which they stand as surrogates. The symbol may be responded to in the same manner as that for which it stands. Apples, for example, may be responded to as objects to be picked and eaten; they also may be talked about. In Situation I, the apples are constantly present in the field. In Situation II, they are symbolically present.

[4] They express affectively toned attitudes towards situations, actions, or objects. The question whether symbols are ever wholly neutral is perhaps debatable. Kenneth Burke discusses this problem and makes the distinction between poetic and semantic meaning (*Philosophy of Literary Form,* p. 138ff.). "The semantic ideal would attempt to *get a description* by the *elimination* of attitude (p. 147)." Concerning the attainment of this "ideal" Burke expresses considerable doubt. "The best thing to be said in favor of the semantic ideal is that it is a fraud: one may believe in it because it is impossible (p. 159)." All language is inherently poetic (in Burke's sense) because it steers action, and action is never neutral. This is its orienting function. The farmer's hostile attitude is indicated by reference to a nonpresent shotgun, and the man's orientation by the debunking metaphor, "trigger-happy." It appears that symbolic devices have a special potency for establishing a framework for action. Friendly or unfriendly aspects are identified, and a course of action implied which may or may not take place. Its direction at least is indicated. The farmer *threatened* action. The man *planned* (symbolically) to buy apples from the farmer. The ritual shaking of hands was a symbolic action which, so to speak, set the stage for a new orientation of the relationships between the farmer and the man. On the other hand, the action may be specifically *directed*. The words on the sign instructed trespassers to keep out of the orchard.

[5] Symbolic techniques enable individuals to share experience; that is, to participate in each other's attitudes and motives, and to understand each other's intents and meanings. The Masonic insignia restructured the situation so that the farmer and the man could vicariously share each other's experiences and motives. They were enabled to enter into each other's past experiences. We may assume that each individual reacted to

the insignia in the same manner as he intended the other person to react. This is Mead's "significant symbol." It has the unique characteristic of eliciting responses in the user which are the same as those elicited in "the other."

These, then, are some of the important characteristics of symbolic devices. Actually, of course, we are dealing with an enormously complex process that has many aspects. The number of uses to which these processes are put by man in the business of living is without limit. Any summary statement can only indicate in a general way their functions in human societies. But we may say with assurance that the use of symbolic processes enables man to select, identify, and manipulate aspects of a situation, generalize about it, express attitudes toward it, relate it to other situations in the past and in the future, direct his own and the actions of others in it, and evoke in himself and others similar attitudes and tendencies to action.

SELECTED PUBLICATIONS BY DR. FEARING

"Psychology and the Films," *Hollywood Quarterly*, vol. 2, 1947, pp. 118–121.

"Some Sources of Confusion," *Journal of Social Issues*, vol. 3, 1947, pp. 2–7.

"Summary: (Mass Media: Content, Function and Measurement)," *Journal of Social Issues*, vol. 3, 1947, pp. 58–60.

"Influence of the Movies on Attitudes and Behavior," *Annals of The American Academy of Political and Social Science*, vol. 254, 1947, pp. 70–80.

"The Effects of Radio and Motion Pictures on Children's Behavior," in *Redirecting the Delinquent*, 1947 *Yearbook*, National Probation and Parole Association, pp. 78–93.

"Motion Pictures as a Medium of Instruction and Communication: An Experimental Analysis of the Effects of Two Films," *University of California Publications in Culture and Society*, vol. 2, no. 3, 1950, pp. 101–202.

"The Structure of Opinion: A 'Loyalty Oath' poll," *Public Opinion Quarterly*, vol. 14, 1950–51, pp. 729–743. (With D. Wilner.)

"A Selected and Annotated Bibliography in Communications Research," *Quarterly of Film, Radio and TV*, vol. 6, 1952, pp. 283–315. (With Genevieve Rogge.)

"Toward a Psychological Theory of Human Communication," *Journal of Personality*, vol. 22, 1953, pp. 71–88.

"Social Impact of the Mass Media of Communication," in *Mass Media and Education, The Fifty-third Yearbook of the National Society for the Study of Education, Part II*, 1954, pp. 165–191.

"An Examination of the Conceptions of Benjamin Whorf in the Light of Theories of Perception and Cognition," in Harry Hoijer (ed.) *Language in Culture* (U. of Chicago, 1954), pp. 47–81.

QUESTIONS

1. For what reasons does Fearing emphasize that "human communication" cannot be understood in terms of simple engineering or mechanical analogies? Do you agree or disagree with his major premise? Why?

2. "In communicating, I make public something that has hitherto been private," writes Fearing. In what kinds of communications situations and by what means might a person unwittingly communicate to another something he wants to keep private? Does a poet who employs a highly personalized set of private symbols "communicate" in the sense that Fearing means?

3. Distinguish between "physiognomic" and "geometric technical" perception. Why can the physiognomic mode never truly be eliminated from any concept of language behavior in human communication?

4. Keeping in mind the several aspects of Dr. Fearing's paper, would you say it is easier for an Eskimo to communicate with members of his group than for a person living in the United States to effectively communicate with someone else from his city? Is it easier for a member of a rural community in Arkansas to communicate with a neighbor than for a New Yorker to communicate with another Manhattanite? Why?

5. Why does Fearing stress the importance of Arnheim's statement: "It is the function of the metaphor to make the reader penetrate the concrete shell of the world of things by combinations of objects that have little in common but the underlying pattern"?

W. Phillips Davison

On the Effects of Communication [*]

THE FOLLOWING ESSAY by Dr. W. Phillips Davison brings into sharp focus a number of the concepts that are presented in the selections by Wright and Fearing. As the author justifiably points out, although our knowledge of communications effects has increased steadily in the last two decades, it is often difficult to relate some findings of the researchers to those of others, and even more difficult to relate "communications research" per se to the larger body of knowledge about human behavior.

Davison's purpose in this article is to show how communications serve as a link between individuals and their environments. In turn, this suggests to him that the effects of mass communications should be viewed in terms of the role they play in enabling people to bring about more satisfying relationships between themselves and their environments.

In a more detailed manner than either Wright or Fearing, Davison examines the role of attitudes as guides to action. By understanding the habits, stereotypes, attitudes, maxims, generalizations, and facts that human beings accumulate in the course of their experience we can begin to analyze why people have "opinions."

Davison suggests one important caveat about studying the effects of communications, which should be carefully heeded by all students. Although he has cited the "experimental" research of Hovland, Janis, and Kelley at Yale as important for our understanding of the effects of communication, Davison has reservations about communication research conducted in the classroom or laboratory, because, he points out, the effects of communications on the subjects do not go beyond the classroom or "experimental" situation. The subjects are not ordinarily rewarded for maintaining a consistent opinion, nor are they penalized for changing their opinions, as is frequently the case in the world outside the classroom. This is a problem which is not restricted to communication research alone, but rather applies to much of the experimental research of psychologists and other

* Reprinted from the *Public Opinion Quarterly* (1960), pp. 344–360, by permission of the author and the publisher.

behavioral scientists. Davison's point is well taken and bears our closest scrutiny.

It is his view that the communicator can influence attitudes or behavior only when he is able to convey information that may be utilized by members of his audience to satisfy their wants or needs. This is one reason why mass communicators find themselves in a different position when they try to effect persuasion outside their own group than when they are communicating directly to a group of which they are members and in which they have some control. For, mass communicators generally, do not control aspects of the environment that are significant to their audiences. Of course, in a totalitarian situation such as the Third Reich in Germany, Goebbels' high status in party affairs gave him about as much power as any mass communicator has ever possessed.

Davison emphasizes one further point that strikes us as most valuable, namely, that the audience of the communicator should not be considered a "passive recipient," "a lump of clay" to be molded by some master persuader. As he puts it, "Audiences, too, can drive a hard bargain."   D.M.W.

MR. DAVISON is currently Senior Research Fellow at the Council on Foreign Relations. He has been editor of Public Opinion Quarterly, and has written numerous articles in the field of public opinion and communications.

Quantitative studies conducted in recent years, many of them laboratory experiments, have made it possible to formulate an impressive number of propositions about the effects of communication. Progress has also been made in collecting and systematizing these propositions, and in putting them to work in education, public relations, advertising, and other fields.[1] The qualitative literature on the effects of communication has been less well explored. Much of it still lies unrecognized in historical treatises, biographies, and the writings of reporters in all eras. Attempts to systematize or derive propositions from the relatively small segment of qualita-

1. One of the most comprehensive summaries is the chapter by Carl I. Hovland, "Effects of the Mass Media of Communication," in Gardner Lindzey (ed.), *Handbook of Social Psychology* (Addison-Wesley, Cambridge, Mass., 1954). Literature summarizing a greater or lesser portion of what is known about the effects of communication and applying this knowledge to a variety of problem areas is now so voluminous that only a few examples can be given: Erik Barnouw, *Mass Communications* (Holt, New York, 1956); W. L. Brembeck and W. S. Howell, *Persuasion—A Means of Social Control* (Prentice-Hall, Englewood Cliffs, N.J., 1952); Rex F. Harlow, *Social Science in Public Relations* (Harper, New York, 1957); *Mass Communication and Education,* National Education Association, Educational Policies Commission, 1958.

tive experience that has been sifted have been made largely in the literature of rhetoric, political communication, and psychological warfare.[2]

While knowledge about communication effects has increased steadily, although unevenly, many of the insights gained have tended to remain discrete. It has proved difficult to relate propositions to each other, and to the larger body of knowledge about human behavior. Some of the effects produced by communication have been identified and found to be associated with certain characteristics of the audiences being studied, but it has less often been possible to specify why these relationships rather than other ones have existed. Nevertheless, several major steps in the direction of linking the accumulated knowledge about communication effects more closely to social and psychological theory have been taken recently by Festinger; Hovland, Janis, and Kelley; Katz and Lazarsfeld; and others.[3] The most comprehensive proposal for a theoretical structure—at least in the case of mass communication—has been made by Klapper, who accounts for many of the observed variations in response to identical communication stimuli by the role played by certain mediating factors, such as audience predispositions, group affiliation, and opinion leadership.[4]

The purpose of this article is to suggest another method of interpreting the existing body of knowledge about the effects of communication. According to this mode of interpretation, communications serve as a link between man and his environment, and their effects may be explained in terms of the role they play in enabling people to bring about more satisfying relationships between themselves and the world around them.

In order to introduce this approach to the study of communication effects it will be necessary to restate briefly some familiar, even though

2. Aristotle's *Rhetoric* is still a widely used text in courses on public opinion and communication. A brief summary of experience in psychological warfare is presented by John W. Riley, Jr., and Leonard S. Cottrell, Jr., in "Research for Psychological Warfare," *Public Opinion Quarterly*, vol. 21, 1957, pp. 147–158. The principal anthologies on political communication and psychological warfare also include collections of qualitative as well as quantitative data on effect: William E. Daugherty and Morris Janowitz, *A Psychological Warfare Casebook* (Johns Hopkins Press, Baltimore, 1958); Daniel Lerner, *Propaganda in War and Crisis*, New York, Stewart, 1951; Wilbur Schramm, *The Process and Effects of Mass Communication* (U. of Illinois Press, Urbana, Ill., 1954).

3. Leon Festinger, *A Theory of Cognitive Dissonance* (Harper, New York, 1957); Carl I. Hovland, Irving L. Janis, and Harold H. Kelley, *Communications and Persuasion: Psychological Studies of Opinion Change* (Yale U. Press, New Haven, 1953); Elihu Katz and Paul F. Lazarsfeld, *Personal Influence: The Part Played by People in the Flow of Mass Communication* (Free Press, New York, 1955).

4. Joseph T. Klapper, "What We Know about the Effects of Mass Communication: The Brink of Hope," *Public Opinion Quarterly*, vol. 21, 1957, pp. 453–474.

not uncontroversial, assumptions about the needs of man and the ways these needs are satisfied.

BEHAVIORAL "EFFECTS" AND THEIR CAUSES

Our first assumption is that all human actions and reactions, including changes in attitude and knowledge, are in some way directed toward the satisfaction of wants or needs. That is, whatever we do is in response to some conscious or subconscious requirement or purpose. This is not to say that the action in question is always the most appropriate one, or that actions taken to satisfy one need may not work against the satisfaction of another. Nevertheless, it can be maintained that all actions can be traced to needs, that these in turn can be related to more generalized needs, and so on.[5]

There have been many attempts to draw up lists of basic human needs and wants. The physical requirements for human existence—food, clothing, and shelter—are fairly well agreed upon. Lists of other desiderata that people pursue vary widely in their degree of generality and in their terminology, but there is a heavy degree of overlapping when it comes to values such as power, security, love, and respect. Cooley, for instance, captured in a few words several of the most widespread forces motivating human action when he wrote: "Always and everywhere men seek honor and dread ridicule, defer to public opinion, cherish their goods and their children, and admire courage, generosity, and success." [6] Lasswell lists eight goals which he finds pursued in nearly all cultures, although some are emphasized more in one culture than in another: power, respect, affection, rectitude, well-being, wealth, enlightenment, and skill.[7] Festinger suggests that the existence of inharmonious attitudes or conflicting

5. The definition of needs or motives can, of course, easily be reduced to absurdity if one attempts to achieve extremes either of generality or of specificity. At one extreme, all actions can be explained as efforts to relieve some type of tension, or as ultimately traceable to one single "drive"; at the other extreme, the explanation refers only to the immediate object of the action: e.g., the reason I buy a magazine is because I want a magazine. Intermediate levels of description, at which categories of specific actions can be related to more generalized needs, seem to be the most fruitful for purposes of social inquiry. (Cf. Gardner Murphy, "Social Motivation," in Lindzey, op. cit., p. 608.)

6. Charles Horton Cooley, Social Organization (Free Press, New York, 1956), p. 28.

7. Harold D. Lasswell, Power and Personality, New York, Norton, 1948; also Lasswell and Abraham Kaplan, Power and Society (Yale U. Press, New Haven, 1950), especially pp. 55–58.

elements of knowledge within an individual (a state that he labels "dissonance") produces a striving for consistency on the part of that individual, and that dissonance is thus a motivating factor in its own right.[8] A large number of lists and observations concerning human wants and needs could be cited. Indeed, consideration of the forces motivating human action and (to view the other side of the coin) the qualities that people pursue has always been one of the most persistent interests of those who have studied man's behavior. These forces and qualities vary from individual to individual and from culture to culture, but nearly all students agree that they can be identified—at least on a descriptive level— and that they are useful in explaining human actions.

Our second basic assumption is that man's wants and needs are dependent for their satisfaction on his environment. Some requirements can be satisfied from within the individual in the first instance—for example, some tensions can be relieved by yawning or stretching—but our self-sufficiency is exhausted when we must satisfy the more fundamental desires of which these tensions are an expression. Most of our needs or wants can be satisfied only if we are able to manipulate parts of the world outside ourselves, or to adjust in some way to this environment. In the case of requirements for food or clothing the sources of satisfaction are in our physical environment; needs for affection, esteem, or even self-respect, can ordinarily be satisfied only by other people. Our desires for some other goals, such as security and power, can be met in part from our material and in part from our social surroundings. Actions thus occur when we attempt to satisfy needs by manipulating or adjusting to certain aspects of the environment.[9]

Just as it is possible to subdivide needs or motives almost infinitely, if one should wish to engage in this exercise, the content of the environment could be arranged and rearranged in an impressive number of categories. For our purposes, however, it may be most useful to mention four aspects of the environment, as it is experienced by human beings: the physical, the social, the expected, and the imagined. Some may object that the latter two categories are of a different order from the first two (and overlap the first two because expectations and imagery include content from the real environment). This objection can be conceded or it can

8. Festinger, *op. cit.*

9. Kornhauser and Lazarsfeld observe, in another context, that any action is determined on the one hand by the total make-up of the individual and on the other by the total situation in which he finds himself. Explanations must refer both to the objective and the subjective. See Arthur Kornhauser and Paul F. Lazarsfeld, "The Analysis of Consumer Actions," in Paul F. Lazarsfeld and Morris Rosenberg, *The Language of Social Research* (Free Press, New York, 1955), p. 393.

be disputed; a decision either way makes no difference to the argument that follows.

Different kinds of people depend on each of these different aspects of the environment for the satisfaction of their needs to varying degrees. The farmer's requirements are filled to a larger degree from the physical realm than, say, those of the entertainer, who is as dependent for success on the approval of other people as the farmer is on the weather. The young student may live largely in the world of the future, the mystic in the realm of the supernatural. To some degree, all of us orient our activities toward environmental circumstances in all four categories.

The trend of recent research has been to stress increasingly the importance of the social environment for most people. Satisfaction of physical needs often turns out to be largely a means to the end of achieving a relationship with the social environment that will satisfy other needs. From Veblen to the motivation researchers, students have emphasized that in the process of obtaining food, clothing, and air-conditioned shelter we usually are attempting to bolster our status in the community or elicit approval from the neighbors, or are in some other way orienting our actions toward the social environment. The willingness of human beings to bind their feet, wear corsets, or observe stringent diets, where norms or customs provide that such behavior will be socially rewarded, seems once again to underline the importance of adjustment to the social environment at the expense of the physical.

Our third assumption is that human attention is highly selective.[10] From birth, people learn that satisfaction of their needs is dependent more on certain aspects of their environment than on other aspects. They therefore focus their attention on these aspects. As wants and needs become more complicated the important aspects of the environment become more numerous, but in view of the almost infinite complexity of the world the selective principle remains and becomes even more rigid. We don't often examine the pattern on the wallpaper, listen to the ticking of the clock, or notice what color socks one of our colleagues is wearing, because we don't need this information.[11]

10. William James refers to this "narrowness of consciousness" as one of the most extraordinary facts of our life. "Although we are besieged at every moment by impressions from our whole sensory surface, we notice so very small a part of them." *Psychology—Briefer Course* (Holt, New York, 1892).

11. A familiar classroom illustration of the selectivity of perception is for the instructor, half-way through the period, to cover his necktie with a large handkerchief and then ask the students what color the tie is. Ordinarily, fewer than half the students will be able to name the color correctly. This is, of course, as it should be, since there is usually no reason why they should pay attention to the color.

In view of the importance of the social environment for the satisfaction of most people's needs, we would expect that this would occupy a heavy share of their attention and be involved in a large proportion of their actions. This seems to be the case, although reliable information about the quantitative division of attention is difficult to obtain. Nevertheless, indirect evidence is afforded by such indices as the prominence of the social environment in informal conversations and in the content of people's worries and problems.[12]

ATTITUDES AS GUIDES TO ACTION

A fourth assumption is that people gradually accumulate and carry around with them a substantial quantity of information about those aspects of the environment that are important to them. This information, in the form of habits, stereotypes, attitudes, maxims, generalizations, and facts, has been accumulated in the course of their experience. In the past it has helped them to satisfy some of their needs, or they may think that it will be useful in the future. With the aid of these stored impressions people are able to decide easily and quickly what actions are appropriate in most of the situations in which they find themselves.[13]

The existence of the various aspects of this internal picture of the world has often been noted. Habits take us up and down stairs in our own houses, guide us to our offices in the morning, and do much of the work of driving our cars, leaving our consciousness free for other things. Stereotypes, as Walter Lippmann has pointed out, are also useful in reducing the burden on our capacities of perception: "For the attempt to see all things freshly and in detail, rather than as types and generalities, is exhausting. . . ." [14] Lippmann refers to these images as "pictures in our heads." Cantril mentions the "assumptive form world" that we build up on the basis of past experience. Festinger sees the body of our attitudes and beliefs as constituting a fairly accurate mirror or map of reality.[15]

An attitude is particularly important as a labor-saving device, since it

12. *Cf.* Samuel A. Stouffer, *Communism, Conformity, and Civil Liberties* (Doubleday, New York, 1955), especially pp. 58–71; also Jeanne Watson, Warren Breed, and Harry Posman, "A Study in Urban Conversation: Sample of 1001 Remarks Overheard in Manhattan," *Journal of Social Psychology*, vol. 28, 1948, pp. 121–133.

13. *Cf.* Hadley Cantril, *The "Why" of Man's Experience* (Macmillan, New York, 1950), pp. 66, 77.

14. Walter Lippmann, *Public Opinion* (Penguin, Baltimore, 1946), p. 66.

15. Cantril, *op. cit.*, pp. 103–104; Festinger, *op. cit.*, p. 10. An application of Cantril's approach in a study of policy makers in seven countries has been made recently by Lloyd A. Free, *Six Allies and a Neutral* (Free Press, New York, 1959).

usually provides some key to the behavior that is appropriate when we encounter the subject of the attitude or when it comes up in conversation.[16] If we regard another person as "a good man" or "a bad man" this gives us some crude but useful guidance as to how we should act toward him. Likes and dislikes regarding food provide an even more obvious guide to behavior. Very frequently, attitudes have little relevance to action toward the object of the attitude itself, but instead provide a key to the proper behavior in a given social group. Thus people may be for or against a given foreign country (or baseball team) because this is the attitude one should display in the group in which they move, although they have little idea of what the country (or team) in question is actually like.

When attitudes, stereotypes, and the other forms of information that we have internalized are based on little experience and serve a minor need they tend to be lightly held and easily changed. When they are based on extensive experience and and/or serve a deeply felt need, it is difficult to affect them. But if a person's needs change, or if his environment is altered, then he usually has to abandon at least some of his stored-up information, since this leads him to follow lines of action that are inefficient in gaining for him a satisfactory adjustment to his environment.[17]

Changing one's attitudes, stereotypes, and so on, is additionally complicated by the necessity of maintaining as much consistency as possible within this body of internalized information. If two stored-up cognitions indicate two inconsistent courses of action the resulting conflict may be painful. A not excessively painful conflict can be observed in the case of the man in the coffee advertisement, who snaps: "I love coffee, but it keeps me awake." He "snaps" because of the discomfort caused by the inconsistency between his attitude and his experience. Fortunately, his problem can be solved by drinking caffeine-free coffee. The position of the man who is persuaded of the virtues of Presidential Candidate A,

16. M. Brewster Smith, in connection with an intensive study of opinions toward Soviet Russia, found one function of attitude to be that of providing a person with an evaluation of the salient aspects of his world. "The greater the extent to which this evaluation takes account of the important harms and benefits that he may expect from his surroundings, the more adequately will it serve his adjustment in the longest run." (*Functional and Descriptive Analysis of Public Opinion,* Harvard University, 1947, pp. 34ff.) Unpublished doctoral dissertation.

17. In his autobiography, Benjamin Franklin reports that at one time he was a vegetarian and considered the taking of fish a kind of unprovoked murder. On a voyage from Boston to Philadelphia, however, his ship became becalmed off Block Island and the crew diverted themselves by catching cod. When the fish came out of the frying pan, they smelled "admirably well." "I balanced some time between principle and inclination till I recollected that when the fish were opened, I saw smaller fish taken out of their stomachs. 'Then,' thought I, 'if you eat one another, I don't see why we mayn't eat you.' So I dined upon cod very heartily. . . ."

while his family and friends continue to admire Candidate B, is likely to be more difficult. One set of attitudes leads him to support his candidate in conversations; another set impels him either to recognize that Candidate B has some virtues or to remain silent. Recent voting studies have found that persons subject to these "cross-pressures" are most likely to shift their opinions during a campaign.[18] Changing one important attitude, stereotype, or piece of information may necessitate an exhausting process of adjustment in other cognitions and even patterns of action. Most people would like to avoid this and therefore make important changes only when forced to do so.[19]

COMMUNICATION AS A LINK
TO THE ENVIRONMENT

Habits, attitudes, and an accumulated stock of knowledge about those aspects of the environment that concern us most go a long way toward shaping our actions, but this stored-up information must be supplemented by a flow of current data about the world around us. The more complicated our needs and the more shifting the environment, the greater our requirements for current information become.

We need this current information for several different reasons. Some of it tells us about changes in the physical or social environment that may require an immediate adjustment in our behavior (a colleague is annoyed; our house is on fire). Other incoming information is stored in one form or another as of possible utility in the expected environment (Main Street is going to be turned into a four-lane highway; a vacation always costs more than you expect). It is probable, however, that a large proportion of our current informational intake primarily serves the purpose of reassuring us that our existing action patterns, attitudes, stereotypes, and so on, are indeed correct—i.e., that they are likely to satisfy our wants and needs.

Most of this information can be acquired by direct observation or personal conversation. The immediate physical surroundings are subject to our scrutiny. In the family, in the neighborhood, and on the job we learn about the most important things by observing, by talking to people, or by overhearing others talk among themselves. But there is still some important information that cannot be acquired at first hand. If a person enters employment in any skilled capacity, if he takes his citizenship

18. Bernard Berelson, Paul F. Lazarsfeld, and William M. McPhee, *Voting* (U. of Chicago, 1954).

19. *Cf.* Smith, *op. cit.:* "Since his attitudes are inextricably involved in his psychological economy, . . . [a person] cannot alter them without at the same time carrying out more or less complicated readjustments" (pp. 37–38).

seriously, or if he seeks to broaden his knowledge in almost any sphere, he tends to pay at least some attention to the media of mass communication. This attention to the mass media does not necessarily diminish his participation in personal conversation; on the contrary, it may give him more to talk about.[20]

Our attention to the mass media, as to other aspects of the world around us, is highly selective. We scan the newspaper headlines and select a few stories to sample further or even to read in full. We can expose ourselves to only a very small proportion of the available radio fare, and when it comes to magazines and books our attention must be selective in the extreme.

All the information that we are exposed to through personal experience or the mass media can be divided into three categories according to our behavior toward it: some we seek out eagerly; some we attend to on the chance that it may prove useful; some we attempt to exclude because we have reason to believe that it would make satisfaction of our wants and needs more difficult.[21]

In this formidable task of sorting incoming information we are assisted by habits and attitudes, many of them culturally defined, just as habits and attitudes assist us in other aspects of our behavior. On the basis of past experience (either our own or that of others that has been handed on to us) we believe that useful facts are most likely to come from a particular person or group, or are to be found in a given newspaper, in certain radio programs, or in other specified information sources. Conversely, we know, or sense, that there are some sources of information that are likely to make it more difficult for us to satisfy our requirements, and we make strenuous efforts to avoid exposure to these. Students have often noted the tendency

20. At least, this is the case with opinion leaders in many fields, who typically belong to more organizations, have more social contacts, and in general are more gregarious than others. They also are likely to follow the mass media appropriate to their sphere of interest. *Cf.* Elihu Katz, "The Two-step Flow of Communication," *Public Opinion Quarterly,* vol. 21, 1957, pp. 61–78.

21. Principal mechanisms of exclusion appear to be nonperception (the small boy simply doesn't hear his mother tell him to keep his hands out of the cookie jar); distortion (we note that crime in our town is due mainly to visitors from outside); and, most commonly, forgetting (many people have trouble remembering how little money is left in their checking accounts). All these exclusion mechanisms have been described in connection with systematic studies: e.g., Frederic C. Barlett, *Remembering* (Cambridge U. P., New York, 1932); Gordon W. Allport and Leo J. Postman, *The Psychology of Rumor* (Holt, New York, 1947); Eunice Cooper and Marie Jahoda, "The Evasion of Propaganda," *Journal of Psychology,* vol. 23, 1947, pp. 15–25. Distortion is, however, not only a mechanism for excluding information. It can also be used to make some information more useful or more comprehensible.

of the listener to turn off his radio when a speaker of a political party he opposes comes on the air.

A related category of devices that help us select for attention those communications that are likely to contain useful information might be called "indicators." We learn that (at least in some newspapers) the more important news is likely to be given larger headlines than the less important news. Certain tones of voice indicate urgency; others indicate sincerity. Some colors and symbols signify danger. These and many other indicators help us to give our attention to communications that are likely to be important to us, although we not infrequently find that a widely accepted indicator has been used by someone who wants to direct our attention to a message of very little importance to us.

By these and other sorting processes, we try to obtain useful information from the stream of communications. For most of us, information about our personal social environment, or information that we can use in this social environment, is important, and we give particular attention to learning about anything that may affect our relationship to those with whom we live and work. Most of us are particularly interested in knowing what other people think about us and what they think about each other. We also like to have information about those aspects of the physical environment that affect our needs, or are likely to affect them, and information that may be professionally useful, but for most of us these categories, although important, are in the second rank.

In connection with the relative attention given "personally useful" as opposed to "professionally useful" information, a small experiment conducted by the author may prove suggestive. Forty-nine government officials concerned with foreign affairs, most of them with about fifteen years' experience in this area of activity, were exposed for twenty seconds to a poster showing ten greatly enlarged newspaper headlines, and were asked to read these headlines over to themselves. No reason for the request was given. Immediately afterward, they were asked to write down as many of the headlines, or approximations of the headlines, as they could remember.[22]

The original hypothesis behind this experiment was that the officials would be most likely to remember those headlines that referred to matters with which they had been professionally concerned. This was not the case. The headline that was remembered most often was a dramatic one of a type that would be likely to provide conversational material. The next two

22. The forty-nine responses were obtained from several smaller groups. This made it possible to vary the order in which the headlines were presented. With minor exceptions, the rank order of the headlines in each subgroup remained the same.

apparently had to do with personal interests of many of the respondents. Next came matters of professional interest, and at the bottom came matters that apparently were of little personal or professional interest to most of the men. These results are shown in Table 1.

Table 1—Frequency with Which Headlines Were Recalled by Forty-nine Officials Concerned with Foreign Affairs

Headline	Number of Mentions
Fallen Jet Is Hit by Train on Coast	29
LSU Rated No. 1 in Football Polls	28
Stock Offerings Rose Last Month	25
UN to Withdraw Group in Lebanon	23
Tunisia Will Buy Arms from Reds	16
Easing of Tension over Berlin Seen	13
Soviet Asks Curb on Atomic Planes	7
Railroads Yield on Tax in Jersey	7
Transport Unity Urged as U.S. Need	7
West Tries to End Nuclear Impasse	5
	160

To summarize our thesis thus far, it may be said that communications provide a link between the individual and the world outside himself. But they do not link him with all aspects of his environment; this would be impossible in view of the limited capacity of the single human being for attention and action. Instead, each person must somehow select for attention those communications that deal with aspects of the environment that are most likely to affect his needs.[23] In this selection process he is aided by habits and attitudes, as well as by his ability to choose consciously. If it were possible to judge objectively whether a person's selection of environmental aspects about which to inform himself was "good" or "bad" from the point of view of satisfying his basic needs, it would probably be concluded that most people choose fairly well but that there is always room for improvement.

23. The same communications may be used in various ways to satisfy different needs. On the basis of a study of children's attention to comics and TV programs, the Rileys observed that "the same media materials appeared to be interpreted and used differently by children in different social positions." The principle of selectivity was also illustrated by this study. Peer group members, for example, appeared to select materials from the media which would in some way be immediately useful for group living. (Matilda White Riley and John W. Riley, Jr., "A Sociological Approach to Communications Research," *Public Opinion Quarterly,* vol. 15, 1951, p. 456.) Similar observations were made by Merton in his study of Kate Smith's marathon drive to sell war bonds by radio. Listeners who perceived the same aspects of the broadcast sometimes "used" this information in different ways. In other cases people's attention to different aspects of the performance could be related to their psychological requirements. See Robert K. Merton, *Mass Persuasion* (Harper, New York, 1946).

The fact that we tend to perceive and remember things that are important to us is neither startling nor novel. It underlies many psychological tests and its implications have been taken into account by social workers, students of public opinion interviewing, and psychotherapists. It is also taken into account, although not always consciously formulated, by practical politicians, teachers, and many others.[24] The reason for going over this familiar ground here is that, in the opinion of the author, it provides a useful link in the chain of relationships between communication and action.

COMMUNICATIONS AND BEHAVIOR

It has been maintained above that the explanation of most human actions, at least those of interest to the social scientist, should be sought in people's efforts to establish a relationship with their environment that is likely to satisfy their needs. According to this way of thinking, a communication cannot properly be said to produce behavioral effects itself, since it merely serves to link the individual to some aspect of his environment, thus enabling him to react to it or manipulate it.

One might express the environment-communication-action relationship in its simplest terms as follows: a given situation exists in the environment; this situation is reported by a communication that comes to the attention of the individual; the individual then adjusts his behavior in a manner calculated to help satisfy some want or need. Or, to translate this formula into experiential terms, we come into our house alone on a dark night; we hear a voice growl "stick 'em up—I gotya covered"; we probably then do as advised or else try to escape. In taking this action we are reacting not directly to the communication but to the situation we think exists in the environment—i.e., a burglar with a gun. If we know that our eight-year-old son is home or that someone has left the television on, we will respond to an identical communication in a different manner.

Communications can lead to adjustive behavior in those exposed to them in at least three ways. First, they can report an actual or expected change in the environment, or a previously unknown fact about the environment, that is important to the person at the receiving end of the communication: a death in the family, the poor financial condition of a local bank, or the fact that a favorite clothing store will start its annual sale next Wednesday.

24. The politician who mingles with the crowd, looking friendly and receptive but saying little, "just to see what people have on their minds," is practicing somewhat the same technique as the nondirective interviewer or the psychologist who administers a projective test.

Tactical psychological warfare communications during World War II were often of this type. They attempted to influence the behavior of enemy personnel by telling them about developments (or developments to be anticipated) in the military situation: "You have been cut off"; "The units defending your flank have already surrendered"; "Stay away from rail junctions—they will all be bombed." Application of this principle in advertising is even more familiar: "Now for the first time you can buy Product A with a leather carrying case"; "Hurry and order your copy of Book B before the limited edition is exhausted."

A second way that communications can lead to behavioral adjustments is by pointing out an existing feature of the environment (not a change or a completely new fact) and reminding the individual that his needs would be served if he adjusted his behavior in a given manner. Much of the strategic propaganda in World War II was of this type: Axis personnel were told again and again about the overwhelming economic superiority of the Allied powers, and were advised to surrender to avoid senseless destruction. Allied audiences, for their part, were reminded of the great victories that the Axis forces had already achieved, and were urged to give up—also to avoid further destruction. In some cases, these communications may have contained information that was new to recipients of the propaganda, but in most instances leaflets or broadcasts served merely to remind people of facts they knew already and of needs they had already experienced. Similarly, many consumer items have been used for a long time in substantially the same form, but this does not deter advertisers from calling attention to the virtues of these products and trying to persuade people that it is to their advantage to buy them.

Communications that serve as reminders—either about conditions in the environment or about needs—have been observed to lead to substantial behavioral responses. Election studies have shown that those who lean toward a particular political party are more likely to get out and vote if they are exposed to this party's propaganda. Reminders may also strengthen existing attitudes by providing information that is in accord with them. These phenomena of activation and reinforcement were observed, for instance, in the election study of Lazarsfeld, Berelson, and Gaudet in Erie County, Ohio.[25] They are also likely to come into play on any hot day when we see a sign showing a picture of an ice-cold beverage and telling us where it may be obtained.

The third way in which communications may cause a behavioral adjustment is by bringing to a person's attention a new way of patterning his relationships to the environment. Those who have experienced a religious

25. Paul F. Lazarsfeld, Bernard Berelson, and Hazel Gaudet, *The People's Choice* (Columbia U. P., New York, 1948).

conversion or adopted a new philosophy may see the same environment about them, but they interpret it differently. Their basic needs may not have changed, but they find that a new pattern of behavior will serve these needs better than the pattern they had followed previously, or the relative emphasis they place on different values may have changed. A similar reorganization of behavior is sometimes brought about by education. Such organizing principles do not, of course, have to be presented *in toto* by specific communications; they sometimes are worked out by the individual on the basis of exposure to many diverse communications.

In all three cases, assuming that the information in question is perceived as "useful," immediate behavioral adjustments may take place, or (when immediate action is not appropriate) the information contained in the communications may be stored in the form of attitudes or remembered facts to guide future behavior.

In some respects, a communication is thus analogous to a conductor of electricity, whose characteristics influence the work done by the electricity only insofar as the conductor is a good or a poor one. The "conductivity" of a communication seems to be influenced primarily by two factors: whether or not it is clearly organized, uses the language best understood by the audience, etc.; and whether or not it is set off by the proper "indicators" and takes advantage of the communication habits of the audience.

Most research results on the effects of communication can be translated into these terms, although it is usually necessary to supplement the reported data with unsupported assumptions and untested inferences in order to trace the steps of the hypothesized process. For instance, a recent study sponsored by the United States Information Agency in Greece found that those Greeks who were favorably predisposed toward the United States were more likely than those who were not so predisposed to notice and remember a series of United States–sponsored newspaper advertisements.[26] Furthermore, the advertisements, which dealt with basic human rights supported by both Americans and Greeks, appeared to have the effect of strengthening the pro-American attitudes of those who held such attitudes already.

To interpret these observations in accordance with the scheme suggested here, we would have to assume that those affected by the advertisements were people who had found that information about the principles of democracy or about Greek-American ties had tended to satisfy certain of their needs in the past. It may have reassured them of the correctness of their decision in voting for a party supporting Greece's NATO ties. Some of them may have had relatives in the United States. Similar information

26. Leo Bogart, "Measuring the Effectiveness of an Overseas Information Campaign: A Case History," *Public Opinion Quarterly*, vol. 21, 1957, pp. 475–498.

may previously have helped them to maintain good relations with those among their associates who had similar attitudes or to defend themselves against the arguments of those opposed. The number of possibilities is very large. In any event, their experience had taught them to be on the lookout for—or at least not to resist—information of the type offered in the advertisements.

We also have to assume that the communications habits of those who noticed the advertisements were such that they looked upon the newspaper as a valuable source of information, and that the advertisements were written in a manner that easily conveyed meaning to the readers.

Very similar observations were made as a result of a postwar information campaign to make Cincinnati United Nations conscious. After an intensive six months' effort to inform people in the area about the United Nations, it was found that the people reached by the campaign tended to be those who were already interested in and favorably disposed toward the world organization.[27] In this case, to follow the interpretation suggested here, we would have to assume that the population of Cincinnati could be divided into those who had some use for information about the United Nations and those who did not. Most of those for whom such information was useful had already assembled at least some information from sources available to them prior to the campaign, but the campaign enabled them to obtain a little more. Those who had no use for information about the United Nations, however, continued to have no use for it and therefore disregarded the campaign along with other content of the communication flow for which they had no use.

Studies reported in the large body of literature on experimental modification of attitudes through communications can also be interpreted in these terms. To take a very simple example, subjects are sometimes given attitude tests, then exposed to communications for or against an issue or a political figure, and finally retested. If the issue or the political figure is one that is relatively unknown to them, their attitude changes in the direction of the communication are likely to be great.[28] If, on the other hand, the subject of the communication is one with which they already are well

27. Shirley A. Starr and Helen MacGill Hughes, "Report on an Educational Campaign: The Cincinnati Plan for the United Nations," *American Journal of Sociology,* vol. 55, 1950, pp. 389–400.

28. *Cf.* A. D. Annis and Norman C. Meier, "The Induction of Opinion through Suggestion by Means of 'Planted Content,' " *Journal of Social Psychology,* vol. 5, 1934, pp. 65–81. In this experiment a pronounced change in attitude toward a little-known Australian prime minister was achieved through exposure to material about him "planted" in a campus newspaper. One must assume that a much smaller change would have been achieved if the individual concerned had been better known to the respondents.

acquainted their attitudes are likely to change little or not at all. In the former case, the communication may be the only link or the most important link with a sector of the environment that hitherto has been largely unknown to them. Therefore, when they are faced with the necessity of expressing an opinion about this subject, they are forced to rely on information from the experimental communication. Conversely, in the latter case, the communication is only one of several links with this aspect of the environment, and when it comes to expressing an opinion, information that has already been stored from other sources may be quite adequate.

That utility influences the retention and also forgetting of facts is indicated by two observations of widely varying nature. McKown at Stanford (in an as yet unpublished study) found that the ability of a reader to conjure up a personal image of the supposed writer of a research report correlated highly with his ability to recall the content of the report. In this instance, the possibility that the report's contents might be useful in social relations as well as in professional activities appeared to result in its making a stronger impression.

The other observation comes from the experience of an interviewer of Soviet military personnel who had been captured by the Nazis. Many of the Soviet soldiers reported that they had been in Poland when Russian forces occupied the Eastern half of that country in 1940 and had been amazed at the high standard of living they found. Then, when they returned to Poland during the Soviet advance in 1944–45, they again had been amazed at the high standard of living. When the interviewer expressed surprise at the fact that they reported being amazed twice, his respondents explained that it had been wise to forget what they had seen in 1940.

A small experiment was conducted by the author to contrast the effectiveness of a communication in influencing an attitude that had little basis in knowledge or experience with the almost total inability of a communication to influence an attitude that was rooted in a substantial body of knowledge or personal experience. Sixty-nine government officials with an average of fifteen years' experience in foreign affairs were given tests to establish their attitudes on a four-point scale toward the United States foreign service and toward two German politicians.[29] They were then exposed to a speech (purportedly by a retired foreign service officer) sharply criticizing the foreign service and also to a speech (by a political scientist) highly praising *one* of the German politicians but not mentioning the other.

The results of the experiment were as expected. On the "after" test designed to elicit attitudes toward the foreign service, only one respondent

29. The attitude tests were given in three groups and the responses totaled later.

appears to have shifted his rating by one point on the scale. (The possibility of compensating changes exists, but is very slight.) Most of these officials had had personal experience with the foreign service over a period of years, and had built up attitudes of considerable stability. Even though the criticisms made in the speech were shared by many of them, these criticisms had already been taken into account in their thinking and consequently gave them insufficient reason to revise the image of the foreign service they had already formed.

Although not unexpected, the results regarding the two German politicians—von Brentano and Erhard—were more interesting. Responses on these questions were divided into two groups: those from men who had had experience with reference to Western Europe and those from men who reported no such experience. With regard to Erhard, about whom no communication was presented, the scale ratings on the "before" and "after" tests were identical (or there were compensating changes, which is unlikely). The results in the case of von Brentano showed a pronounced influence of the persuasive communication among those with no Western European experience, while it had almost no influence in the case of those who were European experts. These results are shown in Table 2.[30]

Table 2—Evaluation by 69 Foreign Affairs Experts of the Choice of von Brentano as Foreign Minister of the German Federal Republic before and after Reading a Speech Praising Him.*

	Before	After
Those with Western European experience:		
Excellent	12	14
Good	16	16
Satisfactory	4	4
Poor	2	1
No opinion	4	3
Those with no Western European experience:		
Excellent	5	18
Good	11	10
Satisfactory	5	1
Poor	0	0
No opinion	10	2

* The question was: "In 1955, Dr. Heinrich von Brentano was appointed Foreign Minister of the German Federal Republic. On the basis of what you know about Dr. von Brentano, would you say that this choice was excellent, good, satisfactory, or poor?"

30. The question used to divide respondents into experts and nonexperts on Western Europe did not discriminate perfectly, as the four "no opinion" responses of the experts in the "before" test indicate. If a more accurate division could have been obtained, the changes probably would have been even fewer among the experts and more pronounced among the nonexperts.

Experiments such as this offer certain difficulties of interpretation, since they make use of communication habits that do not play a role in other situations. When confronted with a communication in the classroom or laboratory, the subject usually makes the conscious or subconscious assumption that the instructor or experimenter wants him to pay attention to it. Furthermore, by the time he has reached high school or college he presumably has the habit of paying attention in the classroom. Therefore, he may assimilate information that in another context he would regard as not having sufficient utility to justify his attention. For instance, in the case reported in Table 2 it is unlikely that most of those who were not experts on Western Europe would have read the speech about von Brentano if they had not been specifically asked to do so. Another aspect of the classroom or experimental situation is that it does not ordinarily reward an individual for maintaining a consistent opinion (as is usually the case in other situations) or penalize him for changing his opinion. Indeed, the opposite may be the case. Emphasis on keeping an open mind may even predispose him toward exposure to information that he would otherwise ignore, and may encourage him to revise his opinions in the light of new data. In experimental situations where subjects have been rewarded in some way for maintaining a consistent opinion, observed changes have been considerably less. Finally, in experimental situations, the social setting of the respondent is often ignored. We usually pay little attention to his relations with the other respondents or with the experimenter; yet these relationships may exercise an important influence on his responses. To translate these remarks into the terms that have been used above, we might say that in the experimental situation a subject's needs are often different from those in other situations and therefore somewhat different habits, including communication habits, are appropriate to this situation.

SOME IMPLICATIONS FOR PERSUASION

This way of looking at the effects of communication suggests that the communicator can influence attitudes or behavior only when he is able to convey information that may be utilized by members of his audience to satisfy their wants or needs. If he has control of some significant aspect of his audience's environment, his task may be an easy one. All he must do is tell people about some environmental change or expected change that is important to them. For example, he may offer a large sum of money to anyone who does a certain thing. If he is a merchant, he may sell a product at a very low cost. We all have control over an aspect of the environment that is significant for members of the primary groups to which we belong—our own behavior.

Most communicators are in a more difficult position when they are trying to effect persuasion outside their own group, since they do not control aspects of the environment that are significant to their audiences. Furthermore, they usually do not have a monopoly of the channels of information, and must ordinarily assume that people have already located sources of information about aspects of the environment that are important to them. To influence behavior under these conditions the communicator's information must be more accurate or otherwise more useful than information from competing sources. He can, it is true, sometimes build on tendencies toward action that are already present by reminding people of existing needs and of how they may be satisfied. But to bring about any basic behavioral changes is very difficult. Attitudes and behavior patterns that are based on extensive information or on personal experience are likely to have already proved their utility and to be tough and highly resistant to change. Furthermore, the capacity of people to disregard information that is not useful (either because it is irrelevant or because it conflicts with already established patterns of thought and action) appears to be almost unlimited.[31]

This approach to the study of communication effects also suggests that soundly based knowledge about the principles of persuasion will be attainable only as a result of basic advances within psychology and sociology. A better understanding of the way people perceive their social environment and how they adjust to it appears to be particularly important. The advances that can be made independently in the field usually labeled "communication" are likely to be limited and tentative.

Nevertheless, communication studies, while they cannot stand alone, contribute to our understanding of human needs and the way these are satisfied. A substantial quantity of information on the various ways communications are utilized by different people is already available but has not been systematically organized. For most Americans, for example, news carried in the press of a totalitarian country is not very useful because of its incompleteness and inaccuracy. But for the citizen of such a country this news may be vital to preferment or even survival, since it lets him know what the power holders *want* him to believe.[32] Similarly, it has frequently been observed (e.g., in studies of prejudice) that communications

31. The communicator may be able, however, to *make* his information useful—the very fact that certain people are talking about a subject makes this subject relevant for others.

32. *Cf.* Paul Kecskemeti, "Totalitarian Communications as a Means of Control," *Public Opinion Quarterly,* vol. 14, 1950, pp. 224–234. Some case material that illustrates Kecskemeti's observations very well is presented by Alex Inkeles and Raymond A. Bauer in *The Soviet Citizen* (Harvard U. P., Cambridge, Mass., 1959), p. 175.

from within the group have more effect on attitudes than identical communications from outside the group. This seems to be true in cases where the utility of the information to the recipient is not in its objective content but in the fact that a member of his group believes it.

Finally, this approach emphasizes that the communicator's audience is not a passive recipient—it cannot be regarded as a lump of clay to be molded by the master propagandist. Rather, the audience is made up of individuals who demand something from the communications to which they are exposed, and who select those that are likely to be useful to them. In other words, they must get something from the manipulator if he is to get something from them. A bargain is involved. Sometimes, it is true, the manipulator is able to lead his audience in to a bad bargain by emphasizing one need at the expense of another or by representing a change in the significant environment as greater than it actually has been. But audiences, too, can drive a hard bargain. Many communicators who have been widely disregarded or misunderstood know that to their cost.

SELECTED PUBLICATIONS BY DR. DAVISON

"More than Diplomacy" and "Voices of America," two chapters in Lester Markel (ed.), *Public Opinion and Foreign Policy* (Harper, New York, 1949).

"The Role of Research in Political Warfar," *Journalism Quarterly,* Winter 1952.

"An Outline for the Study of International Communication," in Wilbur Schramm (ed.), *The Process and Effects of Mass Communication* (U. of Illinois Press, Urbana, Ill., 1954) (with A. L. George).

West German Leadership and Foreign Policy (Harper, New York, 1957) (joint editor with Hans Speier).

Twentieth Anniversary Issue of *Public Opinion Quarterly,* devoted to *Twenty Years of Public Opinion Research* (Guest Editor).

The Berlin Blockade—A Study in Cold War Politics (Princeton U. P., Princeton, N.J., 1958).

"The Public Opinion Process," *Public Opinion Quarterly,* Summer 1958.

"Pragmatic Approaches to Political Communication," *World Politics,* October 1959.

"A Public Opinion Game," *Public Opinion Quarterly,* Summer 1961.

QUESTIONS

1. In the light of Davison's contentions, how might the article, "On the Effects of Mass Communications," as a communication in itself, have an impact on (your) attitudes?

2. Considering Davison's "basic assumptions," what are the primary needs and wants of the organism? What role do *communications* play in relation to needs and wants?

3. Discuss the role of typical attitudes among students (*a*) at the University of Mississippi during the Meredith admission battle, and (*b*) at your university during the same period.

4. As a Democrat, you continually turn the sound off during Republican political announcements on television. What principles are involved here?

5. How can communications lead to adjustive behavior? What principles are involved? Cite examples which illustrate them.

6. Are the following conclusions valid in the light of Davison's discussion? (*a*) Whether communication is good or poor depends on its organization solely and not on its ability to take advantage of the communications habits of the audience. (*b*) The communicator's audience is an impassive recipient. Discuss.

7. You are given an attitude test—reference, the 1964 Senatorial campaign in Massachusetts. You are then exposed to a five-minute "paid political announcement" compiled by the Kennedy-for-Senator Committee. Finally, you are retested. What might be your attitude change (*a*) if Kennedy were relatively unknown to you prior to the exposure to the film (*b*) if you were serving as head of the Boston University chapter of "Youth for Kennedy?"

8. Davison says that communications can lead to adjustive behavior in those exposed to them in at least three ways. What are these? Can you think of other ways, not cited by Davison, in which communications affect us?

9. The author shows that foreign affairs experts (with no Western European experience) were affected in their evaluation of Dr. Heinrich von Brentano after reading a speech praising him. Yet, as Davison points out, such laboratory "research" has its limitations. What are they?

Charles R. Wright

Functional Analysis and Mass Communication *

BECAUSE THE FOLLOWING essay by Professor Wright deals with a highly complex set of variables, it may, at first reading, appear quite formidable to grasp in its entirety. We urge its careful and painstaking study, however, for a better understanding of the combinations of functions and dysfunctions which the mass media may assume.

Granted that the mass media are important contemporary social phenomena, we should then welcome ways of examining their consequences upon our society. As Wright points out, functional analysis has as its concern just such an examination of the effects (or functions) of any given social phenomena, in this case the mass media, which affect the operation of a social system.

The increase in sophistication in communications theory in just a decade or two can be seen by comparing Harold Lasswell's well-known paradigm for the study of mass communications with the one Wright proposes in his article. From Lasswell we learned to study mass communications by examining the following: "Who says what to whom (how), and with what effect?" To this "formula" Wright has added the concept that there can be latent (unintended) functions as well as manifest (intended) functions of a mass-communciated event. For example, thousands of boys manifestly watch exploits of the astronauts on television or read explicit accounts in Life magazine by Glenn, Carpenter, Shirra, and colleagues; many of them may aspire to a career in space flight or engineering because of the latent consequences of these communications. Of course, when the government makes a special effort to exploit the successful

* This is a revised version of a paper contributed to the Fourth World Congress of Sociology, Milan and Stresa, Italy, September 1959. It is my pleasure to acknowledge an indebtedness to Herbert H. Hyman, Leonard Broom, Mary E. W. Goss, and Raymond J. Murphy for their thoughtful and critical readings of earlier drafts of the paper. [Reprinted from *Public Opinion Quarterly*, 1960, pp. 605–620, by permission of the author and the publisher. Copyright 1960 by Princeton University.]

"shots" by astronauts' participation in parades, personal appearance and other publicity, the communication is also manifest.

Wright also has added to his paradigm the notion that not every communication has positive value from all points of view for the social system in which it occurs, or for the groups or individuals which comprise that system. Quite clearly, the announcement of the Cuba quarantine by President Kennedy in his speech of October, 1962 to the nation was received by most of his listeners in a positive manner; but to those who feared that this action was too drastic and that it might precipitate a nuclear conflict with the Soviet Union such a speech was a dysfunction. For the readers of Pravda or Izvestia who saw in the speech either a "defeat" to their country's status or a possible provocation which might lead to a nuclear war, it was also highly dysfunctional. Thus, as Fearing pointed out in his article, the communicatee or interpreter of the mass-communicated "event" will perceive it as functional or dysfunctional, depending on the way it affects him.

Wright, then, poses the basic question of communications in this way: "What are the manifest (and latent) functions (and dysfunctions) of mass-communicated surveillance (news), correlation (editorial activity), cultural transmission, and entertainment for society, subgroups, individuals and cultural systems?"

The best way to determine whether a "theory" has any relevance for us is to try to apply it. By taking an event reported in the newspaper or over the radio-television media and comparing it with Wright's partial functional inventory (Tables I and II) we can "test" his paradigm. One has only to examine a Sunday issue of the New York Times to perceive that it serves interests of and functions for its readers, ranging from working the crossword puzzle in the magazine section to perusing the travel advertisements (entertainment) to reading the dire, threatening news from the borders of India or Viet-Nam or the Berlin Wall (surveillance). The surveillance function of the Times' vast reportorial resources is supplemented by its critical or correlation function, in which the raw magnitude of the day's or week's events are made manageable to its readers.

But there are, of course, some hundred million American readers on a Sunday who do not "need" or "want" the thorough surveillance facilities of the New York Times. For many, it is enough that the mass media present them with relatively much entertainment and little surveillance.

Surely, we all know individuals who prefer not to know too much about the world's turmoil, since such knowledge may have a definitely dysfunctional and threatening impact on their equilibrium. As Wright points out, "One function of mass-communicated entertainment is to provide respite for the individual which, perhaps, permits him to continue to be exposed to the mass-communicated news, interpretation, and prescriptions so necessary for his survival in the modern world."

It seems to us that Wright's approach toward understanding the multiple uses to which the mass media are put is an important contribution. As we learn more about the varied gratifications (and annoyances) that people experience from getting the "news" we shall be better able to ascertain the effects of mass communications upon a given society.   D.M.W.

DR. CHARLES R. WRIGHT is Associate Professor of Sociology at the University of California at Los Angeles, and is the author of a widely used book on the characteristics of the media, Mass Communication: A Sociological Perspective (Random House, New York, 1959). During 1963 he was Organization of American States Professor of Sociology in Chile. Prior to his faculty affiliation at U.C.L.A., Dr. Wright was a research associate at the Bureau of Applied Social Research at Columbia University and a member of the sociology department of that university.

This paper discusses certain theoretical and methodological points relevant to the growth of a functional theory of mass communications. In recent years various studies have explicitly or implicitly used a functional framework for examining different aspects of mass communications. The current discussion occasionally draws from such studies to illustrate the problems at hand, with no attempt, however, at a comprehensive survey of the field. Three specific topics are explored here:

[1] Items suitable for functional analysis. There is a need for specification and codification of the kinds of phenomena in mass communication which have been, or can be, clarified by means of the functional approach, together with formal statements of the basic queries which are raised in each instance. A few examples of such basic functional queries—there are others, of course—are presented in the first section.

[2] Organization of hypotheses into a systematic functional framework. Future research and theory would be helped by the introduction of a larger organizing framework into which can be fitted a variety of hypotheses and findings about the functions and dysfunctions of mass communication. One such organizing procedure—*a functional inventory*—is proposed in the second section.

[3] Rephrasing hypotheses in functional terms. Additional hypotheses need to be formulated in terms which are specifically related to such important components of functionalism as, for example, functional requirements and the equilibrium model. A few hypotheses of this sort are suggested in the third section.

What is meant here by "mass communication"? In its popular usage the term refers to such particular mass media as television, motion pictures, radio, newspapers, and magazines. But the use of these technical instruments does not always signify mass communication. To illustrate, a nationwide telecast of a political speech is mass communication; closed-circuit television over which a small group of medical students observe an operation is not. Modern technology, then, appears to be a necessary but not sufficient component in defining mass communication, which is distinguishable also by the nature of its audience, the communication itself, and the communicator. Mass communication is directed toward relatively large and heterogeneous audiences that are anonymous to the communicator. Messages are transmitted publicly; are timed to reach most of the audience quickly, often simultaneously; and usually are meant to be transient rather than permanent records. Finally, the communicator tends to be, or to operate within, a complex formal organization that may involve great expense.[1]

SUBJECTS FOR FUNCTIONAL ANALYSIS

Functional analysis, to a great extent, is concerned with examining those consequences of social phenomena which affect the normal operation, adaptation, or adjustment of a given system: individuals, subgroups, social and cultural systems.[2] To what kinds of social phenomena can functional analysis be applied? The basic general requirement, according to Merton, is "that the object of analysis represent a *standardized* (i.e., patterned and repetitive) item, such as social roles, institutional patterns, social processes, cultural pattern, culturally patterned emotions, social norms, group organization, social structure, devices for social control, *etc.*"[3] This basic requirement, however, is very broad. Hence a necessary first step in the application of functional analysis to mass communications consists of *specifying* the kinds of "standardized item" with which the analyst is concerned. As a step in this direction several of the more obvious types of item are distinguished here.

First, at the broadest level of abstraction, mass communication itself, as a *social process,* is a patterned and repetitive phenomenon in many

---

1. A fuller discussion of the characteristics of mass communication appears in C. Wright, *Mass Communication: A Sociological Perspective* (Random House, New York, 1959).

2. Types of systems to which functional analysis can be applied are developed in R. K. Merton, *Social Theory and Social Structure* (Free Press, New York, 1957), chap. I.

3. *Ibid.,* p. 50.

modern societies; hence it is suitable for functional analysis. The basic question at this level is: What are the consequences—for the individual, subgroups, social and cultural systems—of a form of communication that addresses itself to large, heterogeneous, anonymous audiences publicly and rapidly, utilizing a complex and expensive formal organization for this purpose? Thus formulated, however, the query is so gross as to be unmanageable empirically, and essential evidence cannot be obtained.[4] Obviously it is useful to have comparative data from several societies in which mass communications are absent or developed to varying degrees, e.g., underdeveloped *versus* industrialized societies; pre-modern *versus* modern periods of the same society. But it is hardly possible to analyze the consequences of the dissimilar communications systems under such circumstances; their effects cannot be readily separated from those resulting from the host of other complex organizational differences between the societies under study. There remains, of course, the possibility of a speculative "mental experiment" in which the analyst imagines what would happen if mass communication did not exist, but such hypotheses are not empirically verifiable.[5]

Nor are the difficulties reduced if the analyst delimits the problem by considering concrete communication structures rather than the abstract total mass communication process. Lazarsfeld and Merton have underscored such difficulties with reference to the analysis of the social role of the mass media:

> What role can be assigned to the mass media by virtue of the fact that they exist? What are the implications of a Hollywood, a Radio City, and a Time-Life-Fortune enterprise for our society? These questions can of course be discussed only in grossly speculative terms, since no experimentation or rigorous comparative study is possible. Comparisons with other societies lacking these mass media would be too crude to yield decisive results and comparisons with an earlier day in American society would still involve gross assertions rather than precise demonstrations. . . .[6]

Functional analysis at this level, then, appears currently to be dependent primarily on speculation, and holds little immediate promise for the development of an empirically verifiable theory of mass communication.

4. For one discussion of methods of testing functional theory see N. S. Timasheff, *Sociological Theory* (Random House, New York, 1958), pp. 229–230.

5. For a discussion of the dangers in such an approach see M. Weber, *The Theory of Social and Economic Organization,* translated by A. Henderson and T. Parsons (Free Press, New York, 1947), pp. 97–98.

6. P. Lazarsfeld and R. Merton, "Mass Communication, Popular Taste and Organized Social Action," in L. Bryson (ed.), *The Communication of Ideas* (Harper, New York, 1948), p. 98.

A second major type of functional analysis, slightly less sweeping than the first, considers each particular *method* of mass communication (e.g., newspapers, television) as the item for analysis. An early example is an essay by Malcolm Wiley, in which he asks, "What, then, are the functions performed by the newspaper? What are the social and individual needs that it has met and still meets?" As an answer, he isolates six distinguishable functions: news, editorial, backgrounding, entertainment, advertising, and encyclopedic.[7] Sometimes the analyst focuses on the interrelations among several media as they affect total communication as a system. Janowitz's study of the role of the local community press within a metropolitan setting provides a case in point. Janowitz found, among other things, that the community weekly newspaper does not simply duplicate the services of the larger metropolitan daily but plays a quite distinct role, such as providing information about local residents, local issues, and neighborhood organizations.[8] Touching on several media, one might ask: What are the functions and dysfunctions of multiple coverage of the news by television, radio, and newspapers? Opportunities to test hypothesized functions at this level are available when circumstances provide societies in which a particular medium is absent (e.g., countries without television) or when the normal operation of a medium is disturbed (e.g., by a strike), providing one can account for the influence of factors in the situation other than the absence or malfunctioning of the mass medium.

As a third major instance, the functional approach can be used in the *institutional* analysis of any mass medium or organization in mass communication, examining the function of some repeated and patterned operation within that organization. Here, clearly, there is a good possibility of obtaining essential data for empirical verification of hypotheses, through case studies, comparative analysis of differently organized media, or direct experimentation. Warren Breed's study of the middle-sized daily newspaper illustrates such institutional analysis.[9] Breed examines, among other things, the ways in which the paper's presentation of the news is affected by such institutionalized statuses in the newsroom as publisher, editor, and staff member, and by the professional norms and regularized activities surrounding the newspaperman's work.

Finally, a fourth type of analysis—and one which we believe offers great promise for the development of a functional theory of mass com-

7. M. Wiley, "The Functions of the Newspaper," *Annals of the American Academy of Political and Social Science,* vol. 219, 1942, p. 19.

8. M. Janowitz, *The Community Press in an Urban Setting* (Free Press, New York, 1952).

9. W. Breed, "The Newspaperman, News, and Society," Columbia University, 1952, unpublished doctoral dissertation.

munications—treats the question of what are the consequences of handling the *basic communication activities* by means of mass communication. What is meant by basic communication activities? Lasswell notes three major activities of communication specialists: "(1) the surveillance of the environment; (2) the correlation of the parts of society in responding to the environment; (3) the transmission of the social heritage from one generation to the next." [10] Modifying these categories slightly and adding a fourth—entertainment—provides a classification of the major communication activities which concern us here. Surveillance refers to the collection and distribution of information concerning events in the environment, both outside and within any particular society, thus corresponding approximately to what is popularly conceived as the handling of news. Acts of correlation, here, include interpretation of information about the environment and prescriptions for conduct in reaction to these events. In part this activity is popularly identified as editorial or propagandistic. Transmission of culture includes activities designed to communicate a group's store of social norms, information, values, and the like, from one generation to another or from members of a group to newcomers. Commonly it is identified as educational activity. Finally, entertainment refers to communication primarily intended to amuse people irrespective of any instrumental effects it might have.

It goes without saying that each of these four activities predates mass communication, and in some form each is still conducted on a "nonmass" basis in every society. But where mass media exist, each activity is also conducted as mass communication. In its simplest form, then, the question posed here is: What are the consequences of performing such activities through mass communication, rather than through some other form of communication? For example, what are the effects of surveillance through mass communication rather than through face-to-face reporting? What are the results of treating information about events in the environment as items of news to be distributed indiscriminately, simultaneously, and publicly to a large, heterogeneous, and anonymous audience? Similarly, what are the consequences of handling prescription, interpretation, cultural transmission, and entertainment as mass-communicated activities? Thus formulated, the basic query of functional analysis at this level calls for—at the least—an *inventory* of functions of mass-communicated activities, a subject to which we turn now.

10. H. Lasswell, "The Structure and Function of Communication in Society," in Bryson, *op. cit.*

TOWARD A FUNCTIONAL INVENTORY
FOR MASS COMMUNICATIONS

Functional analysis does not restrict itself to the study of useful consequences. On the contrary, several types of consequences are now recognized in functional theory, each of which must be taken into account if an inventory is to be complete. For example, Merton distinguishes between consequences and the motives for an activity.[11] Clearly, these two need not be, and often are not, identical. To illustrate, a local public health campaign may be undertaken to encourage the people in the area to go to a clinic for a check-up. In the process of pursuing this goal, the campaign may have an unanticipated consequence of improving the morale of the local public health employees, whose everyday work has suddenly been given public attention.[12] Results that are intended are called *manifest* functions; those that are unintended, *latent* functions. Not every consequence has positive value for the social system in which it occurs, or for the groups or individuals involved. Effects which are undesirable from the point of view of the welfare of the society or its members are called *dysfunctions.* Any single act may have both functional and dysfunctional effects. For example, the public health campaign might also have frightened some people so much that they failed to report for a check-up.

Combining Merton's specification of consequences with the four basic communication activities provides a fuller query that serves to guide the inventory. Stylized into a "formula," the basic question now becomes:

	(1) manifest	(3) functions	
What are the	and	and	of mass communi-
	(2) latent	(4) dysfunctions	cated

(5) surveillance (news)	for the	(9) society
(6) correlation (editorial activity)		(10) subgroups
(7) cultural transmission		(11) individual
(8) entertainment		(12) cultural systems?

The twelve elements in the formula can be transformed into categories in a master inventory chart which organizes many of the hypothesized

11. The cited distinction and others to be discussed are from Merton, *op. cit.*
12. An example of such an unanticipated consequence can be found in R. Carlson, "The Influence of the Community and the Primary Group on the Reactions of Southern Negroes to Syphilis," Columbia University, 1952, unpublished doctoral dissertation.

and empirically discovered effects of mass communication. Its essential form is illustrated in the accompanying chart, in which some hypothetical examples of effects have been inserted. A full discussion of the content of the chart cannot be undertaken here, but the method of organization will be illustrated through a limited discussion of certain functions and dysfunctions of mass-communicated surveillance.[13]

Consider what it means to society and to its members to have available a constant flow of data on events occurring within the society or in the larger world. At least two positive consequences or functions occur for the total society. First, such a flow of information often provides speedy *warnings* about imminent threats and dangers from outside the society, e.g., impending danger from hurricanes or from military attack. Forewarned, the population might mobilize and avert destruction. Furthermore, insofar as the information is available to the mass of the population (rather than to a select few) warnings through mass communication may have the additional function of supporting feelings of egalitarianism within the society, i.e. everyone has had an equal chance to escape from danger. Second, a flow of data about the environment is *instrumental* to the everyday institutional needs of the society, e.g., stock market activities, navigation, and air traffic.

For individuals, several functions of surveillance can be discerned. First, insofar as personal welfare is linked to social welfare, the *warning* and *instrumental* functions of mass-communicated news for society also serve the individual. In addition, a number of more personal forms of utility can be identified. For example, in 1945, Berelson took advantage of a local newspaper strike in New York City to study what people "missed" when they did not receive their regular newspaper.[14] One clearly identifiable function of the newspaper for these urbanites was as a source of information about routine events, e.g., providing data on local radio and motion picture performances, sales by local merchants, embarkations, deaths, and the latest fashions. When people "missed" their daily papers they were, in fact, missing a tool for daily living. A third function of mass-communicated news is to bestow *prestige* upon the individuals who make the effort to keep themselves informed about events. To the extent that being informed is considered important by the society, people who conform to this norm enhance their prestige within the group. Often those individuals who select local news as their focus of attention emerge as

13. A fuller discussion appears in Wright, *op. cit.,* from which the following section is drawn.

14. B. Berelson, "What 'Missing the Newspaper' Means," in Paul Lazarsfeld and F. Stanton, editors, *Communications Research 1948–1949* (Harper, New York, 1949), pp. 111–129.

Partial Functional Inventory for Mass Communications

	SYSTEM UNDER CONSIDERATION			
	Society	Individual	Specific Subgroups (e.g. Political Elite)	Culture
1. MASS—COMMUNICATED ACTIVITY: SURVEILLANCE (NEWS)				
Functions (manifest and latent)	Warning: Natural dangers Attack; war	Warning Instrumental	Instrumental: Information useful to power	Aids cultural contact Aids cultural growth
	Instrumental: News essential to the economy and other institutions	Adds prestige: Opinion leadership	Detects: Knowledge of subversive and deviant behavior	
	Ethicizing	Status conferral	Manages public opinion Monitors Controls	
			Legitimizes power: Status conferral	
Dysfunctions (manifest and latent)	Threatens stability: News of "better" societies	Anxiety Privatization Apathy Narcotization	Threatens power: News of reality "Enemy" propaganda Exposés	Permits cultural invasion
	Fosters panic			
2. MASS—COMMUNICATED ACTIVITY: CORRELATION (EDITORIAL SELECTION, INTERPRETATION, AND PRESCRIPTION)				
Functions (manifest and latent)	Aids mobilization	Provides efficiency: Assimilating news	Helps preserve power	Impedes cultural invasion
	Impedes threats to social stability	Impedes: Overstimulation Anxiety Apathy Privatization		Maintains cultural consensus
	Impedes panic			

Dysfunctions (manifest and latent)	Increases social conformism: Impedes social change if social criticism is avoided	Weakens critical faculties Increases passivity	Increases responsibility	Impedes cultural growth

3. MASS-COMMUNICATED ACTIVITY: CULTURAL TRANSMISSION

Functions (manifest and latent)	Increases social cohesion: Widens base of common norms, experiences, etc. Reduces anomie Continues socialization: Reaches adults even after they have left such institutions as school	Aids integration: Exposure to common norms Reduces idiosyncrasy Reduces anomia	Extends power: Another agency for socialization	Standardizes Maintains cultural consensus
Dysfunctions (manifest and latent)	Augments "mass" society	Depersonalizes acts of socialization		Reduces variety of subcultures

4. MASS-COMMUNICATED ACTIVITY: ENTERTAINMENT

Functions (manifest and latent)	Respite for masses	Respite	Extends power: Control over another area of life	
Dysfunctions (manifest and latent)	Diverts public: Avoids social action	Increases passivity Lowers "tastes" Permits escapism		Weakens aesthetics: "Popular culture"

local opinion leaders in their community, while people who turn to events in the greater society operate as cosmopolitan influentials.[15]

Lazarsfeld and Merton have suggested two other functions of mass communication which seem to be especially applicable to mass-communicated news: *status conferral* and the enforcement of social norms (*ethicizing*).[16] Status conferral means that news reports about a member of any society enhance his prestige. By focusing the power of the mass media upon him society confers upon him a high public status. Hence the premium placed upon publicity and public relations in modern societies. Mass communication has an ethicizing function when it strengthens social control over the individual members of the mass society by bringing their deviant behavior into public view, as in newspaper crusades. The facts about norm violation might have been known already privately by many members of the society; but the public disclosure through mass communication creates the social conditions under which most people must condemn the violations and support public, rather than private, standards of morality. By this process, mass-communicated news strengthens social control in large urbanized societies where urban anonymity has weakened informal face-to-face detection and control of deviant behavior.

Surveillance through mass communication can prove dysfunctional as well as functional for society and the individual. First, uncensored news about the world potentially *threatens* the structure of any society. For example, information about conditions and ideologies in other societies might lead to invidious comparisons with conditions at home, and hence to strains toward change. Second, uninterpreted warnings about danger in the environment might lead to *panic* by the mass audience. For example, in Cantril's analysis of the effects of the radio program "Invasion from Mars," the belief that the radio story was actually a news report contributed to the panic reaction by many listeners.[17]

Dysfunctions can be identified on the individual level too. First, data about dangers in the environment, instead of having the function of warning, could lead to heightened *anxieties* within the audience, e.g. war nerves. Second, too much news might lead to *privatization:* the individual becomes overwhelmed by the data brought to his attention and reacts by turning to matters in his private life over which he has greater control.[18]

15. Cf. R. Merton, "Patterns of Influence: A Study of Interpersonal Influence and of Communication Behavior in a Local Community," in Lazarsfeld and Stanton, *op. cit.,* pp. 180–219.

16. Lazarsfeld and Merton, *op. cit.*

17. H. Cantril, H. Gaudet, and H. Herzog, *Invasion from Mars* (Princeton U. P., Princeton, N.J., 1940).

18. For a discussion of the feeling of social importance that marks privatization, see E. Kris and N. Leites, "Trends in Twentieth Century Propaganda," in G. Ro-

Third, access to mass-communicated news might lead to *apathy*. Or he may believe that to be an informed citizen is equivalent to being an active citizen. Lazarsfeld and Merton have given this dysfunction to the label of *narcotization*.[19]

One also can analyze functions and dysfunctions of mass-communicated news for smaller subgroups within the society. To illustrate, such news activity might prove especially functional for a political elite insofar as the free flow of news provides information which is useful to the maintenance of *power* by this group. Furthermore the publicity given to events within the society facilitates the *detection* of deviant and possibly subversive behavior, as well as providing an opportunity to *monitor* (and perhaps control) public opinion. The attention which the news media give to political figures and their behavior can, in turn, enhance and *legitimize* their position of power, through the process of status conferral. On the other hand, mass-communicated news may prove dysfunctional to such a political group in a variety of ways. The news which reaches a mass audience may undermine or threaten the political power elite, as for instance when news of losses during wartime contradict the leaders' claims of victory or when enemy propaganda deliberately aims at undermining the rulers' power.[20]

Finally, one can canvass the impact of mass-communicated news on culture itself. Among the possible functions here are the enrichment and variety which are introduced into a society's culture through mass-communicated information about other cultures, as well as possible growth and adaptability of culture as a result of such contacts. On the dysfunctional side, such uncontrolled news about other societies can lead to cultural invasion and weakening of the host culture.

While present space does not permit a full discussion of possible functions and dysfunctions of the other three communication activities—correlation, cultural transmission, and entertainment—a few hypothesized functions and dysfunctions are illustrated in the accompanying chart. Such examples demonstrate the usefulness of this form—or some equivalent method—of organizing hypotheses and findings about the effects of mass communications.[21] We turn now to our third, and final, point of

heim, editor, *Psychoanalysis and the Social Sciences* (International Universities Press, New York, 1947).

19. Lazarsfeld and Merton, *op. cit.*

20. Cf. H. Speier, "Psychological Warfare Reconsidered," in D. Lerner and H. Lasswell, editors, *The Policy Sciences* (Stanford U. P., Stanford, Calif., 1951).

21. For one instructive analysis of the effects of edited news coverage, see W. Breed, "Mass Communication and Socio-cultural Integration," *Social Forces*, vol. 37, 1958, pp. 109–116, reprinted in this volume on pp. 183–200.

discussion: the desirability of rephrasing or formulating additional hypotheses about mass communication in terms especially central to functional theory.

FORMULATING FUNCTIONAL HYPOTHESES

Not all effects of mass communication are germane to functional analysis, only those which are relevant and important if the system under analysis is to continue to operate normally. The basic pattern of functional analysis has recently been characterized by Hempel as follows:

The object of the analysis is some "item" i, which is a relatively persistent trait or disposition (e.g. the beating of the heart) occurring in a system s (e.g. the body of a living vertebrate); and the analysis aims to show that s is in a state, or internal condition c_i, and in an environment presenting certain external conditions c_e such that under conditions c_i and c_e (jointly to be referred to as c) the trait i has effects which satisfy some "need" or "functional requirement" of s, i.e., a condition n which is necessary for the system's remaining in adequate, or effective, or proper, working order.[22]

Hempel also elaborates the basic terms in this schema. The item i, for example, may be one of several such items forming a class I, any one of which is functionally equivalent to any other; that is, each has approximately the same effect of fulfilling the condition n necessary for the system to operate properly. One can argue, that, if at any time t, system s functions adequately in a setting of kind c, and s can function adequately in setting c only if condition n is satisfied, then some one of the items in class I is present at t. The item i (or its equivalent) is a functional requirement of s, under the conditions stated.

What constitutes a state of normal operation remains, as yet, undefined and poses one of the most difficult problems in functional theory. Rather than assume that only one state represents normal operation, Hempel suggests that it may be necessary to consider a range of states, R, that defines adequate performance relative to some standard of survival or adjustment. Specification of the standard, then, poses a problem the solution to which may vary from case to case. One solution, however, may come from the study of the system itself, if the analyst employs an equilibrium model or general hypothesis of self-regulation of the system. This hypothesis, overly simplified, asserts that the system will adjust itself by developing appropriate traits which satisfy the various functional requirements that arise from changes in its internal state or environment.

22. C. Hempel, "The Logic of Functional Analysis," in N. Gross, editor, *Symposium on Sociological Theory* (Harper, New York, 1959), p. 280.

In the study of any given system *s*, then, the standard of survival or adjustment,

. . . would be indicated by specifying a certain class or range R of possible states of *s*, with the understanding that *s* was to be considered as "surviving in proper working order," or as "adjusting properly under changing conditions" just in case *s* remained in, or upon disturbance returned to some state within the range R. A need, or functional requirement, of system *s* relative to R is then a necessary condition for the system's remaining in, or returning to, a state in R; and the function, relative to R, of an item *i* in *s* consists in its effecting the satisfaction of some such functional requirement.[23]

To illustrate the third essential step in functional analysis of mass communication (i.e., phrasing of hypotheses and propositions) let us apply some of the above ideas about self-regulation to one aspect of mass communication: surveillance. Let the items *i* represent such varied forms of mass-communicated news as television newscasts, newspaper stories, radio news reports, and motion picture newsreels; together they comprise a class of items I, mass-communicated surveillance. Assume, for the sake of the example, that these items are functionally equivalent forms of news. Let the *individual* be the unit or system with which we are concerned. And let conditions *c* be those of a modern society, in which many events of importance to the individual occur beyond the immediate environment which he can observe first-hand. Then proposition 1 is:

1. If the individual *s* is to maintain a state of adequate or normal operation R, in a society C in which events of importance to him occur outside the immediate observable environment, then there must be available to him some sufficient form of mass-communicated news *i*.

Normal operation needs to be defined, of course. We might, for example, define such a state as one in which the individual has sufficient information to cope with the environment. Or we might define adequate or normal operation as a state in which the individual *thinks* that he has sufficient information about events in the environment. Arbitrarily we select the latter definition here, since our next concern will be with predicting the probable behavior of the individual when he is disturbed from the normal stage. We assume that such purposive behavior is motivated by the individual's definition of the situation as well as by the objective situation itself.

With this subjective definition of normalcy, then, proposition 1 can be rephrased as follows:

23. *Ibid.*, p. 296.

2. If at any given time *t* an individual *s* is operating in a normal state R (i.e., he thinks that he has sufficient information about events in his environment), and this state can be achieved in a modern society only if the individual has access to mass-communicated surveillance I, then some form of mass-communicated news *i* must be present and available to him at time *t*.

And the hypothesis of self-regulation predicts that:

3. If the individual is disturbed from his normal state R (i.e., he comes to think that he does *not* have sufficient information about events in the environment) by the removal of or interference with *i* (the previously adequate form of mass-communicated news), then the individual will react by seeking the functional equivalents of *i* (i.e., another source of mass-communicated news), in order to return to his normal state R.

What are the circumstances under which such a hypothesis could be tested? One method consists of experimentally manipulating the forms of mass-communicated news *i* available to the individual, perhaps disturbing the normal pattern by removing or interfering with *i* for an experimental group of individuals but not for a matched control group. Then the analyst could examine the behavior of the individuals involved. The hypothesis of self-regulation would lead to the prediction that the deprived individuals would now turn to alternative *i*'s in order to continue to meet the necessary conditions for normal operation.

A second method consists of taking advantage of natural disturbances in mass-communicated surveillance. Berelson's study of people's reactions to a newspaper strike is a case in point.[24] Surveillance, of course, is only one of the many services which the daily newspaper provides for the reader. Nevertheless, for some readers this appeared to be a very important function, and these people found themselves greatly disturbed by the loss of their customary source of information about international, national and local events. Under such circumstances of sudden deprivation, one would like to know the new communications behavior of the individuals involved.

Still a third method consists of analyzing the behavior of people who are differentially located in society with respect to their access to specific forms of mass-communicated news. What alternative form of surveillance has been employed by people for whom a certain type of mass-communicated news is not ordinarily available? Several possible groups might be compared instructively here, such as literate *versus* illiterate members of the society; immigrants knowing only their native language *versus* citi-

24. Berelson, *op. cit.*

zens; people wealthy enough to have television and radio receivers *versus* those who are not.[25]

To conclude our discussion of functional propositions we shall introduce one further complexity. Thus far we have treated each communication activity (surveillance, correlation, cultural transmission, and entertainment) as if it existed in isolation from the others. Obviously, in a total communication system any mass medium may perform any one or several of these activities; and the performance of one activity may have consequences for the others. Our concluding proposition is that many of the functions of one mass-communicated activity can be interpreted as *social mechanisms* for minimizing or counteracting the dysfunctions produced by another activity, in order to keep the system from breaking down.

To illustrate, suppose we accept the proposition that in a modern society the individual's need for surveillance must be met through the process of mass communication. At the same time, however, the mass-communicative features of this activity have effects on the individual that may be dysfunctional. For example, large amounts of raw news may overwhelm him and lead to personal anxiety, apathy, or other reactions which would interfere with his reception of the items of news about the environment necessary for his normal operations. What happens that helps prevent such dysfunctional effects of mass-communicated news from interfering with the basic functions? To some extent such dysfunctions are minimized by the practice in modern societies of handling the second communication activity, correlation, also by mass communication (see our chart). Not all the events in the world get reported to the listener or reader through mass communication. There is a constant process of selection, editing, and interpretation of the news as it appears in mass-communicated form, often accompanied by prescriptions on what the individual should do about the events reported.

But even edited news can have dysfunctions when mass-communicated, such harmful effects as might come from the content or nature of the information itself. For example, news about war or international

25. People also may turn to word-of-mouth sources of information as alternatives to mass-communicated news, of course. As examples of instructive analyses relevant to this point see P. Rossi and R. Bauer, "Some Patterns of Soviet Communications Behavior," *Public Opinion Quarterly*, vol. 16, 1952, pp. 653–670; R. Bauer and D. Gleicher, "Word-of-mouth Communication in the Soviet Union," *Public Opinion Quarterly*, vol. 17, 1953, pp. 297–310; *Communications Behavior and Political Attitudes in Four Arabic Countries* (Bureau of Applied Social Research, New York, 1952); and O. Larsen and R. Hill, "Mass Media and Interpersonal Communication in the Diffusion of a News Event," *American Sociological Review*, vol. 19, 1954, pp. 426–443.

events sometimes increases personal tensions and anxiety which, in turn, leads the individual to reduce his attention to the news (hence disturbing the normal state of equilibrium). From this perspective, it is significant that the same mass media which provide surveillance and correlation often serve as a source of entertainment in a mass society. Indeed, the entertainment aspects of events may be interspersed with or woven into the news itself, in such forms as human-interest stories, oddities in the news, scandal, gossip, details of private lives, cartoons, and comic strips. One function of mass-communicated entertainment, then, is to provide respite for the individual which, perhaps, permits him to continue to be exposed to the mass-communicated news, interpretation, and prescriptions so necessary for his survival in the modern world. At present, such an assertion is only conjectural. There is no reason, however, why future audience research might not bear directly upon the functional issue at hand, especially as such research illuminates the multiple uses to which the mass media are put and the varied gratifications and annoyances that people experience while getting the news.[26]

SELECTED PUBLICATIONS BY DR. WRIGHT

Applications of Methods of Evaluation, Co-author with Herbert H. Hyman and Terence K. Hopkins (U. California Press, Berkeley, 1962).

Public Leadership, Co-author with W. Bell and R. J. Hill (Chandler Press, San Francisco, 1961).

Mass Communications: A Sociological Perspective (Random House, New York, 1959). (Japanese edition published in 1960; Spanish and Italian translations in press.)

QUESTIONS

1. Describe the four components Wright uses in defining mass communications.

2. How does functional analysis apply to a given social system?

3. What are the six functions of the newspaper, according to Malcolm Wiley?

26. For a recent discussion of some possible studies of the "uses" of mass media see E. Katz, "Mass Communications Research and the Study of Popular Culture: An Editorial Note on a Possible Future for This Journal," *Studies in Public Communication,* no. 2, 1959, pp. 1–6.

4. Explain the three major activities of communication specialists mentioned by Lasswell.

5. Distinguish between manifest functions and latent functions.

6. Describe examples of dysfunctions in mass communications with reference to (1) international relations, (2) crime.

7. Discuss at least two positive functions the mass media perform for society and its members by making a constant flow of data available on events occurring within the society or in the larger world. How can these positive functions be transformed into negative ones?

8. Compare Fearing's theory of communications with Wright's *functional analysis* of the mass media. Would Fearing agree with Wright's statement: "If the individual is to maintain a state of adequate or normal operation in a society in which events of importance to him occur outside the immediate observable environment, then there must be available to him some sufficient form of mass-communicated news"?

Elihu Katz

Communication Research and the
Image of Society: Convergence
of Two Traditions [1][*]

THE FOLLOWING REPORT *does two things of significance for us: First, it reviews a body of literature on the way in which communications affect members of social groups. It points out that the body of literature under review strongly suggests that communications from the mass media are not directly effective on most members of the "mass" but rather have an effect only after they have been transmitted or legitimized by local initiators and leaders. That is to say, in terms of this analysis, it is misleading to think of an undifferentiated mass or public or vast crowd directly affected by the mass media—rather the mass media act through those local people who set intellectual or physical styles for particular groups. It is not entirely clear, in terms of the work that has been done, so far, whether the public are often aware of what the mass media are saying but do not act until the local leaders have approved and ratified the mass-media recommendations, or whether the local leaders act as transmission belts. As a guess, it seems likely that there is some variation from one to the other of these situations. It should be pointed out that the "local leaders," the style-setters, in one area or subject are not necessarily leaders or style-setters in another and that some of those who actually initiate or pass*

1. This is a revision of a paper prepared for the Fourth World Congress of Sociology, 1959, and is part of a larger inventory of research on social and psychological factors affecting the diffusion of innovation supported by the Social Science Research Committee of the University of Chicago and the Foundation for Research on Human Behavior. Thanks are due to Martin L. Levin, who has assisted with this project, and to Professors C. Arnold Anderson and Everett M. Rogers for helpful criticism.

* Reprinted from *American Journal of Sociology,* vol. 65, no. 5, March, 1960, by permission of the author and the publisher. (Copyright 1960 by the University of Chicago Press.)

on changes would not normally be called "leaders," e.g., the teen-age girls who are first to seize upon new fashions and pass them on to their mothers and aunts.

Second, the article shows that a totally independent group of scholars, working in a different field, have found the same "two-step" flow of influence operating. Students of innovation in agricultural practices in this country have found that, in general, new techniques are most effectively spread through local style-setters and innovators rather than through direct appeal to the mass of farmers. This finding tends to confirm the impression that we are here confronted with a general social process—that innovations are generally spread through some such two-step flow process rather than going directly and immediately to a crowd or mass.

The writer, who has much of his life been concerned with candidate selection, is reasonably sure that normally candidates become public figures in the same fashion: here and there a local innovator or political style-setter is persuaded to support a given candidate and after enough of them have talked with their friends and neighbors, then and only then is appeal to the masses ordinarily useful.

Of course, two or even three swallows do not prove the existence of a summer, though they may strongly suggest it. The mere fact that in general, and chiefly in the United States, the two-step flow of influence has been demonstrated in two situations does not enable us to be certain about what happens elsewhere or in other circumstances. Perhaps a Castro or Peron appealed directly to the masses in the first instance; though we may doubt it, we can not honestly say, "Certainly, no." Perhaps in Communist China the introduction of new agricultural practices takes place directly from the top to the mass without the need for intermediaries; though again we may doubt it. I am not even aware of studies in Puerto Rico or French Canada which show that the process Katz describes takes place among the peasants there; though I strongly suspect it does. All of which is merely to say that here, as so often elsewhere, in the study of human behavior in general and mass communications in particular, we need careful studies, replicating in new areas or in different times original studies. If the examples just cited seem pedestrian (perhaps readers of this book are not much interested in the way in which a new variety of cherry came to be grown in Puerto Rico or how new fishing techniques were disregarded in that island, although these are important economic matters) or impractical (can Yankee students study Castro's Cuba empirically and impartially?), there are exciting and practical possibilities—is the "Negro revolution" in the United States the crusade for desegregation, exemplifying or contradicting Katz's point? Do such long-established political heroes as Muñoz Marin in Puerto Rico or Smallwood in Newfoundland or de Gaulle in France exemplify or contradict the thesis? Berelson (503–509) *to the contrary withstanding, there is ample room for significant and interesting studies of public opinion and communications now, here, today, on such problems as these.*   L. A. D.

DR. KATZ *is associate professor of sociology at the University of Chicago. This article is a product of the author's continuing concern with the design of research on the flow of influence and, especially, with the processes of mass and interpersonal communication relevant to the diffusion of innovation.*

Research on mass communications has concentrated on persuasion, that is, on the ability of the mass media to influence, usually to change, opinions, attitudes, and actions in a given direction. This emphasis has led to the study of campaigns—election campaigns, marketing campaigns, campaigns to reduce racial prejudice, and the like. Although it has been traditional to treat audience studies, content analysis, and effect studies as separate areas, there is good reason to believe that all three have been motivated primarily by a concern with the effective influencing of thought and behavior in the short run.[2]

Other fields of social research have also focused on the effectiveness of campaigns, a prominent example being the twenty-year-old tradition of research by rural sociologists on the acceptance of new farm practices. Yet, despite this shared concern, the two traditions of research for many years were hardly aware of each other's existence or of their possible relevance for each other. Indeed, even now, when there is already a certain amount of interchange between them, it is not easy to conceive of two traditions that, ostensibly, seem more unrelated. Rural sociology suggests the study of traditional values, of kinship, primary relations, *Gemeinschaft;* research on mass communications, on the other hand, is almost a symbol of urban society.

The recognition that these two traditions of research have now begun to accord each other is, in large measure, the product of a revision of the image of society implicit in research on mass communications. Thus, although the convergence now taking place has surely proceeded from both directions, this paper attempts to present the story from one side only.[3]

2. This point is elaborated in Elihu Katz and Paul F. Lazarsfeld, *Personal Influence: The Part Played by People in the Flow of Mass Communication* (Free Press, New York, 1955).

3. It would be interesting if a rural sociologist would tell it from his point of view. In any case, this meeting of traditions is timely, in view of the pessimism expressed by C. Arnold Anderson's "Trends in Rural Sociology," in Robert K. Merton *et al.* (eds.), *Sociology Today* (Basic, New York, 1959), p. 361. Anderson regards research on diffusion as the most sophisticated branch of rural sociology.

COMMUNICATION RESEARCH AND THE
IMAGE OF SOCIETY

Until very recently, the image of society in the minds of most students of communication was of atomized individuals, connected with the mass media but not with one another.[4] Society—the "audience"—was conceived of as aggregates of age, sex, social class, and the like, but little thought was given to the relationships implied thereby or to more informal relationships. The point is not that the student of mass communications was unaware that members of the audience have families and friends but that he did not believe that they might affect the outcome of a campaign; informal interpersonal relations, thus, were considered irrelevant to the institutions of modern society.

What research on mass communications has learned in its three decades is that the mass media are far less potent than had been expected. A variety of studies—with the possible exception of studies of marketing campaigns—indicates that people are not easily persuaded to change their opinions and behavior.[5] The search for the sources of resistance to change, as well as for the effective sources of influence when changes *do* occur, led to the discovery of the role of interpersonal relations.[6] The shared values in groups of family, friends, and co-workers and the networks of communication which are their structure, the decision and the networks of members to accept or resist a new idea—all these are interpersonal processes which "intervene" between the campaign in the mass media and the individual who is the ultimate target. These recent discoveries, of course, upset the traditional image of the individuated audience upon which the discipline has been based. Moreover, there is good reason to

4. Cf. similar conclusions of Eliot Freidson, "Communications Research and the Concept of the Mass," in Wilbur Schramm (ed.), *The Process and Effects of Mass Communication* (U. of Illinois Press, Urbana, 1954), pp. 380–388, and Joseph B. Ford, "The Primary Group in Mass Communication," *Sociology and Social Research*, vol. 38, 1954, pp. 152–158.

5. For a review of such studies see Joseph T. Klapper, *The Effects of the Mass Media* (Bureau of Applied Social Research, New York, 1949); relevant excerpts from this document appear in Schramm (ed.), *op. cit.*, pp. 289–320. G. D. Wiebe suggests reasons why marketing campaigns fare better than others, in "Merchandising Commodities and Citizenship on Television," *Public Opinion Quarterly*, vol. 15, 1951–52, pp. 679–691. See also Paul F. Lazarsfeld and Robert K. Merton, "Mass Communication, Popular Taste and Organized Social Action," in Wilbur Schramm (ed.), *Mass Communications* (U. of Illinois Press, Urbana, 1949), pp. 459–480.

6. This parallels the discovery of the relevance of interpersonal relations in other modern institutions, especially in mass production.

believe that the image of society in the minds of students of popular culture needs revision in other dimensions as well.[7] But these remarks are concerned only with the discovery that the mass audience is not so atomized and disconnected as had been thought.

INTERPERSONAL RELATIONS AND MASS COMMUNICATIONS

Given the need to modify the image of the audience so as to take account of the role of interpersonal relations in the process of mass communications, researchers seem to have proceeded in three directions. First of all, studies were designed so as to characterize individuals not only by their individual attributes but also by their relationship to others. At the Bureau of Applied Social Research of Columbia University, where much of this work has gone on, a series of successive studies examined the ways in which influences from the mass media are intercepted by interpersonal networks of communication and made more or less effective thereby. These were studies of decisions of voters, of housewives to try a new kind of food, of doctors to adopt a new drug, and so on.[8] Elsewhere, studies have focused on the relevance of such variables as relative integration among peers or membership in one kind of group rather than another.[9] These studies are rapidly multiplying.

A second strategy is the study of small groups; indeed, a number of links have been forged between macroscopic research on the mass media and the microscopic study of interpersonal communication.[10]

But, while research on small groups can provide many clues to a

7. See Edward A. Shils, "Mass Society and Its Culture," *Daedalus,* vol. 89, 1960, pp. 288–314, for a critique of the common tendency among students of communication to conceive of mass society as disorganized and anomic.

8. For a review of these studies see Elihu Katz, "The Two-Step Flow of Communication: An Up-to-Date Report on an Hypothesis," *Public Opinion Quarterly,* vol. 21, 1957, pp. 61–78.

9. For a recent systematic exposition of a number of these studies see John W. Riley, Jr., and Matilda W. Riley, "Mass Communication and the Social System," in Merton *et al.* (eds.), *op. cit.,* pp. 537–578, and Joseph T. Klapper, "What We Know about the Effects of Mass Communication: The Brink of Hope," *Public Opinion Quarterly,* vol. 21, 1957–58, pp. 453–474.

10. E.g., Carl I. Hovland, Irving L. Janis, and Harold H. Kelley, *Communication and Persuasion* (Yale U. P., New Haven, 1953), chap. v, "Group Membership and Resistance to Influence," and John W. C. Johnstone and Elihu Katz, "Youth Culture and Popular Music," *American Journal of Sociology,* vol. 62, 1957, pp. 563–568. For a review of the implications of research on the small group for the design of research on mass communication see Katz and Lazarsfeld, *op. cit.,* Part I.

better understanding of the role of interpersonal relations in the process of mass communications, it focuses almost exclusively on what goes on *within* a group. The third strategy of research, then, was to seek leads from research concerned with the introduction of change from *outside* a social system. Here the work of the rural sociologists is of major importance.[11] For the last two decades the latter have been inquiring into the effectiveness of campaigns to gain acceptance of new farm practices in rural communities while taking explicit account of the relevant channels of communication both outside and inside the community.[12] Yet, despite the obvious parallel between rural and urban campaigns, it was not until after the "discovery" of interpersonal relations that the student of mass communications had occasion to "discover" rural sociology.

INTERPERSONAL RELATIONS AND RURAL COMMUNICATION

If the assumption that interpersonal relations were irrelevant was central to the research worker on mass communications, the opposite was true of the student of rural campaigns. And the reasons are quite apparent: rural sociologists never assumed, as students of mass communications had, that their respondents did not talk to each other. How could one overlook the possible relevance of farmers' contacts with one another to their response to a new and recommended farm practice? The structure of interpersonal relations, it was assumed, was no less important for channeling the flow of influence than the farm journal or the county agent.[13]

---

11. Relevant also is the anthropological study of underdeveloped areas where social structure may sometimes be taken into account along with culture in explaining the acceptance of change; e.g., see Benjamin D. Paul (ed.), *Health, Culture and Community: Case Studies of Public Reactions to Health Programs* (Russell Sage Foundation, New York, 1955).

12. For reviews of research in this field see Subcommittee on the Diffusion and Adoption of New Farm Practices of the Rural Sociological Society, *Sociological Research on the Diffusion and Adoption of New Farm Practices* (Lexington: Kentucky Agricultural Experiment Station, 1952), and Eugene A. Wilkening, "The Communication of Information on Innovations in Agriculture," in the forthcoming volume by Wilbur Schramm (ed.), *Communicating Behavioral Science Information* (Stanford U. P., Stanford, Calif.). A recent bibliography on *Social Factors in the Adoption of Farm Practices* was prepared by the North Central Rural Sociology Subcommittee on Diffusion (Iowa State College, Ames, 1959).

13. Yet rural sociologists have justifiably berated their colleagues for not taking more *systematic* account of interpersonal structures (e.g., Herbert F. Lionberger, "The Diffusion of Farm and Home Information as an Area of Sociological Research," *Rural Sociology*, vol. 17, 1952, pp. 132–144.

Why did relationships among members of the audience figure so much more prominently in research on new farm practices than in research on marketing campaigns, campaigns to reduce prejudice, and the like? Consider the following explanations.

It is obvious, in the first place, that rural sociologists define their arena of research, at least in part, by contrast with the allegedly impersonal, atomized, anomic life of the city. If urban relationships are "secondary," rural life must be somewhere near the other end of the continuum. Hence primary, interpersonal relations—their location, their sizes and shapes, and their consequences—are of central concern.[14]

Second, research on mass communications, linked as it is to research on opinions and attitudes, is derived more directly from individual psychology than sociology. Students of rural change, on the other hand, have a sociological heritage and a continuing tradition of tracing the relations of cliques, the boundaries of neighborhoods, the web of kinship and the like.[15] Only recently has sociological theory begun to have a cumulative impact upon research on mass communications.

Rural sociologists, moreover, who study the adoption of new farm practices are, typically, in the employ of colleges of agriculture, which, in turn, are associated with state colleges and universities. The locale of operations is somewhat more circumscribed, as a result, than it is in the case of the student of urban mass media. The student of the adoption of new farm practices is not interested in, say, a representative national sample. Sometimes, therefore, he will interview all the farmers in a given county or a very large proportion of them, and this makes it possible to collect data on the relations among individual respondents, which, obviously, is impossible in random cross-sectional sampling where respondents are selected as "far apart" from each other as possible. By the same token, the investigator of rural communication is more a part of the situation he is studying; it is more difficult for him to overlook interpersonal influence as a variable.

Finally, a fact, related in part to the previous one, is that the rural sociologist has been primarily interested in the efficacy of the local agricultural agency's program, and, while the local agent employs the mass

14. See the propositions concerning the systems of social interaction in rural, as contrasted with urban, society in Pitirim Sorokin and Carle C. Zimmerman, *Principles of Rural-Urban Sociology* (Holt, New York, 1929), pp. 48–58.

15. The work of Charles P. Loomis is outstanding in this connection; on his approach to the relationship between interpersonal structures and the introduction of change see Loomis and J. Allan Beegle, *Rural Sociology: The Strategy of Change* (Prentice-Hall, Englewood Cliffs, N.J., 1957). Sociometry has played an important role in this development.

media as well as personal visits, demonstrations, and other techniques, his influence is plainly disproportionately effective among the more educated and those enjoying prestige in the community and considerably less so among others. Research workers soon were able to suggest, however, that the county agent's effectiveness for a majority of the population may be indirect, for the people he influences may influence others. This idea of a "two-step" flow of communication also suggested itself as a promotional idea to magazines and other vehicles of mass communications, but it was not actually studied—perhaps because it was more difficult to define operationally—until rather recently.[16]

SOME CONSEQUENCES OF CONVERGENCE

That research on mass communications and on the diffusion and acceptance of new farm practices have "discovered" each other is increasingly evident from the references and citations in recent papers in both fields.[17] The realization of the shared interest in the problem of campaigns—or, more accurately now, in the shared problems of diffusion— has evidently overcome academic insulation. From the point of view of students of mass communications, it took a change in the image of the audience to reveal that the two traditions were studying almost exactly the same problem.

Now that the convergence has been accomplished, however, what consequences are likely to follow? First of all, the two will be very likely to affect each other's design of research. The problem of how to take account of interpersonal relations and still preserve the representativeness of a sample is paramount in studies of mass communications, while that of rural sociologists is how to generalize from studies of neighborhoods, communities, and counties. What is more, despite their persistent concern with interpersonal relations, students of rural diffusion have never mapped the spread of a particular innovation against the sociometric structure of an

16. For mention of the claims of communicators that members of their audiences are influential for others see one of the earliest pieces of research on opinion leaders: Frank A. Stewart, "A Sociometric Study of Influence in Southtown," *Sociometry*, vol. 10, 1947, pp. 11–31.

17. E.g., Everett M. Rogers and George M. Beal, "The Importance of Personal Influence in the Adoption of Technological Changes," *Social Forces*, vol. 36, 1958, pp. 329–335, and Herbert Menzel and Elihu Katz, "Social Relations and Innovation in the Medical Profession," *Public Opinion Quarterly*, vol. 19, 1955–56, pp. 337–353. More important, perhaps, is the "official" recognition of the relevance of research on mass communications in the 1959 bibliography of the North Central Rural Sociology Subcommittee, *op. cit.*

entire community; paradoxically, a recent study deriving from the tradition of research on mass communications has attempted it.[18] Clearly, both fields can contribute to the refinement of research design, and their contributions, moreover, would have implications not only for each other but for a growing number of substantive fields which are interested in tracing the spread of specific innovations through social structures. This includes the work of students of technical assistance programs, of health campaigns, of marketing behavior, of fads and fashions, and the like.

Second, the convergence has already revealed a list of parallel findings which strengthen theory in both. Several findings that seem most central are:

[1] In both urban and rural settings personal influence appears to be more effective in gaining acceptance for change than are the mass media or other types of influence. A number of studies—but by no means all—have found that there is a tendency for adopters of an innovation to credit "other people" with having influenced their decisions.[19] What is of interest, however, is not the precise ranking of the various sources of influence but the undeniable fact that interpersonal communication plays a major role in social and technical change both in the city and on the farm.

18. See James S. Coleman, Elihu Katz, and Herbert Menzel, "The Diffusion of an Innovation among Physicians," *Sociometry*, vol. 20, 1957, pp. 253–270. See also the reports of "Project Revere," e.g., Stuart C. Dodd, "Formulas for Spreading Opinions," *Public Opinion Quarterly*, vol. 22, 1958–59, pp. 537–554, and Melvin L. DeFleur and Otto N. Larsen, *The Flow of Information* (Harper, New York, 1958). Extensive work on informal cliques as facilitators and barriers to interpersonal communication in rural communities has been reported by Herbert F. Lionberger and C. Milton Coughenor, *Social Structure and the Diffusion of Farm Information* (University of Missouri Agricultural Experiment Station, Columbia, 1957).

19. Typically, the respondent is asked to recall the sources influencing him, arrange them chronologically, and then select the one which was "most influential." The shortcomings of this are obvious. There are many exceptions, but a sizable number of studies have reported that the influence of "other people" is more influential than other sources. See, e.g., Herbert F. Lionberger, *Information-seeking Habits and Characteristics of Farm Operators* (Missouri Agricultural Experiment Station Research Bull. 581, Columbia, 1955); E. A. Wilkening, *Adoption of Improved Farm Practices as Related to Family Factors* (Wisconsin Agricultural Experiment Station Research Bull. 183, Madison, 1953); Marvin A. Anderson, "Acceptance and Use of Fertilizer in Iowa," *Croplife*, II (1955); George Fisk, "Media Influence Reconsidered," *Public Opinion Quarterly*, vol. 23, 1959, pp. 83–91; and Katz and Lazarsfeld, *op. cit.*, Part II. The more important question, however, is under what conditions certain sources of influence are more or less likely to be influential. Different innovations, different social structures, and different phases of the process of decision and of diffusion have been shown to be associated with variations in the role of the media. The latter two factors are treated below.

[2] When decision-making is broken down into phases (e.g., becoming aware of an innovation, becoming interested in it, evaluating it, deciding to try it, etc.), the mass media appear relatively more influential in the early informational phases, whereas personal influences are more effective in the later phases of deliberation and decision. The tendency in both traditions is no longer to look at the media as competitive but, rather, as complementary by virtue of their function in various phases of an individual's decision.[20]

[3] The earliest to accept an innovation are more likely than those who accept later to have been influenced by agricultural agencies, mass media, and other formal and/or impersonal sources, whereas the latter are more likely to be influenced by personal sources (presumably, by the former).[21] Furthermore, the personal sources to which early adopters respond are likely to be outside their own communities, or at a greater distance, than are the personal sources influencing later adopters.[22] The orientation of early adopters—"cosmopolitan," "secular," "urbanized," "scientific" (to choose from among the terms that have been employed) —also reveals an openness to the rational evaluation of a proposed change and a willingness for contact with the world outside their communities.[23]

20. Cf. James S. Coleman, Elihu Katz, and Herbert Menzel, *Doctors and New Drugs* (Free Press, New York, 1960), with such recent rural studies as Rogers and Beal, *op. cit.;* James H. Copp, Maurice L. Sill, and Emory J. Brown, "The Function of Information Sources in the Farm Practice Adoption Process," *Rural Sociology,* vol. 23, 1958, pp. 146–157; and Eugene A. Wilkening, "Roles of Communicating Agents in Technological Change in Agriculture," *Social Forces,* vol. 34, 1956, pp. 361–367. Earlier formulations tended to *infer* the psychological stages of decision-making from the typical sequence of the media reported by respondents, but more recent formulations define the phases of decisions and the media employed in each phase independently. The studies cited above representing the most advanced approach to this problem are also considering the consequences of the use of media "appropriate" or "inappropriate" to a given stage of decision.

21. This, of course, is the "two-step" flow of communication, a conception which finds support in the studies reviewed by Katz, *op. cit.;* Rogers and Beal, *op. cit.;* Lionberger, *op. cit.;* and F. E. Emery and O. A. Oeser, *Information, Decision and Action: Psychological Determinants of Changes in Farming Techniques* (University of Melbourne Press, Melbourne, Australia, 1958).

22. Cf. Coleman, Katz, and Menzel, *op. cit.,* with E. A. Wilkening, *Acceptance of Improved Farm Practices in Three Coastal Plain Counties* (North Carolina Agricultural Experiment Station Technical Bull. 98, Chapel Hill, 1952), and James Copp, *Personal and Social Factors Associated with the Adoption of Recommended Farm Practices* (Kansas State College, Agricultural Experiment Station Research Bull., Manhattan, 1956).

23. See Bryce Ryan and Neal Gross, *Acceptance and Diffusion of Hybrid Seed Corn in Two Iowa Communities* (Iowa State College, Agricultural Experiment Station Bull. 372, Ames, 1950), and Emery and Oeser, *op. cit.* The latter, however, suggest that, under certain conditions, personal contact may be more impor-

Many of the studies support the notion of a "two-step" flow of communication in which innovators are influenced from outside and in which they, in turn, influence others with whom they have personal contact.

This is not to claim that there are no differences between communication in urban and rural society or that the direction of the difference between the two kinds of communities may not be essentially as originally perceived by social theorists. Nor is it claimed that all research findings are mutually compatible. Instead, the purpose of this paper is to call attention to the image of society implicit in two fields of research on communication, pointing to the influence of such images on the design of research and on "interdisciplinary" contacts, and to call attention to a few remarkably similar findings in these heretofore unrelated fields, suggesting that the study of communication will surely profit from their increasing interchange.

SELECTED PUBLICATIONS BY DR. KATZ

Personal Influence: The Part Played by People in the Flow of Mass Communication (Free Press, New York, 1955), with Paul F. Lazarsfeld.

"The Two-Step Flow of Communication: An Up-to-date Report on an Hypothesis," *Public Opinion Quarterly,* vol. 21, no. 1, 1957, pp. 61–78.

"The Social Itinerary of Technical Change," *Human Organization,* vol. 20, no. 2, 1961, pp. 70–82.

SUGGESTIONS FOR FURTHER READING

Freidson, Eliot, "Communications Research and the Concept of the Mass," in Wilbur Schramm (ed.), *The Process and Effects of Mass Communication* (U. of Illinois Press, 1954), pp. 380–388.

Riley, John W., Jr., and Matilda White Riley, "Mass Communication and the Social System," in Robert K. Merton et al. (eds.), *Sociology Today* (Basic, New York, 1959), pp. 537–578.

Lionberger, Herbert F., *Adoption of New Ideas and Practices* (Iowa State U. P., Ames, 1960).

Rogers, Everett M., *Diffusion of Innovations* (Free Press, New York, 1962).

QUESTIONS

1.   "Interpersonal communication plays a major role in social and technical change both in the city and on the farm." (*a*) Is this statement of any particular significance? When? (*b*) What are the implications of this statement for students of mass communication?

---

tant for early adopters even though they, in turn, are primary sources of influence for those who follow their lead.

2.   Under what circumstances did students of mass communication "discover" rural sociology?

3.   A and B are exposed at different times to a new idea. A heard about it through the mass media. B heard about it from A. Which one would be most likely to accept the new idea first? Under what circumstances? Of what concept is this an example?

PART III

THE COMMUNICATOR
AND HIS AUDIENCE

Raymond A. Bauer

The Communicator and the Audience *

HAD BAUER not already used his title "The Communicator and His Audience" we might well have called our entire book "Communicators and Their Audiences." For Bauer is here making in particularly cogent fashion the point to which we return again and again: the communicator says what he has to say because of his notions about his audience(s). In most cases, his notions of his audiences and their expectations and understandings are more or less correct. Pool and Shulman, in a following article (pp. 140–158) indicate what kinds of notions one particular class of communicators have in mind. White's Gatekeeper Study (pp. 160–171) has become a classic because he demonstrates the process of selection used by "gatekeepers" in the communication process, and this selection is determined of course in part by the notions about audiences. As Breed (pp. 86–200) makes clear, communicators may in some instances be more influenced by their immediate audience of superiors and colleagues than by the "mass" audience "out there" somewhere. Dexter (pp. 397–409) shows that the old problem of democratic political philosophy, the relationship of a representative to his constituents, can also be well interpreted in terms of a communicator-audience relationship.

This article, like that by Dexter (pp. 397–409), is related to the recently published Bauer-Pool-Dexter volume on American Business and Public Policy (Atherton, New York, 1963). That volume (except for Part I) is an attempt to describe a complex web of communicator-audience relationships, involving Congressmen, big businessmen, small businessmen, State Department employees, lobbyists, and "interested citizens." The way in which social role and position affect the interpretation of communications in all these categories of people is the book's major emphasis; there is particular concern with the degree to which choices about what to listen to and what to say are made in terms of social position and role. This last point, the authors

* Revision of a paper delivered at the tenth anniversary of the founding of the Department and Laboratory of Social Relations, Harvard University, Feb. 9, 1957. [Reprinted from the *Journal of Conflict Resolution*, vol. 2, no. 1, March, 1958, pp. 67–77, by permission of the author and the publisher. Copyright 1958 by the *Journal of Conflict Resolution*.]

suggest, is particularly important, because often if forced to concentrate on a particular subject, individuals might believe the same thing and vote the same way, regardless of immediate experience. But minor variations in recent social experience—foreign travel, for example— may somewhat alter what they choose to attend to; and the choice of what to attend to is, among busy "decision makers," often likely to determine what gets done.   L. A. D.

DR. BAUER is currently Professor of Business Administration at the Harvard Graduate School of Business Administration. A social psychologist, he received his Ph.D. from Harvard in 1950. He has also taught in the Industrial Relations Section at Massachusetts Institute of Technology, and in 1955–56 he was a fellow of the Center for Advanced Study in the behavioral sciences. He has conducted research in communications, marketing, and decision making.

If we may judge by the glee with which physicists greeted the recent demolition of one of the theoretical underpinnings of their trade, it would seem that limited chaos is a sign of health in a science. When old models prove too simple, we expand them and add new variables. In the short run we are delighted when our work substantiates our theories. In the long run, however, it is the discarding of theories and assumptions that marks the milestones of advance. On these grounds, research in the field of social communications may be viewed with a great deal of satisfaction. A high proportion of individual pieces of research are so inconclusive that they have forced on us these ever more elaborated models of the communications process. To cite just one major example: It is now generally conceded that the Erie County study of the 1940 elections compelled us to discard certain simple assumptions about the direct impact of the mass media upon the mass audience. The idea of the "two-step flow of communications" was introduced, and this initiated a search for opinion leaders. But opinion leaders proved not to be a single class of persons all of whom exercised their influence in the same way. We are now thrown back on looking for networks of interpersonal communication. Not only has the communications model been expanded, but the study of informal communications has now blended into basic psychological research on interpersonal influence and sociological studies of the primary group.[1]

The same sort of revision is gradually taking place with respect to the classic formula of communications research: "Who says what to whom and with what effect?" Originally, communications research implicitly gave the major initiative to the communicator. The main question

1. This trend is excellently and extensively reviewed by Elihu Katz and Paul Lazarsfeld in the first portion of *Personal Influence* (11).

asked was: What sort of communications and media are most effective and under what circumstances? It would be incorrect to say that the audience was *ignored,* but it was certainly accorded very little initiative. Audiences (if I may use this term to embrace also "readers") have, however, proved intractable. They make their own decisions as to whether to listen or not to listen. Even when they listen, the communication may have no effect, or it may boomerang. Increasingly, researchers have had to shift their attention to the audience itself to find out what sorts of people they are dealing with under what circumstances.

I would like to go further and suggest that in the future we may come to regard the audience more and more as a system of response potentials and the communication as a signal which triggers off the response highest in the hierarchy. Or, to shift language a bit, what was once regarded as a "stimulus-bound" situation looks more and more like a "response-bound" situation. I am not proposing that this is all of what happens in *all* communications, but I *am* proposing that we are likely to find that it is profitable to look at a high proportion of communications not as *changing* behavior but as triggering the organism to do what it was very likely to do in any event. If this view of the audience is correct, it is of course not the result of, nor can it be tested by, any single crucial experiment; it is rather the reflection of the impact of a long series of research findings.

Our own attempts to understand a series of problems in the field of international communications have suggested to us the desirability of entertaining seriously the following propositions concerning the role of the audience in communications: (I) The audience influences the way in which the communicator organizes new information and thereby what he himself may remember and/or believe at a later point in time. (II) A communication once completed has an existence external to the originator. It is a sample of his behavior which he must often reconcile—as a result of social or of internal pressure—with other behavior. On this latter point we need only remember the story of Franklin Roosevelt's asking Samuel Rosenman to reconcile one of his early speeches with later policy. After some deliberation, Rosenman told FDR that the only solution to his dilemma was flatly to deny having made the first speech. (III) Communications are seldom directed to a single manifest audience. Secondary audiences or reference groups, usually internalized and often imaginary, are important targets of communication and may at times play a decisive role in the flow of communications.

These propositions are not new discoveries. They may be found in the sociology of C. H. Cooley and of G. H. Mead, the psychiatry of Harry Stack Sullivan and others, and the essays of writers on communication.

The rationale for presenting them in this context is twofold. First, practical problems of communications research have suggested to us their utility; second, it appears that it is presently possible to bring to bear on these propositions more systematic data than have been employed in the past. Much of what I have to say will consist of reporting work we have done and are planning to do and of pointing to established areas of research and to individual studies which contribute with varying degrees of directness to the testing of these propositions, their implications, and their practical significance.

I. EFFECT OF THE AUDIENCE ON ORGANIZATION AND RETENTION OF MATERIAL

Our first proposition is that audiences influence the way in which a person organizes new information and thereby what he himself may remember and/or believe at a later point in time.

The functional approach to perception and remembering which has been so attractive to social psychologists in the past decades has led them to investigate the relationship of man's needs and interests to the way he perceives and remembers the "blooming, buzzing confusion" around him. Is it not equally plausible that one will organize new information in terms of its intended use in interpersonal relations, that a person who intends to communicate on a topic will organize and remember material on that subject as a function of his image of the audience he has in mind?

This question was posed by Harry Grace in a paper published in 1951 (8). He asked subjects to remember an array of objects which they were later to report to an experimenter. Some of the subjects were told that the person to whom they were to report was a woman; the control subjects were told nothing about the characteristics of the person to whom they were to report. It was anticipated, since some of the items might be "embarrassing" to report to a woman, that those subjects who were briefed on the sex of the experimenter would remember fewer of these items than would control subjects. Grace's data were not so conclusive as one might hope for, but he had nevertheless posed a meaningful question.

As often happens, the same question occurred to us without our having been aware of Grace's earlier work. While we were trying to organize our thoughts concerning the impact of foreign travel on American businessmen, Ithiel Pool suggested the possibility that a person might never formulate his impressions of a foreign country systematically until he was in the position of having to communicate them to someone else. In this event, the first audience to whom he addressed himself would influence the way in which he would organize his information and the terms in which he would couch his conclusions. In this way the audience would influence what he would later remember and believe. Let us consider the position of a man confronted with a new batch of information or with old unorganized knowledge, i.e., items of information which he has not previously related to each other. He is now in a position in which he views this information, whether "old" or "new," as something he may have to communicate to another person. He has a set to communicate to an audience of which he has a specified image. It is a basic assumption of both content analysis and effective public speaking, as well as the object of commonsense observation, that the communicator adapts his statements to his audience, taking into consideration its interests and expectations for purposes of more effective communication. That this set to communicate may affect what he later remembers is given plausibility by the voluminous experimental literature on the effect of set on perception and retention (cf. Ref. 15, pp. 562ff.).

One of the major problems of design in studies of the influence of set on remembering has been to prevent rehearsal of the material between periods of recall. From the standpoint of communications research, we would assume that such rehearsal is precisely what happens in the real-life situations in which we are interested. Therefore, it presents no design problem. Cooley long ago spelled out the process that we would guess to be at work. The anticipated audience would serve as—in Cooley's words —an imaginary interlocutor with whom the subject would hold internal conversations in anticipation of the eventual communication (Ref. 4, esp. pp. 61–62). In the course of these internal conversations the material ought to be "reworked" to bring it closer to the form in which it was intended to be communicated. Cooley contended that the human personality is formed via such internal conversations with audiences real and imagined. Our goals are more modest. We should like to know what happens to the particular batch of new or newly organized information about which we have been talking. Is retention of this information indeed affected by the person's image of the audience to which he expects to communicate? The audience, in a fashion, coerces the individual into playing a role. Does this also mean, as the work of Janis and King on the influence of role-playing on attitudes (9, 13) suggests, that the subjects' attitudes are changed in this process?

We have so far undertaken only one piece of research directed at the question of the influence of the audience on what is remembered of new, incoming information. This was an experiment reported by Claire Zimmerman and myself (19). The design evolved out of a joint Harvard-MIT seminar consisting of Dr. Zimmerman, Ithiel Pool, Jerome Bruner, George Coelho, and myself.

The experimenter presented herself in the classrooms of a number of colleges and universities, as a representative of one of two fictitious organizations: the National Council of Teachers, identified as interested in improving the teachers' lot, or the American Taxpayers Economy League, identified as interested in saving taxpayers' money. Her organization, she said, was seeking speakers to address its members on the topic of teachers' pay, and she had arranged with the instructor to have them write sample speeches during class time one week from that day. In the meantime, she said, her organization was also interested in how well people remembered material on this topic. She then read a short passage to them—in half the instances favoring, and in the other half opposing, teachers' pay raises. There were thus four groups of 18 persons, each involving all possible combinations of materials and "audiences" both favoring and opposing raises in teachers' pay. She then asked the subjects to write from memory the passage she had just read to them, as close to verbatim as possible. On returning the next week she asked them again, before writing the sample speech, to write down the passage as literally as they could. This was an experiment in remembering, but under conditions where the subjects anticipated communicating the material to an audience of specified characteristics.

Our prediction was that, at the end of a week, subjects would remember more information in those instances in which the passage and the intended audience were on the same side of the issue (we called this a situation of "congruence") than they would if the passages to be remembered and the audience for whom they were to write a speech were in conflict (a situation we labeled "incongruent"). Thus a subject would remember more arguments in favor of raising teachers' pay if he were anticipating a favorable audience than if the intended audience were interested in saving the taxpayers' money. There were no differences among the groups in their initial recall immediately after the presentation of the material. However, there were differences in the expected direction at the end of the ensuing week. Our hypothesis was supported comfortably beyond the 0.01 level of statistical significance. Schramm and Danielson have since replicated the basic experiment at Stanford University, using as subject matter a quite different issue, that of lowering the voting age to 18. The results once more hold up beyond the 0.01 level (17).

A subsidiary hypothesis was that this "audience effect" of selective remembering would be maximal for persons primarily concerned with the audience and minimal for persons primarily involved in the subject matter. The complete design mentioned above was carried out both on graduate students of journalism (supposedly oriented by selection and/or training to be sensitive to the characteristics of the audience) and on students in teachers' colleges (presumably highly involved in the issue of teachers' pay). The basic hypothesis held up for both groups. But the effect, as predicted, was greater among the graduate students of journalism. The difference in effect was, again, statistically significant beyond the 0.01 level. The journalism students' rate of forgetting in a situation of "incongruence" was *double* that in a situation of "congruence." These results appear to be not only statistically but practically significant (see Table 1).

Table 1—Mean Angles Corresponding to Percentage Losses for All Groups Between First and Second Recall Trials *

	TAX AUDIENCE		TEACHERS AUDIENCE	
STUDENTS OF	Incongruent Raise Salary Arguments	Congruent Do Not Raise Salary Arguments	Incongruent Do Not Raise Salary Arguments	Congruent Raise Salary Arguments
Journalism	55.44	26.85	54.79	27.30
Teaching	40.05	26.81	41.09	25.88

* From Zimmerman and Bauer (Ref. 19, p. 244).

Since the completion of this experiment, several other pieces of work starting out on entirely different tacks have been done which testify to the effectiveness of a set to communicate on the organization and retention of information. Zajonc, in a study directed at an understanding of cognitive process (18), has found that persons who anticipate communicating a body of material organize it differently from persons who anticipate being communicated *to* on the same subject. Furthermore, by specifying that the other persons (i.e., those to whom the subjects are supposedly going to communicate or who are going to communicate to the subjects) are opposed to the subjects' own position on the issue, he was able to effect still further changes in the organization of the material. Thus in Zajonc's work, not only is the communicative set *per se* found relevant, but the qualitative image of the intended audience is also of importance to the way in which new information is handled.

Jones and Aneshansel (10) became interested independently in the question of the relative influence on retention of experimental subjects' own values and their intention to use controversial material for communication. They told some of their subjects that they were going to have to use the material presented to them in rebuttal to arguments with which they were to be confronted later. Their subjects remembered significantly more material counter to their own values when they were told they would have to use this material in an argument. Under control conditions the usual results were found. Subjects remembered more material in line with their own beliefs.

These several findings all seem to say that it is possible to affect what a person will recall of new information by telling him he will have to communicate on the subject and that his image of the audience will affect what is remembered. This indicates that the audience can, in fact, have an enduring effect on the communicator that extends beyond its influence on the form and content of individual messages.

Is it "perception" or "remembering" that is affected? All these studies suffer from the usual difficulty of distinguishing between perception, retention, and recall. In the instance of the Jones and Zajonc studies a very early effect was observed which might possibly reflect the initial organization of incoming material, i.e., perception. In the Zimmerman experiment, however, there was no observed effect on initial recall of the material. But there was a pronounced "audience effect" at the end of a week. This suggests that conscious or unconscious rehearsals of the anticipated speech resulted in accommodation of the newly acquired information to the values and expectations of the intended audience. It makes sense in light of this to look at the intended audience as an induced reference group of high salience. Presumably one's habitual reference groups regularly evoke similar internal conversations, although this process is somewhat more difficult to study.

However, we must again complicate matters. Image of the audience, information, and communicator's values appear to be in a state of active interrelationship in which any one of the elements may affect any one or combination of the others. Communicators committed strongly to the subject matter may "distort" their image of the prospective audience to bring it more in line with either their own values or the content of the incoming information and thereby reduce the "audience effect." Thus the teachers' college students were more likely than the journalists to report "objectively incongruent" audiences as "neutral" with respect to the material they were given to memorize. Furthermore, those subjects who "neutralized" an incongruent audience remembered most of the material. Because of the limited number of cases that fell in these categories, the differences in Zimmerman's data are not statistically reliable and, in fact, some of the findings are presently ambiguous. They do, however, suggest this line of speculation.

Whereas it was previously proposed that reference groups, by acting as internal audiences, affect what one remembers (and possibly one's attitudes), it seems likely also that the individual's image of a reference group is formed and changes in the process of these internal conversations. On controversial issues, this may eventually produce a schematization of reference groups in which positive reference groups are seen as "all white" and negative reference groups are seen as "all black." This proposition, also, seems amenable to systematic study.

There are indications also that the set to communicate may have a dampening effect on the impact of the individual's own values. Most of the experiments on the influence of personal values on remembering and perception accept implicitly the position that pleasurable material will be remembered better than disagreeable material. That which is consonant with the individual's personal values is taken tacitly by most of the investigators to be pleasurable to the individual. Direct test of the proposition that agreeable material will be better remembered has produced conflicting results in quite a number of experiments (cf. Ref. 15, pp. 571ff.). The possibility that positive results of the influence of personal values on remembering and perception may be due, at least in part, to greater familiarity with consonant material may be bypassed for the moment in deference to a point more crucial to the present argument. Reinforcement of one's self-image or ego-defense is only one of the possible motives that may influence one's set toward incoming information. This is already implied in the notion of "perceptual vigilance" with the suggestion that under some circumstances the threshold for so-called "contravaluant" material will be lowered. Jones and Aneshansel make the same argument I am making now and say: "The functionalist might suggest that we examine the total context in which perception (or learning) takes place, in an effort to determine those conditions which promote lowered thresholds for threatening material (perceptual vigilance) and those which promote higher thresholds (perceptual defense)" (Ref. 10, p. 27). It will be remembered that in their experiment positively valued material was better remembered in the control situation, but negatively valued material was better remembered by the experimental subjects who were told they were going to have to use the material in a later argument. Zimmerman's data also indicated that when subjects were given instructions that they would have to communicate on the topic of the material they were to memorize, this set to communicate dampened the effect of the subjects' personal values. Teachers-college students, for example, remembered material opposed to raising teachers' pay as well as they remembered material favoring raising teachers' pay. Pending more direct evidence, it is reasonable to assume that a majority of them favored high salaries for the profession they were about to enter.

To summarize the discussion of this point, I have presented evidence, argument, and speculation to the effect that one's image of the audience to which material is to be communicated affects how this material is organized and/or retained. The influence of the communicative set seems on occasion to offset the role of the individual's personal values and beliefs. However, the audience does not operate independently either of the content of the information in question or of the communicator's values. In some instances the communicator apparently accommodated his image of the audience so as to reduce the perceived incongruence between it and his values and information. Other investigations, of course, have indicated that under some circumstances his values influence what he remembers.

Present evidence is at best not definitive. We have in plan further experimentation to test on larger samples some of the findings which are statistically unreliable; to ascertain to what extent Zimmerman's results reflect forgetting in any meaningful sense as opposed to a response set induced by the fact that the subjects were actually prepared to write a speech; to determine how lasting is the "audience effect" on what is remembered and whether or not attitudes are influenced. Our comparison of teachers-college students with journalism students was a lucky shot in the sociological dark but tells us less of the psychological factors which may be involved. It will be necessary to look into the psychological characteristics which differentiate persons of varying degree of "audience susceptibility" and audience resistance.

II. COMMUNICATION AS PERSONAL COMMITMENT

It is a commonplace that people on occasion say things other than precisely what they feel in their hearts. In psychological literature this circumstance has been memorialized in the distinction between "private" and "public" attitudes. Even the most honest and thoughtful person, confronted by different situations, will, quite sincerely, say different things on the same topic. What is relevant to one person in one situation is not what is relevant to another person in another situation. A disingenuous politician may well argue that he does not preach civil rights in the South because his audience is not interested in the topic. Regardless of the motives involved or the amount of disparity between private belief and public statement, the fact remains that a statement once made constitutes some degree of personal commitment.

It is easy to see how a public figure may be haunted by some utterance of his and be forced to extremes of ingenuity to reconcile it with other of his statements. We need but recall the incident mentioned previously when President Roosevelt asked Rosenman to explain away an earlier speech of Roosevelt's on balancing the budget. More pertinent for us, however, is the possible effect of such commitments on the communicator's own attitudes.

Probably the most relevant body of research is that on compliance to group norms. Students of group dynamics have devoted a considerable amount of attention to the conditions under which an individual will shift his belief—at least on the overt level—to conform to the majority opinion in his group. It was Festinger who, a few years ago, called attention to the fact that overt compliance to group norms is not synonymous with covert compliance, i.e., change in private opinion (5). It is therefore interesting to note that in a recent book Festinger devotes two chapters to the discussion of the conditions under which forced compliance leads to change of private opinion (Ref. 6, chaps. iv and v). He cites experimental work of McBride and Burdick and Kelman's work on the effect of response restriction on opinion change (12).

My own work on political loyalty in the Soviet Union (discussed in Ref. 1), and Bettelheim's earlier study of Nazi concentration camps (2) offer clinical evidence of opinion change when individuals are forced by external circumstances into a given line of behavior. In the light of this work on the effect of forced compliance on opinion change, it is reasonable to hypothesize that the audience, by evoking a commitment from the communicator, may have the second-order effect of causing him to accommodate his own beliefs to that commitment. This process, it would seem, is continuous with the one referred to above in which the audience affects the way in which the communicator organizes and retains information. The difference, however, is that one effect occurs in anticipation of the communication and the other follows after it. While it is easy to draw this distinction analytically, it may be difficult to draw empirically in practical situations, if an individual is involved in several successive communications.

From our contact with elite communications in this and other countries it seems to us that occurrences like the following sometimes take place. A prominent man is invited to deliver a ceremonial speech. In some instances a subordinate may draft the speech, and the speaker is rather indifferent to the content. He only wants it to be a good speech, appropriate to the occasion—that is, not blatantly divergent from his own values. On occasion the speech makes quite a hit, and the speaker is invited to make more speeches on the topic. Soon he is committed even in his own mind to this position and becomes an active advocate of it.

This sort of occurrence is probably rare among the general populace. However, among elite communicators of the sort we have been studying, this may be a problem of genuine practical significance. We have been struck with the frequency with which a public figure, bent on holding or gaining a position of influence, will deliberately seek out issues which may interest his constituency. When he hits on a successful issue and is rewarded, he becomes a vigorous proponent of that issue and in many cases converts himself even more firmly to that belief. This is exemplified in the instance of one ardent congressional spokesman for protectionism who told us that he had tried several issues on his constituency but found them uninterested until he evoked an enthusiastic response to a speech in favor of high tariffs. He has since made this his business.

We have no immediate research plans in this area. But, because of its seeming significance among elite communicators, it appears that we ought to take a closer look at the potential coercive force of the audience in evoking commitments and producing attitude change.

III. REFERENCE GROUPS AS SECONDARY AUDIENCES

Our third and final point is that messages are seldom directed to a single manifest audience but that reference groups, acting as secondary audiences, have an influential and occasionally a crucial role in the flow of communications. The importance of secondary audiences is a matter of common experience and has often been commented on anecdotally. Anyone who wishes to refresh himself on their role in everyday life need only leaf through a few casually selected doctoral theses. It has been my experience in reading them that I could identify certain pages written for Professor A, for Professor B, and certain others for Professor C, even though none of these gentlemen obviously was going to read the thesis.

As I have said, the importance of secondary audiences has been commented on frequently in anecdotal fashion but seldom studied systematically. Systematic work on reference groups—to which I am referring in this context as potential secondary audiences—has been confined largely to their influence on the attitudes of the subjects under investigation. But, unless we consider the interview situation in which the attitudes were evoked as an instance of communication, there has been little direct research on the role of reference groups or secondary audiences in the flow of specific messages. Daniel Lerner has pointed out (14) that the reviews of *The American Soldier* were influenced by the reference groups of the reviewers. More recently, Herbert Gans has presented a case study of the role of the reference groups of various movie-makers in the production of the movie *The Red Badge of Courage* (7). But such examples are few.

In an attempt to get at the actual role played by secondary audiences in the flow of communications, Irwin Shulman, a research assistant at MIT and a journalist himself, interviewed newspapermen immediately after they had finished writing a story for their newspapers. At first he asked, "Who reads stories like this?" In response to this question he got stock answers derived from the newspaper's readership surveys. Then he shifted to asking, "While you were writing this story did you think of any person or group?" The answers to this question were quite different from those to the former question. The persons or groups of whom they actually thought while writing the story were seldom the "average middle-class man who buys this newspaper." The number of interviews was not sufficient for statistical analysis. Yet the qualitative evidence suggested that there was a patterning to these secondary audiences with respect to the type of communicator and story involved. Let me put the case more conservatively: There was in these interviews at least enough evidence that these secondary audiences are more than "noise" in the communications system to encourage us to continue the investigation.

The fact that many, possibly not all, journalists in Shulman's sample thought of secondary audiences while writing did not by any means demonstrate that these secondary audiences influence the content of what is written. An experiment was conducted with journalism students who were asked to write news stories out of a set of disjointed facts (16). The conditions of the experiment and the findings are too complicated for brief summariztaion. However, Pool and Shulman demonstrated that the reference groups and persons evoked were systematically and predictably a function of the material presented to the subjects of the experiment; and, much more interesting, the distortions which occurred in the handling of the material were a systematic function of idiosyncratic images which individual subjects imagined.

Both the results of Zimmerman's experiment, suggesting internal conversation in rehearsal of a speech, and Shulman's and Pool's work indicate the utility of thinking of reference groups as internalized audiences which are targets of imaginary conversations. While the existence of negative reference groups has been mentioned in the literature, almost all attention has been paid to positive reference groups. Reference groups have usually been treated as groups whose acceptance is sought or who are used as positive yardsticks for self-assessment. Our own orientation and data suggest that negative reference groups should be given more serious attention and that reference groups should be regarded as groups which one wants to influence in *any* fashion, whether it be to gain their approval or to persuade them to one's own position.

IV. CONCLUSION

The general import of these remarks is that there is something to be said for expanding our model of the communications process. I have proposed the utility of three propositions and presented evidence for both their plausibility and their practical import. These three propositions are, in summary, (I) images of audiences, both real and imaginary, external and internal, affect the way in which we organize and retain information and what we believe; (II) the audience often commits the speaker to a public position to which he may subsequently accommodate his private belief; and (III) finally, one seldom has in mind a single audience, and secondary, reference-group audiences may often exert the determining influence in the organization and retention of information, as well as in the flow of communication. In the simplest words, the communicator may actually be addressing himself to someone other than the manifest audience.

It will be remembered that our interest in this expanded model of communications was generated by concern with the practical problem of the impact of foreign travel on American businessmen. It is our belief that this view of the communications process will continue to have practical implications in the field of international relations. In the recent conduct of our own foreign policy, observers have commented, the utterances of American officials, while ostensibly directed abroad, were actually directed at domestic American secondary audiences. Also, in international relations audience *images* play a crucial role. Negotiators between nations, in all probability, carry in their heads highly stereotyped images of their opposite numbers. Their absorption and retention of information will be much affected by the intervention of these images. Coelho has, partially out of the stimulus of these ideas, done a doctoral dissertation on the role of audience images as reference groups in the accommodation of Indian students to the United States (3).

While we may talk about such practical implications abstractly, it will take a considerable amount of empirical work to establish what part audience images actually play in international affairs.

SELECTED PUBLICATIONS BY DR. BAUER

"An Analysis of the Influences on Recall of a Controversial Event," *Journal of Social Psychology*, 1941, pp. 211–228. (With John C. Eberhart.)

"Opinion in Relation to Personality and Social Organization," *International Journal of Opinion and Attitude Research*, Winter 1949–1950. (With Henry Riecken.)

"The Influence of Foreign Travel on Political Attitudes of American Businessman," *Public Opinion Quarterly*, Spring 1956. (With Ithiel de Sola Pool and Suzanne Keller.)

"The Effect of an Audience upon What is Remembered," *Public Opinion Quarterly*, Spring, 1956. (With Claire Zimmerman.)

"Brainwashing: Psychology or Demonology?" *The Journal of Social Issues*, vol. 13, no. 3, 1957.

"Limits of Persuasion," *Harvard Business Review*, September–October 1958.

"Executives Probe Space," *Harvard Business Review,* September–October 1960.
"America, Mass Society and Mass Media," *Journal of Social Issues,* vol. 16, no. 3, 1960. (With Alice H. Bauer.)

REFERENCES

1. Bauer, R. A., "Brainwashing: Psychology or Demonology," *Journal of Social Issues,* vol. 8, no. 3, 1957.
2. Bettelheim, B., "Individual and Mass Behavior in Extreme Situations," *Journal of Abnormal and Social Psychology,* vol. 38, 1943, pp. 417–452.
3. Coelho, G., *Acculturative Learning: A Study of Reference Groups,* Harvard University, Ph.D. thesis, 1956.
4. Cooley, C. H., *Human Nature and the Social Order* (Scribner, New York, 1902).
5. Festinger, L., "An Analysis of Compliant Behavior," in M. Sherif and M. O. Wilson (eds.), *Group Relations at the Crossroads* (Harper, New York, 1953).
6. ———, *A Theory of Cognitive Dissonance* (Harper, New York, 1957).
7. Gans, H. J., "The Creator-Audience Relationship in the Mass Media: An Analysis of Movie-making," in B. Rosenberg and D. M. White (eds.) *Mass Culture* (Free Press, New York, 1957).
8. Grace, H. A., "Effects of Different Degrees of Knowledge about an Audience on the Content of Communication," *Journal of Social Psychology,* vol. 34, 1951, pp. 111–124.
9. Janis, I. L., and B. T. King, "The Influence of Role Playing on Opinion Change," *Journal of Abnormal and Social Psychology,* vol. 49, 1954, pp. 211–218.
10. Jones, E. E., and Jane Aneshansel, "The Learning and Utilization of Contravaluant Material," *Journal of Abnormal and Social Psychology,* vol. 53, 1956, pp. 27–33.
11. Katz, E., and P. Lazarsfeld. *Personal Influence* (Free Press, New York, 1955).
12. Kelman, H. C., "Attitude Change as a Function of Response Restriction," *Human Relations,* vol. 6, 1953, pp. 185–214.
13. King, B. T., and I. L. Janis, "Comparison of the Effectiveness of Improvised v. Non-improvised Role-playing in Producing Opinion Changes," *Human Relations,* vol. 9, 1956, pp. 177–186.
14. Merton, R. K., and P. Lazarsfeld (eds.), *Continuities in Social Research: Studies in the Scope and Method of "The American Soldier"* (Free Press, New York, 1950).
15. Osgood, C. E., *Method and Theory in Experimental Psychology* (Oxford U. P., New York, 1953).
16. Pool, I. de S., and I. Shulman, "Imaginary Audiences and the Creative Process," Cambridge, 1957 (mimeographed). See the following article in this Reader.
17. Schramm, W., and W. Danielson, "Anticipated Audiences as Determinants of Recall," *Journal of Abnormal and Social Psychology,* vol. 56, 1958, pp. 282–283.
18. Zajonc, R., *Cognitive Structure and Cognitive Tuning,* University of Michigan, Ph.D. thesis, 1954.
19. Zimmerman, Claire, and R. A. Bauer, "The Influence of an Audience on What is Remembered," *Public Opinion Quarterly,* vol. 20, 1956, pp. 238–248.

QUESTIONS

1.   What new variables has Bauer introduced or discussed that have an influence on a person or group's set to communication? What other variables of this kind have been introduced thus far in this text? In related readings?

2.   Select several objective newspaper articles or verbatim reports on speeches or press conferences delivered by political figures. Note the following in each: On the basis of the speech and current political situation did the speaker have a secondary audience in mind? If so, what kind? Is there any indication that the audience anticipated by the speaker affected his position? If so, in what way?

3.   Formulate a basic signal-response communication model and develop it by use of Bauer's three propositions. Keep in mind his impatience with elaborate models.

Ithiel de Sola Pool and Irwin Shulman

Newsmen's Fantasies, Audiences,

and Newswriting *

THIS ARTICLE, and those by White, Gieber, Dexter, and Breed, go together. They all point out that news is written in terms of the newswriter's conception(s) of the audience. Taken together, they show that the conception of the audience originates in the personality (temperament) of the newswriter and his immediate social environment.

The theoretical approach underlying the articles with which we are here currently concerned—those by Gieber, White, Breed, Pool and Shulman, and by Dexter on Congress—has been most thoughtfully worked out by Arthur F. Bentley (with John Dewey) in An Inquiry Into Inquiries (Beacon Press, Boston, 1954),[1] The Knowing and the Known (Beacon, Boston, 1949), and Behavior, Knowledge, Fact (Principia, Bloomington, Ind., 1935). Bentley's interpretation of social relationships rests upon the notion of "transaction"; he develops the point that relationships between any persons or groups of persons are often profitably studied as relationships between roles and statuses.[2]

* This study was sponsored by the Foundation for Research on Human Behavior through a grant to the communication research program of the Center for International Studies, MIT. It was also supported in part by Air Force contract AF49(638)486 and by funds from the Ford Foundation. The work was done at MIT and in part at the Center for Advanced Study in the Behavioral Sciences. Eugene Walton contributed substantially to the research.

Reprinted from the *Public Opinion Quarterly,* vol. 23, 1959, pp. 145–158, by permission of the authors and of the publisher. (Copyright 1959 by Princeton University.)

1. An historical note: most of these writers were not consciously influenced by Bentley's work; rather their approach fits into and is illuminated by Bentley's approach.

2. For two other examples of the transactional approach see R. Bauer, I. Pool, and L. Dexter, *American Business and Public Policy* (Atherton, New York, 1963), on the relationship between foreign travel and views on tariffs, pp. 166ff., and L. Dexter, "The Representative and His District," *Human Organization,* 1957,

Bauer's discussion of the communicator and the audience applies the transactional approach to the theory of mass communications— each "side" behaves as it does in terms of its orientation towards the other, that is in terms of its notion of its own role and status and of that of the other "side." Pool and Shulman in their study make Bauer's approach more concrete by suggesting that communicators may have several different audiences in mind. At a more elementary level, even for those who think they are totally uninterested in theory, Pool and Shulman make a contribution by demonstrating how communicators' selection and emphases are determined in part by "the pictures in their heads" of those who are going to read and listen.

In all probability this kind of analysis could profitably be carried further to demonstrate that news selection is made in terms of the total life experience of the writer or editor. For example, it might be interesting to investigate whether and how a newsman's writings may be influenced not only by his present but by his past social environment, especially if his roles in the two environments differed markedly. For instance, how does a graduate of a school of journalism, where there has been considerable emphasis on giving the public significant information, reconcile his conception of the kind of news his teachers would have wanted with the somewhat different emphases of colleagues or editors on some newspapers which have, as Breed points out, very particular policies to push? Or how about a newspaperman with considerable orientation towards "getting the story" who is employed by a business firm or a government organization as a public relations officer with the understanding that unfavorable stories are to be played down or, where possible, suppressed?

The White, Gieber, Breed, and Pool and Shulman studies all deal with newspapermen; no doubt, they apply to communicators in other media also—not only to radio news departments or to mass media but to literature and science. The selection of articles for the present collection has no doubt been influenced by the editors' picture of the teachers and students who might use the book and of the reviewers and publishers' employees who would pass on it.

In fact, scholars who wish to undertake inexpensive and potentially very valuable research might apply this method to poets, novelists, radio writers, scientific popularizers, editors of academic journals, and writers of textbooks.

A word may be said therefore about the technique employed in this study by Pool and Shulman. It is based upon that of Harold D. Lasswell in Psychopathology and Politics, 1930, and Power and Personality, 1948; Lasswell was concerned with finding out, for instance, what preconceptions led judges to emphasize one aspect of the law

reprinted in Bobbs-Merrill Political Science series, and in R. Peabody and N. Polsby (eds.), *Perspectives on Congress* (Rand McNally, Chicago, 1963).

rather than another in their decisions and sentencings. He utilized the Freudian psychoanalytic approach—including the personal interview, largely with orientation towards fantasy material—for his purpose. Quite regardless of whether one accepts or rejects or modifies psychoanalytic theory, its interview technique is very useful for the study of communicators' conceptions of audiences or of audiences' conceptions of communicators; it can be used to throw light on, for example, what sort of readers or listeners are thought about in preparing a given document or speech.   L.A.D.

DR. ITHIEL DE SOLA POOL is Professor of Political Science at the Massachusetts Institute of Technology. He was educated at the University of Chicago where he earned his Ph.D. in 1952. He was a study director at the Hoover Institute of Stanford University from 1949–53. Since then he has been at MIT, where from 1959–61 he was chairman of the Political Science section.

IRWIN SHULMAN was educated at McGill University and has an M.S. from the University of Wisconsin. Formerly a newspaper reporter, he is now with the Canadian Broadcasting Corporation as Supervisor of Research Analysis. His current work involves studies of audience sizes, of programs, and of sequences of programs in different regions of Canada against varying types of TV competition.

Most studies of communication address themselves to the problem of how the message affects the audience. In the communication process, however, effects go both ways: the audience also affects the communicator. The messages sent are in part determined by expectations of audience reactions. The audience, or at least *those audiences about whom the communicator thinks,* thus play more than a passive role in communication. The present study concerns this feedback.

What we are here describing is a reference group phenomenon. "Imaginary interlocutors," [1] who may also be described as reference persons, enter the author's flow of associations at the time of composition and influence what he writes or says.[2]

1. A term used by Charles Horton Cooley, *Human Nature and the Social Order* (Scribners, New York, 1902).
2. The importance of such reference persons in communication is suggested by a great deal of recent social science research. Samuel A. Stouffer *et al., The American Soldier* (Princeton U. P., Princeton, N.J., 1949); Edward A. Shils and Morris Janowitz, "Cohesion and Disintegration in the Wehrmacht," *Public Opinion Quarterly,* vol. 12, 1948, pp. 300–306, 308–315; Bernard Berelson, Paul Lazarsfeld, and William McPhee, *Voting* (U. of Chicago, 1954); Elihu Katz and Paul Lazarsfeld, *Personal influence* (Free Press, New York, 1955); Ithiel de Sola Pool, Suzanne Keller, and Raymond A. Bauer, "The Influence of Foreign Travel on Political Attitudes of American Businessmen," *Public Opinion Quarterly,* vol. 20, 1956, pp. 161–176; George Coelho, *Changing Images of America: A Study of*

In an earlier article our associates, Claire Zimmerman and Raymond A. Bauer, showed that the character of the audience one expects to address affects what one remembers of the materials available for a speech. Facts which were perceived as incongruent with the attitudes of the prospective audience were often forgotten over a period of one week; approximately twice as many facts were remembered and thus available to be communicated when the audience was expected to be favorable to them.[3] A replication by Wilbur Schramm and Wayne Danielson has confirmed these results.[4] In those experiments, however, there was not direct evidence of how the subjects were thinking about audiences; one audience was experimentally induced. It was assumed that this would, as it did, have some impact on the subjects.

In the present study we sought to ascertain empirically something about the population of reference persons who actually flowed into the consciousness of a communicator as he communicated (rather than assume that we had induced a particular audience) and also to ascertain whether those spontaneously produced images influenced a communication in the way that we know an experimentally induced audience does.

The study proceeded in three phases. First we conducted thirty-three exploratory interviews with newsmen. On the basis of the hypotheses formed in the interviews, we constructed a controlled experiment in which the subjects were journalism students. The final phase, two years later, was a reinterview with some of the newsmen.

Indian Students' Perceptions (Free Press, New York, 1958); Harold Isaacs, *Scratches on Our Minds* (John Day, New York, 1955); Daniel Lerner, *The Passing of Traditional Society* (Free Press, New York, 1958); Everett M. Rogers and George M. Neal, *Reference Group Influence in the Adoption of Agricultural Technology* (Iowa State College Press, Ames, 1958); Bryce Ryan and Neal C. Gross, "The Diffusion of Hybrid Seed Corn in Two Iowa Communities," *Rural Sociology,* vol. 8, 1943, pp. 697–709, have all shown that those groups whose opinions are important to a person and whose respect he wants influence his communications in a very direct fashion. Such studies fall into two groups: those which ask direct questions about personal influence, e.g., whose opinions do you respect, whom would you consult, etc., and those which attempt to infer the importance of a reference group from the fact that an individual's behavior approximates the modal behavior of the group, e.g., in the voting studies it was found that the friends of most Republicans are Republicans, the friends of most Democrats, Democrats. But neither of these previous approaches nails down evidence on whom respondents actually thought about as they reached a decision, and how much difference that made.

3. Claire Zimmerman and Raymond A. Bauer, "The Effect of an Audience on What is Remembered," *Public Opinion Quarterly,* vol. 20, 1956, pp. 238–248.

4. Wilbur Schramm and Wayne Danielson, "Anticipated Audiences as Determinants of Recall," *Journal of Abnormal and Social Psychology,* vol. 56, 1958, pp. 282–283.

The interviews, after the first few, proceeded in a standardized fashion. Mr. Shulman would arrive at a newspaper office by previous appointment at a time when the newsman to be interviewed was still working on some copy. He would wait until the story was finished and begin the interview immediately thereafter. (The absence of a time gap is crucial to the success of the interviewing technique we developed.) Shulman would then go through the text paragraph by paragraph, asking the reporter to recall in detail all the persons who at the time of writing had come to his mind. Respondents varied greatly in the extent to which they could produce recall. However, enough material was gathered to enable us to sense certain recurrent patterns. Let us examine what these were, for they provided the hypotheses we tested in the experiment.

Supporters and critics. Single interviews generally showed consistency in the kind of image produced. A defensive respondent might deny that he thought of anyone but the characters in the story; another respondent would mention a whole series of persons threatened by ill fate whom he would like to help; while a third might list "fakers" and "crooks" whom he would like to punish.

The variable in the writer's flow of associations which appeared to influence most markedly what he wrote was the affective relationship that he conceived to exist between himself and his imaginary interlocutors. Some respondents thought about persons who were disliked, critical, or hostile; others thought of persons who were liked, supportive, or friendly. Thus, for most of our respondents, the act of writing seemed to provide one of two alternative kinds of gratification. For some, writing provided the opportunity to bestow pleasure on readers, who would reward them for it by admiration and affection. For others, the gratification came from awareness of the weapon of words which they had in their hands and the damage that it could do to the "bad guys."

Both the gratification of winning affection and the gratification of aggression are predicated upon the power of the printed word. They involve a fantasy of someone's reading the text and being strongly moved by it. The reporter himself may be a shy man, but behind the protective moat that separates him and his piece of paper from the world, he can indulge in fantasy about overcoming all sorts of toils and troubles and ending up either with love or with triumph.[5]

The two sets of fantasies are in part opposed and in part similar. They both presuppose danger and hostility, but they meet it in the one case by denial and ingratiation and in the other by counterattack. *Our overall hypothesis was that newswriters would be better able to communicate*

5. Guy Swanson, "Agitation through the Press: A Study of the Personalities of Publicists," *Public Opinion Quarterly,* vol. 20, 1956, pp. 441–456.

stories which fit their particular strategy of self-enhancement than stories which did not.

Some illustrative quotations from the interviews. It might be well at this point to examine quotations from some typical interviews of both kinds. A columnist who had just written a story on muscular dystrophy stated that he had "an intense desire to write and write entertainingly." He saw his readers as "people with a sense of humor. . . . If I stopped a man in the street and told him what I wanted to write, if he said, 'What do you want to do that for?' I would probably drop it. . . . You'd be dead if you didn't know what is interesting. If it's read, it's a success." "If I can humanize a person who is generally regarded as stiff and formal, I may create a warm attitude toward that person." "I have to please widely." "I try not to ridicule even a person like X. . . . [That] would make people mad." "Readers like to relax. . . . I get a fair amount of mail and phone calls, most of it enthusiastic." The columnist was aware of restraining himself from mentioning directly that muscular dystrophy might be hereditary because of the effect on families with a history of the ailment. But then he did allude to it and explained that the family without it "would say 'how lucky *we* are.' I felt it might cause some people to think 'We haven't very much but we are pretty lucky.' " With regard to a passage quoting a patient as saying he would not get better, "I had some pretty disquieting feelings about this. . . . This might be a little cruel." "The [paper] didn't say it; he did. . . . I expected people to be mad or disagree with him."

In that interview the gratification of the writer was revealed to be the fantasy of people reading what he writes with pleasure. In his eyes if you don't please them you are "dead"; people would get mad. If you do they will be enthusiastic. This interview also illustrates what happens when such a writer has to deal with incongruent material—material which could make his readers uncomfortable and unhappy. By his own admission that material gave him disquieting feelings and made him hesitate to say certain things. It made him put things in quotes which he might otherwise have said directly, and it made him rationalize the "cruel" things he did say by thinking of the people who would be happy that they had been spared. Perhaps the fact that this man is a columnist and specializes in rosy human interest stories is a result of these emotional predispositions, for he himself says that he would not make a good "hard-driving" reporter.

Let us look at two other cases, interviews with newsmen whose professional role has not become specialized on writing to keep people happy and who nevertheless show the same motivation strongly. The first was a foreign affairs specialist of the press and radio who had just finished writing on the Hungarian and Suez crises, which were then taking place.

The lead referred to "wanton massacres." The writer indicated he was having second thoughts about the accuracy of the dispatches on the actual size of the massacres. "I started the lead about the political situation, then discarded it, a thing I rarely do." He thought another passage "would have a potentially unsettling effect on the listener." About another passage: "I was also aware that this would relieve some isolationist fears." He felt that the reference to Dulles' illness might not hurt Republican chances; it would remove from the scene an unpopular man. Once again we have a writer who has hesitations about including items which might cause or suggest harm and who wants to include items which will reassure.

Our other example of reporters of this type was a general assignment reporter. He had just written a piece concerning a missing Army machine gun. "I thought of the potential danger to the public . . . someone using the gun with reckless abandon . . . people being mowed down by bullets." But the missing gun was defective, and he was very aware of wanting to stress this fact, reassuring readers that the gun was not dangerous. He had no desire to increase the impact of the story, or to scare people. "I wanted to make sure the readers would not be . . . unduly alarmed—this was calculated to reassure the readers." He hated guns, knew nothing about them, and did not want to know anything about them. He had recently won an award for a series of articles on safety and expressed concern at road death statistics. He said about the reporter who had phoned in the facts on the machine gun: "He's a good newspaperman, but I felt he was being extra-long-winded." Here we have a story which our man, with his fear of violence, would himself have played down, so he felt some conflict with the importance another reporter gave it. He strove to reassure his readers: indeed, the first two words of the lead labeled the gun as defective, even before noting that it was missing.

Now let us turn to some interviews where the other common pattern of gratification is illustrated. These are interviews with writers who think not of persons they wish to please and protect but of hostile persons toward whom they, too, feel hostile. Such writers are ruminating on the power of their pen to destroy.

For example, a general assignment reporter who had written a story on a suicide was not concerned to spare anyone from pain. "The first thing that came into my mind . . . was that the boy was from Xtown. I thought of his classmates from Xtown who might read this, and I made sure to refer to Xtown in the lead. . . . I thought I would call his father if there was any more to the story—and I thought of his father in a negative way, how to avoid having to do this." (It should be emphasized here that, as we noted above, having an aggressive fantasy does not at all mean that the reporter is willing to perform the aggressive act in person; the aggres-

sion may be confined to the privacy of his writing desk. He thinks of
calling the father but shies away from really doing so. It is the aggressive
fantasies and their effect on writing with which we are here concerned.)
"I know when there are these problems you can usually pin it down to the
parents." He continued with his fantasy of the bad news hurting people.
"Every senior at the high school he attended would be cognizant; the news
would spread by word of mouth; the teachers there would know about it."
Then, talking about himself, he indicated some awareness of his tenseness,
saying that he would not feel happy "sitting in front of a TV set with a
bottle of beer."

Another general assignment reporter had just finished three short
crime stories. The first was on the conviction of a public housing official.
"I thought the story would be of interest to the thousands of people who
live in housing projects. . . . I thought (laughter) that it would reinforce their beliefs that everyone who works for a public housing project
has his hand in the till. But actually before I got to that stage, the first
thought that was in my mind was why X (a fellow reporter who had supplied the material) didn't write his own damn copy properly. . . . The
man did not go to jail; either he has political pull or a hell of a big family
or something like that." Story two concerned a killer who did go to jail.
Our respondent said, "[If the killer] could have afforded the lawyers that
other people could have . . . he might have gotten off with less than
five years. . . . There is a lot of injustice in justice." As to readership
of the story: "Some people may read this one accidentally while they're
looking for the comics or the obituaries." The third story concerned shoplifting. "The police claimed the women were part of a ring . . . while
actually all the women were accused of was a $100 theft. Actually, I be-
lieve that the story of the ring is probable, though. I think that shoplifting
goes on on a tremendous scale. . . . The stores could stop it if they really
wanted to . . . no sympathy for the stores . . . public has to pay for
these goods indirectly when they buy something else."

Each of the stories written by our last respondent had only one or two
short paragraphs. They followed highly conventional journalistic format.
It is hard to see how the writer's personality and fantasies affected the
copy in any way. This instance helps us to make an important point. The
author's private fantasies are clearly not the only things that affect the
character of what he writes. An experienced professional newsman will
have acquired great facility in turning out a standard product for each of
the many kinds of routine story of which so much of the news consists.
The more experienced, the more professionally skillful, a newsman, the
less important may be his own fantasy life in determining much of what

he writes. The role of fantasy grows with every factor that gives greater freedom to the writer. In the above illustration, a longer text would have done so. Other factors would be more unusual stories, the greater latitude of format provided by the feature story, or a less well organized and professionalized newspaper.

Let us turn to one last example in which the reporter's desire to mete out punishment apparently did affect the distribution of emphasis in the article. This story concerned level crossings, and the point which received unusual stress was a finding that both the railroad and the town were at fault in a series of accidents. "I thought immediately of prospective readers in the town of X. . . . I know that what happens at the crossings is the people's own fault as well as the railroad. . . . I thought that the residents of the town of X would find some impact in learning 'We were at fault too.' " "I didn't have any concepts of bereaved relatives or anything of that sort. . . . Mrs. Y (who was killed) had another woman in her car, . . . they were probably talking, and . . . she had been oblivious." Then, speaking of the railroad's spokesman: "He is a man subject to the foibles of most humans." Clearly, our respondent took the opportunity here to hand out blame, stressing that theme over other aspects of the story.

The interviews, of which the above were examples, suggested an hypothesis, namely, that reporters who have supportive images in mind would have trouble reporting unpleasant facts, and that reporters who have hostile images in mind would have trouble reporting pleasant facts. The interviews we have just described suggested this, but in field interviews it is not possible to determine the direction of causality. The kind of story written by a reporter might have determined his images, or the images the kind of story, or both might be a function of the man's career assignment, and that in turn might be influenced by his personality. In order to separate out some of these influences we designed an experiment to be conducted with journalism students under controlled classroom conditions.

THE EXPERIMENT

Four sets of facts were drafted, each providing the material for a news story. Within each set the facts were then scrambled so as to require rewriting to constitute a good story. Two of the stories described events which our subjects would presumably find pleasing; we shall call these "good news." Two of the stories described "bad news." In each pair, one of the stories concerned events at Boston University, where our subjects were enrolled, and one of the stories concerned events overseas.[6] The topics were a blindness cure discovered at BU, a successful Asian good-will baseball trip by the Brooklyn Dodgers, a tuition raise, and the Suez crisis.

The subjects, assembled in their regular class hour, had a mimeo-graphed set of facts distributed to them as a class assignment and were given twenty minutes to rewrite it. Each student received only one of the four sets of facts, the distribution being made in a random fashion. The total number of subjects was 132, or thirty-three students writing on each story.

As soon as he had finished writing his story, each subject turned to a questionnaire. The first question asked the subject to list all the persons who had happened to come to mind while he was writing the story. The directions emphasized that the respondent should list everybody he thought of, not just persons relevant to the story. The mean number of images listed was seven. The subject was then asked a number of questions about himself and about each image person he had listed. Most importantly, he was asked to check on a 6-inch scale ranging from "very approving" to "very critical" each of the persons he had listed. The specific instruction was: "Try to reconstruct very carefully how you felt, as you were writing the story, about the extent of agreement or disapproval expressed by the people you thought of toward what you were writing." This scale permitted us to compute for each subject the mean degree of approval or criticism of him which he conceived his image persons to feel.

HYPOTHESES AND EVIDENCE

[1] The first hypothesis confirmed by this experiment was that persons writing about good news tend to produce supportive images, while persons writing about bad news tend to produce more critical ones. This is in a sense the obverse of the hypothesis which interests us. It is concerned not with the effect which free associations, as an independent variable, may have on what is written, but rather with the effect of the material about which one is writing (as an independent variable) on the mood and thoughts of the writer.[7] We find, as we might expect, that bad

6. The authors wish to thank Dr. David M. White of the Division of Journalism of Boston University for his help in this project.

7. The reader may desire a fuller census of the kinds of images which our subjects reported as having come to mind. The students listed 247, or 28 percent of all the images, as possible readers. In the interviews with newsmen 17 percent of the 510 images were of readers. Of the 580 identifiable persons listed on the stu-

news produces dysphoric associations, good news euphoric ones. The only interest in this result is that bad news not only produces images of persons who are less well liked (we asked that, too) but also of persons who are viewed as being more often critical of the author, a conclusion which is not completely obvious. The data supporting this result are contained in Table 1, which is based on 129 usable questionnaires.

Table 1—Mean Scores of Subjects on Approving or Critical Character of Their Images for Each Assigned Story

	Mean Score *
"Good news" stories:	
Close event	1.4
Overseas event	1.6
"Bad news" stories:	
Close event	2.3
Overseas event	2.5

* The scores represent distance along the 6-inch scale from 0, very approving, to 6, very critical.

[2] We turn now to the more significant question, whether there is also a reverse direction of effect: If we hold constant the effect of the stimulus materials, do the images which a particular person produces predict what he will write? Clearly, even though bad news tends in general to elicit critical images, there will be some individuals who produce strongly supportive images despite the fact that they are handed bad news to write about, while others given the same assignment will produce even more than the usual quota of critical images. So, too, with good news; the

---

dent questionnaire study, 107 were characters in the story (12 percent) and 242 were personally known (29 percent of classifiable), including 31 family members, 129 others known well, and 82 others known more casually.

The largest group as yet unaccounted for are those who are not actually characters in the story but are persons who have been involved in related situations. For example, the Suez Canal story did not mention Nasser, but he might easily come to mind. The preponderance of such related persons may be indexed by the correlation of the locale of the story and the locale of the images, as shown in the following table:

Locale of Images by Locale of Story

	Locale of Story	
Locale of Image	University	Foreign
University	107	10
Local	47	11
United States	125	124
Foreign	15	229
	294	364

mean of the images will be supportive, but there will be a distribution. Our procedure was to take the distribution for each of the four stories and divide it by natural breaking points into three segments: the modal individuals, those whose images were more supportive than normal for that story, and those whose images were more critical than normal for that story. The result was the assignment of the subjects to three groups, namely, 23 persons who produced unusually supportive images, 86 modal persons, and 20 persons who produced unusually critical images. The question to be answered was whether the stories written by the 23 persons who produced unusually supportive images would be more accurate on good news and less accurate on bad than those written by the 20 persons who produced unusually critical images.

The stories written by the 43 deviant individuals were subjected to content analysis. The analysis was designed to explore a highly subjective matter, how far the writer, in writing the story, had distorted or modified the facts given him. In order to make this evaluation of the stories reasonably objective, we did two things. We broke down the judgment of distortion into three separate judgments, and we had the judgments made independently by two expert judges (former practicing newspaper reporters who had returned to graduate study in the behavioral sciences). We asked each judge to indicate for each story (1) whether there had been significant rearrangement of the order of the facts given, (2) whether any significant information had been added to that given, and (3) whether any significant information had been omitted.

One judge was considerably stricter than the other, which permitted the construction of a three-point scale of change in the story instead of the usual dichotomy, changed-unchanged. On a highly changed story both would agree that it was changed; on a slightly changed story A would call it changed, and B would call it the same (the direction of disagreement being almost always the same); on a still less changed story both would call it unchanged. Unreliability would consist of a reversal of the direction of disagreement in the middle category. Let us illustrate by reference to deletions. Of the 43 analyzed stories, both judges agreed with regard to 11 that there had been significant deletions, and both agreed with regard to 17 that there had been none. Thus they disagreed on 15 stories. But of these 15 stories there was only one instance in which the usual direction of disagreement between the two judges was reversed, i.e., there was only 1 coding discrepancy regarding deletions. There were 5 regarding additions and 4 regarding changes in order.

The three-level scale of change allows for greater sensitivity of the scale and greater confidence in our assessment of the extreme cases than would a dichotomy. We shall label changes which both judges agreed were significant (++), those one judge thought significant (+o), and those both agreed were not significant (oo).

We want to compare the amount of change under two experimental conditions which we shall label congruent and incongruent. We have, it will be recalled, segregated those individuals who produced an unusual preponderance of supportive images (given the story event on which they were writing) from those who produced an unusual weight of critical ones. These two groups of persons were not simply responding in an average way to the facts of the story, but were giving expression to some autonomous tendencies of their own. A congruent situation is one in which the story event and this autonomous tendency reinforce each other. Thus the two congruent situations are the one in which a story concerns good news and the images are unusually supportive and the one in which the story concerns bad news and the images are unusually critical. The two incongruent situations are the one in which supportive images are produced despite bad news and the one in which critical images are produced despite good news. As Table 2 shows, we have 15 instances of congruent behavior and 28 of incongruent.

Table 2—Congruent and Incongruent Cases

	Congruent	Incongruent	Total
Bad news	7	15	22
Good news	8	13	21
	15	28	43

Table 3 provides the evidence for our major hypothesis: *Where a person's images are incongruent with the character of the event being described, his accuracy in reporting is reduced.* More precisely, persons who have supportive images in their flow of associations do a more straight-

Table 3—Accuracy of Reporting in Congruent and Incongruent Cases

	Definitely Changed (++)	Intermediate Change (+0)	Unchanged (00)
Changes in order of facts *	22	12	9
Congruent situation	4	5	6
Incongruent situation	18	7	3
Additions †	13	14	16
Congruent situation	2	5	8
Incongruent situation	11	9	8
Deletions ‡	11	15	17
Congruent situation	1	5	9
Incongruent situation	10	10	8

* $\chi^2 = 6.95$ $p = .015$ (one-tail test).
† $\chi^2 = 4.23$ $p = .06$ (one-tail test).
‡ $\chi^2 = 5.68$ $p = .024$ (one-tail test).

forward job of reporting good news and a less precise job of reporting bad news than do persons who have critical images in their associations. Those persons with predominantly critical images in their associations do a more straightforward job of reporting bad news and a less precise job of reporting good news than do persons who have supportive images. It is important to emphasize that accuracy of reporting turns out to be a function of the relation between the image flow and the events being described, not just a function of the image flow. Plausible hypotheses that thinking about critics or thinking about supportive characters in and of itself produces more accurate reporting turn out not to be sustained. The important point is the congruence between the character of the news event and of the images in the flow of associations.

Table 4—Accuracy of Reporting in Congruent and Incongruent Cases, Bad and Good News Separately

	Definitely Changed (++)	Intermediate Change (+0)	Unchanged (00)
Changes in order of facts: *			
Bad news	14	3	5
Congruent	3	0	4
Incongruent	11	3	1
Good news	8	9	4
Congruent	1	5	2
Incongruent	7	4	2
Additions:†			
Bad news	8	9	5
Congruent	2	3	2
Incongruent	6	6	3
Good news	5	5	11
Congruent	0	2	6
Incongruent	5	3	5
Deletions: ‡			
Bad news	7	7	8
Congruent	1	1	5
Incongruent	6	6	3
Good news	4	8	9
Congruent	0	4	4
Incongruent	4	4	5

* For comparison of bad news total with good news total, $\chi^2 = 4.72$.
† For comparison of bad news total with good news total, $\chi^2 = 4.06$.
‡ For comparison of bad news total with good news total, $\chi^2 = 0.92$.

Table 4 indicates that the above hypothesis does indeed hold up for both good and bad news. In short, the results summarized in Table 3 are not an artifact arising from the presence of a massive effect in one of the two types of situation and not in the other. Of course, the numbers in

Table 4 are generally too small to attain independent significance. What is important, however, is that they all are in the direction required by the main hypothesis. Our explanatory discussion must therefore take account just as much of the fact that it was hard for subjects thinking of critics to be accurate about good news as that it was hard for subjects thinking about supportive characters to be accurate about bad. The familiar hypothesis that people distort unpleasant facts is not an adequate explanation of the findings. Our explanation must also take account of the discovery that some of our respondents had a tendency against accurately reporting *pleasant* facts.

There is, it is true, a definite, though not always statistically significant, tendency for bad news to be more extensively distorted than good news (compare the total in the Definitely Changed column of Table 4). That is hardly surprising. The surprising result is the stronger tendency for either kind of news to be distorted when not congruent with the individual's image flow.

IMPLICATIONS OF THE FINDINGS

Our data have revealed three tendencies to be simultaneously and independently operating in the writing process: (1) Good news tended to elicit images of supportive persons, bad news, images of critics. (2) Where the images elicited were congruent with the kind of news, the reporting was more accurate than where the images were incongruent. Good news was more accurately reported in the presence of supportive images, bad news in the presence of critical ones. (3) Good news was more accurately reported than bad. Proposition 2 is the novel one, and the one which interests us here. It is also the one that was suggested by our interviews.

How can we explain the fact that accuracy of reporting is low on good news and bad news alike when the news is incongruent with the tone of the reporter's fantasies? Let us consider some possible explanations.

Reference group theory, at least in simple form, does not fully explain what we found. The simple reference notion is that persons behave in ways which will be approved by those whom they value highly. But for many of our respondents negative reference groups were controlling. Their communication behavior was designed to punish and offend individuals they disliked; it was not designed to win approval from those they liked.

A reference phenomenon was indeed in operation. The potential effects of the communicator's behavior were tested by him by fantasy reference to people's expected reactions. But the process was more dynamic than simply following imaginary leaders. It involved adopting dissonance reduction strategies to sustain an established mental picture of the world. Each respondent had a basic fantasy which related him to the world, either as a recipient of rewards from it or as a battler against it. His actions as a communicator sought to sustain this image.

But dissonance reduction alone is not an adequate explanation of our results either. There could be an infinity of mental dramas relating a communicator to his imaginary reference audiences, and just as many ways for him to distort his communication so as to make his behavior consonant with the point of each drama. We found, however, only two main types of mental drama arising in the newswriting situation: (1) winning of favor from the reader and (2) verbal aggression to demolish him. These patterns correspond to what one might expect from familiar political science hypotheses such as those developed by Lasswell from Freudian notions. The newswriting situation, like political oratory, is an instance of one-way communication to a secondary audience. The gratifications arising from such activities are largely deference and power, either real or fantasied. The communicator is the teacher, instructor, guide, i.e., the authority figure over a passive audience. And since the audience consists of secondary contacts, at best, notions of power and deference replace and symbolize more tangible and intimate rewards. Thus one result of our study is that the fantasies of our writers as they write are polarized around the power which their pen gives them, power to command affection, or power to destroy.

Bringing together these various strands of theory we are led to a possible, though admittedly speculative, picture of what may have been going on as reporters accurately or inaccurately relayed good or bad news. A reporter with a flow of unusually supportive imaginary interlocutors may have great need for support from reference persons. In a wish-fulfilling fashion, he may regard his act of bringing good news as performing a favor which will be rewarded by gratitude and affection. He may fear that bringing bad news will alienate him, and he may therefore distort it, either to soften its edge or because anxiety engendered by having to report it makes him less efficient.

Conversely, a person with a flow of unusually critical imaginary interlocutors may be engaged in a mental debate in which he aggresses against and triumphs over his critics by giving them bad news unblunted. News is a weapon in his hands. He may report good news inaccurately, for it does not serve the purpose of his fantasies.

One more empirical finding is relevant to the above speculations. It is the consistency over time of a man's imaginary interlocutors. How far are the persons thought about a matter of mood and how far a matter of personality? Our reinterview with the newsmen two years later was designed to throw some light on this matter. With the attrition over two years from an already small sample, the numbers become very low. However, the repetition of the same procedure with the same individuals suggests that temperament may be a more important factor than mood. Respondents tended to display the same image patterns in both interviews, even though they rarely remembered what the earlier interview was about and the stories they were writing were, of course, always somewhat different. If that is so, then the most plausible explanation of the results we obtained would treat the population of interlocutors in the writer's mind as a personality variable.

Our results could conceivably have practical implications, but these depend upon some of the unanswered questions on which we have been speculating. Could one, for example, increase the accuracy of reporting by deliberately drawing attention to certain kinds of audience figures? It is not clear from our results that that is the case. A person who spontaneously thinks of critical images may be a better reporter for bad news, but it is not clear that subjecting to critical images a person who by temperament (if it *is* a temperamental matter) spontaneously thinks of supportive images will improve his accuracy. Such a manipulation might frighten him and thus reduce his accuracy. Our results, however, suggest that there is an important area here for exploration, and one which might possibly have practical implications.

One should also keep in mind that what we have been describing here as accurate reporting is not always a result to be desired. If all our results could be restated in terms of imaginativeness rather than accuracy, the overtones of what we have said would be reversed. The persons who handed back exactly the facts that had been handed to them, and in much the same way, were conforming to one set of values particularly important in journalism—straightforwardness or accuracy of reporting—but they were failing to meet another set of preferred values concerning creative writing—originality and imagination. Possibly incongruity of the events described with the structure of the author's image flow promotes the latter qualities.

These are questions which have heretofore been largely neglected by scientific students of public opinion. Except on the psychiatrist's couch, the flow of mental images has not been extensively used in research. The simple instrument of asking respondents to name who or what had just come into their minds, while obvious in the light of its use in psychiatry, has not been in the standard battery of techniques of behavioral science research. Perhaps a reason has been that the content of free associations seemed relatively inaccessible to careful experimentation. A subject's report of his associations cannot be independently validated, and he has many obvious motivations for distorting them. We have no illusions that the reports of free associations which we received are either very reliable or complete. Whatever the shortcomings, however, the successful use of such data in this study seems to show that at least a portion of the image flow can be recaptured even on a questionnaire, and a sufficient portion to give useful results on at least some topics.

SELECTED PUBLICATIONS BY DR. POOL

The Comparative Study of Symbols, Hoover Institute Studies (Stanford U. P., 1952).

The Prestige Papers, Hoover Institute Studies (Stanford U. P., 1952).

Symbols of Internationalism, Hoover Institute Studies (Stanford U. P., 1951).

Trends in Content Analysis (U. Illinois Press, 1959) (editor).

American Business and Public Policy (Atherton, New York, N.Y., 1963) (co-author with Raymond Bauer and Lewis A. Dexter).

Kuomintang and Chinese Communist Elites, Hoover Institute Studies (Stanford U. P., 1952) (Co-author).

American Businessmen and International Trade: Code Book and Data from a study on Attitudes and Communication (Free Press, New York, 1960) (Co-author).

"Variety and Repetition in Political Language," in Heinz Eulau, Samuel J. Eldersveld, and Morris Janowitz (eds.), *Political Behavior* (Free Press, New York, 1956).

"TV: A new dimension in politics," in Eugene Burdick and Arthur J. Brodbeck (eds.), *American Voting Behavior: How the People Participate in Politics* (Free Press, New York, 1959).

"Studies in Political Communication," *The Public Opinion Quarterly,* vol. 20, no. 1, Spring 1956 (editor of issue).

"Who Gets Power and Why," *World Politics,* October 1949.

"Content Analysis for Intelligence Purposes," *World Politics,* April 1960.

"Public Opinion and the Control of Armaments" *Daedalus,* Fall 1960.

"Free Discussion and Public Taste," *Public Opinion Quarterly,* Spring 1960.

Communications and Values in Relation to War and Peace; Report to the Committee on Research for Peace (Institute for International Order, Program of Research, New York, 1961).

QUESTIONS

1. State Pool and Shulman's hypothesis on the relation between the reporter's images of the character of the event he is describing and the accuracy of his report. Does the hypothesis involve any difference from the idea that the reporter "objectively" records "all the important news that's fit to print"?

2. The authors suggest that "imaginary interlocutors" enter the reporter's flow of associations at the time of composition and thereby influence

his writing. Two main types of mental drama occur in the process of newswriting depending upon the reporter's orientation to his imaginary audience. (*a*) What are these two types of orientation? (*b*) How might the possession or lack of a by-line affect each of these two orientations? (*c*) Can you think of other types of audience reaction which produce this kind of feedback?

3. Interview three or more students who have recently written a term paper or thesis for the same professor; determine what conceptions of the professor's requirements they have. Preferably, you should select a professor of whom you know little. It would be desirable also to select students who do not know each other well; why? After comparing the students' conceptions of the audience, see how their conceptions compare with the professor's picture of himself as audience.

4. Interview: (*a*) people in your college publicity office (for instance those responsible for preparing the college catalogue), (*b*) students or parents of students who are considering entering the college. See if you can apply the Pool and Shulman approach profitably to analysis of these interviews.

5. To what degree would you expect (*a*) poets, (*b*) original scientists to be influenced by conceptions of the audience? by conceptions of their own status and role in relation to the audience?

David Manning White

The "Gatekeeper": A Case Study in the Selection of News *

IN 1949 IT SEEMED fairly obvious to the writer that even as the body of theoretical concepts on the nature of mass communications was evolving, an important notion was being overlooked. Through the development of a germinal suggestion from an important study by the late Kurt Lewin, it became apparent that (1) the flow of any news items would be through certain channels and, more important, (2) that certain places within these channels would serve as "gates" through which given news items might or might not be admitted.

Thus, with the cooperation of a patient editor, who was curious enough to see what kind of "gatekeeper" he might be, we studied closely the manner in which he functioned at his "gate." Analysis of the reasons given by our "Mr. Gates" for rejecting various types of news stories indicated how highly subjective and reliant upon value-judgments based on the gatekeeper's own set of experiences, attitudes and expectations the selection of "news" actually is.

Dr. Walter Gieber, through numerous articles and monographs, has added substantially to the whole area opened by the original "gatekeeper" essay. In an original paper written for this volume, "News Is What Newspapermen Make It," Gieber summarizes the major findings of these studies. It is noteworthy that in 1956 when Gieber studied the telegraph editors of 16 Wisconsin dailies he was discomfited to learn that (1) the editors were "passive," i.e., they played no real or active role as communicators and made no truly critical examination of the incoming wire news, and (2) that as communicators these 16 editors had no "real perception of their audience." When Gieber replicated his Wisconsin study with a similar group of small-city dailies in Indiana, he found the same

* The author acknowledges the suggestions of Dr. Wilbur Schramm during the preparation of this paper, also the assistance of Mr. Raymond F. Stewart.

Reprinted from *Journalism Quarterly*, vol. 27, no. 4, Fall, 1950, pp. 383–390, by permission of the author and the publisher. (Copyright 1950 by the Association for Education in Journalism.)

phenomenon and, as he puts it, he was, if anything, more discomfited. For if, as Wright has suggested in his essay (pp. 93–108), a major function of the newspaper is the purposeful surveillance of the environment for the reader, then it would appear that this function was only being met fortuitously.

Subsequently, Gieber made an extremely valuable analysis of how a set of gatekeepers handle local civil liberty news. Here again he found that although the reporters were able to rationalize their concepts of audience needs, they were less successful in "knowing" their audience. The argument that Gieber makes is that far too often the press (via its "gatekeepers") has lost sight of its proper goal: to "serve" the audience. The means, e.g., the news-gathering machinery and bureaucracy, too often, Gieber states, determine the ends. Thus, Gieber has elaborated on the initial gatekeeper concept to explore the social forces which bear on the making of news; for, short of understanding them, he believes, we cannot understand what news really is.

Other writers, such as Warren Breed, Roy E. Carter, Jr., Douglass Cater, Robert Judd and Ken Macrorie, have touched on aspects of the "gatekeeper" process without necessarily using the phrase. Certainly, Leo C. Rosten's valuable study of the Washington correspondents in the mid-1930's should be read by any student concerned with the gatekeeping function. How valuable it would be were Dr. Rosten, or someone he might designate, to replicate this early study with newsmen working in our capital today. (See p. 174, n. 3.)

Wilbur Schramm, commenting recently on studies of this sort,* said, "Participant observer studies are clearly called for." Certainly, we agree with Schramm that the kind of inquiry reported in this volume by White and Gieber might well be replicated many times over, with other "gatekeepers," before the gatekeeping process is understood. Certainly, a number of hypotheses remain to be explored. For example, as an editor grows older and remains at his desk from one decade to the next, does he become more rigid in his view of what is "good" copy and what is not? Further, the relationship between the theory of cognitive dissonance and a gatekeeper's choice of one press association's story over another's might prove valuable to analyze. A study, for example, of a Soviet national (or an American, for that matter) who works for the Information section of the United Nations might prove quite revealing in terms of the gatekeeping function. It is to be hoped that the inclusion of the following two essays in this volume may stimulate further explorations into this area of mass-communications study.   D. M. W.

* Wilbur Schramm, "Challenge to Communications Research," in R. O. Nafziger and D. M. White (eds.), *Introduction to Mass Communications Research* (Louisiana State U. P., 1963).

DAVID MANNING WHITE has been Research Professor of Journalism at Boston University since 1949. Dr. White previously held teaching posts at the University of Iowa, William and Mary College and Bradley University. His interest in communications research was initiated by studying with Wilbur Schramm at the University of Iowa, where he earned his Ph.D. From 1954 to 1957 he was Chairman of the Council on Communications Research of the Association for Education in Journalism. His major professional interest has been the analysis of various mass cultural phenomena (e.g., the comic strip) in American society.

DR. WALTER GIEBER is Associate Professor of Journalism at San Francisco State College. He was educated at the University of Wisconsin, where he took his Ph.D. He has taught at the University of Indiana and at the University of California. His major research interests have focussed on the sociology of journalism.

It was the late Kurt Lewin, truly one of the great social scientists of our time, who applied the term "gatekeeper" to a phenomenon which is of considerable importance to students of mass communications. In his last article,[1] before his untimely death, Dr. Lewin pointed out that the traveling of a news item through certain communication channels was dependent on the fact that certain areas within the channels functioned as "gates." Carrying the analogy further, Lewin said that gate sections are governed either by impartial rules or by "gatekeepers," and in the latter case an individual or group is "in power" for making the decision between "in" or "out."

To understand the functioning of the "gate," Lewin said, was equivalent to understanding the factors which determine the decisions of the "gatekeepers," and he rightly suggested that the first diagnostic task is the finding of the actual "gatekeepers."

The purpose of this study is to examine closely the way one of the "gatekeepers" in the complex channels of communication operates his "gate."

Wilbur Schramm made an observation central to this whole study when he wrote that "no aspect of communication is so impressive as the enormous number of choices and discards which have to be made between the formation of the symbol in the mind of the communicator, and the appearance of a related symbol in the mind of the receiver."[2] To illustrate this in terms of a news story let us consider, for example, a Senate hearing on a proposed bill for federal aid to eductaion. At the hearing

1. Kurt Lewin, *Channels of Group Life,* Human Relations, vol. 1, no. 2, p. 145.
2. Wilbur Schramm, *Mass Communications* (U. of Illinois Press, 1949), p. 289.

there will be reporters from the various press associations, Washington correspondents of large newspapers which maintain staffs in the capital, as well as reporters for local newspapers. All of these form the first "gate" in the process of communication. They have to make the initial judgment as to whether a story is "important" or not. One has only to read the Washington stories from two newspapers whose general editorial attitudes differ widely on such an issue as federal aid to education to realize from the beginning of the process the "gatekeepers" are playing an important role. The appearance of the story in the Chicago *Tribune* and the Chicago *Sun-Times* might well show some differences in treatment. It is apparent that even the actual physical event of the Senate hearing (which we might call the *criterion event*) is reported by two reporters in two different perceptual frameworks and that the two men bring to the "story" different sets of experience, attitudes, and expectations.

Thus a story is transmitted from one "gatekeeper" after another in the chain of communications. From reporter to rewrite man, through bureau chief to "state" file editors at various press association offices, the process of choosing and discarding is continuously taking place. And finally we come to our last "gatekeeper," the one to whom we turn for the purpose of our case study. This is the man who is usually known as the wire editor on the nonmetropolitan newspaper. He has charge of the selection of national and international news which will appear on the front and "jump" pages of his newspaper, and usually he makes up these pages.

Our "gatekeeper" is a man in his middle 40s, who after approximately 25 years' experience as a journalist (both as reporter and copy editor) is now the wire editor of a morning newspaper of approximately 30,000 circulation in a highly industrialized Midwest city of 100,000. It is his job to select from the avalanche of wire copy daily provided by the Associated Press, United Press and International News Service what 30,000 families will read on the front page of their morning newspapers. He also copy edits and writes the headlines for these stories. His job is similar to that which newspapermen throughout the country hold in hundreds of nonmetropolitan newspapers.[3] And in many respects he is the most important "gatekeeper" of all, for if he rejects a story the work of all those who preceded him in reporting and transmitting the story is negated. It is understood, of course, that the story could have "ended" (insofar as its subsequent transmission is concerned) at any of the

3. By far the majority of the approximately 1,780 daily newspapers in this country are in the smaller cities not on the main trunk wires of the press associations. Their reliance on the single wire "state" operations which emanate from the larger cities thus places great responsibility in the hands of the wire editor.

previous "gates." But assuming the story has progressed through all the "gates," it is obvious that this wire editor is faced with an extremely complicated set of decisions to make regarding the limited number of stories he can use.

Our purpose in this study was to determine some preliminary ideas as to why this particular wire editor selected or rejected the news stories filed by the three press associations (and transmitted by the "gatekeeper" above him in Chicago) and thereby gain some diagnostic notions about the general role of the "gatekeeper" in the areas of mass communications.

To this end we received the full cooperation of "Mr. Gates," the above-mentioned wire editor. The problem of finding out what Mr. Gates selected from the mass of incoming wire copy was not difficult, for it appeared on the front and "jump" pages of his newspaper each morning. Actually, we were far more concerned with the copy that did not get into the paper. So for the week of February 6 through 13, 1949, Mr. Gates saved every piece of wire copy that came to his desk. Instead of throwing the dispatch into the waste basket once he had decided not to use it, he put it into a large box next to his desk. Then at one o'clock when his pages were made up and his night's work through, Mr. Gates went through every piece of copy in the "reject" box and wrote on it the reason why he had initially rejected it, assuming that he could recall the reason. In the cases where no ascertainable reason had occurred to him he made no notations on the copy. Although this meant that Mr. Gates had to spend between an hour-and-a-half and two hours each night at this rather tedious phase of the project, he was perfectly willing to do this throughout the entire week.

When Mr. Gates had turned over the raw material of his choices for the week period, we tried to analyze his performance in terms of certain basic questions which presented themselves. These questions are applicable not only to this particular "gatekeeper," but with modifications to all of the "gatekeepers" in the communications process. Thus, after determining what wire news came in during the week in terms of total column inches and categories, we measured the amount of wire news that appeared in the papers for that period.

Assuming that five lines of wire copy are equivalent to a column inch in a newspaper, Mr. Gates received approximately 12,400 inches of press association news from the AP, UP and INS during the week. Of this he used 1297 column inches of wire news, or about *one-tenth,* in the seven issues we measured. Table 1 shows a breakdown by categories of the wire news received and used during the week.

It is only when we study the reasons given by Mr. Gates for rejecting almost nine-tenths of the wire copy (in his search for the one-tenth for

Table 1—Amounts of Press Association News Mr. Gates Received and Used During Seven-Day Period

CATEGORY	WIRE COPY RECEIVED		WIRE COPY USED	
	Col. In.*	% of Total	Col. In.*	% of Total
Crime	527	4.4	41	3.2
Disaster	405	3.4	44	3.4
Political				
State	565	4.7	88	6.8
National	1722	14.5	205	15.8
Human interest	4171	35.0	301	23.2
International				
Political	1804	15.1	176	13.6
Economic	405	3.4	59	4.5
War	480	4.0	72	5.6
Labor	650	5.5	71	5.5
National				
Farm	301	2.5	78	6.0
Economic	294	2.5	43	3.3
Education	381	3.2	56	4.3
Science	205	1.7	63	4.9
Total	11,910	99.9	1297	100.1

* Counting five lines of wire copy as one column inch.

which he has space) that we begin to understand how highly subjective, how reliant upon value-judgments based on the "gatekeeper's" own set of experiences, attitudes and expectations the communication of "news" really is. In this particular case the 56 wordings given may be divided into two main categories: (1) rejecting the incident as unworthy of being reported, and (2) selecting from many reports of the same event. (See Table 2.)

Thus we find him rejecting one piece of wire copy with the notation, "He's too Red." Another story is categorically marked "Never use this." dealt with the Townsend Plan, and because this "gatekeeper" feels that the merits of the Townsend Plan are highly dubious, the chances of wire news about the Plan appearing in the paper are negligible. Eighteen pieces of copy were marked "B. S."; 16 were marked "Propaganda." One interesting notation on a story said "Don't care for suicides." Thus we see that many of the reasons which Mr. Gates gives for the rejection of the stories fall into the category of highly subjective value-judgments.

The second category gives us an important clue as to the difficulty of making choices of one piece of copy over another. No less than 168 times, Mr. Gates makes the notation "No space." In short, the story (in his eyes) has merit and interest, he has no "personal" objections to it, but space is at a premium. It is significant to observe that the later in the

Table 2—Reasons for Rejection of Press Association News Given by Mr. Gates During Seven-Day Period

Reason		Number of Times Given
Rejecting incident as worthy of reporting		423
Not interesting (61); no interest here (43)	104	
Dull writing (51); too vague (26); drags too much (3)	80	
No good (31); slop (18); B. S. (18)	67	
Too much already on subject (54); used up (4); passed—dragging out;* too much of this; goes on all the time; dying out	62	
Trivial (29); would ignore (21); no need for this; wasted space; not too important; not too hot; not too worthy	55	
Never use this (16); never use (7)	23	
Propaganda (16); he's too Red; sour grapes	18	
Wouldn't use (11); don't care for suicide stories; too suggestive; out of good taste	14	
Selecting from reports of the same event		910
Would use if space (221); no space (168); good—if space (154); late —used up (61); too late—no space (34); no space—used other press service; would use partially if space	640	
Passed for later story (61); waiting for later information (48); waiting on this (33); waiting for this to hatch (17); would let drop a day or two (11); outcome will be used—not this; waiting for later day progress	172	
Too far away (24); out of area (16)	40	
Too regional (36)	36	
Used another press service: Better story (11); shorter (6); this is late; lead more interesting; meatier	20	
Bannered yesterday	1	
I missed this one	1	

* In this and other cases where no number follows the reason, that reason was given only once.

evening the stories came in, the higher was the proportion of the "no space" or "would use" type of notation. As the evening progresses the wire editor's pages become more and more filled up. A story that has a good chance of getting on the front page at 7:30 or 8 o'clock in the evening may not be worth the precious remaining space at 11 o'clock. The notation "Would use" is made 221 times, and a similar one "Good— if space" is made 154 times. Other reasons which fall into the mechanical category are "Used INS—shorter" or "Used UP—this is late." Even in this category, though, we find subjective value-judgments such as "Used AP—better story" or "Used INS—lead more interesting."

Now that we have some preliminary knowledge of the manner in which Mr. Gates selects or rejects news for his front and "jump" pages, it might be interesting to examine his performance for a specific day. In Table 3 the amount and type of news which appeared on the front and

**Table 3—Column Inches Devoted to Content Categories in
February 9, 1949, Issue ***

Category		Front Page and Jump
Local		3.50
Crime		5.00
Disaster		9.75
Political		41.25
Local	9.75	
State	19.50	
National	12.00	
Human interest		43.75 †
International		23.00
Political	11.50	
Economic	11.50	
War	.—	
National		24.25
Labor	19.25	
Farm	.—	
Economic	5.00	
Education		.—
Science		6.00 ‡

* Banner not included.
   † About one-half of this amount were Cardinal Mindzenty stories, which, because of the human appeal, were classed as Human Interest.
   ‡ Three column picture not included.

"jump" pages edited by Gates for February 9, 1949 is presented. Table 4 shows the total number of dispatches (classified as to type of story) received but not used.

During this particular week the Cardinal Mindzenty trial was receiving wide play from newspapers throughout the land and the press associations were filing many stories covering all phases of the case. So in making a comparison of the dispatches received and the stories which appeared it should not be surprising to note that Human Interest news was used most. Yet even in his treatment of the Mindzenty case, Mr. Gates used highly subjective reasons in his selection of stories. Particularly interesting in this connection is his remark on an Associated Press story which he rejected with the comment *"Would pass, propaganda itself."* The story dealt with a statement by Samuel Cardinal Stritch, who said, "It is very unfortunate that our news agencies are not giving their sources of information in their day-by-day reports on the trial of Cardinal Mindzenty. It should be made clear that restrictions have been made on a few American correspondents who have been present at the trial." It is obvious that Mr. Gates resented the implication by Cardinal Stritch that the press associations were not doing all they could to tell the Mindzenty story. The com-

Table 4—Number of Pieces of Press Association Releases Received But Not Used February 9, 1949

Category	Received before Front Page Was Made Up	Received after Front Page Was Made Up	Total Received For Day
Local	3		3
Crime	32	1	33
Disaster	15		15
Political			22
Local	1	2	
State	10	2	
National	6	1	
Human interest	65	14	79
International			46
Political	19	5	
Economic	9	1	
War	10	2	
National			37
Farm	2		
Labor	13	1	
Economic	17	4	
Education	3	2	5
Science	5	2	7
Total for day	210	37	247

ment which Mr. Gates put on a United Press story dealing with Cardinal Stritch's statement, "No space—pure propaganda," illustrates his sensitivity on this particular point. And when the story came to his attention for the third time that evening as an International News Service dispatch he again rejected it, this time with the statement "Would pass." Perhaps his feeling of anger against the story had cooled by this time, but Mr. Gates still considered the story worthless.

Political news enjoyed the second largest play. Here we begin to have an indication of preference, as political news ranked only fifth in the "dispatches received" department. Political news seems to be a favorite with Mr. Gates, for even if we subtract the almost ten inches given to a local political story it ranks second in play.

While a total of 33 crime stories was received, only five column inches of crime appeared on the front and "jump" pages of Mr. Gates' paper. The obvious conclusion is that crime news, as such, does not appeal to this wire editor. But it should be noted that no "big" crime stories broke that day.

As one examines the whole week's performance of Mr. Gates, as manifested in the stories he chose, certain broad patterns become apparent. What do we know, for example, about the kinds of stories that he selected in preference to others from the same category? What tests of subject matter and way-of-writing did Mr. Gates seem to apply? In almost every case where he had some choice between competing press association stories Mr. Gates preferred the "conservative." I use this expression not only in terms of its political connotations, but also in terms of the style of writing. Sensationalism and insinuation seemed to be avoided consistently.

As to the way-of-writing that he preferred, Mr. Gates showed an obvious dislike for stories that had too many figures and statistics. In almost every case where one news agency supplied a story filled with figures and statistics and the competing agency's story was an easier going, more interpretative than statistical type of story, the latter appeared in the paper. An indication of his standards for writing is seen in Table 1, where 26 stories were rejected as being "too vague," 51 rejected for "dull writing" and 61 for being "not interesting."

Another question that should be considered in this study (and subsequent ones) is: Does the category really enter into the choice? That is, does the wire editor try to chose a certain amount of crime news, human interest news, etc.? Are there some other divisions of subject matter or form which he chooses in this manner, such as a certain number of one-paragraph stories?

Insofar as this "gatekeeper" is representative of wire editors as a whole, it does not appear that there is any conscious choice of news by categories. During this particular week under examination an emphasis on the Human Interest type of story was seen mainly because of the large news appeal of the Cardinal Mindzenty story. It would be most interesting and valuable to ascertain how a wire editor determines what one issue or type of story is "the" story of the week. Many times that decision is made by "gatekeepers" above him, or by "gatekeepers" in competing media. Can a wire editor refuse to play a story "up" when his counterpart in the local radio station is playing it to the hilt? Likewise, can a wire editor play down a story when he sees competing papers from nearby metropolitan areas coming into his city and playing up the story? These factors undoubtedly have something to do in determining the wire editor's opinion as to what he should give the reading public the next morning. This brings up the rather obvious conclusion that theoretically all of the wire editor's standards of taste should refer back to an audience who must be served and pleased.

Subsequent to Mr. Gates' participation in the project to determine the "reasons" for selecting or rejecting wire stories during a week, he was asked to consider at length four questions which we submitted. His answers to these questions tell us much about Mr. Gates, particularly if they are collated with the "spot" reasons which came under the pressure of a working night.

Question 1: "Does the category of news affect your choice of news stories?"

The category of news definitely enters into my choice of stories. A crime story will carry a warning as will an accident story. Human interest stories provoke sympathy and could set examples of conduct. Economic news is informative for some readers and over the heads of others. I make no attempt to hold a rigid balance in these selections but do strive for variety. The category of news suggests groups that should be interested in a particular story, that is, teachers, laborers, professional people, etc. Wire service reports can't keep a strictly balanced diet and for this reason we could not attempt it. For the most part, the same thinking applies in the selection of shorts, although some are admittedly filler material.

Question 2: "Do you feel that you have any prejudices which may affect your choice of news stories?"

I have few prejudices, built-in or otherwise, and there is little I can do about them. I dislike Truman's economics, daylight saving time and warm beer, but I go ahead using stories on them and other matters if I feel there is nothing more important to give space to. I am also prejudiced against a publicity-seeking minority with headquarters in Rome, and I don't help them a lot. As far as preferences are concerned, I go for human interest stories in a big way. My other preferences are for stories well-wrapped up and tailored to suit our needs (or ones slanted to conform to our editorial policies).

Question 3: "What is your concept of the audience for whom you select stories and what sort of person do you conceive the average person to be?"

Our readers are looked upon as people with average intelligence and with a variety of interests and abilities. I am aware of the fact we have readers with above average intelligence (there are four colleges in our area) and that there are many with far less education. Anyway, I see them as human and with some common interests. I believe they are all entitled to news that pleases them (stories involving their thinking and activity) and news that informs them of what is going on in the world.

Question 4: "Do you have specific tests of subject matter or way of writing that help you determine the selection of any particular news story?"

The only tests of subject matter or way of writing I am aware of when making a selection involve clarity, conciseness and angle. I mentioned earlier that certain stories are selected for their warning, moral or lesson, but I am not inclined to list these reasons as any test of subject matter or way of writing. The clarity trio is almost a constant yardstick in judging a story, especially when I often have three of a kind, AP, UP and INS. Length of a story is another factor (or test) in a selection. The long winded one is usually discarded unless it can be cut to fill satisfactorily.

It is a well-known fact in individual psychology that people tend to perceive as true only those happenings which fit into their own beliefs concerning what is likely to happen. It begins to appear (if Mr. Gates is a fair representative of his class) that in his position as "gatekeeper" the newspaper editor sees to it (even though he may never be consciously aware of it) that the community shall hear as a fact only those events which the newsman, as the representative of his culture, believes to be true.

This is the case study of one "gatekeeper," but one, who like several hundred of his fellow "gatekeepers," plays a most important role as the terminal "gate" in the complex process of communication. Through studying his overt reasons for rejecting news stories from the press associations we see how highly subjective, how based on the "gatekeeper's" own set of experiences, attitudes and expectations the communication of "news" really is.

QUESTIONS

1.   If you were repeating this research, what questions would you ask the "gatekeeper" that White did not ask?

2.   By comparing different versions of the same story which appear in two or more daily newspapers, can you discern any changes in the respective versions which indicate the "gatekeeping" function? If so, try to hypothesize what were the reasons why the "gatekeeper" played the story as he did. Compare an Associated Press and a United Press International version of the same story.

3.   If the transmission of a message about a "criterion event" is altered at several steps (from the "encoding" of the first "gatekeeper" to the "decoding" of the receiver) is it possible to get a "true" picture of a "happening," unless you witness it yourself?

4.   The reader of a news story, TV viewer, etc., also may be said to be exercising a "gatekeeping" function in that he refuses to accept certain cues, responds quickly to others, etc. This, of course, is clearly related to what psychologists term "selective perception." If you doubt this, write on a sheet or two of paper as many of your *attitudes* and *opinions* as you can think of at one sitting, e.g., I don't like people who drive big, ostentatious automobiles. Then look again at the last newspaper you thought you had read quite thoroughly. Observe to what extent you have read those things that were customarily meaningful to you, or which did not conflict with your prejudices or predispositions.

5.   A fruitful area for your own "gatekeeper" study would be to study the managing editor and/or city editor of your campus daily or weekly. By checking an "interview" story, for example, as it appears in your college newspaper with (1) the interviewer, (2) the reporter, and (3) the managing editor of the newspaper, you can determine to what extent the "gatekeeper" principle may apply to even this limited transmission of a message.

Walter Gieber

News Is What Newspapermen
Make It

Interest in the gatekeeper study is founded on what at first blush seems to be an utterly simple notion: news is what newspapermen make it. Well then, how do newspapermen make news? The answer is as complex as any attempt to assay a social institution and its resident occupations.

There is no argument here with the premise that our society has a significant concern with the role of the press and its impact in the community. But, there may be some argument over which comes first, the horse or the cart. Most critiques of the press are concerned with the effects on society of the press—for example, its impact on "public opinion," as though the press were an autonomous force. It seems to me that the examination of the press must start where the news begins—*within* the institution of the press, *within* the walls of the newsroom or any other place where a newsman gets and writes his stories.

To a sensitive, thoughtful newspaperman, writing the news story is a singularly personal experience. For despite what "professional" or "ethical" controls he enforces upon himself, or for that matter, the bureaucratic controls that are thrust upon him, the news story is—or should be—a product of his disciplined perception and his evaluation of the environment, of the social arena from which the story and its characters come, and of the bureaucratic climate in which it is written. The contemporary literature of the newsman is rich in personal, informal insights into the intimate nature of news-gathering experience.[1]

But if a newspaperman were to look over the body of mass-media research of the past 25 years, he would be amazed at the paucity of

1. Only a few books can be mentioned here: Eric Sevareid, *Not So Wild a Dream;* Joseph and Stewart Alsop, *The Reporter's Trade;* Vincent Sheean, *Personal History;* Webb Miller, *I Found No Peace;* Kenneth Stewart, *News Is What We Make It.*

literature on the newsgathering process.[2] In 1937, Leo C. Rosten completed *The Washington Correspondents*,[3] a classic study of the "psychology" of the reporter. More than a decade later, the publication of David M. White's gatekeeper study (pp. 161–172) gave impetus to research in a critical area—the channels of mass communications themselves. What happens to news stories as they are handled by newsmen within these channels?

The gatekeeper study is an empirical, systematic examination of the behavior of those persons who at various points control the fate of news stories. Who are the gatekeepers? They are the newsmen employed by a news-gathering bureaucracy; they are the sources of news outside of the news bureaucracies; they are the members of the audience who influence the reading of other members of the audience (recall the two-step flow of communications). All these persons are gatekeepers at some point. This paper, however, concentrates primarily on the newsmen and their sources.

The conceptual underpinnings of "gatekeeper" studies can be found in particular among those studies of human behavior which take place among the professions and within bureaucratic institutions. The most helpful analytic schemes have come from Kurt Lewin's social channel and field theories, Robert K. Merton's, among others', discussions of role behavior within reference groups and Bruce Westley's and Malcolm MacLean's model for communication research.[4]

The methodology of the gatekeeper study was well adapted to White's purpose; for our purpose here, however, we prefer the techniques of the depth interview and participant-observation.

The goal of the gatekeeper study is hopefully to make a contribution toward a better understanding of the behavior of mass-communications specialists, ultimately toward a sociology of the journalist. David Manning White's more immediate goal was an attempt to explain some of the facets of behavior within the complexities of the networks of news gathering.

White's conclusion, "how subjective news really is" poses the question "how subjective?" Let's start with the telegraph editor as did White. A press association, as a news network, provides a series of telegraph editors

2. And this includes press history, according to Allan Nevins, "American Journalism and Its Historical Treatment," *Journalism Quarterly*, 36:411–422, Fall 1959.

3. New York: Harcourt, 1937.

4. Kurt Lewin, *Field Theory in Social Science*, edited by Dorwin Cartwright, New York: Harper & Brothers, 1951; Robert K. Merton, *Social Theory and Social Structure*, Revised, New York: The Free Press of Glencoe, 1957; Bruce H. Westley and Malcolm S. MacLean, Jr., "A Conceptual Model for Communications Research," *Journalism Quarterly*, 34:31–38 (Winter 1957).

with a common budget of news items; the "flow" of communications up to and through the gate area, the telegraph desk, can be measured; the behavior (selection of items) of the editors can be compared and contrasted.

If one takes his clue from Lewin, one can define "subjectivity" in this case as the telegraph editor's perception of his own values, the values of the newsroom and the values of his audience, the newspaper readers. The gatekeeper's selection in accordance with "subjective" value criteria is limited by the number of news items available, their size and the pressures of time and mechanical production.

In 1956, the author selected 16 Wisconsin dailies receiving only the Associated Press wire.[5] No major differences in news selection and newspage display were found among the wire editors. They did differ, however, in the explanations and rationalizations of their role behavior.

But I also found that, in each case, it was possible to approach what was a prediction of selection. If the editor's selection was regarded as a sample, statistically speaking, of the incoming wire budget, his "draw" was excellent. Moreover, through testing the editor's decisions on a group of "test" news items and by watching his selection for several days, it was possible to project what he would do on a selected operational day.

Common to all the telegraph editors were the pressures exerted by the reality of the newsroom bureaucratic structure and its operation. The most powerful factor was not the evaluative nature of news but the pressures of getting the copy into the newspaper; the telegraph editor was preoccupied with the mechanical pressures of his work rather than the social meanings and impact of the news. His personal evaluations rarely entered into his selection process; the values of his employer were an accepted part of the newsroom environment.

In short, the telegraph editor was "task oriented"; he was concerned with goals of production, bureaucratic routine and interpersonal relations within the newsroom.

Two bald, discomforting facts became apparent. First, in his communication behavior, the telegraph editor was passive. He was playing no real and active role as a communicator; indeed, the press association was more instrumental in making the selection than the telegraph editor. An active communications role seemingly would cause the newsman to come to grips—what Joseph and Stewart Alsop call *engagé*—with the environment. There was some evidence that the telegraph editor, a desk-bound newspaperman, may have different motivations leading to the difference

5. Walter Gieber, *The Telegraph Editors: A Study in Communication Behavior,* Ph.D. dissertation, University of Wisconsin, 1956, and "Across the Desk: A Study of 16 Telegraph Editors," *Journalism Quarterly,* 33:423–432 (Fall, 1956).

in occupational choice from that of the reporter. It may be that he was lazy or, more acutely, he became lazy because his executives did not encourage him to be otherwise. At any rate, he made no critical evaluation of the incoming wire news.

Second, as a communicator he had no real perception of his audience and, therefore, was not truly communicating to it. If the major function of the newspaper is the meaningful and purposeful surveillance of the environment for the reader and, thus, the fulfillment of his communications needs and expectations, then this function was only fortuitously met.

A discussion of "subjectivity" in news selection must take into account the limitations imposed by bureaucratic pressures.

These conclusions, based on a study of small-city telegraph editors,[6] were discomforting. Several further questions remained because, first of all, telegraph news filters to the telegraph editor through a long series of news networks controlled by other gatekeepers who are responsive to the demands of a diversity of newspapers; second, the press association budget carries a wide range of stories and thus a large variety of socially meaningful symbols. Thus, the question arises: What "subjectivity" would be found if local news items were involved and the variety of symbols restricted? To put the question another way: Can news stories which carry socially evaluative symbols exert the pressure to force their way through "gate areas"? The opportunity to examine this question came with a study of the gatekeepers of local news of civil rights and liberties.[7]

Having made a content analysis of news of civil rights and liberties,[8] I had noted the relative paucity of *local* stories. This, in 1958, was at a time when local spokesmen for civil rights were proclaiming that, despite large regional events and major court and legislative actions, Western cities were not free of violations of civil rights and liberties. If this were true, what was happening to local stories on these issues? Obviously, content analysis could not explain the reasons for such missions.

6. The author replicated the Wisconsin study with a group of small-city dailies in Indiana. The results were not published; they were, if anything, slightly more discomforting.

7. Walter Gieber, *Gatekeepers of News of Civil Rights and Liberties: A Study of the Fate of Local News Stories,* Department of Journalism, University of California, 1958; "How the 'Gatekeepers' View Local Civil Liberties News," *Journalism Quarterly,* 37:199–205 (Spring, 1960); "Two Communicators of the News: A Study of the Roles of Sources and Reporters," *Social Forces,* 39:76–83 (October, 1960).

8. The Civil Liberties and Rights Project of the Association of Education in Journalism.

In view of the marked social value given to symbols of civil liberties
and rights—at least among a number of vocal publics—it seemed to me
that relevant stories would create among gatekeepers a variety of strong
evaluative (subjective) responses: The gatekeeper's values may be consonant or in conflict with (*a*) the values in the story, (*b*) the values of
the newspaper—which in turn may be in conflict or consonant with the
values of the story, (*c*) the perceived values of the audience—which in
turn may be consonant or in conflict with the values of the newspaper.

Using the same set of stories, in this case persons involved in civil
rights activities, I went to both the sources of the news and to the reporters; I found that the two "gatekeepers" of this single channel (source
to reporter) of news were operating at different levels of discourse.

The sources tended to communicate in connotative terms. Civil liberties and civil rights were discussed in a tone and context of great urgency;
the *public had to know* about relevant events and attenuating symbols.
But the sources had little notion of the ways in which the press works.
And they had little knowledge of the mass-media audience. In essence,
they were attempting to communicate in terms of their own values and
assuming that the audience shared these values. They saw consonance
among the stories, themselves and the public and believed themselves
frustrated by a dissonant press.

The reporters, with few exceptions, *personally* held the same general
values as the sources but publicly did not so convey them. Moreover, news
of civil liberties and rights had to compete with other stories. In handling
relevant news stories, the reporters tended to use denotive symbols (names
rather than values; action rather than meaning; controversy rather than
consensus). Although the reporters also held a *rationale* of audience needs
(that it needs to know the facts), they too had little knowledge of their
readers. They appeared to be oriented primarily to problems of the craft
and the newsroom.

The reporters' major complaint was the lack of opportunity to write
any story the way they saw it. The reporters were cognizant of the social
meaning of events which took place in the community. No matter how
feeble their awareness of the news interests and needs of their audience
happened to be, they were aware of numerous events which required full
reporting even if only in purely denotative symbols. The sad fact was that
although many reporters were aware of their environment and, both
personally and professionally, had a wide knowledge of the background
of civil rights events, they had little opportunity to report fully on them.
They charged that their employers did not allow them sufficient time to
write full reports, often because they were preoccupied with a frantic

gathering of trivia, failing to distinguish items of broader social significance. The reporters could, then, only discuss these issues among themselves and, in a few instances, write on them for magazines of small
circulation.

The reporters' major concern was with the "climate" of the newsroom: they recognized themselves as employees of a news-gathering
bureaucracy in which rewards came from their editors and colleagues. The
value system of the newspaper (news policy) was not considered a problem; the reporters accepted it as part of bureaucratic structuring. They
were more inclined to complain of inconsistency in or lack of policy. In
fact, the main charge against their employers was the failure to give the
reporters a chance to exploit their craft and the failure to actively maintain surveillance of the environment.

The fate of the local news story is not determined by the needs of
the audience or even by the values of the symbols it contains. The news
story is controlled by the frame of reference created by the bureaucratic
structure of which the communicator is a member.

The reporters recognized the evaluative nature of symbols of civil
rights and liberties items, but these were only one set of symbols among
many demanding attention; moreover, they believed that transmission of
relevant events is enhanced by denotative symbols, arguing that the readers
would get the point if "name" were given more attention than a "principle." (And they may well have a point.) Accordingly, they were unlikely to present fully an evaluative release. The reporters saw dissonance
between themselves and the sources over the definition of news and they
saw incongruity between their own craft expectations and the reality of
the newsroom.

The civil liberties study further explored a basic problem in the
transmission of news—the problem of the bureaucratic frame of reference. The press holds a basic tenet that it must remain aloof from the
influences of other institutions—sources, public relations experts and
others desiring to reach, or to avoid, the "public." It is likewise well
known that other institutions—and all persons eager to reach or avoid the
"public"—exert pressures on the press to get it to behave as they would
like. Politicians and governmental bureaucrats are traditionally the most
notorious for applying such pressures on the press.

In point of fact the press and its reporters have not remained pristine
by any means. Indeed, one can envision three possible relationships between the sources of the news and the reporters: (a) the reporters remain
independent of the sources; (b) the reporters and the sources find areas
of collaboration for their mutual benefit; (c) the sources "absorb" and
dominate the reporters, or vice versa. With this in mind, the author

studied the relationships between reporters and the elected and appointed officials in a small California city.[9]

Both sources and reporters hailed the press as the champion of democratic society. Both supported "open" channels of communication. Both claimed a principled interest in the public weal; but it was at this juncture that basic differences arose. The sources saw themselves as *custodians* of the welfare of the community and its voters; the reporters saw themselves as *protectors* of the "public." (I may as well mention that both had hazy, stereotyped perceptions of the "public.") Each group developed its own perception of its public role, its own frame of reference for its communications, and claimed for itself the primary role of communicating to the public.

For the sources the frame of reference was the "city." Any communication reaching the public had to be cleansed of any information that might upset the community consensus. All communications had to enhance the consensus. Naturally, all attempts to "protect" from publication the utterances and records of the individual source were well rationalized as contributions toward consensus.

Inasmuch as the press is the major communication artery to the voters, the sources' major objective was to assimilate the press into their frame of reference. Their method: suasion and sociability.

The reporters saw themselves in an independent "distributive" role. Their frame of reference was the "beat" which included themselves, the sources and the "public." On the one hand, fiercely rationalizing their "watchdog" function on government; on the other, the reporters, nonetheless, were passive; they rarely "dug" for a story and remained content to accept releases or to record public meetings. They shared with their sources an admiration for "efficient" city government and tended to avoid stories about latent conflicts within the community. Overt conflict at a meeting between sources and voters, or among sources, was another matter —it was fair play. More important, the reporters had interpreted the symbol of the "public" to apply narrowly only to a strong "in-group" loyalty to "the city" as opposed to the broader community. Their best stories were written when the "city" was in conflict with an "outside" agency. Indeed, the reporters would cooperate—and did cooperate—with the sources in suppressing or postponing publication of a story in order to protect "the city" from threats from "outsiders."

Thus, the reporters, by giving up any real independence of surveillance and critique and by allowing themselves the comfort of "in-group"

9. Walter Gieber, *The City Hall Reporter and His Sources,* a paper prepared for the Media Analysis Section, Association for Education in Journalism, August, 1960.

community loyalties, willy-nilly have moved into the area of collaboration with their sources.

While I acknowledge that a great deal more research must be accomplished before the full dimensions of the nature of news communications are known, this generalization can be made from our research: News does not have an independent existence; news is a product of men who are members of a news-gathering (or a news-originating) bureaucracy. But the question remains: how "subjective" is the news? Very much so, in my opinion. This answer implies a particular definition of "subjective." If one means expression of the individuality of the communicator, the answer is that there is *some* subjectivity. It appears to me that the reporter's individuality is strongly tempered by extrapersonal factors. Although no one expects the newsman to have the freedom of the artist, the professional communicator often does see himself as a craftsman possessing the right to "tell the story as he sees it." But craft freedom, which would encourage individual role development and critical evaluation of the news, is controlled by the news-gathering bureaucracy. The "splendid isolation" necessary to the craftsman does not exist for the newsman.

The press—and by delegation, the individual newsman—rightfully has the institutional license to gather and make public the news. Society rightfully can expect the press to maintain critical surveillance of the social arena and to provide an independent appraisal of the environment. This requires, it seems to me, the press to remain free from undue influences from other social institutions. And it means that the individual reporter must remain independent from pressures from sources and free as far as possible from such pressures from the news bureaucracy which would interfere with his craft of full and critical reporting.

The ultimate *rationale* of the press—the reason for its license—is to serve the audience. The news-gathering machinery and the news-gathering bureaucracy are the means; the audience needs are the goals. In the telegraph editor survey, the means all but replaced the goals. In the civil liberties study, both the sources and the reporters rationalized audience needs but neither seemed to know the audience; both communicators shared responsibility for a communications breakdown resulting from their antagonistic frames of reference; each was communicating thought by the means of his bureaucracy. In the city hall study, the communicator allowed himself to be caught in a frame of reference which was only in part of his own making; the proper goals were all but forgotten.

News is what newspapermen make it.

But until we understand better the social forces which bear on the reporting of the news, we will never understand what news is.

SELECTED PUBLICATIONS BY DR. WHITE

Mass Culture, the Popular Arts in America (Free Press, New York, 1957) (co-editor).

Introduction to Mass Communications Research, 2nd ed. (Louisiana State U. P., 1958) (co-editor).

Publishing for the New Reading Audience (Government of Burma Press, Rangoon, 1958) (co-editor).

Identity and Anxiety (Free Press, New York, 1960) (co-editor).

The Funnies: An American Idiom (Free Press, New York, 1963) (co-editor).

From Dogpatch to Slobbovia: The—Gasp—World of L'il Abner (Beacon Press, Boston, 1964) (editor).

Elementary Statistics for Journalists (Macmillan, New York, 1954) (co-author).

SELECTED PUBLICATIONS BY DR. GIEBER

The Telegraph Editors: A Study in Communication Behavior, Ph.D. dissertation, University of Wisconsin, 1956.

"Across the Desk: a Study of 16 Telegraph Editors," *Journalism Quarterly,* vol. 33, pp. 423–432, Fall 1956.

Gatekeepers of News of Civil Rights and Liberties: a study of the fate of local news stories, Dept. of Journalism, U. of California, 1958.

"How the 'Gatekeepers' View Local Civil Liberties News," *Journalism Quarterly,* vol. 37, pp. 199–205, Spring 1960.

"Two Communicators of the News: A Study of the Roles of Sources and Reporters," *Social Forces,* vol. 39, pp. 76–83, October 1960.

SUGGESTIONS FOR FURTHER READING

Breed, Warren, "Newspaper 'Opinion Leaders' and Processes of Standardization," *Journalism Quarterly,* vol. 32, pp. 277–284, Summer 1955.

———, "Social Control in the Newsroom," *Social Forces,* vol. 33, pp. 326–335, May 1955.

These two articles by Breed are based on Dr. Breed's doctoral dissertation, "The Newspaperman, News and Society" (Columbia University, 1952). The first examines the "arterial process" in which the news editors of larger newspapers and the wire services influence the judgments of other gatekeepers. The second concentrates on the multi-faceted pressures of social controls over the journalist in the newsroom.

Carter, Roy E., Jr., "Newspaper Gatekeepers and the Sources of News," *Public Opinion Quarterly,* vol. 22, pp. 133–144, Summer 1958. A valuable inquiry into the different patterns of the interaction between the newspaperman and his sources.

Cater, Douglass, *Fourth Branch of Government* (Houghton, Boston, 1959). The author shows how the reporter (a gatekeeper) has become a participant in the affairs of government. Most of all, Cater sharply defines the basic difference between the role of the reporter and his source; the reporter's role is "distributive" and the source's role is "assimilative."

Judd, Robert, "The Newspaper Reporter in a Suburban City," *Journalism Quar-*

terly, vol. 38, pp. 35–42, Winter 1961. This depth study emphasizes the dangers of the "passive" gatekeeper.

Macrorie, Ken, "The Process of News Reporting," *Etc.,* vol. 13, pp. 254–264, Summer 1956. An interesting study of a "gatekeeper" who approaches a story with a "hypothesis."

Rosten, Leo C., *The Washington Correspondents* (Harcourt, New York, 1937). A classic study of the gatekeeper.

QUESTIONS

1. In his study of city hall reporters and their sources, Gieber noted that the two held distinctly different frames of reference. Describe them. In spite of their different frame of reference, the reporters appeared to be seeking the comfort of "in-group" community loyalties. How may this tbe explained? Where the *source* of news is a strong in-group (such as local government), is there a greater tendency for reporters to "collaborate" with the *source?* What other examples of strong in-group sources can you think of? Under what circumstances might they compel collaboration?

2. Gieber is extremely critical of the telegraph editors he studied. Why? Can you think of possible means of alleviating the problems Gieber outlines?

3. Gieber feels that "splendid isolation" (freedom from restrictive aspects of the news-gathering bureaucracy) simply does not exist for most reporters. Set up a symposium for your class in which you invite three reporters from local daily newspapers. As moderator of the symposium, summarize Gieber's argument and see whether the reporters confirm or deny Gieber's hypotheses. Can you think of further evidence which might support or undermine his argument?

4. "The news story is controlled by the frame of reference created by the bureaucratic structure of which the communicator is a member," according to Gieber. Interview the managing editor of a local daily (or invite him to class for a group interview) and ask him to describe the news-gathering function of his staff. Compare his analysis of the reporter's role with that given by Gieber, by the reporters in the symposium suggested above.

Warren Breed

Mass Communication

and Sociocultural Integration [*]

"A LITTLE LEARNING is a dangerous thing; drink deep or taste not of the Pierian spring. . . ." This point, made several centuries ago by Alexander Pope, may be addressed as fair warning to the reader of Breed's article. Those who half-understand it may misinterpret it, rather dangerously. Like Gieber, Breed considers some of the areas where the news may not be fully reported. Whereas Gieber views this primarily negatively as a departure from the ideal of the objective and independent newsman who provides full surveillance of his environment, Breed indicates that omission to report the news fully may be the result of a responsibly made decision in good conscience and may function positively to maintain individual and social virtues. Breed points out that the mass-media value respect for convention, public decency, orderliness, as well as the accurate reporting of significant events. Accurate reporting is sometimes sacrificed to these other virtues of respect, decency, and order, that is, the mass media have often placed more emphasis on some value other than truth—which is to say there are conflicts of values.

This violates the popular conception that newspapers ought always to print the truth, the whole truth, and nothing but the truth (although the New York Times more modestly and accurately dedicates itself to "all the news that is fit to print"). This popular conception is shared by many students and teachers of journalism, and, other things being equal, is probably believed by most publishers, editors, and reporters. But, as Breed shows, in concrete situations, other things often are not equal. In a brilliant unpublished manuscript by Stanley

[*] Expanded version of paper read at the 1956 meetings of the American Sociological Society. Gratitude is expressed in the Tulane University Council on Research for funds granted, and to William L. Kolb and David Riesman for a critical reading of an earlier draft.

Reprinted from *Social Forces*, vol. 37 (1958), pp. 109–116, by permission of the author and publisher. (Copyright 1958 by University of North Carolina Press by assignment from the Williams and Wilkins Company.)

Bigman, and in equally competent interviews on the same episode by
Stewart E. Perry,[1] the following is reported:

Shortly after the Supreme Court decision ordering school desegregation, a Border City school board did in fact abolish segregation.
In protest an active group stayed out of school and tried to organize
riots. But the newspapers, with the support of most of the goodwill
organizations in the community, gave the episode very little coverage,
played it down, and really did not let the public know what was happening. The newspaper executives pointed out that if they had published "the truth"—reported the event "straight" according to the
usual criteria of news value, as they might have done on an issue of
less moral weight such as athletics or dress—they might have caused
the failure of desegregation and certainly would have hurt the community and the country. National reporting, a few years later, of
similar events in New Orleans almost certainly had precisely the
effect there which these men feared—and avoided—in Border City.

"Truth" and "true reporting" in other words are sometimes dangerous. It is suggested at this point that the student reflect whether
accurate reporting at his college or university would under all conditions be desirable. One of the greatest Universities in the world for
years reportedly told new employees in its public relations office that
its first business was to keep unfavorable news out of the papers and
only secondarily to get favorable news in. The University of Chicago
in particular suffered from bad publicity; it lost a great sociologist
due to World War I hysteria aggravated by the mass media. Later
the University's administration had to spend many man-years of effort
fighting charges of un-Americanism, due to the extensive publicity the
mass media gave these charges (in the early Walgreen episode). It
also lost considerable reputation because of the widely reported Loeb-
Leopold and Heirens cases. In these instances the greater the truthful
reporting of newspapers, the more distracted the University was from
its purpose: the pursuit and transmission of basic truths.

So, the decision of what truths to report and what truths are too
uncomfortable or dangerous to be reported is a very difficult one to
make. The cynic will say that newspapers, in underplaying or suppressing news, do not live up to their ideal values. But in a world in
which people cherish different moral values, in concrete cases they
must sometimes choose between values. For sometimes they cannot
be all applied together! This is the dilemma of conscience, the dilemma of living in a complex world. Thus, "What may at first blush
appear to be the immoral decision of a designing conniver, may, on
further examination, turn out to be the moral decision of a highly

1. Stewart E. Perry, "The Conflict for the News Editor in Desegregation Disturbances," *Psychiatry*, 26 (1963) pp. 352–367.

conscientious man, forced to make choices in a concrete situation."
This was said about politicians but can be equally true of mass media
executives.

Breed points out that home-town newspapers generally speak
well of the home town, and of its leaders. For is not the value of
permitting people to keep their self-respect as great as the value of
reporting the truth? To turn from the local to the national scene,
were those more or less publicly implied by Senator McCarthy to
be homosexuals not severely hurt? And who was the better (be Mc-
Carthy right or wrong) for the publicizing of this information? That
is to say, the value of charity ("the greatest of these is charity")
often runs athwart the value of truth in news.

The point of all this is that determination of what to publish and
how to publish constantly involves moral decisions, based on guesses
about the consequences of the communications. In view of the time
schedule of the media, these decisions and the guesses on which they
are based often have to be made very quickly and without scholarly
articulation. Most of the examples Breed cites are, in the nature of
the case, concerned with protecting the dominant values and interests
of American society in recent years. Most of these values and interests may be called "conservative." From this one should not, however, be led to suppose that "liberals" are faced with fewer value conflicts in handling news. Any reader of PM or The Nation during and
just after World War II who will look back upon them today will
be startled by the manner and extent to which they slanted or suppressed news to support a "liberal leftist" point of view. The "progressive" press exposes suppressions of news which might be favorable
to conventional middle-of-the-road or conservative positions; but such
rightist publications as The National Review sometimes show where
national media have suppressed or slanted news that would favor
extreme conservatism and hurt the middle-of-the-road position. Since
the majority of sociologists tend to be a little left of center, it is
natural that they should notice particularly distortion and slanting of
the news against their position. Were as many sociologists to sympathize with Senator Goldwater as do with Governor Stevenson, they
could probably find extensive documentation of distortions on the
other side. Such documentation would not at all invalidate the points
made by Breed but only show that the great mass media of this country are overwhelmingly middle-of-the-road. It is unfortunate, however,
that Breed had no similar set of anticonservative distortions on which
to report, because his report makes the press sound more biased
towards the right than is probably the case.   L. A. D.

DR. BREED, Associate Professor of Sociology at Newcomb College,
Tulane University, is interested in mass communications and public
opinion, and also in social organization and disorganization. He was a

newspaper reporter 1938–41 and received his Ph.D. in sociology at Columbia University in 1952.

That a key problem facing any society is the maintenance of order and social cohesion has been the thesis of Durkheim, Weber, and many sociologists, especially the functionalists.[1] Not only is the division of labor and of roles necessary ("functional integration"), but also "normative integration"—consensus over a value system.[2] Should consensus fail, anomie is said to result, such as was found in Harlan County, Kentucky, following the sudden onset of industrialization, France in the 1930's, and Shanghai in 1948.[3]

Just which sociocultural elements and combinations thereof will provide societal order, then, is a generic problem of great scope. The one independent variable to be analyzed here is the mass media, in cases which find the media facing the dilemma of publishing or not publishing material which may injure popular faith in the society or its institutions. That controlled communication may promote order has been widely suggested, both in theoretical generalizations and in empirical work. Speaking of divisive forces, E. C. Devereux has said, "Such head-on conflicts are prevented also by various barriers to communication embedded in the social structure; taboo'd areas simply are not to be discussed, and hence the conflict need not be 'faced.' "[4] In discussing cohesive factors in American society, Robin Williams said: "It is as if there is a tacit agreement not to express or to become aware of what would be dysfunctional. We need careful research in this area, for observation already shows the existence of a mass of specific devices for thus suppressing disruptive elements. We suspect that a study of areas of blocked communication would often reveal conflicts that remain nondisabling only so long as they are kept from overt crystallization."[5]

One such study will be reported below. Many previous studies have

1. See Kingsley Davis, *Human Society* (Macmillan, New York, 1949).

2. Ronald Freedman, Amos Hawley, Werner Landecker, and Horace Miner, *Principles of Sociology* (Holt, New York, 1952), chaps. 4, 5.

3. See P. F. Cressey, "Social Disorganization and Reorganization in Harlan County, Kentucky," *American Sociological Review,* vol. 14, June 1949, pp. 389–394; Georges Gurvitch, "Social Structure of Pre-War France," *American Journal of Sociology,* vol. 48, March 1943, pp. 535–554; Robert E. L. Faris, *Social Disorganization* (Ronald, New York, 1955), p. 65.

4. Edward C. Devereux, Some Notes on Structural-Functional Analysis (hectographed), pp. 3–4.

5. Robin M. Williams, Jr., *American Society* (Knopf, New York, 1951), p. 529.

touched on these "areas of blocked communication" or reflect on them by reporting what is not blocked. Thus functions of the media for aiding in the creation of a new consensus in societies undergoing urbanization are shown by Thomas and Znaniecki,[6] Redfield,[7] Helen M. Hughes,[8] and Tocqueville,[9] while Riesman [10] has compared these functions for his three "directedness" types of society. Brinton [11] has suggested that the Greek oracles performed a consoling, conservative role in Ancient Greek society.

These and other studies offer a picture of the latent functions of the media somewhat as follows: By expressing, dramatizing, and repeating cultural patterns, both the traditional and the newly emerging, the media reinforce tradition and at the same time explain new roles. Members of the society thus remain integrated within the sociocultural structure. As a form of adult socialization, the media are seen as guarantors that a body of common ultimate values remains visible as a continuing source of consensus, despite the inroads of change.[12]

The maintenance of cultural consensus is most apparent in simpler societies, where folklore of a single ideology is dominant. For complex societies, the issue is as old as the argument between Plato and Aristotle over the functions of art for man and society, Plato taking the "functionalist" view for stability.[13] More recently, Wirth,[14] and Lazarsfeld and Merton [15] have asserted that the media maintain cultural consensus by

6. W. I. Thomas and Florian Znaniecki, *The Polish Peasant* (Knopf, New York, 1927), vol. 2, 1367–1396.

7. Robert Redfield, *Tepoztlan* (U. of Chicago Press, 1930), pp. 1–14.

8. Helen MacGill Hughes, *News and the Human Interest Story* (U. of Chicago Press, 1940).

9. Alexis de Tocqueville, *Democracy in America* (Knopf, New York, 1948), vol. 2, 111–114. For further comment relating the press to early American class structure, see "The American Press: I. How It Has Come into Being," London Times Literary Supplement (Sept. 17, 1954), p. lxx.

10. David Riesman, *The Lonely Crowd* (Yale U. P., New Haven, 1950), chaps. 4, 9.

11. Crane Brinton, *Ideas and Men* (Prentice-Hall, Englewood Cliffs, N.J., 1950), p. 79.

12. Davis has made a parallel statement with regard to the dangers of too much specialization, rationality, and emphasis on achievement, in education. *Op. cit.,* pp. 218–222.

13. See Herbert Weisinger, *Tragedy and the Paradox of the Fortunate Fall* (Michigan State College Press, 1953), pp. 238–73.

14. Louis Wirth, "Consensus and Mass Communication," *American Sociological Review,* vol. 13, February 1948, pp. 1–15.

15. Paul F. Lazarsfeld and Robert K. Merton, "Mass Communication, Popular Taste and Organized Social Action," in Lyman Bryson (ed.), *The Communication of Ideas* (Harper, New York, 1948), pp. 95–118.

reaffirming norms. Janowitz[16] found that Chicago weeklies maintain local consensus by emphasizing common values rather than attempting to solve "values-in-conflict" problems. Similarly, in studying the plots and audience of a daytime serial ("Big Sister"), Warner and Henry concluded that the primary social (as distinguished from psychological) function of the story "is to strengthen and stabilize the basic social structure of our society, the family." [17]

Putting the foregoing in a different way, Albrecht [18] has reviewed studies of literature (popular and classical alike) and classifies the imputed functions into three categories. There is the "reflection" hypothesis (literature reflects society); its converse is that literature "shapes" society with powerful influences. The third is the "social control" hypothesis, that literature maintains and stabilizes society. The latter is most closely under examination here.

Thus writers for years have held that the media serve certain societal and cultural purposes by bringing people into community relations and aiding their socialization into approved forms of behavior. The media have done this by "singing the praises" of vital cultural themes, according to these writers, in a *positive* recounting of the group's ideals.

Such findings are the result of conventional content analysis, which proceeds by studying a given content. The present study turned the question around: What is not printed or broadcast? The procedure was to compare newspaper content with another type of description of the American urban scene: the community study. Some eleven studies [19] were pe-

16. Morris Janowitz, *The Community Press in an Urban Setting* (Free Press, New York, 1952).

17. W. Lloyd Warner and William E. Henry, "The Radio Day Time Serial: A Symbolic Analysis," *Genetic Psychology Monographs,* vol. 37, February 1948, pp. 3–71, esp. p. 64.

18. Milton C. Albrecht, "The Relationship of Literature and Society," *American Journal of Sociology,* vol. 59, March 1954, pp. 425–436.

19. The studies, with a code for each, were: A. B. Hollingshead, *Elmtown's Youth* (Wiley, New York, 1949), (E); R. S. and H. M. Lynd, *Middletown* (M) and *Middletown in Transition* (MIT) (Harcourt, New York, 1929, and 1937); W. L. Warner and P. S. Lunt, *The Social Life of a Modern Community* (Yale U. P., New Haven, 1941), (YC); A. Davis, *et al., Deep South* (U. of Chicago Press, 1943), (DS); James West, *Plainville, U.S.A.* (Columbia U. P., New York, 1945), (Pvl); Albert Blumenthal, *Small Town Stuff* (U. of Chicago Press, 1932), (Mvl); Joseph H. Fichter, *Southern Parish* (U. of Chicago Press, 1951), (SP); John Useem *et al.,* "Stratification in a Prairie Town" (PT) and C. Wright Mills, "The Middle Classes in Middle-sized Cities" (CC), both in Logan Wilson and W. L. Kolb (eds.), *Sociological Analysis* (Harcourt, New York, 1949); W. F. Whyte, *Street Corner Society* (U. of Chicago Press, 1943), (SCS).

rused, and each time a statement was made which to the best of his knowledge the present writer believed would not be featured in that city's press,
a note was made. In addition to this "reverse content analysis," data were
gathered from other sources, including Dave Breger's book presenting
cartoons rejected by popular publications,[20] and data gained in the writer's
interviews with newspapermen. Thus two types of data are used: items
from the eleven community studies which are believed would not be
featured in the media, and cases of known suppression. It is acknowledged that one cannot give a statistical account of such negative and
presumed items, but as compiled they present a pattern of regularity fit-
ting a consistent theoretical construction.

"Mass media" is here used broadly, embracing most of the press,
radio, television, motion pictures, popular magazines and songs. The
"quality press," such as the *New York Times* and *Harper's,* which does
not reach the mass, is not included. It is true that most intellectuals consider the media vulgar, trivial, commercial, and oversimplified. Regardless
of the validity of this view, it is not pertinent here, the focus being on
functions of the media for society.

To review the argument so far, other writers have said the media
maintain sociocultural consensus by precept through dramatizing proper
behaviors. Our findings will indicate that they do this also by omission:
they omit or bury items which might jeopardize the sociocultural structure and man's faith in it. This is the hypothesis under investigation. To
the extent that a hypothesis containing such global variables can indeed
be tested, considerable supporting evidence was found.

FINDINGS

The findings of the "reverse" content check, consisting of more than
250 items, clustered around central institutional areas. By far the most
frequent finding focused around the politicoeconomic area. Roughly two-
thirds of the items presumably "buried" by the press were of this type.
Religion ranked second, with about one-fifth of the total. The remaining
notes were concerned with such areas as justice, health, and the family.
(Here it should be said that shortly after the perusal of community
studies started, the subject of the family was dropped, on the grounds that
this is a clearly "private" area, of concern to the sociologist, but to much
less degree to the newspaper.) A discussion of the several "areas of protection" follows.

20. Dave Breger (ed.), *But That's Unprintable* (Bantam, New York, 1955).

BUSINESS ETHICS

The most frequent item screened out of the press dealt with the politicoeconomic area. More specifically, the typical behavior involved an elite individual or group obtaining a privilege through nondemocratic means. Some examples (the citation and page are given for each case):

Propertied interests prevent tax increases, force low physical and educational standards at high school (E 121–47); Rotarians, with the aid of newspaper, control election to school board (E 123); city grade crossing project abandoned when manufacturers find it would disturb loading (M 488); power and light company owned by prominent men, remains smoke nuisance (M 489); X family buys land, city paves streets (MIT 350–51); banks manipulate wires behind scenes to keep smaller business elements in line (CC 448); businessmen, fearing rise in wages, discourage heavy industry from coming to town (DS 256, 337; M 419; MIT 80); employers insert antisocial security literature in pay envelopes (MIT 361–62); business leaders, promising an open shop to General Motors for bringing its plant back to city, get 50 percent increase in police force, paid by taxpayers (MIT 35–39); chamber of commerce has power over community affairs, wielded by "contacts" and manipulation (CC 447); leading Democrat holds many mortgages and notes, thus his word on how to vote carries weight (Pvl 89); no sample ballots printed, reportedly for fear of decline in Republican straight-ticket voting (MIT 417–18); small gamblers arrested in "cleanup," large ones let alone (MIT 332–38; SCS 127); X family members hold some censorship power over books, teachers, and speakers at college and YMCA (MIT 83–85); advertising tends to be caveat emptor (M 475); the press is discreet about manipulation behind the news (MIT 375). Such events need not happen frequently; once may be enough to acquaint the townspeople with the power structure.

More generally, other nondemocratic privileges were cited as follows: favoritism and unequal opportunity, descending by class rank and ethnic prestige—in jobs (M 50–52; MIT 67–73; E 362–74; Pvl 26–27; SCS 273; PT 460–63; DS 424–25 and passim; Mvl 341); in schools (M Part III; Mvl 341; E passim; YC 361–62; SCS 106); in treatment by police (PT 463; DS 510–13; YC 373, 427); in access to health care (M 137; PT 458) in opportunities for upward mobility (M 66–68; MIT 70–72; PT 455; CC 449; Pvl 134–41; E 272–73; DS chap. 8; YC passim). Perhaps the most striking fact is that the word "class" is almost entirely absent from the media.

These data suggest that when favors are granted to elite groups and individuals, mostly from the higher levels of business, little "news" results.[21] Further data could be marshalled from many other sources, such as Floyd Hunter's study of the power wielders in "Regional City"[22] and the several reports in Robert S. Allen's *Our Fair City*.[23]

RELIGION

Members: low attendance at services (SP 138, 152; Mvl 354; Pvl 142; M 358); extreme differentials in religious participation (SP 55, 68, 188–89); attitudes of skepticism and disbelief of members (Pvl 142; M 329); increasing nonreligious character of church meetings (Pvl 163; M 399–404); upper-class resentment at lower class membership in their church (PT 461).

Clergy: ministers express bitterness over obstacles to their work, shortage of rewards forthcoming (M 347, 350; Pvl 149, 163); ministers forced to play "good fellow" role (M 344); ministers frustrated in reaching out into the community (M 352–54).

Churches in the community: rivalry between churches, replacing earlier "union" spirit (M 333; Pvl 146); churches contributing less to civil charity works (Mvl 359; M 461–62; MIT 296; Pvl 147); churches ranked in hierarchy of class and wealth of church (YC 356–59; Pvl 134; M 402); undertaker sends expensive gifts to pastor at Christmas (SP 129); churches resist scientific training in agriculture and modernized school curricula (Pvl 163–218).

Other data can be added. Religious cartoons banned for publication ranked third most frequent in Breger's account; even such a serious film as *Androcles and the Lion* mutes Shaw's irreverence while stressing the boy-girl romance; almost every newspaper has a weekend section devoted to church activities, but religion—doctrine, faith, ritual—is seldom mentioned. It should be noted that religion is of double significance to social integration: it is not only a value in itself but it justifies and rationalizes other sentiments which bring order to a society.

21. This may be partly because controversy creates news more than the absence of controversy and the granting of favors is less apt to create controversy than many other aspects of life.—L. A. D.

22. Floyd Hunter, *Community Power Structure* (U. of North Carolina Press, 1953), esp. pp. 87–111, 183–189.

23. Vanguard, New York, 1947. For an exception to the pattern, see Dallas Smythe, "Reality as Presented on Television," *Public Opinion Quarterly*, vol. 18, Summer 1954, pp. 153–155.

THE FAMILY

Since most of the "unprinted news" items related to the categories of business and religion (and "family" items were not counted because of the unlikelihood of their becoming public and therefore news potential), data for the rest of the categories will be drawn from a variety of sources. That the family is an institution without which society would perish is a belief reflected in the media. The most obvious datum is the withholding of the media's blessing to extramarital sex relations. By far the largest category of unprinted cartoons in Breger's compilation (68 out of 183) dealt with adult sex. Moreover, editors of "slick" magazines, according to Simmons, consider the family "more sacred than church or country." [24] Mother as the "madonna" has long symbolized this sentiment.[25] One datum epitomizes the preferred treatment shown mother. A reporter told the writer how that same day he had covered a story about a baby undergoing an emergency operation. The mother he said, actually showed little concern for the baby, but "made eyes at the internes like she was auditioning for a movie." The baby died, but the story, written by this reporter, spoke of "the soft-voiced young mother, waiting quietly in a bedside vigil, praying. . . ." The operation for abortion, when performed under proper surgical conditions, has been shown to be safely reserved for *scientific* (not popular) publication.[26] Neither has birth control received a good press. The media stress virtues such as duty, obedience, and affection. A number of these conclusions are verified in studies by Warner and Henry, and Albrecht.[27]

PATRIOTISM

Patriotism, or national ethnocentrism, is a value protected by the media. When an individual is accused of disloyalty, favorable discussion of him by the media is sharply checked. He cannot be dramatized as an individual or a leader, only as a "controversial" person under suspicion. American soldiers overseas may violate norms involving persons and property for which they would be publicly punished in this country, but

24. Charles Simmons, *Plots That Sell To Top-Pay Magazines* (Funk, New York, 1952), p. 101.
25. Robert F. Winch, *The Modern Family* (Holt, New York, 1952), p. 378.
26. Edwin M. Schur, "Abortion and the Social System," *Social Problems,* vol. 3, October 1955, pp. 94–99.
27. Milton C. Albrecht, "Does Literature Reflect Common Values?" *American Sociological Review,* vol. 21, December 1956, pp. 722–729.

the press here minimizes overseas derelictions. In other countries, they are "representatives" of our nationality and thus in a quasi-sacred position.[28] United States intervention in the internal affairs of other countries is not stressed; the Guatemala "revolution" of 1954 is a good example. (The Cuba intervention of 1961, on the other hand, was not only unsuccessful but received full publicity; in accordance with the present thesis, it brought a serious and prolonged crisis to the United States.) The media, when depicting history, glorify American deeds and heroes and minimize deviations. Wars are won in the media by courage and character, the role of technological strength being deemphasized. Finally, this value can be epitomized by the Unknown Soldier, to whom ultimate reverence is accorded.

THE COMMUNITY

A tendency toward "local enthnocentrism" or "civic pride" is also found in the media. The progress, growth, and achievements of a city are praised, the failures buried.[29] A reporter told the writer that his city's community chest quota had not been reached for several years, but neither he nor any other reporter mentioned it. A southern reporter said he had been assigned to report on the progress of a new citrus venture nearby; he tried to praise the struggling farm, but could not justify it and the story was never printed. The "chamber of commerce attitude" is well exemplified in "Magic Middletown," where the papers carry "booster" pleas from civic clubs and officials such as "You must think that there is no finer town in the whole United States" (M 487). Much of this is caused by the desire for new industry, but not all: "Middletown wants inveterately to believe in itself, and it loses no opportunity to reaffirm its faith in itself" (MIT 433). And, "above all, Middletown people avoid questioning the assumed adequacy of the reigning system under which they live" (MIT 449). Studio audience participants on the air regularly boost their home town. The Hollywood film *Cover Up* surprisingly exemplified this pattern. A town's "meanest man" meets with violent death, and both the sheriff and an outside private detective discover he was murdered by the town's beloved old physician, who died quietly soon thereafter. The detective is persuaded by the sheriff and others to report suicide. The citizens were explicit about the town's need for the doctor

28. For some exceptions and discussion, see "The Soldier Reports," and a note by Dwight McDonald, in *Politics,* October 1945, pp. 294–295. The Girard Case in Japan was an outstanding exception.

29. See John R. Seeley *et al., Community Chest* (University of Toronto, 1957).

as an exemplar of goodness—and besides, the decision to evade came at Christmas time!

Two other community studies highlight the same pattern. In an Alabama town, " 'Dirty linen' is not washed in public." [30] And even more poignant is the function of illusion-maintenance illustrated in a small town in New York State: "There is silent recognition among members of the community that facts and ideas which are disturbing to the accepted system of illusions are not to be verbalized. . . ." [31]

HEALTH AND DOCTORS

Health is a vital matter, especially since some therapy is effected not so much by medicine and skill but by the patient's faith in the doctor. Since this faith performs positive functions, the maintenance of the physician's prestige by the media is a contribution. Several reporters have told the writer that physicians are almost never shown in a bad light by the press, and the treatment of doctors in other media such as daytime serials is often worshipful. A Mississippi reporter told how white ambulance drivers took an injured Negro boy to three hospitals late one night before a doctor would examine him, and the boy died at 5 A.M. The reporter wrote the whole story, but the doctors' derelictions were edited out. Suppose the boy had been white? "He probably would have gotten better attention, but I'd say from past experience that doctors are influential in keeping such things out of the paper." Nurses, too, are needed, and recruitment is spurred by glorifying, not mirroring, their role. Our perusal of community studies located two items relevant here: medical society condemns citizens' committee proposal for free out-patient clinic to reduce heavy medical relief costs (MIT 394–96); TB specialist needed, local doctors forbid outsider's entry (M 443).

OTHER VALUES

Justice is an undoubted value, particularly in times when courts are deciding between life and death and also on private business and public welfare. Judges are treated with respect by the media, even at times after serious criticism. The bitter criticism of the Supreme Court in 1957 was a marked reversal of form.

The dignity of the individual also seems respected in the media. Libel

30. Solon T. Kimball and Marion Pearsall, *The Talladega Story* (U. of Alabama Press, 1954), p. 18; see also pp. 51, 61, 89, 91, 147.

31. Arthur J. Vidich and Joseph Bensman, *Small Town in Mass Society* (Doubleday, New York, 1960), p. 308; see also pp. 32, 43, 46, 103 and 297–311.

laws are certainly part of the explanation, in addition to criticism over the invasion of privacy. Media operators attempt "not to hurt anybody"; this was the first rule given the present writer by his first editor. Small-town papers print "folksy" trivia, but as the Mineville editor pointed out, it was never malicious gossip (Mvl 180–81). Radio and TV commentators frequently offer the irrelevant but warming bouquet about a sports or entertainment celebrity that "he's a great guy." The exceptions are criminals, "characters," and "stuffed shirts." The latter are targets for Groucho Marx, who interestingly to the present thesis has called himself "America's laxative." When published gossip exceeds certain bounds, there is widespread indignation, as with certain columnists and "confidential" magazines.

Other "delicate" areas protected by the media doubtless exist. Newspapers in the South, for example, rarely refer to "white supremacy" or "Jim Crow," whereas northern papers may do so.[32] Other areas of value might include youth, ethnic groups, death, hard work, and certain aspects of education. Hollywood refers to this type of discretion as "licking."

Summarized, it appears that the media typically screen out such items as these: elite individuals or groups, usually business-based, gaining advantage in a privileged manner; shortcomings in religious behavior, such as lack of piety or respect by parishioners, discontent shown by the clergy, or "human weakness" in church relationships; doctors acting in selfish rather than professional fashion; anything calling into question national or community pride or integrity; shortcomings in mother, judge, or other institutions or unpleasant role deviations. This is a knotty list, making classification difficult. The list is not exhaustive and there certainly are exceptions in the various media, and changes over time.

DISCUSSION

What, then, are the functions of the media for sociocultural structure? Taking the "social" plane first, it appears that "power" and "class" as structural strata are protected by media performance. Business leaders, doctors, and judges stand high in class rank, and are among the groups which sometimes possess the power to utilize "undemocratic" means to their ends. This finding is no surprise, as critics have for centuries noted the disproportionate power of elites and the winking by the media at their actions.

Yet power and class are not the whole answer. Do mothers have "power," and overseas GIs, members of churches and the Unknown Sol-

32. Warren Breed, Comparative newspaper treatment of the Emmett Till Case, *Journalism Quarterly*, vol. 35, Summer 1958, pp. 291–298.

dier? It seems also that *cultural* patterns are likewise given protection by the media. Values of capitalism, the home, religion, health, justice, the nation and the community are also "sacred cows." Furthermore, the disinclination of the media to talk about social class has a cultural as well as a social aspect; class, being social inequality, is the very antithesis of the American creed. (Since this report was first written, the topic of class has been creeping into the media, and into paperbacks like Vance Packard's *The Status Seekers.*)

The media, then, withdraw from unnecessarily baring structural flaws in the working of the institutions. They are an insulating mechanism in the potential clash between two powerful modes of behavior, the normatively ideal way and the persistent pragmatic way.[33] The pattern presents a good fit to the theoretical statements of Devereux and Williams, cited above, as to the nature of "areas of blocked communication." Furthermore, the pattern appears to be a case of Merton's patterned (or institutionalized) evasion,[34] and is likewise related to what Linton and Kluckhohn have called "covert culture." [35]

At the level of community, the media are not only protecting particular "pressure" groups, as is well known, but are also protecting the community *from* particular groups with a disruptive purpose. As Davis [36] has pointed out, the community's ends are more ultimate than those of any constituent group within the community and it therefore must not be partial. Seen as organs of the community, rather than as spokesmen for a subgroup, the media are serving the end of unity.

The media are obviously not the only mechanism promoting consensus; one functional alternative is humor. Edmonson,[37] studying humor among Spanish-Americans of the Southwest, found strong inhibitions on

33. Ignorance as an incentive for continued conforming behavior is discussed in Wilbert E. Moore and Melvin M. Tumin, "Some Social Functions of Ignorance," *American Sociological Review,* vol. 14, December 1949, pp. 787–795.

34. Robert K. Merton, *Social Theory and Social Structure* (Free Press, New York, 1957), pp. 343–345. See also Robin M. Williams, *op. cit.,* chap. 10, and Talcott Parsons and Edward A. Shils, *Toward a General Theory of Action* (Harvard U. P., Cambridge, 1951), pp. 174–175.

35. Clyde Kluckhohn, "Covert Culture and Administrative Problems," *American Anthropologist,* vol. 45, April–June 1943, pp. 213–227. He speaks of "the extraordinary convergence" on this topic, among Sumner, Chapin, Sapir, Sorokin, Warner, Pareto, Parsons, and Whitehead. He could add Merton, and also A. M. Lee ("façades").

36. Davis, *op. cit.,* p. 312.

37. Munro S. Edmonson, Los Manitos, dissertation, Harvard University, 1952. In a paper read at the 1958 meetings of the American Sociological Society, Peter B. Hammond cited anthropologists' interest in "The Functions of Indirection in Communication" such as joking, and suggested further leads. For an analysis of

jokes about certain subjects, such as religion, Hispanidad (the glorification of the Spanish tradition), and father and father-in-law (the kinship pattern is patriarchal). In the area of religion jokes were permitted about certain themes, such as religious duties and the saints, but no jokes were uncovered about core areas: the Eucharist, Good Friday, and the *Penitente* movement. While no detailed comparison of these findings with those concerning the media is possible here, they appear to be complementary.

Are media personnel aware that they are performing this function? Perhaps many are, but for present purposes the question is not relevant: subjective motivation and objective consequences need not be related.[38] It is probable that spokesmen for various institutions who do public relations work intensify the existing awareness of media personnel as to the importance of their respective institutions to the society.

THE MEDIA POINT OF VIEW

Since we are studying media performance in relation to cultural values, it is well to consider the particular situation of the media to check on the validity of the comparison. The press will print a "delicate" item when it enters the public ken, as with most police and court records and formal statements or charges brought by a responsible group or individual (i.e., not a "crank"). The press, for instance, could not suppress the 1938 indictment and conviction of Richard Whitney. The news, however, tended to dissociate Whitney from investment bankers as a group, and he was made to seem an exception to the rule; news about other bankers implicated was not featured.[39] Television dramas occasionally portray a businessman as villain, but the focus is on individual morality, not the institution. Newspapers are inclined to print—but not feature—news of structural faults as contained in investigations of campaign financing, lobbying, concentration of economic power, etc.

What has been described as the withdrawal of the media from delicate subjects is typical, not mandatory, and many exceptions occur. Certain media at times broadcast themes which refute the hypothesis presented

---

concealment of information, misrepresentation, impression management, symbols of ceremony and many other forms of inhibited communication, see Erving Goffman, *The Presentation of Self in Everyday Life* (U. of Edinburgh Social Sciences Research Center, 1956).

38. Merton, *op. cit.*, pp. 60–61.

39. See I. F. Stone, "Quesions on the Whitney Case," *The Nation*, vol. 148, Jan. 14, 1939, pp. 55–58. There are obviously many exceptions and more subtlety than indicated here; see Irving Howe, "Notes on Mass Culture," in Bernard Rosenberg and David M. White (eds.), *Mass Culture* (Free Press, New York, 1957), pp. 501–502.

here (although such an "adult" medium may no longer be a "mass" medium). Functional analysis as used here tends to be static rather than dynamic and processual; it is admitted that many exceptions occur and that shifts of focus toward and away from a given elite or value occur in different periods. Such shifts could be documented elsewhere, but it remains that despite change and variety, certain patterns have been noted which show much constancy. It also appears that an exceptionally frank program like a Mike Wallace interview makes viewers uncomfortable; "the exception proves the rule" that public media do not challenge basic institutions by exploring flaws in the working of the institutions.

Thus the mass media have very different purposes and contents than the quality press, the protest press (organs of minority groups, etc.), and art. Art (like education) is (relatively) free to criticize what it will, including institutions and values. Whether or not the consensus that is protected by media evasion is a good consensus or a pseudo-consensus is a most significant question (that is, the media may be protecting "bad" as well as "good" values) and calls for further study on the sociocultural, as well as the individual, plane. Some of the evasions may be arguable as responsible contributions to consensus, while others take the form of rationalizations for the derelictions of elites. Some may restrict freedom and individual choice, and others may reduce the potential for adaptation and goal-attainment in a society. One finds much to deplore in the media, but the latent functions claimed here should not continue to be overlooked by students of social integration.[40]

THREE RELATED OBSERVATIONS

[1] Besides values and kinds of behavior, we have seen that certain specified individuals receive favorable treatment: doctors, business leaders, judges, mothers, clergymen, GIs overseas, etc. This leads to the proposition that leaders personify or embody the values related to their office.[41] Thus the media, in avoiding criticism of the incumbents, are again supporting the existing cultural structure. Contrariwise, should a leader's deviation become a public scandal, it is possible that a "domino effect" will endanger faith in the institution he represents as well. Whether people respond to such a failing in specific or diffuse ways is an empirical question; exploratory interviews suggest that both occur. For example,

40. By 1962, several intellectuals have found the media not to be totally "bad" for society. See citations in Joseph R. Gusfield, "Mass Society and Extremist Politics," *American Sociological Review*, vol. 27, February 1962, pp. 19–30.

41. See Orrin E. Klapp, "Heroes, Villains and Fools as Agents of Social Control," *American Sociological Review*, vol. 19, February 1954, pp. 56–62.

to such a "shattering" question as "What would you think if you discovered the Archbishop had a harem?" some respondents expressed shock about the individual only, others said they might question all religion, and one respondent pointed the way to anomie: "If they can do it, everybody can." The Hollywood production code follows the diffuse theory: "The reason why ministers of religion may not be comic characters or villains is simply because the attitude taken toward them may easily become the attitude taken toward religion in general." [42]

[2] The values of religion, as Durkheim said, are linked to *social processes* taking the form of ritual. Durkheim maintained that rituals, with their repeated, rhythmic, tangible form served to concretize and reinforce religious beliefs. While the analogy is far from perfect, it may be that the mass media also, by the repeated, patterned "ritual" of their dissemination—every month or week, day, hour, etc.—serve a similar function in the conservation of sociocultural resources. One comes to expect a certain joke from Jack Benny, a "Tiny Tim" story at Christmas, a boy-gets-girl story in magazine and movie, etc. People may not so much "learn" from the media as they become accustomed to a standardized ritual. [43]

[3] In this sense of discretion, we can perceive a similarity between mass communication and personal communication. Tact, the use of the white lie, and the studied avoidance of stating unpleasant facts may be characteristic of all social (as distinguished from scientific) communication. Perfection is a severe model for human behavior, and the use of discretion enables the structure of relationships—however genuine—to survive in the face of strain. What Malinowski called "phatic communication" [44] can thus also be found in formal mass communication.

An important difference between personal and mass communication is the lack of feedback available to permit questions and discussion of problematic points in the latter. Thus while a Sunday School teacher might show that David fell victim to temptations of the flesh (as when he sent the husband of a woman he coveted to die in battle), the young pupils can work out any anxieties in the ensuing primary-group discussion; this is not possible with the mass media, hence their withdrawal from consideration of such issues.

42. For an illuminating discussion of the conservative functions of the various media codes see Wilbur Schramm, *Responsibility in Mass Communication* (Harper, New York, 1957), pp. 286ff.

43. See Bernard Berelson, "What Missing the Newspaper Means," in Paul F. Lazarsfeld and Frank N. Stanton (eds.), *Communication Research 1948–1949* (Harper, New York, 1949), pp. 111–129.

44. Bronislaw Malinowski, in C. K. Ogden and I. A. Richards, *The Meaning of Meaning* (Harcourt, New York, 1936), pp. 315–316.

SELECTED PUBLICATIONS BY DR. BREED

"The Harrisburg Community and Its Newspapers," Columbia University Bureau of Applied Social Research, 1950 (with J. M. Stycos).

"Social Control in the Newsroom? A Functional Analysis," *Social Forces,* vol. 33, May 1955, pp. 326–335.

"Newspaper 'Opinion Leaders' and Processes of Standardization," *Journalism Quarterly,* vol. 33, Summer 1955, pp. 467–477.

"Comparative Newspaper Treatment of the Emmett Till Case," *Journalism Quarterly,* vol. 35, Summer 1958, pp. 291–298.

"Analyzing News: Some Questions for Research," *Journalism Quarterly,* vol. 33, Fall 1956, pp. 467–477.

"Pluralistic Ignorance in the Process of Opinion Formation," with Thomas Ktsanes, *Public Opinion Quarterly,* vol. 25, Fall 1961, pp. 382–392.

"Development of Pluralistic Opposition Groups in Crisis Situations," in A. W. Gouldner and S. M. Miller, *Applied Sociology* (forthcoming).

"Group Structure and Resistance to Desegregation in the Deep South," *Social Problems,* vol. 10, Summer 1962, pp. 85–94.

SUGGESTIONS FOR FURTHER READING

Head, Sydney W., "Content Analysis of TV Drama Programs," *Quarterly of Film, Radio and Television,* vol. 9, 1954–55, pp. 175–194.

Noel, Mary, *Villains Galore—the Heyday of the Popular Story Weekly* (Macmillan, New York, 1954).

Friedsam, H. J., "Bureaucrats as Heroes," *Social Forces,* vol. 32, March 1954, pp. 269–274.

Demant, U. A., "The Unintentional Influences of Television," *Cross Currents,* vol. 5, 1955, pp. 220–225.

Coffine, Thomas E., "Television's Impact on Society," *American Psychologist,* vol. 10, October 1955, pp. 630–641.

Berlo, D. K., and H. Kumata, "The Investigator: The Impact of a Satirical Radio Drama," *Journalism Quarterly,* vol. 33, 1956, pp. 287–298.

Janowitz, Morris, *The Community Press in an Urban Setting* (Free Press, New York, 1952).

Inglis, Ruth A., "An Objective Approach to the Relationship between Fiction and Society," *Am. Soc. Rev.,* vol. 3, August 1938, pp. 526–533.

Hughes, Helen MacGill, "The Social Interpretation of News," *Annals,* vol. 219, January 1942, pp. 11–17.

Herzog, Herta, "Motivations and Gratifications of Daily Serial Listeners," in W. Schramm (ed.), *The Process and Effects of Mass Communications* (U. of Illinois Press, 1954), pp. 56–61.

Bigman, Stanley K., "Rivals In Conformity," *Journalism Quarterly,* vol. 25, June 1948, pp. 127–131.

Warner, W. Lloyd, and William E. Henry, "The Radio Daytime Serial: A Symbolic Analysis," in B. Berelson and M. Janowitz, *Reader in Public Opinion and Communication* (Free Press, New York, 1950), pp. 423–437.

QUESTIONS

1.   Prior to the Cuban quarantine "crisis" of October, 1962, the Department of Defense maintained strict censorship on certain phases of

the event. Newsmen were incensed with the Kennedy administration for this action. Consider arguments for both sides: the government and the press.

2. Breed states, "By expressing, dramatizing, and repeating cultural patterns, both the traditional and the newly emerging, the media reinforce tradition and at the same time explain new roles." What did Alexis de Tocqueville see in the America of the 1830s which indicated to him that media would aid in the creation of consensus in the United States?

3. Explain Breed's notion of "reverse content analysis."

4. What areas of news did Breed find were most likely to be "buried" by the press?

5. Compare Breed's summary of what the press does and/or does not do in maintaining consensus with his earlier study, "Social Control in the Newsroom: A Functional Analysis," *Journalism Quarterly*, vol. 33 (Summer, 1955), pp. 326–335. Precisely what correlation between the two studies exists?

6. Breed says, "The media . . . are an insulating mechanism in the potential clash between two powerful modes of behavior, the normatively ideal way and the persistent pragmatic way." Frame examples of areas and forms in which such clashes may occur. Do you think this role of the media is ultimately beneficial or dysfunctional? Why?

7. Can the reporter avoid making judgments of value? If he cannot avoid making judgments of value, what kind of "objectivity" can he attain? How?

8. Is scrupulous accuracy any guarantee of objectivity?

9. Should editors and reporters consciously concern themselves with long-range editorial policy, or should they strive merely to be as objective and accurate as possible on a day-to-day basis? (*Note:* Carefully considered, this is a very difficult question, a subject for an essay rather than for a brief answer.)

10. What kinds of journalists might be expected to object to or resent what points made by Breed?

PART IV
LOOKING AT THE MEDIA

Ben H. Bagdikian

Why Dailies Die *

IN THE FOLLOWING essay a noted reporter and analyst of the printed media describes why so many newspapers in the United States have "died" since World War One's highwater mark. The fact that in the past 40 years the number of cities with competing newspapers has decreased almost 90 percent, that in 95 percent of the cities of this country there are no competing newspaper managements, or that in only 24 cities are there papers that compete during the same part of the day raises serious questions about the role of newspapers in our society.

Mr. Bagdikian is aware that there might be several causes for this phenomenon. Several years ago William Allen White sounded the tocsin about newspapers becoming merely an industry; here Bagdikian examines the forces that are squeezing many papers out of competition. He uses a newspaper in Jackson, Mississippi for a "case study" on how an older, mediocre newspaper survived an attempt on the part of Jacksonians to "improve" their available communications. The significant point to consider is that when the advertisers of the community failed to support the new competing afternoon journal, which called itself "The Newspaper Owned by the People," it was a doomed operation.

Although any citizen or group of citizens who are dissatisfied with the newspaper situation in their respective cities are free to start a new enterprise, there are very few, if any, who are inclined to do so today.

What do people really want from their newspapers? Bagdikian cites an extremely interesting study by Stanley K. Bigman, who surveyed 600 former readers of the Washington Post and of the Washington Times-Herald after the two had merged. Bigman found that the main remnant of loyalty of the Times-Herald readers was to the comic strips, whereas the loyalty of the Post readers was first for its editorial policy, then for its news coverage. Although the "average"

* Reprinted from the *New Republic*, April 26, 1962, pp. 7–13, by permission of the author. (Copyright 1962 by Ben H. Bagdikian.)

Times-Herald reader hated the Post's internationalist, liberal political stand, within three months of the merger 90 percent of them were reading the combined Post and Times-Herald. The readers of the ultraconservative, McCarthyist Times-Herald were willing to accept the Post, which resourcefully retained all of the Times-Herald's "funnies" and other successful features.

The experience in Washington would seem to suggest that people do not necessarily buy newspapers which editorially carry the "line" of which they approve. The era of the strong party press in the United States had reached its zenith in the early eighteenth century. The owners of the Washington Post gambled on the premise that they could get most of the readership of a newspaper that was as nearly opposite to it as any paper could be—and they won their bet.

Another study by Stanley K. Bigman should be read in connection with Mr. Bagdikian's article. In the Journalism Quarterly (vol. 25, June, 1948, pp. 127–131), Bigman studied two competing dailies in a medium-sized Pennsylvania city and showed that although owned by different publishers, the two papers were essentially "rivals in conformity." Bigman discovered a tacit understanding between the papers that certain professions and occupations were more credible than others. In short, the mere fact of competing newspapers in a community does not ensure that all of the news in the community will see light.

Although there are grounds for pessimism about some trends in the current newspaper scene in this country, we know that certain newspapers of very high quality are also highly successful. Bagdikian shows how the decision of the New York Times during World War II to use its sparse newsprint for a maximum amount of news brought it an unbeatable circulation lead over the New York Herald-Tribune. There is substantial evidence that if a local paper fails to give its readers what Bagdikian describes as "a sense of personal concern unfolding with public affairs" and neglects to give its readers such stories reliably and understandably, they will turn for information to other media, for example to magazines like Time or U.S. News, radio and television, or to weekly or suburban dailies.

Bagdikian also reports on the increasing number of chain newspapers in this country—four times as many as 40 years ago. But even more threatening to newspaperdom than any zealous chain-newspaper publisher waiting to tempt a bored heir or a group of indifferent stockholders, or to absorb small independent papers on the brink of failure, is the tendency of most newspapers to give the news an ever increasingly smaller proportion of space. In the past quarter century the proportion of advertising has increased from 40 percent to more than 60 percent today. As Bagdikian points out, in some papers "hard news" contributes only one page in 24.

This article and the one by Theodore Peterson (pp. 250–260) on the plight of magazines suggest that those media of communication in this country face severe problems in the years ahead.   D. M. W.

BEN H. BAGDIKIAN *is one of this country's most astute analysts of the mass media. He served for several years as chief Washington correspondent of the Providence Journal, and recently became a contributing editor of the Saturday Evening Post. The article in this volume will be incorporated in a forthcoming book by Mr. Bagdikian on the newspaper and its role in American society. Among his previous studies is a penetrating analysis of Time magazine.*

In terms of community leadership, the Jackson (Mississippi) *Daily News* must be one of the worst newspapers in the United States. In ordinary news coverage of its own city it is not the worst but it is pretty bad. For national and international news it is one of the more flippant newspapers in a state capital. Its circulation has failed to keep up with the city's growth in population, education and wealth. It has little impact beyond its immediate area.

The proprietors of the *News* are disliked by enough Jacksonians so that seven years ago [1955] nearly 900 of them subscribed a million dollars to start a competing afternoon newspaper—the Jackson *State Times.*

All over the United States bitter politicians, unhappy merchants and grumbling subscribers have yearned for, or at least talked about, such a revolution.

On January 16, 1962, the Jackson *State Times,* "The Newspaper Owned by the People," sold its subscription lists and "goodwill" to its hated competitor and went out of business.

The death of the Jackson *State Times* is symptomatic of the larger epidemic that has been sweeping American journalism for 40 years, cutting down, decade after decade, the number of newspapers in the country at large and the variety available to any city. In 1920 there were 552 cities with competing daily newspapers; today there are fewer than 60. There are 1,700 daily papers, but 95 percent of cities have no competing newspaper managements and in only 24 cities do papers compete during the same time of day. Local monopoly on printed daily news is normal in the U.S.

This numbing normalcy usually is attributed to conspiracy and conflict among robber baron publishers, to "rising costs," to public apathy, or to the petrification of what used to be a human profession by the stony infiltration of big business.

These causes are real. Publishers do conspire, sometimes explicitly and more often through the telepathy of common experience, for greater mutual profit. Costs have risen. Readers often seem apathetic, though this is hard to distinguish from a sense of powerlessness. And metropolitan newspaper publishing more and more has taken on the attributes of an industry.

But there are underlying forces, some unique in this country and some unique to the newspaper business, that are more potent than all of these:

[1] The United States, unlike other large industrial societies, is organized on a local basis. The central institutions of the people—schools, police, property tax powers, urban development, political leadership—are controlled in each place by the citizens in that place. As a result the daily press in America is essentially a local press.

[2] American daily papers, like those everywhere, are not paid for by their readers, who barely support the cost of delivery. The rest, 75 to 80 percent of the total, is paid for by advertisers who purchase white space in the paper at rates based largely on circulation.

[3] These two facts—each paper rooted to its own metropolitan area and the bulk of its income dependent on as large a sale as possible within that area—have created powerful pressures to sell at least one paper to every household in its zone. To do this a paper must appeal not to a specialized audience but to a wide variety of tastes and interests; it becomes a publication of multiple functions—news, opinions, entertainment, advertising. No one of these elements is enough to sell a newspaper to every family, but a combination may be.

[4] Two important steps in the mechanical production of newspapers are almost a century apart in technology. The composing room, where written words are cast into raised metal letters in preparation for printing, has had few radical innovations since the turn of the century; production per man-hour has changed little in 75 years. But presses and folding machines have changed enormously in capacity and speed; each pressman produces far more than he ever did before. This means that production costs for a 24-page paper of 20,000 circulation are about the same as for a 24-page paper of 40,000 circulation, except for the small additional cost of presstime, paper and ink and wear and tear for the last half of the run for the larger paper. Mass production pays.

[5] Advertisers are quite aware of this. Their prime concern is: how much does it cost to get one line of advertising into the hands of one reader? Thus if the publisher charges the most attractive rates he can and the advertiser buys the most economical space, money flows to larger papers even without collusion.

The result is an almost irresistible trend to monopoly, toward one plant with one overhead. Where there is competition it tends to be an armed truce, one paper in the morning field and the other in the afternoon, and all waiting for any sign of instability that will lead to final, efficient consolidation. Or a city may be large enough to support specialized papers like the tabloids (of all sizes) in New York and Boston. Where there is outright competition it is a tug-of-war in equilibrium. The balance may come from equal circulations and advertising revenues, or from outside money making up for deficiencies on one side. But each side knows that, as in a tug-of-war, once the friction of fixed position has been overcome and one side begins to pull ahead, the acceleration in his favor becomes irresistible. Competing local publishers read their circulation and advertising statistics like fathers watching the temperature of a feverish child, as well they might. Most of them feel in their bones that there is no longer any second place in community newspaper publishing.

WHAT HAPPENED IN JACKSON

It is not likely that the rebellious band who started the Jackson *State Times* in 1955 had such things in mind. Their new paper seemed unbeatable. Jackson had grown from 22,000 people in 1920 to over 100,000 in 1955. A postwar boom brought enlarged per capita wealth. In 10 years the percentage of school-age children in higher grades had doubled. All this meant more and more potential newspaper readers in Jackson.

The city's existing papers had failed to keep up, either in manner or content. For a generation the city was involved in a printed battle between the Hederman family, large landholders who owned the morning *Clarion-Ledger,* and Major Fred Sullens, a bizarre, witty, and flamboyant firebrand who edited and partly owned the afternoon *Daily News.*

Major Sullens had no mild opinions. He and a Governor wrestled and spilled blood in the lobby of the Walthall Hotel. When another Governor he disliked, Theodore Bilbo, visited Holland, the Major announced in the *Daily News* that the Governor was such an uncontrollable ladies' man that when he landed the Dutch band played "God Save the Queen."

Of all the Sullens hates, the fiercest was for the Hedermans. He accused them of using the *Clarion-Ledger* to promote their own interests at the expense of the public good, of slanting, suppressing or inventing the news. For years the foremost fact in Jackson journalism was the Hederman-Sullens feud. In 1954 when the Hedermans bought a controlling interest in the *Daily News* the city was shocked. About 20 business leaders decided to start a new afternoon paper. These were bond dealers, retail merchants, insurance executives, bankers and car dealers. Cab drivers and waitresses joined to buy shares, the smallest holding $10, the largest $25,000, for a total of $1 million.

Like many nonnewspaper groups—and not a few within the trade—they mistook the printed paper for their only product and the first edition of the *State Times* as their automatic triumph.

The errors, at least by hindsight, are staggering. The first publisher was a respected college president who, unfortunately, had no experience with newspapers. The editor, eventually, was a part-time employee who spent most of his time in another city. The group spent $400,000 on a new building and another $400,000 to furnish and equip it, yet they did not consider using new offset photographic reproduction systems which smaller papers can use to bypass the composing room (being used by a new competitive daily in Phoenix, Arizona). Before the first edition came off the presses, the million dollars was gone.

The *State Times'* competitor, the *Daily News*, was not vulnerable because its owners were unpopular but because it was not much of a newspaper and, together with its more solid morning sister, the *Clarion-Ledger*, it had failed to exploit the special advantages of a paper operating in a central city. With easy income from the dense metropolitan area, a paper can afford to extend its coverage to outer areas where there is less revenue per square mile but where long-range profit lies. Such a spread creates larger circulation to reduce overhead and raise advertising rates; it ties together the metropolis and the surrounding countryside in a news and marketing network of benefit to all; and it keeps out other papers. The *Clarion-Ledger* with 51,000 circulation and the *Daily News* with 41,000 might have radiated outward from the capital and dominated the state. Instead, out-of-state papers invaded inward and occupied Mississippi except for isolated pockets like Jackson. The Memphis papers, *Commercial Appeal* and *Press-Scimitar*, sell 72,000 papers daily in northern Mississippi. The New Orleans papers, *Times-Picayune* and *States-Item*, sell 20,000 in southern Mississippi. The outsiders maintain full-time news bureaus in Jackson and more than 75 part-time correspondents throughout their circulation areas in Mississippi, more aggregate manpower and more circulation in the state than any Mississippi paper, including the biggest of all, the Hederman papers. There are days when there is more hard news about Mississippi in the Memphis and New Orleans papers than there is in the *Daily News*. One assumes this is profitable: neither the Tennessee nor the Louisiana paper is known to be obsessed by a desire to lose money.

So an original plan of the new Jackson paper to outflank its competitor by hiring part-time correspondents throughout the state and trucks to get the papers out made sense. But they succumbed to their central error: they misjudged how much time and how much money is required for a paper to take root, especially under the shade of an established plant.

Within 18 months the statewide plan was withdrawn and the local *State Times* staff cut in half.

The new paper was superior to the *News* in selection and display of serious news, in identifying community problems and discussing alternatives in an atmosphere of reason. It exposed some routine political hijinks in state and city hall. The *State Times* was no progressive social pleader; it was economically conservative, racially segregationist (though not violent, like the *Daily News*) and broke no Jackson mores. The *Daily News* remained the provincial personal journal of its editor, a former photographer under Major Sullens but, alas, no Sullens. Where the Major was spirited, witty and outrageous, his successor is merely outrageous, with an inclination toward bathroom humor.

But the most noticeable area of competition between the two papers was in syndicated features. The *Daily News* and *Clarion-Ledger* had a total of 97 comic strips and cartoon panels a day, the *State Times* had 21 comic strips. Both had the full panoply of columnists, canned features and boilerplate "women's features" to garnish grocery and fashion ads.

The *State Times* limped from crisis to crisis. It lost a reliable $150,000 a year and a total of $1.5 million in its lifetime. This is not novel for early proprietorships of newspapers. When George and Dorothy Backer bought the *New York Post* in 1939, though it was an old paper in an ideologically sympathetic city, they lost $1.25 million the first year and smaller amounts annually until the eleventh year, after which the *Post* has consistently made money. Generally speaking, older papers established 40, 50 or 100 years ago with small investments (after all, Adolph Ochs took over the *New York Times* only 66 years ago with a borrowed $75,000) have been able to grow with reinvestment of money and credit from their growing papers and cities. But for new papers, facing giants already full-grown, some drive other than conventional desire for profit must sustain the prolonged effort. If virtue is rewarded in the newspaper business, it takes its time.

UNREADY FOR THE LONG ORDEAL

Established papers, even shoddy ones, have custom on their side. The habit of reading a particular newspaper in a particular way is one of the deeply ingrained personal practices Americans learn from childhood. The multiple attractions of the poorest newspaper entwine themselves in the daily lives of the subscriber, whether it means the reflex of scanning Page One, or surveying the life and times of Dick Tracy, or studying the ballscores. Readers shun withdrawal symptoms; barring sudden elimination, there is no answer but to dangle the new papers and wait—sometimes for a newer generation of readers.

Nothing in the *State Times'* finances or corporate organization prepared it for this kind of expensive ordeal. A strong man in control, with money behind him, skill in newspapering, convictions about his role, and a sturdy front when times are rough, is what a new paper needs. The *State Times* board of directors consisted of 50 men, many of them advertisers, all of them called upon regularly to make up the deficits. The tenuous balance that keeps competing papers from coalescing into monopoly is maintained or upset at times by psychological warfare. Rumors of failure or decline can stimulate advertisers to throw their lot with the expected victor. But when the *State Times* was in trouble, everyone knew it. Its circulation stayed far below its competitor's, between 26,000 and 21,000. (A similarly rebellious paper in Lima, Ohio, the *Citizen,* catapulted by a strike against the absentee-owned and eccentric Hoiles paper, the *News,* survives: the two papers have almost the same circulations.) With the *State Times'* failure to equal the *News* circulation, the near-equal advertising linage in 1956 showed a growing gap until in 1961 the new paper had 6 million lines and the older one almost 9 million.

The Hedermans steadily reduced advertising rates, offering a Thrifty Contract, a not-so-secret weapon of any morning-evening combination management. A common kind of advertising cost $2.34 an inch in the morning *Clarion-Ledger* and the same amount in the afternoon *News.* The *State Times* charged $1.97. But the combined papers offered to run such an ad in the morning paper for $2.34; if the same ad were used it could run in the afternoon paper for 42 cents. Thus, the advertiser got for 42 cents in a paper of 40,000 circulation, what he had to pay $1.97 for in a paper of 25,000 circulation.

"That," said the last publisher of the *State Times,* O. A. Robinson, "is what broke our back."

Yet it was a practical thing for the opposition to do. It cost them less to use the same ad in both papers so they could charge less. If it didn't they had the resources of associated properties—real estate, a third paper in Hattiesburg, radio and television stations, a job printing plant—to subsidize the fight.

The *State Times* went through all the worst fates of failing papers. To absorb the losses it was turned over to the corporation of one of the original backers, R. L. Dumas Milner whose Dumas Milner Corporation encompasses products like Pine Sol, Perma Starch and large auto dealerships. The paper became a tax loss subsidiary on the parent corporation, a parlous state for any social institution. In spring of 1961 when the parent corporation decided to issue public stock for the first time, the paper was transferred from the corporation to Milner personally. He warned merchants to support the paper or it would die. Either they didn't believe him or they couldn't resist the advertising bargain in the *News*. A few, sensing the paper was on its last legs, made their peace with the opposition. The last edition was published January 16, 1962.

About a week later the afternoon *Daily News,* newly reestablished as a monopoly, presented this Page One: Lead story, a bank robbery in a town 50 miles away; second lead, the editor's standing column of jokes and promotion; next to it, "Neighbor Boy Admits Slew Mother, Tot," a UPI story from Denver with no local significance; next to that "Stomps Baby to Death," a UPI story from Chicago with no local significance; dominating the top of the page a four-column photograph of a trapped robber in Los Angeles with no local significance; still above the fold, "Bare-Breasted Belles Debated," an AP story from Malaya about "brown-skinned women in their normal state of seminudity," the most prominent foreign news displayed.

This is the paper that survived in Jackson. Do bad papers drive out good? Is there a positive or negative relationship between quality and survival?

There are risks in generalizing about 1,700 newspapers. Daily publishing is a $3 billion industry, but it continues to be an economically blurred one. The American press is a conglomeration of isolated business duchies, each secretive about its balance sheet and income statement and therefore subject only to provincial and internal talents of analysis and not national or dispassionate ones. Consequently, much remains to be learned about the selection process that ordains one paper to survive and another to die. But some factors are obvious. Perhaps the plainest is the will and the wealth of the paper's owner.

WHY DO PAPERS SELL?

But what if the will and wealth of two competing owners are equal? (They never are, but the hypothesis may be useful.) Given the flow toward monopoly in any city, and given the fact that the balance tips in favor of the paper with the larger circulation, the winner will be the man who best perceives what it is that welds a paper securely to the largest possible audience. This is not a simple perception. Publishers and editors themselves argue over what makes people buy newspapers.

Many social critics, for example, overlook the fact that advertising, quite aside from its revenue, is reading matter of compelling interest to a large number of readers. Marshall Field's prewar New York paper, *PM,* without advertisements, eventually had to assign reporters to write up department store and grocery prices as news. But advertisements are not unique or primary; they follow circulation, not vice versa. Papers devoted entirely to advertisements are throwaways, with minimal profit to both advertiser and publisher.

Nor is it possible to overlook entertainment, sports, and guides to broadcasting, movies and other diversions as ingredients in the decision of a reader to buy a particular paper every day. But given two competitors trying to concoct a winning combination, the entertainment elements are for the most part available from national syndicates by the yard, like sausage, and while there is a first-come first-served advantage, if a publisher spends enough he can develop a mass of popular syndicated features. But these do not guarantee his survival. When Robert McCormick's isolationist, McCarthyist, ultraconservative *Washington Times-Herald* began losing its grip—despite the fact it was tied with the *Evening Star* for readership in Washington—it was sold to the third-place internationalist, liberal *Washington Post.* A social scientist, Stanley K. Bigman, surveyed 600 former readers of the original papers and found that the leading element in the loyalty of *Times-Herald* readers was the comics (29 percent liked these more than anything else); the leading elements of loyalty of *Post* readers were editorial policy (38 percent), followed by news coverage (35 percent). The merged paper shrewdly kept the *Times-Herald* comics and most of its syndicated columnists. Though the typical *Times-Herald* reader hated the *Post's* politics, within three months of the merger all but 10 percent of them were reading the new *Post & Times-Herald,* which went on to dominate the Washington field. Syndicated material is transferable.

But the success of a newspaper publisher depends on more than features. Any moderately talented Junior Achievement Club can contract to get them printed. The most enduring element in success is a paper's editorial-reportorial staff. It takes years, even decades to build a staff of quality, to give it unified direction and consistent high performance, but during this building process some significant side effects occur, important to corporate survival:

1. The staff becomes an operating organism with a force of its own, attracting to it young people in its own image and drawing from them what they see in the paper; and

2. The readers, growing up with what they see, come to expect what they have seen; in one generation a newspaper can create its own audience.

The emphasis on quality of news runs counter to a vestigial strain in American journalism: the idea that the giants of early mass circulation—Hearst, Pulitzer, Scripps—originally ran circuses in print and that any realistic, hard-boiled publisher directs his paper at a circus-minded reader.

Proprietors dominated by this notion today usually overlook three things:

1. Hearst, Pulitzer, and Scripps originally were screaming champions of the underdog, calling for such radical measures as public ownership of utilities, higher taxes on the rich, and more labor unions. If they were irresponsible in handling news, it was in a context of vigorous support for the aspirations of the mass reader. Since then most publishers (except for Pulitzer and a few others) have changed political sides. Circuses for the benefit of bankers lack a certain popular appeal.

2. The early builders of mass circulation generally paid a great deal of attention and money on building talent in their news staffs. Much of the result was not responsible news, but it was highly talented and shrewdly designed for the semiliterate, politically naïve citizen who may have been buying a daily paper for the first time.

3. The original Hearst-Pulitzer audience no longer exists. Neither do papers that are exactly like the original Hearst and Pulitzer, but the audience has changed faster than the papers. The parlor maid moving her lips as she reads the latest scandal is a reader-figure that dominates many journalistic minds. But the parlor maid has disappeared. In one generation the American population has moved from rural areas into big cities and suburbs, the number of adults who attended high school has doubled, the number of white collar workers has doubled, and where before the war a 30 percent minority of families earned more than $3,000 a year, now a majority of 70 percent do so (both measured in 1950 dollars). All of these characteristics, according to a 1959 Bureau of the Census survey, are those of high newspaper readership.

At the same time, swelling city life has involved its citizens in an urgent concern with highways, urban development, shifts in employment and national programs affecting employment, with school building and programs, and given them a sense of personal concern unfolding with public affairs. There is some evidence that even if most readers don't read all such stories every day, they value the presence of such stories in their papers for the times and circumstances when they do wish to read them. If the local paper fails to give them such news reliably or understandably, the city-dweller can now buy news-magazines or one of the national newspapers, or he can spend more time with radio and television, or he can buy the growing suburban weeklies and once insignificant suburban dailies, which are today filling in the areas that the big metropolitan papers fail to cover adequately.

Emphasis on news is demonstrably profitable in some cases—if one waits long enough and assumes accompanying good business management. Before World War II, the *New York Times* and the *New York Herald-Tribune* had about equal circulations. When their newsprint was fixed by ration during wartime, the *Tribune* decided to use its newsprint for a maximum amount of advertising (*i.e.,* immediate profits). The *Times* decided to use its newsprint for a maximum amount of news spread out to the largest possible circulation. The *Tribune* since then has never caught up with the now seemingly unbeatable *Times,* which has a circulation of 680,000 against the *Trib's* 356,000.

The same happened with smaller competitors in smaller cities. In St. Petersburg, Florida, the *Independent* and its competitor, the *Times,* had equal prewar circulation. The *Independent* concentrated its wartime newsprint on ads, the *Times* on news and circulation. In addition, after the war the *Independent* was bought by the Canadian newspaper tycoon, Roy Thomson, who frankly admits that all he cares about in newspapers is to make money. At the same time the proprietor of the *Times,* Nelson Poynter, almost compulsively filled his paper with foreign and national news, pressed vigorous local coverage, and combed the country for reportorial talent. Today the *Independent* is losing from $100,000 to $250,-000 a year and has 34,000 circulation; the *St. Petersburg Times* makes a comfortable profit and has 114,000 circulation.

Kenneth R. Byerly, of the University of North Carolina, studied dailies in cities under 50,000 population and reported in the trade magazine, *Editor & Publisher,* on "blue ribbon" papers—those that sell more copies than their city population and therefore are presumably outstanding commercial successes: "Two factors most often mentioned in success stories of the 'blue ribbon' newspapers in this study were the maintenance of alert stringers and branch offices in far-flung circulation areas and strong editorials on local affairs." That newspaper is hard to kill whose audience has been trained to high expectations, attuned to the special product of the paper's own staff.

This is the significance of the collapse of the *Washington Times-Herald* and of the steady shrinkage of the Hearst empire: their staffs and their editors were constitutionally incapable of understanding or of explaining reality to the American population in the second half of the 20th Century. It is the significance of the growth of the *New York Times* and the *Wall Street Journal*—steady reinvestment in staff and their tools (for the *Times* $11 million of its $18 million net income from 1953 to 1960 was reinvested) and a discipline that keeps the staff attuned to reality.

Investment in quality of reporting can never be demonstrated as profits in any given year. It usually diminishes dividends. Yet papers with such a reinvestment seldom die and those that do not invest steadily are among the most vulnerable. In a stable monopoly a reduction of effort in staff and leadership can go unpenalized for years in terms of corporate existence or, for a time, dividends. Yet, when a testing time comes—an economic slump with readers tempted to stop buying a paper, or intrusion of outside papers and news-magazines, or pressure by other advertising media, or the grim reaper of a rich absentee buyer—the paper that has been living off syndicated news and features has no depth of strength and no unique product to throw into the battle. And when the call to battle is sounded, it is too late to start building.

The kind of discipline and restraint that builds a staff—and the other functions of the paper with it—is seldom the creature of the normal instincts of businessmen from other fields, but arises from one man moved by some desire other than quick financial return.

Yet such men are mortal, too, and once-strong papers can die, as did two branches of the Rothschild banking family, from a lack of sons or a lack of kings to serve.

The sons of successful shapers of newspapers, like the heirs to all wealth, are beneficiaries of success and victims of it, too, susceptible to the conservatism of those who find the world readymade and the timidity of those knowing they did not make it. Or to what William Allen White called "the unconscious arrogance of conscious wealth." Successful publishers are forever praying that they will have sons and that these sons will be willing and able to inherit a completed institution and make it grow in a society that is still changing. And lacking sons they gaze with hope upon sons-in-law, one of the more important relationships in American newspaperdom, from Philip Graham of the *Washington Post* and Orvil E. Dryfoos of the *New York Times* on down.

Lacking strong, competent and dedicated personal heirs, leadership of newspapers tends to be dissipated to a variety of indifferent heirs or bank trustees or lawyers whose instincts are not to throw themselves into the building of an institution but to the administration of an estate. With Malthusian arithmetic, with each passing business generation the paper's ownership, if left to ordinary inheritance, becomes divided into ever smaller pieces until no one body of shareholders has the power or the personal involvement to enforce creative growth. Management, usually protected by business monopoly, tends to fall to pleasing personalities, adventurers or fiscal caretakers.

THE NEWSPAPER CHAINS

There are also newspaper chain operators, who conduct their newspapers—with a few notable exceptions—as minimal expense, minimal performance properties, who keep dossiers on locally owned papers going down hill, or being split by family fights. Such operators have the centralized financial resources to tempt a bored or bitter heir or a dollar-minded trustee or a group of indifferent stockholders. The chains are picking up the crippled giants at an increasing rate. Forty years ago there were 31 chains with 153 papers; in 1960 there were 109 chains with 560 papers that controlled almost half of all American circulation. This has been the fate of once-good papers from Portland, Oregon, to Springfield, Massachusetts.

A chain may merely have the quality of patience. In Cincinnati in 1952 employees of the leading paper, the *Enquirer,* took court action to prevent the paper's sale to their competitor, a paper owned by the Taft family. When the employee-owned and operated *Enquirer* then pulled ahead with phenomenal success, the Tafts gave up and sold their paper to the third and least impressive paper, a Scripps-Howard daily. When the employees of the *Enquirer* fought among themselves, Scripps-Howard quietly bought up a controlling interest and today Cincinnati is for all practical purposes controlled journalistically by a chain.

Or, a paper can die for a lack of kings to serve. The *Boston Transcript* is often offered as proof that a paper of high quality cannot survive. But the *Transcript* served a small and special audience, the elite of Boston who controlled their kingdom. For decades it was profitable to advertise at high rates in the *Transcript* to get a message into the hands of the king. But with the crash and the New Deal, this elite lost its power and so did the paper that served them. It took a few years to die, but the *Transcript* was doomed in 1929.

And what of the huge papers, fat in pages and long in advertising linage, that falter and consolidate, like the *Los Angeles Mirror* (Chandler-owned) and the *Los Angeles Examiner* (Hearst-owned)? These two papers were recently suspended, leaving, by remarkable coincidence, the afternoon field exclusively to the *Los Angeles Herald-Examiner* (Hearst-owned) and the morning field to the *Los Angeles Times* (Chandler-owned).

Los Angeles has special problems of a sprawling and fragmented metropolis, but its newspapers' ability to grapple with it was clouded by two influences: a failure to remain engaged with the political and social realities of their readers, and a curious tendency of newspapers to choke themselves with paper.

For years the Chandlers ran their papers as personal organs of political and social opinion, the richest in linage but among the least responsive to the people they served. The *Times* is changing rapidly for the better, partly by evolution and partly because the *New York Times* will soon publish on the West Coast and take away thousands of frustrated serious readers. The *Examiner* had Hearst's disease: the former city editor in telling CBS what makes "a great newspaper" recounted such spectacular murder stories as "the Dahlia case . . . the Overell case."

The other curse of the fat papers is that although it is more efficient to print papers of consistent size in large quantities, at present advertising rates the profit begins to go down per page as each individual paper gets fatter. Large circulations attract advertising so that not only do papers go to more people, but each paper has more pages to accommodate all the ads. In 1945, with newsprint $78 a ton, papers of 100,000 or more circulation averaged 22 pages, and used 205,000 tons of paper a month. Ten years later, with newsprint at $126 a ton, papers averaged 40 pages, and were using 420,000 tons a month. Their outlay for paper—the biggest single item papers pay for—had gone up more than 230 percent. National advertising rates on a per subscriber basis rose in that same period only 39 percent and advertising revenues only 59 percent. Today average daily paper size is over 43 pages. Publishers of most large dailies have been giving away paper.

THE SQUEEZE ON NEWS

At the same time, the news has been getting a smaller proportion of the added space. Not only must the poor reader struggle with hundreds of pages and grope through square yards of advertisements for his news, but the farther back he gets in the paper the smaller his reward, something both publishers and advertisers ought to worry about. In 1940 papers gave 40 percent of their space to advertising. Now advertising gets 60 percent. Additional pages are added on most papers with a ratio of one column of news to seven columns of ads. But even this "news" usually isn't; a 96-page-plus paper has to have most of its pages preprinted, so what small non-advertising space there is gets imperishable "features," much of it designed to create a "buying mood." As a result, real news occupies an average of only 38 percent of non-advertising space in big city dailies, or 15 percent of the whole paper. In some papers hard news is only one page in 24.

A prudent publisher need not be impelled by altruistic motives to meet his social obligation, though such an impulse is a commanding one in men who make great papers. Where a daily fails to provide good local reporting it is also failing to exploit its potential as a carrier of advertising in the widest market area. Where it fails to present adequate national and world reporting, it is in danger of losing a small but profitable portion of its audience to the newsmagazines and to the spreading serious national papers.

Dailies have died for many of the same reasons that automobile companies have died—the economy of bigness and the profits of impersonal technology. But good newspapers are not yet impersonal in their operation or their product. To a remarkable degree the more distinguished and often the most profitable newspapers continue to be human institutions, led by a dedicated chief and cushioned against the lapses of hierarchical change by a strong staff with its own momentum. The inexorable attrition leading to local monopoly has not always been consistent and at certain times in certain places events have conspired to kill better papers while lesser ones survived. But if there is any principle beyond such happenstance it is that the notable survivors have been those impelled by an institutional rather than a purely commercial zeal and have avoided estrangement from the social realities they are supposed to report.

QUESTIONS

1. Which of the various reasons hypothesized for the increasing mortality of daily newspapers in this country seems most plausible to the author of this article? Do you agree with him? Can you think of other possible reasons he did not discuss?

2. Invite the publisher of the newspaper in your city to discuss with your class the problems involved in producing a newspaper that is both profitable and meritorious. Ask him to define what he feels a "good" newspaper can and should do and how well his own paper fulfills these goals. Perhaps, if you are a long-time reader of his newspaper you will have disagreed with his interpretation of goals or the performance of his newspaper. Does he alter your views at all?

3. Kenneth Byerly of the journalism faculty at the University of North Carolina is cited by Bagdikian as saying, "That newspaper is hard to kill whose audience has been trained to high expectations, attuned to the special product of the paper's own staff." How do you interpret this remark?

4. Another finding in the Byerly study reported above is that "blue ribbon" newspapers carried strong editorials on local affairs. Why would a strong editorial stand on local affairs seemingly carry more favor with readers than one on national or international affairs?

5. Would you agree with Morris L. Ernst in (*The First Freedom*) that the decreasing number of daily newspapers in this country constitutes a strong threat to American society? Explain your answer with evidence which supports or refutes this view. If you agree with Ernst's view, what do you think might be done to reverse the tide?

Alex S. Edelstein and J. Blaine Schulz

The Leadership Role

of the Weekly Newspaper as Seen by

Community Leaders:

A Sociological Perspective *

IN PREVIOUS ESSAYS *in this volume we have examined in some detail the ways in which the communicator perceives his audience (Bauer, Pool and Shulman), and how the communicator serves as a "gate-keeper" of news (White, Gieber, Breed). The next essay views the communications process from a different perspective. It is concerned with how the audience perceives the communicator. The authors have selected a special segment of the audience, the community leaders of a small city. Some of the questions they ask are: What is the extent of the leadership role accorded to the newspaper editor by the leaders of the local community, and how nearly does the newspaper's performance fit this role expectation? Do community leaders feel that the newspapers should play the same role in situations of consensus as in those of controversy?*

This, of course, leads one to try to find out if and how the editor's performance of his role fits the expectations of the community leaders. How much of his work is guided by the norms and ideals of journalism, how much by his sense of community identification, and finally, how much by his perception of the power structure of his community?

By employing techniques derived from Floyd Hunter's panel-of-experts device, Edelstein and Schulz determined who were the community leaders of Grangeville. The characteristics of these leaders

* This research grew out of the several studies of weekly newspaper leadership directed by the senior author, who wishes to express his appreciation to Dr. Merrill Samuelson of the School of Communications, University of Washington, for many helpful suggestions and discussions.

compared generally with community leaders of other rural or semi-rural communities.

In this pioneer study the authors have also indicated areas for further investigation, not only in the small community, but for newspapers in larger cities. Accordingly, we believe, the following essay—prepared especially for this volume—will prove to be a valuable addition to the increasing number of studies on social control of the press.   D. M. W.

DR. ALEX S. EDELSTEIN is an associate professor of communications and chairman of graduate studies in the School of Communications at the University of Washington. His interests include the community press, the weekly newspaper and its setting, and the role of the newspaperman. His writings have appeared in the Journalism Quarterly, Public Opinion Quarterly, Nieman Reports, Gazette, and the Columbia Journalism Review. His most recently completed studies have been in the field of student political behavior.

J. BLAINE SCHULZ is a former weekly newspaper editor and publisher, has been a teacher of journalism, and presently is a member of the staff of the Portland Oregonian.

The past decade has seen some heartening progress toward the achievement of sociological perspectives on the role and status of the newspaperman and on social factors which influence the selection of newspaper content. Breed,[1] Stark,[2] Carter,[3] Gieber,[4] White,[5] and others have done valuable functional analyses of social and organizational control in the newsroom, of contrasting perceptions of the role and status of the newspaperman and his news sources, and of factors bearing upon the

1. Warren Breed, "Social Control in the Newsroom: A Functional Analysis," *Social Forces,* vol. 33, 1955, pp. 326–335. Breed discusses how one newspaper influences another in "Newspaper Opinion Leaders and Processes of Standardization," *Journalism Quarterly,* vol. 32, Summer 1955, pp. 277–284.

2. Rodney W. Stark, "Policy and the Pros: An Organizational Analysis of a Metropolitan Newspaper," *Berkeley Journal of Sociology,* vol. 7, 1962, pp. 11–31.

3. Roy Carter, "Newspaper 'Gatekeepers' and Their Sources of News," *Public Opinion Quarterly,* vol. 22, 1958, pp. 133–144. See also "The Press and Public School Superintendents in California," *Journalism Quarterly,* vol. 31, 1954, pp. 175–185.

4. Walter Gieber, "Across The Desk: A Study of 16 Telegraph Editors," *Journalism Quarterly,* vol. 33, 1956, pp. 423–432. See also "How the Gatekeepers View Civil Liberties News," *Journalism Quarterly,* vol. 37, 1960, pp. 199–205, and "The City Hall Beat," *Journalism Quarterly,* vol. 38, 1961, pp. 289–297, with Walter Johnson.

5. David Manning White, "The 'Gate Keeper,' A Case Study in the Selection of News," *Journalism Quarterly,* vol. 27, 1950, pp. 283–290. The "gatekeeper" research was stimulated by White, in the context of Kurt Lewin's work. See "Channels of Group Life," *Human Relations,* vol. 1, 1947–48, pp. 143–153.

editor's selection and display of news—the so-called "gatekeeper" studies. Breed has also used functional analysis [6] to demonstrate how newspapers omit or bury stories which attack the sociocultural structure or the community's faith in it.

All of these studies have one thing in common: they focus attention upon the interaction of idealized journalistic norms and ethics with socially and organizationally determined norms of the larger community in a variety of conditions and status levels. Such studies are of great potential value to the mass media and its professionals, for they promise to establish reference points from which more intelligent judgments can be made about the newspaperman in his social setting. Many important questions need to be answered. How does the newspaperman's concept of his role operate to limit or enhance his effectiveness in his relationship with his peer group (in the newsroom), in his interaction with his news sources (presumably at all status levels) and in response to a variety of reading publics (where perception of their needs becomes crucial)? As Carter put it, there is an inescapable premise that the nature of oneself and others affects strongly the kind of interaction that will occur in a given situation.

Such considerations prompted this investigation into the leadership role accorded weekly newspaper editors by the power structure of the local community. Studies of the community power structure have shown that individuals within it often tend to overestimate their own influence upon community affairs and similarly to underestimate the influence of others.[7] One would expect this misperception to be characteristic of newspaper editors, who are guided in many of their actions by loyalties to journalistic traditions of leadership and to the newspaper's role as "watchdog" of government. What is the extent of the leadership role accorded to the newspaper editor by the power structure of the local community, and how nearly does the newspaper's performance fit this expectation of role? How much of the editor's behavior is guided by journalistic norms, his sense of community identification, or his perception of the power structure of the local community and its needs?

The data to be presented here are based upon a case study of one community. It describes the attitudes of the community leaders toward the

6. Warren Breed, "Mass Communication and Socio-Cultural Integration," *Social Forces,* vol. 37, 1958, pp. 109–116.

7. See Alfred O. Hero, *Opinion Leaders in American Communities* (Studies in Citizen Participation in International Relations, vol. 6, World Peace Foundation, Boston, 1959). The author reports "conversations" with authors and cites studies of Fitchburg, Mass., and "Southtown." See F. A. Stewart, "A Sociometric Study of Influence in Southtown," *Sociometry,* vol. 10, 1947, pp. 11–31, 273–326.

leadership function of the weekly newspaper. The authors fortunately have available to them data from an unpublished study by two University of Washington professors which provides a generality that case studies do not usually provide.[8] When put together with additional data bearing upon the attitudes of the general population toward the leadership function of the weekly newspaper,[9] it is hoped that together they will constitute the beginnings of a systemic study of role, power, and status relationships that operate to control the leadership function of a newspaper in a small community. The focus of this paper, however, will be upon this case study of a single community.

The community chosen for study, Grangeville, is a city of approximately 3,600 population located about 30 miles from Seattle, Washington. It serves also as a trade center for an additional 6,500 persons who live in the suburban and farming countryside. Originally settled by Scandinavian and Anglo-Saxon nationalities, Grangeville is a conservative community, not unlike many American communities of the same size and economic character.

I. DESCRIPTION OF METHOD

The method used to select community leaders was an adaptation of the work of Hunter,[10] Fanelli[11] and others. In his study of the power structure of Regional City, a large Southern industrial community, Hunter[12] selected leaders for study from prepared lists of leading civic, professional, and fraternal organizations, and from governmental personnel, business leaders,[13] and "society" and "wealth" personalities sug-

8. Robert McGregor Shaw and P. Lee Irwin, "Comprehensive Survey of Washington Weeklies; Report No. 6," June, 1960. (Mimeographed.)

9. Alex S. Edelstein and Joseph Contris, "Attitudes of the General Population Toward the Leadership Function of the Weekly Newspaper." (In preparation.)

10. Floyd Hunter, *Community Power Structure* (Chapel Hill: U. of North Carolina Press, 1953), p. 11.

11. A. Alexander Fanelli, "A Typology of Community Leadership Based on Influence Within the Leader Subsystem," *Social Forces,* vol. 34, 1956, pp. 332–338.

12. Hunter, *loc. cit.*

13. Hunter tested and rejected the door-to-door random method of interviewing householders as a means of finding community leaders. Interestingly, however, Fanelli later successfully used the random-sampling method, also used by Merton in identifying "influentials" in a variety of relationships. See Robert K. Merton, "Patterns of Influence: A Study of Interpersonal Influence and of Communication Behavior in a Local Community," in Paul F. Lazarsfeld and Frank Stanton (eds.), *Communications Research, 1948–49* (New York: Harper & Bros., 1949). See also Peter H. Rossi, "Community Decision-Making," *Administrative Science Quarterly,* vol. 1, 1957, p. 428.

gested by "expert" sources. In Regional City, more than 175 persons selected the top 40 leaders. Each person was permitted to add to the list any person he considered as powerful or more powerful than persons already on the list. Thus Hunter provided the basic methodology: (1) a panel of experts and (2) the so-called "snowball technique" of adding persons to this list.

The panel-of-experts technique was validated in the community of Cibola, where Schulze and Blumberg [14] used selections from three groups of experts in an effort to determine if the same leaders would be nominated by different experts. [15] The results showed that despite the fact that the three panels of experts (heads of voluntary associations, public leaders, and economic dominants) occupied different positions and played dissimilar roles in the social structure, each category perceived substantially the same set of persons as most influential in the affairs of the community. However, because there is some disagreement with this conclusion in the behavior of certain *subgroups,* the generalization should be limited to that extent. [16]

Because of the small size and homogeneity of *Grangeville*—the name adopted to describe this predominantly rural community—it was decided to combine three of the most significant elements of leadership into a single "identifying" question. These elements of identification were determined to be: (1) respect for the person's opinion; (2) his power to affect decision-making; and (3) the extent of his personal participation in community events. Examples are cited from the literature:

Respect—"Now, who would you say are the five people in Bakerville *whose opinions on community affairs you respect most?*" [17]

Decision-making—"[Who would you say are] the most important people in town *when it comes to making decisions* about local public affairs here in Community A?" [18]

14. Robert O. Schulze and Leonard U. Blumberg, "The Determination of Local Power Elites," *American Journal of Sociology,* vol. 63, 1957, p. 291. It should be noted that in Schulze's discussion of "The Role of Economic Determinants in the Community Power Structure" he points out that in Cibola there was an absence of any neat, constant and direct relationship between power as a potential for action and power in determinative action. See *American Sociological Review,* vol. 23, 1958, pp. 8–9.

15. See also C. Wright Mills, *The Power Elite* (Oxford U. P., New York, 1956).

16. Hero, *op. cit.*

17. Fanelli, *op. cit.,* p. 333.

18. George Belknap and Ralph Smuckler, "Political Power Relations In a Mid-West City," *Public Opinion Quarterly,* vol. 20, 1956, p. 75.

Participation—"Select the five names from the list that *you would want to work with you* on a committee directing a community project." [19]

The elements were combined as follows:

"First of all, I am going to ask you to name the top ten leaders in this community in the order of their importance. These can be people who are *influential,* who are *active,* who make *decisions,* who hold *power*—to sum it up—people who have an effect upon what is done in this city."

The broad definition of leadership left interviewees with few questions as to what was meant by "leader." In practically every instance, respondents answered the question unhesitatingly.

Essentially, Hunter's panel-of-experts technique was utilized in Grangeville. A prior list of thirty "most probable" leaders was prepared by two of the three partners who published the *Grangeville Record,* the weekly newspaper, as they were presumed to be knowledgeable sources.[20] The "Snowball" technique then was employed, wherein interviewees could add names to the starter list. However, interviewees were not shown the starter list for fear of biasing the selection.[21] There appeared to be no critical loss of nominations as a result of this method in either the top, secondary or third levels of leadership. This was shown by a clustering of votes in the top groups. There was, however, an anticipated "tail-off" effect. Depending on the size of community, experience shows that the number of top leaders should fall between 3 and 25, while the secondary level should range from 10 to 60. In Grangeville, five top leaders received 24–36 of the 46 votes; nine secondary leaders received 12 to 18 votes, and nine tertiary leaders got 5 to 9 votes. However, the data that will be presented here represent 46 leaders of varying degrees of popularity.[22]

An indication of the extent to which Grangeville leaders identified

19. Fanelli, *op. cit.,* p. 334.

20. Delbert C. Miller, "Industry and Community Power Structure: A Comparative Study of an American and an English City," *American Sociological Review,* vol. 23, 1958, p. 10. Miller affirms that public relations officials, newspaper reporters, and certain government officials constitute the most qualified panel-raters. The publishers are "reporters" in the real sense of the term.

21. See Ernest A. T. Barth and Baha Abu-Laban, "Power Structure: And the Negro Sub-Community," *American Sociological Review,* vol. 24, 1959, pp. 69–76. Barth's experience suggested that a prepared list of leaders not be shown to respondents because of possible bias.

22. Hero, *op. cit.* See also E. R. Hooker, "Leaders in Village Communities," *Social Forces,* vol. 6, 1928, pp. 605–614.

by this method compare with leaders identified by other studies is seen in Table 1.

Table 1—Comparison of Grangeville Leaders with General Characteristics of Rural or Semirural Communities [23]

General Characteristics of Leaders	Characteristics of Grangeville Leaders
Most born into community or resided there for generation.	Most lived in community for generation or more.
Most born into upper-middle class homes; inherited wealth.	44 percent earned $10,000 or more per year; data for other criteria not collected.
Most have college educations.	38 percent graduates and graduate work; 72 percent attended college.
Few under 45 years of age or over 60.	Only 1 in 5 in lower age group; 1 in 8 over 60.
Protestant, Anglo-Saxon background.	Majority of Protestant faith. Two ministers among 46 leaders.
Members of business or proprietor class—owners of large farms, ranches, rural factories, food processing plants.	84 percent in business or professions.
Occasionally a civic, professional or other leader, but tends to have business, family, wealth ties.	Only 3 of 46 were public officials of any kind.
Lawyers when office-holders or powers "behind the throne."	Few lawyers.
Important owners of newspapers sometimes in top group.	Editor in top group.
Women not found in top group.	No women in group.

Although data for all comparisons are not available, it can be seen that Grangeville community leaders were typical of community leaders of rural and semirural communities.

An additional and extremely interesting measure of validity was afforded by a record of interactions of leaders. Each leader on the panel had been asked to rate the others as leaders in social activities, wealth, community participation, power, and decision making. It was predicted that those who scored the highest (the top leaders) would interact as a small elite.

The sociogram below (Fig. 1) demonstrates the degree to which this interaction of top leaders did occur. The top-rated leader received and gave votes to each of the other four top leaders; thus he had four shared choices. The others each had two or three shared choices.

23. To achieve a stability of response, a "second panel" was used. This included members of the starter list and those with two votes. There was a high similarity of characteristics in such factors as age, sex, length of residence in the community, educational, economic and social status.

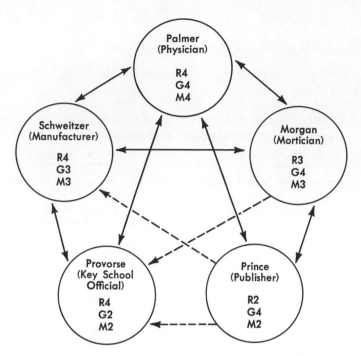

Figure 1. Grangeville's top five leaders of criteria of social activities, wealth participation, manipulation, and mutual interaction.

First figure in the circle (R) = number of votes received from the other four "top" leaders. Second figure in the circle (G) = number of votes given to other four "top" leaders. Third figure in the circle (M) = number of mutual choices made within the "top five" leadership group. Solid lines indicate mutual or shared choices; dotted lines indicate votes given by a leader but not shared. (*Note:* Names given are fictitious, but represent specific leaders in Grangeville.)

It became a matter of some interest also to determine whether the top leader was primarily a person in the community who commanded respect, was participant, was a power wielder, an influential, or a decision maker.

To determine this, community leaders were asked to name the "top leader." Colloquial phrasing was employed; "experts" were asked to name "The Biggest Man in Town." The term deliberately was not defined.

In this ranking process the top three men in the voting also were named most often as "biggest man in town," but the first and second leaders in the voting switched positions in the ranking process.

The controlling factors in this shift appeared to be those of power and decision making. The "biggest man" in the ranking process (Schweitzer) held important appointive and elective posts both locally and statewide which enabled him to make important decisions. Furthermore, he owned and managed a local manufacturing company, which gave him economic power. As shown in the sociogram, he was not high in socialization. In contrast, the top rated leader in number of votes (Palmer) was a doctor who obviously commanded "respect," was an extraordinarily active "participant" in community affairs, and was clearly an "influential." But while the doctor was rated a leader by most of the panel, he was clearly not the most powerful.

Once the community leaders had been identified, interviews were carried out to determine the attitudes of leaders toward the leadership role of the newspaper. Leaders were asked to evaluate the newspaper's generalized leadership role and its actual performance in both consensus and conflict situations.

II. ATTITUDES OF COMMUNITY LEADERS IN CONSENSUS AREAS

Community projects were selected as one vehicle by which the roles of both editors and leaders could be fully expressed. Editors tend to view community projects not only as an opportunity for leadership but also as newsmaking—their stock in trade, while community leaders see themselves as custodians of community values and as decision makers in areas that affect the community as a whole or its basic institutions. Thus there was an ideal balancing of roles for the editors.[24]

Each leader was asked (1) to recall three specific community projects,[25] (2) to describe what the actual performance of the newspaper had been, and (3) to evaluate what its role should be in activities of this kind.

Only one community leader in the panel of 46 said that it was the newspaper's role to initiate such projects. The majority, about 59 percent, said the newspaper should work jointly with community leaders to initiate such projects, while 39 percent said the newspaper's role was to provide publicity—not to initiate projects.

With respect to actual performance, leaders implied that the newspaper exercised less initiative than leaders were willing to concede to it.

24. Five types of projects were mentioned. The most frequently cited were physical improvements, 48 percent; other improvements, 23 percent; celebrations, 22 percent; personal recognition, 4 percent; fund raising and miscellaneous, 3 percent.

25. For a discussion of consensus and conflict content in a community (neighborhood urban weekly) newspaper, see Alex S. Edelstein and Otto N. Larsen, "The Weekly Newspaper's Contribution to a Sense of Urban Community," *Journalism Quarterly*, vol. 37, 1960, pp. 489–498. Related aspects of the same research are discussed in the work by the same authors, "Communication, Consensus, and the Community Involvement of Husbands and Wives," *Acta Sociologica*, vol. 5, 1960, pp. 15–30.

Only 30 percent of the leaders said that the newspaper had played the role of working jointly with them in initiating projects and getting them underway. In contrast, 59 percent had given the newspaper this degree of participation. Similarly, 62 percent of the leaders said the newspaper did no more than provide publicity, but only 39 percent would have limited them to this role. Interestingly, the community leaders expressed almost unanimous approval of the newspaper's actual policies. This suggests that while the leaders acknowledged and accepted the journalistic norms, they found it unnecessary to defer to them in practice.

One can speculate from the types of projects mentioned—physical improvements to the community, the community development program, and various kinds of community observances—that the leadership was anxious to maintain the existing role relationships.

Table 2—Rank Order of Frequency of Comments by Community Leaders on Leadership Role of the Newspaper

Rank Order	Typical Comment
1	Newspapers should reflect the ideas of the whole community in a nonpartisan manner.
2	No one group or individual has the corner on ideas.
3	Other groups have the specific job of providing leadership.
4	The newspaper should merely "point up" the need where it sees a need for improvements.
5	The newspaper or the people can get hurt if the newspaper is treading on toes.
6	The newspaper should not be dictatorial or try to direct a community.
7	Newspaper people are in a better position to get around more and have access to more information than the average person.
8	Because of its small size, the weekly newspaper doesn't have time to take the initiative.
9	The newspaper might be suspected of promoting its own interests in backing certain projects.

Finally, leaders were asked to recount how they actually had initiated specific projects and gotten them underway.

The pattern seemed to be: (1) get together with key people; (2) seek the necessary organizational support; (3) take the project to the local newspaper to discuss it and get its help in publicizing the project. The responses afford insight into the classification of the editor as a member of the leadership structure. It is reflected in the essentially journalistic practice of attending meetings and the status role of seeing community leaders "personally" about projects that are developing.

In summary, community leaders felt the newspaper was performing its role in consensus areas within the limits they had defined for it. Few leaders believed the newspaper should initiate projects. While they were willing to accept some degree of participation, they actually preferred the role of publicity.

III. ATTITUDES OF COMMUNITY LEADERS IN CONTROVERSIAL AREAS

As was the procedure for study of consensus activities, leaders were asked to describe three controversies that had arisen in the past year.

It was expected that leaders would be critical of the controversial content of the newspaper, viewing it as a threat to community consensus and leadership, and the hypothesis was confirmed. Two out of three leaders said the newspaper should publish controversy only when it could not avoid doing so. Only one of three leaders said that the newspaper should take the initiative in bringing controversies to public attention.

It was apparent that many of the leaders—a majority of them businessmen—were aware that controversy was a marketable commodity in a weekly newspaper. If controversy could not be avoided, they were willing to sanction newspaper action in airing it. As businessmen, it is probable that many leaders perceived also the advantages of deferring to the press in controversial areas, for it permitted them to escape personal identification with matters that might bring in their wake economic or social reprisals. However, this involvement does not fully explain the extent of the deference of the power structure to this journalistic "norm." Evident in the interviews was the theme that society was imperfect and that some legitimized means of expressing conflict was desirable. Leaders were willing to concede this role to the newspaper if certain that the editor would not threaten the community structure or its basic values. However, there was a clear desire on the part of the leaders to limit the newspaper's attention to controversy, as reflected in statements summarized in Table 3.

Table 3—Statements of Leaders on Newspaper's Role in Controversy

The newspaper should just present the facts.

The newspaper should present both sides.

The newspaper should report on the events after meetings are held and others have made decisions on controversial issues.

The newspaper should play down or drop some controversial comments for the good of the community.

Editors should give their opinions as members of the community only, not as members of the newspaper.

The newspaper can't afford to go against community opinion; someone—the newspaper or the people—gets hurt.

Controversy is bad for the community.

It was interesting to observe that the leaders of Grangeville felt they had made substantial concessions to the journalistic norms in matters of controversy. Most of them perceived the newspaper as expressing itself quite freely on issues. Three of five leaders said the newspaper commented on such issues "always" or "most of the time." The same number (60 percent) conceded that controversies were "very important" news.[26] However, statements calling for "just the facts," "both sides," and "let others make the decisions"—as seen in Table 3—tesify to the desire of the leaders to limit this kind of content both in quantity and "level" of discussion. Only one of three leaders, for an example, said that editorials were "very important," suggesting that leaders did not want the editors to comment, speculate upon, or propose solutions to controversial issues in the newspaper.

It was evident that community leaders in *Grangeville* felt that the newspaper had performed within the permissive limits of the role that had been prescribed for it.[27] Where 84 percent of the leaders said they had commented to the editor about his treatment of "consensus" stories, only 57 percent said they had commented about controversies. Where leaders had ranked "key people in the community" and "organizations" as the first sources of information on "consensus" content, they ranked the newspaper as the first source of "controversial" news. Table 4 reveals the degree of consistency between the role prescribed for the newspaper by the leadership structure and the estimate by leaders of the manner in which the newspaper actually had performed.

Table 4—Prescription of Leadership Role for Newspaper and Percentage Estimates by Leaders of Performance of Role

Statement	Role Prescription for Newspaper	Estimate by Leaders of Performance
Newspaper should take the initiative in publicizing controversies	32.0	35.0
Newspaper should publicize controversies only when others have discussed them	53.0	49.0
Newspaper should play down or exclude controversies	10.0	11.0
Don't know	5.0	5.0
Totals	100.0	100.0

Thus the role assigned to the newspaper in areas of controversy was similar to that accorded to it in consensus activities. Leaders prescribed the reporting function rather than encouraging initiative in bringing

26. News of business, farming and industry was rated *most* important (80 percent); community projects were rated *very* important or *most* important by all leaders.

27. Merton describes "functionally optimum degree of visibility" as being that degree of privacy required for optimum functioning of the society. This would prescribe a permissiveness on the part of the editor sufficient to permit the community leadership to operate at an optimum level; similarly it would require that community leaders provide a degree of permissiveness sufficient to permit the newspaper to meet its ideological commitments. See Robert K. Merton, *Social Theory and Social Structure* (Free Press, New York, 1957), p. 345.

controversial issues to public attention. However, there was an important difference which should be noted. While the newspaper exercised less initiative than leaders said should be permitted it in consensus situations, the leaders seemed satisfied. However, while the leaders demanded a less active role for the newspaper in controversial areas, the publisher appeared to assert himself fully, yet won praise for his performance. One might say that while there was social distance between role prescription and role performance in consensus activities, there was a strong consensus in conflict activities. This suggests that in Grangeville a division of labor existed, one in which the newspaper was conceded the validity of its journalistic role as watchdog of the community [28] while the leaders preempted the initiative in consensus areas.[29]

That this arrangement was functional is indicated by the generalized response of the leaders to a question asking them to evaluate the newspaper's performance. Some 46 percent said the newspaper always did a good job, while another 50 percent said the newspaper did a good job most of the time. The acceptance of the editor into the top level of the power structure provides the most convincing evidence of the efficiency of the newspaper as an instrument of social control and as a link in the communications network upon which the community power structure leaned substantially for cues in shaping its own actions and policies.

POSTSCRIPT

It must be noted that in Grangeville the publisher was identified by the top leadership structure as a community leader and that the publisher correctly perceived the identity and roles of those at the apex of power structure. Questions may reasonably be raised about the generality of the data, for a number of studies indicate that publishers tend to be at the secondary and tertiary levels of leadership in small communities. The efficiency of our adaptation of the "snowball technique" for identifying community leaders, the similarity of their characteristics to leaders of other rural communities, and the appropriateness of sociological theory are conditions that lend some assurance that Grangeville and its leaders are not atypical. Nevertheless, some question remains as to the idiosyn-

28. See Herbert Brucker, *Freedom of Information* (Macmillan, New York, 1949), p. 70, for a diagramatic relationship of the individual, the press, and the government. Brucker sees the interdependence of these relationships in a context of equilibrium.

29. The study of the general population sees a "dual surveillance" role for the press and government; it is reluctant to concede the "watchdog" role exclusively to the press. In this the general population prescribes the reporting role for the newspaper, much in the pattern of community leaders.

cratic nature of the publisher. How typical was he in his interaction with leaders?

Two sources of data were available to test this proposition. The first, a short questionnaire, was administered by the authors of this study to a group of weekly newspaper editors at the annual spring meeting of the Washington Newspaper Publishers Association in Seattle.

Some 41 publishers were asked the same question that had been asked of community leaders: How do you think your newspaper should, in general, handle community controversies? As will be discussed later, this essentially journalist-editor group of publishers had a stronger view of leadership in controversial areas than did community leaders, yet the difference is not dramatic, as seen in Table 5.

Table 5—Comparisons of Responses of Community Leaders and Journalist-editors on Newspaper's Role in Handling Controversial Activities

Statement	Replies of Leaders N–46	Replies of Journalist-editors N–41
The weekly newspaper should take the initiative in publicizing controversies	32.0	51.0
The weekly newspaper should publicize controversies only when others have discussed them	53.0	37.0
The weekly newspaper should play down or exclude controversies	10.0	12.0
Don't know	5.0	
Totals	100.0	100.0

Essentially the same question was asked by Shaw and Irwin in a series of extensive personal interviews with 117 weekly newspaper publishers in the state. The questionnaire covered a broad range of problems, one section of which was devoted to the attitudes of editors toward the leadership function of the newspaper and the editor's view of the impact of the community power structure upon the newspaper's policies. Shaw and Irwin found that the editors who had the clearest perception of the power structure tended most to work with community leaders before "initiating" any community project. Thus working jointly with community leaders appears to be typical for what we will call the "community editors." These editors described their formula for getting things done as follows: (1) Get a feeling for community attitudes; (2) Talk over the project with community leaders; (3) Work personally "behind the scenes" with leaders and others; (4) Employ the newspaper to publicize activities and keep the project underway. There can be seen a remarkable similarity to the mode of operation of community leaders, suggesting that a procedure well understood by the editor and community leaders is being followed.

The journalist-editor was characterized by a much stronger identification with journalist ideology. He was characterized by a conviction that all facts should be printed [30]—expressed as "holding a mirror up to the community"—and a sense of rivalry with community leaders was described by some editors as in the nature of an "armed truce." While the journalist-editor took pride in his ability to "needle" community leaders, the "community editor" was concerned with maintaining "spirit and harmony," an expression of consensus. While "printing all the facts" was viewed by journalist-editors as a professional imperative, it meant to community-editors printing "only those facts that stressed the good points of the community," nor would community editors print controversy, they said, until it "reached a point of concern."

Similarly, the few claims made for the "power of the press" were made by journalist-editors. Community editors agreed that editorials, by themselves, were ineffective except when written to "create an atmosphere" for later action. The Grangeville editor was clearly a community editor, but how typical was he? Shaw and Irwin estimate that the proportion of weekly newspaper editors expressing journalist-editor ideology was no more than one in five, *but even in this group few acted on that premise.* Thus it was more verbalized than acted upon.

There is an implied generality to our study of Grangeville which deserves further examination and possible refinement. Certainly, one conclusion must be reached: The power structure of the community must be considered by the editor in any program that he may visualize for the community, whether it be in the area of controversy or acceptance. This does not mean that there is no place for newspaper initiative or no time for crusading for programs, no matter what the preferences of the power structure. There are definite indications that a permissive environment does exist for journalist ideology. At the same time, the editor must understand the functional aspects of social organization and its accompanying hierarchy of power and values. Accurate role perceptions not only help the editor to achieve his editorial purpose but actually enhance his capability for leadership.

30. This points to the dysfunctional nature of journalist-editor ideology. Intended to promote community welfare, it often breaks down operational and communication networks. Merton points out that the leaders and the press must rely upon each other for reliable cues as to the needs of the community. See also George C. Homans, *The Human Group* (Harcourt, New York, 1950) to whom Merton acknowledges this observation.

SUGGESTED READING

Social control studies of the press may be summarized under four headings: (1) environmental, (2) craft-centered, (3) technical-physical; and (4) person-nel-testing. Where footnote references already have been made to a study, only the author's name and the footnote number will be used for identification.

1. ENVIRONMENTAL STUDIES

Breed (1)* explains how policy is "communicated" in the newsroom, modes of acceptance and rejection by newsmen, and consequences for the newspaper and newsmen. In a *Journalism Quarterly* article, Breed (1) demonstrates how the emphasis given a story by one newspaper affects the way in which it is played by another newspaper.

Breed (6) discusses the "sacred cows" of the newspaper—what is *not* printed, and the significance of these omissions in maintaining sociocultural values.

Stark (2) describes stresses between "pros" and "locals" in a newsroom with rigid political party outlook but with fixed requirements for craft competence.

Carter (3) describes different role and content prescriptions held by newsmen, hospital administrators, and school superintendents and the stresses that result from these varying perceptions.

2. CRAFT-CENTERED STUDIES

White's (5) original newspaper gatekeeper analysis of "Mr. Gates" combines craft-orientation and Lewin's concepts in this reflection of "newspaper culture."

Gieber (4) in 1956 saw the newspaper as an "open gateway" in which the wire editor perceived his readers as stereotypes and himself was a copy-fixer who evaluated news according to wire service criteria. Gieber's (4) 1960 study of gatekeepers and civil liberties news sees the reporter as guided by news policy—both positive and negative—and by craft training which governs perception of news. Gieber and Johnson (4) describe interaction between journalist roles and news sources, who view themselves as links in a communications system. Reporters are subjected to stress in their perception of their own need to get craft-defined "news" and the sources' need for community consensus.

Valleau (see John F. Valleau, "Oregon Legislative Reporting: The Newsmen and Their Methods," *Journalism Quarterly*, vol. 29, 1952, pp. 158–170) describes the interaction between journalistic roles and Oregon legislators in the covering of Oregon politics.

Related to craft-centered and environmental studies is an experimental study of "Communicator Performance Under Cognitive Stress" (*Journalism Quarterly*, vol. 39, 1962, pp. 169–178) in which the authors (Bradley S. Greenberg and Percy H. Tannenbaum) demonstrate that newsroom environment adversely affects performance of reporters as a function of cognitive stress.

* Numbers in parentheses refer to numbered footnotes in the present paper.

3. TECHNICAL-PHYSICAL STUDIES

There have been a number of "flow" studies of the news, most notable of which is that by the International Press Institute, *The Flow of the News* (Ganguin & Laubscher, Zurich, 1953). Each has implied "gatekeeper" considerations, but the emphasis is on the *mechanics* of control rather than on environmental or psychological factors. See especially the following:

Robert J. Cranford, "Effects of the Teletypesetter Upon Newspaper Practices," *Journalism Quarterly*, vol. 29, 1952, pp. 181–186.

George A. Van Horn, "Analysis of AP News on Trunk and Wisconsin State Wires," *Journalism Quarterly*, vol. 29, 1952, pp. 426–436.

Scott M. Cutlip, "Content and Flow of AP News—From Trunk to TTS to Reader," *Journalism Quarterly*, vol. 31, 1954, pp. 434–446.

Ralph D. Casey and Thomas H. Copeland, Jr., "Use of Foreign News by 19 Minnesota Dailies," *Journalism Quarterly*, vol. 35, 1958, pp. 87–89.

4. PERSONNEL-TESTING STUDIES

There have been a variety of studies done of the characteristics of newspapermen and their satisfaction with the job, the most widely used of which include the following:

Francis V. Prugger, "Social Composition and Training of the Milwaukee Journal News Staff," *Journalism Quarterly*, vol. 18, 1941, pp. 231–244.

C. Harold Stone, "An Objective Personnel Study of Metropolitan Newspapermen," *Journalism Quarterly*, vol. 30, 1953, pp. 448–467.

Robert L. Jones and Charles E. Swanson, "Small-City Daily Newspapermen: Their Interests and Abilities," *Journalism Quarterly*, vol. 31, 1954, pp. 38–55.

Robert L. Jones, "A Predictive and Comparative Study of Journalism Personnel," *Journalism Quarterly*, vol. 31, 1954, pp. 201–214.

Charles E. Swanson, "Agitation Through the Press: Study of the Personalities of Publicists," *Public Opinion Quarterly*, vol. 20, 1956, pp. 441–456.

QUESTIONS

1. On the basis of this pilot study of a small community, do you feel that the "gatekeeper" on the weekly newspaper plays a substantially different role than his counterpart on a daily newspaper?

2. If you were the editor of the Grangeville *Record,* whose opinions on community affairs would most likely "influence" your thinking, those of Schweitzer, the manufacturer, or Palmer, the doctor? In what ways do the power wielders in a community use the mass media, and do you think it is more difficult in a community where there are competing media channels?

3.   Only one community leader in Grangeville felt that it was the news-
       paper's role to initiate community projects, e.g., physical improve-
       ments to the community. Nearly 40 percent of the leaders said the
       newspaper's role was to provide "publicity" and not to initiate projects.
       If you were the editor how would you go about to reclaim the obvi-
       ously more important role?

4.   On the basis of what you know of the role played by the editor of
       the Grangeville *Record,* do you feel that the community would be a
       "loser" if the newspaper, for some reason, was unable to continue
       publishing? In what ways do you feel this hypothetical suspension of
       publication would affect the communication network upon which the
       power structure of the community appears to lean for cues in the
       shaping of its own actions and policies?

5.   How does the use of the sociogram by the authors of this study help
       us to understand the power structure of the Grangeville community?
       Can you think of other ways in which the sociogram might be em-
       ployed in communications study?

6.   Community leaders generally are willing to let the newspaper serve
       as the institutional means of expressing conflict in the community.
       What happens, in your opinion, when the community leaders feel
       that the editor is threatening the structure of the community and/or
       its basic values? What actions would the leaders institute to make the
       editor fall into line?

7.   Interview an editor of a weekly newspaper in your area to see if his
       general role is similar to that of the editor in Grangeville. Determine
       whether the role of his newspaper is essentially to maintain con-
       sensus in the community or to serve as an "initiator" of important
       community affairs.

Harold Mendelsohn

Listening to Radio

THE FOLLOWING discussion is of value first because it shows the difficulty of applying to the effects of the mass media the distinction between "information and instruction," on the one hand, and "mass culture and entertainment," on the other. Mendelsohn's study of listeners as they respond to radio demonstrates that this distinction is not based on the experience of the listener but on a theorist's a priori division of experience. For example, he shows that the radio, whether giving "news" or helping improve a listener's mood, "brackets the day" and establishes its "mood." The authors in this anthology have, on the whole, distinguished between types of content in political and intellectual terms. But Mendelsohn, looking at the "basic psychological" functions served by the mass media, shows that for a good many listeners at least such distinctions are meaningless. We could, in fact, take Mendelsohn's point much further and suggest that, in all probability, the reports of such disparate events as a world series and a hotly contested political convention have the same psychological significance for many listeners. Another significant contribution of Mendelsohn's article is the verification of the notion that mass media may become personalized; radio is, he tells us, viewed by the listener as a "companion" and so is personified. Although this is probably more frequent with radio than with other mass media (except small-circulation magazines), it does apply to the other mass media as well. Mendelsohn's original report upon which this discussion is based shows in considerable detail how a number of New York City stations are personalized by their listeners.*   L. A. D.

---

* The population used in the specific study which Mendelsohn here reports was selected as follows:

There was a quantitative subsample of 1,000 drawn from 3,294 phone numbers, selected by an elaborate process of randomization, from the 19 telephone directories in the New York-New Jersey metropolitan area. Only one person was interviewed in each household, and only persons over 13 were interviewed; weighting procedures were used to ensure an adequate representation of the population distribution. The specifications called for 1,000 interviews, 550 of them with current listeners to WMCA, 200 with former but not current listeners, and 250 with nonlisteners to that station. Attrition was due to the relatively low proportion of

Mendelsohn's findings are particularly significant for this volume in that they indicate the difficulty in drawing the line between "sociable face-to-face" contacts and "impersonal" mass media.

DR. HAROLD MENDELSOHN, *represented previously in this volume on pp. 29–34, was a Senior Research Officer of the Psychological Corporation in New York City at the time this study of radio was conducted. He is now Professor and Director of the Research Department of Radio-Television-Film at the School of Communication Arts, University of Denver.*

THE NEED FOR A FUNCTIONAL APPROACH

The very fact that radio has survived the keen competition of television suggests that the two media probably serve quite different functions for their audiences. Yet the empirical literature on the explanations for radio listening in a society that has been saturated with television is sparse indeed.

Some of the functions that radio currently serve for its listeners are obvious and have been well documented.[1] For example, it is clear that radio entertains people, informs people, provides suitable background "noise," allows people to carry out other tasks while being either entertained or informed, fills in "dead time," dissipates boredom. The catalogue is familiar and can be expanded almost infinitely. If further research in this area is not to fall into the trap of "redocumenting the obvious," it must of necessity examine the totality of the radio listening experience. It must not only describe the obvious uses to which the listener puts radio, but it must also seek to uncover the more subtle and oftentimes unacknowledged functions that listening to the radio serves the individual. That is to say, the proper study of the functions of radio today (and for that matter of any social phenomenon) necessitates examination of its manifest as well as latent properties and attributes within the context of given situ-

listeners in the original group of 3,294 and to the normal causes of difficulty in getting interviews—refusals, interviewer dropout, respondent nonavailability, etc.

A qualitative subsample (the qualitative subsample was interviewed intensively on a "quasi-conversational" basis) consisting of 101 selected current listeners to WMCA, 23 former listeners, and 26 listeners to stations other than WMCA. The qualitative subsample was not selected on an area basis: the full report indicates its general representativeness of significant segments of the Greater New York population.

1. See Joseph T. Klapper, *The Effects of Mass Communication* (Free Press, New York, 1960) for a general discussion, and W. N. McPhee and R. Meyersohn, *Futures for Radio* (Bureau of Applied Social Research, Columbia University, New York, 1955), for a specific discussion.

ations. This is the essence of functional analysis as the term is used in this paper.

The discernment of the manifest-latent functions of radio in our contemporary scene is an extremely difficult one due to the somewhat overwhelming presence of television. As the great mass audience increasingly shifted total time spent on radio listening to television watching, the immediate salience of radio seemed to fade further away from the consciousness of people. Yet the radio is almost ubiquitous, from which it can be conjectured that it continues to perform a variety of functions which are not served by other media.

The lack of immediate and apparent salience of radio to its listeners forces the researcher in this area to rely on the tools of intensive qualitative research to uncover the various psychological "uses" the listener makes of radio and the kinds of gratifications he derives from it. Of much of this the listener himself is unaware, and thus to the naive question, "Why do you listen to radio?" he more often than not replies simply, "In order to hear the news and to listen to the music I like."

Obviously this is not enough to explain the choice of radio over the many other possible sources of information and entertainment. The answer to *why* an individual listens to radio can be found through intensive probing of his psychological needs, attitudes, motivations, preferences, and habits.

SOME FINDINGS FROM A STUDY OF RADIO LISTENERS IN NEW YORK CITY

In studying the AM radio audience in New York City late in 1961, the author had the opportunity to explore in depth the variety of functions, beyond the provision of entertainment and news, that radio currently serves.[2] The following are some highlights from the findings of the study, along with illustrative quotations from it.

Most of the listeners interviewed in the study (78 percent) considered radio to play an important role in their everyday lives.

Radio's overall role is one of an "important and versatile presence" that can stimulate, and yet relax; that can be intimately companionable, yet unobtrusive; that can bring into focus the great events of the world out-

2. The research, "Listening To Radio Station WMCA—A Study of Audience Characteristics, Habits, Motivations, and Tastes" was conducted for Radio Station WMCA in New York while the author was Associate Director of Research of The Psychological Corporation. The three-volume study is based on intensive interviews with 150 radio listeners in the New York metropolitan area plus 1,000 interviews with an area probability sample of listeners in telephone homes in the same locale.

side, and at the same time admonish Junior to wear his galoshes because of the imminence of a storm. A suburban housewife said:

"To me when the radio is off, the house is empty. There is no life without the radio being on. As soon as I get up at six thirty, the first thing I do is turn it on. I get the seven o'clock news. Radio to me is company, pleasant. I feel that if there is news happening, I know about it. It's on even when I vacuum or when the machine is going, even though I can't hear it when they are on. The minute I'm through, I want the radio. I also listen to records which I could do by putting a stack of records on, but this would not do for me what radio does, because this way I get news which I can't get from records and the music I want to hear. I like both kinds of music, popular as well as rock-and-roll. I like getting traffic conditions. This is very important when you live in the suburbs as I do."

RADIO "BRACKETS" THE LISTENER'S DAY

Radio serves as an accompaniment to the rhythms of the day's activities. To many listeners, radio "brackets" the day. First, it "cues in" the listener in the mornings, thereby preparing him for his encounters with the outside world, with reports about the events of the previous night, the status of the world today, and the possible threats to his normal routines. The cueing function of morning radio very often helps to set the listener's mood and his frame of mind.

"I like to know what to expect. These days with things as uncertain as they are, every little thing can affect my business. Even the weather can affect us. So I listen to the radio in the morning to find out what's in store. Sometimes when I wake up grouchy, radio puts me in a better mood. It starts me off on the right foot."

Where morning radio serves a general alerting function that "sets" the listener psychologically, the function of nighttime radio is generally reassuring and more pacifying—the threatened storm came and went; a new avenue for negotiating with the Soviets seems to be opening up; the immediate tensions of the work day have been somewhat abated. The listener in effect writes "finis" to the day's happenings, and before he drifts off to sleep, tunes in his radio as his last activity of the day. Often this is a clock radio which, while lulling the listener to sleep, is preparing itself to alert him once again to the next day's encounters.

THE "COMPANIONSHIP" FUNCTION OF RADIO

Generally speaking, radio functions as a diverting "companion," and it helps to fill voids that are created by (1) routine and boring tasks and (2) feelings of social isolation and loneliness.

To the harried mother whose environment is child- and work-centered for the good part of the day, radio introduces an "adult" element that is perceived to be both companionable and diverting.

"I listen to the radio from the time I get up until I go to bed. It regulates my day and it keeps me company. I can do other things at the same time, cook, clean, and still hear it all the time. I do everything with it and because it's in the kitchen I'm in there with it almost all day. Also, when you are home with children, the day seems to have no beginning and no end, and radio really helps to break it up a little."

To the individual who by virtue of either his occupation or incapacity is cut off from much social participation during the normal course of the day, radio serves as a reliable, nonthreatening, pleasant human surrogate that sustains him by keeping him "in touch" with the "realities" of normal social life. A truck driver commented:

"It makes my driving easier. I drive a truck all day and if I didn't have the radio, I'd go batty. I find driving more enjoyable when I hear nice music."

THE "MOOD" FUNCTIONS OF RADIO

Corollary to radio's major function as a companion is its adaptability to the listener's mood or psychological frame of mind at any given time. The wide variety of radio stations available to the average listener affords him the opportunity to select programs that either (1) correspond to his state of mind or (2) can effect a change of mood in the listener.

"If you are in the house a lot, you can relax. . . . If it's a topic on social affairs it will relax you in that it makes you think more. . . . Also, music is very good, it's relaxing. . . . My first choice is rock-and-roll and then, classics. . . . *It depends on the mood.* . . . There is a time for everything. Rock-and-roll keeps me happy, classical is good to relax with when you are reading."

The two basic mood functions of radio—that of sustaining and creating desired psychological climates—to a great degree affect the listener's choice of kinds of stations and programs. This is particularly true, in regard to music. If the listener is looking for active mood accompaniment, he will seek out music that is in his words "peppy and lively." "I like rock-and-roll. It's lively; it's what keeps you going. It's just what I like; it's good waker-upper music." On the other hand, if the listener desires to eliminate an unpleasant or disagreeable mood tone, he will seek out the "releasing" music that he considers to be "relaxing." "I like to relax with semiclassical music. Actually, I like waltzes best. I just love them. They make me feel so good—particularly when I am overly tired and need a change. Waltzes make me feel as if I am flying or soaring. They do give me a lift."

It is interesting to note that no particular form or style of music is considered to be any more suitable for active moods or for "relaxing" than others. Consequently, classical music, jazz, rock-and-roll, operetta, country music, all are considered to be equally appropriate to the two functions.

RADIO AS A CONVEYOR OF NEWS AND INFORMATION

Thus far the discussion of the functions radio performs has been in terms of the gratifications to the individual listener. These gratifications are indicative of the *manifest* "entertainment" functions of radio. What qualifications does the conveying of news and information provide?

In times of crises people turn to radio as a source of immediate news in an effort to "keep up" with events as they occur. Thus, for example, 44 percent of the WMCA listeners in the Qualitative Sample reported that they tune in their radios "especially to hear the news."

The possibility of surfeit with the very frequent presentation of news (often the same news) is remote. Listeners simply do not seem to get enough news. Whether the "newcast" is a warmed-over version of what was already heard, whether it adds one or two "new" details, or whether it reports "news"—does not seem to affect the listening habits of the listener. Consequently, 80 of the 100 WMCA listeners who were interviewed intensively claimed they would not switch off a given station's news broadcast—even though they had chosen that station to listen to music and had already heard the news.[3]

"I just leave it on. I may not listen, but I leave it on. I sometimes hear the same news six or seven times a day, and I usually do hear it without making any attempt at listening, unless there is something new; then I perk up my ears. I never get a morning newspaper and I depend on the radio for the news during the day until late afternoon or evening."

LISTENERS' VICARIOUS AND IDENTIFICATORY PARTICIPATION IN NEWSWORTHY HAPPENINGS

In addition to enjoying a sense of being "informed" at all times, radio news and information broadcasts allow the listener to participate vicari-

3. Nearly half (47 percent) of the 100 WMCA listeners who were interviewed in the qualitative sample claimed to depend "a great deal" on radio as a source for news.

ously in the great events of the day. In a world of overwhelming complexity where the role of the individual in shaping events is becoming ever more remote, "keeping up" with the news easily becomes a substitute for being actively involved in the issues and events of the day.[4]

On a smaller scale, radio provides information that is of immediate personal utility to the listener, who may be affected by a strictly local event such as an emergent storm, a traffic tie-up, or a strike in the local plant.

"To me, radio gives me the latest happenings. Just what happened at the time it happens. To me news timeliness is very important. At times I am in forefront of news or part of the news. Right now as a police officer, because of my job, I am very interested in the hurricane. I am on alert now so news is very important. As a rule, the radio is on at all times that the TV isn't on."

THE "SOCIAL LUBRICATING" FUNCTION OF RADIO

Just as radio allows the listener to "participate" psychologically in the news events of the day, it also allows him to share with others a wide variety of events of common interest and concern. The listener uses radio to bind him closer to other listeners like himself merely by virtue of having been a witness to the same happenings. To many listeners these shared experiences become foci of attention and conversation.

In this process, much of the "talk" content of radio broadcasts serves as a "social lubricant" by providing listeners with things to talk about. It serves as a rather harmless catalyst in making casual communication between people easier. Consider, for example, the following statement by an adult female listener: "The current events on radio help me to discuss with my husband in the evening."

To the teen-ager who is often particularly in need of approved social cues, radio's role in providing him with such cues is significant. As one teen-ager remarked, "It's a means of communication, because so many teen-agers listen to radio, to rock-and-roll. So, I guess I could call it a

4. To some extent, this dynamic explains the popularity of "talk" shows on radio. One New York station, WOR, devotes the larger part of its daily log to "talk" shows. Generally, these programs center about activities of a minor sort with little or no social or political consequence. Yet, the talk show conveys the notion of serious activity in which "important" individuals are involved. By attending to the "adventures" of these individuals *qua* individuals, the listener enjoys a feeling of participation and is reassured that the days of individual enterprise are not gone forever. On television, the old Jack Paar show and its receptivity by audiences epitomized this dynamic.

conversation piece. If it's a record we feel is good, it's up to us to make it a good record. So, we talk about it and buy it to make it a hit. It's a way of getting teen-agers who don't like to read papers, gives us some idea of what's going on in the world. I feel it gives us our own place. Like my mother likes Galen Drake, Dorothy and Dick, that gives her her place. I like rock-and-roll and at a party, rock-and-roll is there. Nine out of ten teen-agers like it. It gives us that in common."

FUNCTIONS OF INDIVIDUAL STATIONS
FOR LISTENERS

Just as audiences listen to radio programs to meet a variety of needs, expectations and gratifications, the programming of stations is in part determined by the way it meets listeners' requirements. The WMCA study demonstrates that the "one-station-only" listener is merely a fiction. Rather, a radio listener is likely to tune in a number of different radio stations at varying times of the day. Why a listener will select one radio station at one time and another at some other time depends largely on what the station will do for him at a given time under given circumstances.[5]

The data on the relative functional attributes of the ten AM stations in New York were obtained through a sorting technique whereby radio listeners were asked to match some forty function statements to a reproduction of the AM dial. Statements ranged from "When I want to find out about the weather as quickly as possible, I usually listen to _____" through "When I am feeling blue and down in the dumps, I usually listen to _____" to "When I want to listen to a station that cares about the little guy, I usually listen to _____."

THE FOUR MAJOR FUNCTIONS OF INDIVIDUAL RADIO STATIONS

The data obtained from this research show that the same listener more often than not actually selects different radio stations for the following:
  1. Utilitarian information and news
  2. Active mood accompaniment

5. Recently much discussion about the influence of "images" of specific stations has appeared in the literature. It appears to the author that the concept of "image" is an extremely vague one, and that there has been no demonstration that "image" plays a role in actually motivating listening to a given station. To the contrary, it appears that "images" of radio stations are more the result than the cause of listening to a given station.

3. Release from psychological tension and pressure
4. Friendly companionship

The analysis of the responses indicated that as far as listeners were concerned, none of the ten AM stations in New York City were able to fulfill more than two of the four functions very successfully.

Furthermore, those who listened to certain stations primarily for utilitarian information and news rarely listened to these stations for release from psychological tension and pressure. The reverse held true: stations that were tuned in primarily for psychological release were not tuned in for information and news. It is interesting to note that of the two radio stations rated "high" on psychological release function play mainly soothing background music, the other mainly hard and fast rock-and-roll.

Of the two stations that were mentioned most frequently as providing friendly companionship, it is not surprising to find out that one was an "all talk" station.

Two stations were listened to most frequently for active mood accompaniment; yet neither of them scored well with regard to their use as primary vehicles for psychological release for the same listener.

It is clear from these data that a listener selects different radio stations in accordance with the functions he expects them to perform. It is also obvious that the listener does not expect any one station to fulfill all four major listening functions equally well. Consequently, the dial-twisting phenomenon that radio researchers have noted since serious investigation in this area began is neither pure random activity on the one hand, nor is it particularly guided by the "image" of a given station on the other. Rather, switching from one radio station to another by the same listener reflects a quest for satisfaction of specific needs that, first, radio itself appears to satisfy effectively and, secondly, that one specific radio station can satisfy more effectively than another.

SOME GENERAL OBSERVATIONS

Radio plays an important part in the everyday lives of some, probably many, people.

The importance of radio lies more in its ability to fulfill certain psychological needs than in the amount of time that is spent with the medium.

Among the more important psychological functions that are served by present-day radio are the "regulation" of the ebb and flow of the listener's day; the provision of friendly, diverting companionship; versatility in accommodating the diverse and ever-changing moods of the listener; the ability to "involve" the listener in the great and small events of the day;

the provision of commonly shared experiences that can facilitate interpersonal experiences and also that can cement the solidarity of various
subgroups (e.g., adolescents, young couples, the aged) within a mass
audience.[6]

Just as radio itself satisfies a wide variety of listeners' psychological
needs, specific radio stations are tuned in for their ability to gratify listeners' needs.

At least four principal functions are performed by the radio stations
studied:

    1. A utilitarian information and news function
    2. An active mood accompaniment function
    3. A psychological release function
    4. A friendly companionship function

QUESTIONS

1.   What does Mendelsohn mean by the "bracketing" role of radio for
      the listener?

2.   What does Mendelsohn mean by the "social lubricating" function of
      radio? Do you think that radio serves more as a facilitator of interper-
      sonal relations between teen-agers than between, say, older people?
      Is radio unique in this function, or do others of the mass media, e.g.,
      movies, comic strips, magazines, also perform this role? To what

---

6. Research conducted after the WMCA study seems to support the observation derived from New York area radio audiences that radio still plays a significant
role in the lives of many people throughout the country. For instance, *Broadcasting,* vol. 63, Sept. 17, 1962, p. 35, contains a CBS Radio sponsored study conducted by Motivation Analysis, Inc.

Research was conducted in seven U. S. cities—New York, Chicago, Boston,
Philadelphia, St. Louis, San Francisco, and Los Angeles. One thousand adults who
listen to radio at least 15 minutes daily, equally divided among men and women,
were interviewed via telephone in *each* of the seven cities. Findings showed:

    1. That adults spend an average of 3½ hours per day listening to radio.
    2. ". . . about 22 percent [of the listeners] have a great interest in new in-
       terviews, discussions, sports and similar talk features, and also have a
       minimum-to-moderate interest in music but do not tune to radio primarily
       for music."
    3. An additional 12 percent say they listen to radio for news only.
    4. Further, 16 percent claim they tune in radio to hear what they consider to
       be classical and semiclassical music.

These findings show that at least half the radio listeners in seven major American cities *actively* seek out the kind of fare that by any definition lends significance
to their lives.

extent might radio and other media serve a contrary function, limiting the quality and intensity of interpersonal communications?

3. Four major functions are cited by the author. Can you add to the four he used?

4. How many functions does radio perform for you personally? Compare your utilization of radio with that of your parents, your younger brother or sister. Do you listen to radio in a different pattern from your younger days, and do you envision yourself using radio differently as you grow older?

5. The author posits that radio serves a "mood" function, to sustain and create appropriate psychological climates for the listener. Can you remember the mood you were in when you last heard the radio? How does your own personal use of radio conform to the author's hypotheses?

Theodore Peterson

From Mass Media to Class Media [*]

IT IS A TRUISM that the type and variety of magazines an individual reads are a projection of his educational background, cultural interests and many other variables. In the following essay by Dean Peterson of the University of Illinois College of Journalism, several related enigmas about magazine publishing in the United States are solved, and in so doing the author tells us considerably about the mass media in general.

Why are some magazines growing at a rapid pace, while other extremely familiar and widely circulated titles of just a few years ago have gone out of existence? Collier's, Woman's Home Companion, American, Coronet—only recently these four alone had a combined circulation of nearly 14 million readers; today they no longer exist. As Dr. Peterson points out, more than a quarter of the 47 magazines that had circulation in excess of one million a decade ago, have vanished from the scene. Were they unable to adjust to a shift in the public's taste, or were the variables involved more complex? Dr. Peterson suggests that the basic problems may be traced as far back as 1890, when certain publishers discerned that mass production was beginning to stimulate a boom in advertising. With the consequent change in direction of producing magazines not only for the educated well-to-do but rather for the growing middle class, the magazine publishing business was revolutionized.

There is ample evidence that the magazine field can and should be considered among the mass media. Nearly four billion copies of magazines are distributed annually, which means an average of about 22 individual copies of magazines each year are bought for every man, woman, and child in the country. Herbert Mayes, former editor of McCall's, believes that his magazine alone will be bought by some 11 million women in 1965, and this would not, of course, match the total circulation of Reader's Digest, with its more than 14 million readers.

* Reprinted from *Challenge,* the Magazine of Economic Affairs, vol. 10, no. 6, March 1962, by permission of the Author and Publisher. (Copyright 1962 by Institute of Economic Affairs, New York University.)

Nevertheless, Professor Peterson points out that although we will probably continue to have our supermagazines with millions of readers, the big successes in the years ahead will be among "magazines that pinpoint their appeal to some clearly defined audience with special tastes, needs, or interests." A case in point, but one which will win us no kudos in the court of world culture, is Playboy, which was aimed, according to its publisher Hugh Hefner, as the "young, urban male market." In eight years Mr. Hefner has parlayed his original investment of $7,600 into a complex of corporations worth nearly $20 million. It might also be noted that a host of would-be imitators of Playboy lost a great deal of money for their backers. Likewise, any number of magazines over the past three decades have attempted to catch the flavor (and the audience) of the New Yorker, but none has succeeded.

In this perceptive essay, which summarizes the major trends in the magazine world, Professor Peterson shines the lamp of objectivity on several shibboleths current in the discussion of periodicals. For example, by showing that advertising revenues for magazines seem to have grown at about the same pace since the advent of television as before, he indicates that the magazine dropouts will have to find a better explanation for their failure instead of merely crying, "television." Such insights enable us to assess more realistically the role of magazines in the spectrum of mass communication.

D. M. W.

DR. THEODORE PETERSON is dean of the College of Journalism and Communications at the University of Illinois. He holds his B.A. from the University of Minnesota, his M.A. from Kansas State University, and his doctorate from Illinois. He was the 1963 president of the Association for Education in Journalism and is on the education committee of the Magazine Publishers Association.

In October, 1961, *Coronet* magazine died, a month short of its twenty-fifth anniversary. At that time it had more than two million subscribers (most of them attracted by bargain offers) and single-copy sales of about 750,000 a month. It had made considerable gains in advertising linage and revenue in 1960. Even so, it had been running at a loss—$600,000 a year, according to trade reports. In short, its situation was similar to that of many other magazines.

Coronet's fall, however, was a mere thud compared with the loud crash that Crowell-Collier Publishing Company sent reverberating through the industry in 1956 when it killed off *Collier's, Woman's Home Companion* and *American,* with a combined circulation of well over 11 million. But it made enough noise to remind publishers of the essential mortality of their offspring.

It was a reminder they scarcely needed. Twelve of the 47 magazines that had circulations of at least one million a decade ago are gone today. In recent months, to strengthen their hold on readers and advertisers, both *Life* and *Saturday Evening Post* have come up with drastic design changes. Even before December, when Curtis Publishing Company told stockholders that its operating loss for the previous nine months had been more than $11 million, insiders knew that the publisher of *Ladies' Home Journal, Saturday Evening Post* and other magazines was having a hard time. Probably every publisher has worried to some degree about the economic health of the industry.

Just what is the condition of magazine publishing today? How has it fared in the past dozen or so years since television emerged as a major competitor for advertising and audiences? What is the outlook for the future?

In some ways, the industry seems in remarkably robust health. Advertising revenues in 1960 were $941 million, an all-time high. And indications are that the 1961 revenues are only slightly behind this record. Forecasters expect present advertising income to double by 1975. Individual magazines continue to pull in advertising grosses that would have made publishers of an earlier day envious. *Life* alone in 1960 had advertising receipts substantially larger than the combined total for the 30 magazines that led in advertising revenues in 1925. Just one issue last November, the pre-Christmas peak, brought in $5,202,000, a sum that many a major publisher of the 1920s or 1930s would have considered a good showing for the entire year.

Circulations, too, are at an all-time peak, and there is little evidence that they have approached the saturation point. Even the Television Bureau of Advertising, scarcely an agency to give comfort to a competitor, has acknowledged that increases in magazine circulation have kept a pace or two ahead of increases in the population.

Despite those encouraging signs, however, publishers have good cause for gloomy days and fretful nights. Two out of every five consumer magazines are running at a loss, according to the industry's own estimates, and profits for the remainder have slid alarmingly downward in the past decade. In 1950, 35 of the largest publishers had average profits, after taxes, of 4.3 percent. By 1960 that figure had fallen to 1.7 percent, and in 1961 it was almost certainly lower.

Most of the troubles afflicting magazines, some commentators say, stem from the spectacular growth of television as a competing medium in the past 15 years. TV now penetrates 90 percent of American homes, and today the typical youngster leaving high school has spent more time before his family's set than in the classroom. Advertising billings of networks and local stations climbed from virtually nothing in 1947 to about $1.8 billion in 1961.

Actually, however, researchers have found little proof that television has seriously diminished the amount of reading done by the public. What it apparently does curtail is certain *kinds* of reading. TV evidently cuts into reading time once given to fantasy and escape, but it does not seem to affect reading for information. That is the assumption of magazine editors who have drastically reduced their fiction offerings while expanding the space devoted to nonfiction. And it is the conclusion reached by Dr. Edwin Parker of the Institute of Communications Research at the University of Illinois in several of his investigations.

Parker found that TV has made inroads into the time that children spend on such escapist fare as comic books, movies and radio; it does not seem to have cut into their use of such informational media as books, newspapers and magazines. The same general pattern seems to hold for book reading among adults, according to a still-unpublished study Parker has made of the effects of television on library circulations in Illinois. On the average, TV reduced circulations by just slightly more than one book per capita per year—and that drop was in fiction. Parker found no change in the circulation of nonfiction attributable to TV, although it has increased as a result of other factors.

Nor is there any really convincing proof that television has deprived magazines of advertising revenues. The $941 million that advertisers spent in magazines in 1960 was about 52 percent more than they spent in 1947, when TV began its meteoric rise. No one can say, of course, how much more money they would be spending in magazines today if television had never come along.

But, by some standards, the advertising income of magazines seems to have grown at about the same rate since the advent of television as in the past. Except for dips in 1949 and 1958, revenues have grown at a steady pace since the 1930s. From 1935 through 1950 the number of dollars that magazines took in from advertising closely paralleled consumer expenditures on goods. That ratio has not fallen in the age of television. If anything, it has slightly increased.

The real banes—and boons—of magazine publishing go back to the 1890s, when a few publishers saw that mass production was beginning to stimulate a boom in advertising. To take advantage of it, they produced magazines, not for the educated well-to-do, as most publishers had in the past, but for the growing middle class. This approach revolutionized the publishing business.

The principle on which these publishers operated, and which they have bequeathed to their successors, is really quite simple. The publisher typically sells his product at less than production cost. By holding down the price to readers, he hopes to build a large circulation; that circulation can bring him enough advertising money to cover his costs and to provide him a profit as well.

In practice, however, the system rarely works that simply. Things over which the publisher has little or no control can quickly convert the black ink in his ledgers to red. If advertisers curtail their budgets, his large circulation is a liability instead of an asset. Seldom can he cut his costs far enough or fast enough to keep income and outgo in balance. His costs, in fact, are quite rigid since he cannot drastically alter his product if he expects to hold his readers and reattract advertisers.

Since the publisher must have a following among advertisers as well as among readers, even editorial success carries its dangers. He may have millions of readers, as *Coronet* did, but not enough advertising to make a profit. And if circulation jumps ahead rapidly, advertising rates may lag behind. The classic case is that of *Life* in its early days, when circulation bounded so far ahead of advertising rates that the magazine lost $5 million in a year and a half.

The whole system makes the publisher especially vulnerable in a period of rising costs. And publishers will tell you glumly how much their basic costs have gone up since 1950—paper by 31 percent, printing by 44 percent, postage by 89 percent, salaries by 41 percent.

Today fierce competition has intensified these inherent problems. Although publishers have been scrabbling for large circulations since the 1890s, television has made some of them more concerned than ever about reaching mass audiences. Television can deliver a mammoth audience to the advertiser at a comparatively small cost per viewer. Some publishers, fighting TV on its own ground, have gone after mammoth audiences of their own. The A. C. Nielsen Company, a professional audience-counting firm, reports that *Reader's Digest* now reaches 27 percent of all adults in the U.S., *Life* more than 25 percent, *Look* 21 percent and *Saturday Evening Post* approximately 18 percent.

Fifty magazines now have circulations of one million or more, and for 29 of them the million is simply a floor. Ten have sales of between two million and four million; four between four million and six million; and six between six million and eight million. One, the *Reader's Digest,* which increased its circulation guarantee by one million during 1961, has sales of more than 13 million.

But it is not just television that magazines are battling in their fight for numbers. The leaders are struggling among themselves for supremacy, even for survival. The most dramatic internecine warfare in recent years has been among the women's magazines. A decade ago, *Ladies' Home Journal,* the queen, sat primly on her throne, and advertisers paid her tribute to the tune of about $22 million a year. At her feet were *Woman's Home Companion* and *McCall's.* In 1956 the *Companion* vanished, its advertising far too lean for its circulation. Two years later *McCall's,* under its aggressive new editor, Herbert Mayes, set out to depose the *Journal.*

Mayes gave *McCall's* a new dress, crammed its fat issues with works by well-known authors and loudly proclaimed its changes among advertising agencies. Speaking confidently of sales of 11 million by 1965, he has already pushed *McCall's* ahead of the *Journal* in advertising and circulation. Ad income is almost three times what it was a decade ago. Some issues are hitting sales of eight million to give advertisers a bonus circulation of a million over the base at which rates are pegged. The *Journal* has retaliated by promising advertisers that it will deliver them readers at the same cost per thousand. Throughout the tussle, the magazines have screeched at one another in most unregal fashion.

Magazines have waged their circulation war at heavy cost. Publishers now can build large circulations only at considerable expense, by luring readers with bargain offers. Most major magazines offer new subscriptions at reduced rates, usually at about half the regular price. And such bargain subscriptions make up a large share of the circulations of many magazines. More than 99 percent of the new subscriptions and renewals for *Reader's Digest* in the first half of 1961 were at reduced rates. For *Life* the figure was 75 percent, for *McCall's* 59 percent.

Some magazines have picked up readers by taking over the subscription lists of publications going out of business. *Look* took over the unexpired *Collier's* subscriptions in hopes of adding a million to its circulation: *Reader's Digest, Saturday Evening Post, Ladies' Home Journal* and *Holiday* have divided up *Coronet's* subscription list.

One reason for all this is that single-copy sales have fallen considerably in recent years. During World War II newsstand sales accounted for about 55 percent of the circulations of *Life* and *Look;* today they account for less than 10 percent. For magazines generally, single-copy sales are at about their 1950 levels, although total circulation has risen by about 21 percent.

The mad race for circulation, some publishers think, is inherently unhealthy. "The lesson for other magazines is to stop chasing numbers," said the editor of *Coronet* upon the demise of that magazine. "If the numbers game continues, it will destroy many more magazines."

Advertisers, too, are concerned about the practice of capturing new readers at any cost. Increasingly, they have complained that they are being called on to bear too large a share of the publisher's cost, the reader too little.

Since circulation costs money unless it pulls in a corresponding volume of advertising, some magazines have had to dip into their reserves or tap other sources of income to stay in business. Several leading publishers have branched out into other areas as profits in their industry have slumped.

Time Inc., which has owned TV stations since 1952, has expanded its broadcasting operations at home and abroad in the past year [1961]. It has also aggressively entered the book publishing field. *Reader's Digest* last year added a record club to its book club. Meredith Publishing Company has long had broadcasting stations and a book department besides its *Better Homes and Gardens* and *Successful Farming*. In the past two years it has bought up several trade, text, and technical book publishing firms and has begun selling teaching machines and related materials. Macfadden Publications last year acquired new interests in radio stations, pay television and paperback books.

In their preoccupation with sheer numbers, some observers think, magazines have renounced one of their traditional strengths—the ability to attract a highly selected audience for the advertiser. In December [1961], Fairfax Cone, advertising agency head, said that the huge circulations magazines boast about are not really very impressive. He pointed out that the advantage of numbers lies clearly with TV, and that the unassailable advantage of magazines is their selective market.

America no doubt will continue to have its super magazines of multi-million circulation. But the big successes in the years ahead quite probably will be among magazines that pinpoint their appeal to some clearly defined audience with special taste, needs or interests.

The plight of the circulation leaders with their high costs, high risks and low profits should discourage anyone but the most venturesome from starting a new publication of broad appeal. A mass-oriented publication needs millions of readers before it can even begin to divert the attention of advertisers from television. It needs an almost prohibitively hefty bankroll to get it started and to keep it going until it attracts advertiser and reader followings—if it ever does.

In contrast, a publisher can experiment with a specialized magazine at much lower cost. If his experiment fails, as it well might, he may be able to count his losses in the thousands or hundreds of thousands instead of in the millions. But if the publication finds a receptive audience that advertisers want to reach, the backers may get a good return on their investment.

The case of *Playboy* offers a striking example. Its publisher, Hugh

Hefner, recently remarked: "In our own case, we happily decided to try reaching and entertaining the young, urban male market, and in eight years *Playboy* has blown our personal investment of $600, plus a borrowed additional $7,000, into a complex of corporations, the present value of which must be somewhere in the neighborhood of $20 million, with most of the expansion still ahead."

Strange as it may seem, television has helped to give publications with sharply limited audiences a new reason for existence. TV and the mass magazines are aiming at a substantial proportion of the total population, and they are bound by the tastes, interests and beliefs of the great majority. They cannot afford to explore at great length and depth subjects of concern to just a minority, even a sizable minority. They have left a big place for specialized magazines that can give the hi-fi fan or the boating enthusiast or the sports car buff the specialized information that he wants and in the desired detail.

Vernon C. Myers, publisher of *Look,* has neatly summed up the case for the specialized magazine: "As education, income and leisure time have continued to rise, the interests of the American people have ranged more broadly and more deeply into more subjects than ever before. Hence, it's not surprising that many new magazines are appearing to cater to specific needs and interests."

And appear they have. In the past year publishers have hopefully launched or planned dozens of new magazines aimed at modest followings among persons interested in campus life, antique airplanes, the effects of environment on human life, high fashion, FM listening, the problems of growing old, European travel and a good range of other subjects, some bordering on the esoteric. The very titles of some of the new magazines reflect their limited appeal—*Asia, Back Stage, Candlepin Bowler, Country Club Woman, Pool Life, Private Pilot, Show, Ski Life, Tape, Underwater.*

Odds are strong, of course, that a high proportion of the magazines started in the past year or two will fail. Some already have. Some of those projected were abandoned before their first issue. Some were begun with more faith than finance, and still others seem to have woefully overestimated their potential.

Yet publishers of sharply focused magazines can take a good deal of encouragement from what has been happening to their kind of publishing in the era of the picture tube. Specialized magazines, especially the chiefly informational ones, have made some of the greatest gains in circulation and in pages of advertising. Magazines beamed at highbrow audiences have soared ahead while those attuned to less educated segments of the public have definitely lost ground.

Take, for example, *Scientific American*. It was a feeble publication, long past its prime, when two young journalists bought it for $40,000 in 1947. Their aim was to bridge a gap between the educated layman and scientists working at the outposts of discovery. Their contributors have included 25 Nobel Prize winners and scientists such as Albert Einstein, Jonas Salk, Linus Pauling and James Van Allen. In 14 years, circulation increased sevenfold to 300,000 and advertising income 63 times to some $4,667,000.

Their story is more dramatic than most, but what happened to *Scientific American* has been happening on a lesser scale to other magazines. Consider a few figures. Between 1950 and 1960, total magazine circulations increased by 21 percent, the number of pages of advertising by 10 percent. In that same period, the combined circulations of the major newsweeklies—*Newsweek, Time, U.S. News & World Report*—climbed by 89 percent, their advertising pages by 27 percent. Two monthly magazines usually identified with the intellectual elite—*Atlantic* and *Harper's* —raised their combined circulations by 50 percent, their advertising pages by 85 percent. *Saturday Review's* sales were up by 145 percent, its advertising pages by 63 percent.

On the other hand, the three leading mass circulation weeklies and biweeklies—*Life, Look* and *Saturday Evening Post*—carried 30 percent fewer advertising pages in 1960 than in 1950, although their revenues had grown as a result of rate increases.

As existing magazines of special purpose have been pushing ahead, they have been joined by a flock of newcomers. *The Reporter* was launched in 1949 to interpret national and international affairs. More recently *Current* has come along to combine excerpts from speeches, documents and other sources into coherent discussions of current issues and *Atlas* provides an interesting sampling of the world's press. *American Heritage, Horizon* and *Wisdom* have been started for cultured and affluent readers. *Sports Illustrated* in 1954 began reporting the "wonderful world of sport" for fans who do not have to sit in the bleachers.

Meanwhile magazines that drew their readers from the lower educational levels have been dropping behind. The combined circulations of five leading "confession" magazines last year were only 90 percent of what they were in 1950. Those of four top movie fan magazines were 53 percent.

Publishing for closely knit interest groups neither guarantees big profits nor provides immunity from the ills that have killed scores of magazines in recent years. Yet, for more than three decades, the *New Yorker* has shown that a magazine can earn a comfortable living by worrying less about the number of it readers than about the kind.

The *New Yorker* has never pretended to be a magazine for everyone; its pitch is to the sophisticated, urban reader with money. Although it gently reminds readers when their subscriptions are about to expire, the *New Yorker* has little use for circulation campaigns and bargain offers. It counts on people who want it to seek it out. Yet its circulation has grown steadily, and is renewal rate is one of the highest in the industry.

The *New Yorker* likes advertisers, but it does not fawn over them. It has been turning down some $250,000 worth of advertising a year because the products would not appeal to its readers, or because the copy and layout were below its standards, or because space was unavailable. Late in 1959 it announced that it would hold advertising to 5,000 pages in 1960 because it could not obtain high-quality editorial matter to balance more than that. Grumbled one advertising executive: "Their salesmen do not see you, they grant you an audience; their advertising departments do not sell advertising, they accept it."

The *New Yorker* has made money every year except for the first faltering three. Its 1960 profits after taxes were 10 percent of its revenues of $18,606,488. That is a record many a publisher would envy.

Some magazines ares growing lustily; others show signs of decay; still others are only memories. There is little likelihood that new mass circulation magazines will appear. But, by and large, the prospects for specialty magazines seem bright.

SELECTED PUBLICATIONS BY

DR. PETERSON

Magazines in the Twentieth Century, U. of Illinois Press, 1956, rev. ed., 1957. (Winner of Sigma Delta Chi Award for Distinguished Research about Journalism.)

Four Theories of the Press, U. of Illinois Press, 1956, with F. S. Siebert and Wilbur Schramm. (Winner of Kappa Tau Alpha Research Award.)

"The American Magazine: An Assessment," *The Cresset,* vol. 24, September 1961, pp. 7–10.

"The Changing Role of Journalism Schools," *Journalism Quarterly,* vol. 37, Autumn 1960, pp. 579–585.

"A Criticism of Press Criticism," *Christian Century,* vol. 76, Sept. 16, 1959, pp. 1048–1051.

"The Economics of Magazine Publishing: The Role of the Publisher," *Current Economic Comment,* vol. 14, August 1952, pp. 52–60.

"Estates in Conflict," in "The Press Looks at the Church" series, *Christian Century,* vol. 79, July 18, 1962, pp. 883–885.

"Magazine Publishing in the U.S.," *Gazette* (Amsterdam), vol. 6, no. 2, 1960, pp. 105–117.

"Magazines," in *Collier's Encyclopedia Yearbook,* 1961, pp. 368–369; 1962, pp. 360–362.

"The Minority Magazine in a Mass Media Culture," *The Cresset,* in press.

"Those Hardy Perennials: Magazines," *Think* 23 (August 1957), pp. 11–14.

SUGGESTIONS FOR FURTHER READING

Bogart, Leo, "Magazines Since the Rise of Television," *Journalism Quarterly*, vol. 33, Spring 1956, pp. 153–166.

Cort, David, "Face-Lifting the Giants," *The Nation*, vol. 193, Nov. 25, 1961, pp. 424–426.

Gehman, Richard, "How to Start a New Magazine," *Writer's Digest*, vol. 41, November 1961, pp. 15–19, 53–56.

Gillenson, Lewis W., "The Struggle for Survival," *Columbia Journalism Review*, vol. 1, Spring 1960, pp. 34–38.

Kobak, James, "Magazines—Crisis in Recession," *Media Scope*, June 1958, pp. 23–27.

"Magazine Paradox: Are They Thriving or Dying?" *Business Week*, Jan. 19, 1957.

Mathieu, Aron, "Man Against White Space," in Mathieu, Aron (ed.), *The Creative Writer* (*Writer's Digest*, Cincinnati, 1961), pp. 457–527.

Porter, William, "The Quality Magazines and the New American Reader," *Gazette*, vol. 6, no. 3, 1960, pp. 305–310.

The Profitable Difference: A Study of the Magazine Market, Its Size, Quality and Buying (Magazine Advertising Bureau of Magazine Publishers Association, New York, 1960). A much-discussed research report designed to show that magazines reach not only a huge market, as TV does, but a better one.

"Rival Magazines Near Hair-Pulling Stage," *Business Week*, Oct. 1, 1960, pp. 88–92. Review of bitter battle between *Ladies' Home Journal* and *McCall's*.

Shaffer, Helen B., "Reading Boom: Books and Magazines," *Editorial Research Reports*, vol. 2, no. 23, Dec. 20, 1961.

Wirsig, Woodrow, "Will the Big Magazines Kill Each Other?" *Harper's*, vol. 224, May 1962, pp. 73–80.

QUESTIONS

1. *Coronet* magazine folded one month short of its twenty-fifth anniversary with a circulation of more than two million subscribers and single-copy sales of about 750,000 a month. (*a*) Why did it fold? (*b*) What is the effect of television on magazine advertising revenue? On magazine content? (*c*) Is the effect always the same? Under what conditions might it differ?

2. With reference to the "numbers game" does the advantage lie with television or magazines and why?

3. What has happened to specialized magazines in the ten year period 1950–1960, as compared with mass circulation magazines? How does Peterson explain these changes?

4. What is the author's forecast for mass media magazines? For class media magazines? Do you think it plausible? Why or why not?

Charles Winick

Teen-agers, Satire, and *Mad* *

IT HAS FREQUENTLY happened in the history of social science that a
few scholars have undertaken to investigate habits, traits, and practices which are generally regarded, even by their colleagues, as vulgar,
unscholarly, trivial. Thus many political scientists in the 1920s were
scandalized by Lasswell's [1] attention to propaganda and to the irra-
tional factors in political behavior, and in the early 1930s a leading
state university expelled from its faculty a psychologist (later of great
distinction) because he studied actual dating customs among young
people in the state. In fact, universities and colleges were generally
very slow to accept sociology as a respectable subject for study, apparently because it dealt with ordinary people's ordinary and often seemingly "vulgar" behavior; indeed, Oxford University, for instance, has
hardly yet admitted that sociology is a proper, intellectual discipline.

The point of the foregoing remarks is not to condemn past
scholars but to suggest that the opportunities of the present may lie
in investigating precisely those areas which seem vulgar, improper, or
corrupt.[2]

Few scholars of whom we know are more vivaciously aware of this
point than Dr. Winick. The list of his publications shows that he
has indeed "made a major effort out of [what are generally regarded
as] minor matters" [3] in the fields of mass communications and culture.

* Reprinted from the *Merrill-Palmer Quarterly of Behavior and Development,*
July, 1962, pp. 183–203, by permission of the author and publisher. (Copyright
1962 by the Merrill-Palmer Institute.)

1. Indeed, a reviewer, Walter L. Whittlesey, a Princeton professor, in the *American Political Science Review* (vol. 29, 1935, pp. 500–501), stigmatized Lasswell's
great study on the psychological basis of political behavior as "the droppings of
English sparrows"; (For another citation of this review, see p. 502 below, introduction to Berelson.)

2. A comparative analysis of epithets of disgust and disdain applied to political
or intellectual enemies among different groups is one example which comes to mind
as of great potential value.

3. Along the same lines, at Boston University one of the editors of this book
has just completed a three-year study of the social implications of comic strips.
See David Manning White, *The Funnies: An American Idiom* (Free Press, New
York, 1963).

One example of this emphasis is to be found in the following article. Satire as a means of reflecting, communicating, and perhaps altering prevailing orientations is his subject. But instead of dealing with literary classics which are respectable due to time and fame, he analyzes the magazine Mad. Satire is often used as a means of saying or implying what is dangerous, unwise, or embarrassing to say directly. Consequently satire is one of the literary modes most likely to communicate or instruct in significant political or social attitudes. It can and does happen, however, that the writers have concealed even from themselves what they are communicating or teaching; perhaps because they are too timid to clarify their purposes, or because they simply do not care and are merely "selling" their product. It would be an interesting follow-up to Winick's study to see how far Mad's editors, contributors, and enthusiastic readers would accept his analysis.   L. A. D.

DR. CHARLES WINICK has had much experience in studying various aspects of public response to significant changes and events. Among the subjects he has studied are: how people respond to a perceived threat to a community, methods of withdrawal from stress, responses to an anxiety provoking stimulus in a group, the content of celebrity fan mail, how communities react to an innovation, how the public uses popular magazines, the content of popular reveries, what the television censor censors, how celebrities respond to the pressures on them, travel in fantasy and fantasy needs of young people. Since 1957 he has conducted a course on mass response to social change ("The Face of the Crowd") at New York University.

This is a report on some aspects of American teen-agers' perception of their world via a content analysis and some interviews with regular readers of the satirical magazine *Mad*.

Goethe once observed that nothing shows a person's character more than the things at which he laughs. This thought has recently been translated into psychiatry by measures of personality, based on a patient's ability to respond to humor (Redlich, Levine & Sohler, 1951) and on his favorite joke (Zwerling, 1955). How people respond to satire should be a revealing clue to their character, because satire is the form of humor most concerned with comment on the norms of a society. Jonathan Swift's epitaph on his Dublin grave, "Where savage indignation can no longer tear his heart," suggests the nature of the satirist's work; expressing savage indignation, usually stemming from a firm sense of morality. There have been times in a literature—as in the age of Pope—when satire was the dominant literary form. Some satirists, like Lord Byron, have become international celebrities as a result of their wit.

Although satire has often flourished in America since James Russell Lowell first acclimated it, the writers and artists of today do not seem to respond with satire; in contrast to the tradition of Americans like Mark Twain, Thorstein Veblen, Kin Hubbard, E. W. Howe, Robert Frost, and Sinclair Lewis.

Television performers have generally addressed their satire to peripheral themes, rather than to the central social concerns of our times. It is possible that sponsors have feared that claims made for their products would suffer if linked with the derision of satire. Another contributor to the decline in satire seems to be a decrease in the incidence of "wisecracks," an almost indigenous form of satire. Satirical movies are seldom made, or are usually unsuccessful commercially even when successful artistically.[1] The character actors who provided humor and satire in movies have almost completely disappeared.

Although satirical magazines for adults flourish in other countries, the United States has no such magazines.[2] Today the only satire magazine published in this country which has any considerable circulation is *Mad*, a magazine in comics format, which is geared toward adolescents.

Why adult satire has not been successful in the last several decades can only be a subject for speculation. The areas of national life in which ridicule is acceptable have diminished steadily. The preoccupation with un-Americanism, and, thus, with Americanism, can only be seen in perspective if we consider how we might feel if we heard of "Englishism" and "un-Englishism" and "Frenchism" and "un-Frenchism." James Thurber, who began as a satirist and spent his last years as a moralist, commented that it is almost as if patriotism were a monopoly by Americans (Thurber, 1958). Such a climate is not one that fosters satire. Another possible reason is that satire is like a soufflé. It must be done well; and there is no audience for an average performance.

Other reasons for the decline in American satire may reflect larger cultural trends. The American audience for even better-than-average satire may be smaller than the European audience, because Americans read less than Europeans. Even in the theater, American audiences do not go to satire, unless it is set to music, in contrast to European audiences, who enjoy the work of satirical dramatists. It is, therefore, less surprising that the only viable format for American satire is *Mad*, which is in comic-book format.

1. For example, *Beat the Devil* (1954), or Preston Sturges' films.

2. Writers like Anatole France, G. K. Chesterton, Oscar Wilde, G. B. Shaw and A. P. Herbert have contributed to European satire magazines. They include France's *Bizarre* and *Le Canard Enchainé*, England's *Punch*, Germany's *Simplicissimus*, Italy's *Candido*, *Travaso* and *Marc Aurelio*, and the Soviet Union's *Krokodil*.

Satirical magazines other than *Mad* have only limited circulation.[3] There are many college satire magazines, but few enjoy much extramural circulation. Many imitate *Mad,* while disdaining it. The *New Yorker* used to be a satirical magazine; but only a diminishing proportion of its content is satirical or even humorous. Perhaps the only format in which American satire has continued to appear over the decades is the editorial page political cartoons (e.g., Herblock). Some satirical cartoonists (e.g., Jules Feiffer, Saul Steinberg) have achieved commercial success.

The absence of a national, adult satirical magazine, at a relatively prosperous time like the present, is puzzling, because such magazines seem to flourish with prosperity. *Puck,* which established the traditional text and cartoon format of so many other satire magazines, was most successful during the Gilded Age. The satirical magazine *Life,* at its peak in the 1920s, had a circulation of 250,000 (Peterson, 1956). *Life* was a major vehicle for satirists, and ran articles on subjects like Anthony Comstock, trusts, and Christian Science. *Judge* also reached its top circulation of 250,000 in the 1920s. In the same decade, *Vanity Fair's* famous satirical "We Nominate For Oblivion" department was widely influential. One *Vanity Fair* cartoon, at the time of Japan's attack on Manchuria, showed the Japanese emperor pulling a rickshaw containing the Nobel Peace Prize. It was headed "Unlikely Happenings." The cartoon elicited a formal protest from the Japanese government. The *American Mercury,* which was a magazine of irreverence as well as of satire, reached a peak circulation of 77,000 copies in 1927, under H. L. Mencken's editorship. It is possible that satire could flourish in the 1920s because of the widespread awareness of institutions like "speakeasies" and "gangsterism" which so conspicuously flaunted current morality.

In that same period, *Ballyhoo* gleamed more brightly than any previous American satirical magazine. By the time of its sixth issue in 1931, *Ballyhoo* had reached a circulation of two million. It was read by adults and developed an array of rings, ties, and other objects sold by the magazine. The magazine inspired a successful Broadway show "Ballyhoo Revue." A number of advertisers paid to be satirized in the magazine. Thus, one manufacturer paid to have his radio identified as the one which gave you "all the crap in the world at your finger tips." *Ballyhoo* made a

---

3. Among the satirical magazines published recently, *Cracked* and *Sick* are imitators of *Mad; Caterpillar* published only a "preview" issue; *Ad Lib, Trump,* and *Bounty* collapsed after one, two, and three issues, respectively; considerable time has elapsed since *Ape* and *Babel* published their first issue; the future of *Monocle* is uncertain; and *For Laughing Out Loud, 1,000 Jokes,* and *Help,* which are published regularly, can be classified as satire only with difficulty. *The Realist* is more of a free-thought publication than a satirical magazine.

household word of "Elmer Zilch," a silly-looking man whose picture it displayed prominently. All the editors on the masthead were called Zilch. The creator of *Ballyhoo* could not account for its success (Anthony, 1946). Its success is probably attributable to a combination of a shock reaction to the depression, the public's reaction against advertising as the most visible symbol of our economy, and to the psychological spark of its "slapstick" approach.

MAD

Mad has some characteristics of *Ballyhoo*. Advertising and other media are among its major targets. It has a masthead on which "Fumigator," "Bouncer," and "Law Suits" are among the staff titles listed. It sells special identifying materials. It has a character somewhat like Elmer Zilch in "Alfred E. Neuman," who is a foolish-looking boy often shown in the magazine. He usually appears with the caption, "What—Me Worry?" He is always grinning, has tousled hair and a missing tooth. The face was originally used in an advertising slide at the turn of the century and adopted by *Mad* several years ago. His name was given him by a member of the magazine staff. Neuman has become a symbol of the magazine, just as Zilch became associated with *Ballyhoo*. The name "Melvin" appears occasionally, as does an avocado plant called "Arthur," and a child in a cart. The nonsense word "potrzebie" appears from time to time in the magazine. On one recent cover, Alfred E. Neuman's girl friend, "Moxie," who looks much like him, is dressed as a drum majorette. She is beating a drum on which there is a picture of Neuman with a black eye.[4] The drum belongs to Potrzebie High School, the Latin motto of which is "Quid, me vexari?" (i.e., "What—me worry?").

Mad started in 1952 as a comic book which lampooned other comics (e.g., *Superman*) and sold at the regular comic price of ten cents. It changed its format and raised its price to twenty-five cents in 1955. Its format of the extended comic magazine story differs from the text emphasis of earlier satire magazines, although its vocabulary level is fairly high. An average story has perhaps ten panels covering three pages, and an average issue has 17 stories. Some authors are well-known comedians like Steve Allen and Orson Bean. Its circulation has increased steadily and in 1960 reached 1,400,000, of which 97 percent are sold on newsstands. The magazine receives over 1,500 fan letters a week. Surveys have indicated that the bulk of the readership is probably concentrated among high school students, although there is some readership in colleges and among

4. December, 1959.

adults (Gehman, 1960). Fifteen *Mad* anthologies have been published successfully. There are few areas of the country in which it does not enjoy some popularity, although it is most popular in urban areas. *Mad's* stemming from comic books was probably responsible for its initially having more boy than girl readers, but both sexes are now equally represented among its readers. *Mad's* ability to institutionalize satire and to develop an audience seemed to provide a clear-cut opportunity to study some parameters of satire's appeal to teen-agers.

CONTENT ANALYSIS

A content analysis of the magazine was conducted in order to determine the relative incidence of various kinds of subject matter. All eight issues published during 1959 were examined and each story was placed into one of eleven subject categories, which had been established on the basis of preliminary analysis of previous issues. Table 1 gives the incidence of each theme.

Table 1—Content Analysis of Issues Published in 1959

Theme	Proportion of Total Percentage
U.S. leisure time activity, other than media	21
Advertising	19
Magazines, newspapers and radio	18
Television	10
Biographies of noted persons	10
Movies	6
Transportation	5
Politics and international relations	4
Business customs	3
Special groups in the population	2
Education	2
Total	100

Each of the categories shown in Table 1 represents a satirical treatment of a subject; laughing at it by using its established vocabulary or trappings. Although satire includes both the understatement of *irony* and the exaggeration of *parody,* there is less irony than parody in *Mad.* However, much of *Mad* is in the form of parody, since it treats the same subject as the original but burlesques its style. Thus, the category "Advertising" would include what appear to be real advertisements. Readers who know the original can easily recognize that the manner of presentation of the advertisement is satirical.

For example, one story classified as advertising was called "The Hip Persuaders," and presented "hip" versions of ten, very familiar, advertising campaigns, each one treated in one panel.[5] One such advertisement showed a man wearing earphones with antennae coming out of his spectacles and about to put a wicked-looking pizza pie into his shining teeth. The headline read, "He lays on only *GLEEM,* the choppergrease for cats who can't sand after every scoff." The reader can respond to this on three levels. He can recognize the well-known advertisement which recommends a toothpaste for people who can't brush after every meal. He can also identify "hip" people who are in touch with the secret language of a deviant subculture. He can also comprehend the translation of the advertising slogan into "hip" language.

Another popular format for a *Mad* story is like Fielding's approach in *Jonathan Wild,* in which the actions of a highwayman are described in mock admiration, in the language usually bestowed on statesmen; and the satire consists in the linking of disparates.

An example of such high satire is "The National Safety Council's Holiday Weekend Telethon," in which a telethon is the theme.[6] An announcer urges people to go out and get themselves killed in a highway accident, so that the Safety Council's quota for the holiday weekend will be met. Drivers are told that the program will pay their toll if they crash into another car while on a toll bridge. Children are told that they can contribute to the total even if they have no automobile by going out and playing on a highway after dark, when it will be easier for them to be hit. Similar appeals are used throughout the rest of the story (i.e., "The family that drives together—dies together." As in *Jonathan Wild,* the mood is sustained; viewers of the telethon are urged not to tie up the lines by telephoning nonfatal accidents, because only fatal accidents can be used. As the story progresses, the number of deaths listed on the scoreboard mounts.

Over half of *Mad's* contents are concerned with leisure and adult mass media. The central role of media in socializing adolescents makes this major theme of *Mad* of special interest. The leisure and media activities and problems of adolescents, however, receive little coverage. Other adolescent problems are either not treated or treated without much gusto. Thus, the teen-age reader can enjoy his spectatorial role as he reads about how sick and silly is the rest of society. One possible reason for the relative absence of satirical material of direct interest to adolescents is that adolescents may have difficulties in perceiving comic elements in situations in which they are involved.

The teen-ager can laugh at those younger than himself, as well as those who are older. One article on magazines for younger children, for ex-

5. April, 1959, pp. 20–22.
6. January, 1959, pp. 11–13.

ample, featured a magazine called "Pedal Trend, The Tricycle Owner's Magazine," with articles on customizing tricycles, the *Grand Prix de Disneyland,* and similar subjects.[7] Much of the satirical material on younger people is not separate but is worked into the details of the panels of stories on other subjects. Thus, one panel in a 14-panel story on "halls of fame" dealt with a copywriter who wrote advertisements for babies, with slogans like "ask the kid who wets one." [8] The artist who regularly draws a child in a cart in his stories never offers an explanation of why the child is there.

PERSONAL INTERVIEWS WITH READERS

Although readers of *Mad* range from eight-year-olds to college students and adults, the most typical *Mad* reader is a high school student. Personal interviews were conducted in 1959 with 411 regular readers of *Mad* with a mean age of 16.2, in order to determine the readers' attitudes toward the magazine, pattern of reading, and participation in other typical activities of teen-agers.[9] The respondents were asked questions on stories they would have published in *Mad* "if editor," what they liked most about it, how they read an issue, with whom they discussed it, how often they read magazines for teen-agers and comic books, and how they liked rock-and-roll music. The sequences of questions was rotated in order to minimize the effect of the sequence of questions. Background data on other and previous media use were also obtained.

Stories in Mad *if editor.* The average respondent gave eight stories which he would run "if editor," with a range from four to 22. The responses were coded into the categories developed in the content analysis. Most respondents cited stories which had already appeared in *Mad.* Table 2 gives their specific choices.

There was a high degree of agreement between what actually appeared in *Mad* and what the readers would put in the magazine.[10] The only

7. January, 1959, 15.
8. June, 1959, 34.
9. The sample was selected by administering a screening questionnaire on reading habits to the total population of a high school which services a large and fairly heterogeneous population in the metropolitan New York area. A personal interview was conducted with each student who met the criterion of a regular reader (i.e., having read at least five of the last eight issues). The age range was 15.2 to 17.7. There were 218 boys and 193 girls. Weighting equally the three criteria of residence, parents' income and father's vocation, 102 were classified as lower class, 243 were described as middle class, and 66 upper class. In terms of their school performance they were divided into those doing relatively well (82), average (241), and relatively poor (88).
10. The Spearman rank correlation coefficient between the content analysis by theme and what the readers would put in the magazine was .69. Student's *t* was

major category which *Mad* readers said they would like to see in the magazine and which had not been previously coded was Alfred E. Neuman. In the content analysis, there was no category for Neuman because he has not been the subject of stories, although often figuring in them.

Table 2—What Readers Would Put in Issue of Mad If They Were Editor

Theme	Proportion of Total Percentage
Advertising	17
Business customs	14
Leisure time activity, other than media	14
Movies	12
Alfred E. Neuman	11
Education	7
Biographies of noted persons	6
Television	5
Transportation	4
International relations	4
Special groups	3
Magazines, newspapers, and radio	2
Miscellaneous	1
Total	100

Readers would, however, like more of some subjects and less of others. They want more satire on business customs, education and movies and less attention to other mass media. Respondents expressed no interest in seeing problems of adolescence like parents, vocational choice or sex, treated by the magazine. Its readers seem to prefer that matters close to them not be satirized, with the exception of movies and education, which are both relatively external institutions. The magazine occasionally carries articles on parents, in which parents and the family are presented as being relatively unattractive.[11]

Cross-tabulations by sex, status, and school performance yielded no significant differences, except that more boys than girls selected the business customs area ($p < .01$). Boys might be expected to be more aware of business. Their interest in business customs may reflect adolescents' special fascination with adult business behavior; much of which *Mad* has helped them to perceive as foolish and immoral. The readers may regard such stories as clues and "how to" guides to the world of business which they may soon be entering. Some readers may want stories on business because

.98. As another check on the relationship between the content and the readers' preferences, the coefficient of concordance between the two ranked groups was computed to be .568. Snedecor's F (1.26) confirmed that there was no significant degree of variation in rank between the two groups of themes.

11. For example, a story on "How to Deal With Parents from Ages 21 to 60" in the December 1960 issue, pp. 39–47.

of the inadequacies of high school instruction on business and their feeling that this is an important and mysterious area of American life that they do not understand. Others may want more on business, because the work done by their fathers is increasingly removed from the children's "ken" and less product-oriented, so that the children have a relatively dim impression of just what their fathers do in the business world.

The interest in movies reflects teen-agers' extreme "movie-going" activity; only the 15–19 age group has increased its movie-going in the last ten years (Opinion Research Corp., 1957). The teen-age 11 percent of the population accounts for approximately half of all movie tickets. Movies are important for teen-agers as the traditional "safe" date. It is also possible that the procedures whereby the movie stars of today are made into stars, have been so widely publicized that teen-agers are cynical about the techniques of making stars, and would like to see them satirized. There is often so little to say about the artistic qualities of some movie stars that their publicity stresses how they were "discovered," and teen-agers may wish to see more satire on this aspect of the movies.

The interest in education perhaps reflects readers' feelings that the subject should get more treatment in *Mad,* so that they might have a better vocabulary for laughing at it. Another possibility is that some teen-agers feel that their schools and teachers are quite inadequate, and that the sensationalist criticism of education in popular media is wide of the mark. *Mad's* integrity might seem to these teen-agers to make it an ideal vehicle for candid and informed criticism of the schools.

Since the respondents are regular readers, their general acquiescence in *Mad* content is not surprising. It is curious that readers did not mention major social issues of our time, like "desegregation" and "atomic war," as subjects for satire. There seems to be a tacit understanding that there are some subjects which are best left alone, even satirically. The readers may sense that the traditional *Mad* procedure of satirizing both sides of a controversy would lead to obvious difficulties in the case of desegregation. Some may be apathetic about the issue while others may be so ego-involved in it that they would not want it satirized. Teen-agers may be so fatalistic about nuclear war that they could not face even a satirical treatment of the subject.

What liked about Mad? The reasons given by the respondents for liking *Mad* were coded into several categories. The average respondent gave approximately four reasons. The proportion citing each reason is shown in Table 3.

The respondents described the appeal of the magazine mainly in generalities and the third person. Relatively few responses refer to the reader's response in the first person ("relaxing, makes me laugh, fun, cheers me up"): In view of the complex and perhaps threatening nature of satire and of humor, it is hardly surprising that the readers did not verbalize many details of the magazine's appeal. Over half of the reasons cited clearly refer to the magazine's satirical and witty content.

Table 3—What Readers Like About Mad

Reason	Proportion of Readers Who Cited Reason Percentage
Makes fun of and satirizes things	44
It's funny, comedy	37
Stories on famous people	25
Like everything in it	24
Makes me laugh	22
Makes fun of itself	22
The ads	21
Tells how things work	19
Not afraid to attack things	19
It's crazy	19
The jokes	19
Alfred E. Neuman	18
Has current events	18
Well done, well written	17
Not like other magazines	17
The stories	16
It's fun	12
It's relaxing	8
It's silly	7
Cheers me up	2
Miscellaneous	2
Total	388

One reason for liking *Mad* ("famous people, how things work") is its role as socializing agent. Some teen-agers may be learning skills for functioning in our society by acquiring the procedures for survival in America today which are spelled out in witty detail by *Mad*. They may, thus, covertly be learning rules for antisocial behavior, while overtly laughing at those engaged in such behavior. *Mad* has carried seventeen different articles with titles beginning "how to," and many other articles with similar themes. At their best, they range from the bitter satire of Schopenhauer's enumeration of the many ways to win a controversy without being right (1942) to the inspired buffoonery of Rabelais' Panurge's debate with "a great English scholar" (1952).

Reading *Mad* may thus be a kind of problem-solving activity. The teen-ager may feel that he is learning to emulate "gamesmanship" while laughing at it. He can be an inside "dopester" while chivying inside dopesters. It would be analogous to, for example, a reader of Ovid's *Art of*

Love or Castiglione's *Book of the Courtier* studying them for the apparent purpose of ridiculing love-making and the courtier's life, respectively, but actually sopping up much "how to" information on these subjects. Thus, a recent *Mad* article on the "Practical Scout Handbook" is a parody of the *Boy Scouts' Handbook* in terms of various social situations.[12] A discussion of scout teamwork urges the reader to keep on the alert for accidents, so that he can call an ambulance and then a lawyer. The reader is advised to act surprised if the lawyer offers him part of his fee, but to turn him in to the police for "ambulance chasing" if he doesn't. The reader can thus smile at the advice; which is typical of the literalist content of much of *Mad*. He can also experience dislike of people who behave in this way, while at the same time absorbing the advice. The same appeal can be seen, for example, in recent books which deplore prurience and consist largely of examples of prurience to which the reader can feel superior while enjoying them.

Few respondents said that they discuss the details of their enjoyment of the magazine with their peers. They said that they did often discuss it in general terms (i.e., "did you see the last issue, did you see the story on —?"). There appears to be no specific social context of teen-agers within which the magazine is unusually likely to be discussed.

A number of respondents (22 percent) praised the consistency of the magazine, which manifests itself in *Mad's* making fun of or attacking itself in "house" advertisements. Such advertisements seem to say, "We can't criticize others without criticizing ourselves." A typical advertisement urges readers to buy a picture of Alfred E. Neuman, so that street cleaners may be kept busy gathering up the pictures when they are thrown out. An anthology from the magazine is called "The Worst from *Mad*" and refers to "sickening past issues" from which it is culled. The editors run their own pictures and laugh at them. These are examples of what many readers perceive as the infectious high spirits and enthusiasm with which the magazine is edited. Such enthusiasm seems to have a special appeal for young people, who are likely to respect competence in any form and apparently interpret the self-mocking advertisements as expressions of consistency and competence. The respondents commenting on how well written *Mad* was (17 percent) also are praising the competence of the editors. The implication may be that the authors of *Mad* are professional enough to have absorbed all the skills of the people they are satirizing, but have chosen to use their expertise in making fun of society and even of themselves. Inasmuch as there is considerable agreement that a distinctive feature of juvenile delinquency is its celebration

12. October, 1961, 43–47.

of prowess (Matza, 1961), it is possible that the teen-age reader perceives *Mad* as a kind of delinquent activity which has somehow become successful; and, thus, one way of demonstrating prowess by antisocial activity.

Relatively few readers (3 percent) volunteered any features of the magazine which they did not like. These features were relatively independent of their enthusiasm for the magazine. Thus a reader liking a great many features might still mention some which he did not like. Alfred E. Neuman heads the list of least-liked features; one half of those who expressed some dissatisfaction did so because Neuman "runs too often," "looks too dopey," and similar reasons.

Cross-tabulations—by sex, socioeconomic status, and degree of success at school—of the various reasons for liking the magazine did not yield any significant differences, with two exceptions: Alfred E. Neuman and current events.

Of the 74 respondents who cited Alfred E. Neuman as a reason for liking the magazine, 56 percent were in the group which was not doing well at school ($p < .01$). It can be speculated that the less successful students are more likely to identify with Neuman because he conveys a feeling of failure, defeat, defensiveness, and uninvolvement. His nonworry slogan has a "let the world collapse, I don't care" quality, and his appearance suggests stupidity. One fan admiringly said that "If Alfred E. Neuman jumped off the Empire State Building, he would be laughing." A few readers thought that Neuman was a functionary of the magazine, although he does not appear on the masthead. It is possible that his silliness and appearance of being someone who doesn't know any better, helps to make the magazine more acceptable, by making its attack less committed.

An adolescent who is doing well at school might enjoy the magazine because of its "joshing" of the very symbols of status and achievement to which he is attracted. The less effective adolescent may like *Mad* because of Neuman, who represents fecklessness and nonachievement. The magazine may thus appeal to teen-agers at opposite ends of the scale of achievement for quite different reasons, while giving each one a chance to feel superior.

Most of the respondents (71 percent) who commented on the magazine's basing its stories on current events, were in the group which was doing relatively well at school ($p < .01$). The more alert readers, thus, seem to derive pleasure from their ability to recognize the relationship between an actual happening and its being satirized by *Mad*. A few called such consonance between *Mad* stories and current events to their parents' attention, perhaps as one way of making their parents feel that the magazine has some educational value. It might be speculated that the identification of such current events material may help to assuage guilt feelings which the magazine's satirical content may evoke.

Even though doing well at school does have some status among teen-agers, it is more important for them to achieve good grades by appearing to do little work *without* making any special efforts to get good grades (Coleman, 1959). Adolescents' group norms operate to keep effort down. Therefore, if a *Mad* reader can scoff at his elders and society, by seeming to learn something about current events, he is deriving multiple dimensions of satisfaction.[13]

How read an issue. Another question put to respondents was intended to determine their traffic through the magazine. Over half (62 percent) of the regular readers go through *Mad* soon after getting it. Twenty-eight percent read the magazine in two or three sittings. Ten percent read it intermittently. Readers often reread their favorite articles.

The large proportion of respondents who read *Mad* through is another confirmation of the loyalty of its readers, which is not unexpected in view of adolescents' fierce loyalties to group, team, and school.

It can be speculated that one way in which the group can give vent to nonconformism is by regular readership of a magazine which largely mocks the adult world. This is a world which the magazine's readers have not yet engaged directly, but which they are approaching during a period when they are trying to learn who they are and what their feelings are. By enjoying satire on this adult world, they can approach it while mocking it. They can also mock the world of younger children.

This ability of adolescents to take a socially acceptable medium, the format of which involves conformity to group norms—like a comic magazine or rock-and-roll—while using the medium to express hostility and aggressiveness, is in line with what is known about adolescents' needs. They want both, to belong and not belong, to have and have not, to enjoy but also to attack.

The very name of *Mad* implies not only aggression ("mad at") but also the foolishness ("mad as a hatter") of much civilization. This kind of ambivalence—enjoying media which imply conformity while at the same time using them to rebel against it—is a special kind of escape, which is strongly developed in adolescents.

---

13. In spite of the great success of *Mad*, it would not be safe to assume that all teen-agers are interested in laughing at the ways of adult society. The largest selling teen magazine is *Boy's Life*, sponsored by the Boy Scouts, with a circulation of 1,790,000. Magazines like *Boy's Life* and *Scholastic* were not included, because they have institutional affiliations and are not bought on the open market. The magazines tabulated were *Dig, Teen, Flip, Hep Cats, Modern Teen, Seventeen, 16, Datebook, Teen Parade, Teens Today,* and *Teen World.*

Adolescence has long been known to be a period of contradictions, and of the growing awareness of contradictions. Materialism and idealism, egoism and altruism, and sociability and loneliness are among the contradictory feelings, which are likely to be emerging simultaneously. A major problem of adolescents is how to express their hostility while seeming not to do so. One noted expression of this conflict was "Hound Dog," probably the most successful single phonograph record ever made. This rock-and-roll record sold 5,500,000 copies, almost all to teen-agers. Its lyrics represent pure hostility, although the format in which it is expressed is the socially acceptable one of the rock-and-roll record. Elvis Presley, the nonpareil exemplar of the rock-and-roller's hostility toward the adult world, is the first performer in history to make a long-playing record that sold over one million copies. Another example of adolescents' ability to use media in this way is the extent to which they will *seem* to read all of a school circulated magazine (i.e., *Reader's Digest*) which has both serious and humorous material, but will pay attention to the jokes and cartoons, and largely ignore serious material.

This ability to *express* aggressiveness seems to have found some relatively recent outlets, but the *presence* of the aggressiveness has often been noted by other investigators. The most intensive study ever made of adolescent fantasy—using cartoon-like picture stimuli—found that its major theme was aggression, which was described as "practically universal" (Symonds, 1949). Even "mild" boys and girls told extremely aggressive stories, with considerable destructive violence. There were over three times as many themes of "aggression" expressed by the adolescents studied, as "eroticism," the next most popular theme. Anxiety, Oedipal conflict, moral issues, success striving and turning stories into jokes, were other common themes; all of these elements can be found in *Mad*.

A study conducted before the "heyday" of comic books suggested that high school students are less likely to respond to pictorial humor than to verbal and intellectual humor (Harms, 1943). *Mad* would seem to represent a combination of these elements. The use of the comic format may help to remove some sting from the aggressive content for some readers because of the association of comics with "kid stuff." Another reason for the special appeal of the comic format is suggested by previous studies of adolescent humor, which report that visual presentation of humorous material facilitates the ability of adolescents to respond to it (Omwake, 1937). Many adolescents have had much experience with the comic format in their preadolescent years. The great majority (89 percent) of the respondents had read comic books before *Mad*. A convincing case could probably be made for the comic book's having supplanted the fairy tale as a major carrier of our culture's ethos to young people! *Mad,* along with some other comic books, is not permitted in schools by many teachers and even by some parents in their homes, thus adding the lure of the forbidden to the magazine.

During the interviewing, a number of respondents referred to *Mad* as "our magazine." They meant that *Mad* expressed their point of view so effectively that they had almost a proprietory feeling about it. *Mad* reinforces membership in the teen-agers, peer group—it's the "thing to do." As one respondent said, "All the kids read *Mad*. The cats and the frats both make it." This suggests that the less, as well as the more, staid teeners enjoy it. There is so much interest in *Mad* that one fan has published a complete cross-index to the magazine (von Bernewitz, 1961). It is likely that this in-group feeling is strengthened by the several personalities in the magazine who are never explained: Neuman, Arthur, the plant, the child, and potrzebie. A number of the respondents mentioned that they had "discovered" these features by themselves. Their having done so seemed to contribute to their feeling of being a member of an in-group.

Practically no respondent referred to the magazine's commercial success, which did not seem to have made much of an impression on readers. Many explicitly commented on the extent of peer-group readership as a positive feature. "Most of the other kids read *Mad*" and "we swap old copies back and forth," were typical comments. The wide readership of the magazine by other teen-agers helps to legitimize its appeal; especially in the face of the considerable opposition to it by parents and other institutionalized figures of authority. Readership of *Mad,* thus, reinforces membership in a kind of ritual nonconformity.

This use of media to obtain membership in an in-group of outsiders is one way in which the adolescent can make tolerable his need both to assent and dissent. It is perhaps this sensitivity and response to the near-intolerable which has helped to make what is now called "sick" humor, an established part of adolescent humor. Stories like, "I stepped on my mother because I wanted a stepmother" have been told by teen-agers for decades. A similar kind of gallows humor appeared in World War II among French adults faced with the extreme situation of the Resistance. It is probably no accident that this kind of "sick joke" has appeared among American adults, coterminously with the near intolerable situation of the threat of atomic annihilation.

A special appeal of a magazine of satire like *Mad* is that *the satirist can say things which even a reformer or critic cannot easily say. It may be easier to laugh at something than to discuss it objectively.* The adolescent both wants to make contact with the symbols of success in the outside world, as some do by autograph collecting and fan clubs, and, at the same time, wants to believe ill of them. *Mad* provides its readers with an opportunity to "go away a little closer" from some important American institutions.

This hostility seems to have a special need to find expression in high school and college students. They enjoy the absurd and satirical, as well as the opportunity to release pent-up emotional energy, and feelings of superiority (Kambouropoulou, 1930). Satire may have a special appeal to relatively young people, because it can be viewed psychoanalytically, as a reflection of the inner dependence of childhood, which is projected onto noted individuals and institutions, in order to attack them (Bergler, 1956). Satire is often described metaphorically as "biting," because it is a method of communication for persons who respond orally. It can be regarded as a weapon of the weak; and adolescents may regard themselves as being relatively weak. *Mad* offers an apportunity for a kind of counter-phobic, defensive reaction to social institutions. The adolescent readers of the magazine face the prospect of going out into the adult world, not with anxiety but with an opportunity for gratification through laughter, as they achieve symbolic mastery over the adult world by continually assuring themselves that its institutions and personalities cannot be taken seriously (Wolfenstein, 1957). The gratification comes from reenacting mastery over anxiety (Kris, 1938), for which the *Mad* story provides the occasion. It is traditional to say that adolescents "quest for new people to love and new forms of functioning." By its exposés of the latter, *Mad* gives its adolescent readers new targets for their ambivalence.

ENTHUSIASM SCORE

Even within a group of such regular readers of the magazine, it was considered useful to obtain a measure of comparative degree of enthusiasm. Each interview was read through independently by two analysts, who considered how the magazine was read, what the respondent said about it, the respondent's feeling tone about the magazine, and the extent of his ego involvement in it.[14] The interviewee was rated on a scale with one representing the lowest and ten the highest score. The range of scores was from four to ten, with an average of 8.0.

Boys had an average enthusiasm score of 8.7, girls of 7.8 ($p < .05$). The upper class readers had a score of 8.6, middle class readers also averaged 8.6, and lower class readers 7.1 ($p < .01$). The group which was doing relatively well at school averaged 8.2, the average students 8.4, and the poorest students averaged 7.5 on enthusiasm. The difference

14. Acknowledgment is made of the cooperation of Regina Pezzella and Elliott Winick.

between the poorest students and each of the other two groups was significant ($p < .05$).

The readers whose families are faring better economically and who are better students, thus seem to like *Mad* better. Why? We might speculate that these students are likely to be expecting, consciously or otherwise, to be assuming more active and significant roles in their society and community once they leave school and college. Similarly, boys are likely to be more aware of their potential involvement with and functioning in the community than girls, because the boys face decisions on jobs and military service. The very closeness of these groups to the opportunity of functioning in our society may make them more than usually alert to the dissonances and moral ambiguities of society. It is this kind of alertness which makes satire possible.

It is no coincidence that our wealthiest universities have also spawned some of the best college satire and humor magazines (e.g., Columbia *Jester*, Vassar *Igitur*, MIT *Voo Doo*, Stanford *Chaparral*, Harvard *Lampoon*). The student body at the Yale Law School in New Haven, which is perhaps as sensitized to power as any American student body, created *Monocle*, which is the only American political satire magazine. Thus, universities with students likely to achieve power also have publications which sneer most enthusiastically at manifestations of power. These publications represent one method of absorbing role strain on the part of groups other than the lower class marginal groups, which have traditionally showed strain in adolescence. How cautious even such elite groups may be, can be seen in a recent issue of *Monocle,* in which *over half* the contributors use pseudonyms.[15] The editors dedicate the issue to the contributors' skill in selecting pen names! It is a vivid commentary on satire in our time, and a magazine of satire in which most of its authors do not wish to be identified. The caution of these contributors to Yale's *Monocle* make especially relevant George S. Kaufman's observation, that "satire is what closes in New Haven."

Another possibility for the greater interest in *Mad* of the higher socioeconomic groups and better students is that satire is the end result of indignation, and indignation is based on the awareness of standards. The higher status and education group may be more aware of the standards which contemporary society is implicitly said to be violating by *Mad*, because of its greater exposure to literature, other art forms, and other facets of society.

The existence and success of *Mad* does not necessarily mean that from an adolescent's point of view there is more to satirize today than

15. Summer-Fall 1960.

there has been in the past. What it does mean is that this particular kind of satire has found a market at this time, because it serves some significant function for the teen-agers who are its primary market. There have been some changes in the life situation of teen-agers that probably contribute to their greater receptivity to satire. The number of teen-agers increased from 15 to 20 million during the 1950s. They currently spend ten billion dollars a year and are the targets of many marketers, so that they are more aware of marketing. They save their money less than previous generations did, start dating earlier, and marry earlier. Teen-age girls spend $300 million on cosmetics each year. The first magazine specifically for teen-agers, rather than for boys *or* girls, appeared in 1955.

The 1950s appeared to provide a climate that was especially hospitable for the approach of a satirical magazine. Cynicism among the middle classes was certainly a significant characteristic of the post-World War II national mood; to which, on another level, the late Senator McCarthy responded. *Confidential* strengthened this mood by becoming the most successful magazine in American history, with its exposés of "irregularities" among the famous. This combination of factors may have helped to contribute to the mood of criticism of society, which is necessary for satire. A clue to how teen-agers feel about the morality of their elders can be obtained from the comments of teen magazines on the charge that their leading television master of ceremonies, Dick Clark, had accepted "payola." None of the magazines that commented on the charge had anything adverse to say about Clark, because they saw nothing wrong in payola.

The teen-agers of the 1950s are the "war babies" of the World War II period. Not only were their fathers often away, but their mothers were likely to be working. Even after the war, many teen-agers of the 1950s may have grown up in suburban communities, where fathers were at home less often than the fathers of previous generations. The effect of moving from one place to another, which 20 percent of the population engages in each year, may be related to the feelings of deracination that many teen-agers experience; and that may have contributed to teen-agers' feeling more critical of their elders, and closer to each other.

Inevitably, the success of *Mad* and the new sick comedians during the same decade suggests some comparison between the two.[16] *Mad* and the new comedians are both nihilistic, and level their burlesque at so many targets that they hardly seem to have any time or energy left to deal with alternatives to the lunacy they attack. They must both therefore continue

16. It is an interesting commentary on our culture's attitudes toward satire, that these comedians have been completely unsuccessful in their attempts to be called "truth" comedians.

to charge harder at their targets. They both engage in irony and reinforce their audience's feeling of being "in." Both see corruption everywhere. Both enjoy attacking mass media. The sick comedians, however, regularly attack intolerance, domesticity, religion, and self-improvement, which are seldom butts of *Mad*. Although politics represents a target for the sick comedians, it constitutes a small proportion of *Mad's* content. *Mad* actually does not comment on substantive political matters, but deals with personalities in politics. Thus, it might joke about Senator McCarthy's heavy beard, President Eisenhower's golf, or President Kennedy's haircut, but not about their policies.

It is curious that, with the possible exception of the sick comedians, satire has not found a market among adults since *Ballyhoo*. In a democracy in which the dissident voice may be a sign of healthy differences in points of view, and awareness and examination of alternatives, *Mad* has not only entertained dissident theories but made them feel at home and helped to get them into millions of homes. Its very success, however, may have a boomerang effect. As *Mad* achieves greater success and recognition as a vehicle for teen-agers, adults may reinforce their image of satire as a juvenile medium. Satire as an adult format may thus become less possible in this country for this generation. Another possibility, of course, is that the millions of teen-agers who have read *Mad* may develop into adults who will constitute a ready audience for sick comedians and other satire. It is also possible that the reason teen-agers enjoy *Mad* is that school has sensitized them to standards, but today's nonschool, adult world is so normless that adults cannot respond to an art form that implicitly is based on departures from the norm. Yet another possibility is that the magazine's continuing attacks on so many targets will give its satire almost a good-natured quality, and thus ultimately blunt its impact. For at least the next few years, however, it appears likely that *Mad* will maintain its unique status of being respected, if not quite respectable.

SELECTED PUBLICATIONS BY DR. WINICK

Trends in Human Relations Research (Anti-Defamation League, New York, 1955).

Dictionary of Anthropology (Cassell, London, 1956).

"Is Society the Patient?" *Journal of Educational Sociology,* vol. 30, no. 2, 1956, pp. 106–112.

"A Realistic View of Motivation Research," in Dan H. Fenn (ed.), *Management in a Rapidly Changing Economy* (McGraw-Hill, New York, 1958), pp. 169–189.

Taste and the Censor in Television (Fund for the Republic, New York, 1959).

"Status, Shoes, and the Life Cycle," *Boot and Shoe Recorder,* vol. 156, Oct. 15, 1959, pp. 101, 199–203.

"The Folklore of Shoes," *Boot and Shoe Recorder,* vol. 156, Oct. 15, 1958, pp. 98–99, 190–194.

"Art Work Versus Photography: An Experimental Study," *J. Applied Psychology*, vol. 43, no. 3, 1959, pp. 180–182.

"Leisure, The Problem That Isn't," *Leisure*, vol. 1, no. 1, 1960, pp. 25–27.

"The Relationship Among Personality Needs, Objective Factors, and Brand Choice: A Reexamination," *Journal of Business*, vol. 34, no. 1, 1961, pp. 61–66.

"Direction, Salience, and Intensity of the Effects of an Intergroup Education Experience," *Journal of Intergroup Relations*, vol. 2, 1961, pp. 49–55.

"How People Perceived 'The Mad Bomber,'" *Public Opinion Quarterly*, vol. 25, no. 1, 1961, pp. 25–38.

"Space Jokes As Indication of Attitudes Toward Space," *Journal of Social Issues*, vol. 17, no. 2, 1961, pp. 43–49.

"Censor and Sensibility: A Content Analysis of the Television Censor's Comments," *Journal of Broadcasting*, vol. 5, no. 2, 1961, pp. 117–136.

"The Diffusion of an Innovation Among Physicians in a Large City," *Sociometry*, vol. 24, no. 4, 1961, pp. 384–396.

"An Experimental Study of Some Factors in the Recognition of Slogans,"

Journal of General Psychology, vol. 65, 1961, pp. 339–351. (With Jacob Goldstein.)

"Fan Mail to Liberace," *Journal of Broadcasting*, vol. 6, no. 2, 1962, pp. 129–142.

"Differential Recall of the Dream As a Function of Audience Perception," *Psychoanalysis and the Psychoanalytic Review*, vol. 49, no. 1, 1962, pp. 53–62.

"The Public Image of the Museum in America," *Curator*, vol. 5, no. 1, 1962, pp. 45–52.

"Celebrities' Errancy As a Subject for Journalism: A Study of *Confidential*," *Gazette*, vol. 7, nos. 3–4, 1962, pp. 329–334.

"Thoughts and Feelings of the General Population as Expressed in Free Association Typing," *American Imago*, vol. 19, no. 1, 1962, pp. 67–84.

For the Young Viewers (McGraw-Hill, New York, 1962). (With F. Rainsberry and R. Garry.)

"Preference for Individual Digits," *Journal of General Psychology*, vol. 67, no. 4, 1962, pp. 271–281.

"A Content Analysis of Orally Communicated Humor," *American Imago*, 1963.

BIBLIOGRAPHY

Anthony, N., *How To Grow Old Disgracefully* (Eagle Books, New York, 1946), p. 126.

Bergler, E., *Laughter and the Sense of Humor* (Intercontinental Medical, New York, 1956), pp. 161–165.

Coleman, J. S., "Academic Achievement and the Structure of Competition," *Harvard Education Review*, vol. 29, 1959, pp. 330–351.

Gehman, R., "It's Just Plain Mad," *Coronet*, vol. 48, no. 1, 1960, pp. 96–103.

Harms, E., "The Development of Humor," *Journal of Abnormal Sociology*

and *Psychology*, vol. 38, 1943, pp. 351–369.

Kambouropoulou, P., "Individual Differences in the Sense of Humor," *American Journal of Psychology*, vol. 37, 1930, pp. 268–278.

Kris, E., "Ego Development and the Comic," *International Journal of Psychoanalysis*, vol. 19, 1938, pp. 77–90.

Matza, D., "Subterranean Traditions of Youth," *Annals of the American Academy of Political and Social Science*, vol. 338, 1961, pp. 102–118.

Omwake, L., "A Study of the Sense of

Humor," *Journal of Applied Psychology,* vol. 21, 1937, pp. 688–704.

The Public Appraises Movies (Opinion Research Corporation, Princeton, N.J., 1957), p. 12.

Peterson, T., *Magazines in the Twentieth Century* (U. of Illinois Press, Urbana, Ill., 1956), pp. 147–152.

The Portable Rabelais (Viking, New York, 1952), pp. 306–310.

Redlich, F., J. Levine, and T. P. Sohler, "A Mirth Response Test," *American Journal of Orthopsychiatry,* vol. 21, 1951, pp. 717–734.

Schopenhauer, A., "The Art of Controversy," in *Complete Essay of Schopenhauer* (Wiley, New York, 1942), pp. 1–98.

Symonds, P. M., *Adolescent Fantasy* (Columbia U. P., New York, 1949).

Thurber, J., "A Subversive Conspiracy," *The Realist,* vol. 1, no. 1, 1958, pp. 25–26.

von Bernewitz, F., *The Complete Mad Checklist* (Published by the Author, Silver Spring, Md., 1961).

Wolfenstein, M., "A Phase in the Development of Children's Sense of Humor," in *The Psychoanalytic Study of the Child,* (International Universities Press, New York, 1957), vol. 6, pp. 336–350.

Zwerling, I., "The Favorite Joke in Diagnostic and Therapeutic Interviewing," *Psychoanalytic Quarterly,* vol. 24, 1955, pp. 104–114.

QUESTIONS

1. What clues does *Mad's* satire give as to American character and culture?

2. Is there any American satirical parallel of *Mad* for an adult audience? How do you account for this?

3. What functions for teenagers would you say are served by *Mad's* laughter at the adult world? Do these functions seem contradictory? Discuss.

4. Does *Mad* succumb to the so-called demands of conformism or "Americanism" by watering down its satire on such controversial issues as desegregation or nuclear testing? Why so or why not?

Martin U. Martel and George J. McCall

Reality-Orientation and the Pleasure Principle: A Study of American Mass-Periodical Fiction (1890-1955) *

THE ESSAY THAT FOLLOWS *may well be at this moment the most original contribution in the Reader. It may well prove to be, also, the most difficult for many readers.*

This difficulty may arise in part out of the very originality of the contribution. We urge therefore that readers make a special effort to master it.

One reason we have included it in this volume is that we think that, if carefully studied, it will give a vivid awareness of what it is like to tackle problems of scientific exploration—of how exciting and how tough such exploration can be.

But it may be encouraging to point out some of the reasons why new, original work is likely to be hard reading. First, of course, it is unfamiliar. But, second, the original formulations of a new idea are always likely to be rough and clumsy. The early automobile, by way of analogy, appears incredibly clumsy alongside the 1964 model. The modern reader of Waverley, or of any of Sir Walter Scott's later historical novels—however much he may enjoy them—will nevertheless be startled to note how little command Scott had of the literary techniques that present-day historical novelists seem to know almost "instinctively." So, also, with scientific work; it is unlikely that the first effort in a particular direction will be clear, technically polished,

* Published for the first time in this volume. An earlier version was presented at the annual meetings of the American Sociological Association, September 1961. The research reported here was made possible originally through financial aid from the Institute of Gerontology at the State University of Iowa. Much of the present analysis was carried out under a grant from the Social Science Research Center at Cornell University. Of many who have given us valuable criticism and assistance, we are particularly indebted to William O. Aydelotte, Elihu Katz, W. W. Morris, William Porter, and Samuel F. Sampson.

and obvious. (The history of science is full of instances where discoverers and discoveries were rejected and ridiculed. One reason is simply that the early discoverers were rarely trained writers, and were therefore hard to understand.)

A third reason why much original work is hard to read lies in the nature of many discoverers and inventors. They are so concerned with improving their discoveries and perfecting their analyses that they find it temperamentally very hard to sit back and finish up a polished job of exposition. Certainly, this is one difficulty with the paper that follows. This project has been under constant revision for a long period of time, and it is almost impossible to do the optimum job of explanation and exposition while one is rearranging one's ideas and techniques. But this is part of the nature of many discoverers—the denseness and difficulty of most of John Dewey's books, or of the earlier work of Harold D. Lasswell, may be attributed to the same situation—Dewey and Lasswell simply had too many ideas, too frequently, to focus on issues of clarification and exposition. Since this is a common phenomenon among scholars of great originality, it is probably desirable that those becoming familiar with the world of scholarship should deliberately be exposed to some examples of this sort of tough and difficult reading—even where it might be possible by an extensive editing to simplify it.

Two points should be remembered by those who are tackling the article:

1. The present essay is primarily a description of how a study was set up; but in the process of this description, there is a review of the literature on readership and studies of magazine content which in and of itself is of greatest value.

2. This study resembles Winick's study of Mad magazine (pp. 262–282) but goes even further in showing how entertainment items of mass culture communicate and represent even in the process of entertaining. Put another way, this study is an application of the point in Wright's article (pp. 93–108) about the distinction between the manifest and the latent aspects of communication. Although the manifest aspect of the stories Martel and McCall study is to entertain, the latent aspects which their technique permits them to explore are numerous and significant.

Much of the difficulty of this article stems from its central virtue; namely, that the authors take the reader right along with them through all the painstaking probing, questioning, and rechecking that is inherent in starting a new line of research. Such a procedure is of great value in understanding research methods and in developing some skill at estimating the validity of new approches. In fact, it may be said that the greatest value of the article lies precisely in its detailed presentation of the rationale behind a new use of a particular technique of communications research, in this case content analysis—and in the way it shows how this technique can perhaps be used to exploit the rich stores of social and historical information which lies concealed in the accumulated stacks of mass communications products, even in that seemingly very unlikely source of such information, the magazine short story.*

Aside from making a powerful case for a new approach to certain types of sociological and historical research, and in addition to its obvious great values as a bibliographic guide to studies of magazine literature, the article offers three principal contributions to students of mass communications:

1. The second section contains an elaborate and rather intriguing theory of the manner in which certain story contents are determined by prosaic social forces rather than by "artistic considerations." This theory, based upon modern sociology, affords an interesting comparison and contrast with earlier Marxian efforts to show that art is a "direct reflection of reality." Although the authors were aware of the ideological implications of this point, their interest in it herein focuses on its relevance to the validity of their inferential techniques. Nevertheless, readers with an interest in the sociology of art may find the theory of interest in itself.

2. Closely intertwined with the theory just described, but more prominent in the third and fourth sections of the article, is a novel social-systems view of the role of the mass magazine in the development and functioning of advanced industrial society, particularly in America. This "middle mass" view avoids simply taking one side or the other on the old question of whether mass media "lead" or "follow" the society in their portrayals, and the authors manage to present some unique data bearing on their more differentiated statement of this question. They conclude, in part, that the magazines were an important progressive force on many issues during the first decades of the twentieth century but that the culture at large has "caught up" with them in most respects at mid-century. However, the authors caution, there are—and were—other problems on which the polarity is reversed or on which no consistent difference over time is discernible.

3. The article presents a provocative alternative to the "elitist" view (of Dwight MacDonald, for example) that the mass media cater to the "lowest common denominator" uniting the audience. Utilizing some early results from their new content-analysis technique and comparative data on the United States population, Martel and McCall buttress a common denominator argument but are led to

---

* If this essay happens to be noticed by any professional historian, we suggest the real importance of the Martel-McCall approach for historiography.

conclude that the appeal is made rather to the highest common denominator.

But perhaps the most valuable feature of this article is that these
contributions to mass communications research are not presented as
ends in themselves but to serve as vital links in a complex web of
evidence constructed as a means of gaining further knowledge of societies and the manner in which they change and develop. If this
point is kept in mind while reading the article, the student may find
it both less taxing and more rewarding than it might otherwise appear
on first encounter.   L. A. D.

DR. MARTEL, chairman of the Department of Sociology at Arizona
State University, has done research in sociological methodology, content analysis and in problems concerning the relationships between
technology, the group structures of society and social values. He has
taught sociology at the University of Washington, State University
of Iowa, and Cornell University.

GEORGE J. MCCALL was completing his doctoral work at Harvard University at the time this article was written and is now teaching social
psychology in the sociology department of the University of Iowa at
Iowa City. There, as at Harvard previously, he offers courses in symbolic interactionism, field methods, and sociological theory.

SYNOPSIS

One of the hardest problems for the social researcher is that of obtaining information about broad social changes which work themselves out
over a period of generations. Generally speaking, the difficulties are more
acute the further into the past one seeks to go, and the more one is concerned with the ordinary patterns of life in society rather than with larger-
scale events which are more likely to become matters of public record.

This paper is a by-product of an investigation concerned with changing social roles and values in American society during the past century.
Due to the paucity of more direct sources of information, an exploratory
study was made of the possibility of using the portrayals of community
life in samples of magazine fiction stories as valid indicators of various
changes of interest. For analytic purposes, these samples were chosen from
popular magazines published in selected years since the 1880s, and many
different aspects of story portrayals were examined. In order to include
a wide range of sociological variables in the analysis and still maintain
reasonable standards of reliability, a highly structured content-analysis
procedure was developed. This necessitated the standardization of a detailed Codebook and Coding Schedule.

The objective has been to develop systematic criteria which could distinguish between the representative and unrepresentative components of story portrayals, under diverse social conditions. As a starting point, a very gross theoretical model was formulated, hypothetically stating conditions under which portrayals of actual changes would occur. The model focuses on the type of communication system in which stories are presented; the kinds of appeals made by writers and editors to the readers; and also the literary conventions of style, plot and composition governing the stories themselves. Through the analysis of points of correspondence with reality and distortion of it in the stories sampled from various periods, the attempt has been made to evaluate and improve the statement of theoretical criteria in the original model.

The present paper concentrates on the problems and rationale of the study and is divided into four main sections. The first section takes up some general considerations involved in seeking to infer social conditions from fictional portrayals and includes a brief summary of the findings of earlier studies on this subject. The second section outlines the theoretical formulation with which this investigation began. Section three summarizes the procedures adopted for sampling and analyzing stories, with mention made of some main difficulties encountered. The final section discusses findings to date on the main patterns of correspondence with reality and distortion of it in magazine story portrayals. These findings underscore the essentiality of taking adequate account of complexities of group structure and relations between groups in order better to understand the content selections of mass communication systems.

A. THE ETHNOGRAPHIC UTILITY OF FICTION DESCRIPTIONS

As indicated, the research upon which this report is based was originally undertaken to obtain information about changes in the family, work, and leisure roles of American adults during the past century before the main impetus to urban industrialization developed. We were led to consideration of magazine fiction stories as possible data sources on these role changes largely through a process of elimination, after alternative sources had been tried and found wanting. Ideally, we would have liked to have had a combination of community ethnographies and nationwide surveys, conducted at regular intervals throughout our period, which would have provided more direct information of known representativeness. However, few studies of either kind were conducted before World War II, and the available few were inadequate for our purposes. Other, more conventional, documentary sources also failed to meet our requirements in one way or another. For example, census reports and official documents provide much valuable information on the population and economy but offer little on prevailing patterns of community life. Nonfiction articles in newspapers and magazines seemed too preoccupied with the immediate, the unusual, the controversial, and the problematic—in short, with everything but the accepted practices most taken for granted during a period. We decided that we might do best to focus initially on the descriptions of contemporary social life in the more "realistic" types of fiction stories,[1] published in magazines that had maintained widespread circulation among broad readership groups over a period of many decades.

Now there are, of course, long-standing precedents for the use of fiction materials in social research. Historians often have made use of dramas and legends as data sources on the ancient Greeks or other past societies. Similarly, anthropologists studying primitive societies have drawn upon myths and folk tales for indications of cultural attitudes and values. And in recent decades social scientists have on occasion turned to popular fiction for evidence of changes in beliefs and practices in complex societies.[2] The studies closest to our present interest have focused on

1. A focal problem throughout this paper is that of *"realism"* in fiction, and the reader will encounter a number of related terms, such as "ethnographic validity," "ethnographic utility," "authenticity," "reality-correspondence," "reflection," "distortion," etc. There are two main usages here which we have tried to keep separate throughout, with something less than complete success.

The first usage (for which we have endeavored to reserve the bare terms "realism" and "realistic" in the text) is in the sense of the well-known *literary tradition* (see footnotes 8 and 9).

The second usage—our own concern with the problem—is quite restricted, falling entirely within the purview of the feasible aims and methods of the sciences. Moreover, we have limited this usage to the "social level," ignoring questions about the psychological, biological, or chemical "realism" of the stories. "The social level" we have interpreted as comprising the range of interests of sociology, social anthropology, economics, political sciences, and other fields that deal with the organizational patterns of society and the interrelations among groups. In a general way, then, our notion has been that *a fictional portrayal of society should be considered more "realistic" the more closely it approximates a complete and accurate description by the standards of the various social sciences.* This is the sense in which "ethnographic realism" and its synonyms will be employed hereafter.

2. The earliest study of this kind that we know of, which employed systematic methods of investigation, is that of Hornell Hart; reported in *Recent Social Trends,* Chap. 8, "Changing Social Attitudes and Interests" (McGraw-Hill, New York, 1933). Hart compared magazine fiction-stories with nonfiction articles for evidences of religious, family and sexual attitudes during the period from 1900 to 1930. Subsequent investigations which we have taken as background include

types of fiction that have attained popularity, rather than on single works or those of an individual author. They assume in various ways that the characteristics common to large numbers of stories that have proved popular with readership groups during an era, are likely to reflect in some way the values, aspirations, practices, frustrations, or conditions of life prevailing among the groups from which the readers were drawn.

The particular aspects of fictional works that have been taken as indicators of readership characteristics have varied considerably, as has the precise nature of the correspondence assumed. Heroes and villains have long been thought to embody, respectively, the positive and negative values of an era. Plot tensions have been regarded as expressions of widespread anxieties, with plot resolutions expressing both the hopes of a period and the optimism that these hopes will be fulfilled (e.g., the "happy ending" versus other resolutions). Time-space locales have sometimes been interpreted as reflections of interests, concerns, and attitudes toward change (emphasis on the past, for example, being taken as indicative of "traditionalism" or of a "sense of decline"). Stylistic preferences also have been explored for their sociological contents, in terms of correspondence to speech patterns of different social classes or the frankness with which various aspects of social life are discussed.[3]

Most promising for our own interests were numerous suggestions that certain ("realistic") types of fiction stories might, *in their background descriptions of community activities,* provide some fairly direct reflections of accepted social practices. And if such an assumption could be made for stories published in widely selling magazines, their use seemed to offer

---

Patrick Johns-Heine and Hans H. Gerth, "Values in Mass Periodical Fiction, 1921–1940," *Public Opinion Quarterly,* vol. 13, 1949, pp. 105–113; William O. Aydelotte, "The Detective Story as a Historical Source," *Yale Review,* vol. 39, Autumn, 1949, pp. 66–95; and H. J. Friedsam, "Bureaucrats as Heroes," *Social Forces,* vol. 32, 1954, pp. 269–274. Also highly suggestive to us, although they do not strictly deal with "popular fiction," were Leo Lowenthal's analysis of selected European novels and dramas in *Literature and the Image of Man, 1600–1900* (Beacon, Boston, 1957), and the study of religious "best sellers" from 1875 to 1955 by Louis Schneider and Sanford H. Dornbusch, *Inspirational Books in America* (U. of Chicago Press, 1958).

3. Something of the range of possible interpretations of correspondences between fictional works and societal characteristics is suggested in Max Lerner, *America As a Civilization,* Chap. 11, "Arts and Popular Culture" (Simon and Schuster, New York, 1957). For systematic discussions of more basic theoretical approaches to the relationship involved, see Milton C. Albrecht, "The Relationship of Literature and Society," *American Journal of Sociology,* vol. 59, 1954, pp. 425–36, and H. D. Duncan, *Language and Literature in Society* (U. of Chicago Press, 1953).

a number of distinctive methodological advantages over books or other fiction sources.[4]

Several considerations made it plausible to think that popular magazine fiction might have some ethnographic utility. (The term "ethnographic" is used here in its ordinary anthropological sense, to refer to descriptions of the accepted beliefs and practices of a people.)[5] To begin

4. Since publication occurs at regular intervals, items are likely to be selected with editorial cognizance of cultural attitudes during a relatively delimited period, in contrast with books, where the time period of reference is far more variable. Also, successful magazines ordinarily depend upon a *continuing* readership to a high degree (as opposed to books which may be published on an *ad hoc* basis); and editorial policy is likely to be responsive to the interests, values and sensibilities of readers. If readership patronage is successfully maintained, presumably the editorial appeals made have had some success. A further advantage is that, relatively speaking, there is a fair amount of information available on readership and editorial policy for major American magazines. While the available facts always leave much to be desired, it is possible to analyze magazine contents with some knowledge of the communication process in which they were presented, on both the readership and editorial side.

5. In seeking clarification of the requirements for adequate social description, we found it expedient to borrow from our anthropological colleagues and take as our basic model the ethnographer-observer working among the primitives. As a methodological standard, this "primitive model" had advantages for us, despite the fact that our immediate interest has been solely in complex societies that have evolved to the point of magazine fiction: one of these is worth particular emphasis.

The model pointed to an investigative situation in which *direct observation* is most often taken as a standard for valid description. Actually, even in anthropological studies of primitives, very little social research is done through direct observation of the phenomena that are described. The basic reason for this is the extraordinary time demands that such a method involves. Roughly speaking, we can say that it takes one man-hour of observation to record one man-hour of behavior, and one lifetime to record a generation. Most social research, including conventional ethnography, depends for its coverage upon the indirect testimonies of "informants" whom a social researcher may call upon through interviews, questionnaires, or historical documents.

The informant, then, is in effect deputized as a substitute observer, and the researcher's portrayal becomes dependent upon the *informant's* observational abilities and his direct access to the phenomena of interest (always subject to the researcher's critical skill in discerning the more dependable testimony from the "fiction").

Thus from the perspective of our model one could think of fiction writers as deputized informants of a specific type, to whom an ethnographer might resort in lieu of his own first-hand observations. The "stories," correspondingly, could be regarded as something like "recorded interviews" obtained from the informants. Granted that by conventional ethnographic standards these "interviews" had certain peculiarities: among them, that the informants were deputized *post hoc* and their accounts were acknowledged fictions. There also were the difficulties that the investigator could not choose his deputies, nor have any say in the questions asked

with, casual inspection of magazine stories published since the latter part of the nineteenth century showed that they often contained a good deal of ethnographically relevant material. Characters were presented in recognizable types of community settings and social situations. Portrayals of characters often included their occupation, marital status, family membership, nationality background, and other important social identities. The social relations and activities depicted covered many of the social roles that an ethnographic report on community life would contain. There were also varied indications of the values and preferential attitudes of story characters, in the statements made about their thoughts and conversations and their reactions to one another. In addition, there seemed to be a certain internal coherence to the social descriptions appearing in the more realistic stories—what might be termed a "socio-logic" in their construction. Activities of characters fitted their social statuses, at least in very general respects, and the activities themselves seemed to relate quite naturally to the scenes and situations in which they occurred.

Just as an ethnographer pieces together a portrayal of community lifeways by observing how people act in recurrent situations and listening to their conversations, it seemed possible to think of the analogous construction of a composite *"Storyville"* portrayal, based on the "case descriptions" of recurrent events in samples of stories.[6]

Of course, the mere presence of such descriptions in stories did not at all mean that they could be accepted as *valid* representations of social life. While the same may be said of ethnographies, there are certain fundamental differences between a scientific report based on observation and a work of fiction, and these differences affect the confidence one can have in their authenticity. For one thing, the *aims* of the two are not the same, although the degree of difference may vary greatly. The scientific observer is committed to present accurate descriptions while the fiction writer may have no such objective. In fact, the latter is likely to be an outright "liar," who falsifies his data to make it more interesting and describes incidents which are purely "literary inventions." Equally striking are the differences in *methods*. The ethnographer steeps himself in the milieu of the people he describes, having first (hopefully) undergone systematic training in observational procedures. The writer may be a "sensitive" person,

---

in the interviews. Most frustrating to him, he had to put up with "Editorial Chieftains" as go-betweens; and could not even intrude to probe or cross-examine the witness for clarification.

6. It seems essential, however, that even a simple-minded approach to the problem must take serious account of the structural complexity of the total society in which a publication medium operates, both as this affects the "reality" that is portrayed, and also in relation to the editorial constraints on the medium.

but he rarely has any formal methodological training and may write of situations with which he has had little or no direct familiarity. To make matters worse, while the ethnographer strives for reportorial *objectivity,* some writers are notorious for their indulgences in "subjectivity" and "bias" (from a scientific standpoint). Then too, *stylistic norms* of fiction writing leave much to be desired by scientific standards of clear reporting. The writer is likely to eschew the use of standardized terms and notation, may even deliberately cultivate linguistic ambiguities, and certainly would never use charts, tables, or footnotes. In these and other respects, fiction is likely to make very poor ethnography.[7]

7. In order to clarify our standards for gauging social realism, we asked what the requirements would be for an "ideal ethnography," which focused on the social values and more generally accepted role practices of a population. The answer in a general way seemed to hinge on four basic criteria: (1) *comprehensiveness* in describing main subgroups and patterns; (2) *discriminateness* in distinguishing major variations in patterns both among subgroups and by occasion; (3) *accuracy* in the classification of the patterns for different groups and individuals; and (4) *systematization* in tracing out the connections between elements. Conversely, it seemed one could designate four deadly "sins" of misrepresentation, which might be referred to as: (1a) *selective omission,* if something essential is left out; (2a) *stereotyping* or indiscriminateness, where characteristics are included but important distinctions are not noted; (3a) *factual errors,* or inaccurate classifications; and (4a) *distortion,* where the elements might be included correctly but their linkages are not. To a large extent it appeared that these violations of reality had a necessary order of succession. The second sin listed presupposed the first transgression to a degree; the third could be fully avoided only if the earlier temptations had been withstood; and the last perversion climaxes the earlier iniquities.

More precisely, the modes of misrepresentation stem from four logically dependent steps in the process of adequate classification and characterization of a unit. (1) "Comprehensiveness" involves the adequacy of the list of variables or property concepts used in a description. (2) "Discriminateness" is a matter of the precision of the categories of the variables, and the validity of the breaking point between them. (3) "Accuracy" is of course putting cases observed into the appropriate categories, which becomes a statistical problem cumulatively as the number of cases grows larger; and (4) "Systematization" concerns the relations ascribed between the variables or, more precisely, between their categories. To illustrate, briefly, consider a population of men and women with a list of status variables including sex, age, employment, social class, and so forth. We would have *"selective omission"* if an ethnography overlooked age or employment; *"stereotyping"* if the relevant variables were used, but in a misleading manner (e.g., the category "employed" made no distinction between full-time and part-time workers, or most people were lumped into a broad middle class); *"factual errors"* if the full- and part-time categories were used, but the workers were mixed up; and *"distortion"* if the links between sex, age, class and employment were misrepresented through omissions or commissions.

Beyond these four criteria, which are matters of elementary logic, we thought the ideal ethnography should fulfill yet another important requirement, which cuts across the preceding group. (5) It seemed of the utmost importance that the

There were, however, various kinds of evidence in *support* of the claim that *some* degree of ethnographic validity could be expected in works of fiction, including those in popular magazines. Of major importance was the development of "literary realism" in the nineteenth century as a dominant movement in fiction writing. In a general way, this movement fostered the acceptance of scientific goals as being relevant to works of fiction, particularly in their portrayals of society. The point to us was that with the realism movement, the goal of authentic social description became, to writers, publishers, and the reading public, an explicit desideratum in certain kinds of fiction writing.[8] This did not, of course, mean that other types of fiction—fantasies, whimsical episodes, or tales with conventionalized formulas involving overt distortions of ordinary life (e.g., detective stories)—were simply discontinued. What seems to have happened is that the "realistic" story and novel emerged as differentiated literary types, subject to editorial controls against sociological misrepresentations. There were numerous indications that readers took it upon themselves to do much of the "editorial controlling," by complain-

description have a sense of proportion, in reflecting the relative importance of elements in the cultural scheme of things. We thought of the exemplar ethnography as analogous to a "relief map," with high mountain ranges for the primary social values and roles, their height and breadth being commensurate to the importance of elements. The goal was to mold the contours to form a proportionate representation, and most of all not to overlook the Himalayas. The proportionality criterion seemed especially critical, since we were well aware that no ethnography can ever hope to be complete; there is always selectivity of variables (criterion 1) as is true of geographic maps. In fact, the ideal ethnography could be thought of as a composite of all conceivable maps blended into a coherent whole. We did not want to say that *any* selectivity was a perversion of realism, a position that would simultaneously throw all social scientists and cartographers out of work while abandoning ethnographic realism in literature as a hopeless cause. It still seemed reasonable, however, to ask that an incomplete, selective portrayal have some sense of proportion, and to take points away for glaring misrepresentations.

8. The broad movement toward social realism in literature very closely parallels the rise of the social sciences in its emergence, and shares many of the specific objectives of the latter. At certain points the two movements are difficult to distinguish, as in the case of the "naturalism school" associated with Émile Zola. As conceived by Zola, the novel became a special kind of sociological research report with data anecdotalized and ordered in the form of a story. It should "reflect the process of research and observation, as in a laboratory. Characters were to be conceived in accordance with psychology, sociology, and the laws of heredity. They were to be placed in an accurately constructed environment, representing a segment of time and space, and their conduct was to evolve naturally from the interaction of their personalities and environment. . . . Fancy, subjectivity, the personal eccentricity of the writer were to be excluded from the creative process." [Lillian H. Hornstein (ed.), *The Reader's Companion to World Literature* (Mentor, New York, 1960, p. 491).]

ing in no uncertain terms if a work of the realistic type falsely described an institution or locale with which they were familiar. It seemed, then, that controls on social realism operated with greatest efficacy for stories presented as of the kinds of communities in which their readers lived.

In terms of our interest in creating ethnography out of fiction, the advent of literary realism seemed auspicious. If one could assume that stories were written during a period with some concern as to their descriptive accuracy, then our task seemed more reasonable. And it appeared that this assumption holds to some degree for periodical fiction in the United States since at least the decade of the 1880s. It was then that William Dean Howells, as editor of the *Atlantic Monthly,* became the celebrated champion of the realistic movement, against "the forces of Victorian prudery and sentimentalism," as some say.[9] The movement was clearest in the fiction written for persons of high cultural status—readers at that time, for example, of expensive, elite-oriented periodicals like *Century, Harper's,* and *Scribner's,* as well as Howells' *Atlantic.* However, there were many indications that the realistic mode was also gaining currency in the more popularly oriented magazines during this period. There was, of course, no direct information about the concepts of literary realism held at that time by various classes of readers. (And in fact, as far as we know, no systematic data of this kind have *ever* been obtained for *any* readership groups.) But we had scattered evidence that many popular magazine editors were coming to *assume* a preference for fictional realism among their readers, and to guide their selections accordingly. A commitment to social realism was particularly evident among several editors of *Cosmopolitan,* the *Saturday Evening Post,* and some of the other magazines that were to become the main circulation leaders early in the present century.[10] In the words of George H. Lorimer—*Post* editor from 1897

9. The classic account of this development is Vernon L. Parrington's *The Beginning of Critical Realism in America, 1860–1920* (Harcourt, New York, 1920); especially Chap. 3, "Victorian Realism." Other references on which we have depended are Alfred Kazin's more recent work, *On Native Grounds* (Doubleday-Anchor, New York, 1957), and Wilbur L. Schramm's essay, *Realism in Contemporary American Literature: An Historical Survey* (U. of Iowa Press, Iowa City, 1952).

10. The most valuable general reference on American magazines during the nineteenth century is Frank Luther Mott's encyclopedic survey, *A History of American Magazines* (Harvard U. P., Cambridge, 1957). Four volumes have been published to date, covering the period up to 1905. Although he is not fully explicit on the point, Mott indicates in various ways that realistic fiction in the broad present sense was a recognized form in the middle-range publications by the 1880s, gradually replacing the "chocolate fudge" stories that predominated earlier. (See Vol. III, Chap. 9, and Vol. IV, Chap. 8.) Two related trends that he reports are of significance to us: (1) a growing preference for native American writers at this

to 1936, who guided it to a dominant position among popular magazines —a basic purpose of fiction was "to reflect existing manners and conditions, in short, life as it is." [11]

There were, of course, many other purposes. For popular magazine fiction, the ruling editorial purpose decidedly was one of entertainment, of stimulating a reader's interest sufficiently so that he would continue as a patron. The appeal to "interest" seemingly meant that materials were selected which in some way departed from the mundane patterns of everyday life—the very patterns which we have been seeking. Such departures seemed most likely in the "stories" *per se* (i.e., the plots, the kinds of incidents selected, the order of presentation, the emphasis given to various incidents, and the outcomes or "endings"). On the basis of our initial browsings, it appeared that the plausible realism would be found largely in the descriptions surrounding the main narrative actions of the story. In fact, it appeared that many stories in the realistic mode derived their dramatic impact precisely from the juxtaposition of a somewhat novel tale against a quite ordinary, familiar backdrop. *If so, we could think of distilling out the background components, while ignoring or trying to control for the plot variations. This was the kind of strategy we finally accepted,* but we were aware of many complications. Stories do not easily divide into "foreground" and "background." Both are often contained in the same sentences and characterizations, and with varying emphasis even in a single story. Also, we were plagued by the question of how much the selective distortions of the story plots would slant and warp the remaining contents.

Some complexities had been pointed up by previous studies of magazine fiction, in which the contents were systematically examined from a sociological viewpoint. None had explicitly distinguished stories in the realistic mode from others—a distinction we were coming to feel was of basic importance. However, one or two seemed implicitly to have some such notion in mind. The studies conducted had all indicated many strong elements of correspondence between story portrayal and social reality. However, they had also reported a variety of misrepresentations and distortions.

Most suggestive was a study by Albrecht, which systematically ex-

---

time over British and European writers who had been favored earlier; and (2) the increasing popularity of short stories as rivals to the novel and serial.

11. From a letter cited by John Tebbel in *George H. Lorimer and the Saturday Evening Post* (Doubleday, New York, 1948), p. 48. Lorimer's success in achieving this policy, incidentally, is attested to in Robert E. Park's wry comment on newspaper reporting in the 1920s: "The *Post* writes the news in the form of fiction, while the daily press frequently writes fiction in the form of news."

amined the way in which a number of widely held marital and family values were depicted in short stories from magazines appealing to different social strata. His analysis was carried out on magazine volumes for the year 1950, when a good deal of information already was available on American family values, based on community studies and opinion surveys, which could then be compared with the story portrayals. Also, surveys had been made on magazine readership so that periodicals could be selected grossly to represent known segments of the population. (The magazine sample he chose consisted of the *Atlantic* and the *New Yorker* for the "upper level," the *American* and *Saturday Evening Post* for the "middle level," with *True Confessions* and *True Story* for the "lower level.")

The family values upon which Albrecht focused were conceptualized on a highly abstract level. They included some values known to be publicly upheld throughout much of the population (e.g., "Marriage should be based on personal affection and individual choice," and "sex should be contained within wedlock"). Also included were some more controversial positions (e.g., "Marriage should be monogamous and permanent, but if mates are very unhappy, divorce is sanctioned"). The stories selected were those with relevant value content, and presumably were limited to contemporary American settings. As each story was read, instances of approval or disapproval of the predesignated value positions were recorded.

Albrecht reported overwhelming approval for those values most widely upheld throughout American society, especially in middle-level magazines. (For example, the approval percentages for the first two values mentioned were, respectively, 96 and 90 percent in the total sample. In the middle-class sample, there was complete unanimity.[12])

On a quite different ethnographic level, Berelson and Salter had analyzed the portrayals of "majority Americans" compared with portrayals of members of various ethnic and racial minorities, in representative samples of short stories in magazines for 1937 and 1943. (Their

12. Milton C. Albrecht, "Does Literature Reflect Common Values?" *American Sociological Review,* vol. 21, 1956, pp. 722–729. He concludes: "The overall quantitative evidence of our sample favors the conclusion that the cultural norms and values of the American family are strongly upheld in the short stories of wide-circulation magazines, even though they represent distinct reading levels." (p. 724.) It should be mentioned that Albrecht made separate analyses of the support shown for the selected values in main story plot themes as well as in other components. He indicates that while the "background" statements conformed to the values, the plot themes varied greatly in relation to them, with further marked differences among the three magazine levels.

magazines were drawn from the "middle" and "lower" levels.[13]) The findings indicated reality-correspondences in many aspects of the differential portrayals of majority and minority characters and in the relationships between them. The characters identified as native white Protestants, for example, had higher economic and occupational statuses than Negroes and white minorities. They monopolized the higher military ranks in the World War II stories, and both marriage and dating tended to follow ethnic lines of differentiation. There also were hints of social realities of another sort in the occasional prejudices explicitly stated by majority characters in reference to minorities, though these reportedly were infrequent. At the same time, the findings showed numerous elements of misrepresentation. Stories tended to idealize characters with majority identities, giving them a very disproportionate share of the leading roles and most favorable portrayals. By contrast, the negative characteristics of Italians, Jews, Negroes, and other minorities (where they were portrayed at all) were grossly exaggerated in a stereotypically prejudicial manner.

Other investigations had examined changes in story portrayals over a period of decades, comparing them with social trends. Here again there were evidences of broad parallels between the two, as well as many discrepancies. Hart, for example, compared the treatment of religion and sexual taboos in stories (in "middle-" and "lower-level" magazines) from the early 1930s and the beginning of the century. He reported a considerable decline in religiosity and sexual inhibitions of heroes and heroines— trends that he along with others had documented for the American population during this period.[14] Gerth and Johns-Heine examined changes in distributions of hero-statuses and locales in stories from the 1920s and 1930s, comparing a depression period with one of economic prosperity. Their magazines, selected for readership diversity, were the *Atlantic, Country Gentleman, Ladies' Home Journal,* the *Post,* and *True Story.* In accord with societal trends, they reported a decrease in heroes from business and industry, with a corresponding increase in heroes in professions and service occupations; they also report something of a shift away from urban locales in several periodicals.[15] (Interestingly, while the decline in urban settings was strongest in magazines with a predominance of

13. Bernard Berelson and Patricia J. Salter, "Majority and Minority Americans: An Analysis of Magazine Fiction," *Public Opinion Quarterly,* vol. 10, 1946, pp. 168–197. The sample included *American, Collier's, Cosmopolitan, Ladies' Home Journal, Saturday Evening Post, True Confessions, True Story,* and *Woman's Home Companion.*

14. H. Hart, *op. cit.,* especially pp. 407–408 and 419–420.

15. Johns-Heine and Gerth, *op. cit.,* Table 2.

urban readers, the reverse trend—decline in rural settings—appeared in *Country Gentleman*.) Their analysis also highlighted thematic and other differences among the various magazines and showed many changes which had little or no direct correspondence to changes in the society or among the respective readership groups.[16]

In sum, from the previous studies of magazine story contents, it seemed clear that stories often contain many valid ethnographic components and, further, that in some respects these are sensitive to broad social changes. However, it was equally clear that *no uniform correspondence could be assumed,* and that one could be seriously misled in making inferences from story portrayals to societal facts. The correspondences that had been indicated varied widely among different types of magazines, stories, and story elements.

It was evident that any serious use of fiction works for the study of social change would require development of *discriminative criteria* which would specify the conditions under which various portrayals could be accepted as more or less reliable social indicators. The findings and interpretations of previous investigators contained many suggestions as to what some of the main conditions might be. However, we were unable to find in the existing literature any fully explicit or systematic formulations of criteria such as our problem required.

Accordingly, our first research task became one of seeking more systematic criteria for uncovering what valid ethnographic needles there might be in different sorts of fictional haystacks. In effect, this has meant the development and testing out of a rudimentary theory that would discriminate and account for the differential correspondences between fictional descriptions and their societal counterparts.

B. SOME DETERMINANTS OF THE ETHNOGRAPHIC VALIDITY OF FICTION

Assuming that the degree of ethnographic realism in fiction varies greatly, our initial problem was to begin to specify the *conditions* where

16. Another suggestive study along this line was made by Inglis, comparing the changing employment statuses of *Post* heroines in romantic stories from 1901 to 1935—a period in which employment of women increased in the society. She reports a corresponding increase among the heroines, although the specific employment rates were far from identical, and the heroines had a penchant for more glamorous occupations than most members of the labor force. (Ruth A. Inglis, "An Objective Approach to the Relationship between Fiction and Society," *American Sociological Review,* vol. 3, 1938, pp. 526–531.)

it is most likely to occur. While our immediate interest was in the fiction works appearing in popular magazines, it was important that insofar as possible these conditions should be stated without restriction to the unique characteristics of American magazines in their present historical form. Such statement was necessary if we were to compare works from different historical periods, where the fiction media and their conditions of dissemination might vary widely. It was also our hope that the formulated criteria could in time be used on samples of fiction from other societies, thereby permitting comparative investigations of changes in social roles and values on a cross-societal basis.

Our theoretical strategy in approaching the question was to work from the simple to the more complex. As a first step, we tried provisionally to delimit a *class of fiction works* that seemed reasonably likely to include valid ethnographic components, at least in certain respects. To keep matters simple, the class was deliberately defined in fairly extreme and oversimplified terms, always stating the "high" values of the variables involved. It was hoped that if the class as formulated was even partly on target, the necessary corrections and refinements could be progressively discovered through a detailed comparison of stories falling *within* the formulated domain, with stories that were excluded from it.

The provisional formulation of our domain was based upon a number of suspicions (i.e., hypotheses) as to the most important determinants of the ethnographic portrayals presented in fiction stories and of the validity of these portrayals. These "determinants" seemed crucially to involve (1) the *type or "mode" of fiction* story, in terms of conventional understandings by writers and readers as to characteristics of story plots, stylistic usages, heroes and villains, etc.; and (2) the *publication medium* viewed as a process of communication between writers and their readership groups.

1. TYPES OF STORIES

Fiction stories, like any other form of conventional communication, depend for their meaning upon shared norms and expectations relating to their purposes. It seemed clear that differences in purposes or in conventionalized restrictions could greatly affect the validity of societal portrayals in numerous respects. For example, in extreme the *aim* of fiction writing might be to deliberately misrepresent certain features of society, whether for serious ideological purposes or merely to divert or entertain. Familiar instances are found in various types of detective stories, Westerns, and the like, with *stereotypic plot formulas* incorporating highly conventionalized distortions of social life that presumably are well understood by readers. To the extent that such formulas are operative, one would have to be cognizant of them to avoid being misled. A related consideration is the norms accepted concerning the *stylistic use of language* itself, which might varyingly correspond to popular usage. In general, it seemed reasonable to think that ethnographic authenticity would be greater the more the literary style was prosaic, approximating ordinary speech in the society. Alternatively, departures from the vernacular through "poetical" language, along with rhetorical or whimsical manipulations of content and context, seemed likely in and of themselves to introduce elements of social distortion.

After consideration of a number of such factors, we attempted to spell out the aspects of literary form which seemed likely to maximize the ethnographic realism of fiction. We felt that such realism should be greater in a given work, the more the following conditions hold:

(*a*) The *goal* of "ethnographic realism" is part of the definition of its purposes, as understood by writers, editors, and readers. (This, of course, does not exclude other purposes insofar as these do not contradict that of realistic description.)

(*b*) It "tells a *story*" about human characters, having recognizable *social identities* corresponding to those of the *modal group of readers* and of persons in conventional counter-roles.

(*c*) The story is presented as occurring in types of *communities* and *settings* familiar both to writers and to many readers. Ideally, the time settings are *contemporary* with the writing of the story.

(*d*) The *story-plots* do not follow *conventionalized formulas* which stereotypically require departures from actual activities familiar to the main readership groups.

(*e*) The story is presented in *prosaic language,* avoiding poetical, rhetorical, or other marked deviations from ordinary discourse.

(*f*) The main incidents are described in a *"naturalistic" context,* avoiding recognized contexts of supernaturalism, fantasy, and the like.

Even within these restrictions on literary form there is a great deal of leeway for variation in social content. Consequently, we were led to a consideration of some further determinants of ethnographic realism in fiction works—namely, the nature of the communication process in which these works are constituted, disseminated, and controlled.

2. CHARACTERISTICS OF PUBLICATION MEDIA

Let it be said at once that at no time have we ever thought of trying to predict the contents of works by an individual writer. We collected works by such a large number of writers that no individual's eccentricities could exert determining influence. This selection of works was further restricted to those published for circulation among a "mass audience"— that is, an audience not necessarily large in number, but one in which the members are territorially dispersed and most of whom do not know one another (or the writers and publishers) on a personal basis. In this sense, the works had to be presented through a "mass communication" process, subject to editorial selection, by publishers and editors aiming for patronage in any anonymous market. We further assumed that the publication medium was one of several competing media, all of which were not under the monolithic control of a single person or tightly knit ideological group, as might occur in a police state. Each of the independent media, then, operates in a competitive "free market" and has continually to appeal to its consumers if it is to win and hold their patronage.[17] Under these conditions, it was thought that *consumers* (as well as writers, editors, and publishers) would effectively exert some degree of editorial control over the contents of the medium.

One crucial fact in this connection is that in complex societies it is the rarest thing for any communication medium (or mode thereof) to

17. Our present use of the "free market" model incorporates several key ideas from the analysis of mass communications by Talcott Parsons and Winston White in "The Mass Media and the Structure of American Society" (*Journal of Social Issues,* vol. 16, no. 3, 1960, pp. 67–77). The authors present a highly generalized concept of the "market" and "market determinants," which is applied to mass-communication media and political parties as well as to economic exchanges in the more restricted sense. They argue that in a free society, all three agencies are faced with similar requirements in having to appeal successfully for diverse patronage to remain "in business" or "in office." Thus, the consumer's purchasing power is seen as analogous to the political vote, in its policy-control implications.

This might be the place to credit our main theoretical sources. The underlying model of society is derived most directly from the "social-systems approaches" of Talcott Parsons, especially in *The Social System* (Free Press, New York, 1951), and of Robin M. Williams, Jr., in *American Society* (Knopf, New York, 1960). Also in the immediate background are the works of Robert E. Park on newspapers, publics, and collective behavior (with Ernest W. Burgess) in *Introduction to the Science of Sociology* (U. of Chicago Press, 1921), and his collected articles in *Society* (Free Press, New York, 1955). More directly on mass communications, we have drawn liberally upon Raymond A. Bauer and Alice C. Bauer, "America, Mass Society and Mass Media" (*Journal of Social Issues,* vol. 16, no. 3, 1960, pp. 3–96); numerous articles in Bernard Berelson and Morris Janowitz, *Reader in Public Opinion and Communication* (Free Press, New York, 1950), Elihu Katz and Paul Lazarsfeld, *Personal Influence* (Free Press, New York, 1955), Theodore Peterson, *Magazines in the Twentieth Century* (U. of Illinois Press, 1956); much in Bernard Rosenberg and David Manning White, *Mass Culture* (Free Press, New York, 1959), and Edward Shils' essay, "Mass Society and its Culture" (*Daedalus,* vol. 89, 1960, pp. 288–314).

come anywhere near obtaining patronage from representatives of all subgroups in the society. There is *selective patronage* in numerous respects, even for the most popular media. It seemed reasonable to assume tha magazine-writers and producers, to the extent to which they were aware of selective patronage at a given time, would be *oriented primarily to their reader patrons* rather than to the population at large. And further, that their ethnographic reality controls might be expected to be strongest when fictional descriptions dealt with those characters, activities, and situations *most familiar to modal readership groups.* (Of course, the ·producers of fiction might well misperceive the true nature of their readership groups, in which case this control process would operate in an unrepresentative manner.)

Considerations of this sort sharply raised the question of just how tenuous it might be to assume that fiction in magazines (or any other medium) could be taken to reflect the lifeways even of readership groups, to say nothing of those of the larger society. The compelling fact was that *readers neither write nor edit* the stories or communication items to which they are exposed. They selectively *react,* at best, and this is always "after the fact" in the case of fiction-publication in magazines. Thus it appeared that readership control of content selections (including "reality-control") must always be indirect, and any assumption of its operation in a given case rather precarious.

Nonetheless, it seemed reasonable to believe that, under certain conditions more than others, readers (as patrons) might well be assumed to influence the content-selections of a medium. The most important of these conditions seemed to be that (1) a periodical had had a *continuing readership* that (2) had been *maintained successfully* for a period of time sufficiently long so that (3) the *success of producers in "appealing" to their readership groups* had been amply demonstrated. This did not, incidentally, seem necessarily to require a huge circulation. A merely substantial but increasing circulation among certain readership groups might show quite as well the success of appeals to the patron-groups.

Two further aspects of readership selectivity seemed important as determinants of content. First, that magazines and other communication media appeal differentially not only to societal subpopulations, but appear to make *specialized* appeals to readers in terms of *selective identities,* relating to certain of their social roles more than others. (For example, among contemporary American magazines, appeals are varyingly directed toward homemakers, hobbyists, playboys, members of occupational groups, of ethnic groups, and of political opinion segments, to mention just a few.) Thus, it seemed useful to think of any readership as a *social system* composed of individuals who share a selected set of identities and roles, but are connected only through common participation in that channel of the communication process constituted by the periodical in question. Appeals to the same concrete population, for example, could be made by involving different combinations of identities, and readership responses accordingly might be expected to vary with the identities worked. That is, Mr. X might read magazine Y as a would-be "playboy," magazine Z as a member of a particular political group, and magazine Q as an employee in a particular industry.

A second aspect of readership selectivity is the *situation* in which a periodical (or unit of another medium) is "consumed," as this factor affects the possibility of preserving the boundaries of segregative readership groups. For example, a magazine received in the home (or a daytime TV program), unless it is directed almost exclusively to adults or to children, is restricted in its contents by the fact that "mixed company" may be present in the consumption situation. As a result, material considered unfit for exposure to one or other of the groups may be omitted entirely.

These considerations, then, suggested that even a provisional treatment of the determinants of the social content of fiction had to give cognizance to the role identities in terms of which readerships are defined and patronage sought, and to the social situations in which the media contents are ordinarily available.

Finally, there were *writers, editors, and other controllers* to take into account, as the "efficient conditions" affecting content selections at a given time. No matter how much one could assume that editorial policy was oriented toward readership appeal, their direct influence on story contents through writing, selecting, and censoring could never be ignored. Both *deliberate and inadvertent* "biases" on the part of these personnel could affect the social content of the stories at various points along their trajectory from personal idea to widely read story, including the possibility of total omission from such a trajectory. At the same time it seemed reasonable to think that there are *limitations* on the extent to which the descriptions appearing in fiction stories can be deliberately manipulated.

Story descriptions say *far more,* ethnographically, than writers can keep in mind at once for conscious manipulation. Accordingly, the greatest editorial influence lies in the selection of the main story themes and a limited number of characteristics of the activities and characters described. Moreover, there was reason to believe that stories are much less subject to editorial manipulation in these respects than is *nonfiction*.

On the other hand, we had many indications of specific ways in which fiction *is* manipulated and censored. As an example at the level of explicit policy, Lorimer of the *Post* held to one iron-clad rule, that "there must never be an off-color situation, an indecent word or suggestion in a *Satur-*

day Evening Post story. The rule was broken twice." [18] Similarly, the decline in the number of business heroes in the wake of the depression was partly the result of a shift in explicit editorial policy, and even today writers inclined to focus on more mature characters are instructed to concentrate on the problems of young adults. At a less deliberate level, the magazine writer attempting to create a more or less believable story is usually confined to elements within the accidental limits of his own experience (and knowledge).

These, then, were some of the main aspects of the communication process which we regarded as affecting the content selection and ethnographic validity of magazine stories. More specifically, we felt that the prospects of finding some amount of ethnographically valid content in stories (which conform to the literary conventions of realism, as discussed above) should be greater to the extent that the following conditions hold:

(*a*) The stories appear in publications having a *continuing, core readership* at a given time.

(*b*) Readership *patronage* is sought in a *free market,* where the reader's patronage of the publication is not officially required on the basis of his membership in political, religious, ethnic, or other groups to which he belongs (as opposed to official publications of groups which involve a "captive audience" and whose editorial policy may be less subject to readership sanctions). In the free-market case, readership sanctions are expressed most centrally through voluntary patronage, which can be terminated at any time.

(*c*) The publication has been in existence *long enough for readership patronage* to be expressed.

(*d*) The *contents of the publication* are consciously edited in an attempt to *"appeal"* to selective readership groups and to maintain their patronage.

(*e*) These *appeals* are made to readers in terms of a varied set of their *roles and identities,* including certain of their *primary community roles* (e.g., family member, worker, etc.). Where appeals are made in terms of highly segmental roles, validity can be assumed only *within the limits of those roles* (for instance, if the main appeal is to the identity of "political intellectual," stories are likely to be slanted accordingly).

(*f*) *Readership groups* express *specific sanctions* toward content elements by means more informative than simple patronage, such as letters to the editor, etc.

18. Tebbel, *op. cit.,* p. 47.

(*g*) *Non-readership groups* (such as the state) do *not* exert substantial influence on story contents, directly or indirectly.

(*h*) *The situations of consumption* do not require that the contents be edited with an eye toward persons outside the main readership group who might nonetheless be exposed to them (e.g., children in the home).

(*i*) *The writers and editors* have social backgrounds similar to those of the modal readers and are familiar with their culture patterns.

Clearly the two sets of favorable conditions stated in this section greatly restrict the range of fiction stories regarded as likely to have some degree of ethnographic authenticity. It is doubtful that one could ever find a large class of stories which met all these criteria simultaneously. Our intention was not to rule out the use of all other materials for ethnographic content analysis, but to call critical attention to certain factors which are likely to produce more or less *generalized* social distortions in fiction stories. However, these factors do not in themselves specify which elements *within* realistic stories can be taken as having ethnographic validity. Such specification was one of the main problems for our empirical research, and we shall turn to some preliminary results on the question in the concluding section, after indicating something of our research methods in the next few pages.

C. SAMPLING MAGAZINE STORIES AND CONTENT-ANALYSIS PROCEDURES[19]

Research is a chain of compromises—sometimes between conflicting methodological ideals, but more often between such ideals and human practicalities. Given the inevitable limitations of time and resources, the fundamental compromise at every step is between *intensity* and *extensity* of investment. This dilemma applies to every aspect of investigation, including the number and diversity of cases one can sample, the range of variable characteristics considered for each case, and the thoroughness with which each characteristic is examined. The larger the number of cases, the less attention one can pay to each (and, unfortunately, *vice versa*).[20]

19. Technical aspects of the method problem will be treated more fully in subsequent articles. The emphasis throughout this paper is on the overall rationale *behind* the method rather than on particular details.

20. This dilemma becomes particularly acute when, as in the present study, standardized methods for dealing with one's variables have not yet been developed. One then has to decide how much to invest in the development and per-

In the present investigation, having decided to try our luck with realistic stories in popular magazines, we were faced with three preliminary sets of decisions.

(1) There was the problem of *which magazines to select,* in terms of the criteria favorable to realism as mentioned in the preceding section. Ideally we would have liked to include magazines appealing to many different readership groups, and going back as far as "realistic" stories were contained and the minimum information existed on conditions of publication. It also was important that magazine samples for different periods be as comparable as possible in various respects.

(2) Related was the problem of *selecting stories* within sampled magazines—a question again both of numbers and range. Our central interest was in stories in the realistic mode presented in contemporary American settings familiar to their readers and writers. However, we also were interested in types of stories which departed in various respects from the ideal conditions of our model, and wanted to systematically compare the societal portrayals in different types of stories.

(3) Our third problem was the *range of variable components* of social portrayals to be included in the analysis of each story, and the thoroughness of the examination. Our dilemmas here were heightened by the complexity of our original research problem. We wanted to include, for each period examined, many different aspects of the family, work, and leisure roles defined. For example, we wanted information about the activities carried out together by family members, and their obligations to one another; about authority relations between husbands and wives in different matters; about whether careers were favored for women in various circumstances (and, if so, what kinds were preferred); about the importance given to a man's occupational success (and how "success" was conceived); and about whether various types of leisure pursuits were carried out within the family or neighborhood. It was our conviction, moreover, that the significance of role patterns of these kinds could not be understood adequately without considering the *relations* between them and their relative importance. (That to understand career patterns for women, for example, one has to know the priorities given to careers compared with marriage or parenthood.)

Concretely, then, our dilemma was that the more different role patterns we included in our examination of each story, the more we would have to limit the number and range of our sampled stories and

---

fection of methods, always a relative matter anyway. Obviously, the investment must be sufficient to ensure some minimum degree of dependability, but if all one's resources are spent on method development, one may never reach even provisional answers to the substantive questions with which one began.

magazines. There was the further problem that the larger the number of role characteristics included, the more difficult it would be to maintain adequate standards of comparability in analyzing different stories from diverse historical periods.

The line of compromise we adopted gave highest priority to the range of social roles and values. As a result, we have been forced to severely limit the extensity of our samples of magazines and stories, as well as the number of time-periods from which the samples were drawn. Also as a result, we were led to invest a great deal of offort into the development of standardized methods for analysis of stories, so as to maintain reasonable standards of comparability while taking account of a very large number of variables.

SAMPLING MAGAZINES AND STORIES

Prime Magazine Sample. Our most intensive analysis has been limited to magazine stories published during three selected years, falling approximately at the beginning, the end, and the midpoint of our period. (These stories are referred to as our "Prime Sample," and the specific years chosen are 1890, 1925, and 1955.) The specification of these times was of course determined by the availability of periodicals with fiction stories in the realistic mode, where some minimum of information was available on circulation, editorial policy, and conditions of publication. Also, we decided initially to eliminate volumes published during periods of national military or economic crises, since our interest was mainly in the more stable patterns of community life, and we had problems enough without taking on the added complexities entailed. (In a supplementary sample subjected to much less intensive analysis, some comparisons with crisis years have been made as indicated below.)

Specific magazines chosen were limited initially to those that had maintained at least a fairly broad circulation among "middle-class" readers, with some minimum of editorial comparability throughout the period concerning selections of fictional items. Also, in keeping with our theoretical criteria previously mentioned, we sought magazines appealing to their readers in terms of a fairly wide range of basic roles and identities, and with as much editorial diversity as possible to minimize the impact of particular editors, publishers, or readership appeals.

While it proved impossible to find periodicals that did not depart significantly from our ideal criteria, there appeared to be four magazines which did least violence to them over the period defined. The four which we finally selected were *American, Cosmopolitan, Ladies' Home Journal* and *Saturday Evening Post.* Of all American periodicals with middle-

class, "general interest" appeal, these appear to be the group that maintained the broadest circulation over the longest period of time with goodly
numbers of realistic stories before the year 1890.[21]

21. Our study approximately spans the period of ascendency and dominance
of the general-interest, popular magazine as a national communication medium in
the United States. There were of course numerous periodicals from the colonial
period on. Newspapers were already thriving in several burgeoning cities along
the Atlantic coast, and a few literary magazines like *Atlantic, Harper's* and *Scribner's* had gained dependable followings among a comparatively small, elite readership, concentrated mostly in the Northeast. Other types of magazines were
published for church groups, farmers, political dissenters, as well as other subpopulations. But the more successful publications had quite limited circulation
by present-day standards (before 1885, to sell 100,000 copies was considered spectacular), and most circulation leaders seem to have succeeded by appealing to
distinctive "minorities."

It was during the 1880s that the era of the popular magazine began. While
many of the social and economic forces involved are not well understood, several
major factors clearly played an essential role. Among these, the spread of the
railroads across the continent, the lowering in 1879 of postal rates for periodicals,
and a series of radical advances in techniques for inexpensive mass printing (including low-cost reproduction of photographs and illustrations) were of major
importance. Equally important was the rising standard of literacy among the population through the public high school, coinciding with the advent of large-scale
production of clothing, pharmaceuticals, household goods and other commodities
manufactured for a national market. Education created an expanding market for
literature at the same time that industry was seeking nationwide advertising media
that would reach the largest number who could afford the new products. Under
these conditions, some enterprising publishers saw the potentiality for a new type
of inexpensive magazine that could be financed through advertising revenue if only
sufficiently large circulation could be attained.

Of a number who tried, very few succeeded, and no single magazine reached
a circulation of a million before 1900. However, those that became the largest
"sellers" of the first third of the twentieth century were almost all in contention
with rapidly expanding sales by the 1890s. Cyrus Curtis is frequently credited with
setting the pattern for the emerging industry. His *Ladies' Home Journal* (founded
in 1886 and first edited by his wife) was selling a half-million copies by 1890 and
showed remarkable growth in succeeding decades. In 1897 Curtis took over the
Saturday Evening Post, a magazine founded in the 1820s but floundering at the
time, and made it the largest selling man's magazine within a few years. *Cosmopolitan* began publication in the 1890s under publisher-editor Edwin Walker.
While its sales have been considerably less than the two Curtis giants during most
of our period, it had reached the half-million mark by 1905 when William Ran-
dolph Hearst purchased it and built it up much further. Somewhere in-between
was *Frank Leslie's Monthly* (predecessor to the *American,* as it was renamed in
1905 after a change in ownership), which also began to reach out for a circulation
of hundreds of thousands during this time. Its main impetus, however, was to
come after 1911 when its ownership was assumed by the Crowell-Collier Company,
which also was then publishing *Collier's* and the *Woman's Home Companion.*
These were the leading national magazines in the general-interest category that

Within the sampled magazines, we limited our selections to short-stories (i.e., omitting novels and serials) that could be considered "realistic" in the present sense, where the main incidents described were presented in American settings contemporary to their time. Thus, to begin with we eliminated all stories set in other times and places; those that clearly were expressed as whimsy, fantasy, or in supernatural contexts; and also those that were written to certain stereotypic plot formulas with well-understood sociological distortions (e.g., detective stories, Westerns, and the like). It must be said that we found a number of stories that were not excluded by these criteria, which still seemed of doubtful acceptability by realistic standards. In order to avoid imposing our own biases on the selection of our sample, we held to the rule of *including* all marginal cases that were not eliminated by our explicit definition of realistic fiction.

The first ten realistic stories in each sampled volume were selected for our most detailed analysis, giving us a total of forty stories per sample year. The numbers of stories were of course decided in terms of statistical requirements for the analysis we had planned, and represented the smallest sample defensible for our purposes.

A Supplementary "Student Sample." Partly to overcome various limitations of our Prime Sample, a second and considerably larger sample of stories was analyzed with the help of an advanced sociology class. This *Student Sample* was intended to include all the volumes from our first sample, but differed in that it also contained: (1) four additional volume years (1905; 1917; 1937; and 1943), including periods of military and economic crisis; and (2) selections of "nonrealistic" stories that were excluded from the first sample, which still described contemporaneous American communities. The analyses were carried out as part of a course assignment, with pairs of students assigned to each magazine volume so that their story selections and analyses coulld be compared. Since it was not possible to provide the students with the training required for use of our detailed methods of content-analysis, a "short-cut" analysis procedure was devised for their assignment that was restricted to a small number of the variables included in the Prime Sample. As a result, it has only been possible to use the Student Sample findings in a supplementary manner.[22]

were gaining popularity before the present century began, were still being published in the 1950s and published significant amounts of fiction throughout the period. (See Mott, *op. cit.,* for further details.)

22. The Student Sample was limited to *American, Ladies' Home Journal,* and *Saturday Evening Post.* The fourth magazine (*Cosmopolitan*) was eliminated. Within each sampled volume (i.e., from years 1890, 1905, 1917, 1925, 1937, 1943, and 1955) the first ten realistic stories with contemporary American settings were selected for analysis, the same as in our Prime Sample. In addition, the first five stories excluded from the previous category also were included in this sample.

ETHNOGRAPHIC CONTENT-ANALYSIS OF FICTION

For the stories included in our Prime Sample, our core analysis consisted of character-by-character examination of the major roles and relationships described (for each character in his relations with each of the others). Perhaps the distinctiveness of this kind of approach may best be understood by contrasting it with the ordinary way in which most of us "read" a work of fiction, where emphasis is placed on the plot sequence or "story." By contrast, our analysis led us for the most part to ignore the narrative sequence in a story, and the varying dramatic emphasis placed by the author on the incidents described. Instead, our attention was focused on the background descriptions of the relations between characters and some more general portrayals of community life—regardless of the emphasis these may have received. Another contrast is that, in so far as possible, we attempted to classify the role definitions and values attributed *to the characters,* disregarding the explicit evaluations occasionally presented by the writers (speaking for themselves) as well as the favorability with which the writers portrayed their various characters. Thus, it might be said that the "heroes" and "villains" were given "equal votes" in our Storyville survey, with our main concern directed toward the evaluations they placed on one another.[23]

The large number of variables that we attempted to include created difficulties. For example, the information we sought from each story included numerous characteristics of the communities portrayed; a good

---

The students were not informed of the stories we had selected from these volumes, so that difficulties in deciding which stories were "realistic" could be uncovered. It might be said that, despite very limited instruction on this point, an overall agreement of better than 85 percent was realized in this sample.

23. There are of course many difficulties in taking this position. Obviously, stories are the creations of their writers, and the evaluations made by characters of one another may be indirect expressions of those of writers. We might, then, think of characters as being like "puppets" on a stage, at all times manipulated by their masters. The problem, however, is far more complex where literary works of fiction are considered under the conditions outlined in the second section, above. If "realistic fiction" has any social meaning in the sense that has been suggested, the author is partly constrained by the conceptions of readers and editors to portray relations in a manner that fits "naturally" into the context presented. Within this fictional mode, there is then frequently a considerable difference between the values expressed from the standpoint of various characters and those attributable to the writers, although the distinction, to be sure, is often blurred. Perhaps it should be said that a supplementary analysis has been made of various components of story plots in different sample years, and the results have been compared with those of the ethnographic analysis.

many status descriptions for each story character; and (actually) hundreds of different classifications of the family, work and leisure orientations attributed to each character in each of his social relations. A single story might of course only describe a limited number of the characteristics on our list, but it was important to check whether or not each one was described. This was necessary if we were to be reasonably sure that a characteristic was *absent* from a given story.

With so many variables, it became a difficult task merely to keep all the relevant characteristics in mind while reading the statements in a story bearing on each story character or relationship. The further problem was of course to maintain comparable standards of classification from one story to the next, and to do so by objective criteria which any other researcher could apply for himself. The complexity of our analytic task led us to invest a great deal of effort into developing a standardized procedure that would insure at least minimum comparability throughout our classifications. Our efforts in this respect might well be compared with those of a psychological tester, seeking to develop a standardized "test" procedure which could be used with reasonable consistency on many different cases.

The standardization of our approach required, to begin with, the development of a Codebook containing: (1) the theoretical definitions of each of our variables and its categories; (2) explicit definitions of the *units* in the stories to which the varibles applied; (3) the *sequential order* in which each classification judgment was to be made; (4) the kinds of statements in the stories on which the various classifications were to be based; and (5) the *more general conditions* under which the story reading and classifications were to be carried out. Like any other type of rational analysis procedure, the problem basically required taking what was at the outset a vague complexity and breaking it down into explicitly indicated sequences of parts.

Our Codebook has been developed and revised over a period of years, and still is under revision. We found, however, that by the end of the first year we had worked out a preliminary version that permitted us to analyze story portrayals in terms of several hundred variables per character with substantial agreement in our separate classifications. (Copies of this Codebook dated February 1960 are available on request to the senior author at Arizona State University.) This version has proved quite workable in permitting us to analyze the stories in our Prime Sample, taking into account considerably greater complexities of portrayal than has been attempted in previous studies of a comparable sort.

In order to apply the analysis procedure outlined in our Codebook, it further was necessary to devise a Coding Schedule (or booklet), in which the classifications made for each story could be recorded in an orderly manner. The complexity of our analysis problem again intruded to make this task far more difficult than is usually true; and it was not until a satisfactory format and code had been worked out that our method became fully operational.[24]

Armed with these paraphernalia, perhaps reminiscent more of survey research than the traditional content-analysis of fiction, we proceeded to the task of analyzing the 120 stories in the Prime Sample that has been described. The application of our method remains tedious. For example, a full workday is required on the average for the basic analysis of a single magazine story of ordinary length. However, the results from our labors to date have amply rewarded us for the time invested. Perhaps the most compelling reward has been the acquisition of a number of findings on multivariate complexities in story portrayals, that simply were "invisible" to us through "reading" of the stories. These only came to light after our microscopic analysis of each story had been completed, and the results were collated for the various sample years.

D. REALITY–ORIENTATIONS AND DISTORTIONS IN STORYVILLE PORTRAYALS

After the selected stories had been read and analyzed, following the procedures that have been indicated, statistical summaries were made of various portrayal features for each sampled magazine and year. For ease of reference, we will refer to the summary descriptions emerging from a given sample as the "Storyville portrayals" for that sample. It should be noted that these portrayals represent statistically reconstituted profiles, obtained by assembling the separate classifications made and recorded while reading the individual stories. While in all cases the profiles are based upon the actual statements appearing (or not appearing) in the stories, one cannot simply equate the Storyville portrayals with the "pic-

24. The schedule booklet developed consists of 13 pages of blank tables, with horizontal rows assigned to characters. Each page is used for a different set of variables that is listed across the top (i.e., as "column headings"), and listed moreover in the order in which the corresponding classifications are to be made. Each story character is assigned the same row throughout the booklet (a process made easier by extending a "flier" from the last page of the booklet, on which the name of a character occupying a given row is entered). Thus by reading through the booklet on a given row one can obtain the profile of a given character, or by glancing down a column on a particular page one can see how a variable distributes among the characters in a story. The Schedule has been precoded for IBM processing, and has proved quite usable for transcription to cards or tape. (Again, copies are available on request to the senior author at Arizona State University.)

tures" of social life that a reader of the stories would obtain in practice. One reason for the partial discrepancy is that many of our classifications give equal weight to any statement relevant to a given variable of interest, regardless of the dramatic prominence the statement might have received in the narrative story. Another reason, as mentioned before, is that our approach focused upon the activities and values attributed to the characters in the stories, largely disregarding the writers' evaluations of them —something to which a reader ordinarily would be highly sensitive.[25] In

25. It might be said that the "ethnographic content analysis" approach that was adopted, which sought to extract background descriptions from the stories, treated the dramatic prominence of a portrayal as a "random variable." A relevant description was given the same attention whether it was part of the mainstream of events in the narrative or merely an incidental part of the "setting." At the same time, several attempts were made to take account systematically of prominence variations, in order to appraise their bearing upon the validity of the story descriptions. This was done in different ways for different types of variables. For example, the prominence given to various social statuses was controlled for, indirectly, by recording the dramatic importance of the characters to which various statuses were ascribed. (Characters were grouped into three main *prominence categories*—"Stars," "Supporting Players," and "Bit Players"—based upon their overall importance in the narrative. The categories were formulated with meanings analogous to those in discussions of motion pictures or the theatre, with marginal cases rounded to the higher category.) Thus, it has been possible to examine the relative prominence, say, of "widowhood" compared with "being married" or "divorced" by looking at the incidence of these respective statuses among the principals, the bit players, etc., as shown partly in Tables 2 and 3. The dramatic favorability with which various statuses and other characteristics were treated also was examined in a similar way, by ratings made of the characters. This procedure is of course far less satisfactory than the more refined approach of separately rating each characteristic for dramatic importance or favorability. (Sociologists will recognize the familiar difficulties of "ecological correlations" in our method of handling status prominences by ratings of characters.) More direct ratings of prominence were made for some of our variables concerned with role-activities, but we failed to carry out these ratings systematically for many variables in our list. As a result, we have only partially been able to weigh the Storyville portrayals to correspond more closely to the emphases in the stories.

A more basic reason for the discrepancy between the composite portrayals and the story contents arises from the emphasis we placed upon standardization of the theoretical definitions of our variables. What this meant is that for the most part, the classifications recorded for the stories were made in terms of *our* theoretical categories rather than those of the writers, and our categories varied greatly in their correspondence to those found in the stories.

The same kind of gap is found, for example, if an interviewer uses a standardized set of question-responses, and seeks to place the responses to his questions into a preformulated set of categories. Partly as a check on the validity of our structured classifications, several attempts have been made to check our categorizations against the explicit statements made in the stories, recorded approximately in the writers' words. This kind of consistency check might be compared with the

order to make the correspondence between the Storyville portrayals and the readers' "pictures" a precise one, it would be necessary to weigh the profile features proportionally to their dramatic emphasis and treatment in the context of the stories. This is only partially done in the discussion that follows.

Our analysis of reality orientations and distortions in the Storyville portrayals was framed in terms of our model of an "ideal ethnography" which has been discussed above. Thus, we thought of the story portrayals as materials that an ethnographer might use in seeking to describe the values, role patterns or other social characteristics of the American population or its subgroups at various times. Assuming that he composed his ethnography solely on the basis of these materials, and interpreted them at "face value" as comprehensive, discriminate, and accurate accounts, we asked how far and in what ways his ethnographic account would be selectively incomplete or misleading. More specifically, our aim was to isolate main patterns of distortion in the portrayals by comparing the story descriptions with corresponding facts of social life as documented by other sources.[26] Beyond this, the attempt has been made to clarify the

---

use of "open-ended questions" in survey research, where the open responses are weighed against the more structured classifications.

26. Our analysis has been handicapped by a special form of the "dark alley versus the lamppost" dilemma. (The reader will recall the tale of the inebriated gent who lost his wallet in a dark alley, but was found searching for it near a corner lamppost because "it was lighter there!") In keeping with our original longitudinal interest in studying changing social roles and values, we wanted to check the accuracy of the relevant Storyville descriptions in our sampled volumes. The difficulty has been the lack of comparative sources with adequate validity, particularly for the earlier years of the period. This, as was mentioned, was precisely the reason for our interest in magazine fiction sources in the first place.

Finding no simple way to overcome this validational dilemma, we have resorted to a double-barrel strategy. Over one barrel we have followed the "lamppost strategy" of making comparisons for those variables and years where reliable comparative information exists. This has meant, for example, giving particular emphasis to status characteristics of our Storyville populations which could be compared with Census or other official reports from 1890 on (e.g., age, sex, educational, occupational, and residence characteristics). On the "dark alley" side, we have tried to check the social role and value portrayals of greatest interest against a variety of data sources and expert judgments, where often the sources compared are no more dependable as indicators than the story descriptions themselves. Each set of comparisons has basic limitations then, and even taken together they fall considerably short of the standards one would prefer.

Lacking direct validations of portrayals at the most crucial places, we have turned to an "inductive" strategy, seeking to develop *generalizable criteria* of portrayal validity which could be applied during historical periods where no specific comparative sources are available. This was, of course, the motivation behind the development of the provisional theoretical model discussed in the second section

more *generalizable determinants* of portrayal validity by examining the relationships between distortion patterns and the conditions of publication and dissemination of the magazines during various sample years. Our hope has been to specify determinants which could *explain* the patterns of distortion evidenced in our samples, and which could also be extended to *predict* the more or less valid components of entirely new fiction samples. It must be said at once that our comparative analysis is still far from complete, and that our findings to date do not begin to provide explanatory or predictive criteria of this kind in a very precise sense. There are, however, several promising leads as to the directions from which such criteria may in time be had.

What follows is a "sampler" of our comparative findings, selected so as to (1) illustrate something of the complexity of the problem of disentangling the valid from the invalid strands in Storyville portrayals, and also (2) highlight some of the main generalizations emerging from the analysis. These generalizations especially point to the importance of the selective composition of the magazine readership at various periods, and of the specialized "appeals" directed toward the population subgroups from which the majority of readers were drawn, as determinants of content selections in the stories. Perhaps the most general conclusion suggested is that *the stories must be viewed as differentiating modes of communications within the society, addressed to certain "in-groups" to the relative exclusion of other "out-groups,"* if the selective validity of their social portrayals is to be made comprehensible. These Storyville in-groups correspond very closely to the changing composition of the readership during the period, although the relationship indicated is very complex and differs for different types of story contents. In order to examine some of the detailed findings bearing on this relationship, some characteristics of the magazine readers will have to be mentioned.

of this paper, which tentatively specified some characteristics (of fiction stories and communication media) that might affect the validity of ethnographic portrayals in general. Starting with samples of magazines and stories selected in terms of the criteria from the model, our Storyville analysis was designed to clarify further the *kinds of story portrayals* that are more or less valid.

MAGAZINE READERSHIP CHARACTERISTICS [27]

If the readership of our four magazines is taken together and compared with the American population from the 1880s on, it is clear that a broad cross-sectioning of the population is represented throughout the period. The readers include men and women at all stages of adult life, drawn from many different occupations, income and education levels, religious and ethnic backgrounds, political viewpoints, geographic regions, and types of communities. In these respects, there is much internal diversity.

At the same time, viewed externally, it is equally clear that the readers are far from constituting a representative sample of the American population. Many sizable subgroups are virtually excluded or greatly underrepresented, with some important changes occurring in these during the period of interest. To begin with, the readership throughout is restricted to the literate, "English reading" segments of the population, a restriction that excludes the most recently arrived immigrants along with older subgroups that were not Americanized in this sense. While we do not have specific information on the point, there can be little doubt that in the early decades the readers were mainly native whites of North European extraction who were Protestant in their religious affiliation. As the period unfolds, the readership undoubtedly becomes increasingly diverse in its ethnic and religious makeup, with Catholics and Jews whose forefathers came from other parts of Europe more frequently represented as their proportions in the Americanized population grow larger.

Ethnic factors are by no means the only important criteria of readership selectivity. Within the changing white, Americanized core, the magazine readers are disproportionately from the "middle-class" adult group, somewhat more highly urbanized than the overall population, and also somewhat above the national averages in schooling, income and social standing. Disproportionately few seem to have been drawn from rural fundamentalist sects, urban nonconformists, intellectuals, and the very

27. Our estimates of readership characteristics have been based upon a variety of sources. Actually, we have only been able to obtain specific information about the readers of the specific sample magazines for the last of our sample years (1955). Data for this year were provided to us by Daniel Starch and Associates of Mamaroneck, N.Y., one of the oldest commercial research organizations concerned with mass communications; these data were based on two nationwide interview surveys. Estimates for earlier years have been based upon published readership surveys for the period since the 1930s (e.g., they give information about readers of *groups* of periodicals but are not broken down by specific magazines), and upon circulation figures and expert judgments for the earlier period.

poor. In the earliest years, it further appears that readers were unduly concentrated in the larger cities along the Eastern seaboard and were relatively higher in income and education compared with the averages than is true later on. As the period unfolds, it seems a fair surmise that the readership came to resemble the general population more closely in these respects, as it does in its ethnic and religious makeup. One point to see is that the growing representativeness in the former respects is as much the result of changes in the population as in the readership. That is, if we will not be misunderstood, we might say that the population comes to resemble the readership over the period more and more as general educational and economic standards and urban concentrations increase. While the readers also seem to have gained in these respects, speaking in "absolute" terms, their relative advantage seems to decline fairly steadily.

One final characteristic needing mention is that women seem to have constituted the majority of the magazine readers during all sample years, and this seems particularly true of *fiction* readers.[28] The magazines differ in their relative patronage by men and women and have changed in this respect during the period covered. The *American* and *Cosmopolitan,* for example, seem to have had their earliest success as family magazines read by men and women, but became increasingly oriented to the woman reader from the 1920s on. In contrast, the *Post* seems to have undergone something of a cycle since the 1880s. First published as a family magazine, it was reorganized in 1897 as a man's periodical and continued in this way for two decades or so. During the 1920s it was reconverted to its original status, apparently because the publishers discovered a growing popularity with women. Throughout these vacillations in the overall appeal to the sexes by the magazines, it appears that women have been the main fiction consumers (with the exception of the *Post* during its masculine era), and that editors have been aware of this fact and guided their selections accordingly. There are in fact many indications that fiction reading as such has been defined as a rather feminine preoccupation by

28. One major gap in our data, for all sample years, has been the unavailability of information specifically dealing with fiction readership for our sampled magazines. From various sources it appears that fiction in our magazines has been written primarily for women since the decade of the 1930s at least. There also are suggestions that this has been true to some degree throughout our entire period (and there is of course little doubt concerning *Ladies' Home Journal*). However, we have many indications that *Cosmopolitan* and the *Post* attempted to balance their fictional appeals between both sexes in the earlier decades, perhaps on the partly mistaken assumption that this could successfully be done. If this can be assumed, then from the standpoint of the "conceived" audiences of fiction for our four magazines taken together, it appears that women have become a more prominent reference group as the period progresses.

Americans since colonial times, to be engaged in by men only under special conditions and to a more limited degree. While certain types of fiction have of course been produced strictly for male consumption, it often appears that stories of this type are strenuously constructed to emphasize the "hair on their chests," and therefore their appropriateness for the masculine reader.

STORYVILLE MISREPRESENTATIONS AND READERSHIP SELECTIVITY

In a great many respects the patterns of misrepresentation and distortion in Storyville portrayals of American life seem to reflect the selective composition of the magazine readership. The relationship involved is exceedingly complex, and so far we have been unable to formulate a strong enough hypothesis to eliminate all the loose ends. In bold outline, however, it appears that *the stories are pervasively slanted so as to overemphasize those characteristics of the readers that are common to them as a group.* More specifically, a two-sided relationship is indicated between portrayal distortions and readership selectivity.

1. The stories tend to greatly overrepresent those identities, understandings, values and interests most widely common to various readership subgroups. Correlatively, they tend selectively to avoid reference to sources of contention, division, and cleavage between readership subgroups.
2. A further tendency is to overemphasize those characteristics which most differentiate the readership from the remainder of the population, in a manner that enhances the relative position of the readers.

In both respects it might be said the tendency is to accentuate the boundaries of a readership "in-group" by emphasis upon common characteristics at the expense of differences and also by emphasis upon characteristics which set the readers apart from various "outgroups" in the population. The first part is the "common denominator" emphasis that has often been noted for popular magazines as well as other mass-communication media aimed at heterogeneous audiences. *The more distinctive point to emerge from our analysis is the second part—that there also are "out-group differentiations" in the portrayal distortions, and that the two sides of the boundary-delineation process must be viewed in their interrelations.*

There is a related complication in certain instances where a "common characteristicism" does seem to be indicated, contrary to the charges of some who indiscriminately have attacked such a tendency in the mass media. It does *not* uniformly appear that the stories appeal to a *lowest* common denominator or anything of the sort. At some points, in fact, the tendency seems much closer to seeking a highest point of commonality.

Emphasis on Common Experience. Most fundamental as a restriction on the representativeness of the Storyville portrayals of American social life is the confinement of the stories overwhelmingly to events and symbolic expressions familiar to the largest number of readers. While our evidence in support of this contention is highly indirect, in several broad but compelling respects the case is almost indisputable. The restriction to the familiar is shown in the first place by the language usages in the stories. Apart from the invariable limitations that all of the sampled stories are written in English—a factor that can all too readily be taken for granted because of its familiarity, leading us to ignore the many biases thereby represented (e.g., in portrayals of non-English-speaking subgroups)—the story descriptions of characters and social events make little use of the richness of the language.

For the most part, the kind of English used is that of the urban American adult: one with some education but decidedly less than the "highly educated" people of his time. If we ignore some of the specifically literary conventions that the language exhibits (commented upon much earlier), it further appears that the story descriptions most often are expressed in language of the sort used with strangers rather than close acquaintances, when "mixed company" is present. (While there are, to be sure, some uses made of variable ethnic, occupational and other "dialects," especially in depictions of conversations and thoughts of the characters, these are far less evident than the roles and statuses of the characters would suggest.)

The emphasis upon language usages within the narrow range that has been suggested is one of the clearest examples we have of common characteristic emphasis in the stories, corresponding to the broader commonalities of the readership group. On the whole, the subgroup usages receiving selective emphasis seem fairly well chosen to fit the range with which most readers would have been comfortably familiar. While the selected modes of expression may, therefore, be fairly reliable for describing characters resembling the more typical magazine readers, and especially for descriptions within the kinds of situations where the language resembles the appropriate speech, these modes in and of themselves are likely to produce distortions to the extent either of these two conditions do not hold. Applied to characters with statuses excluded from the readership circle, for example, the likelihood is that the descriptions would represent in-group stereotypes of the respective outsiders, far more lacking in authenticity than comparable in-group portrayals. Similarly, we well might expect the language modes to be more adequate for the description of relations between "relative strangers" than between more intimate associates—an important possibility since the stories devote much attention to the latter and fairly little to the former. Where relations between parents and children or spouses are described in such a mode, one might reasonably ask if the descriptions might not provide more valid indications of the way in which these personal relations would be *discussed among relative strangers* rather than how they are defined or enacted by the intimates themselves. If this conjecture is reasonable—and we suspect that it is—then the relevant Storyville portrayals would have to be partly discounted as indices of the kinds of social events seemingly described, although they still could provide useful ethnographic data within the narrowed range of their validity.

Table 1—Proportionate Emphasis on Fiction in Selected Magazine Volumes (1890–1955), with Time-Place Locales of Short Stories, Percentages by Year *

Fiction, Locales	1890	1905	1917	1925	1937	1943	1955
Nonfiction items	77	62	69	67	58	62	65
Fiction items	23	38	31	33	42	38	35
Short stories	15	25	24	26	21	16	16
(Percent Distribution of Short-story Locales)							
United States Locale	65	77	84	83	81	70	91
Past	6	10	17	7	18	3	13
Contemporary	59	67	67	76	63	67	78
Future	0	0	0	0	0	0	0
City	27	46	64	66	51	30	65
Town	27	19	14	31	22	28	20
Farm area	19	8	8	16	14	12	7
Other Countries	35	23	16	17	19	30	9
Britain, Europe	28	10	16	17	6	17	3
North and South America	7	10	3	0	0	3	0
Africa, Asia	0	3	6	0	6	10	6

* Student Sample, including all types of short stories from the *American, Ladies' Home Journal,* and *Saturday Evening Post.* Stories were selected consecutively starting with the first January issue until various quotas were filled. The 1890 *Post* volume was unobtainable, so the closest year (1885) was substituted. Percentage values for "fiction" and "nonfiction" refer to the respective numbers of titled items in sampled issues, weighted very roughly for length. The latter figures have been compared with detailed line counts from 1937 on, provided by the Lloyd H. Hall agency, with a surprisingly close correspondence shown.

A second indication of the story emphases upon the familiar is shown in the story locales and in their changes during the period investigated (Table 1). The predominance of American locales in all of the story samples is itself indicative in this connection. More interestingly, however, are the changes in frequency with which various foreign locations occur. For example, between 1890 and 1917 there is a considerable shift away from European stories. Not shown in Table 1 is the fact that most settings in the first sample year were in Britain, and all were in Northern

Europe. If we accept the contention made earlier that the original readers were mainly of Anglo-Saxon or related backgrounds, but that by 1917 the readers were starting to increase in ethnic diversity, then the trend from European to American settings is at least compatible with the changing background of the readers. We hardly would mention so tenuous a relationship were it not supported by contextual analysis of the stories pointing to very gross cultural resemblances between the British and New Englanders in the 1890 stories and also the later changes in foreign locations as partly hinted at in the table. Another illustrative chip of evidence is offered by regional changes in American story locations (not in Table 1). In 1890 the stories are mostly set in the North Atlantic states, and few take place west of the Mississippi. In line with demographic dispersions of the readers, the stories "migrate" westward as the period develops, but the North Atlantic still predominates in 1955.

Perhaps it should be emphasized that while the *directions* of change in locations that have been mentioned correspond to apparent changes in readership familiarity, there is no close comparability in the *rate* of change. This point is further supported by the variations in urban versus rural locations in the American stories (Table 1, again). We might also note here, since this is our first opportunity to mention data relating to it, that the changing prevalence of urban locales does not uniformly or clearly support our second contention mentioned at the beginning of this section (that portrayals exaggerate the points of distinctiveness of the readership). While this pattern is shown in the years 1905, 1917, 1925 and 1955, there are unexplained fluctuations which do not fit the expectation. The most glaring contradiction appears in 1890, when our information is that the readers were mostly situated in New York, Philadelphia, and other Eastern cities, and held their greatest urban predominance than of any time during the period. Nonetheless, the majority of American story locales were in towns or rural areas, as if to spite our hypothesis.[29] While the distributions of locales in regional and other

29. In defense of a worthy hypothesis that does find impressive support from other comparative findings below, it might be worth mentioning two extenuating circumstances that may eventually lead to a more sturdy, "dynamic" reformulation of it. The hypothesis, as well as our readership data, suffers from temporal ambiguities. In arguing that portrayals will emphasize the distinctive differences between the readership group and the population, and that this might apply to story locales, the question is left open as to how long a difference must exist under various conditions to become distinctive. A further problem from the magazine publication side is that, particularly in 1890, all of our magazines but the *Post* had only been in operation for a few years, and the latter was faltering. It may be that the writers and editors were not yet operating in a determinate publication context reflecting *current* readership inclinations.

aspects offer slightly better support, the claim certainly is not clearly substantiated as concerns the story locales. That the contention still holds for some range of story contents is indicated below in the comparisons from which it was derived.

In numerous other ways it appears that the stories feature the common experiences of their readers. This pattern is shown, for example, in the selective distributions of roles described in the stories as enacted on various levels of social organization and with varying degrees of responsibility and authority. The largest number of roles receiving emphasis are carried out in family groups, local neighborhoods, with friends, or at work in a relatively small work group. While occasional roles are described which involve executive responsibilities in larger business firms, there is rarely any attention given to political activities or other action carried out in the national society or in larger-scale communities within it. (In our Prime Sample of 120 realistic stories in American settings, only two stories give any attention to roles of this kind.)

Moreover, where work roles or other differentiated roles are described, the descriptions mainly emphasize those generic aspects which an outsider could readily comprehend, with perhaps some sprinkling of specific details for flavor.

"In-Groups" and "Out-Groups." Several different methods have been used to explore the ways in which "in-groups" and "out-groups" are distinguished in our stories, and to compare the in-group boundaries with the readership composition. One approach has been simply to ask what kinds of characters (in social status terms) are "admitted" to the stories at all, and, if admitted, how frequently. Further refinements were added by examining the prominence and favorability with which various types of characters were portrayed, following the lead of some previous studies that have been mentioned. Thus, we asked who was more or less eligible for a "starring role," or conversely, who was most likely to be relegated to a background position if admitted at all, or given the "villain's treatment" in the story portrayal. Beyond this, our most detailed analysis has focused on the sociometric structures of the Storyville populations, much in the manner of sociometric studies made in actual communities which examine the association patterns attributed to different characters and their evaluations of one another. The latter analysis, which has proved the most rewarding, is extremely complex and can only be alluded to here. Its main results, however, are foreshadowed by the findings on the changing sociological casting of the "stars" and other players as partly summarized in Tables 2 and 3.

The findings for the realistic stories in our Prime Sample reveal a very gross correspondence between the makeup of the Storyville and the readership populations in each sample year. It is here that we see most clearly the tendency mentioned, for the stories to accentuate those characteristics which distinguish the readership from everybody else in the population. This tendency is shown most convincingly for the 1955 sample, where our most systematic analysis was possible (Table 3). However, it also derives support from a number of changes in the readership from one sample year to another.

The coincidence between readership composition and boundaries of the Storyville in-groups is most strikingly evident in terms of racial, ethnic, and religious identities.[30] In 1890 the story population, like the readership, primarily consists of native white Protestants from North European backgrounds. Among the few exceptions are a Negro couple that is hardly mentioned, three characters who are explicitly Catholic, and a few immigrants of either Scottish or German background.

The increasing ethnic diversity of the readers has its reflection in the 1925 stories. These contain a much wider ethnic scattering, including more than a few Irish and Jewish characters; some Italian and Scandinavian immigrants in addition to more Germans; and one Amish community. There also are several more Negro characters than before, and they are given more prominent, complex and favorable portrayals. This is the period in which the "ethnic story" was in vogue in American popular magazines. While the white minorities are less numerous in Storyville than our estimates would have it for the readership (and far less numerous than in the total population), many have leading roles in the stories, and they in fact appear twice as frequently (i.e., 20 percent) among the stars as among the less prominent characters. And, it further appears that (with the probable exception of the Amish) at least the white minority characters are selected from groups that were becoming fairly numerous among the readership. We might say then that Storyville here contains something of a "balanced ticket" in relationship to the readership group, still weighted to be sure in favor of the majority.[31]

There is another side to the ethnic portrayals in Storyville of 1925. In numerous ways the minority characters are segregated from the majority circle. They are, for one thing, largely restricted to their own stories and story scenes; their contacts with the majority largely are confined to business or other formal associations; and their friendships, courtships,

---

30. Racial and ethnic statuses have been omitted from Table 2 since the former are so homogeneous and the latter are too diverse for specific statistical significance of any kind, with a story sample as small as the present one.

31. Among the white characters, the main exception is the Amish group which only appears in a single story, and is the ethnic group portrayed as having the least contact of any personal sort with the majority.

Table 2—Percentage Distributions of Social Statuses for (1) All Adult Characters, and (2) "Stars" only: with (3) Mean-Differences in Favorability-Scores for Status Categories; by Sex and Year *

STATUSES	MALE CHARACTERS									FEMALE CHARACTERS								
	1890			1925			1955			1890			1925			1955		
	(1)	(2)	(3) d_i†	(1)	(2)	(3) d_i	(1)	(2)	(3) d_i†	(1)	(2)	(3) d_i†	(1)	(2)	(3) d_i	(1)	(2)	(3) d_i
Sex	54	46	−.01	64	54	−.03	60	60	+.03	46	54	+.01	36	46	+.03	40	40	−.03
Age																		
Child	1	0	—	1	0	—	5	3	—	7	5	—	1	0	—	3	0	—
Adolescent	2	2	—	1	0	—	3	5	—	2	2	—	9	12	—	5	2	—
Young adult	53	83	−.03	43	55	+.04	53	65	.00	47	83	+.05	51	70	+.09	63	86	−.01
Middle age	36	9	.00	47	39	−.08	34	19	.00	38	5	−.04	35	13	−.05	24	12	−.08
Older person	8	6	.00	8	6	+.07	5	8	+.10	6	5	−.07	4	5	+.05	5	0	+.25
Social Class																		
Upper class	37	41	+.02	33	35	−.01	17	21	−.02	38	41	+.03	34	41	+.05	16	14	−.15
Upper middle	19	25	−.03	28	21	+.01	32	36	+.05	12	17	−.05	23	24	+.03	22	31	−.14
Middle class	35	32	.00	33	39	+.05	47	41	+.09	39	39	+.14	38	35	+.06	60	52	+.04
Lower class	9	2	−.33	6	5	−.03	4	2	.00	11	3	+.03	5	0	−.02	2	3	—
Total adult characters	199	33	186	228	49	213	194	51	190	159	33	120	129	42	121	126	33	119
Occupation																		
Business; officials	43	43	+.15	55	47	−.07	53	46	+.03	39	45	−.17	36	48	+.06	37	33	−.05
Professionals	14	8	+.20	20	21	+.15	24	23	+.06	5	0	+.37	2	4	—	21	27	+.12
Clerical workers	6	12	−.13	8	10	−.05	8	13	−.12	5	11	—	28	30	+.01	26	33	+.04
Laborers (nonfarm)	10	4	.00	12	10	+.08	12	16	.00	33	33	+.09	30	9	+.18	16	7	+.16
Farmers	27	33	−.02	5	12	+.10	3	2	+.29	18	11	+.37	4	9	—	0	0	—
Total characters	147	26	140	190	49	187	160	44	158	35	9	34	48	23	48	43	15	40

	(1)	(2)	(3)	(1)	(2)	(3)	(1)	(2)	(3)	(1)	(2)	(3)	(1)	(2)	(3)	(1)	(2)	(3)
Schooling																		
College	33	44	+.07	14	16	+.07	34	45	+.02	8	4	−.17	6	12	+.37	21	35	−.08
High school	40	51	+.04	62	72	−.02	64	58	+.02	62	94	+.04	68	78	+.01	67	64	.00
Elementary school	27	7	−.21	24	12	+.11	2	2	—	30	0	−.16	26	10	+.12	12	1	—
Total characters	116	29	115	211	49	206	184	49	181	124	33	119	126	42	119	115	33	113
Marital status																		
Single	56	70	+.02	42	64	−.03	46	50	+.03	47	66	−.01	42	44	+.10	43	46	.00
Married	38	21	.00	50	25	−.01	46	38	+.09	38	23	−.02	44	31	−.10	43	45	−.05
Divorced	2	3	—	1	2	—	3	10	−.25	1	6	—	1	9	—	4	4	−.58
Widowed	6	6	−.01	7	8	+.09	5	2	+.15	14	6	+.12	13	15	+.14	10	4	+.24
Total characters	149	33	145	133	45	132	111	48	106	153	33	149	119	42	117	118	33	114

* Main sample, including the first 10 "realistic stories" with contemporary U.S. settings in each year's volume of the *American, Cosmopolitan, Ladies' Home Journal* and *Saturday Evening Post*. (The 1885 *Post* substitutes for 1890.) With the exception of "age" distributions, all figures are limited to adult characters. The characters were classified as "stars," "supporting players" and "bit players" in terms of their importance in a story. Column (2) refers only to every adult character by age, social class and ethnic status through liberal use of "marginal categories" (as described in the Codebook); and without exception all were classifiable by sex. The figures for the first three status variables are more variable, the separate totals are presented. Since the numbers that could be classified by occupation, schooling, and marital status variables refer approximately to the indicated total numbers of adult characters.

† Favorability scores (d_t): the scores in col. (3) are based on ratings of how favorably a character was portrayed in a story. A 7-point rating scale was used, with scores ranging from +1.00 (for exceedingly favorable portrayals) to −1.00 (for extreme villains, and zero for neutral portrayals. For purposes of "mass communication," the summary scores in the table have been given the same value range, and can be interpreted in essentially the same manner for groups. Actually, these scores compare the mean favorability score for each status category (e.g., upper-class men in the 1890 sample) with the mean for all adult characters in that year's sample. Thus, the d_t value of +.02 for the 1890 upper-class men indicates that their average portrayal was a shade more favorable than that for the entire sample; while the extreme of −.33 for lower-class men that year indicates predominantly negative portrayals—the lowest favorability score in the table. Scores are presented as comparison (or "mean differences") in this way to take account of changes in overall favorability of portrayals in different sample years.

Table 3—Statuses of Magazine Readers and Story Characters, Compared with U.S. Adult Population (1955), by Sex *

	MALES				FEMALES			
	Percent of U.S. Popu-lation	Percent Difference from U.S. Population			Percent of U.S. Popu-lation	Percent Difference from U.S. Population		
		Readers	Characters			Readers	Characters	
STATUSES		Readers	All	Stars		Readers	All	Stars
Sex	49	−12	+11	+11	51	+12	−11	−11
Race								
White	90	+ 8	+ 8	+ 9	90	+ 8	+10	+10
Age								
10–17	16	− 5	−12	−10	15	− 5	−10	−13
18–25	11	− 1	− 1	+ 2	13	0	+11	+22
26–35	19	+ 4	+21	+30	19	+ 5	+22	+32
36–55	33	+ 4	+ 5	−11	32	+ 3	− 8	−20
56 and over	21	− 1	−13	−11	21	− 3	−16	−21
Schooling								
College	16	+17	+14	+17	14	+15	+ 8	+24
High school	39	+12	+25	+26	46	+11	+21	+16
Less than high school	45	−29	−39	−43	40	−26	−29	−40
Employment								
Women	—	—	—	—	30	+ 2	+ 4	+13
Occupation								
Business, officials	13	+ 9	+40	+33	6	+ 2	+31	+27
Professionals, technicians	8	+10	+16	+15	12	+ 8	+ 9	+14
Clerical workers	12	+ 6	− 4	+ 1	36	+15	−10	− 2
Laborers (nonfarm)	56	−20	−44	−40	42	−22	−36	−25
Farmers	11	− 5	− 8	− 9	4	− 3	− 4	− 4
Marital status								
Single	20	+ 2	+26	+30	13	+10	+30	+33

* Characters are from "realistic" stories with contemporary U.S. locations in the *American, Cosmopolitan, Ladies' Home Journal,* and *Saturday Evening Post.* The figures on statuses of readers and characters are percentage differences between the respective percentage values and those for the U.S. population (e.g., an estimated 37 percent of adult readers were men—presented as "—12 percent" compared with 49 percent males among U.S. adults).

Readership data were provided by the Daniel Starch Agency, based on national surveys in 1954 and 1955. U.S. population data are Census figures for nearest available years. Status distributions refer to groups over 18 years old, except "Schooling" (where 26 years is the lower limit) and "age" as indicated.

and marriages are of course contained within their own circles. The overall in-group suggested—that is, all the characters admitted to the stories (as contrasted with the Storyville minority in-group which corresponds to the majority readership), is then highly differentiated internally, and quite far from an ecumenical unity. The tendency toward internal solidarity, however, is still maintained in various ways. This is shown, for example, by the fact that most points of dramatic contention relating to the minority characters are concerned with their relations with their own kind. If their intimate associations are constrained to their Storyville ghettoes, so too are their conflicts. Moreover, the ethnic barriers are invariably portrayed as being supported by the minority groups on their own initiative. The point is illustrated most strikingly in the Amish story, in which the boundary maintenance is threatened by a young Amishman who falls in love with an outsider, apparently of nondescript majority identity. Obsessed by his infatuation, he leaves his home community to seek and win the lady of his affections, only to find that she is somewhat vulgar upon closer acquaintance. In the end, he returns to the fold with the warm approval of his kinsmen, the girl next door, and presumably the writer himself.

This is not at all to suggest that the stories give "separate-but-equal" treatment to minority characters. Many portrayals are prejudicially stereotypic from the standpoint of the minorities, although the degree of hostility is not great. This is true, it should be noted, despite the fact that at least several of the writers of the minority stories share the minority statuses of their characters. In presenting their stories in terms of majority stereotypes in these cases, the writers appear to be catering to their majority audiences, like the Negro performers in vaudeville who gained success with white audiences by caricaturing members of their own race.

In the 1955 sample, the emphasis on ethnic and religious minorities is greatly reduced and their relations with the majority are changed. No Catholic or Jewish characters are found in our sample who were explicitly classifiable in these terms, although some hints of these identities appear in references made to a "black Irishman," a sharp television producer, and other mentions of this kind. There are a few Negro characters, one Eurasian woman, two Polish immigrants, and a slightly larger number of Italians and Scandinavians than in 1925. The latter two groups receive the most pronouncedly ethnic portrayals in the sample, with differentiation from the majority in-group somewhat implied. The barriers upheld, however, are really slight by comparison with before, and interestingly they are strongest with relation to older characters. In several stories, the children of white immigrant minority parents marry or otherwise move into the majority circle, in sharp contrast to the earlier years. We have no identifiable cases where such an entry cuts across major religious or racial lines, but even here the force of social distance is greatly reduced. Easy acquaintanceship is portrayed, albeit still within fairly formal situations, between a Negro character and a white married couple, and also between a *Ladies' Home Journal* heroine and the "black Irishman" mentioned, an eminent scientist toward whom she develops a crush. (The lady already is safely married, so that problems of intermarriage are averted.)

In sum, our last sample year reveals the persistence of ethnic and racial differentiations within the readership in-group, but these have become more subtle and mild. In the perspective of our period, there seems to be a broad trend toward assimilation of white ethnic and religious minorities into what is initially a strict majority circle, still considerably short of integration at the end, and seemingly in line with readership developments. Somewhat more friendly and equalitarian acceptance for non-whites is indicated in formal situations, but color lines remain in force in 1955, as also appears through self-segregation in the readership group.

The distinguishing social statuses of the readers are emphasized in the Storyville in-groups in many other ways. Equal in importance, perhaps, are the relative absence of children and adolescents, of persons with less than high school education, and of manual laborers. In these and other coinciding respects, where differences between modal readers and the population are most striking, it appears quite consistently that the over-representation of distinguishing marks of the readers is greatest among the leading story characters, although it also is shown for the story populations as a whole (Table 3, especially).

At the same time, we want to note that the correspondence shown is not uniformly simple for any of the status variables, if all of their categories are taken into account. Thus for education, in 1955, while the pattern of exaggeration of readership distinctiveness holds for the "elementary school" group, the number of "college persons" is very close to the readership. When the educational distributions for the three sample years are compared, moreover, there is an up-down-up-again cycle in the frequency of college-educated characters that does not simply correspond to any readership changes of which we are aware (Table 2). A further problem appears when the changing age distribution of characters is examined. In 1955, for example, older characters are greatly under-represented in the sample, although their proportion among the readers is approximately that in the overall population. Then again, there is the decrease in middle-aged women characters over the sample period, and the irregular shift in the middle-aged men, which do not correspond to known or likely changes in the readership group.

When the status distributions mentioned for the characters are related to the sociometric structures, a somewhat more orderly picture emerges, but the irregularities noted still are not resolved and several new complications appear. One new complication that has particularly intrigued us is that several underrepresented readership subcategories, which do not fall under our hypothesis, show up as *isolates* excluded from the intimate majority circle in the stories. A case in point is the aged men in the 1955 stories, who have no reciprocal affectional attachments with characters in the in-group in any of the stories in which they appear. In several cases they are described as being closely attached to their children or other younger adults, without, however, a reciprocation. The only reciprocal relations described for them are with children, oldsters, or others outside of the in-group. The portrayals of farmers in 1955 also show something of this pattern. In both cases the excluded characters are portrayed in a favorable, almost idealized manner, but are not fit for intimate relations. The patterns for the aged and the farmer both seem to hang on the fact of former inclusion in the in-group, with much higher status in the past, followed by status loss and a movement toward exclusion. The trend may be fruitfully contrasted with that noted for the formerly excluded ethnic minorities that *gain* in acceptance and social standing.

Storyville Values and Interests. It often has been argued that mass communications, in their "common-denominator" appeals for broad, heterogeous patronage, give exaggerated emphasis to those values and interests most widely supported in the society. We have mentioned before that Albrecht's study of family values in stories from magazines for 1950 offers qualified support for this position. His findings also indicate that the correspondence involved is not always uniform, and that differences exist among magazines published for different social strata.

The present analysis has not proceeded very far as yet in systematically examining the validity of value portrayals in our story sample. However, we have scattered indications that *Storyville portrayals of social values may be most determinately valid where they are attributed to the minority in-group of the stories,* and become more stereotypic and less dependable where they pertain to other groups. This suggestion seems generally in keeping with some of Albrecht's speculations. It appears that more than anything else the stories are responsive to the values strongly upheld by the readership majority, and that, conversely, they are not responsive to the values of groups excluded from the readership. We are not denying, in taking this position, that powerful minorities may have imposed their viewpoints on the magazines through political or economic means. There are indications, however, that this control has proven tenuous where the viewpoints do not at least partially coincide with those of the readership.

Some illustrations of the possible influence of readership values on the stories, where these values are at variance with those of large subgroups outside of the readership, are presented in Table 4. We hedge our interpretations of the correspondence to readership values since the most

Table 4—Mean "Liberal-Conservative" Ratings of Adult Male and Female Characteristics on Ten Divisions of Liberalism, with Percent of Major Characters Classifiable on Each Division, by Years

CHARACTERISTICS	MEN			WOMEN		
	1890	1925	1955	1890	1925	1955
1. Provincialism (−1) Cosmopolitanism (+1)	+.51(30)*	+.63 (24)	+.59 (17)	+.42 (35)	+.29 (36)	+.64 (18)
2. Puritanism (−1) Fun morality (+1)	+.43 (67)	+.65 (97)	+.71 (47)	+.43 (93)	+.72 (96)	+.65 (59)
3. Male supremacy (−1) Sex equality (+1)	+.26 (76)	+.65 (97)	+.63 (56)	+.21 (96)	+.70 (98)	+.66 (64)
4. Technological conservatism (−1) Technological progress (+1)	+.28 (5)	+.67 (32)	+.73 (24)	+.18 (6)	+.49 (26)	+.75 (3)
5. Prudery (−1) Sexual freedom (+1)	+.22 (51)	+.63 (88)	+.54 (44)	+.08 (71)	+.57 (93)	+.57 (60)
6. Political laissez-faire (−1) Welfare statism (+1)	.— (0)	+.21 (11)	.— (0)	.— (0)	−.09 (11)	.— (0)
7. Age supremacy (−1) Equality (+1)	−.36 (16)	−.10 (15)	−.17 (12)	−.22 (30)	−.18 (27)	−.03 (9)
8. Marriage as sacrament (−1) Rejection of marriage (+1)	−.45 (51)	+.09 (84)	+.22(40)	−.51 (74)	−.06 (94)	+.18 (55)
9. Familialism (−1) Autonomy of kin (+1)	−.48 (48)	−.34 (77)	−.31 (28)	−.54 (90)	−.49 (99)	−.43 (51)
10. Religious fundamentalism (−1) Agnosticism-atheism (+1)	−.48 (39)	−.31 (21)	−.42 (6)	−.63 (48)	+.01 (31)	−.38 (5)

* Prime sample. Figures in parentheses refer to percentage of characters ratd in a given year. Other figures are mean scores, based on a 7-category scale. For convenience in presentation, the mean values have been converted to a numeral scale with the range ±1.

suggestive data concern the changes in values shown, and we already have mentioned our uncertainties as to the readership composition in the earlier years, not to speak of their values.

The table shows the mean ratings for all (ratable) story characters on ten broad value dimensions, pertaining to areas in which important sub-group differences are known to have existed in American society during our period. The areas of disagreement, for instance, include "religious fundamentalism," "the sacramentalism of marriage," "sexual prudery," "laissez-faire ideology," and "puritanism" (as opposed to what is some-times called the "fun morality"). It should be noted that the main figures in the table are adjusted mean scores, presented in a scale running from "+1.00" at the liberal extreme to "−1.00" at the conservative extreme for each value area. It also should be pointed out that the limiting values of the scales deliberately were made very extreme and that mean scores with values of .30 or greater (in either direction) show a fairly pro-nounced value predominance among the Storyville population that could be rated on the respective value areas. Separate scores are given in the table for male and female characters in each story sample, with the per-centage of characters rated shown in brackets.

The most striking indication of value correspondence to a readership majority, that probably is much at variance with the viewpoints of the general population, is shown for the 1890 sample. Particularly in four of the ten value areas ("provincialism," "puritanism," "sexual prudery," and "male supremacy"), the values supported in Storyville seem far more "liberal" than those usually assumed to have been upheld by the majority of the population at the time. Recalling our assumption that the reader-ship then was far more urbanized and formally educated than the popu-lation, and further assuming that this would indicate more liberal values in these respects as a correlate, stories here seem to reflect the viewpoints of their readers in at least partial opposition to those of major groups outside of the readership. This correspondence continues to be supported for the 1925 and 1955 samples, although the claim that distinctive reader-ship values are supported become more tenuous as the distinctiveness of the readership itself becomes less marked.

The distributions of the remaining six value dimensions indicated in the table do not conform to the pattern of emphasizing distinctive reader-ship values. In various ways they suggest the operation of other selective mechanisms, beginning with the fairly obvious tendency toward avoid-ance of controversies within the readership group. The latter tendency is apparent, for example, in the infrequent mention of political viewpoints in the stories, and also in the relative absence of religious viewpoints in 1925 and 1955, respectively shown in the table by the small number of characters classified on the "laissez-faire" and the "religious fundamentalism" dimensions. In this respect, the stories conform to the taboo on discussion of religion and politics so widely found in more direct communicative relationships between persons of diverse social backgrounds. The avoidance of the controversial also is illustrated by selective omissions in the role-behaviors described for the story characters. Among the most striking illustrations are the virtual exclusion in the stories of any references to promiscuous or otherwise intimate sexual behavior, despite the emphasis given to romantic relations between the sexes in the stories; and also the very low occurrence of divorce, although many stories center around marital frustrations and estrangements and it is often realistically difficult to understand why the married couples in question choose to remain together as the story endings have it.

CONCLUDING NOTE

Our discussion has emphasized the correspondence between patterns of ethnographic misrepresentation in "realistic" magazine fiction portrayals of American society, and the selective nature of the magazine readers. The main conclusion suggested is that stories from each sampled period are built around a Storyville in-group with social characteristics resembling those of the readership majority; that Storyville portrayals greatly overrepresent the importance of the readership subgroups in the population; and that the portrayals of characters and social events primarily express those understandings, interests, and values which are most widely common to (and distinctive of) the readership. In terms of our original question of portrayal validity, there is the strong implication that discriminate analysis of Storyville portrayals must begin by distinguishing story in-groups from story out-groups and their respective characterizations. The most directly valid portrayals would seem to be found in the values attributed to the in-group characters, where the social situations described are most analogous sociologically to those pertaining to the communication medium, and further, where the roles described are congruent with the primary "identity-appeals" made to the readership (e.g., family roles in family magazines). Alternatively, portrayals of subgroups not included within the readership majority circle seemingly should be treated with suspicion as being more indicative of majority stereotypes than valid reflections of the subgroups' orientations. It further appears that the portrayals most consistently appearing in a story sample provide more valid reflections of the *ideals and aspirations* of the modal in-group than of either their actual attitudes or behavior.

The relationship suggested between the values of in-groups in the stories and in the readership is far from one of simple correspondence. It does generally appear that story values are likely to be at least compatible with those of the readership majority, but the reflection provided is highly selective, and subject at all points to pressure-group influence as well as other intervening factors. The methodological implication is then that the precise justification of inferences from Storyville portrayals to readership characteristics requires detailed information about the specific intervening conditions which may intrude between the two.

Among the "other factors" that our comparative analysis suggests, are the influences of writers, editors, publishers and advertisers. Contrary to some allegations, our analysis does not support the claim that Storyville portrayals positively reflect the propagandistic manipulations of any of these subgroups at points where their values might differ substantially from the readership majority. Thus, there is comparatively little "capitalistic" ideology in the stories on the one hand, or "bohemianism" on the other, beyond minor shadings that are evident on occasion. It appears that both the writers and the economic controllers exert their influence primarily through a "veto" power, indicated by numerous otherwise puzzling omissions of readership values and concerns. One might say, then, that both constitute minority subgroups from the standpoint of their influence on story contents, whose overt influence is limited by the need to appeal to readership values, but who, like other minorities, can exercise censorship power. A more adequate formulation of the determinants of Storyville selections would incorporate these influences. In fact, the story portrayals might be said to represent a "negotiated compromise" between the values of these various masters, in which, however, the readership majority through "purchasing power" has the decisive vote, within broad limits.

PUBLICATIONS

Martel, Martin, "Some Controversial Assumptions in Parsons' Approach to Social Systems Theory," *Alpha Kappa Deltan,* vol. 29, 1959, pp. 53–63.

McCall, George J., "Symbiosis: The Case of Hoodoo and the Numbers Racket," *Social Problems,* vol. 10, 1963 (Spring), pp. 361–371.

Dr. McCall is also collaborating with J. L. Simmons in the preparation of a volume on the interactionist approach to personality.

QUESTIONS

1.   What do the writers mean by "ethnography"? How does the conception apply to their article?

2.   As indicated in the introduction, there are several different ways in
      which this article might be structured. Outline the article as it is, then
      make two alternative outlines for the same material.

3.   Where is the work heading? The authors suggest that this article is
      chiefly a methodological introduction to later substantive work. What
      would you expect to find in their later articles?

4.   How would you set about applying the same ethnographic approach to
      the study of (*a*) radio commercials and (*b*) documentary type detec-
      tive stories? What problems would be raised in such efforts which
      Martel and McCall did not have to face?

5.   Suppose you were to make a similar study of historical novels such as
      those of Walter Scott, G. A. Henty, Thomas Costain, or of "Wild
      West" stories—whose ethnography would you be studying? Can you
      conceive any advantage under any circumstances in studying historical
      or Wild West fiction in the magazines Martel and McCall selected
      for their purposes rather than studying contemporary-type fiction?

6.   Advanced students wishing to undertake serious papers could very
      profitably send for the Codebook which Professor Martel (Depart-
      ment of Sociology, Arizona State University, Tempe, Arizona) will
      make available to them, and try to work on a project of the sort sug-
      gested in the text.

PART V

SOCIAL INSTITUTIONS STUDIED IN TERMS OF COMMUNICATION THEORY: SOME EXAMPLES

W. Lloyd Warner

The World of Biggy Muldoon:

Transformation of a Political Hero *

AS THE BIBLIOGRAPHY and citations show, the essay that follows is taken from a book which is part of a series about "Yankee City" in the 1930s.[1] One of the major points that Dr. Warner and his associates suggest throughout the series is this: "Yankee City" had been within the memory and experience of men then living, relatively autonomous—that is, business and industry within Yankee City were, in the early 1900s, controlled in large measure by Yankee City people, conscious of the other residents of Yankee City, themselves enmeshed in the Yankee City social pattern and tradition. In the volume on labor relations in Yankee City, The Strike,[2] in particular, the Warner team show how much Yankee City changed between the 1890s and the 1930s in this regard. By 1930, business, industry, and the trade union movement alike were, on the whole, managed, controlled, and directed by outsiders to whom Yankee City meant very little and to whom its special customs and traditions meant nothing. To be sure, the "market," the "consumer," and the supplier of raw materials for Yankee City's factories and mills had always been remote and impersonal; but management and labor, which in 1900 were for the most part within Yankee City, had by 1930 become similarly impersonal.

* Reprinted from *The Living and the Dead*, Yale University Press, New Haven, 1959, by permission of the author and the publisher. (Copyright 1959 by Yale University Press.)

1. See below, p. 357. It is now no secret that "Yankee City" is Newburyport, Massachusetts, and that several of John Marquand's novels deal with the same social scene as is portrayed by Warner et al. It is no secret either that the Mayor, described in the following article, is "Bossy" Gillis—one of the most durable political figures in Massachusetts life, who thirty years later is still off-and-on a strong mayoralty candidate. Those who wish to check the Warner account can do so by studying the reports on Gillis in newspapers and magazines of the thirties, especially the Boston press.

2. The full title of this study is indicative of its emphasis: it is: *The Social System of the Modern Factory—The Strike: A Social Analysis*.

Yankee City, according to Warner and his associates, showed the social consequences of "this division of labor" as analyzed by the eminent French sociologist Emile Durkheim in a classic study of that subject.[3] Durkheim suggests that industrialization through the division of labor increases the impersonality of immediate, local relationships while at the same time vastly enlarging the number of meaningful relationships conducted at a distance.

So far as we know, the initial interest of the Yankee City researchers in mass communications was not very great. They came to their field work first, greatly influenced by Durkheim's sociological theories [4] and second, by theory derived from the study of small, primitive tribes by anthropologists. Initially, they were concerned with social symbols and their meanings, with the effects of industrialization, and especially with the nature and relationship of social classes in Yankee City and the United States.

These three interests, however, resulted in what could well become a classic contribution to the study of mass communications—the essay that follows. By chance, during the period of their study and utterly independent of it, Newburyport became the center of national (and to a slight extent even international) attention, because of its mayor, whose early career is described below. Mayor Gillis, indeed, probably gave Newburyport more national attention than anybody and anything else associated with the city for the past ninety years. And, to the upper- and middle-class families of Newburyport, Gillis represented the same sort of social menace that conservatives and reactionaries elsewhere imagined in candidates like Franklin D. Roosevelt, Fiorello H. La Guardia, Robert M. La Follette, Huey Long, or Upton Sinclair.[5] Yet so far as the substance of what he did was concerned, Gillis in no way challenged (as all the men mentioned to some extent did) any nationally established political system or way of doing things; and after all, Newburyport is one of several thousand small cities in the United States which elects a mayor every two or four years and it is safe to say that during the last thirty years no other small town Mayor has received as much concentrated and sensational publicity as Gillis (excluding mayors of New York, possibly no other big-city mayor either).[6]

3. Emile Durkheim, *De la division du travail social,* 8th ed., F. Alcan, Paris, 1893; available in English translation (Free Press, New York, 1960).

4. Found also in his *Rules of Sociological Method* (Free Press, New York, 1950).

5. Upton Sinclair, the novelist, ran for governor of California on the Democratic ticket on an "End Poverty in California" platform in 1934 in one of the very few American elections in which a Socialist position was seriously put forward by a major party candidate.

6. A few exceptions may have occurred. James M. Curley of Boston and Jasper McLevy of Bridgeport unquestionably received more lifetime publicity nationally,

Of more immediate interest to Warner and his associates—who, we must note, were studying the local Newburyport community—was how Gillis's challenge, which was in the area of manners and zoning restrictions and had no bearing on central city services or the tax rate, became such a pleasurable scandal to many citizens of Newburyport.

In addressing themselves to this question, Warner and his associates, because of their interest in the influence of symbolic and historic patterns in Newburyport, started out with the idea that Gillis could be explained in the same way as a seemingly similar Newburyport figure of the early nineteenth century—"Lord" Timothy Dexter, author of "A Pickle for the Knowing Ones." "Lord" Dexter scandalized the upper classes much as did Mayor Gillis, and became in his own time a figure of some regional notoriety.

But whatever the similarities may be between Gillis and Dexter, one difference soon becomes apparent. Gillis was the creation of the mass media. Not, of course, Gillis the man in face-to-face contact with his enemies, nor Gillis the mayor in the day-to-day performance of his municipal responsibilities—but Gillis the legend, Gillis the public figure, and ultimately, Gillis the candidate for mayor, without the normal political backing that comes from organizations and contacts. It is this last point that is the central theme of Dr. Warner's paper.

The way in which metropolitan newspapers "created" Gillis the legend is a striking parallel to the industrial and economic developments which Warner and his associates discuss elsewhere in the series. For, in the area of local politics and of political legend, just as in the areas of business and industry, large outside influences focus, organize, and direct local concerns. But Warner, as an anthropologist interested in legends, recognizes more persuasively than most commentators on the mass media that, in large measure, they are selling not "news" in the sense of facts but heroes and dragons, buffoons and saints, angels and devils. But the tradition of factual news reporting limits, constricts, and guides the mass communicators just as the tradition of the medieval morality play limited, constricted, and guided its authors —they find it far easier to create the sensations for which they strive when the characters fit the part. Gillis, in this sense, was a godsend, a "natural"; he played the part of the comic hero, the shrewd, virile semibuffoon, providing, in "Lord" Dexter's own words, "a pickle for the knowing ones," that is, a challenge to established, proper upper-class people. His very appropriateness as a comic buffoon arose out of the fact that he was in no sense or manner a challenge at any basic level. He had no program of "robbing the rich to aid the poor," of high taxes, of municipal socialism—he was not, basically, any threat

---

but Gillis' publicity peak was probably greater than Curley's, and certainly greater than McLevy's.

to national values—and therefore it was possible to blow him up many times larger than life by selective reporting. He commanded the press, for a time, much as—over a much longer period—the artist Salvador Dali has; but he differed from Dali in that he had no conscious sense of public relations and just happened to fit. With the wartime developments, Gillis accordingly faded from national attention; he was no longer "news."

But the legendary Gillis had both national and local appropriateness. The set of challenges and complaints which he was making to the well-to-do residents of big houses, the bankers, and the lawyers, and the descendants of sea captains, who were Newburyport's most important people, expressed the feelings of the less important people in the city. And the entire massive Warner study demonstrates why there were many people in Newburyport eager to express resentment and disdain for the well-to-do and proper who supposedly ran their city. So long as Gillis's protests were merely individual ones, such as any local "sorehead" makes, he did not mean much to his fellow citizens; but the mass media put Gillis's complaints within a dramatic framework and made him a symbol of their own complaints. There have been throughout American history a number of such symbols of resentment, resentment which is not in itself seriously revolutionary— "Pitchfork Ben" Tillman, for instance, who expressed the resentment of the Southern back country farmers in the 1890s at the cautious conservatism of the President by threatening to stick a "pitchfork" in the softest portion of the Chief Executive's ample anatomy. But, until the twentieth century, most of these figures won their support and following by a direct, local appeal. Gillis's career is significant because it shows how the mass media can create and dramatize such a public figure, guided in his case (and in most cases) more by canons of what makes news than by any intention of creating such a figure.*

L. A. D.

DR. WARNER, University Professor of Social Research at Michigan State University, was Professor of Sociology and Anthropology at the

---

* In our judgment, the late Senator Joseph McCarthy was an example of the same sort of protest figure. His attack on widespread treachery in the government, his attempt to identify State Department employees with homosexuality ("the lavender lads"), and similar conduct was not in any very serious respect an attempt to uncover Communists in government, but it did represent a protest by the suspicious, the underprivileged, the small towns, against the seeming control of government by people from the big universities and big cities, with different tastes and folkways. Some graduate student who wants to undertake a serious research analysis might do well to trace McCarthy's career in detail, using Warner's analysis of Gillis as a model. See Douglas Cater, *The Fourth Branch of Government* (Houghton, Boston, 1959), and Richard Rovere, *Senator Joe McCarthy* (Harcourt, New York, 1959).

University of Chicago from 1935 to 1959, and prior to that a member of the Harvard Business School faculty. His main work has been in the sociology of American communities. His early research was on symbolic behavior and social organization among the Australian aborigines. He for many years worked on the Yankee City research, which has resulted in a series widely known as The Yankee City Series. Professor Warner has also done research in the mass media.

MASK FOR A HERO

Biggy Muldoon's fight with Hill Street was played before two highly interested audiences. The *local* ones, the citizens of Yankee City, consisted of those who participated as actors in the drama and those who, acting as a kind of chorus, watched and commented as the plot unfolded. Among them were the Hill Street crowd, the lace-curtain Irish, and the ordinary little people, Yankee and ethnic, who lived down by the river. For the *national* audience Yankee City itself, through the symbols of the mass media, became a stage where a human drama of intense interest was being played, yet no one of that audience was directly involved. Each member of it vicariously experienced what happened by reading about it in the great metropolitan papers and magazines, seeing it in a newsreel, or hearing it over the radio. Biggy became a topic of dinner-table conversation, barbershop gossip, a part of gay and ribald talk in the speakeasies throughout the nation.

The Yankee City audience at first viewed him as one kind of character in the plot: a public personality fashioned by events and through experiences with members of the town. Later they saw him and the other members of his drama in a different light, characters whose lines had been rewritten by the national media of communication. Here he became something more than he had been and was applauded accordingly. The local effect of this outside influence was considerable. It was felt directly, for about half the newspapers sold in Yankee City came from metropolitan sources.[1]

To the local audience, despite its laughter, this was a serious play, a tragedy or a drama of triumph according to the time and necessities of those who watched. If so minded, they could laugh, and laugh hard, when Biggy made his opponents ridiculous; but beneath the laughter, and often beside it, were anxious feelings that what was happening demanded sober consideration. The responsibilities of the citizen were involved in what should be felt about each event.

For the audience in the world beyond Yankee City, Biggy's drama

1. See "Yankee City Series," Vol. 1.

was either light comedy or slapstick. The hero could be liked and enjoyed by everyone because he laid his paddle across the fat posteriors of the rich, upset the self-respect of the respectable, and dumped their power and authority on the floor. Yet no one needed to feel responsible for what happened; everyone could have fun. Childhood fantasies of kicking adult authority in the pants, of breaking loose from subordination and the restraint of respectability, were vicariously felt. For the general audience Biggy was the little guy, the "small fry" in them, still rebelling against the jail-like constraints of adult responsibility. He was also the embodiment of their distrust and concern about the rigid moral attitudes of the middle class. But above all he was a symbol of revolt against the imposition of these moral restraints by the powerful middle class; through him, without fear of punishment, they had a good time raising hell before the pained gaze of the respectable.

In Yankee City a part of the figure of Biggy Muldoon was inescapably true, real, an actual person—but in Memphis or Peoria or Pittsburgh he was a glorious clown or a figure of light comedy, though still the hero of the show and a man his audience could respect. They liked and trusted him as "an honest man doing his damnedest." Second thoughts that might arise in the minds of the serious about not wanting "that kind of thing to happen in my town" could be easily dropped because Biggy was not there. For many, perhaps most, it was easy to say, "what this town of ours needs is a Biggy Muldoon, maybe he'd stir things up and get rid of the damned stuffed shirts and crooked politicians who are running things." For such people in Yankee City the trouble with Biggy was that he was in Yankee City.

For many in both audiences Biggy's actions, his friends, and his enemies had been transformed into something more than a drama by the metropolitan papers and national mass media. Perhaps the whole might be called a contemporary collective ritual, its participants characters in a collective rite in which everyone symbolically participated. The characters under different names have appeared in thousands of plays and legends and stories, told straight or with humor, that everyone has heard and seen. The hero, dominant and positive symbol· of countless folktales—lodged securely in everyone's pleasant private fantasies and the mythical embodiment of a people's hopes—as champion of the oppressed goes forth to battle. He attacks the position of the powerful few and of those who arouse the fears and anxiety of the many. Those in power fight back, and with their superior weapons capture the hero, incarcerate him, and for a time defeat and disgrace him. But one knows that by his indomitable courage and herculean determination, and with the help of the little people, he will once again attack the fortresses of the mighty, in the end defeating his enemies and winning a great victory for the common people. This drama, continuously modified to meet the needs of the time, older than the records of history, is a public myth often capable of empirical validation, and a private fantasy deeply embedded in the conscious imagery of all Americans.

For a brief time, in the heyday of Biggy's fame, Yankee City became one of the many small stages where America watches the current but passing heroes of the national scene act out a drama whose cast and plot express the varying sentiments, values, and symbolic themes of our people and the system of social relations which organizes and controls us. Through newspapers, magazines, radio, and motion picture, events in that city were conveyed to the world in the form of a drama which did not necessarily correspond in cold fact to what those events and persons really were; nor did its representations present an exact image of the social world of Yankee City.

The contemporary storytellers whose mass art maintains the living continuity of myth and legend in our society and contributes to the integration and persistence of the culture work under far more difficult circumstances than the storytellers of bygone days. Formerly, fables, legends, and myths could be told as if they were true—because they *should* be true, and the imaginations and fantasies of their audiences unquestioningly accepted them. Heroes and villains and their plots and solutions conformed to traditional convention, and for the audience as well as the storyteller who entertained them, defined the proper role of each character and determined how these symbolic beings should be related to each other. The artist and the members of his audience, although different persons, were products of the same social matrix, with closely corresponding beliefs, values, and expectancies about each other and the world in which they lived. The symbols and themes used to arouse anxiety or assuage fear, and the masks and ritualistic plots of the drama which evoked the hopes and fears of their audiences, needed only the artistry of the entertainers and the sanction of conformity to the conventions of the culture to be assured eager acceptance.

The audience believed a tale or a drama was true and conformed to *their* reality if it fell within the confines of sanctioned collective representations. The close fit of the private image and the public symbol provided the conviction of reality while arousing the private emotions of the individual and at the same time controlling them. The collective representations were evaluated beliefs sanctioned by the whole moral and social order. Their private fantasies being controlled more fully by the collective representations of their society, early storytellers easily projected their private imagery on the tales they told and into the folk dramas they presented. Their own private images often were no more than minute individual variations of those in the public domain. Consequently the need of evidence, of induction and rational empirical testing, was greatly reduced.

Today the reporter is trained to be objective, accurate, and to get the facts about the people and events that make a news story. The more recently developed mass media use these same criteria and insist on rules of evidence as guides for their field men who report on current events. The instant repercussions of a modern libel law, as well as the potential embarrassments inherent in a modern system of communications only too ready to point out and publish any discrepancies of facts, sharpen this rule.

Despite the intrusion of modern canons of accuracy and the infusion of the spirit of rationality into newspapers and other mass media, a casual listing of the prevailing selection of stories and the simplest analysis of the criteria of a "good story" that will hold readers and perhaps build circulation demonstrate that the "objective" coverage of what happens every day to the people of the world is dominated by the basic wishes, the hopes and fears, the nonlogical symbolic themes and folk beliefs of the people who buy and read the papers. The degree of rationality and accuracy exhibited in the news stories of a paper or magazine is in direct relation to the degree of rational values of its audience. The audiences of mass media vary by age, sex, education, social class, urbanity, and many other social characteristics. Those who have been trained to respect rationality and objective reporting and to expect accurate coverage of events usually read papers and magazines which carry more stories of this character and have corresponding policies. Even these papers print news accounts often filled with evocative, nonlogical symbols rather than logical and empirical ones—symbols arousing the feelings and cultural beliefs of the reader rather than pointing out the factual flow of human actions in the event reported.

The fact is, the contemporary newsman must tell his story much as did his progenitors. His tale must arouse and hold the interest of his readers; he must hold out the same kind of symbols to their fears and hopes as did his predecessors. There must be villains and heroes in every paper, and the story lines must conform to the usage of suspense, conflict, the defeat of evil, and the triumph of good that have guided the good sense and artistry of past storytellers and controlled their audience's ability to respond.

But today the reporter must put the mark of empirical truth on the story—over the whole of his plot, its *dramatis personae,* and its solutions —as if it all really happened. He must believe (or pretend) that the facts, rather than the story, speak for themselves. Although the events of the news story may have all occurred in the form in which they are set forth, the relations of the major and minor characters, the arrangement of the incidents, and the symbols used to refer to them must be part of the storyteller's art. The news report is consequently composed of fact combined with the thematic materials supplied by the reporter and the conventions and traditions of his profession as well as those of his readers and his society. An exact correspondence between the scientific reality of what has actually happened and the story of what is supposed to have happened is not necessarily a test of the story's capacity to convince its readers. The mask of empirical truth is often present only for the easier acceptance of the nonlogical "truths" of contemporary popular arts. The empirical facts of an event for those who write and read may be no more than a passing illustration of the deeper evocative "truths" of the nonlogical symbols of our culture.

BIGGY MULDOON AND THE MASS MEDIA

The symbolic transformation of Biggy began with the paid advertisements he placed in the local paper when he first challenged his enemies to answer his charges of injustice and foul play. He thus unknowingly began his public transformation from the inconsequential boy from the wrong side of the tracks to the American citizen who has not been given a fair chance. In one of his first political ads Biggy told everyone that all he wanted was an opportunity to show his "true worth." Later he said that his enemies, the high and mighty "codfish aristocrats," were conspiring to destroy the rightful chance of every American to be somebody. "There is a little crowd of bankers and aristocrats in this old town," he reiterated throughout the campaign, "who don't want anbody else to have a chance but themselves. They have run this town long enough. They don't want me to have a chance. That's what the row has been. They've ridden me." When he became mayor he added, "Now, I'm going to ride them. I'll repeal their zoning law and go after that permit."

He told the people along the river and anyone who would listen that the zoning law his opponents used to stop him from putting the gas station on Hill Street was a law to protect the people on Hill Street, not the people of Riverbrook. The clammers (almost entirely Yankee and lower-lower-class) were being deprived of their livelihood, he said, because no one had come to their assistance; but he, Biggy, would be their champion, lead them, and force the state to purify the polluted waters of the river and make their clams fit for sale and human consumption.

These efforts were the first suggestion of his transformation into the hero who championed the poor. But as Biggy himself has said, it is doubtful if they would have been sufficient to elect him. Just before the election a further development in his symbolic transformation occurred which lifted him out of himself and made him something more than the man, Biggy Muldoon. This was the story, previously mentioned, which appeared first in the metropolitan press, then in hundreds of other papers, thus beginning the transformation of Biggy into a real public hero. It changed the campaign of local fact and fancy into what was also a battle between positive and negative national stereotypes, symbols now identified with Biggy which both friends and enemies tried to use to capture the imagination and votes of the people. The story was published in a Boston paper a few days before the election, a two-column, front-page news item with Biggy's picture, recounting the incidents—now dated by a year or so—of the circus posters, the chamber pots, and the house of Hill Street. It will be remembered that outwardly, until the mayoralty election, his acts in themselves, dramatic as they were, had done little to advance Biggy's political aspirations. It is certain that very few persons thought of what he had done on Hill Street as important enough to make him a successful candidate for the highest political position in the community. Yet the emotional foundations for this had been established.

The man who wrote the story, a former resident of Yankee City, having full knowledge of what had happened during the time Biggy had attempted to remove the house and establish his filling station, had considerable insight into the episode.

Biggy Muldoon [the article began], Yankee City's thirty-one-year-old bad boy, perpetual foe of mayors, city councilmen, police chiefs, fire chiefs, judges, and other symbols of law and order, once more threatens the serenity of this quiet old city.

Conservative citizens are just recovering from Biggy's antics of last summer when he entertained motorists along the Yankee City Turnpike with displays of circus posters, imitation gravestones, and genuine old-fashioned chamber pots on the old Sampson property on Constitution and Hill Streets. And now when everything seems set for a long quiet winter Biggy proceeds to furnish these same conservative citizens with material for new nightmares by threatening to get himself elected mayor.

In facing the question of issues that might elect Biggy and capture the votes of the city, the author of the piece found it difficult to formulate a suitable answer.

If someone should ask why Biggy's candidacy is so serious at this time, the only appropriate answer is, ask me another. Perhaps it is because he represents the wild and reckless spirit of youth and has caught this prim city in a moment when she is tempted to do a little high stepping. Perhaps it is because he is a self-confessed grudge candidate and there are so many people in the town who have grudges of their own to work out.

Take, for instance, the clam diggers of Riverbrook. They sit outside their picturesque shanties these sunny autumn days and hurl imprecations at the law which says they shall not dig clams in the Yankee City harbor because its waters are polluted by the waste from the big manufacturing cities up the river. Who wouldn't have a grudge under such circumstances? Well, along comes Biggy Muldoon and he tells them that if he is elected mayor he will build a new sewer at a cost of more millions than Yankee City can raise by taxation in a decade, and that when that is done they can dig their clams. Even though they know the boy is talking through his hat they like his audacity.

The writer retold the story of the Sampson house. He told it dramatically and clearly in a form not uncomplimentary to Biggy, adding that "tearing down the stone wall which flanked the turnpike was a public-spirited act because it improved vision at a dangerous corner." But he went on to say that after these exhibitions Biggy's candidacy was regarded as another joke, that

. . . the citizens laughed when they learned that in a harangue at Smith's Cafe—a speech which was not recorded in the newspapers but which reached every voter nevertheless—he had declared that when elected he would commit the police chief to an old man's home and designate the deputy chief official keeper. Biggy despises the fire marshal, too, and another promise was that he would replace that official with a certain business man in whose establishment mysterious fires occur with exasperating regularity. The very efficient policeman who recently arrested Biggy for loitering on the corner was to be assigned to the cemetery beat, "where he will have a lot of other dead ones for company."

It is possible that the story in the Boston paper would not have provoked the developments that rapidly followed had not Biggy responded with an extraordinary advertisement in the local paper. He wrote it—his enemies said with the help of others but Biggy said "with the help of my own pencil"—partly in fear that the irony and gentle leg-pulling of the news story might do him harm. He also believed that such important news coverage indicated that his powerful enemies were responding because he had hit them where it hurt. He addressed himself to "Mr. Voter and Taxpayer."

I have harpooned the whale.

I am using its oil in the machines that will carry you to the polls to vote for me.

Such bombastic fiction brought fame to said Barnum.

As the pup in Aesop's Fables. The codfish aristocrats give way.

They acknowledge they have lost, the substance is grasping at the shadow.

Wake up! Wake up! staid old Yankee City. Defeat the invisible king of Shylocks that has ruled our city the past thirty years. Let the shop whistles blow at seven every morning by casting your vote for Thomas Ignatius Muldoon for Mayor December sixth.

Bring health, prosperity, and employment to all.

THOMAS IGNATIUS MULDOON

The ad aroused everyone. Literary critics who admired Herman Melville and Walt Whitman, historians and writers who knew and loved the culture and lore of the glorious days when Yankee City and other ancient New England towns were great seaports, responded with delight. For everyone who loved New England it stimulated deep feelings about the period when her merchant princes built and sent her ships to trade in the Indies or hunt Moby Dick in distant seas, when her able seamen manned vessels that brought Yankee daring and economic enterprise to the whole earth. No New Englander, particularly a native of Yankee City, could remain indifferent to the impact of its symbols.

Despite their criticisms of the grammar and syntax everyone knew and, better yet, felt what Biggy meant. The metaphors may have been a bit involved, but "harpooning a whale" and "the good old oil," "Shylocks," and "codfish aristocrats" are all solid parts of our traditional equipment.

The attack on Biggy now had to shift, for the drama was no longer confined to the local scene. Immediately following this advertisement his opponent addressed a personal letter to him in the local paper. Unfortunately for the writer, despite the factual points made, its mockery and lofty air were not easily appreciated; it embarrassed more than it pleased. The crude implications of the. bad grammar, the joking about "happy laborers," the supercilious air of a superior person addressing his inferiors validated Biggy's contentions as to the common man needing a common man to represent him. The general effect was further to enhance his reputation as champion of the little people.

Dear Thomas [the letter began]:

The Yankee City bad boy write-up you got in the Boston papers was wonderful. You got your picture in and everything. We never did think you was so bad [said the writer invidiously], even after you used your youthful strength in beating up a man of Mr. Flaherty's age. Oh, Thomas, please repeat that ad about the health and happiness you are to bring to us sleepy old residents of Yankee City. Just think of it: that could only be exceeded by the wonderful prosperity that you would bring to our factories. In our fancy we hear the cheerful blowing of the whistles every morning of the year. The happy laborers tripping lightly to their labors with songs of praise of our Biggy on their lips, all the long happy day. After we elect you and make our factories prosperous you must promise not to overlook our clammers. We pray that you give us a mild winter and a nice early spring.

JOHN J. SMITH
Hill Street

The intervention of the Boston and New York and other papers now brought about a drastic change in Biggy's significance and the character of the local political struggle. A vast new national audience suddenly joined the local one. The impact of this force on the community was great, but its effect on Biggy as a public symbol cannot be overemphasized. Biggy the man remained largely the same, but Biggy the symbol rapidly went through mutations and elaborations that made him a national celebrity. Minor aspects of his public personality took new form and grew into dominant themes of the fabricated legend; soon the man Biggy was acting a new role before the new audience the mass authors had created. Although there is only slight evidence of change in his inner world, there is clear proof that the outer man, Biggy's social personality as publicly conceived, changed greatly. New interpreters selected and rejected events in his life and political battles and translated them for national consumption. The camera's eye, the microphone, and the wire services of the news syndicates captured the excitement of the drama and began to recast it into the stereotypes that entertain mass audiences.

As soon as the metropolitan press focused the public's attention on him, Biggy became the "two-fisted, redheaded, hard-working go-getter. He not only calls a spade a spade but he will go further and identify a pick and shovel for you in a manner that leaves nothing to the imagination.

"But don't get the idea that Mr. Thomas Ignatius Muldoon is a harem-scarem gashouse roughneck. His talk and manners may be a bit rough at times but his mental apparatus works as smoothly as a ball bearing in olive oil."

It was no longer easy for Biggy's enemies to ask rhetorical or satirical questions in the local press about his competence and know that the answers from the electorate would always be the ones they wanted.

When his well-placed opponent inquired, "Would you want him for your boss? Would you place him in charge of the city's money? Do you want him to look after the education of your children?" many replied in effect, "Why not? He's a hard-working go-getter, and maybe he didn't go to Harvard but he was educated in our high school and he's smart as hell. Look what he's done to that bunch on Hill Street."

The transfigured, symbolic Biggy and the flesh-and-blood person became inextricably interwoven in the public mind. The real Biggy acting as hero of the plot—developed sometimes by the press, sometimes by Biggy himself—and the symbolic stereotype became one. Moreover, since the local audience now read about Biggy in the metropolitan press, what people thought and did was now determined somewhat by symbols coming from the outside world as well as from the local group. Perhaps Biggy needed no prompting to do what he did as mayor, but the reporters' early delight and extensive coverage of the first acts of the drama shaped the course of events and helped Biggy, his friends, and his foes alike to learn who they were and to define to themselves what they were doing.

His inaugural speech immediately after election brought to Yankee City still more reporters, cameramen from the motion picture companies, and agents of all America's great mass media to record and report what was said and done by the new mayor and those around him, whether friend or foe. The symbol of Biggy as the untamed man from the wrong part of town, the big tough hero of the multitude, the strong and powerful protector of the weak who had no social pretensions, was further delineated, expanded, made more attractive, more understandable and, for a time, more acceptable to the American public.

Despite the fact that he was a person of considerable substance, to some of these legend makers and myth builders he was "the man with only one shirt," the fellow who had "a cheap $25 suit," and "the redhead with the old hat that doesn't fit." These external signs were supposed to represent the inner man and what Biggy was to his community. Such a positive symbolic person, created as a physically powerful man clothed so that he became a person who dressed "just like everyone else only worse," was easy for the masses to understand and someone with whom they could easily identify. "You don't laugh *at* a guy like that," it was said, "you laugh with him, you laugh because you like him. He is the kind of a guy who can take care of himself and he doesn't have to think he is Jesus Christ to do it."

Some news accounts played at length on the relation between Biggy's clothing and his status. Under the heading MAYOR SAYS HE HAS A SHIRT one reported on the experience of a salesman entering the mayor's office.

The silk-shirt salesman was most confident of them all coming in. Going out, and he went out quickly, he was almost indignant. He let his wrath spill over in the hearing of the usual anteroom crowd.

"The mayor was kidding me," he sputtered.

"What did he say?" asked one of the mayor's friends.

"He said he had a shirt."

"Well," said the mayor's friend unsmilingly, "he has."

When Biggy walked out on the platform to make his inaugural speech to a huge crowd overflowing beyond the auditorium through the corridors and out into the street, one of the great metropolitan dailies having a large circulation in Yankee City reported that

Biggy's football physique didn't squeeze with real dignity into his grand new $25 mayor's suit. Biggy's flaming red mop of hair can't be tamed by even such an afternoon as he spent today in Nick's Nifty Barber Shop. Biggy never made a speech before in his life if you don't count the times that he has told this gang or that gang just where to get off and what to expect. So the "big bunch of fellow citizens" out front thought they saw something funny. Biggy opened his mouth to read and then snapped his jaw shut. He jerked loose a half-dozen buttons of his overcoat with one yank. He bent a steely blue eye on the nearest and huskiest laughter. That gentleman never so much as snickered again all evening. Biggy's eye roved, silence followed his glance.

All the press reported his speech and described everything that Biggy and his audience said with great enthusiasm. All used the same symbol in anecdotes and stories, the only difference being the order or emphasis. All played up the point that Biggy now had control over constituted authority, and all made particular reference to what he had to say about policemen. "And best of all," the American public was told, "were the cops, the cops that have 'hunted' Biggy and have 'pinched' him twice and have treated him like a 'bum.' They were all good cops tonight. They stood respectively at attention. They 'Yes, Mr. Mayored' him, and Patrolman Johnny Evans, whom Biggy has promised to 'get,' stood by Biggy's side while Biggy spoke and held Biggy's hat. It was a big night."

Under such headlines as NEW MAYOR TO BE FRIEND OF BUMS other reporters said that Biggy had declared he was "going down to the cop station and tell a few flatfeet something for their own good and 'if I ever hear they are getting too high hat to send out word at night for a prisoner who wants to arrange bail, they will be up on charges. That is what they did to me when I was arrested for bouncing my fist off the then mayor's mug.' "

When Biggy Muldoon announced that he would reward his friends the press changed his expression to meet the demands of the symbol they had helped to create, and to satisfy the appetites of their readers. "What the hell," they had him say, "we won, didn't we? Don't the winners deserve the gravy?"

Within a few days following his inauguration Biggy was in a bitter fight with the city council. "This morning," the big dailies announced, "before the smoke of the press photographers' flashlights had cleared away on the inaugural scene, Biggy called his brand new council into his presence and, in the picturesque and often unpublishable language of which Navy forecastles and Yankee City street corners have made him a past master, told 'em straight from the shoulder 'what is what, who is who, and why, from now on in this man's town.' "

The first meeting with the city council, which still prevented him from getting his permit for a filling station, was reported in the *New York Times* under the following heading and lead lines:

NEW MAYOR, EX GOB, SWABS CITY'S DECK. MAYOR TELLS YANKEE CITY COUNCIL WHAT IS WHAT, WHO IS WHO, AND WHY. WILL PAY OFF GRUDGES. MAN WHO HAD HIM "PINCHED" AND ONE WHO CALLED HIM "PUPPY" ARE OUT OF LUCK.

Within two weeks after his election, two classes of functionaries pushed into the drama of Biggy Muldoon: representatives of the stage and entrepreneurs who thought they saw a chance to make some quick money out of the fame of this new celebrity. The Boston papers played up his Yankee shrewdness at bargaining in this new situation. The headline over one of them summarized a long story: BIGGY LISTENS TO SIREN CALL OF VAUDEVILLE. ISN'T GOING TO GET HIM DIRT CHEAP, HE SAYS, AFTER SEEING AGENT. ANTE MUST BE DOUBLED AT LEAST.

Meanwhile the following wire, one of several, came from a motion picture company. "Your colorful career excellent material for motion picture story. Please wire collect if you are interested in starring in this production to be made in Yankee City." Another headline announced: BIGGY GETS $10,000 THEATRICAL OFFER. MAKES ENGAGEMENT TO JUDGE TWO BEAUTY CONTESTS. The story reported a wire from New York offering him a thousand a week for ten weeks.

Biggy signed a contract with one of the great theatrical producers to appear for a week with *The Connecticut Yankee*, at that time playing in Boston. After being introduced by the star, he made a speech each night. He told them, "Mark Twain was considered erratic and a fool in the days gone by. A lot of persons consider me a fool. But let me tell you if I wasn't the mayor I'd still be making a living. I can always buy gas and I can sell it cheap."

A short time later the country's public prints were reporting new developments in Biggy's career under such headings as these from the *New York Herald Tribune:* BIGGY MULDOON SAILS FOR COAST, PERHAPS IN SEARCH OF BRIDE. MAYOR OF YANKEE CITY SEEKS REST AND QUIET AS HE LEAVES FOR THE WEST. PREDICTING REPEAL OF BAY STATE DRY LAW AND THE ELECTION OF A WET GOVERNOR. The American press generally reported: BIGGY MULDOON IN THE WEST TO FIND BRUNETTE OR REDHEADED WIFE. MAYOR DECIDES TO "GIVE BREAK" TO SOME BEAUTIFUL GIRL. BARS BLONDES BECAUSE THEY ARE "NOT SO GOOD AS HOUSEKEEPERS."

All these stories were part of the publicity that ensued when he was asked to judge beauty contests, dance marathons, and similar exhibitions all over the country. He accepted a large number of these invitations. Wherever he went he was warmly received by the press and the people, and spread the story of his mistreatment, telling his audiences how he stood for the common man and for everyone's having more fun out of life.

He became a symbolic figure of pleasure, of permissiveness. With him millions could vicariously rebel against the restraints of their environment and have a good time. Although he did not drink, prohibiting people from having a drink was not to him a "noble experiment"; he was for everyone's drinking as much as he wanted. He swore and enjoyed gambling with his friends. He liked to have fun. For his great audience he was a "good guy" and a "straight-shooter"—not a hypocrite or a stuffed shirt.

LADY'S FAVORITE AND
MASCULINE SYMBOL

As indicated by the references to blondes and redheads, one of the most striking symbolic transformations of Biggy Muldoon, following his recognition by the national mass media, was his masculine role and his relation to women. It will be remembered that at the time of his election his reputation was such that he felt it necessary to declare publicly, "I'm supposed to be a woman-hater, that's the bunk," and that with the Navy in the Caribbean he had been forced to "jump out of a second-story window to keep my independence."

Editors and those who controlled other mass media soon got the feel of Biggy's potentialities as a sexual symbol. Within a month or two he was being played up as a judge of beautiful women, a man in search of a beautiful bride, an authority on female attractiveness. The businessmen who put on such attractions as beauty contests, marathons, and burlesque shows saw in him a figure that would appeal to male and female alike as a man who knew his way around and was attractive to women. He was regarded by both sexes as a he-man, "not a pretty boy you see in the movies, but a two-fisted guy." Biggy became a powerful masculine sexual symbol for many in the great audience. For the women he was something more than the bad boy who said girls were "like puppy dogs"; multitudes of letters, coyly or openly erotic, poured in on him.

In America the cluster of meanings about the big two-fisted, strong young male who knows what he wants and sets out to get it always evokes positive feeling among many as to his sexuality and potency. In the fantasies of his mass audience Biggy was soon transformed and served as symbol of the untamed male, the great muscular "brute." He became still another example of the libidinal male found in the literature of the superior such as *The Hairy Ape, Lady Chatterley's Lover,* and Robinson Jeffers' "Roan Stallion," or in popular novels, movies, and radio as the truck driver and the husky sailor; or in folk myth and ballad as expressed in the powerful sexuality of the subordinate white or Negro male. Symbolically he was to many the anarchal monad, the free man, free from weakening middle-class morality. In fact, even in middle-class terms Biggy was in many respects a well-reared, proper boy; he was not loose sexually any more than he was loose in other areas of his deportment. His mother's training had stayed with him. He did not drink or smoke and, though not ascetic, his conduct with women was scrupulous and careful. But the women who wrote him from all over the United States saw and responded to another Biggy—the symbolic one created by the press. A Missouri young woman wrote him:

I guess you are beginning to wonder who in the world has the boldness to write to you. I am a widow twenty-six years old. I have a daughter two and a half years old. I have said in the last two years that no man was worthy of my respect. But I changed my mind yesterday when I read the article about you. I said to myself, "there's my ideal man, a man that decides what he wants and then gets it . . ." Have you a sweetheart? I hope not, for maybe if you haven't you will write to me . . . P.S. I wonder if you care if I cut your picture and kept it?

A young mother sent him this note: "Dear Mayor: I have a baby son fourteen months old who is a Red Head and a wow. He's bound to have everything he wants and to have his own way, so I hope you won't feel bad if I call him Biggy Muldoon the second." Biggy replied that it was O.K. with him.

A young lady from Mississippi told Biggy that she "loved his picture and admired his taste for beauty." She went on to say,

I'm a perfect brunette, 5 feet, 4 inches, under thirty (unfortunately a widow) but just the age and with enough experience to be the most loveable and devoted companion you could ever dream of.

Why don't you spend your summer vacation in the good old Dixie state—Mississippi—or Memphis, Tennessee? Sports of all kinds if you like that too. I am anxiously and eagerly waiting for your answer.

Not all Biggy's letters were from women of his own age. Many were from much older women who gave him motherly advice. One began, "Dear Sir: I am an old lady of seventy years and I want to *talk to you* and hope you will take what I say in the same spirit that I mean it, which is very kindly." There followed a long set of moral instructions on how he should act as a man and as a mayor.

On the masculine side there was considerable variety. Although in grammar, punctuation, and spelling the following is not representative of all the letters he received from men, it does indicate some of the interests of a large class who wrote. Mr. Muldoon, Dear Sir:

i have been appointed to see if you could come to speake in this city [an industrial community in New England] in one of the largest hall in the center of the city we have a strick in the cotton mills there are 27,000 on strick and things are bad i thought i would see a good boam to come you might run for governor some day i was one that helped to bring you here to sant Marey smoke talk and we paide you price but that was a church time and the tickets were 75 cents each. you will dou the wright thing if you come remember you are not the only on that wants money just help and you will get used all wright.

hoping to here from you.

Another large group of letters came from people who were asking favors or financial help. Others expressed gratitude for help received. One covered with bright-colored figures of lions and tigers was from the general agent of the wild animal circus whose posters had brought him fame. It began

My dear Sir:

It is my desire first to say, "That's the spirit, Muldoon, and here's wishing you luck and congratulations." As I have just heard your little piece of Oratory over the radio—I am the little fellow that Approached you and asked Your Permission to Tack Cloth Banners on Your Garage for the West Show and you Helped Give me a Reputation by not only letting me tack Your Garage but you also gave me Permission to Tack Our Cloth Banners on Your Residence on the Boston-Portland Highway Which Caused our Show to get a world of Publicity which is a Star in my Crown and practically made me as a circus press representative.

The newspapers shifted Biggy, the symbol, from the man who was calling certain ethnic groups "guys who weren't white people" to a man who said every American was just as good as anybody else. It also seems probable that Biggy himself, in response to his new situation, had modified his position. By the time he got ready to run for president, he declared,

I hope some of this radical hatred may be wiped out. What difference does it make what we are, whether we are black men, white men, red men, or green men? I judge a man as a man if he pays his bills. You know what they used to say about the man from the South of Ireland a few years ago in Yankee City. I hate to tell you. Now they make as good citizens as anybody else. After the Irishers came the Wops, then the Greeks, then the Armenians. And now you can't tell what they are. They became as good Americans as the rest of us. So I say don't hold nothing against no man. Consider yourself as good as anybody else. That is what I do.

A summary review of a few of the comments appearing at that time in newspapers throughout the United States gives an impression of the kind of composite symbol Biggy had become for the American public. The *New York Times* said that "although his theory that 'the winners deserve the gravy' is not new in politics, it at least is refreshingly frank." The *Kansas City Post* said, "As any soldier knows, women are the silly sex as far as gobs are concerned—Mayor Biggy Muldoon's official behavior promises to be deplorable, but he will get away with it. The women of Yankee City like the women of other towns will forgive him on the grounds that he is picturesque." The Lincoln, Nebraska, *Star* characterized him as an "honest, frank, outspoken, two-fisted mayor, much different from most of his contemporaries." The South Bend, Indiana, *Tribune* editorialized, "He occupies a position which many persons at some time or other wish they held. Many a citizen has told himself, 'Now if I were mayor of this town,' when a traffic man gets rough or some ego-ruffling act is committed by a public servant!" The whole situation as far as Biggy's own career is concerned was well summarized by the *New York Herald Tribune:*

The redheaded ex-"gob," has the distinction of having aroused nation-wide interest in an ordinary filling station in Yankee City. What newspaper has not carried accounts of the multitudinous developments centering around the filling station? . . . It is difficult to begrudge him his victory. Granting his comic-strip qualities, his obvious unfitness for the position of mayor of old Yankee City, one cannot but admire his amazing courage and persistence. He has shed a veritable sea of troubles. He has emerged unbowed with unshaken purpose from a thousand contests. And despite everything, his spirits are high, his vocabulary is as untamed as ever. Probably it would be well if the "big bugs" called off their war on the indomitable redhead. Biggy has threatened to run for governor. Given plenty of violent opposition, another fine or two, and a few more jail sentences, and he might be elected.

Biggy the man, living and acting out his life in Yankee City, had largely disappeared in the enlarged and greatly modified heroic mold into which his life had been re-formed by the public press and other mass media. Although each part of the popular figure was founded on elements of fact, the few quotations from the letters of his public make clear that his meanings for them, although intensely personal, express the collective values, the hopes and fears, the wishes and anxieties of the American people.

SELECTED PUBLICATIONS BY DR. WARNER

A Black Civilization (Harper, New York, 1958).

The Yankee City Series (with varying co-authors; consisting of volumes on *The Social Life of a Modern Community*, 1941; *The Status System of a Modern Community*, 1942; *The Social System of American Ethnic Groups*, 1945; *The Social System of the Modern Factory: The Strike; A Social Analysis*, 1947, and *The Living and the Dead: a Study of the Symbolic Life of Americans*, 1959, all published by Yale U. Press).

Social Class in America (Harper, 1960). (With Marcia Meeker and Kenneth Eells.)

American Life, Dream and Reality (U. of Chicago Press, 1953).

Big Business Leaders in America (Harper, New York, 1955). (With James Abbeglen.)

The American Federal Executive (Yale U. Press, 1963) (With others.)

Democracy in Jonesville; a Study in Quality and Inequality (Harper, New York, 1949).

SUGGESTIONS FOR FURTHER READING

Radcliffe-Brown, A. R., *The Andaman Islanders* (Cambridge U. Press, London, 1938).

Durkheim, Emile, *Elementary Forms of the Religious Life* (Free Press, New York, 1947).

Freud, Sigmund, *Totem and Taboo* (Penguin, 1938).

Lee, Alfred M., *The Daily Newspaper in America* (Macmillan, New York, 1937).

Mead, George H., "Behavioristic Account of the Significant Symbol," *Journal of Philosophy*, vol. 19, 1922, pp. 157–163.

———, *Mind, Self, and Society from the Standpoint of a Social Behaviorist* U. of Chicago Press, 1934).

QUESTIONS

1.   Discuss the rise and fall in the magnification of Biggy's image by the national communications media. Can you think of other instances of the same sort of development? Discuss.

2.   List the basic elements which made Biggy "good copy."

3.   "The degree of rationality and accuracy exhibited in the news stories of a newspaper or magazine is in direct relation to the degree of national values of its audience." Discuss this statement in relation to present-day criticism of newspaper or television content. Is it an argument for or against "higher standards" in newspapers? or TV?

4.   Consider the similarities and differences in the appeal to audience shared by Biggy and Adolf Hitler. Briefly discuss the transformation of the Führer with particular attention to folk symbolism.

Donald F. Cox

Clues for Advertising Strategists *

COX'S REVIEW OF THE LITERATURE bearing on advertising strategy is of necessity a review of the literature on mass communications as it bears on the problem of trying to influence people. Many of the essays in this book are written in what may be called a "contemplative" mood; they describe how things happen. Cox's article is rather "manipulative" in tone; he is saying "If you want to cause certain things to happen, here is how to do it." Therefore he uses the same body of literature in a slightly different way.

Although it happens that he has addressed himself to the problems of the advertiser, much of what he has to say is equally relevant to political propaganda, psychological warfare, or efforts to teach virtuous behavior by exhortation, editorial, and news report. For example, anyone seriously involved in the problems faced by the National Association for the Advancement of Colored People, or for that matter by the White Citizens' Council—or by the Republicans or the Democrats in the next Presidential campaign—or by the John Birch Society or the Communist Party—could translate much of what is here said about selective exposure, selective perception, selective retention, and selective decision, for example, to his own field of concern. Similarly, the effectiveness or ineffectiveness of broadcasts by Radio Free Europe to the satellite nations can be analyzed using such conceptions.

The answers to questions asked from any of the standpoints indicated in the last paragraph might vary from the answers a U.S. advertising man would receive most of the time. But Cox is not primarily concerned with answers; he is concerned with the kinds of questions that can profitably be asked in planning and evaluating an advertising campaign. To a very considerable degree, questions of the same sort can and should be asked about political campaigns or psychological warfare efforts or good-will crusades. As we point out in our introduction to Sorensen's article on psychological warfare (pp. 444-447),

* Reprinted from the *Harvard Business Review,* November–December, 1961, by permission of the author and the publisher. (Copyright 1961 by Harvard University.)

the social barriers to asking rational questions about psychological warfare or political campaigns are great; on the whole, it is easier for an advertising man to be rational about his business than for a campaigner for improved race relations or a candidate for President to be rational about his activity. But even so, the advertising strategist in a big business faces, ordinarily, the kind of difficulties which we describe in our introduction to Sorensen—so much so that market-research specialists not infrequently say "our main obstacle is the client." That is, the client insists on disregarding uncomfortable findings or interprets them (selectively, of course) to fit his own preferences. Because in many business activities there is a dollar-and-cents payoff which is clear and unequivocal, advertising strategists have nevertheless gone further than educators or public officials, for instance, in learning how to conduct effective mass communications—and so everyone interested in influencing through communications can learn something from the kind of analysis Cox here supplies.

L. A. D.

DR. COX is Assistant Professor of Business Administration at the Graduate School of Business Administration, Harvard University. He received his D.B.A. from Harvard and currently teaches there in the fields of marketing and consumer behavior.

Can continued repetition of the same advertising appeal boomerang and cause fewer rather than more people to want your product? "Never," or "almost never," say many advertising textbook writers. Assuming that, except in unusual circumstances, repetition cannot be overdone, they advocate its continued use as an important advertising strategy. However, recent research findings from advertising and mass communications research studies support an opposite conclusion—i.e., that repetition can be, and often is, overdone. In effect, more and more advertising dollars can be spent to drive people away from wanting a product.

I would like to review and to report on some findings of advertising and mass communications research which are relevant to the basic problems faced by the advertising strategist. There are two points to keep in mind throughout:

[1] Important advertising decisions are based on, and to a large extent determined by, certain basic assumptions as to how advertising and the underlying process of mass communications operate.

[2] These basic assumptions are not necessarily in agreement with recent research findings in the area of advertising and mass communications research.

If I seem to be critical of the advertising strategist's thoughts or actions, it is not because I am unsympathetic to the difficulties under which he works. It is because I share his interest in getting the job done better.

One note of warning is in order. The conditions faced by a particular advertiser may be quite different from the conditions on which research findings are based. For example, the subjects used in some of the experimental studies which will be reported were college students who are not entirely representative of the audience to which most advertisers address their appeals.

It would therefore be unwise to accept the findings of any one research study at face value without first determining whether the conditions on which the research is based do apply to the advertiser's particular situation.

It would be equally unwise to reject the research findings unless one is quite confident that the conditions on which the findings are based are quite irrelevant and that if the advertiser's unique conditions *were* substituted, the findings would be different. It is all too easy to reject, out of hand, information which does not agree with our own preconceptions.

CREDIBILITY

A number of recent reports testify to a concern among advertising men that consumers often have less than complete faith in the credibility of advertising. It is a sign of the times that *Printers' Ink* is currently engaged in a "continuing study" of "truth and taste in advertising." [1]

The "credibility" problem confronts not only the obviously dishonest advertiser, but also advertisers who maintain high ethical standards. Some people tend to be suspicious of anyone who is trying to sell something. One way of showing this suspicion is to express disbelief in a company's advertising. But what is the effect of this suspicion? How does an audience react when it perceives a communicator as being high in credibility (i.e., impartial and honest) as opposed to one low in credibility (i.e., biased)?

Carl I. Hovland and Walter Weiss conducted an experiment in which two groups listened to the same persuasive material and were later measured for changes in their opinions. [2] The variable tested was the degree of credibility of the communicator. The communicator presented

1. *Printers' Ink,* July 22, 1960, p. 11.
2. "The Influence of Source Credibility on Communication Effectiveness," *Public Opinion Quarterly,* Winter 1951–1952, pp. 635–650. This information is also reported by Carl I. Hovland, Irving L. Janis, and Harold H. Kelley in *Communication and Persuasion* (Yale U. P., New Haven, 1953).

to one group was introduced in such a way as to appear to be high in credibility (e.g., Dr. Oppenheimer writing about atomic submarines) and the communicator to the second group was made to appear biased and low in credibility (e.g., *Pravda*). As might be expected, when the groups were tested after listening to the communication, there was less changing of opinion in the group which had listened to the low-credibility source.

THE "SLEEPER EFFECT"

The most interesting finding of the study resulted when the subjects were tested four weeks later. At this time the percentage of those exposed to the high-credibility source who had changed their opinions decreased. On the other hand, of those exposed to the low-credibility source the percentage who changed their opinions actually *increased*—what the authors termed the "sleeper effect." In other words, both the positive and negative prestige effects of the source of the communication tended to disappear after several weeks.

These findings were confirmed and extended by the results of a later experiment by Herbert C. Kelman and Carl I. Hovland.[3] Groups of high school students were exposed to communications arguing for lenient treatment of juvenile delinquents. Each group was exposed to the same message, but in one case the communicator was introduced as an impartial and sincere expert (a judge), whereas the other speaker was introduced as a suspicious character who might well benefit from leniency toward young criminals. Attitudes were measured after the communication, and it was again found that initially the "positive" communicator was more influential in changing attitudes.

However, three weeks later the researchers remeasured the attitudes of half of the subjects and found that the effect on attitudes was now about the same for both speakers. Although the listeners had not forgotten the source, apparently they had dissociated the content from the source of the communication. For the remaining half of the subjects, the introductory remarks of the speakers were replayed just prior to the delayed testing (which also took place three weeks after the original communication). It was found that this "reinstatement" of the sources had an effect almost equal to that of the initial communication. In other words, after a period of three weeks the subjects apparently no longer associated the negative or biased speaker with the *content* of the communication and therefore were more likely to agree with the content of his remarks. However, when they were reminded of the biased source, they again

3. "Reinstatement of the Communication in Delayed Measurement of Opinion Change," *Journal of Abnormal and Social Psychology*, vol. 48, 1953, pp. 327–335.

discounted his remarks and were thus much less likely to follow his suggestions.

These findings related to the "sleeper effect" suggest several interesting possibilities in the way of advertising strategy. For example, a coffee growers' trade association which has been trying, by advertising every four weeks or so, to educate housewives in the art of making good coffee might consider the use of concentrated advertising; that is, it might concentrate all advertising which might ordinarily run through a six-month period in one or two weeks. Presumably one of the problems to be faced is source credibility; the housewife's reaction to an ad might be, "They just want me to use more coffee." Yet according to the association's present strategy, advertising is timed to reinstate the communicator every four weeks. This may not be helping the situation! The findings I have reported suggest that in certain situations it might be better for the advertiser to dissociate himself as the source of the message. (Let me emphasize, however, that just because a company is advertising does not mean it will automatically be considered to be low in credibility. Some will be; some will not be. Also keep in mind that advertisers of branded products probably do not want their names to be dissociated from the content of the communication.)

EMOTIONAL APPEALS

A recurring issue in advertising strategy concerns the use of appeals which are primarily "rational" as opposed to appeals which are primarily "emotional."

However, Hovland, Janis, and Kelley cite several studies which support the contention that emotional appeals are superior to rational appeals. However, they also note that other experimental findings "fail to confirm the superiority of 'emotional' appeals and even suggest that such appeals can be less effective than 'rational' ones."

Evidence on this point comes from a study by Irving L. Janis and Seymour Feshbach.[4] They conducted an experiment in which groups of students heard one of three versions of a fifteen-minute talk on dental hygiene. Each version contained the same general information and made similar recommendations, but differed in the strength of the fear appeal used. For example:

> The "strong" fear appeal emphasized the pain caused by tooth decay and was illustrated with slides showing diseased gums.

4. "Effects of Fear-Arousing Communications," *Journal of Abnormal and Social Psychology*, vol. 48, 1953, pp. 78–92.

- In the "moderate" appeal the threats appeared less often and in a milder form.
- In the "minimal" fear-appeal version the more severe threats were replaced by fairly neutral information.
- In addition, the strong appeal emphasized the personal consequences of improper dental hygiene (i.e., "This can happen to you"); the moderate and minimal appeals described the consequences in impersonal language.

The main results of the experiment indicate that the minimal fear appeal was more effective. The net change toward conformity with the recommended hygienic behavior (as reported by the subjects) in the group exposed to the minimal appeal was 36 percent; in the group exposed to the moderate appeal the net change was 24 percent; in the audience for the strong appeal the net change was only 8 percent. These results support the hypothesis that in certain situations appeals which build up a minimal level of emotional tension are more likely to be effective than those which lead to higher levels of tension. Janis and Feshbach suggest that one of the apparent reasons is that subjects exposed to the strong fear appeal showed more resentment toward the communicator and consequently were more likely to reject the communication.

DEFENSIVE AVOIDANCE

Hovland, Janis, and Kelley suggest also the possibility of a mechanism which they call "defensive avoidance." Their hypothesis states that, "when fear is strongly aroused but not adequately relieved by the reassurances contained in a persuasive communication, the audience will become motivated to ignore or to minimize the importance of the threat." [5] While the experimental evidence for this hypothesis is slim, at least none of the data contradict the contention. Furthermore, the hypothesis is consistent with other psychological evidence in the operation of defensive mechanisms.

What is the significance for business? Earlier I suggested that an emotional appeal tends to become less effective as the strength of the aroused motive increases *relative* to the individual's own feelings of certainty that the motive will be satisfied. The role of the rational element in the communications is to spell out, in a believable way, how the advocated course of action can lead to the satisfaction of the aroused motive, and thereby increase the individual's own feeling of certainty of the motive being satisfied.

5. Hovland, Janis, and Kelley, *op. cit.,* pp. 87–88.

If this contention is realistic, the implications for advertising strategy seem clear. Not only must the advertiser be honest and promise no more than his product can deliver; he also must promise no more than a potential consumer thinks his *product* should deliver. To illustrate again:

I have heard of a product which, on the basis of tests, performs exceptionally well. The advertiser, naturally, feels justified in promoting the remarkable achievements of his product. The only problem is that the test results are so remarkable that very few people believe them enough to try his product. While his claims are able to arouse emotions (e.g., the feeling that "it would be a great product—if it worked"), he is unable to provide potential customers with adequate assurance that the product will satisfy the emotions which have been aroused. Since he is unable to convince consumers of the exceptional performance of his product, it is conceivable that he might do better if he claimed less for the product.

BOTH SIDES OF THE ARGUMENT

It is often said that there are two sides to every story, but only rarely do we see or hear both sides of an advertising story. There are occasional advertisers who say, "Other products are good, but ours is better," or, "Other brands cost less, but you get more quality if you buy our brand"; however, in the general run of advertisements these are exceptions rather than the rule. Are there any advantages to presenting both sides of the story? Several interesting experiments have been devoted to answering the question, "Which is more effective, a one-sided or two-sided argument?"

Carl I. Hovland, Arthur A. Lumsdaine, and Fred D. Sheffield presented to groups of soldiers one of two versions of a talk which argued that the war with Japan (after Germany's surrender) would last for at least two years.[6] One version stressed Japan's strength; the other also stressed Japan's strength but gave some opposing arguments dealing with that nation's weaknesses. The soldiers were asked to estimate the probable length of the war before and immediately after listening to the communication.

One of the noteworthy features of this experiment is that the investigators recognized the importance of specifying the conditions under which a variation in appeals is or is not effective. Had they considered their audience to be an undifferentiated mass, and had they tallied their results accordingly, they would have concluded that a one-sided argu-

6. *Experiments on Mass Communications* (Princeton U. P., Princeton, N.J., 1949).

ment was just as effective as a two-sided argument. However, in analyzing the results they split the soldiers into two groups—those initially
opposed to the communicator's position and those initially in favor (but
able to become more extreme in their view). Their findings are summarized in Table 1.

In other words, presenting both sides of the argument is more effective if the individual addressed is initially opposed to the issue, but the
one-sided argument is more effective with those initially favoring the
communicator's position. The implications are clear for advertising
strategy, although it needs to be emphasized that before acting on them
the advertiser should first find out whether and to what extent his
audience is opposed or in agreement with his message.

Hovland, Lumsdaine, and Sheffield also considered the soldier's education as a variable and found that the communication giving both sides
of the argument was more effective with the better-educated group
regardless of initial position, whereas the one-sided presentation was

**Table 1—Net Percentage of Individuals Changing Opinion in Direction
of Position Advocated by Communicator**

	Exposed to One-sided Argument	Exposed to Both Sides
Initially opposed to communicator's position	36	48
Initially in favor of communicator's position	52	23

Source: Carl I. Hovland, "Effects of the Mass Media of Communication," in Gardner Lindzey (ed.),
Handbook of Social Psychology (Addison-Wesley, Reading, Mass., 1954), p. 1079.

primarily effective among the less educated soldiers who were already in
favor of the communicator's position. Here, too, there are implications
for advertising strategy—although it is again important to study the
advertiser's situation first (i.e., the education level of potential buyers).

ADVERTISING "STRATEGY" AND THE
WEAPONS ANALOGY? IS IT VALID?

In listening to some advertising men, and in reading some of their
writings, I am struck by the metaphors they use to describe their advertising strategy. There seems to be a great deal of reference to weaponry and
other symbols of aggression and hostility. They often talk, for example,
of "hitting" people, "taking pot shots," "turning on the heat," "banging
away," "blasting away," and so on. An agency vice-president has said:
"I would consider the use of several different media for short periods of

time too much like using a shotgun when you need the heavy and sustained firepower of a battalion artillery."

Could it be that some members of the audience (the "enemy"?) want to run for cover when this artillery begins to blast away at them in the form of monotonous, irritating, unending repetition of the same jingle, slogan, or whatever other ammunition has been fired at them for the past three to ten years? Can repetition be overdone?

Not according to the textbook writers. Their answer to this question is a qualified "no." Rosser Reeves, the leading exponent of continued repetition of a single successful appeal, maintains that "unless a product becomes outmoded a great campaign will not wear out." [7] Melvin S. Hattwick says that you probably cannot overdo repetition, but if repetition were overdone, it would only lead to " 'overlearning' which . . . is certainly no hindrance to selling merchandise. In fact it is a real aid." [8] Darrell B. Lucas and Steuart Henderson Britt contend that "the surest way for an advertiser to maintain a competitive advantage is to repeat his messages so often that they are always fresh in the minds of the consumers." But they suggest that "repetition of a central theme with variations is more effective than repetition without variation." [9]

The textbook writers offer little directly relevant evidence to support their conclusions. Nevertheless, their counsel does lend unanimous and even vigorous encouragement to the advertiser who would pursue a strategy of continued repetition of the same advertising appeal.

By contrast, communications research offers little evidence which would support the use of excessive repetition of the same appeal to the same audience. For example, Hovland, Janis, and Kelley, after reviewing several experiments, say:

"Repetition does not influence the retention of the information content of a communication in any simple manner. While the usual effect is to increase retention under some circumstances, too-frequent repetition without any reward leads to loss of attention, boredom, and disregard of the communication." [10]

One study they cite found "improvement in retention with increasing repetition up to three or four times. Thereafter, the effect of additional repetition is slight." [P. 249.]

A three-step study carried out by the Schwerin Research Corporation

7. Rosser Reeves, *Reality in Advertising* (Knopf, New York, 1961), p. 32.

8. *How to Use Psychology for Better Advertising* (Prentice-Hall, New York, 1950), p. 244.

9. *Advertising Psychology and Research* (McGraw-Hill, New York, 1950), pp. 80–81.

10. Hovland, Janis, and Kelley, *op. cit.,* p. 247.

combines both laboratory and real-life exposure to commercials (see Table 2):

[1] An audience was invited to view a television program in a theater. During the program break the audience viewed a commercial for a drug product. Immediately after the program the audience was subjected to several tests of recall of the commercial.

[2] The commercial which had been thus tested was then exposed on regular television for a period of two weeks. At that time, another audience (42 percent of whom said that they had seen the commercial

Table 2—Percentage Share of Audience Recalling Brand Name and At Least One Sales Point

| | TEST | | |
COMMERCIAL	No. 1 First Exposure	No. 2 After 2 Weeks	No. 3 After 4 Weeks
A	55	46	36
B	23	25	50
C	32	54	44

Source: "When Should the Effects of Television Advertising Be Measured? Part I: Recall," *Technical and Analytical Review,* Spring 1960, p. 9.

on regular television) was invited to the theater. Like the first audience, these people were exposed to a television program which included this commercial and were then tested for recall.

[3] The commercial then continued to be exposed on regular television for another two weeks, bringing the total period of regular television exposure to one month. At the end of this period, the commercial was again tested with a new audience in the same way as before. Of this third audience 59 percent reported that they had seen the commercial on regular television.

The entire procedure was repeated for two more one-month periods, with two different commercials for the same product and two different audiences (ranging in size from 250 to 730).

Let us call the first commercial "A," the second "B," and the third "C." We see, from the results of one of the measures of recall (shown in Table 2), that Commercials A and C were less effective after four weeks of exposure than after two weeks. It would appear that these commercials had been overexposed. Commercial B is the only one which shows steadily increasing recall. However, this may have happened because Commercial B received only one-third as much exposure on regular television as the other two did.

In another series of studies the Schwerin research group showed commercials for 31 different products to 31 different audiences.[11] After each commercial was shown, the audience was questioned to determine its "competitive preference," i.e., the share of people who want the advertised product. These competitive preference scores were recorded and were compared with the competitive preference scores which were obtained by the same 31 commercials in a second test. The second test (which used different audiences but otherwise was conducted like the first) took place after the commercials had been shown on regular television for periods of from three to thirty months.

These results, too, are not encouraging to the repetitive advertiser. In the case of 77 percent of the products tested, significantly fewer people wanted the product after the second test (i.e., after three to thirty months of exposure on television) than after the first. Because the amount of exposure on regular television was not controlled, these results cannot be considered conclusive. However, they hardly lend support to the strategy of continued repetition of the same advertising appeal. Rather, they buttress the contention of Hovland, Janis, and Kelley that too-frequent repetition of a communication can lead to disregard of that communication. The effect is not merely a matter of diminishing returns, but of *negative* returns. That is to say, excessive repetition can boomerang and cause an actual loss in learning or a negative opinion change.

Although I am unable to relate the results of the measures used by the Schwerin people with sales results, there is some reason to believe that there might well be a positive relationship. If there were such a relationship, then the advertiser who repeats the same commercial to the same audience too often may actually be counteracting the effect on sales of his earlier advertising. Even though his total sales might be holding steady for the time being, sales to that segment of the market which has heard or seen the commercial too often could be sharply reduced.

MEDIA SELECTION

Media selection is one of the thorniest problems of advertising strategy. Ideally, the strategist should develop the most economical media plan which will best fit the many facets of a company's advertising situation and objectives. Unfortunately, he is often in the position of having to consider too many factors and to decide among too many

11. "When Should the Effects of Television Advertising Be Measured? Part II: Changes in Attitude and Behavior," *Technical and Analytical Review,* Summer 1960, p. 1.

alternative media plans—all the while having to base his decision on far too little reliable information. What help does the present state of communications research offer the befuddled media man?

Very little, I'm afraid. There are two basic reasons for this. First, white many media research studies are in fact available, the research methodology employed in many of them is simply not adequate in view of the immense difficulty of media research—especially research on the comparative effectiveness of media. Secondly, some of the very studies which might *eventually* prove to be helpful can compound existing difficulties because they seriously challenge some commonly accepted assumptions about media strategy.

There is considerable evidence which would support the contention that a medium may have persuasive power in its own right. If, for example, we were to present the same commercial on color and on black-and-white television, we might find, as did the Burke Marketing Research organization in 1960, that $1\frac{1}{2}$ times as many color-TV viewers recalled the commercial as did those who viewed it in black and white.[12] We might then conclude that color TV is a more effective medium than black-and-white TV. But we could be wrong.

After reviewing over fifty studies of the comparative effectiveness of various media, the Division of Academic Research Services of the Pennsylvania State University concluded that "the great majority of the studies reviewed (practically all of those made before 1950) suffer from serious defects in design which tend to vitiate their conclusions." [13] Among the defects in study design which were listed in the report was the failure to randomize subjects among treatments.

This particular shortcoming is present in the TV study just mentioned. Although the researchers tried to match viewers of color TV with viewers of black-and-white TV by picking pairs of neighbors—one of whom owned a color set, the other a black-and-white set—there is no guarantee that the neighbors were identical with respect to such characteristics as personality type, education, and intelligence which might account for differential recall. It is possible, for instance, that color-TV owners tend to be more intelligent, or more interested in the programs and products which were televised and hence more likely to recall seeing the commercial.

Unless a study carefully controls for important variables, either by precise matching of respondents or by assigning respondents to an experi-

12. "The Effectiveness of Color vs. Black-and-White Television Advertising," Burke Marketing Research, Inc., 2374 Kemper Lane, Cincinnati. (Mimeographed.)

13. "Studies of the Comparative Effectiveness of Various Media of Communication," 1959, p. 5. (Mimeographed.)

mental treatment (e.g., watching a program on color TV) at random, the results cannot be considered conclusive.

Even when the methodological problems are solved, a difficult problem of comparison remains. The powers of persuasion of any one medium depend not only on the medium *per se,* but on the type of product advertised, the nature of the message, and the types of people to whom you are advertising. While it may be practically possible to detail some of the specific conditions under which one medium is more effective than another, I have encountered little up-to-date published research that would permit useful generalization.

If the findings of recent studies that challenge basic assumptions about advertising media are realistic, some rethinking of the problems of media utilization may be in order.

The medium is often said to be instrumental in "delivering" or "selecting" the audience. But it is more likely, I think, that "audience selection" is the result of the interaction between media characteristics and audience predispositions and that in the final analysis the audience selects the medium rather than vice versa. Available research evidence would seem to support two closely related generalizations about media:

[1] The process of audience selection of media is not random. Any particular medium will have more appeal for some groups than for others.

[2] Within the larger group which is attracted to a particular medium some subgroups will be more attracted than others.

For example, in support of the first generalization, we would expect that doctors would be the primary readers of medical journals. But we must not stop here. Herbert Menzel and Elihu Katz found that most influential doctors in a medical community "were more likely to be readers of a large number of professional journals and valued them more highly than did doctors of lesser influence." [14] By way of contrast, the least influential doctors were more likely to learn of new drugs through detail men, direct mail promotion and periodicals from drug houses.

Similarly, while we would expect most women to be somewhat exposed to mass media, Elihu Katz and Paul F. Lazarsfeld report that opinion leaders are more likely to be exposed to certain mass media (because they read more magazines) than are the women they influence.[15] This study also finds that an opinion leader's sphere of influence is likely to be limited to a specific area such as marketing, fashions, or moviegoing. Interestingly enough, there is a tendency for opinion leaders to be

14. "Social Relations and Innovation in the Medical Profession," *Public Opinion Quarterly,* Winter 1955–56, pp. 337–352.

15. *Personal Influence* (Free Press, New York, 1955), pp. 309–320.

more exposed to media that are appropriate to their own sphere of influence.

In addition to opinion leadership, there are many other bases of differential exposure to mass media. For example, Katz and Lazarsfeld have found highest exposure to "popular fiction" (such as movie and "true story" type magazines and daytime radio and TV serials) among women—

- · who are lower in social status
- · who are less "gregarious" (regardless of social status)
- · who are higher in "anxiety"—i.e., who "sometimes feel blue and depressed," independently of gregariousness

The foregoing studies support two important implications which may conflict with the assumptions held by some advertising strategists. One concerns competition among media; the other concerns the use of the same advertising appeals in media which attract different audiences.

COMPETITION AMONG MEDIA

It is fashionable these days to criticize the "rating game" by which television programs prosper or perish according to their ratings (in cost-per-thousand viewers). I cannot resist joining the critics, and will even go them a step further and criticize the equivalent of the rating game in other media—the use of figures on cost-per-thousand readers, listeners, or passersby as the primary basis for media decisions.

However, the basis of my criticism is different from that of the popular critics. Furthermore, my criticism applies only to those advertising strategists who use cost-per-thousand figures as the primary basis for making either-or decisions among certain "competing" media. It may be that the media attract different audiences or otherwise perform different functions for the advertiser, in which case a decision to buy either Medium X or Medium Y made solely or primarily on the basis of cost-per-thousand readers may be unwise.

It is doubtful whether any media man would admit to using cost-per-thousand figures as the only important basis for marketing media decisions. However, it has been my experience that when "hard" figures (such as cost-per-thousand numbers) are available, they tend to drive out or displace "soft" or less tangible data. Thus, while we may feel that we are weighing all of the important factors, the "hard" dollars-and-cents figures may actually influence a media decision more than we realize they do.

The figures on cost-per-thousand viewers may be a useful starting point in deciding among competing media. Alone, however, they are far from an adequate measure. There are at least two reasons for this:

[1] I have noted that a particular medium may have more appeal for some groups (and subgroups) than others. To the extent that different media aid in attracting specific and relatively different audiences, they do not "compete" so long as those audiences represent potential purchasers of a product. For example, if we are marketing a household product which is purchased by both lower- and middle-class housewives, it might be unwise to make a choice between advertising in either the *Ladies' Home Journal* (presumably middle class) or *True Story* (presumably lower class). The product should probably be advertised in both magazines because their audiences are different.

[2] To varying degrees, media may effectively reinforce one another either through the process of what might be called mutual reinforcement or through complementary reinforcement. By mutual reinforcement I refer to the added effectiveness which results when the same appeal is transmitted to the same audience via several different media. For example, we might predict that if the same audience were exposed to the same appeal on TV, on radio, and in magazines, the effect would be greater than that of triple exposure to any one of the media. Unfortunately, there is little published evidence which would either support or contradict this contention.

Complementary reinforcement may occur when two or more media transmit different appeals or otherwise perform different functions for the same product in communications directed toward the same audience. For example, in a review of a study of the adoption by doctors of a new drug, Elihu Katz reports that commercial media play an "informing" role (i.e., tell the doctors about the drug and its availability) whereas the professional media play a "legitimizing" role (i.e., the prestige of the journal and medical society are associated with the drug).[16] Accordingly, if the advertiser believes that both roles are important to his campaign, he would be unwise to view the commercial media as competing with the professional media.

DIFFERENT APPEALS IN DIFFERENT MEDIA

Typical procedure in developing an advertising campaign seems to be (*a*) set advertising objectives, (*b*) determine a basic advertising appeal which will induce people to take the desired action, and (*c*) develop a media plan which will most effectively deliver the campaign to the right

16. "The Two-Step Flow of Communication," *Public Opinion Quarterly*, Spring 1957, pp. 67–68.

people at the lowest cost per thousand. In effect, a medium is considered as little more than a vehicle which delivers a standard message to a desired audience. The media plan is tailored to fit the advertising message. Except for the way in which it is presented, the message varies little from one medium to another.

It seems plausible to predict, however, that the same factors which make a person more attracted to one medium than to another are also likely to be operative in making him or her more susceptible to specific kinds of appeals which are transmitted in that medium. In other words, not only should advertisers utilize different media to reach specific audiences; they also should consider the possibility of using different appeals in each of the media. For example:

We would expect that the advertiser of the household product previously mentioned might get more "mileage" out of his advertising if he used one kind of appeal in *True Story* and a different kind of appeal in the *Ladies' Home Journal.* Let us assume that he is considering the use of a "fear-arousing" appeal. While this appeal might be effective in the *Ladies' Home Journal,* he probably should not use it in *True Story.* Why? Because we know from the Katz and Lazarsfeld study that readers of *True Story* are more likely to be high in anxiety. Further, we know from the study by Janis and Feshbach that people who are high in anxiety are less likely to be influenced by fear-arousing communications. Putting these two findings together would suggest that our advertiser had better use for some other appeal than "fear-arousing" in the *True Story* ad.

Also, the advertiser should probably avoid the use of two-sided arguments with *True Story* readers whereas he might find two-sided arguments very effective with the presumably better-educated readers of the *Ladies' Home Journal.*

I must admit that for purposes of emphasis I have greatly oversimplified these observations on media strategy. The topic is a challenging one, and I can only urge the reader with unanswered questions to look further into some of the publications that I have mentioned.

I now present a number of studies which support the notion that an advertising audience should not be considered as one large and undifferentiated mass—especially if optimum advertising effectiveness is desired.

INFLUENCING THE AUDIENCE

Basically there are two ways of viewing the audience—what I call the "egotistical" and the "realistic" views. Of these two, the most satisfying to the mass communicator is the first, which enables him to think of the audience as a relatively inert and undifferentiated mass that he can often persuade or influence. It is "egotistical" because it attributes great powers to the communicator and regards the audience as a swayable mass. Proponents of this view would probably hold that if you "hit them hard enough" (or "loud enough, long enough, and often enough"), sooner or later they will buy your product.

Perhaps the "realistic" view is more valid. With it, the audience is regarded as a body of individuals who may respond to a communication or commercial in a variety of ways, depending on their individual predispositions. This view also holds that while the communicator, the communication, and the medium play important roles in the communications process, in the final analysis it is the audience which decides whether (and to what extent) it will be influenced. Further, this view acknowledges the importance of the audience in its own right, through the process of social and personal influence.

Let us examine some evidence which should demonstrate that the "realistic" view is realistic, and the "egotistical" view is egotistical.

CONDITIONS FOR INFLUENCING

In order for an audience to be influenced in the desired manner by a communication, several conditions must be met:

- The audience must, somehow, be *exposed* to the communication.
- Members of the audience must interpret or *perceive* correctly what action or attitude is desired of them by the communicator.
- The audience must remember or *retain* the gist of the message that the communicator is trying to get across.
- Members of the audience must *decide* whether or not they will be influenced by the communication.

We might consider these four conditions—exposure, perception, retention, and decision—as the gateways to effective communication and persuasion.

Communications research has established beyond much doubt that the processes of exposure, perception, retention, and decision do not often occur in a random fashion among the population. To varying degrees, people are predisposed to expose themselves to certain kinds of communications and media and not to others. Different people tend to get different meanings from the same communication. Finally, different people make different decisions as to whether or not they will be influenced.

Since each of these processes involves a selection or choice by individual members of the audience, we may refer to them as *selective ex-*

posure, selective perception, selective retention, and *selective decision.*
Let us first examine some studies which illustrate the operation of the
selective processes, and later discuss the implications of these studies in
the area of advertising strategy.

SELECTIVE EXPOSURE

The conditions under which people engage in selective exposure and
the extent to which this process is operative have not been fully specified
or documented by communications research. However, the general conclusion seems to be that most people tend to expose themselves to communications in which they are interested or which they find congenial to
their existing attitudes and to avoid communications that might be irritating, or uninteresting, or incompatible with their own opinions. The following studies are illustrative:

[1] Danuta Ehrlich, Isaiah Guttman, Peter Schönbach, and Judson
Mills found that new-car owners were much more likely to read advertisements for the car they had just purchased than were owners of the
same make but an earlier model.[17] The new-car owners were also much
more likely to read ads about their own car than they were to read about
other makes. The hypothesis is that the new-car owners were seeking reassurance by exposing themselves to what were, no doubt, very "congenial" communications.

[2] Charles F. Cannell and James C. MacDonald found that only
32 percent of a sample of male smokers were consistent readers of articles
on health (including articles dealing with the relationship between smoking and lung cancer), whereas 60 percent of nonsmoking males read such
articles.[18]

SELECTIVE PERCEPTION

Even when people are accidentally or involuntarily exposed to a communication, they sometimes misinterpret or distort the intended meaning
of the communication. For example, Patricia L. Kendall and Katherine
M. Wolf report a study in which cartoons which were intended to ridicule
prejudice were misinterpreted in some way by 64 percent of the people
who saw them.[19] Misinterpretation was most frequent among preju-

17. "Postdecision Exposure to Relevant Information," *Journal of Abnormal
and Social Psychology,* vol. 54, 1957, pp. 98–102.

18. "The Impact of Health News on Attitudes and Behavior," *Journalism
Quarterly,* vol. 33, 1956, pp. 315–323.

19. "The Analysis of Deviant Cases in Communications Research," in Paul F.
Lazarsfeld and Frank N. Stanton (eds.), *Communications Research* (Harper,
New York, 1949), pp. 152–179.

diced respondents who either saw no satire in the cartoons or interpreted them as supporting their own attitudes. One respondent felt that the purpose of a cartoon intended to ridicule anti-Semitism was "to show that there are some people against the Jews and to let other people feel freer to say the're against 'em too, I guess."

Carl I. Hovland, O. J. Harvey, and Muzafer Sherif presented communications arguing the desirability of prohibition to three types of people—"Drys," "Wets," and those "Moderately Wet." [20] They found that the greater the difference between the attitude of the recipient was to regard the communication as propagandistic and unfair, and even to perceive the stand advocated by the communication as further removed from his own position than it actually was. Conversely, when the distance was small between the recipient's own stand and the position advocated by the communication, the recipient was likely to view the communication as being fair and factual and to perceive it as being even closer to his own stand than it actually was.

Habits also can cause distortion of a communication because people often see or hear that which, on the basis of past experience, they expect to see or hear. Gordon Allport and Leo Postman report that a picture in which a Red Cross truck was shown loaded with explosives was ordinarily perceived by subjects as a Red Cross truck carrying medical supplies (because that is the way it "ought" to be).[21]

In summary, the research cited indicates that under certain conditions people misinterpret or distort a communication so that it will be more compatible with their own attitudes, habits, or opinions.

SELECTIVE RETENTION

There is another way a person can reduce the dissonance or lack of internal harmony resulting when there is a discrepancy between his attitudes and those expressed by a communication with which he is faced. He can simply forget rather quickly the content of the communication! If this process is operative, we should also expect that a person would learn more quickly, and remember for a longer period, communications which are compatible with his own attitudes.

A study by Jerome M. Levine and Gardner Murphy supports these

20. "Assimilation and Contrast Effects in Reactions and Attitude Change," *Journal of Abnormal and Social Psychology,* vol. 55, 1957, pp. 244–252.

21. "The Basic Psychology of Rumor," *Transactions of the New York Academy of Sciences,* Series II, Vol. 8, 1945, pp. 61–68. Reprinted in E. E. Maccoby, T. M. Newcomb, and E. L. Hartley (eds.), *Readings in Social Psychology* (Holt, New York, 1958), pp. 54–64.

contentions.[22] Here it was found that pro-Communist material was better learned and better remembered by pro-Communists than by anti-communists; and the reverse was true for anti-Communist material. Another example of selective retention occurred in an experiment by Claire Zimmerman and Raymond A. Bauer.[23] Given some material which was to be used in preparing a speech, subjects remembered fewer of the arguments which might have been received unfavorably by the audience they were slated to address.

SELECTIVE DECISION

Even when a person has been exposed to a message, correctly perceives its intent, and remembers the main content, he still must decide whether or not to be influenced in the manner intended by the communicator. Because of individual predispositions, different people make different decisions as to whether or not (and to what extent) they will be influenced.

For example, in not one of the studies which I have reported has there been an instance in which every member of the audience made the same decision. In every case, some people decided to be persuaded; others did not. We can only assume that just as certain kinds of communications and to avoid others, they are also predisposed (i.e., more susceptible) to being influenced by some types of communications and appeals and not by others. In the Hovland, Harvey, and Sherif experiment, those whose attitudes strongly favored prohibition were predisposed not to be influenced by arguments against prohibition, and vice versa. Persuasion occurred most often when the individual's attitudes toward prohibition were only slightly different from those advocated by the communication.

The evidence which I have thus far introduced seems to indicate quite clearly that people are very capable of resisting attempts to *change* their attitudes and behavior. If a persuasive communication seems incompatible with their own attitudes, they may avoid it, distort its meaning, forget it, or otherwise decide not to be influenced.

IMPLICATIONS

If these conclusions are valid (as they seem to be), what are the implications for advertising? Although I am unable to offer much in the way of direct evidence, I can put forth two suggestions.

22. "The Learning and Forgetting of Controversial Material," *Journal of Abnormal and Social Psychology*, vol. 38, 1943, pp. 507–517.

23. "The Influence of an Audience on What is Remembered," *Public Opinion Quarterly*, vol. 20, 1956, pp. 238–248.

FUNCTION AND EFFECTS OF ADVERTISING

A great deal of advertising must function either to reinforce existing attitudes and behavior (e.g., maintenance of brand loyalty), or to *stimulate* or activate people who are already predisposed to act in the desired manner (e.g., people who enjoy reading murder mysteries are most likely to be on the lookout for, and to be influenced by, advertising of murder mysteries).

A related implication is that advertising is not, in itself, a cause of audience effects, but rather works with and through various mediating factors such as audience predispositions and personal influence (e.g., word-of-mouth advertising).[24]

It would be a mistake to contend that predispositions are so highly developed and so rigid that attitudes and behavior patterns never change. They do. However, I would argue that *changing* a person's attitudes or behavior (as opposed to *reinforcing* present attitudes or *activating* those already predisposed) is beyond the scope of most advertising except where:

[1] The attitude or behavior involved is of little importance to the individual. People to whom it makes little difference which brand of toothpaste they use are more likely to be influenced to switch brands by toothpaste advertising. Even here, however, some activation of predispositions is involved; people with false teeth are less likely to use any toothpaste.

[2] The mediating factors (predispositions and personal influence) are inoperative. People may be influenced directly by the advertising for a new product because they have not been able to form attitudes which would predispose them against the product.

[3] The mediating factors, which normally favor reinforcement, themselves favor change. If for some reason our friends begin buying color television sets, we are more likely to be influenced by advertising for color TV sets.[25]

If these contentions are realistic, it would then appear that a major function of effective advertising is to "select" people who are already predisposed to buy a product and present them with appeals (appropriate to the types of potential customers) which would hopefully trigger the desired response. In those instances where change of important attitudes

24. See Joseph T. Klapper, "What We Know About the Effects of Mass Communications: The Brink of Hope," *Public Opinion Quarterly,* vol. 21, 1957–1958, pp. 453–474.

25. Points [2] and [3] are taken from Klapper, *op. cit.*

or behavior is the advertising objective, failure is more likely than success unless the advertiser can somehow work with or through the mediating factors.

PREDISPOSITION FACTOR

Now let me offset two generalizations that may shed more light on the predisposition factor:

· Some people or groups are more predisposed than others to be influenced by advertising for a particular product or brand.
· Within that group which is more predisposed toward a particular product, some individuals or subgroups will be more predisposed to be influenced by certain kinds of appeals, while others will be predisposed by different kinds of appeals.

In order to indicate the bases of these predispositions, I will discuss the three groups of factors which interact to make an individual more (or less) predisposed to be influenced by any particular communication: (1) the physical and economic reality which an individual experiences, (2) his personality, and (3) the social environment in which he lives.

Physical and Economic Reality as a Basis of Predisposition. This is the most obvious of the predisposing factors. It is well recognized that a person's income, age, sex, and so on, will predispose him or her to buy certain products and to refrain from buying others. Similarly, products he has owned or now owns may be partial determinants of his future susceptibility to advertising. For some products it is relatively easy to predict, on the basis of physical and economic predispositions, which large group within the population will be most likely to buy.

Within this large group, however, it is sometimes possible to distinguish several subgroups, each of which—though predisposed to buy the product—could best be reached by different communications or different appeals. Taking new owners and old owners of automobiles, for instance, and assuming that both groups were predisposed to buy the same make of auto within the following two or three years, I wonder if an auto manufacturer's advertising would not be more effective if different appeals were made to each group.

Maybe present advertising could be retained to reach both groups and be as effective as could be expected for old owners, but in addition specific appeals could be directed to new owners (by direct mail). This might be effective in giving them greater reassurance at a time when they most need it and thus increase the probability that their next car will be of the same make.

Personality as a Basis of Predisposition. Various studies (such as that by Irving L. Janis et al.[26]) have attempted to show that some personality types are more susceptible to influence than others are. There may be some truth in this supposition, but it is rather difficult to prove that *in general* one person is more persuasible than another. More likely, people are predisposed (on the basis of their habits, attitudes, and motives) to be more susceptible to persuasion on certain issues or by certain kinds of appeals. For example, the study by Irving L. Janis and Seymour Feshbach of fear-arousing appeals aimed at changing dental hygiene practices (discussed earlier) found that people who were high in anxiety were least likely to be influenced by strong fear appeals.[27] Other examples of personality as a basis of predisposition can be found in the preceding discussion of selective exposure, perception, retention, and decision. One further example is the finding of Elihu Katz and Paul F. Lazarsfeld that women who are low in "gregariousness," or who report that they "worry more than others," or who are "sometimes blue and depressed" are more likely to have higher exposure to "popular fiction" (such as movie and "true story" type magazines and daytime serials).[28]

These findings can hardly be considered exhaustive, but they represent an interesting beginning. As the study of personality advances we should expect to see a great many more relationships revealed between personality variables and predispositions to being influenced by certain specific kinds of appeals. The real difficulty at the present time seems to be the lack of reliable and useful tests for measuring individual personality differences. However, just because the effect of personality is not well documented in the research on communications does not mean that it is not important. It may turn out to be the most important determinant of predispositions.

The Social Environment as a Basis of Predisposition. In this age of the "organization man" and the "other-directed" man it is well known, and even accepted that to varying degrees our behavior is influenced by other people and groups. What is not so well known is the *extent* to which our social environment shapes our behavior and attitudes in subtle ways we

26. See Irving L. Janis et al., *Personality and Persuasibility* (Yale U. P., New Haven, 1959).

27. "Effects of Fear-Arousing Communications," *Journal of Abnormal and Social Psychology,* vol. 48, 1953, pp. 78–92.

28. Elihu Katz and Paul F. Lazarfeld, *Personal Influence* (Free Press, New York, 1955), p. 378.

may not even be aware of. When I speak of the social environment as a basis of predisposition, I do not refer to direct, overt attempts by one person to influence another (which is called personal influence); instead I refer to indirect often barely noticeable social influences.

A classic experiment by Solomon A. Asch offers a striking example of the effect of unmentioned group "norms" on individual behavior.[29] Subjects in groups of eight were asked to match the length of a given line with one of three unequal lines. The correct answer was quite obvious, but seven of the eight subjects had been previously instructed to give the same *wrong* answers. In one-third of the cases the person who was not let in on the experiment agreed with the unanimous (though visibly incorrect) majority—even though he "knew" what the correct answer was and even though no overt attempt at influence was made.

Another example of social influence is reported by Francis S. Bourne.[30] He found that women who made negative statements about a food product, but who said the product was popular with their friends, used more of the product than did women who made positive statements about the product, but who said it was unpopular with their friends. In other words, if you know your friends favor a particular brand or product you may be more predisposed to use it yourself.

Bourne offers some evidence which suggests that social influence of this sort is operative chiefly among products which are conspicuous (i.e., both visible and unique). This remains to be seen, but it is fairly clear that in some situations group norms or sentiments play a considerable part in predisposing us to act in certain ways—probably much more so than most of us realize. Since different people belong to different reference groups which may hold varying attitudes toward a particular brand or product, it follows that some groups will be more or less, predisposed to be influenced by advertising for a product than will others.

And within these groups some people may be more susceptible to advertising (or certain appeals) than others. For example, Harold H. Kelley and Edmund H. Volkart found that individuals who least valued their membership in a group were not so likely to resist attempts at influence which were counter to the values of the group.[31]

29. "Effects of Group Pressure upon the Modification and Distortion of Judgements," in E. Maccoby, T. Newcomb, and E. Hartley (eds.), *Readings in Social Psychology,* pp. 174–182.

30. "Group Influence in Marketing Decisions," in Likert and P. Hayes, Jr. (eds.), *Some Applications of Behavioural Research* (UNESCO, Paris, 1957).

31. "The Resistance to Change of Group-Anchored Attitudes," *American Sociological Review,* vol. 17, 1952, pp. 453–465. The findings are summarized by Carl I. Hovland, Irving L. Janis, and Harold H. Kelley, *Communication and Persuasion* (Yale U. P., New Haven, 1953), Chap. 5.

The effect of group norms and other social pressures raises many interesting questions and problems for advertising strategy—questions I cannot now explore. Let me try, however, to offer two generalizations for advertisers to consider:

[1] The fact that the economic and physical reality, the personality, and the social environment act to predispose certain groups to be more, or less, susceptible to influence than others is well recognized by marketing and advertising strategists. Most successful marketing programs begin with an appraisal of "Who buys (or is most likely to buy) the product?" or "To whom will (or does) the product appeal?" In addition, we see a good deal of the practice of selective marketing or market segmentation; that is, producing and marketing products which have a particular appeal for a limited and specific segment of the market.

[2] But only rarely do we notice an advertiser making use *selective advertising;* that is, the use of different appeals about the *same* product to different segments of the market. The research to date clearly suggests that the possibility of making greater use of selective advertising is, for many companies, well worth investigating (and I shall discuss it in more detail later).

Personal Influence. Earlier I excluded personal influence from our discussion of predisposing factors. However personal influence, of course, cannot be long excluded. Not only are members of the audience themselves influenced by mass communications; they also are stimulated at times through personal communication.

Many of the studies of personal influence were stimulated by an earlier study of voting behavior which had suggested a hypothesis called the "two-step flow of communication." According to this theory, ideas "flow from radio and print to opinion leaders and from them to less active sections of the population." [32]

Two pioneering studies which are of particular significance in studying the process of personal influence have been conducted. One is by Elihu Katz and Paul F. Lazarsfeld on the flow of influence among housewives in Decatur in the areas of marketing (food and household products primarily), fashions, public affairs, and movie-going. [33] The other is by Herbert Menzel and Elihu Katz on the spread of a new drug among doctors. [34]

Based on respondents' own assessments (the accuracy of which may

32. Paul F. Lazarsfeld, Bernard Berelson, and Hazel Gaudet, *The People's Choice* (New York, Duell, Sloan & Pearce, 1944), p. 151.

33. Katz and Lazarsfeld, *op. cit.*

34. "Social Relations and Innovation in the Medical Profession," *Public Opinion Quarterly,* vol. 19, 1955–1956, pp. 337–352.

be questioned), the Decatur study concluded that in marketing, personal influence has greater impact than has advertising because respondents reported "more exposure to personal advice than to advertisements; and second, among those exposed to each source, 'most important influence' is more often attributed to people than to formal advertisements." The drug study did not attempt to evaluate relative impact, but did conclude that interpersonal communication and social support are important factors in encouraging doctors to face the risks of medical innovation.

The two studies suggest that influence is related "to the personification of certain values (who one is) . . . to competence (what one knows); and . . . to strategic social location (whom one knows)." [35]

For example, the Decatur study suggests that:

· There is little overlap in opinion leadership, a person tends to specialize in one sphere—e.g., marketing or fashion or movies.
· In marketing, there is a concentration of opinion leadership among "large-family wives" (older women with two or more children).
· Influence flows among people of the same social status and usually among the same age group.
· Women who are "gregarious" are more likely to be opinion leaders.

The Decatur study also shows that opinion leaders are more likely to be exposed to the mass media than are the people whom they influence and also that they are particularly likely to be exposed to the media appropriate to their own sphere of influence. In the case of fashion, it even appears that the opinion leaders are "not only more exposed to the mass media but are also more affected by them in their own decisions." [36] The drug study also showed that "influential doctors were more likely to be readers of a large number of professional journals and valued them more highly than did doctors of lesser influence." [37]

The obvious implication is to advertise to opinion leaders and let them carry the ball from there. Opinion leaders are very interested in a specific sphere, are more exposed to media, and hence are probably more likely to notice and read advertisements appropriate to their sphere of influence. However, just because they are exposed to the advertising does not necessarily mean that they will be influenced by it. (In the Decatur study, only the fashion leaders were.)

Actually, a good case can be made for the proposition that as far as

35. Elihu Katz, "The Two-Step Flow of Communication," *Public Opinion Quarterly,* vol. 21, 1957, p. 73.
36. *Ibid.,* p. 75.
37. *Ibid.,* p. 76.

change is concerned, opinion leaders are more likely to show high resistance than are their followers in many cases. This point was not brought out in the Decatur study, but the drug study noted that it was not the influential doctors who first began using the new drugs, but rather doctors who were relatively isolated from the rest of the medical community. If these innovators were isolated because they were not too highly regarded by the influential doctors, it is not likely that they had a great deal of direct personal influence over the influential doctors.

In studying the process of personal influence (rather than looking at "opinion leaders" as such) we would probably be more realistic if we distinguished between two kinds of leaders—the *innovators* and the *influentials*. Influentials may have considerable personal influence over others in the group but they may enjoy this influence because they recognizably hold the norms and values of the group.

If, as is often the case, the norms of the group favor the status quo, the influentials have an investment in this status quo, hence are more likely to be resistant to change. Unless the norms of the group favor innovation (as in fashion or in some areas of the medical profession), the innovators are very likely to be the deviant or isolated members of the group, none too popular with the rest of the group. However, the innovators may affect the behavior of others (including the influentials) through a process of "social influence by example." For example, in a study of the adoption of hybrid seed corn, Bryce Ryan and Neal Gross discovered that the influential farmers took their cue from innovating farmers after seeing the good results they had obtained.[38] Adoption by most of the others in the community followed adoption by the influentials.

In sum, unless the norms of the group favor innovation, innovating and influencing are two separate processes which are carried out by two different types of people. It is therefore necessary to redefine the simpler notion of opinion leadership in order to take into account two types of opinion leaders—the innovators and the influentials.

The implications of these findings for advertising strategy are not clear. The process of personal influence is undoubtedly of major importance in the marketing of goods and services, yet at the present time only a handful of relevant studies on this important topic are available. It is fairly clear, though, that it is beneficial to have the right people talking about your product, provided they are saying the right things. What should be done in order to encourage this is not self-evident. As a start I would suggest that word-of-mouth activity be used as one measure of

38. "The Diffusion of Hybrid Seed Corn in Iowa Communities," *Rural Sociology*, vol. 8, 1943, pp. 15–24.

advertising effectiveness. In this way, a campaign could be judged partly on the basis of the amount of word-of-mouth activity it stimulated. It may well be that having one person talk about your product to his friends is worth more than having the friends exposed to a commercial or advertisement for the product.

MEASURING ADVERTISING EFFECTIVENESS

What implications does research on mass communications have for testing advertising effectiveness? This is a problem that has always been of concern to advertisers. The research supports two propositions (which, incidentally, confirm what most advertising researchers already know—that measuring advertising effects is a delicate and difficult operation). However, the following propositions, and the research theory underlying them, do more than confirm the obvious; they may help establish a useful basis for measuring ad effectiveness.

In general, the essence of the two propositions is that the connection between a person's factual knowledge and his attitudes or opinions and between the latter and his behavior is not necessarily a direct, one-to-one relationship. More specifically:

[1] It is possible for a person to change his factual knowledge without changing his attitudes or his behavior.

One illustration of this proposition is found in the Janis and Feshbach study of the effect of fear-arousing appeals on changing attitudes and behavior regarding dental hygiene practices.[39] Similarly, a study by Carl I. Hovland, Arthur A. Lumsdaine, and Fred D. Sheffield found that the film *The Battle of Britain* was considerably more effective in changing factual information than it was in changing opinions based on tests before and five days after the film showing.[40]

Does this mean that measures of advertising effectiveness such as the Starch Readership Service and the Gallup-Robinson IMPACT technique are of dubious value? Both services measure name association and recall (i.e., factual information) and research has shown it is possible to effect changes in information without eliciting corresponding changes in attitudes or behavior—or, in other words, without achieving the goals of most advertising. Let us reserve judgment on these measures until we consider the next proposition. At that time they may appear potentially more useful than they do here.

39. Janis and Feshbach, *op. cit.* See also the discussion of the study in *Harvard Business Review,* vol. 39, September–October 1961, pp. 164–166.
40. *Experiments on Mass Communications* (Princeton U. P., Princeton, N.J., 1949).

[2] It is possible for a person to change his behavior without first changing his attitudes (i.e., attitude change may follow behavior change).

ATTITUDE MEASUREMENT

It is often impractical to attempt to relate advertising effects to sales. The closest substitute would seem to be a measure of changes in attitudes produced by an advertisement. The assumption would be that advertising works by first causing changes in attitude that in turn produce changes in behavior. Therefore, since we cannot measure the behavior, the next best thing is to measure that which immediately precedes the behavior— attitudes.

This procedure sounds logical, but unfortunately it so happens that attitude changes may *follow* rather than precede behavior changes. For example, it is possible that a person will see an advertisement buy the product, and then change his attitude toward the product in the direction advocated by the ad. Raymond A. and Alice H. Bauer suspect "that one of the major ways in which mass media influence public attitudes is via the second order effect of having first elicited behavior based on other existing attitudes." [41] If this contention is realistic, measurement of changes in attitudes may not be a valid criterion for evaluating the effectiveness of an ad. For example:

Let us imagine that a number of consumers bought a particular brand of shoe polish after having seen some advertising for that brand, but without exhibiting any measurable change in their attitudes toward the brand. Assume that the advertising was influential, not because it changed their basic attitudes but because it reminded them, at the point of purchase, that the brand existed and they therefore decided to try it.

Suppose the manufacturer was trying to evaluate the effectiveness of his campaign so that he could better focus his advertising efforts. If he had measured the consumers' attitudes before and after advertising (but before they had bought the product), he would have found no change in their attitude toward his brand. He probably would have concluded that the advertising had no effect whatever.

But advertising had, in fact, triggered the purchase by reminding consumers of the brand's existence. The manufacturer would have thus erred in evaluating the effects of his advertising. On the other hand, if he had measured consumers' attitudes before advertising, and again after they had made the purchases (and had changed their attitudes), he would

41. "America, Mass Society and Mass Media," *Journal of Social Issues,* vol. 16, no. 3, 1961, pp. 3–66.

have concluded that advertising had caused consumers to change their attitudes and thus buy his product.

This, too, would have been a mistake and might have led him to the wrong conclusions about how he should advertise his product. If, as we have assumed, the real reason why his advertising was effective was because it reminded people to buy the product, a campaign of "reminder" advertising would be indicated. The manufacturer, however, after studying the results of either type of attitude survey, would probably have concluded that (*a*) the advertising was *not* effective, or (*b*) the advertising *was* effective because it changed consumers' attitudes. This might have led him to the erroneous conclusion that (*a*) he did not have to advertise, or (*b*) that he should launch a campaign which would change people's attitudes.

Unfortunately, it is difficult to find direct evidence in support of the proposition that behavior change can take place without being preceded by attitude change. When Jack W. Brehm asked young women first to rate the desirability of eight products (mostly appliances), then offered them their choice between two of these products, and again asked them to rate the products, he found that after making their choice the subjects showed a marked increase in preference for the product chosen.[42] They also showed a marked *decrease* in their preference for the product *not* chosen. The extent of this decrease in postdecision preference was considerably greater if the subject had initially given both products about the same rating. In other words, the more difficult the choice she had to make, the more likely she was (after the decision) to prefer the chosen product more and the rejected product less.

Similarly, Judson Mills tested students' attitudes toward cheating, then created a situation where some of them were able to cheat during a test.[43] He remeasured their attitudes, and found that those who had cheated became more lenient in their attitudes toward cheating, while those who had not cheated became more severe.

The theory which predicts these kinds of behavior is called the *theory of cognitive dissonance*. This theory was developed by Leon Festinger,[44] and holds that when a person chooses between two or more alternatives, discomfort or dissonance will almost inevitably arise because of the person's knowledge that while the decision he has made has certain advantages, it also has some disadvantages. The girl who chose a toaster in the

42. "Post-Decision Changes in the Desirability of Alternatives," *Journal of Abnormal and Social Psychology,* vol. 52, 1956, pp. 384–389.
43. "Changes in Moral Attitudes Following Temptation," *Journal of Personality,* vol. 26, 1959, pp. 517–531.
44. *A Theory of Cognitive Dissonance* (Harper, New York, 1957).

Brehm experiment did so because she liked it, but she would have liked the iron, too. Also, the cheaters knew there was an advantage to cheating, but they recognized that it was not the right thing to do, hence a disadvantage.

The theory holds that dissonance arises after almost every decision, and further that the individual will invariably take steps to reduce this dissonance. There are several ways in which this can be done, but the most likely way is to create as many advantages as you can in favor of the alternative you have chosen and to think of as many disadvantages as possible relating to the other alternatives. Thus the girl who chose the toaster decided that she really liked it much more than the iron, and so on. The same explanation accounts for the fact that the new-car owners read more ads about their cars than old-car owners.

It is important to remind you: I am not suggesting that attitude changes may not also precede changes in behavior. Undoubtedly they do. However, while the evidence I have offered is only suggestive, there are some grounds for believing that behavior change can take place without being preceded by attitude change. This, combined with the fact that some attitude change almost always follows any important decision or behavior change, makes any attempt at using attitude change to measure advertising effects a delicate and potentially misleading operation.

RECOGNITION AND RECALL

Having built up a little background on dissonance theory, we can now return to the other possible indirect measures of advertising effectiveness —recognition and recall. The theory of cognitive dissonance would hold that when a person faces the chance of being exposed (or is exposed) to knowledge or opinions (i.e., cognitions) which are related to, but in conflict with, some of his own cognitions, dissonance arises. For example, if I own a Ford but suddenly hear an announcer extolling the wonders of a Chevrolet, the cognition that I own a Ford will be dissonant with the cognition that the Chevrolet is a wonderful car. As we know, the theory suggests that I will take steps to reduce this dissonance. But how? I have several alternatives:

· To buy or consider buying a Chevrolet (*selective decision*).
· To turn off the set or otherwise ignore the commercial (*selective exposure*).
· To distort the communication—"Sure, Chevrolet is good, but that model is probably very expensive to operate compared with my Ford" (*selective perception*).

To forget the entire communication very quickly or forget parts of the communication that produce the most dissonance (*selective retention*).

If I am somewhat predisposed to buy a Chevrolet, and if the commercial has been effective in acting on my predisposition, I may take the first alternative—even if it is only so far as to say I will certainly consider a Chevrolet next time. In this case, the advertising has been effective and I am less likely to engage in the alternative defenses. If, however, I am not so predisposed and the commercial has not been effective, then I will certainly try to reduce the dissonance by avoiding the commercial, distorting it, and/or forgetting some or all of it rather quickly.

It would seem to follow, therefore, that measures of exposure and recall can be very useful in evaluating and acting on those people who are already predisposed to buy the product. Therefore, a good measure of exposure and recall should offer valid testimony to the ad's ability to select and act on those so predisposed. The ones who are not predisposed, or who were not acted on, will already have taken steps either to avoid exposing themselves, or to distort or not recall properly all or part of the message.

What criteria then should be met by a good indirect measure of advertising effectiveness? In addition to meeting acceptable standards of research methodology, an indirect measure should:

· *Measure exposure under natural conditions (or allow for the effects of forced exposure).* Any artificial medium must be suspect because it reduces the opportunity for selective exposure.
· *Measure respondents some time (at least a week—preferably two weeks)* after they have been exposed to the communication. This is to allow the process of selective retention to operate.
· *Measure a verbatim playback of the message.* That is, respondents' unaided recollections of the contents of an ad should be recorded *in toto.* It is important to know not only *how much* has been remembered, but also what portions of the message have been forgotten or remembered—what portions are dissonant or consonant, and *with whom.* Respondents can also be identified on the basis of relevant characteristics in order to determine how different types of people react to the advertisement.
· *Measure distortion of the message.* It is important to know what parts of the message are distorted and the nature of these distortions. This would be partially handled by the verbatim playback, but might also require one or two probing questions.

Unhappily, neither the Starch system nor the Gallup-Robinson IM-PACT technique meets *all* of these criteria. But the IMPACT technique does come very close, and with a few slight modifications would meet the suggested criteria. The needed modifications would include delaying the measure of recall for several weeks where practicable, measuring distortion more systematically, and classifying responses by types of respondents.

For those who want high readership or viewership scores, we should note that by measuring recall immediately after exposure, under forced exposure conditions, by probing deeply, and so on, it is possible to achieve inflated results. However, all the evidence indicates that people tend to set up barriers against communications which are incompatible with their own attitudes or which do not interest them. I feel, therefore, that an indirect measure of advertising effectiveness which determines whether or not and to what extent a consumer has engaged in the processes of selective exposure, perception, and retention will be more realistic and hence more valuable to a company in evaluating its advertising efforts.

SELECTIVE ADVERTISING

I would like to close by putting forward an advertising strategy which seems to be supported by much of the research evidence which has been presented—*the strategy of selective advertising*. This strategy is based on two key assumptions:

- Advertising works primarily by reinforcing or otherwise acting upon people already predisposed to act.
- The closer the match between the appeals used and the individual's predispositions, the more likely he is to expose himself to the advertisement, and to act as desired.

Ideally, since we consider people to be different from one another, every individual should be approached with slightly different appeals in order to come closest to matching his predispositions. Obviously, this is quite impractical. What has happened instead is that most advertisers operate at the other end of the continuum; that is, they assume that for practical purposes everyone is more or less alike, and that an appeal which is good for one is good for all.

This approach also may be quite impractical if we think in terms of opportunity cost. It seems that an ideal strategy would involve a compromise somewhere between these two extremes. The advertiser cannot advertise selectively to everyone, but neither should he think that "for all practical purposes" everyone is alike. People are not all alike. However, some segments of the population do have many common characteristics. We would expect much more similarity among people in the same social class than we would among people of different classes. We would also expect more similarity among young people than between people of two age groups, and so on. There are many ways in which the population might be segmented into groups reasonably homogeneous in their predispositions toward any particular product.

GROUP PREDISPOSITIONS

If this is the case, then the task of selective advertising is to select those groups and subgroups which are relevant to the particular product and to match appeals with group predispositions. In other words, a selective advertising campaign would not usually rely on only one appeal or one type of media but would run as many different appeals in as many different media as were necessary to match particular groups which make up the potential market for a product—up to the point where this increased number of appeals maximized the return on advertising investment. Just where the optimum point is located is rather beyond the scope of this article. It seems likely, however, that in most cases the optimum strategy would be to use more than one appeal.

There is still another argument for the use of a variety of appeals. Not only do people differ from one another, but any one individual has many needs which might be satisfied by a product. Dorwin Cartwright suggests that the "more goals which are seen as attainable by a single path, the more likely it is that a person will take that path." [45] In other words, the product is the path by which the person may attain certain goals. Use of a variety of appeals increases the number of goals or needs which the product might be seen as satisfying, and hence increases the probability of triggering off one or more predisposing factors.

In addition, the use of a variety of relevant appeals allows the advertiser to repeat his product story several times in several ways without arousing the wrath of the listener who might be irritated by constant repetition of the same appeal.

Robert K. Merton's analysis of Kate Smith's marathon effort in selling war bonds offers testimony to the power of selective advertising.[46] Merton identified some sixty different appeals used and found that "each new entreaty sought out a new vulnerability in some listeners." As I

45. "Some Principles of Mass Persuasion," Human Relations, vol. 2, 1949, pp. 253–267.
46. Robert K. Merton, Mass Persuasion (Harper, New York, 1946).

have suggested, Miss Smith's use of a variety of appeals was effective in two ways: (1) it offered one person more reasons to buy, and (2) it touched some predisposition in a wide variety of people. An appeal which was not relevant to the predispositions of some would likely trigger off responses in others, and so on.

MYTH OF UNIT MARKETS

To conclude, the strategy of selective advertising would strongly reject the notions that there is but *one* market for a product and that this market can best be reached by *one* appeal which has universal selling power. The strategy of selective advertising would hold that such contentions are myths which have little basis in reality.

Perhaps the day will come when advertisers will abandon their belief in the undifferentiated market and the universal appeal. This day should mark a considerable step forward in the art of advertising strategy.

SELECTED PUBLICATIONS BY DR. COX

"Rational vs. Emotional Communications: A New Approach." (With Raymond A. Bauer), in Leon Arons and Mark A. May, *Television and Human Behavior: Tomorrow's Research in Mass Communication,* New York, Appleton, 1963.

"The Measurement of Information Value: A Study in Consumer Decision-Making," *Proceedings of the American Marketing Association, 1962,* William S. Decker (ed.), Pittsburgh, Pa., 1963, pp. 413–421.

QUESTIONS

1. Media selection is one of the advertiser's greatest concerns. Recently, New York agencies have started using a UNIVAC-type machine to make media selections. Discuss in detail the pros and cons of using such a machine, using Cox's discussions on media as a basis for your discussion. (First, however, you must find out more about such machines and their workings. We suggest *Printers' Ink, Advertising Age,* or *Editor and Publisher.*)

2. Theories of selective exposure, perception, retention and decision point to the advertiser's main contention that advertisements only encourage the buying of given products but do not change the buyers' attitudes. This theory is also easily demonstrated in other fields of persuasion communication. During election time many arguments are adduced to explain why a person should change from one party to another.

Interview friends who voted in the last election and ask them if they switched parties and why (or no) they were influenced in their change. Interpret in the light of the present theory.

3.   Communication models which have been discussed in earlier chapters theoretically account for many phases of communication. Using any model, try to picture the various problems an advertiser must take into account before an advertisement is actually placed before the reader, bearing in mind (1) credibility of advertisements, (2) repetition effects (sleeper effect), (3) media influences, (4) a person's own picture of what an advertisement should contain, (5) selective effects, (6) environmental effects, and finally (7) how it is possible for a person to change his knowledge and behavior of a subject without changing his attitude toward that subject.

Lewis Anthony Dexter

Communications—Pressure, Influence, or Education? *

SUPERFICIALLY, THE FOLLOWING REPORT appears to differ from most of the other articles in this book. For at some point they concentrate on what are obviously mass media—books, radio, TV, etc. Here we are concentrating on what appear to be communications between individuals—from the citizen to a Congressman, from the constituent to his senator. But the kind of mail which we are discussing here is in reality much more like the pseudo-individual advertising testimonials which appear on radio or TV or which most of us receive in our own mailboxes than like letters from friend to friend or counsellor to counsellee. Mail has, on the whole, been neglected as an area of mass communications because in form it resembles personal letters. But when it is planned, organized, stimulated, and directed not to the individual as an individual but an abstract public figure (congressmen, consumer, constituent, or whatever) then it in fact falls within the field of mass communications. To be sure, the mechanical means used in much mail to congressmen is individual handwritten letters; but although the hand may be that of Esau—the ordinary citizen—the words are often those of Jacob—the advertising man, lobbyist, trade association executive, or public relations counsel.

It is important to point out that a good deal of mail to congressmen is in fact individual; [1] Kenneth Gray [2] has made particularly clear

* This is a draft of a chapter based upon "Congressmen and the People They Listen To," copyrighted (hectograph), Massachusetts Institute of Technology, 1955, revised with considerable new material added in Raymond A. Bauer, Ithiel de Sola Pool, and Lewis A. Dexter, *American Business and Public Policy* (Atherton, New York, 1963). I am grateful to Raymond A. Bauer for editorial assistance on this chapter.

1. The weakness of my own articles on mail to Congressmen, listed in the bibliography, and of the present article is that I do not make the distinction between organized mail on legislative issues and personal service-complaint mail quite clear enough. Gray's paper read in conjunction with my work will make that distinction clear.

2. In a paper read at the American Political Science Association meetings,

the way in which a senator or congressman can use the mails as a way
of locating and remedying injustices which are individually experienced and perceived.[3] The interesting thing is that, just as the writer
of advertising testimonials for TV or of direct mail letters for department store advertising often tries to "personalize" what is essentially
a mass communications relationship, so the planners of mail-to-
congressmen campaigns try to make it appear that personal notes
about deeply felt injustices are being written. The shrewd congressman can ordinarily separate the ersatz from the genuine here.

Of course, there are borderline cases—people, for instance, who
are protesting about a personal injustice, which is really felt, but have
been advised through a public relations organization how to write.[4]

Although this article concentrates on mail, it is by no means confined to the mail; we are trying to present in focus the kinds of communications which congressmen are concerned with. Actually, as we
point out, the influence of those colleagues who are regarded as sound
specialists on a given subject is perhaps the greatest influence on most
members; but this kind of consultation with colleagues takes only a
small amount of congressional time as compared with the mail and
visits from or to constituents; and my initial interest was somewhat
too much in the communications which took time and staff time,
rather than with those which influence decisions.   L. A. D.

DR. DEXTER, of Belmont, Massachusetts, is now intermittently with
the Political Science and Sociology Programs, University of South
Florida, Tampa, Florida; has been a free-lance consultant in political
science and sociology and in political public relations; Research Director to Governor Furcolo (1956–57) and Governor Volpe (1960–61)
of Massachusetts; has participated in political campaigns in eleven
states, including congressional campaigns in Pennsylvania, New York,
Missouri, Massachusetts, Illinois, and Maryland.

September 1962 (mimeographed); Gray is currently legislative assistant to Senator Douglas of Illinois.

3. Obviously a pattern of injustice may lead a congressman to think of hearings, investigations, or remedial legislation, even if no such intention exists in the
mind of the complainants.

4. The distinction between the individualized mail and the general mail is in
general that the individualized mail presents a problem with which somebody (not
necessarily the congressman but somebody in authority somewhere) could deal
with as an individual case or problem, whereas the generalized mail demands
changes of legislation or policy. For example, there is usually nothing that a congressman can do about the problem created for a particular textile firm because
it may be thrown out of business due to Japanese competition, without changing
some aspect of legislation or policy; but there is a good deal that can be done to
help a given postal employee who has suffered discrimination because he is physically handicapped, without any change in legislation or policy.

We started out with the notion that public officials would see themselves as under rather constant pressure from those who have a stake in the decisions they make. That seems to be the conventional belief about pressure politics put forth in textbooks and in journalistic accounts. It may in fact be an accurate description of what happens in some cases, such as patronage matters or on getting contracts for highway jobs. These are issues on which the interests of the parties are clear, immediate, unequivocal, vital, and relatively uncomplicated by other relationships with the Congressman which must be considered under the heading of long-run goodwill. But on most general legislation the picture is somewhat different.

The first lesson we learned is that vigorous pushing of an interest is not necessarily regarded as pressure. One of our early talks was with an administrative official who had prepared a report minimizing the defense aspect of foreign economic policy. During the committee hearing he had said with some exasperation to a questioner, "I suppose next you will tell me the toothbrush makers need protection for national defense reasons." (We have changed the product as a disguise.) Angry letters instigated by a lobbyist came to him from all over the country protesting his offense against that minor industry. But when our interviewer asked him, "Did other people put pressure on you in a similar way?" the official "looked . . . incredulously and said, 'Why he (the lobbyist) didn't put any pressure on me.' . . ." Our interviewer insisted but the respondent said vehemently: "No, I didn't have any pressure on me at all; if you are reasonable with these people they are reasonable with you."

"Reasonable," "legitimate," and "threat" turned out to be key words.

We continued to use the word "pressure" for a while in our interviews, but ran steadily into the response: "What do you mean 'pressure'? I wasn't under any pressure. It was all perfectly legitimate."

Or, as Congressman Second from New Anglia [1] told us: "The tariff was No. 2 or perhaps No. 1" in what he heard about from his district. But, he added: "Oh, no, nobody's tried to pressure me. Yes, there've been a lot of letters about the damage they are suffering, but there has been no pressure—*by that I mean no threats.*"

Vigorous representation of a partisan interest turns out to be legitimate *per se,* providing it is "reasonable," i.e., devoid of threat.[2] Said one assistant, talking of organized labor, "It's true the Senator opposed repeal of Taft-Hartley publicly and they criticized him for it. But that was all

1. The districts mentioned herein are deliberately disguised to protect the anonymity of the congressmen.

2. Cf. our fuller report, on this point, Frank Bonilla, "When is Petition 'Pressure'?" *Public Opinion Quarterly,* vol. 20, no. 1, Spring 1956, pp. 39–48.

in the game. Some of them have thought he was sore about the way they took after him, but, hell, he expected it. He wasn't sore."

Most congressmen—and we believe to a lesser extent personnel in administrative agencies—believe strongly and firmly in the right of petition. Furthermore, in very many instances they regard the communications which come into their offices as helpful and instructive. True, persistent pleading of a cause to which the congressman is firmly opposed may eventually have an abrasive effect on his nerves. But, to our surprise, we found many congressmen looking to mail and personal contacts as sources of information on vital issues. This was more true of Representatives than of Senators, who are blessed with more adequate staffs.[3]

We think it fair to say that on general legislative problems communications from constituents are seldom perceived as pressure by the congressman. The Congressman perceives in them little or no element of external threat, which is what makes petition pressure. We have already seen that the constituents from whom the congressman hears are generally friendly. Stable local community groups are bound to their senators and representatives by a variety of issues, and hesitate to alienate them on any single one of them. Recall the farm delegation which approached a group of Southern congressmen and said: "The national told us to pass the word along, we're in favor of Reciprocal Trade, but we shan't get mad if you vote against it."

We repeatedly ran across the theme: "So-and-so has gone along with us on so many issues that we wouldn't think of opposing him because he disagrees with us on this."

The word pressure does exist in congressional parlance. It is used, for example, to explain the opposition's behavior, sometimes described as an opportunistic yielding to pressure. Opportunism and pressure are handy terms to explain why someone else disagrees with you.

Sometimes the term *pressure mail* was applied to mail on the Reciprocal Trade Act. But the term *pressure* (if on oneself) most frequently referred to influence exerted by other Congressmen or by the Administration. An example of such pressure was Mr. Rayburn's injunction to freshman Congressmen on the morning of the key foreign trade votes that to "get along" they had better "go along." What made it pressure was the implied *threat* of disapproval by the powerful Party leadership on whom a junior congressman's fate in Congress may

3. See my discussion of mail and other communications to congressmen in N. Polsby, R. Dentler, and P. Smith (eds.), *Politics and Social Life* (Houghton, Boston, 1963), pp. 485–494.

depend.[4] Similarly, the Administration can apply pressure by threats to withhold patronage. Individual congressmen can also apply pressure by implying that they will not cooperate on other issues with the person being pressured. One congressman said that Representative Cleveland Bailey was "real rough" in attempting to get him to go along on a "protectionist" measure.

But does not the expression of a constituent's view and/or interest incorporate an implied threat to vote against a congressman who disagrees with him? It may. And, in fact, there have unquestionably been individual instances of congressmen who were defeated because of their unpopular stand on a single issue. However, what is important is the fact that while most congressmen definitely respond to mail and other communications, they do not perceive in them in most instances any cause for alarm. One "pro-labor" Senator, out of curiosity, had his staff check up on the writers of 100 letters he received advocating support of a higher minimum wage. It was found that 75 writers were eligible to register, but of these only 33 actually were registered. Furthermore, the letters were advocating his support of a measure on which he had been particularly active, and the content of the mail showed no realization of the stand he had so publicly taken. The Senator could scarcely get excited about these letter writers as either a source of opposition or of support on the basis of that issue. He might, however, respond to their petition as a legitimate request and an opportunity to make some voters among them familiar with him as a person—and to get leads as to where to suggest registration campaigns to labor unions.

Approximately the same result might generally be expected from an analysis of the mail. The reader will remember that most of the businessmen in our sample who had contacted Congress were not aware of the position taken by the man to whom they had written. The probability is that they also did not follow up to see how he voted. Congressman Simpson received a number of letters and postcards in 1953 urging him to vote against the Simpson Bill. We found that even some of the people active in the major interest groups were not aware of how key members of Congress stood on the Reciprocal Trade Act.

In view of such circumstances, it is little wonder that congressmen do not regard issue-oriented communications to them as a source of pressure—in the sense of an active implied threat. However, to say that incoming communications are not perceived as pressure is by no means to

4. We do not consider this to be a contradiction of our earlier statement that in the U.S. Congress party discipline is much less important a factor than in many legislatures.

say that congressmen are not responsive to them, particularly to mail from constituents.

Indeed, the mail is perceived as being the congressman's main source of information on foreign trade policy. Whenever we asked a congressman if he had heard anything about foreign trade policy, he almost inevitably answered in terms of mail. We cannot say whether or not this is true of other issues, but it is our distinct impression that congressmen are far more conscious of what the mail says about foreign trade legislation than they are about any other exposition of foreign trade matters.[5]

Visitors and telephone callers have an impact similar in character to that of mail. They are listened to as indicators of feeling back home. They too, however, seldom "use pressure," nor do the professional lobbyists.

You know all these guys who come in here never talk about issues at all. I've seen lots of them supposedly lobbying. . . . We go out to lunch, but they don't necessarily talk about anything. (We) just know a good guy may be going out of business because he doesn't get more trade or so. It's the spirit that influences.

The "spirit" may be imperfect as a communication medium, but small talk does serve the congressman as a protection against having to reply with a face-to-face "No." Furthermore, congressmen frequently ask questions of visitors in ways which channel their comments in the direction desired. One Congressman asked a delegation whether any of them really, seriously, favored reciprocal trade. They did; but upon receiving this cue that their opinion would be unfavorably received, they talked about other things. The typical business visitor to a congressional office comes in not with one problem, but with several, and in general congressmen are much more experienced and expert at diverting visitors than visitors are in forcing congressmen on a point.

One source of word-of-mouth information is fellow-congressmen and other members of the Capitol Hill work force. The structure of Congress is such that every member has to specialize. As we have noted, the congressman's job is of his own making.[6] The only thing that he cannot do is to try to do all the things the job calls for. Legislation, we noted, is only one of the things on which he may specialize, and if he

5. This is naturally not true of members of the relevant committees, who spend a great deal of time in hearings on these matters.

6. See L. Dexter, "The Representative and His District," Bobbs-Merrill Reprint Series, PS-63, appearing in revised and extended form in R. Peabody and N. Polsby (eds.), *New Perspectives on Congress* (Rand McNally, Chicago, 1963), pp. 3–29.

chooses so to specialize, he can operate effectively only on a part of the legislation which comes before the committees on which he sits. A given Representative or Senator sits on one or two committees, and one will be of particular importance to him. Over a period of years, a capable congressman can become a real expert on the subject matter of his committee assignments. One man becomes a specialist on immigration and another on conservation, one on foreign policy and another on taxes. Among the specialists on any topic, there will be men of different character and viewpoint. Thus congressmen develop an implicit roster of fellow-congressmen whose judgment they respect, whose viewpoint they normally share, and to whom they can turn for guidance on particular topics of the colleague's competence. Each congressman tends to follow the lead not of any one person, but of a roster of specific colleagues sorted by topics.

Members of the House on the whole associate with other congressmen and assistants whose views are like their own. Much of the social life of Congress is passed with other members of the same party and their wives. It is especially from among these friendly associates that a congressman picks out as a mentor on a particular topic a man who is on the appropriate committee and who is a specialist on that topic. Communication with such a person may often be no more than an exchange of two sentences: How should I vote on such-and-such bill? and an answer. Or it may be a validation of the authenticity of a partisan claim, e.g., "Are oil imports really hurting your people?" Occasionally it will be fuller conversation, but even in the usual brief form it may be very effective.

Another source of congressional information is the published word. With regard to reciprocal trade, except for newspapers, this played a very small part in the legislative information system. With two exceptions there was among our congressional interviewees little indication of familiarity with the economists' literature on international trade. On the other hand, perhaps a dozen congressmen referred to some item in the press, and several had evidently obtained ideas from newspaper columns. No respondent mentioned specialized—e.g., business—newspapers. A few did refer to recently issued reports prepared by government agencies or interest groups, but these had been skimmed rather than read. Congressmen seemed to have read somewhat less than had executive department officials whom we interviewed. It must, however, be remembered that there is little available in print which deals successfully with the problem as the congressman faces it, of tariff policy. Essentially what he needs is material which reconciles the claims and desires of his individual constituents with overall problems. What he finds in print is for the most part theoretical and high-level discussions of national interest and economic policy, or else he finds narrowly focused discussions of the situation of a specific industry, but the two types of comments are rarely related.

We might also mention that we can recall nothing to indicate that available nationwide opinion poll data had any appreciable impact on Congress. Members of the Administration were anxious that our survey of business should be published [7] so that they could use the results. (We do not know if they were in fact ever used.) Some Representatives did informal public opinion polls in their own districts. But on the whole, in the Reciprocal Trade controversy, members of Congress paid little attention to general public opinion as it was or could have been ascertained by formal polling techniques.

Despite the fact that on issue after issue the mail has been shown not to be representative—in 1954–55 it was about 10 to 1 protectionist—and despite the fact that there is no reason to suspect that letter writing on any given issue has any relationship to voting or political influence, the mail is nevertheless seen as the voice of the district or state. As is to be expected, many Congressmen and Senators run counter to the mail in obedience to dictates of conscience, party, "special interest," or committee; but when they do so, many of them appear to think they are defying something very significant.

Why is the mail taken so seriously? First of all, members of Congress and their staff spend an enormous amount of time reading and answering mail, and a busy man would be less than human if he were to believe he was wasting this time. Secondly, congressmen much of the time operate in a pretty complete vacuum, uninformed about what their ultimate "employers," the voters in their district or state, really want. The mail gives a feeling, perhaps a spurious one, (a) of receiving instructions on some issues, (b) of being in contact with his constituents, and (c) some notion, again perhaps spurious, as to what is likely to please his constituents and result in his reelection. Thirdly, many junior members of the House, having no important role on major committees, appear to be frustrated at their inability to take any demonstrably effective action on any major issue. Answering constituents' mail is one thing they can do which gives them the feeling of acting effectively. Fourth, writing to one's congressman is an expression of the citizen's right of petition—treasured by most congressmen—from perceived inequities of legislation or administrative action.[8] Finally, some congressmen, whether realisti-

7. This was done in Raymond A. Bauer, Suzanne Keller, and Ithiel de Sola Pool, "The Shift in Business Opinion on the Tariff," *Fortune,* April 1955.

8. A paper read by Kenneth Gray, Legislative Assistant to Senator Douglas of Illinois at the American Political Science Association meetings, September 1962 (mimeographed) presents very capably the individual's use of the mail to remedy

cally or not, appear to regard their correspondence as rational academic discussion of issues of national importance. Much congressional correspondence however serves no visible political or legislative purpose.

But mail is believed only if "genuine." It is not believed if "junk," i.e., press releases or other broadcast mailings, nor if be stimulated. Stimulated mail is not entirely easy to define. In its pure form it consists of virtually identical postcard messages written under the instigation of a single company, union, or interest group. (One company even mailed the postcards for its workers, fearing that they would not know who their congressman was.) Congressmen look for signs of stimulation—similarity of phrasing ("They all used the same argument") or even stationery ("They handed out the paper") and time of mailing ("You could tell the hour or minute someone pushed the button"). Instead it is hard to fool a congressman as to when mail is stimulated. Some organizations urge their members to write in their own words, on their own stationery, and as personally as possible. Congressional assistants tell us that perhaps one in fifty persons who write such a letter will enclose the original printed notice from the organization urging an individualized apparently spontaneous letter. But some mail which would have to be regarded as stimulated in the literal sense does not necessarily have the impact of stimulated mail. Pittsburgh Plate Glass, for example, succeeded in getting people in the community—doctors, lawyers, garage mechanics, school teachers, etc.—to write to their congressmen, and these letters appeared to reflect genuine involvement in the effect on Pittsburgh Plate of foreign competition![9]

Most of the mail sent on the Reciprocal Trade Act was in some sense stimulated. It is our guess that among the Eastern and Southern congressmen, on whom we concentrated our attention, Westinghouse, Dow, Monsanto, and Pittsurgh Plate Glass may have stimulated 40 percent or more of all the mail received on this issue in 1954. In addition, there were the coal, small oil, watch, bicycle, and textile interests, as well as such small groups as the nut and cherry growers. All of this mail was protectionist and outnumbered proreciprocal trade mail about 10 to 1. Mail in favor of reciprocal trade was equally stimulated and perhaps by even fewer prime movers. Our impression is that three-fourths of all anti-

---

injustice and the use of the mail by the individual Senator (under somewhat favorable circumstances) to help remedy injustice.

9. But note that even this well worked-out and individualized effort was not enough to disguise the fact of stimulation. The Congressman who showed us the material and the present authors were fully aware of the campaign or we would not be discussing it in this passage. We doubt that there is much stimulated mail which passes undetected.

protectionist mail was stimulated directly or indirectly by the League of Women Voters.

Stimulated mail and "junk" is discounted (some Congressmen do not even regard it as mail) because it does not appear to arise out of the writer's genuine, spontaneous involvement in the issue.

Congressman to Secretary: "Jane, am I right that we haven't received mail from more than five people on this tariff business?"

Secretary to Congressman: "Yes, except of course, for the pressure groups."

Stimulated or interest group mail is the type of mail which is most likely to be regarded as pressure. (1) It is far from the notion of the individual citizen petitioning. (2) There is little more educational value to 300 similar letters than to one well-written letter. (3) Finally, in particular if the congressman has already made up his mind, stimulated mass mail comes close to being an implied threat to mobilize votes against the congressman, even though, as we have indicated above, there is every reason for him to discount this threat. Yet it cannot be completely discounted. One lobbyist told us a story from an earlier phase in his career when Speaker Bankhead said to him, "Look, I've got 400 letters on this bill." "But, Mr. Speaker," the lobbyist replied, "you known those are stimulated." "Of course they're stimulated," said Bankhead, "but they're there." The person who has been stimulated to write may be organized to cast his vote on the basis of the issue about which he has written. Though we are convinced that the likelihood is not great, a shred of suspicion remains. While the term pressure is not often employed about mail it is almost exclusively applicable to such stimulated mail.

The conventional description of congressmen as under pressure carries with it the implication that the communications addressed to them are an *undesired* burden. But, more often than not, the congressman *welcomes* communication. One Congressman who was having difficulty making up his mind complained that no one came to his office to see him. The only time he saw a lobbyist on that matter was when he sought one out! Still others indicated that on the Reciprocal Trade Act and on other issues they wanted more communication.

Said one newly appointed assistant: "You know I was very much surprised at how few representatives or organizations come around to make themselves known." Said another: "I used to be a lobbyist myself. . . . It is a peculiar thing and rather incredible to me the scarcity of contact with Washington trade association or labor union representatives." The assistant of another who was a key figure in the reciprocal trade fight said: "I absolutely had to beat them over the head at our lobbying organization to find out what I wanted to find out; I had to push and push them on this to get the information." And one Congressman said when asked what he had heard from the lobby groups on his side and whether they had pushed him: "Hell no, it's just the other way around; it's me calling them up and trying to shaft them to get off their fat asses and get out and do something." To many congressmen the interest organization is a source of information about the attitudes of significant groups in his public, a source of research data and speech material, and an unofficial propaganda ally to help him put his own case forward. He talks of "our lobby."

The reader will recall that in *American Business and Public Policy* (*op. cit.*), Part IV on pressure groups, we noted that they became effective when they served as private auxiliaries to Congressmen.[10] The Congressman who told us that he had to telephone "his" lobby to get them going was not telling us a man bites dog story. He was describing a usual state of affairs. For his own career reasons a congressman wants to be a leader of movements with public appeal. He may define as his profession the mobilization of opinion and the propagation of viewpoints on public issues through the mass media. Success in that profession, as in any other depends on creating a product that the public wants and becoming a leading purveyor of it. But as is also true in business or education, the supplier does not wait passively for wants to appear. He helps create them. Businessmen spend billions to create wants for their products. Educators propagate education; they do not wait to be told what the students want to learn. Congressmen promote movements for legislation. Men like Richard Simpson and Cleveland Bailey—not to mention their precursors —gave form and vitality to protectionism as a program for coping with ills. It was in the United States Congress, not somewhere in the hinterland, that the ideological initiative for protection was historically centered. And the men who made themselves national figures by taking this initiative, led—rather than were led—by hired staff men working in association offices.

Thus we note once more that the congressman is not entirely a passive instrument with respect to the communications coming in to him. To a large extent he determines whether or not he is communicated with, in what manner, and on what side of the issue. We have seen that businessmen and interest group representatives tend to communicate with persons who agree with them. We recall the case of Congressman Stubborn who by his obduracy and his vigorous protectionist stand stopped all pro-

10. Cf. Stephen K. Bailey, *Congress Makes a Law* (Columbia U. P., New York, 1950), The Full Employment Act the adoption of which Bailey describes was conceived in the Congress. The liberal congressmen who got it written then pressed the unions and liberal organizations into support of the measure.

reciprocal trade communications from coming to him. He said that no registered voter wrote to him favoring reciprocal trade. That represents but one side of the coin, however.

The other side is that of congressmen who by their manner and conduct communicated their desire for communication. In contrast with Congressman Stubborn, we may consider Congressman Serious Consideration, an indecisive man who called a meeting in his district of people interested in the Reciprocal Trade Act. By indicating his own indecisions he stimulated his constituents to speak up. But by the circumstances under which he called the meeting he virtually ensured it being dominated by persons with protectionist interests.[11] He voted against H.R. 1, the Reciprocal Trade Extension Act of 1955.

Several members of Congress told us, "I tell my people that I want or don't want such and such a type of letter; otherwise I won't pay any attention to it."

Congressman Special has spoken up and down the country and up and down his own district on the evils of a low tariff policy. He has pointed out that in his judgment the Reciprocal Trade Act is an evil product of intrigue advocated by Karl Marx and worked out by Harry Dexter White. He stated that in three months he had received 2,000 letters supporting his position and not one single letter opposing it.

It is true, as we have seen in preceding chapters, that a large proportion of businessmen and a surprising proportion of representatives of interest groups contact congressmen without first ascertaining their views on the issue in question. But this is a relative thing; it is also true that congressmen determine to a large extent both the volume and type of communications that come to them.

In closing this chapter we should underline one additional reason why pressure groups do not appear to exercise so much pressure with regard to general legislation when viewed from Congress as they appear to do when viewed by outside observers. In a preceding section on pressure groups we pointed out that during the Reciprocal Trade controversy in 1953–55, the pressure groups tended to establish liaison only with the congressmen and senators on their own side and act for them as outside men stimulating general public interest in the issue, testifying before committees, or providing staff services for the congressmen and senators. The tactical basis of pressure group activities seemed to be to

11. He asked in effect how the Bill would affect his district and heard from industrial interests in his district. He did not ask how it would affect America's world interests. He did not invite foreign spokesmen or foreign affairs specialists. And he called the meeting in such a way that businessmen, "going to represent the company" found it far easier to attend than others.

stimulate and aid men already on their side to do the job of persuading fellow legislators. For the lobbies putting pressure on uncommitted or opposed congressmen and senators was a minor activity.[12]

12. Was the reciprocal trade situation unique or typical in regard to lobbying? It is instructive to note the items on pressures on Congress which appeared in the press during the preparation of this manuscript (July, 1959). Boston industrialist Bernard Goldfine who had gone out of his way to "maintain good relations" with friends in the national government was convicted of perjury in refusing to disclose to a congressional committee all of his activities. The International Brotherhood of Teamsters had been lobbying against labor legislation before the Congress. When the lobbyist tried to apply pressure in the classical sense saying in effect, "We'll get you," it backfired on him and he apparently ended up with less support than he had at the beginning. (Cf. *Time,* July 27, 1959, pp. 12–13.) In these same few weeks, Robert Kennedy, then counsel for the Senate Rackets Committee, appeared on several TV shows and called for a flood of mail to Congress. His appeal apparently was answered and thousands of letters poured in. But at the very same time a comparable volume of mail was received in protest against the mistreatment of wild horses! One of the results of the Kennedy appeal reported from Chicago was that so many people were calling to find out who their congressman was that a special telephone service had to be installed. In the meantime, Jack Paar, M.C. of one of the TV programs on which Kennedy appeared, shamefacedly reported to his audience that he had telegraphed Senator Javits only to find out that Javits had long been working fervently for the very legislation that Paar urged him to support. During the same period there was a considerable furor over the pressure tactics of missile manufacturers to obtain contracts for themselves. Several weeks of investigation seemed to confirm the fact that little pressure if any had been applied, or at least that the people to whom it was applied did not regard it as pressure. (Cf. "Gates Approves Ex-officers Jobs," *New York Times,* July 8, 1959.)

All in all, actual pressure is likely to backfire and is a dangerous activity. In the case of the missile program, even a moderate amount of self-serving promotion appeared to generate disproportionate counteractivity. Both Goldfine and the Teamsters ended up worse off than they were at the beginning. Kennedy and "Wild Horse Annie" showed that it was possible to stir up a considerable amount of activity in the form of writing to Congress. But both campaigns of letter writing seemed to have more head than beer.

As a footnote to a footnote, we may note that in the spring of 1959, I was asked by a well-known liberal journal to write an article dealing with some aspects of military policy formation; but soon found myself unable to produce what was demanded because the editors took it as a self-evident fact that "illegitimate" pressure or connivance *was* characteristic of the missile and aircraft makers versus the military and regarded an effort by me to ascertain what really was happening as evading "the real issue." At least, that is my interpretation.

SELECTED PUBLICATIONS BY
LEWIS ANTHONY DEXTER

BOOKS

American Business and Public Policy
(Atherton, New York, 1963). (With
R. A. Bauer and Ithiel de Sola Pool.)
*The Tyrannies of Schooling; An Inquiry
Into the Problem of "Stupidity,"* Basic
Books, New York, 1964.

*New Perspectives on State Government
and Politics* (Rand McNally, Chicago,
in preparation).
*Congress and the Legislative Process:
An Analysis of Communications* (title
tentative), Rand McNally (in preparation).

BIBLIOGRAPHY

The point of view stated in this paper
will be developed in a forthcoming
book about Congress, in preparation
by the writer, and in R. Peabody and
N. Polsby (eds.), *New Perspective on
Congress* (Rand McNally, Chicago,
1963). In the meantime, Part V
of *American Business and Public
Policy* by R. A. Bauer, Ithiel de Sola
Pool and L. A. Dexter (Atherton,
New York, 1963) covers much of the
same ground, as does in somewhat
more detail "Congressmen and the
People They Listen To" (copyright by
Massachusetts Institute of Technology, 1955; hectographed; available
Library of Congress and various Uni-
versity libraries, also on microfilm;
Ph.D. dissertation, Columbia Univer-
sity, 1960).

See also the following articles by the
writer: "The Representative and His
District," originally published in *Human Organization,* 1957, now available separately in the Bobbs-Merrill
Political Science Series, and in expanded form in N. Polsby, R. Dentler,
and P. Smith (eds.), *Politics and Social Life* (Houghton, Boston, 1963),
and R. Peabody and N. Polsby (eds.),
New Perspectives on Congress (Rand
McNally, Chicago, 1963); "What Do
Congressmen Hear," appearing in

Polsby, Dentler, and Smith, *op. cit.,* a
portion of which was issued in *Public
Opinion Quarterly,* vol. 20, Spring
1956, pp. 16–27; "Congressmen and
the Formulation of Military Policy,"
in Peabody and Polsby, *op. cit.;* "How
Candidates Lend Strength to Tickets
—Contestable Congressional Districts:
A Table of Variation in Party Strength
in U.S. Congressional Districts, 1946–
54," available at cost from author, 536
Pleasant Ave., Belmont 78, Mass.

The concluding section of Part V in
Bauer, Pool, and Dexter, *American
Business and Public Policy* (*op. cit.*)
contains a discussion of the most relevant literature on Congress.

The general approach to political analysis is best found in numerous readings in Polsby, Dentler, and Smith,
op. cit.

There is not, to the writer's knowledge,
any systematic analysis of either political behavior or the legislative process
as communications—although many
writers, influenced by Walter Lippmann's *The Phantom Public* (Macmillan, New York, 1929), have moved in
this direction. There is certainly no
analysis of the legislative process as
communications.

On the general subject of political letter-
writing, see Leila Sussman, *Dear*

FDR, The Bedminster Press, New York, 1963 (a preliminary report on this is available in L. Sussman, "Mass Political Letter-Writing in America," *Public Opinion Quarterly,* vol. 23, 1959, pp. 203–212).

QUESTIONS

1. Is a congressman or senator as described by Dexter engaged in some mass communications activity? In other words, what justification is there for including this article in this book? Do you think a similar reason would justify including here an article about state legislators in Vermont (see O. Garceau and C. Silverman, "A Pressure Group and the Pressured," *Am. Political Science Review,* vol. 48, 1954, pp. 672–691) or about the government of Andorra?

2. It happens that a number of congressional offices produce autotyped letters which appear individually written on matters of considerable interest (such as postal pay raises, wild-horse bills, Castro). Does this represent any tendency in mass communications? Does it create any difficulty in defining mass communications?

3. In terms of the theory of representative government as you understand it, should a congressman be influenced by the mail he gets? (Be careful about defining "representative" and "influence.")

4. Another aspect of congressional activity, not discussed in the text, is this: Many—probably more than half—of all Congressmen prepare a duplicated newsletter, fortnightly, weekly or monthly, which they send out chiefly to their constituents, telling what they have been doing or reporting on legislation, etc. It is said that Washington newspapermen, eager to do work part-time for small-town newspapers, find these congressional newsletters make their task difficult; editors use such letters as a capitol report. Are congressmen then in terms of their actual function when they do this reporting? Discuss.

5. Think of occasions when you have written to a public figure (if you have), or interview the people you know until you find someone who has. Determine as well as you can what image the writer had in his mind of the kind of response he would get and of why he chose this person rather than others in the same position to write to on the topic.

PART VI

MASS COMMUNICATION, CONFLICT, AND THE STRATEGY OF PERSUASION

Raymond A. Bauer and David B. Gleicher

Word-of-Mouth Communication

in the Soviet Union *

THERE IS A STRONG tendency to believe that through monopoly of communications those who control the media can produce any attention and response desired. Bauer and Gleicher suggest that this is not necessarily the case and indicate some of the limits of mass media as communicators.

It should be noted that the article was first published in 1953 and was based on material collected several years earlier. But since our interest is in the analysis of informal, unofficial oral communication existing side by side with controlled official communications, it does not matter to us if the changes that have recently occurred in the U.S.S.R. government outdate some specific findings.

The discussion made here is developed somewhat further in A. Inkeles and R. Bauer, The Soviet Citizen: Day-to-Day Life in a Totalitarian Society (Harvard U. P., Cambridge, Mass., 1959).

L. A. D.

DR. BAUER, whose biography and bibliography appear on pages 126–138, is Research Professor at the Harvard Graduate School of Business Administration.

MR. GLEICHER currently is a senior staff member of Arthur D. Little, Inc., an industrial research and consulting company, where he works

* This article was a portion of a larger study of Soviet communications behavior undertaken in conjunction with the Harvard Project on the Soviet Social System, sponsored by the Human Resources Research Institute of the Air Research and Development Command, Contract No. AF No. 33 (038)–12909.

We are indebted for the assistance rendered by Jean Briggs and Seymour Katz. Alice and Peter Rossi and Alex Inkeles contributed materially to the form and content of this article by their suggestions and advice throughout all stages of the work.

Reprinted from the *Public Opinion Quarterly,* vol. 17, no. 3, July, 1953, pp. 297–310, by permission of the authors and the publisher. (Copyright 1953 by Princeton University Press.)

primarily on problems concerning the process of technical and social innovation in industrial organizations. Previously he was a research associate at the Bureau of Applied Social Research at Columbia University and at the Center for International Studies at the Massachusetts Institute of Technology. His work in the area of Soviet studies was done while he served as Senior Analyst on the Russian Interview project of the Russian Research Center at Harvard.

One of the outstanding characteristics of communications in the Soviet Union is the extent of control which is exercised over them. The regime attempts not only to determine what information and ideas shall pass through the media, but also who shall have access to what information and ideas. It even makes serious efforts to deprive the Soviet citizen of the sacred privilege of not reading and not listening.

An essential premise of Soviet communications policy is the principle of monopoly. The official media are tightly controlled and organized; the competing media are strictly proscribed. Publication of printed materials contrary to official policy is prohibited and effectively inhibited. Even word-of-mouth communications that involve information and ideas which the regime regards with disfavor are suppressed. It is, for example, possible to receive a severe sentence in a forced-labor camp for telling a joke which has the wrong political implications. The effects of this suppression go beyond the restriction of manifest political word-of-mouth communications because the suppression stimulates an atmosphere of suspicion and fear. Refugees from the Soviet Union state with monotonous insistence "You didn't dare talk to anybody." Yet, despite official sanctions and popular anxiety there is every evidence that there exists in the Soviet Union an important system of informal, unofficial oral communications side by side with the controlled, official media. This paper explores certain of the characteristics and functions of this system of word-of-mouth communications.[1]

This discussion takes as its point of departure the work of Rossi and Bauer on the demographic correlates of communications exposure in the Soviet Union. Here the surprisingly important role of covert media was

1. In the written questionnaires the terms "rumor" and "discussion with friends" were used for separate questions. In coding responses to the oral interviews the category "word-of-mouth" was used to include all such unofficial oral communications. Our practice in this paper has been to employ the more inclusive term "word-of-mouth" except in those instances where we refer to the actual term used in the question wording. Thus, the appearance of the terms "rumor" and "discussion with friends" indicates that we are drawing on answers to the written questionnaire in which these terms were specifically used.

suggested.[2] The data are derived from the same sources as that of the earlier paper, some 2,700 questionnaires, and over 300 oral interviews with Soviet refugees contacted in 1950–51 in Europe and America. All but about eighty of these respondents had left the Soviet Union before the war's end and much of the interview data refers explicitly to prewar experience.

Because of the problem of sample bias involved in the self-selection of our respondents, a word of caution should be inserted against projecting the absolute values of our statistics onto the Soviet population. Statistics derived from these sources are valid for two purposes: (1) they point to the order of magnitude of the phenomena with which we are dealing; and (2) they permit internal comparisons within our sample and make it possible for us to identify group differences which may, with appropriate reservations, be extrapolated back to the parent population.

IMPORTANCE OF UNOFFICIAL SOURCES OF INFORMATION

A wide variety of sources attest to the importance and pervasiveness of informal, unofficial communications in the Soviet Union. Foreign observers comment particularly on the prevalence of rumor. Soviet fiction pictures it as a common social reality, although in tones reflecting official disapproval. The regime itself tacitly acknowledges the importance of such media not only in its propaganda against rumor mongering but, and more directly, in its use of informers, arrests for "alien" ideas, and intellectual "delousing" of Soviet citizens and soldiers exposed to the West. Refugee informants go to great lengths in stressing these aspects of official intervention in the stream of private discussion and observation. More important, however, is the fact that so many of them go on to report that much of what they knew of day-to-day events and policies in diverse areas of Soviet life came to them via the unofficial, word-of-mouth channel.

In the course of the interviews, respondents were asked to indicate their sources of information about what was going on.[3] As Table 1 in-

2. Rossi, Peter H. and Raymond A. Bauer, "Some Patterns of Soviet Communications Behavior," *Public Opinion Quarterly,* vol. 16, no. 4 (Winter 1952–53), pp. 653–670.

3. For this analysis we have three types of data which bear on the use of the various media. (1) The phrase "regular sources" refers to data given in the oral interviews to an open-ended question followed by specific probes on the separate media. Any medium was coded as a "regular" source if, in the coder's judgment, the answer to this question indicated that it was used by the respondent in some meaningful way. (2) The respondent was asked to identify the "most important" of the sources discussed above. Therefore, "most important" source is based on the

dicates, the press was cited by nearly all, with radio being mentioned by 50 percent. The fact is outstanding that 50 percent mentioned unofficial word-of-mouth as a regular source of information. This suggestive statistic is highlighted when we take into account the relative importance

Table 1—Media Cited as Regular and Most Important Sources of Information (Oral Interviews)

	A Regular Sources, Percent	B Most Important Source, Percent	B/A Salience
Newspapers	89	43	0.48
Radio	50	12	0.24
Meetings	19	2	0.11
Personal observation	14	5	0.36
Word-of-mouth	50	33	0.66
Other	*	5	—
Number	(312)	(281)	

of these sources as indicated by responses to the question "Which (of these sources) was the most important?" We find that the press retains its dominant position, being mentioned by 43 percent of our sample as their "most important source." However, close to it in importance and far outweighing the radio is the word-of-mouth source, selected by 33 percent of the respondents. The press and word-of-mouth sources, in fact, account for three-quarters of the citations. It is interesting to note further that of all the regular sources cited, word-of-mouth has the greatest staying power. A rough index of the salience of this medium is provided by the ratio of "most important" to "regular" citations. A ratio of "1" would mean that *all* the people who cite a source as "regular" also cite it as "most important," and to the extent that a source is used but is not salient, its index value would approach zero. This would mean that *no one* who used that particular medium regards it as his most important source. The third column of Table 1 shows that, among the main sources, word-of-mouth is the most "salient" followed in order by the press, personal observation, radio, and meetings.

As so far pictured, unofficial word-of-mouth communication provides a major news source. It might, however, be argued that the people pro-

---

respondent's own statement. (3) On the written questionnaire respondents were asked to rate themselves on the frequency of use of the various media ("frequent," "seldom," "never"). Therefore the use of a medium as a "regular" source implies nothing as to the frequency of its use beyond that it played some meaningful role in the person's communications activity, nor does it have anything to say about the importance of one medium relative to the others. For answers to these other questions we must turn to the other two types of data.

viding these data are anti-Soviet and further, that an appropriate expression of their anti-Soviet orientation would be to stress dependence on unofficial rather than official sources. Were this true, we would expect to find that the respondents who were more anti-Soviet would be more likely to cite frequent use of unofficial word-of-mouth sources. This is not the case. In fact, it is generally the less anti-Soviet of our sample who more frequently cite exposure to unofficial sources.[4] (See Table 2.) Accordingly, we feel warranted in making our earlier statement that unofficial word-of-mouth communication must be considered a major channel for the transmission of news in the Soviet Union.

Table 2—Exposure to Rumor and Discussions with Friends According to Anti-Soviet Sentiment Scores * (Written Questionnaire)

WORD-OF-MOUTH SOURCES	ANTI-SOVIET SENTIMENT, PERCENT			
	Low	Moderate	High	Very High
Rumor				
Frequently	27	17	18	12
Seldom	45	43	38	36
Never	28	40	44	52
Number	(501)	(679)	(542)	(615)
Discussion				
Frequent	28	18	15	11
Seldom	50	51	46	38
Never	22	31	39	51
Number	(511)	(684)	(551)	(620)

* These scores are formed by counting the number of anti-Soviet responses to five questions on the questionnaire.

CLASS VARIATIONS IN THE USE OF WORD-OF-MOUTH COMMUNICATIONS

More interesting than the overall importance of word-of-mouth communications in the Soviet Union are the group differences in use of this medium and the different functions it serves. The groups with which we are concerned here are the major social classes as indicated by the occupation of the respondent.

There are no significant class differences in the proportion of people who cite word-of-mouth as a "regular" source of information. (See Table 3). Once we inquire into the relative frequency of use of word-of-mouth, and its saliency in comparison with other media, however, we find very

4. With one exception which will be discussed below, this relationship holds for all major occupational groups. This finding bears some interesting implications which go beyond the question of the validity of our data.

Table 3—Percentage of Media Cited as Regular and as Most Important
Sources of Information for Various Occupational Groups
(Oral Interviews)

A. REGULAR SOURCES	Professional	Employee	Worker	Peasant
Newspapers	97	93	82	65
Radio	51	60	46	19
Personal observation	16	12	12	23
Word-of-mouth	53	44	48	62
Number	(79)	(99)	(52)	(27)
B. SOURCE MOST IMPORTANT	Professional	Employee	Worker	Peasant
Newspapers	47	52	26	10
Radio	7	14	15	10
Personal observation	5	3	10	5
Word-of-mouth	32	22	41	73
Other	9	9	8	7
Number	(74)	(94)	(39)	(19)
None cited	6	5	25	30
Number	(79)	(99)	(52)	(27)

large class differences. The upper classes reported that they received information by rumor more frequently than the lower classes did. Of the professional respondents to our questionnaire, 52 percent reported "frequent" exposure. Only 13 percent of the peasants made that claim. The trend to greater use of word-of-mouth in the upper groups proceeds in a steady, uninterrupted progression from occupational group to occupational group. A reverse relationship obtains with respect to the relative importance of word-of-mouth in relation to other media (Table 3). Both the upper-class groups—the professionals and the employees—cite the press most often as their "most important" source of information, even though about one-quarter mention word-of-mouth as their major source. Below this occupational level, however, the relative importance of the press drops sharply, and word-of-mouth comes to the fore as the predominant source. For the rank-and-file worker it outweighs the press 41 percent to 26 percent, and 72 percent of the ordinary peasants cite word-of-mouth in comparison to 17 percent who cite the press. Although the number of peasants is small, there is a considerable amount of supporting evidence to indicate that word-of-mouth is their most important source of information.

In summary, the upper classes receive word-of-mouth information more frequently than do the lower classes, but it is relatively less important for them. The lower classes are generally less active in all their communications behavior, but word-of-mouth occupies a relatively more important role for them as a source of information.

An exploration of the factors associated with these differences reveals a good deal about the functions that rumor serves in Soviet society. For the sake of simplicity in presentation, attention will be directed toward the peansantry and urban intelligentsia. The phenomena tend to vary continuously and the concern with the two polar groups should not cause the reader to lose sight of this underlying continuity.

There are three general trends which we find at work: (1) Word-of-mouth may be either a substitute for the official media, or a supplement to and corrective for the latter. The substitutional function is characteristic of groups who have a low level of communications activity; the reverse is true of the supplemental-corrective function, which is found in groups with a high level of activity. (2) By virtue of situational pressures put on persons in responsible positions, and by virtue of their superior access to knowledgeable sources the use of word-of-mouth is generally positively related to involvement in the Soviet system. (3) Highly placed persons, having access to superior sources of information, are also more inclined to credit word-of-mouth with more reliability, than the formal media.

THE PEASANT

The reliance of the Soviet peasantry on informal oral media reflects many factors which are familiar to the readers of recent communications research in backward areas: low educational levels, geographical isolation, the technical inadequacy of formal media in rural areas, and a historically established tradition of oral communication. The peasant has little need to be well informed for the execution of his daily work; his environment does little to stimulate intellectual activity and he has little time or energy for reading. In fact, many of the older peasants exhibit retrogressive illiteracy: they have *forgotten* how to read. To a great extent, the communications behavior of the Soviet peasantry is characteristic of a non-industrial society. In the Soviet case, however, it is important to note that the peasantry is the most disaffected social group and exhibits the greatest indifference to the content of the official media.[5]

The regime is far from unaware that the level of effective voluntary involvement of the collective farmer in the system of communications is low. Though the peasantry is not a key target group, the regime has made appreciable attempts to bring it into the official network of communications. The educational level of the younger generation has been raised,

5. The high degree of disaffection among the Soviet peasantry is a result of a series of factors: the period of collectivization and the enormous dislocations and hardships which followed are remembered vividly by all except the youngest peasants; the result of collectivization has been to lower the standard of living of the peasantry in general; the peasant is particularly resentful of being collectivized and continues wherever possible, to turn back to his individual garden plot.

advances have been made in extending the facilities of the press and radio, and the regime has tried to stimulate the interest and involvement of the rural groups by oral agitation. Despite these measures, young (even the relatively better educated) as well as old collective farmers remain largely untouched by the mass media and express little interest in what is going on in the world around them.

When the regime finds it necessary to inform collective farmers of some event or policy, some official representative conveys this to him directly. For example, one young woman collective farmer who had never read a newspaper or listened to a radio on her collective farm learned about the beginning of the war when the village Soviet convened the field hands in the evening after work and had a spokesman tell them of this event. Typically, another young collective farmer, when asked how he learned about new laws and regulations, answered that the brigadier or the head of the collective farm told him about such things. The regime has even organized a kind of official corps of opinion leaders, largely members of the Party and Komsomol, who serve as spokesmen for the regime in their informal day-to-day personal contacts and who, in addition, are assigned the more formalized task of conveying the content of the official media by such devices as reading the newspapers to groups of field hands during their lunch hours and giving them pep talks in line with current Party or government policy. As one respondent reports, "Teachers used to tell us about things but they usually said just what they saw in the newspaper. They would read the newspapers at night and then tell us about it in the morning."

Despite these direct attempts of the regime to involve the peasantry and other groups in the network of official communications, this group remains predominantly indifferent and isolated. Even official meetings are attended with reluctance. One peasant reports that "Usually one member of our family went to such a meeting and told the others what was said, not in detail, just a little."

This indifferent and frequently reluctant exposure to even the official oral media is the backdrop against which we must view the peasants' participation in the unofficial word-of-mouth network. Within the peasantry the more anti-Soviet individuals make greater use of the unofficial word-of-mouth sources but among other classes, the more anti-Soviet report less contact with this unofficial source. Rural oral communications are more relevant and more appealing to the typical anti-Soviet peasants than to the pro-Soviet minority which makes relatively greater use of the official media. The peasant reported that the bulk of his information was obtained via unofficial word-of-mouth sources. He, however, is not an active communications consumer (he makes no special efforts to obtain information), and the communications he receives in his network differ in kind, in frequency, and in source from those available to others and especially those in the upper Soviet strata.

This network supplies the peasant with much of the information which is legitimate in content; news of agricultural policy, local, national, and international events. His sources are his friends, co-workers, and kin who read and listen to official media and are the middlemen in the rural transmission of official media contents. To a surprising extent, and in contrast to the elite group—the peasant typically learns by word-of-mouth information that is readily available in the official media. One field hand, for example, heard of the Stalin-Hitler Pact in a casual talk with his brigade leader. He first heard of the October Revolution when he "heard people talking." A major function of word-of-mouth is then to act as a substitute for the formal media.

The word-of-mouth network also, and possibly more importantly, supplies the peasant with illicit and otherwise unavailable information; news of economic failures, living conditions in other areas, the extent of hostility toward the regime. Such information provides some emotional satisfaction for the typically anti-Soviet peasant and gives him a more complete picture of Soviet life. The sources of these contents are more varied than those of the official media contents which he receives by word-of-mouth. Prime among these are the people whose work involves travel. As one respondent reports, "In the course of conversation with (people from large urban centers who came to the kolkhoz to recruit industrial workers) you learned something about how people were living in various areas. . . . There were also collective farmers who did seasonal work elsewhere . . . these people had seen living conditions themselves in various areas and were acquainted with them first-hand." Other sources of such information came from fellow collective farmers who had gone to the city markets and from truck drivers who, as in all rural areas, function as carriers of news from the major news centers. With few exceptions the immediate sources for the rural areas are many hands removed from contact with people who handle classified information and even people of less strategic social position but who live in the news centers of the Soviet Union.

This distance from original sources affects both the frequency and range of content of the word-of-mouth news available in rural areas. It also affects their reliability. The original communication is more likely to be distorted the larger the number of intermediaries between original and terminal source. The peasant, being least well equipped to assess the truthfulness of much news, is particularly vulnerable to rumors of low plausibility. For example, one respondent reports that a collective farm in the Ukraine was swept several times by a rumor that the United States had attacked the Soviet Union. These variations in closeness to original sources and in the ability to assess the reliability of the contents received are crucial factors in distinguishing the participation of the peasants and inteligentsia in the unofficial word-of-mouth network.

Among the contents which the peasant receives from this unofficial network must be included the political joke which, in the Soviet Union, provides not only a source of humor but also a deliberate means of communicating opinion and testing the opinions of others.

In general, the word-of-mouth network is the newspaper of the peasant. What little communications activity the peasant has is predominantly in the unofficial network; and what contact he has with the official network is mainly with the system of oral agitation which the regime employs to offset his general isolation from the official network.

THE INTELLIGENTSIA

In marked contrast to the peasantry, the Soviet urban intelligentsia are very interested and active with repect to all the communications media. While exposure to formal media is very high, the urban intelligentsia are also very active users of unofficial oral communications.

The Soviet intelligentsia is in the best position to observe the disparity between reality and the official version of it. Sitting at the news desks of the press, scanning foreign publications, preparing and reading reports, analyzing production figures and plans, observing first-hand the rise and fall of prominent figures, etc., the Soviet intelligentsia see the things which are hidden or distorted in the official media. This experience acts to stimulate awareness that there are information gaps to be filled and helps to specify the gaps, to "nose out" the soft spots of official media content. Because of the circles in which they move, the Soviet intelligentsia are also in the best position to fill these gaps. If a member of this group is in a relatively bad information-locating position himself, he nevertheless is likely to know others who have access to interesting and/or relevant news.

The Soviet intelligentsia are vulnerable to the attention of the heresy hunters and the guardians of the Plan, because of their responsible work assignments. It is to their advantage to be informed on many aspects of official policy, and on anticipated changes in policy which would affect the successful completion of their work assignments. In this sense, the intelligentsia are under pressure to get information much of which is unavailable except in the unofficial network.

All media, but particularly the newspapers, are mobilized for strident and repetitive didactic campaigns which, whether effective as propaganda or not, produce boredom and fatigue—especially among the intelligentsia. This relative paucity of a lighter touch stimulates the intelligentsia to participation in the interchanges of gossip and unpoliticized human interest information which besides providing respite also provide opportunities for the transmssion and reception of other information.

As a result of this constellation of attributes and situations, the Soviet intelligentsia, unlike the peasantry, are active seekers of information supplementary to the official sources and are in a good position to obtain such information. Their use of the unofficial network, however, adds still more differences to this contrast of peasantry's and intelligentsia's use of the unofficial media.

Whereas the peasants' major source of information, in terms of sheer bulk, was word-of-mouth, for the intelligentsia it is invariably the official media. Virtually never do they rely on word-of-mouth to learn something that is readily available in the press. It will be recalled that 33 percent of the intelligentsia respondents said that word-of-mouth sources were the most important. Upon reading through the oral interview we find that by "most important" they were referring not to the sheer amount of information they got—this was provided largely by the official media—but rather to the fact that word-of-mouth provided them with the most *reliable* source of crucial information which they used in conjunction with official media contents. For the peasant, word-of-mouth is a substitute for the press; for the urban intelligentsia it is a supplement. It gives him information that he cannot get from the official media, and, equally important, it helps him interpret these official media. Time and time again our respondents said that the extraction of truth from the official media was an art involving the judicious admixture of some parts of official contents with some parts of "OBS" the abbreviation of "Odna baba skazala," an almost literal translation of our term "old wives tales." They said, for example, "Rumors made it possible to read the newspaper intelligently," or ". . . We read the Soviet papers constantly, but here it is necessary to make certain automatic corrections, so our (next) source was from conversations with people . . ."

Reliance on rumor as a supplement to and corrective for the official media implies a high degree of confidence in one's sources of rumor, something not found characteristic of the peasantry. In fact, throughout their discussions, members of the intelligentsia referred to the greater reliability of word-of-mouth sources in general but most especially with reference to news of political import. More striking, however, is the response to a written question on the reliability of rumor compared with newspapers and magazines. The majority of each class cited rumor as more reliable but there were vast class differences. Some 56 percent of the peasantry regarded rumor as more reliable but fully 95 percent of the urban intelligentsia said that rumor was more reliable than the press (See Table 4). Whatever may be said about the absolute value of these figures, the phenomenon of an urban elite giving so much more proportionate credence to rumor as compared with the considerably more disaffected peasantry is not only surprising but illuminating.

Table 4—Estimates of the Reliability of Rumor and Newspapers for Various Occupational Groups Compared on the Basis of Degree of Anti-Soviet Sentiment

	PROFESSIONAL		EMPLOYEES		WORKERS		PEASANTS	
	Low ASS*	High ASS	Low ASS	High ASS	Low ASS	High ASS	Low ASS	High ASS
Percentage saying some press news is reliable	81	77	76	57	52	35	37	23
Percentage saying no press news is reliable	19	23	24	43	48	65	63	77
Total number	(258)	(71)	(472)	(240)	(221)	(217)	(116)	(145)
Percentage saying rumor more reliable than official media	94	96	87	83	69	74	58	54
Total number	(189)	(46)	(297)	(149)	(126)	(125)	(43)	(61)

* Anti-Soviet sentiment.

Table 4 also clearly indicates that within each class group the most and least anti-Soviet individuals are equally likely to impute greater reliability to the unofficial media. There is, however, no such consensus that nothing in the official media is reliable. The more anti-Soviet persons of each class are much more likely to chastise the official media. Assessment of the reliability of official media is clearly related to one's political attitudes. Assessment of the relative reliability of unofficial media, however, bears no such relationship to political attitudes, but has a marked relationship to social class. Hence, it may be regarded as a direct reflection of the quality of rumors which circulate with the social environment of the rater. The lower classes, whose rumor sources we know to be less reliable than those of higher strata, reflect this reality in their proportionately lesser imputation of reliability to rumor. Conversely, the intelligentsia, nearly to a man, assert the reliability of the rumors which reach them, and, there is every indication that this too is a reflection of reality.

What does the intelligentsia's extensive participation and trust in the unofficial network imply as to their loyalty or disloyalty toward the regime? As we have indicated, much of the stimulus to the intelligentsia's participation in the network comes from the work they do, and the people they know. They are aware of the unreliability of the official media, but, although it complicates their own communications activity, in many instances they nevertheless accept this as a necessary social device for leading the masses to Nirvana. As Rossi and Bauer noted earlier, the people more involved in the day-to-day operation of the Soviet system, more positively oriented toward their work, were the people most active in seeking information of all sorts and from all sources. Comparing individuals *within* class groups, as well as classes themselves it would be the more positively oriented toward the system whose communications activity would be the greatest. As shown in Table 5, this is true of the official media as repre-

Table 5—The Relationship of Anti-Soviet Sentiment to Exposure to Newspapers and Rumor for Various Occupational Groups, Percent

	PROFESSIONAL		EMPLOYEE		WORKER		PEASANT	
	Low ASS	High ASS	Low ASS	High ASS	Low ASS	High ASS	Low ASS	High ASS
Exposure to rumor								
Frequently	40	31	20	9	11	10	5	12
Seldom	42	33	47	36	38	42	19	20
Never	18	36	33	55	51	48	76	68
Number	(254)	(73)	(467)	(184)	(236)	(229)	(124)	(169)
Exposure to newspapers and magazines								
Frequently	89	81	74	61	34	20	15	10
Seldom	11	19	25	34	58	63	59	52
Never	—	—	1	5	8	17	26	38
Number	(259)	(73)	(468)	(244)	(237)	(224)	(121)	(164)

sented by newspapers and magazines; the more anti-Soviet of each class report less exposure. For the unofficial media, however, this relationship holds only for the two upper-class groups and in fact is slightly reversed among the peasantry. In other words, exposure to official media is for all classes an expression of involvement in the system, whereas exposure to unofficial sources implies involvement only for the upper classes. As one descends the occupational ladder interest and communications decrease, the smaller the proportion of one's word-of-mouth information comes from highly placed people, and what one gets via this medium is more and more the result of passive nonavoidance and less a matter of active seeking. Thus use of word-of-mouth ceases to be correlated with involvement in the system. It is possible that, in such sections of society where control over word-of-mouth is less stringent because the regime is less concerned, the more anti-Soviet members of the group become active in circulating derogatory information and opinions via this medium.

The substitutional function of rumor is in no way linked to acceptance of the system (except possibly negatively), but that the supplemental-corrective is integrally related to involvement in the system. If the responses to "frequently" and "seldom" are collapsed for the professional and employee groups, persons low on anti-Soviet sentiment report *some* exposure to rumor much more than do those persons who are high—82 percent to 64 percent for the professional group and 67 percent to 45 percent for the employees.

SUMMARY

The opposition of the regime to the dissemination of information over the unofficial network is such that, if it were feasible, there is little doubt that the network would be suppressed entirely. To the extent that it is a substitute for the official media, the individual is able to avoid exposure to the information that the regime wants to pass on to him. To the extent that it is a substitute and corrective for the official media, it enables him to find out things or form opinions that the regime does not want circulated. On the other hand, it is clear that the populace itself values the unofficial network highly. Viewed in perspective, to what extent may we say that this informal, unofficial system of communications is functional and disfunctional, and for whom?

Clearly the regime regards it as disfunctional, although there are some hints that the regime, on occasion, plants rumors that it wants circulated. Furthermore, refugees state that through its secret informers, the regime does tap this unofficial network as one of its few resources for sounding public opinion. These uses of the unofficial network by the regime, appear to be exploitative accommodations to a situation which is somewhat out of control.

This unofficial communication system also serves some positive *latent* functions for the regime—even though they may be minor. While the unofficial network provides for the circulation of information that the regime would like to suppress, it also effects a certain amount of release of tension that might be harmful to the regime. It also seems likely that, in an appreciable number of cases, people are able to carry out their assigned jobs better by virtue of the information they get via unofficial channels.

For the individual citizen it is almost wholly functional—it supplies him with information that is essential to his survival, it satisfies his curiosity and it provides him with gossip, political jokes, and other diversions not elsewhere available.

In general, however, the operation of the unofficial network is mythbusting. It militates against the regime's ability to convert hostile elements like the peasantry. Even for those loyal adherents whose initial involvement in the rumor network does not stem from disaffection from the system it must, over the course of time, erode their capacity to believe.

Regardless of the extent to which it is functional or disfunctional, the existence of this unofficial network is to a great extent a direct result of the regime's communications policy and of its principles of propaganda. It is the regime itself that is responsible for the elevation of what is ordinarily an incidental information source to the status of a parallel system of communications outside of official control. Viewed from the standpoint of psychological and political warfare, this has very important implications. If we look at the initial Soviet audience or readership which can be reached by radio, leaflet, or informational bulletin it is possible to become overly discouraged. It is necessary to remember that thanks to this independent system of informational communications, now apparently well established in the Soviet Union, the initial audience or readership gets multiplied much more rapidly than it would in another society. It is also important that the most highly placed groups in the system are most convinced of the reliability of word-of-mouth information.

None of these phenomena is peculiar to the Soviet system. The Soviet Union exhibits the characteristic features of all industrial societies, but in addition many segments of the population resemble nonindustrial groups, and the system has certain traits which are peculiar to the Soviet dictatorship. The peasant's communications behavior is not especially unlike that of the mass of the population of most backward areas, and the way in which the urban intelligentsia use word-of-mouth sources to supplement the official media is reminiscent of the use of such sources in American elite circles. Despite the many obviously distinctive Soviet characteristics of the phenomena which we have been describing, in another context, one would be as justified in stressing the continuities with other societies as in stressing the discontinuities.

SELECTED PUBLICATIONS BY MR. GLEICHER

BIBLIOGRAPHY

"Determinants of Voting Behavior," *Public Opinion Quarterly,* Fall 1950. (With Alice S. Kitt.)

The following unpublished research manuscripts were prepared for the U.S. Air Force pursuant to a project on the Soviet Social System: "Political Cleavage in the Soviet Union"; "Party Member Types" (with Anna Weintraub); "The Meaning of Distortion: Causes and Correlates of Hostility toward the Soviet Regime"; and "The Loyalty Problem in the Soviet Military Organization."

QUESTIONS

1.   Interview someone who has been in a heavily disciplined camp or boarding school or in an institution. Find out how "the grapevine" operated in such a setting. What comparisons and differences do you see between this and Bauer and Gleicher's description of communications in the U.S.S.R.?

2.   Does this article raise any doubts about the sociological likelihood of "1984"? Discuss.

3.   List important things you have learned about some organization of which you are a member which were not published until considerably later (if at all) in the mass media, house organs, or even official meetings.

Ithiel de Sola Pool

The Mass Media and Their

Interpersonal Social Functions in the

Process of Modernization *

PROFESSOR POOL'S STATEMENT on the processes of communications in developing countries obviously relates to most of the preceding articles in this volume and in particular to the immediately preceding articles by Dexter and by Bauer and Gleicher. The value of the article is, in our opinion, great. To a very substantial degree the present volume has been influenced by Professor Pool.

These prefatory remarks are made to provide a framework within which disagreement may be expressed. Professor Pool makes a distinction between the attitudes of people having traditional and communist orientations towards truth value as relative to social function in opposition to those brought up within the Graeco-Judaic tradition for whom truth value is an absolute. The point may be somewhat overstated.

In the first place Professor Pool's contacts have been national, metropolitan, and cosmopolitan. Those who have spent much more time on state and local political campaigns and have taught in more locally oriented colleges will be inclined to suggest that Pool's statement be qualified to apply only to cosmopolitan types in the Western nations, or else that it should be put forward in terms of some rather subtle difference of degree.

But, even given his thesis as qualified to apply only to such metropolitan types, there is a second area where questions may be raised. Although there are some things on which such types as scientists,

* Prepared for Seminar on Communications and Political Development, Gould House, Dobbs Ferry, N.Y., Sept. 11–14, 1961. Sponsored by Committee on Comparative Politics of the Social Science Research Council.

Permission given by Princeton University Press for reproduction from Lucian Pye (ed.), *Communications and Political Development*, Princeton U. P., 1963, in which this article (with minor differences) comprises Chap. 14.

Unitarian ministers, Jewish rabbis, university professors of social science, university Presidents, and news reporters for the New York Times or the national broadcasting chains are scrupulous about truth and truth value, it remains to be proved that this is really a general characteristic of these people. Rather, it is equally likely that they have carved out a certain area of professional life and civic responsibility (in the latter case as in the former, different areas for different persons) where the facts, as they understand them, speak for themselves and who says what is much less significant than the thing said. But, on the whole—and this would seem true even in the natural sciences (as David Lindsay Watson in Scientists Are Human * demonstrates) as well as in the news business—there are wide areas in which prestige and authority are far more important than "truth."

Indeed, an attempt to determine when professional men in our society regard "truth value" as sacrosanct and when they regard prestige and authority as an adequate substitute for truth value would make a highly valuable contribution to the sociology of communications.   L. A. D.

A BIOGRAPHICAL statement about Professor Pool appears on page 143. See page 158 for his selected bibliography.

I. COMMUNICATION THEORIES

Characteristic of noncommunist developing countries is a policy which attaches great importance to literacy and the education of children, but little importance to the mass media and which looks down with some disdain on those more popular mass media which do develop at low cultural levels in the private sphere. Characteristic of communist developing countries, on the other hand, is a policy that attaches enormous importance to hortatory communications through the mass media, and which uses these not only for political control but as a major stimulus to the carrying through of development plans.

Behind these divergent investment policies lie two different theories of communication as well as two different theories of economic organization. Our objective is to examine these implicit theories of communication and hold them up against our present social science knowledge about the role of mass media in relation to face to face communication.

* Kegan Paul, London, 1938.

II. DISILLUSIONMENT WITH THE MASS MEDIA

The implicit view about the operation of the mass media which we have been describing as one widely held by elites in noncommunist nations may be labelled that of disillusionment. The media are conceded a potential function of educating people to support urgent national tasks for development, but they fail at it. The media, so it seems, are ineffective agents of action on behalf of the planners. Agricultural advice broadcast on radio seldom gets followed in practice. Exhortations in the press to change established family or social patterns seem to have no results. People may learn that caste discrimination, or a low protein diet, or spitting, or doweries, are disapproved in the modern world but they do not change as the planners exhort them to.

But while the Westernizing leaders become disillusioned about the power of the media in their own hands to engender desired actions, *they simultaneously believe in the vast powers of the hidden persuaders for evil*. It seems that while the media are not effective instruments of constructive action, they have a considerable power to disorient and engender confusion in a society. They engender the revolution of rising expectations, by creating desires for new things about which their readers and viewers learn; however, they do not thereby generate a willingness to take the actions called for to obtain these good things.

Now what we have just described may seem to be a caricature of a jaundiced view of the role of the mass media in development. It is, in fact, however, a view with a firm foundation in social science research. It is true that the mass media alone, unlinked to word-of-mouth communication, fail in producing action, but do create information and desires. We shall document this point later. Here let us simply note that the lukewarm attitude of the governments of most developing countries toward the mass media is a natural concomitant of the weakness of political organization underpinning their regime. Without an effective political organization at the grass roots to provide word-of-mouth support for the messages in the mass media, the latter do not produce desired action results.

From a broader point of view than that of a particular government, the other effects of the mass media, such as demonstration effects or raising of information, may be either good or bad in the long run. But a regime resting on weak political organization can hardly be expected to look with pleasure on forces which introduce shocks to the social fabric, while not facilitating control of the short-run action consequences.

Thus, the theory of communication that underlies the media invest-ment pattern in most noncommunist developing countries is one which says, first, that the media do not seem to produce major changes in action. (That is true if one considers the media alone.) Secondly, other changes in the short run such as changes in beliefs and values unaccompanied by appropriate changes in practices tend to be disruptive. Third, despite the impracticality or dangers of trying to produce changes in the minds of men, it is recognized that such changes are needed for modernization. That is why a seemingly safe investment is made in the very slow-acting medium of education. From the long perspective of history we know how disruptive to the old ways education also may be, but the quick-acting media (press, radio, film, etc.) act in periods coincident with the span considered in political decision making, while education in general does not. For the short run then, this theory says the mass media are not of great importance, and that is correct if one focuses on the objective of pro-ducing action, and assumes that no concomitant strong political organiza-tion is present.

III. THE COMMUNIST THEORY OF MEDIA USE

The communist theory of mass communication differs from that just outlined. Most obviously, it is even more emphatic on the possible nega-tive effects of some messages; oppositional messages are simply banned. Only the approved ideas are in the flow to the public without even slight deviations tolerated.

The communist theory of mass communication, in the second place, while much concerned with the action consequences of propaganda is not quite so exclusively focused on them. Their propaganda rulebook requires that the agitator always exhort to specific actions rather than simply advo-cate attitudes. At the same time communist doctrine recognizes propa-ganda objectives, other than action and objectives, which action-advocating propaganda may serve. The Communists also think of using the mass media to produce characterological change. Also, they are aware of the possibility of using the mass media as organizational devices, for in com-munist theory the media are just an adjunct to political organization.

Let us try to codify communist operational doctrine on this subject.

[1] The important thing about a medium is not what it says *per se* but the social function (*a*) of its existence as an institution, and (*b*) of the statements in it.

[2] Discipline in making the "correct" statement in the media is indeed important, but not primarily because of any direct impact of the

staements made, but rather as a means to producing changes in the direction of discipline and conformity.

[3] Media provide an important activity around which to build organizations. Worker correspondents, discussion groups around key articles, local wall newspapers, etc., involve people deeply in the media.

[4] The media provide an instrument for central direction of organizations dispersed to all corners of a country.[1] The media give the orders of the day to be carried out in face-to-face organization.

[5] Words in the media alone do not effectively change people. It takes a combination of the media and direct personal contact to move people to action. It is only through participation in action that deeply held attitudes are changed. By action, however, these can be changed, even down to changing the basic personality of man.

IV. TRADITIONAL MODES OF COMMUNICATION

In the developing nations, Westernized detraditionalized action-oriented elites without well-organized mass following tend to adopt the first view of the media outlined above—that which we called disillusionment. Certain other elites obviously find the communist doctrine of mass communication genial. Ever since Sun Yat Sen, a surprising number of leaders of developing countries have found the practical political methods of democratic centralism appealing even though they have cared but little about the economics of communism. *Indeed, it is its approach to propaganda and politics which has been the most effective part of Bolshevik doctrine in the underdeveloped countries.* That is not surprising for, in a few important respects the communist doctrine is closer than is the Western approach to the theory of communication which characterizes traditional societies. *It is closer in that it values the social function of a communication above its truth value.*

The similarities that we have just noted between communist and traditional conceptions of communication are not explained by any glib assertation that the communist approach to communication is backward or primitive. The fact that two of the three theories we have been describing are alike on a number of points is better explained by some peculiar and unique features of the third, which sets it apart from most human behavior through all time the world over.

1. Note that the most important magazine in Russia is probably *The Agitator's Notebook,* a journal which gives the two million oral agitators their guidelines for the next few weeks of meetings.

Our third theory rests upon a criterion of objective truth, which is one of the peculiar features of the Graeco-Roman Western tradition. And truth value is a rather curious criterion. It is ruthlessly two-valued and dominated by the law of the excluded middle, something which classical Indian logic, for example, never accepted; statements in the latter system could be simultaneously both true and false. The Western criterion of truth value also assumes that a statement has a validity or lack of it inherent in itself, and quite independent of who says it and why. The Western criterion of truth assumes further that validity can be tested independently of who does the testing provided certain rituals of procedure are followed. Most cultural traditions do not make these assumptions. For one thing, only a society with an unusually high degree of mutual trust in the interpersonal relationships would permit people to accept statements regardless of source. In most societies facts must be validated by an in-group authority before they can be considered credible. Word-of-mouth is therefore more trustworthy than written sources. Distrust of those who are not in one's own family, tribe, or caste, frequently dominates any objective test of truth [2] in non-"modern" societies.

Furthermore, most of mankind does not regard the truth value of statements as terribly important. For most of the the men who have inhabited the earth, the consequences of a statement—e.g., whether it will bring the wrath of God upon you, whether it will help you earn a living, whether it will win a loved one—are considerably more important than whether it matches certain abstract rules of transformability to other statements. The Western tradition is unique in the value it has attached the latter consideration.

A statement is valid in a traditional society if it comes from the right oracle. It is not necessarily everyone's right to judge its validity. There are statements within one's own sphere on propriety and there are those which are outside one's proper role. Daniel Lerner has introduced all of us to the peasant whose reply to the question what would he do if he were someone else—a foreigner, a radio station manager, a politician—is, in effect, "My God! How can you ask me a question like that. I could never be him." [3] The peasant's statement, even in role playing, has no validity. Felix and Marie Keesing document the same point even more extensively in their study of communication behavior in Samoa.[4] There

2. F. and M. Keesing, *Elite Communications in Samoa,* Stanford, Stanford U. Press, 1956; cf. also Thomas Blair, "Social Structure and Information Exposure in Rural Brazil," *Rural Sociology,* XXV, March 1960, pp. 65–75.

3. Daniel Lerner, *The Passing of Traditional Society* (Free Press, New York, 1958).

4. F. and M. Keesing, *op. cit.*

are certain words and certain topics of discussion reference to which is proper only by certain individuals. In Samoa references to those domains in which power is demonstrated by chiefs and talking chiefs is improper for their subordinates. It is not, that the inferior, as in Western dictatorship, is obliged to say approved things. It is rather that it is shocking for him to say anything at all in what is not his proper sphere.

The frequent application of social rather than truth-value criteria in traditional societies is further documented by studies of political movements in them. Lucian Pye has shown how to the Malayan communists the primary criterion applied to communist ideology was the power of the leaders. If the communists seemed likely to win, then what the communist leaders said was valid; if they seemed likely to lose, then what they said was not. It was personal leadership and power that determined the validity of what might be in the mass media.[5]

A study of Cambodia tells us that "information itself is considered sterile by the individual villager until some one of "status" has interpreted it. The individual does not see it as his role to judge the news." [6]

One might cite examples indefinitely. We could talk about honorifics and the problem of communication in Japan where it may become hard to express what one has to say until one has gotten around to finding the words appropriate to the person to whom one is talking.

Our concern here, however, is to consider the significance of these matters to the mass media. The mass media represent a peculiar mode of communication in which one does not know to whom one is talking. Broadcasting or writing for the press is like dropping a note in a bottle over the side of a boat. The man who receives it may be king or pauper, relative or stranger, friend or foe.

There is a problem in a traditional society, though it is not a new problem. All traditional societies have their equivalents of mass media. There is a literature of sagas or folk songs sung to all and sundry. There are assemblages at temples, festivals, or markets where the hawker, priest, or actor addresses himself to a motley crowd of persons of all stations. There are proclamations to the multitude. There are ways of calling out to a stranger in the dark. But for all of these there are established conventions. The rules of etiquette prescribe the form of language in which a folk song is sung. The modern media create a host of new situations for which new conventions must be established. How does one answer the phone or talk on radio or write for the newspapers?

5. Cf. Lucian Pye, *Guerrilla Communism in Malaya,* Princeton, Princeton U. Press, 1956; Edward W. Gude, "Buddhism and the Political Process in Cambodia," ms., 1961, p. 15.
6. Gude, *op. cit.,* p. 14.

The mass media in a stratified society inevitably have the problem of vulgarity in a particularly acute way. They can avoid vulgarity by pretending they are addressing their most cultured listeners. This results in media that use only the highest form of the language and are not understood by the bulk of the population—something that happens extensively in Arab countries. It happens often where the media are in the hands of well-educated civil servants aspiring to be intellectuals. The All-India Radio Management, for example, says that its small village audience is its top-priority audience, but it also often refuses to use those low Hindi forms which the villagers could understand.

Alternatively, the media may seek out their natural mass audience and alienate themselves from their national elite and its goals. They can do this by turning radical or by turning commercial and sensational, or both. Tawdry apolitical yellow publications or movies may well be produced by a largely leftist press corps. Or it may be that the radical publications themselves provide low-level popular culture, some sort of so-called people's art. It takes either a callous unconcern with the values of one's culture *or else an ideology which justifies alternative values* to permit intellectuals, bred among the elite or elite aspirants of any society, to produce the more or less debased materials that can communicate to the masses who share only a watered-down version of the culture.

Granted it is not an insuperable problem. The mass media are also graded and they divide up a national audience among them by taste and cultural level. But a problem does exist. Some media do have to serve the total society. Where there is but a single local newspaper or radio or TV station, dissatisfaction with it is bound to arise in any differentiated society, and especially so in a dual society as any developing society is. Even more important is the fact that highly educated or Westernized elites produce the modern media and give the guidance for them; such men are often unable or unwilling to address their masses, or they are in conflict when addressing them.

Education of the masses so that they will become like their elite is normally hoped for as the answer. But that is obviously an illusory solution. Village schools may produce literacy. They do not thereby reduce the importance of lowbrow highly popularized media—they increase it.

What this signifies is, first that mass education may be expected to create an audience for only the most popularized and simplified media, and second, that media of this kind are the only ones that can serve to induct into modern ways precisely those persons whose familial environment does not push them in the same direction. Education may modernize a child or young man from a household which instills motivation for that goal. It will not effectively modernize the masses.[7] The media, plus associated personal influence on adults, must take over the job at the very low level which is possible.

Media at that low level of popular culture include movies, comics and picture books, and potentially radio and TV. Also particularly effective at this level are the traditional media to which we referred above, and which can be used effectively on behalf of agricultural conservation, or nationalism. The Communists have done a good deal of this, putting out material through traditional storytellers, priests, or players. Some non-traditional parties such as provincial movements in India or that of Prince Sihanouk in Cambodia or of the Muslim Teachers in Indonesia, of course, rely particularly heavily on an organization built up of bards or Maulanas. But experiments have been conducted, and quite successfully, in using such channels for modernizing messages too.[8]

These traditional media are particularly effective because they do involve an organization for word-of-mouth communication. We know that in many traditional societies word-of-mouth is more trusted than the written word, that word-of-mouth, everywhere, is an essential stimulus to action, that it is more adaptable to the variations in style and manner which are so particularly important at least in a dual and transitional society, and we might add here that at the early stages of transition mouths may be more common than newspapers or radios. (Cambodia, for example, has roughly one full-fledged priest for every 80 inhabitants, against one weekly paper in circulation for each 120 inhabitants, one daily in circulation for each 500, and a similar number of radios.[9])

V. THE SOCIAL SCIENCE VIEW OF
MEDIA EFFECTS

In conjunction with development programs, there have been a large number of studies of how to get farmers (and occasionally others) to adopt modern practices. The general finding has been that what occurs when a new practice is adopted is what Katz and Lazarsfeld call the two-

7. Sarah Smilansky, "Evaluation of Early Education," in M. Smilansky and L. Adar (eds.), *Evaluating Educational Achievements* (Educational Studies and Documents, No. 42, UNESCO, Paris, 1961), p. 90.

8. Cf. Y. B. Damle, "A Note on Harikatha," *Bulletin of the Deccan College,* XVII, Poona, for a discussion of the role of such traditional sources in dissemination of ideas about caste. For descriptions of this kind of communication, see Milton Singer, *Traditional India: Structure and Change* (The American Folklore Society, Philadelphia, 1959).

9. Gude, *op. cit.*

step flow of communication.[10] That is to say the mass media do not lead to adoption directly. They create an awareness of the existence of the new practice and they provide guidance to innovating leaders. However, actual adoption of a new practice requires either personal persuasion or personal example by a respected opinion leader. Thus the spread of an innovation can be traced from an initiating center, by direct personal contact out to the periphery. It can also be traced from younger, well-educated, *somewhat alienated* and relatively cosmopolitan individuals in a community to older, highly entrenched, above-average educated individuals with whom the former are in touch, and then finally to other people in the community who follow the leaders. The adoption of an innovation advocated in the mass media has been shown to depend on interpersonal discussion of it.

The last point has been most dramatically demonstrated in a series of UNESCO sponsored studies of radio listening and TV viewing groups. Paul Neurath, for example, conducted a study of village radio broadcasts in India. In the control situations where these broadcasts were listened to by individuals in usual fashion the radio programs had virtually no effect. Where, however, listening groups were organized and discussions of the programs took place immediately after, the suggestions were often followed.[11] The same thing was found with TV viewing groups in France, and in other countries too.[12] Similar results on the role of word-of-mouth communication in clinching media advice have been obtained in marketing studies.

All of these studies add up to the conclusion foreshadowed above, that to stimulate action, mass-media exhortations need to be coupled with the organization of face-to-face leadership. Here, however, we must raise the question of whether exhortation to action is indeed the most important use of mass media in the modernizing process. While many studies have examined how to persuade the citizenry to take specific actions, only a few studies have looked at the role of the media in producing transformations in values and personality. Such changes in values and attitudes, it can be argued, are far more important to modernization than are mere changes in actions.

That is perhaps an unusual view, for it is common to assume that

10. See the article by Katz reprinted earlier in this volume, pp. 110–121.

11. J. C. Mathur and Paul Neurath, *An Indian Experiment in Farm Radio Forums,* UNESCO, Paris, 1959.

12. Henry Cassirer, *Television Teaching Today* (UNESCO, Paris, 1960). Cf. also UNESCO series on Press, Film and Radio in the World Today: J. Nicol, A. Shea and G. J. P. Simmins, *Canada's Farm Radio Forum* (1954); J. Dumaze-dier, *Television and Rural Adult Education* (1956); Anon., *Rural Television in Japan* (1960).

changes in men's actions are the really important objective and that changes in attitudes are but a means toward the desired actions. We would argue, however, that it is the other way around. It is, for example, relatively easy to get peasants to plant a particular kind of seed one foot apart instead of six inches apart. This action can be induced by money payments, by terror, by authority, by persuasion, by proving it to be the will of the gods, and by many other means. But the improvement of one such practice does not mean that the peasant has been in any way modernized. *A far more significant change would be the development of a scientific attitude toward the adoption of new practices.* It is only that kind of internal change in the latent structure of his attitudes that would produce self-sustaining movement toward modernization. Yet the effects of communications in the process of transition has been much studied in relation to specific actions, but only little studied in relation to the much more important matters of values and attitudes.

In this area the most notable contributions have been by Daniel Lerner and David McClelland. They have both put forward the daring thesis that the mass media can have profound characterological effects. Lerner convincingly argues that the media provide the capacity to conceive of situations and ways of life quite different from those directly experienced.[13] That is an essential capacity for functioning in a great society. A great society is characteristically one where every business firm must anticipate the wants of unknown clients, every politician those of unknown voters; where planning takes place for a vastly changed future, where the way people of quite different cultures act may affect one daily. If, as Lerner argues, the media provide the means for emphatically entering the roles that affect a man in a great society, then the characterological contribution of the media to modernization is indeed significant.

McClelland's thesis is that certain types of media content, especially in children's literature, can actually raise achievement motivation, and that high achievement motivation is in turn a major necessary condition for development.[14] If McClelland's results are even partly confirmed they too are vitally important to any theory of development.

Now the interest of the Lerner and McClelland theses for our present paper is that *neither of these depends upon a two-step flow of communication. Neither of them is predicted upon opinion leaders or political organizations paralleling the media.* They are concerned with effects which the media have directly.

This suggests that the conclusion that the effectiveness of the media

13. Lerner, *op. cit.*
14. David McClelland, *The Achieving Society* (Van Nostrand, Princeton, N.J., 1961).

in the process of modernization depends upon their being linked to a well-developed organization of face-to-face influence is too simple. It is not wrong, but it is partial. It is true for certain of the potential effects of the mass media, but not for others. And so we stop here to set up a typology of what the effects of the mass media are.

These effects are of two main kinds: effects upon the individuals exposed to them, and institutional effects arising from the very existence of a mass media system.

Among the direct and immediate effects which exposure to the media may have upon the individuals are changes in:

1. Attention	5. Tastes
2. Saliency	6. Images
3. Information	7. Attitudes
4. Skills	8. Actions

Changes in each one of these may in turn change each of the others: changes in one's actions may change one's attitudes just as changes in one's attitudes may change one's actions; changes in the information one has may change one's distribution of attention or changes in what one attends to may change one's information. Yet it is possible analytically to distinguish these changes and to consider the differences in the conditions for each kind of change.

Various experimental and survey results suggest that the mass media operate very directly upon attention, information, tastes, and images. Election studies, for example, show that the campaign in the mass media does little to change attitudes in the short run, but does a great deal to focus attention on one topic or another.[15] Television studies have shown that medium to have relatively little direct effect on major attitudes, but show it to develop tastes (good or bad) and to provide much image material to stock the mind of the viewer.[16] Harold Isaacs' studies of image formation also support the notion that these scratches on the mind can be picked up casually from the most diverse sources, including literature, movies, etc.[17]

Changes in skills and attitudes are less apt to be brought about by the

15. Paul F. Lazarsfeld, Bernard Berelson, and Hazel Gaudet, *The People's Choice* (Columbia U. P., New York, 1948); Bernard Berelson, Paul F. Lazarsfeld, and William McPhee, *Voting* (U. of Chicago Press, Chicago, 1954).

16. Hilda Himmelweit, A. Oppenheim, P. Vince, et al., *Television and the Child* (Oxford U. P., London, 1958); Wilbur Schramm, Jack Lyle, and Edwin Parker, *Television in the Lives of Our Children* (Stanford U. P., Stanford, Calif., 1961).

17. Harold R. Isaacs, *Scratches on Our Minds* (John Day, New York, 1958).

mass media operating alone. Here the best we can say is sometimes they are, but often they aren't. Usually face-to-face relations with a human being toward whom the learner has considerable *cathexis* is essential for producing changes in those variables. We can, for example, classify attitudes as being of greater or lesser rigidity and saliency. Lightly held attitudes may readily be molded by mass media alone, but not deeply entrenched ones. The experimental literature on the framing of survey research questions is probably as good evidence on this point as any. Responses to low *saliency* questions are shifted readily by question wording, new information, or by almost anything. Other attitudes stand up under any media barrage. Psychotherapy shows that to change deeply rooted attitudes requires the development of an intense relationship with a reference person. So too, the literature on teaching—i.e., the imparting of skills—demonstrates that while many skills can be learned from reading, or TV, or movies, *the learning of difficult matter requires a level of motivation that is only engendered in a relationship with an important reference person who demands the effort.*

Finally, we return to actions—changes in which, as we have already noted are almost always checked with reference persons before an individual embarks upon them.

Changes of all these factors are important in the process of development. But they enter the process in different ways. For example, a conclusion stated earlier in this paper holds, we now see, for some of these kinds of change only. Changes in actions and some skills and attitudes will not be effectively produced by mass media alone; rather the effectiveness of the mass media in influencing them will be a direct function of the effectiveness of political organization to which the mass media are an adjunct.

VI. THE MEDIA AS INSTITUTIONS

There is a vast opportunity for leadership given the politicians by the existence of media. As happened in the West too, the growth of plebiscitarian politics goes hand-in-hand with the growth of the press. The press enables the politician to act on a national scale. It puts into topics the headlines all over the country which are otherwise no part of the experience of the citizens in each separate locality. It makes issues of these topics. It enables the political leader to give the word of the day simultaneously to the whole country on something which the press has made salient for all of it. It makes national parties possible because some issues are the same throughout the country. And a modern media system with wire services does this better than a set of struggling local printing shops putting out newspapers of the sort that used to exist in Jacksonian America.

The press also gives the politicians a recognized national code of procedures by which to confirm status. A highly segmented society is apt to suffer from lack of consensus not only on matters of substance but even on the facts of what has been decided. Anything which establishes a public record of policy decisions, of assignments of prestige (by column inches or anything else), and of responsibilities can be useful. Of course, a party press in which the different papers give very different pictures of the world does not achieve this purpose. But under many circumstances a press consensus enables everyone (including the party leader himself) to know, for example, who is the party leader.

A mass media system permits the unification of a nation in many nonpolitical ways similar to those we have just been describing. The existence of daily price quotations facilitates the establishment of a national market. Media encourage a national art and literature by holding up products to each other. They broaden the relevant reference groups discussions. The same kinds of processes of national organization through the media take place in party politics.

The media are also one of the great educators and employers of a new kind of politician, one who is issue oriented and ideologically oriented rather than oriented to personal identifications. The media provide some of the few mobile professions in many underdeveloped countries. They are miserably paid and grossly exploited ones, but they are professions rigidly tied neither to traditional statuses or castes nor to a Western style educational system. The media thus provide a niche where political men of a new kind can operate in attacking the old elites. The media often provide a livelihood to those politicians while they wait for the opportunities of politics or while they engage in the day-to-day work of political organization. The media create some of the few changes for men who are not notables to become politicians by vocation in poverty-striken countries.

VII. CONCLUSIONS

Neither these points about how the media can give rise to a political class and to political activity, nor the earlier points about how the media generate rising expectations make rapid mass media development seem a happy prospect to leaders attempting to hold together a fragile balance in barely viable states about to explode. But in this field as in others the processes of change are not going to be stopped. The media might be a far more potent instrument of development than has yet been recognized in almost any noncommunist developing nation or by American development planners. But for its potential to be effectively used, its development must also be linked to effective grass-roots political organization.

QUESTIONS

1. The student should notice that the preceding essay is one of the most subtly organized in the book; it is therefore suggested as a profitable exercise simply to outline the argument.

2. Take each major point in the outline and see if you can find any significant related, parallel, or contradictory point in the previous readings. For example, do the previous readings suggest that there is or is not in our society the emphasis on truth value which Pool says there is?

3. Do Bauer and Gleicher suggest that the communist doctrine as interpreted by Pool (*a*) is applied, or (*b*) works in the Soviet Union? Discuss.

4. Would you expect an old-fashioned U.S. political boss to be as disillusioned about the effects of the mass media as might be supporters of a liberal, intellectual candidate like Adlai Stevenson? Discuss.

5. Explain the communist emphasis upon *action* as a necessary correlate of effective propaganda through *mass media* in terms of the point emphasized in the general introduction that people tend to say what is proper, appropriate, and correct for their role, their conception of themselves. Does Cox's article throw any light on this point?

6. Assuming that Pool's distinction between the three approaches to modernization and the use of mass communications is accurate, develop a program of mass communications on integration and desegregation in the United States, using each method.

7. Read a serious account of efforts at modernization in an underdeveloped nation—preferably an account which deals with only one nation —and find out which of the three approaches is used, or how they are mixed (or whether there is a fourth approach towards mass communications).

8. If the United States is engaged in propaganda to underdeveloped nations, which of the three approaches should it use? Why? (*Note:* this question involves a mixture of ethical and practical considerations, and it is important in discussing it to indicate what ethical and practical assumptions you are adopting.)

Robert C. Sorensen

Media Research and Psychological Warfare *

A MAJOR PRESUPPOSITION of the following article is that anyone who is concerned with psychological warfare needs to know what his target groups are and how to appeal to them. Presumably, if he proceeds rationally he will then shape his messages in a way that attracts them.

With appropriate modifications for the difference between warfare and other forms of competition, the same rules should apply to candidates for public office and their advisors, to advertisers, and to people engaged in marketing.

Unquestionably, in terms of sheer rational analysis, Sorensen tells us what should be done. But, in order to do it, certain difficulties need to be overcome.

The first of these difficulties exists chiefly at a moral level, and is very often faced by candidates for public office in this country. It is thought that votes can be won from the opposition by promising something that is clearly silly or that is beyond the candidate's ability to guarantee (such as the promises made by Willkie and Roosevelt in 1940 that American boys would not fight abroad; or by numerous candidates—the most recent prominent example being Nelson Rockefeller in 1962—that taxes will not be raised). Still worse is the belief that votes can be won by conducting a campaign on an issue which most informed people know will hurt the long-range public interest, no matter what the immediate payoff in votes. The nineteenth-century American politicians who conducted a campaign in terms of "fifty-four forty or fight" were in effect promising a war with Great Britain for the sake of gaining some Canadian soil, although in fact they did not reach 54 degrees 40 minutes N. Lat., nor did they fight. Repeatedly, in periods of international crises, the same problem arises; irresponsible promises, such as the guarantee by Lloyd George's supporters that he would "squeeze the Germans till the pips squeak," in

* Reprinted from *Mediascope,* March 1961, pp. 80–92, by permission of the author and the publisher. Original title, "Media Research Can Learn from Psychological Warfare." (Copyright 1961 by *Mediascope.*)

1919, may help domestic victory, but they make constructive compromises more difficult (as Lord Keynes pointed out in his criticisms of the economic consequences of the Treaty of Versailles, designed under the Lloyd Georgian influence). Yet if the target of the managers of Lloyd George's efforts was to win the next British national election, perhaps he chose the "right" appeal.

The second obstacle to making a rational appeal to the target groups is a social and sociological one. Let us assume that a person engaged in psychological warfare or political competition knows what will appeal to certain groups within the opposition. For instance, suppose that, as is unquestionably true, the wisest thing U.S.S.R. psychological warfare could do would be to announce that the U.S.S.R. had outgrown Marxism-Leninism and to recognize that neither Marx nor Lenin knew the kind of people's capitalism which exists in the West today—it would be very wise for the U.S.S.R. to say something of the sort, but extremely risky for those people in the U.S.S.R. who first proposed the idea.

We need only think of the reverse possibility in a U.S. environment. Suppose our overseas broadcasts were to state that, in fact, the United States sees eye-to-eye with the Soviet Union on some point— would there not be grave danger of Congress cutting off appropriations for such broadcasting? Under the threat of what was called McCarthyism, persons who were simply studying Russia and its views —for example, at the Russian Research Center at Harvard—became objects of great suspicion and public attack (the Boston Post conducted a campaign against Harvard's studies in this area in the early 1950s).

And, at a less obvious and still serious level, students of public opinion and researchers in the area are always likely to be more or less suspect. People will think they are disloyal; they report how other people feel, and other people don't feel the way that the top executives or "loyal" people wish them to. For instance, in 1952, as Public Opinion Analyst at the Democratic National Committee, I was asked by the Chairman's office to make an "objective" analysis of how the election would turn out. I inquired several times: did they really want to know what was going to happen? "Yes," was the reply. Accordingly, I wrote up an analysis; and as soon as it was seen by the Chairman's office, I received an immediate call to suppress it, not to let anybody see it. Ironically, and typical of such situations, I erred by giving Stevenson two more states than he actually carried; I was perhaps too loyal for the best analysis.

Of course, sanctions on students of public opinion and researchers in communications need not be very direct. They may simply find their reports disregarded, their attitude portrayed as unduly pessimistic, and themselves accused of "throwing cold water" on the enthusiastic views of colleagues and co-workers.

For most laymen tend to believe that the best psychological warfare is "to hit them hard . . . to tell the truth (as your own side sees it)." Psychological warfare is thus equated with large-scale bombing in which you hit the enemy as hard as possible. Actually, to be effective, it has to be a sort of guerilla infiltration, catching the enemy unawares, taking the target group's preconceptions and preferences into account, and not telling them anything they will not believe.

Psychological warfare thus involves assuming in one respect (and in that respect only) one characteristic of a spy. A spy cannot go about in enemy country speaking out his convictions or preferences; he must say what his enemy believes in order to fulfill his mission. So also psychological warfare, as described by Sorensen, involves the willingness to say much of what the enemy believes in order to get some target groups within the enemy camp to believe the particular things your own side is most concerned with.

But the psychological warfare specialist or public opinion researcher has a difficulty that the spy does not have. The psychological warfare specialist and the public opinion researcher must keep the confidence of their own associates, on a daily basis, while trying to tell these associates the unpalatable facts about what the opposition believes. People speak of the Nazis being great masters of psychological warfare; this was true only to a very limited extent. Most accounts agree that had the Nazis been able when they invaded the Ukraine to talk and act in terms of the Ukrainian attitude towards policy rather than in terms of the Nazi attitude they might have defeated Russia and possibly even won the war. Some people considered Franklin D. Roosevelt a great master of psychological warfare, yet he incurred intense and needless hatred from influential men whose cooperation he needed by attacking them as "economic royalists . . . princes of privilege," and later, according to some analyses, his unhappy insistence upon "unconditional surrender" prolonged the war with Germany for some months. Many Germans were willing to believe they were beaten; but not that they were unconditionally beaten.* Now, Roosevelt and the Nazi leaders in the Ukraine may or may not have realized the cost of what they said and did; but, very probably, they had to say and do precisely those things which Sorensen's analysis would suggest are unwise, in order to retain the confidence of the home front. That is, to retain their home groups, they had to lose crucial target groups.

Of course, in much more elementary matters than this the problem of being overheard by different groups arises—doubtless some South African teachers know that the biological basis of the Apartheid

* Wallace Carroll, *Persuade or Perish* (Houghton, Boston, 1948), gives an extensive presentation of possible negative results from the U.S. verbalization of "unconditional surrender."

laws in that country is nonsense, but they know too that if they criticize these laws, at worst they will go to jail and at best they will lose the confidence and trust on other matters of those with whom they deal.

The excellence of Sorensen's analysis as a starting point lies in the questions it raises as well as in those that it answers. It is a beginning, not an end.

L. A. D.

DR. SORENSEN was from 1954 through 1958 director of audience research for Radio Free Europe in Munich. He has also served as Director of Research for This Week Magazine. Currently he is Vice-President and Director of Research of the D'Arcy Advertising Company in New York City.

It is a habit these days to hail international communications for bringing the world closer together. So be it, but from these same media are fashioned weapons of psychological warfare being fought among several nations throughout this same world. Radio and television, newspapers and magazines, leaflets—all are being employed by many governments to do violence to men's ideas and loyalties in "target countries." It is through mass media that words and deeds accomplish prescribed objectives by conveying various degrees of influence—information, intimidation, example, inspiration, assurance, hope, and deprivation.

Past conflicts permitted only limited displays of psychological warfare. But in recent years nuclear weapons and mass communications have been combined to confound the fate of world civilization with the outcome of what are now euphemistically called "cold wars."

The balance of power in many parts of the world can be tipped by millions of peoples who have demonstrated a growing independence of established concepts of loyalty to their rulers. Populations are amenable to persuasion short of force of arms. The influence of ideas cannot be eliminated through sheer physical suppression at home because their communication from afar cannot be eliminated.

In turn, no government stands still for a calculated effort-by-persuasion to undermine its influence. A redistribution of power and values is often no les onerous than threatened destruction by force of arms.

Media research plays an increasing role in both the operation and assessment of any psychological warfare effort. This has certainly been the case with Radio Free Europe whose audience research effort I headed from 1954 through 1958. Its broadcasts are delivered over a private network of stations and transmitters to five East European countries occupied by the Soviet Union (Czechoslovakia, Hungary, Poland, Romania and Bulgaria). Eighteen hours each day the people in these five countries are provided in their own languages with news and information to provoke questions, ideas, and music for the sake of brain and spirit, and literature to preserve a culture now largely denied them. On a smaller scale, the official Voice of America, Radio Liberty, and BBC are also at work in these countries along with their other world wide commitments.

MEDIA AUDIENCE RESEARCH

It soon became apparent that an analysis of target audiences and regime media might help answer two basic questions: (1) What was the nature of the relationship between Western broadcast media and their audience-publics; and (2) How effective were Western broadcasts and what could be done to increase their effectiveness?

There are three main sources of information in answer to these questions: interviews with refugees and travelers from the target countries, letters from listeners, and a content analysis of communist mass media in the target countries. Each source is employed in part to corroborate the other.

Interviews with refugees inevitably present certain obvious problems. Some refugees tend, even when encouraged otherwise, to tell the interviewer what they assume he wants to hear. Except for occasional "plants" and the usual wanderers, escaping refugees have been willing to accept lethal risks that no typical member of the country's population would take. Access to all refugees, time in which to interview them thoroughly, and availability for continuous interview exposures were among the other problems to be dealt with. In the absence of first-hand contact with the population, the audience sample can never be demonstrably adequate and representative. Yet findings from these sources have been invaluable.

Every refugee must be treated as a case history requiring considerable interviewer rapport, not as a single statistic in a mass sample. Certain questions can be asked, the answers to which can be generalized to apply to people who have stayed behind. Obviously, the fact that refugee X was an anticommunist cannot be assumed for every person at home. But for example: if several refugees were anticommunists, yet criticize Western broadcasts and praise certain regime activities in particular ways, it can only be assumed that many of those who remained behind must have felt similarly.

WHAT INFLUENCES PEOPLE

At first I was interested in audience likes and dislikes, but it became increasingly clear that people were not necessarily influenced by what they preferred. Many radio programs were sometimes to indicate that considerable learning from them had taken place.

What people expected Western media to accomplish was interesting. It surprised some professional anticommunists and some would-be propagandists from the advertising world, that anticommunists in the target countries were not interested in hearing about how bad their living conditions were, how oppressive their rulers were, or how wonderful the Western world was as compared with their own.

Sickened by communist regime propaganda, most of the audience tended to declare "a plague on both your houses" when they felt that the West had only more propaganda to complement that of the Soviet Union. Hope, they felt, was a fine thing, but realism they welcomed most of all.

In part, then, the effectiveness of any Western station is defined in terms of how well it comprehends the limits of people's reactions in a given situation. Responsible Western stations eschew any promises and assurances not only because the international situation forecloses their immediate fulfillment, but because the audience knows this well enough and is intolerant of phantasy. Various groups and ambitions within a target society change in relative significance as time passes; psychological warfare content and technique must change accordingly. The intellectual, for instance, has come into his own as one of the prime targets during the last five years, although during the previous five years he was somewhat neglected for the peasant and church-member who were in fact the leading opponents of communism.

FALLACY OF DIRECT QUESTIONS

Whether and how the output of Western stations was perceived is thus a fundamental question. The questions we asked, therefore, were not confined to how many people were in the radio audience or how often they tuned in to these broadcasts. Like Starch or Politz ad page exposure scores, listening interviews offered no proof that X number of people actually heard or perceived any specific broadcast contents in question. Moreover, it was too easy for the refugee to say what he thought we wanted to hear, *to wit:* "of course we listen and naturally we listen every day." "Pass-along" listeners, broadcast "exposure days," and "total audience" were statistics that I ignored. Our only boxcar statistics were reasonable estimates of Hungarian young people who were shipped off to forcible exile in the wake of their revolution.

Why have people listened to radio broadcasts at all—considering the fact that they could be jailed for listening in groups and persecuted in any case? These were the major reasons offered by Western broadcast audiences: (*a*) The desire for information about events, ideas and people that was deliberately being withheld from media audiences. Radio has provided a kind of bootleg knowledge and culture as well as a basis for evaluating communist media output. (*b*) The desire to seek diversion in what few small ways remained in a drab way of life that was highly structured in time and place. (*c*) The need for asserting one's independence under conditions where minimal collaboration was a necessity and the exercise of one's hostility a dangerous luxury.

RESEARCH INTO COMMUNIST MEDIA

There are no major sampling problems in the content analysis of communist mass media. Transcripts of target country radio broadcasts are available in their entirety through monitoring systems; so are virtually all of the leading newspapers, magazines, and academic journals, along with occasional provincial newspapers. Their systematic examination enabled us to study the number of instances (press and radio items) in which any Western psychological warfare effort was mentioned, the themes employed in these references, and the techniques on our part which apparently did and did not arouse regime officials.

We have also studied the content and techniques of counterattack employed by regime propagandists, and the particular groups of people to whom these usually critical references to Western broadcasts were addressed. Although no complete media audience studies were possible, we have learned within limits the social groups exposed to each newspaper or magazine because the East European press is aimed at very specific groups (e.g., youth, peasants, labor).

Over a period of time the communist-controlled media were mobilized to oppose Western broadcasts in thousands of press and radio items, although almost no references were made in the beginning. Of course, the effectiveness of any psychological warfare effort is by no means always reflected in the frequency with which it is mentioned by the target government. Attacks against a Western station indicate an awareness of its psychological-warfare efforts, to be sure, but they sometimes also signify domestic and personal considerations or represent successful psychological-warfare counteroffensive efforts.

Attacks against a Western station can be occasions for guidance to local "agit-prop" elements, vehicles for rallying support of particular groups, linkage of already discredited ideas and personalities to psychological war efforts through "guilt by verbal association techniques," and exploitation of any errors or vulnerabilities on our part, to name a few examples. Needless to say, these references must be evaluated in terms of the known vulnerabilities of the target regime and known audience reactions.

BREAKING MEDIA MONOPOLY

An examination of communist regime media was vital for one other reason. This involves the very basis for the existence of Western broadcasts—namely, to break the monopoly over mass communications which any communist regime must enjoy if it is going to be truly totalitarian. Such a monopoly exists only when a regime can do and say what it likes without fear of query or contradiction in any communications medium reaching its people. This is a franchise of some considerable worth which no dictatorship abandons lightly.

Western broadcasters have good reason to believe they have broken the monopoly, and that their broadcasts have made a difference in the mass media relationship between the communist regime and captive peoples. The regimes have abandoned the notion that the prerogative of introducing new ideas and issues is theirs alone. (At the same time mass media in these countries are no less the tools of the regimes than they ever were.)

Moreover, a greater effort has been made on the part of media in several of the target countries to give more news and information about the West with seemingly greater objectivity. In addition, news and apologia about internal events which had previously been ignored are occasionally reported, and in sufficient detail to indicate that the regime would prefer its audience to learn first about emotionally charged matters from it rather than from an outside source. Obviously, the regime is also aware that people use Western broadcasts to check the authenticity of regime news releases; this is a goad to greater objectivity. Finally, the subject matter of communist newspapers and broadcasts has gradually broadened to meet the competition of Western broadcasts; some entertainment and jazz are among the concessions that are obviously made to diminish audience interest in culture from afar.

WHAT MEDIA RESEARCH LEARNS

Media research for the advertiser can learn considerably from the challenges confronting media research in the psychological warfare areas. *Above all, the measurement of communications effectiveness is the payoff.* Findings about "total audience" without regard for whether crucial elements of the target population think and act in accordance with prescribed objectives offer only misleading evidence about the results of any psychological warfare undertaking.

Media research in psychological warfare certainly makes these points clear for the "commercial world":

[1] A substantial difference often exists between a medium's prestige and the extent to which audience attitudes are affected by its contact with the medium.

[2] Media do have a differential impact upon the same audience as was proved in cases where contradictory reactions prevailed with respect to similar program content. Differences in image and circumstances of exposure were found to be responsible.

[3] Proof of audience perception of communication content is not demonstrated by its exposure to the eyes and ears of the target group. Lacking any such measurement, at any given time, the broadcaster was hard put to pinpoint any crucial cause and effect relationship between his broadcast and the activities of any specific audience group.

[4] Broadcasters often find that audience reaction varies from that which is predicted; in this case, propaganda content is subject to tactical change in order better to meet policy objectives.

These are but some of the findings whose implications are equally challenging in the study of advertising communications effectiveness before principles of media selection become completely rational.

SELECTED PUBLICATIONS BY DR. SORENSEN

"The Effectiveness of the Oath to Obtain a Witness' True Personal Opinion," *The Journal of Criminal Law, Criminology and Police Science,* September–October 1956.

"The Admission and Use of Opinion Research Evidence," *New York University Law Review,* vol. 28, no. 7, November 1953 (with Theodore C. Sorensen). It was our hope and intention to republish this very valuable article in the present book in the section on Institutions—it is a model of the application of opinion research findings to problems of a profession and management of an institution. Reasons of space unfortunately made this impossible; it is far longer than any other article republished herein.

"Re-Examining the Traditional Legal Test of Literary Similarity: a Proposal for Content Analysis," *Cornell Law Quarterly,* Summer 1952 (with Theodore C. Sorensen).

"The Influence of Public Opinion Polls upon Legislators," *Sociology and Social Research,* 1950.

Social Control, John Marshall Law School, 1948 (with Dr. Thomas D. Eliot).

"Sociological Aspects of Psychological Warfare," in *Contemporary Sociology,* J. S. Roucek (ed.), New York, 1960.

"Local Uses of Wired Radio in Communist Ruled Poland," *Journalism Quarterly,* Summer 1955 (with Leszek L. Meyer).

"Media Research Can Learn from Psychological Warfare," *Mediascope,* March 1961.

"The Economics of Information," *Challenge: The Magazine of Economic Affairs,* vol. 8, no. 7, April 1960.

"New Perspectives in Advertising," in *Ethics, Advertising, and Responsibility,* Francis X. Quinn (ed.), Canterbury Press, Westminster, Maryland, 1963.

QUESTIONS

1.   What are some of the effects of such agencies as Radio Free Europe, the Voice of America, and BBC upon the people who live in Communist-controlled countries? Is there any evidence, besides counterpropaganda broadcasts, that broadcasts from the West are effective?

2.   In terms of Wright's *functional analysis* schema, what are some of the latent, as well as the manifest, functions of psychological warfare? From the point of view of the West, can you think of certain *dysfunctions* which come about through this form of mass communications?

3.   Sorensen states that the "measurement of communications effectiveness is the payoff." How does this statement jibe with Klapper's statement that mass media serve as a mediating nexus and appear mainly to reinforce previous dispositions? What guidelines can the psychological warfare practitioner use to make effective contact with audiences who have lived their entire lives in the closed society of the Communist nations?

4.   Which of the following sources of "feedback" to the Western broadcasts seems to you the most credible: (*a*) interviews with refugees and travelers from the target countries, (*b*) letters from listeners, and (*c*) content analysis of Communist mass media in the target countries? In what ways could they be analyzed collectively to check each other?

5.   Sorensen points out that anticommunists in the target countries were not interested in hearing about how bad their living conditions were or how wonderful the Western world was in comparison with their own. What, then, do the people who listen to Voice of America broadcasts, for example—who risk persecution for doing so—really seek from the broadcasts?

PART VII

THE FRONTIERS OF
COMMUNICATIONS RESEARCH

Bertram M. Gross

Operation *BASIC:* The Retrieval

of Wasted Knowledge *

HERE IS AN ARTICLE which may at first glance appear unrelated to the
main theme of our book. Nevertheless, in our judgment, it is vital to
students of mass communications. In the first place, as the article
itself shows, inability to locate and find needed and relevant information is the greatest barrier now existing to utilizing communications.
In the second place, the conception we have stressed of the relationship between source and audience has considerable promise here.
For, unfortunately, most efforts at information retrieval up to the
present time (e.g., the ordinary library classification systems or abstracts) have been made on the basis of the originator's more or less
arbitrary judgment as to what potential users need, or even more arbitrary guesses about what potential users want. But it is in all likelihood
entirely feasible systematically to apply hypotheses and techniques
about how audiences receive communications,[1] derived from the
studies published or cited in this book, and with them to develop
more effective and acceptable methods of classifying and retrieving
information. For example, the editor of a bibliography or abstract
series (such as Sociological Abstracts) could do a much better job of
classification or cross-classification if he had a clearer picture of his
audience's responses. Still more, such knowledge could help the editor
of a newspaper answer the basic questions: what kind of people will
look for what, where? What kind of people will notice what, where?
What kind of people will be misled by what sort of heading in what

* Based on an address before the Round Table on Information Retrieval in
the Social Sciences, jointly sponsored by Syracuse University and Western Reserve
University, Saturday, July 29, 1961, at the Minnowbrook Conference Center of
Syracuse University, Blue Mountain Lake, New York.
    Reprinted from the *Journal of Communication,* June 1962, pp. 67–83, by per-
mission of the author and publisher. (Copyright 1962 by the National Society for
the Study of Communication.)
    1. The line between mass and nonmass communications largely becomes irrele-
vant at this point.

place? It could also help the head of a large public library. Exactly how such knowledge could be applied we cannot forsee (in fact, our own incomplete knowledge and the limitations of current information-retrieval systems do not enable us to say with assurance that something of the sort has not already been done).

We are convinced that, for example, if any foundation really wished to increase the utilization of certain types of reading materials in public libraries, a highly valuable series of studies and experiments could be conducted on the ways that would-be or potential readers hear about something, learn how to look for it, and actually look for it. Such an experiment could, if adequately financed, be conducted in collaboration with the daily press and the public schools. Whether any such efforts could increase the number of people who read, one cannot tell; certainly, the proposition that media tend merely to reinforce people's tendencies to believe what they would believe anyhow would lead us to doubt such an outcome, but it would be worth making imaginative trials.

Another reason why information retrieval is a particularly important field for the student of mass communications is this: because of the large number of subjects and subject classifications directly related to mass communications analyses (see the article by White, pp. 521ff., on the literature of the field), no one is likely to have a knowledge of all the relevant fields—anthropology, many branches of history, literary criticism, literary history, folklore (which we hardly refer to in this book; but folklore is the folk equivalent of some branches of mass communications—e.g., the advice to the lovelorn), market research, sociology, political science, the technology of communications, the teaching of elementary and high school English, French, Russian, etc. This book almost certainly omits much that might be included, but the administrative task of locating all the pertinent material that may exist, (e.g., in Russian and Japanese) is greater than our present resources will permit. No really adequate analysis of scholarly findings bearing on mass communications is possible until a better method of information retrieval has been standardized. The same difficulty affects every textbook, every summary of a field.

And, finally, the majority of people interested in mass communications are likely to be employed by newspapers, libraries, government offices, market research agencies, or some similar organization—similar in that, although a great amount of communications is sent out, still more comes in, and what is sent out depends on what comes in, how it is handled, and to whom in the organization it is available at the moment of need. Newspaper columnists and book reviewers, for example, rely to a tremendous extent upon their own wide knowledge; they are in and of themselves storehouses of information. But take any series of columns, group of interpretative front-page articles, set of book reviews (even book reviews in such top-notch sources as the London Economist or the New York Times), and then get someone who really knows the subject to discuss these columns or reviews with you, and you are fairly certain to find that, in most cases, the reviewer or the interpretative journalist or the columnist omitted highly significant discussions and citations which might have altered the entire perspective. Indeed, as an exercise on this chapter we suggest a problem calling for the identification of pertinent material apparently omitted by a first-rate newspaper or magazine in a prominent article. It may be that the particular article a particular student selects for analysis cannot fairly be faulted from this point of view, but in order to demonstrate whether it is indeed reasonably immune from such criticism, the student will have to use a good many abstracts, bibliographies, and indices. He is lucky if these are good enough to give him assurance that the article took adequate account of background studies. To be sure, the student is probably not a specialist on the subject of any specific article, but most newspaper men (including columnists) and many book reviewers are not experts either. Yet any journal that wanted to expend the money (and do the job of training) can enormously enhance the likelihood that its writers could locate, coordinate, and use relevant material.

Indeed, an even simpler example is present in most newspaper offices. What used to be called the "morgue" and is now more politely known as the library contains vast amounts of knowledge on many matters which the newsman, harassed and under pressure, needs immediately. He looks in the obvious places, but whoever set up the classification system may not have anticipated his needs or curiosities. Yet, in some (to him) unobvious folder highly relevant information may be found. The better the training and discipline in information retrieval, the greater the awareness of what may be wanted and the better the prospects of adequately utilizing the clipping files and getting the historical background that makes stories meaningful and interesting. And the kind of approach found in White's "gatekeeper" study (pp. 160–172) or in Pool and Shulman's report (pp. 141–158) may increase the possibility of setting up a better method of, in essence, "filing"—better because more relevant to the needs and wants of the immediate users (newspaper reporters and editors) and ultimate consumers (the reading public).

L. A. D.

MR. GROSS, Professor of Administration at the Maxwell School of Citizenship and Public Affairs, Syracuse University, has been a visiting Professor at Hebrew University in Israel, the University of California, and the Harvard Graduate School of Business Administration, where in 1962 he gave the Leatherbee Lectures on "Administration in

Public Affairs." He has been Consultant for the Ford Foundation in India and for the United Nations Korean Reconstruction Adminis- tration. He has also been an adviser to the Israeli Ministry of Finance and a member of the Economic Advisory Staff for the Office of the Israeli Prime Minister. Since 1938 he has held numerous other posi- tions with governmental and international organizations.

When the Arabians snatched Alexandria from the Persian Empire in 640, they fed the furnaces of the public bathhouse—we are told— with books from Alexandria's famous library. The fires blazed for six months.

In May, 1933, in a square opposite the University of Berlin, Nazi-led students burned 20,000 books. The bonfires spread throughout Germany.

We are all shocked by the savage barbarity of the many book-burn- ings in man's brief history on this planet. We know that such destructive- ness has often set back the clock of history. We see it as a tragic waste.

But most of us are blind to our own waste of human knowledge. We proudly go through the ritual of accumulating huge piles of scientific books, journals and reports. True, we do not apply the torch. Like the wood rat with his accumulation of trash, we guard well anything we get our hands on. But we lose track of what we do have. We fail to get many things we should have. The information loss is tremendous. We have not yet heeded Vannevar Bush's warning that "science may become bogged down in its own product, inhibited like a colony of bacteria by its own exudations." [1]

Operation BASIC is a vision of how modern man can create new institutions for the organization of knowledge. It is *a general strategy for assembling scientific and technical information and disseminating it to those who need it, whenever and wherever they need it.*

A. THE INFORMATION CRISIS: LOSS AND OVERLOAD

Before examining Operation BASIC, let us first take a brief look at the information crisis that makes BASIC essential. This crisis may be defined as the *overproduction of information relative to the capacity for its storage, analysis and distribution to point of need.*

One of the reasons for this lack of capacity is the myth of a "body of organized knowledge." According to this myth, every new idea of scientists and researchers is a "contribution" which automatically moves

1. The *Atlantic Monthly,* August 1955. From an address before the American Philosophical Society.

into its appropriate place. This pleasant myth provides a comfortable rationalization for inactivity with respect to the real world's imperfections.

1. THE PAPER FLOOD

How can we measure either the current stock of recorded information or its annual rate of growth?

I doubt that any sophisticated measures are possible. If we use a very crude unit of measurement, we find that the Library of Congress has about 12,000,000 volumes and pamphlets and the Lenin State Library in Moscow a few million more. If we add such things as microfilms, recordings, maps and photographic prints, we reach an aggregate figure for the Library of Congress of more than 35,000,000.

But large as such collections may be, they are still incomplete. They are limited mainly to formal publications. The libraries make little effort to assemble the large number of scientific and technical reports prepared for or in specific organizations. Nor do they provide much information on research projects which are under way and have not yet reached the stage of formal publication.

Although estimates on the annual rate of increase must be just as crude, one thing is clear: the paper flood is rising. One estimate holds that every minute 2,000 pages of books, newspapers or reports are published somewhere in the world. This is enough to fill a thousand feet of bookshelves every day.

In the natural sciences alone about 100,000 technical journals are being published in more than 60 languages. At least two new journals are started every day. A recent Western Reserve University study indicates that over 600,000 documents were published in the natural sciences alone. It is estimated this number would practically double by 1970. In aerospace research doubling is expected in 1965.

The rate of acceleration has been fantastic. According to U.C.L.A.'s Medical Dean Stafford Warren, "More medical research has been published since World War II than in all prior history." [2] Nor has the paper flood been limited to the physical and biological sciences. It has hit the social sciences also—and there, too, it is rising rapidly.

Will the rising flood abate? Are the 40 days and 40 nights nearly over?

No one who knows anything about any field of modern science would delude himself into claiming that abatement is near. The dynamics of modern research and the expansion of population, education and technology decree a continued rise in the flood of paper and other forms of recorded knowledge. Delusion enters when we fail to see that the

2. *Time*, July 7, 1961, p. 56.

present rate of increase in recorded knowledge is *low* in comparison to what we may expect. "We ain't seen nothin' yet." If it is 2,000 pages a minute today, it will be 4,000 pages a minute sometime before 1975. Short of a devastating war, nothing we say or do can stop it.

2. THE SUBMERGENCE OF LIBRARIES

The traditional library has been caught almost totally unprepared by the information crisis of the past decade. It is still worse prepared for the events of the coming decade.

The most obvious impact on the library has been the bursting of physical limitations. There are simply not enough traditional-style shelves, stacks and reading rooms. There are not enough librarians to handle the backlog of cataloguing and classifying.

A more devastating effect has been the bursting of traditional cataloguing systems. This has been described by Jesse Shera as follows: "As library collections grew in magnitude and complexity, as unanticipated relationships emerged among disciplines, and as new disciplines were themselves evolved, the structure of traditional bibliothecal classification began to crumble until not only the structure itself, but the very idea of structure, was condemned." [3]

The pathos of the situation is underscored by the fact that many of today's librarians have been indoctrinated in the idea of providing informational services. They believe that the basic function of the library is not to guard documents but to help people find information. But the important information is the contents of a document—not the title, author and a few generally descriptive words. What do librarians know about content? Their classification systems do little more than help move books in and out of shelves. They are not based on a conception of processing and communicating information. Lacking such a conception, our librarians somehow feel ideally suited to "educate" the people of lesser-developed economies and, under international auspices, to guide them from the frying pan of information scarcity to the fire of an information overload.

3. THE FARCE OF "KEEPING UP"

Nobody, of course, can keep up with *all* the new and interesting information.

Some people may make motions in this direction. Even in the scholarly

3. "Pattern, Structure, and Conceptualization in Classification for Information Retrieval," in *Information Systems in Documentation,* Vol. II (Interscience Publishers, New York, 1957).

disciplines there is an informational KUJ (keep-up-with-the Joneses) syndrome. Fortunately, this involves more pretense than performance. Few things can destroy a person's capacity—or even his sanity—more quickly than excessive informational input.

In our efforts at rational behavior, therefore, we try to keep up with certain selected types of information. Partly, we do our selection with the help of consciously constructed theories, which can vastly augment our intake capacity. Partly, we do it through habit, tradition and spontaneity. In either cause it is the internal "selector system" which makes life, and scientific thought, livable.

But how can we put such a selector system to use? Of all the printed documents relevant to our interest—even excluding the reprints sent us by our best friends—how can we read even a small fraction? What factual basis do we have before reading—to ration our reading?

I recently discussed this subject with the Dean of one of our most prestigious graduate schools. "I find a tremendous sense of guilt," he told me "among our faculty members. Even the best of them seem to feel that they're not keeping up with new developments. They take it to heart, as though it's all their fault. This enlarged sense of personal guilt makes itself felt in all sorts of quarrels and tangles on other subjects."

Without attempting a psychoanalysis of the academic mind, I can buttress the Dean's findings by pointing to certain species of guilt that can readily be observed on any campus. The most obvious is the gearing of one's selector system to an ever more narrow sphere of specialization, a phenomenon often accompanied by a stubborn refusal to trace relationships with other specialties or by a compulsive fixation upon "hard" facts and "rigorous" methodology. Another is a brazen scoffing at "all that nonsense" (a good term for things you do not have time to read or understand). At the other extreme there is the hound-dog who works out his guilt by converting research into search. Perpetually caught in the Sisyphean labor of trying to track down everything that others have done, he loses all capacity for doing anything of his own.

If scientists' systems do not do so well in the face of the paper flood, practical men do much worse. *Fortune* reports that a major electronics firm recently paid $8 million for two potential inventions, only to find out that both ideas had been anticipated by earlier inventors. "When we looked closely at what we were doing," a Du Pont engineer told *Fortune,* "we found we were redesigning the wheel six times a week." [4] One of the reasons for this is that the practical men who manage the world's large organizations are already overloaded by the daily tasks of keeping up with the relevant information within their organizations and in the

4. *Fortune,* September 1960.

immediate environment. Under these circumstances is it any wonder than they cannot by themselves take on the vast job of keeping up with the rising flood of scientific research?

B. THE *BASIC* POSSIBILITY

There can be no single method of coping with a phenomenon so complex as the modern information crisis. Many possibilities—from more help and leisure for scientists to stricter "birth control" over journal publications—will readily spring to mind.

But the most basic possibility—and the one which would provide most support to other acceptable measures—is the full exploitation of modern technology in the development of a co-operative, large-scale program of information retrieval.

1. INFORMATION TECHNOLOGY: ITS REVOLUTIONARY POTENTIAL

In the field of information processing and distribution, as in many other fields, any new machinery or process in operation is, by that token, already obsolete. Nor is any plateau in sight. Information technology— in all its many aspects of engineering, mathematics, logic, linguistics, and general systems theory—is still at an early stage, much like aeronautics in 1913 before World Wars I and II.

At the risk of presenting a myopic view of its revolutionary potential, I shall merely mention some of the possibilities of information technology as applied to the four fields of information storage, search, translation and transmission.

Spectacular achievements have been made in the *storage* of coded information in data-processing machines. Through the use of magnetic tape, notched cards and other devices, unbelievable amounts of data can be stored in computers. Just as dramatic are the possibilities of storing micro-photographic copies of original documents. With modern minification methods it is possible to reduce 10,000 document pages to the size of one page. Thus a photographic copy of a 1,000,000 document library could be stored in a machine the size of one executive desk. Less attention has been given to the more prosaic task of storing original documents. Storage space, obviously, can be conserved by accordion-type shelf-walls. Access can be provided by shelves that move up and down, as well as sideways. Many more potentials could be revealed by the full application of advanced warehousing and inventory-control techniques.

Much more dramatic is the *search* potential of the new technology. Once coded information has been put into computers, any single unit of information can be quickly found by giving the proper instruction to the machine. Any combination of units can be quickly brought together. According to one estimate, it should be possible in one hour to have a machine make a thorough search of the coded equivalent of four million pages of ordinary text (ten billion "binary digits"). This means that no truly revelant recorded knowledge need be lost or ignored. It should also be possible to have an increasing part of the encoding process itself handled by machines.

Machine *translation* from one language to another already holds forth the promise of reducing national barriers to the transfer of knowledge. Machines are already being used in the United States for superficial indexing of Russian and Chinese scientific documents. Many more advanced tasks—including full translations of texts and abstracts—will also be possible. It will thus be possible to store and search in an international code language and receive and answer questions in any major national language.

In the *transmission* of information the physical limits that previously confined us can be largely transcended. Modern reproduction processes can quickly and cheaply provide photographic copies of entire documents or relevant pieces of documents. It will be possible to take incoming oral messages and store them in any form, including the written, without the intermediary of a human transcriber. Outgoing messages can be quickly sent to any part of the world—by teletype, by closed circuit television or radio, or by facsimile printing.

Above all, all of these operations of storage, search, translation and transmission can be developed at extremely low unit costs. The "catch" is that such low costs presuppose a large number of units. On a small scale, the costs of such technology will be extremely high. Moreover, only with large-scale development will it be possible to solve the host of minor problems which render most of today's operations in these fields rather awkward.

2. THE PRIMACY OF SERVICE

One of the reasons for the lack of progress in applying information technology to the information crisis is a widespread fear that such action might lead to the "triumph of technique over purpose." This fear finds justification in the *lack of sufficient attention thus far given to the specific information services that can be designed to meet the specific needs of specified clients.*

This problem has been hard enough to handle in the sphere of the traditional library, where the "file clerk" or "wood rat" propensity of library staff is well known. It was to meet this problem that the Indian philosopher, S. R. Ranganathan, promulgated his five "laws of library science" starting with the shocking proposition that "books are for use." [5] That the Ranganathan philosophy of service has made so little headway in the traditional library should not deter us. Let us see what happens to his principles when we extend them to the "library of the future."

Ranganathan	*My Extension*
1. Books are for use	. . . and so are all forms of recorded knowledge.
2. Every reader his book	. . . and every user of recorded knowledge the information he needs.
3. Every book its reader	. . . every recorded idea its user.
4. Save the time of the reader	. . . and all seekers after recorded knowledge.
Corollary: Save the time of the staff	. . . and the machines.
5. A library is a growing organism	. . . and so is any organization for assembling and transmitting recorded knowledge.

Only if the information-retrieval programs of the future are built on principles such as these will it be possible to raise the present ceiling on feasibility up to the minimum requirements of the information crisis.

3. THE "BASIC" SERVICES, PERIODIC AND SPECIAL

A "philosophy" of service is operationally meaningless unless crystallized into *defined categories of end products, each with specifications designed to meet a given network of client interests.*

Production specification is much easier for an organization whose end products are "hard goods" or the tangible services involved in the storage or movement of things or people. It is quite difficult when the end product is the less tangible service of storing or transmitting information. Here there is a natural tendency for the organization man, tempest-born on a vast sea of intangibles, to focus on any precious islands of tangibility that come into sight. These are the *things*—the equipment, the machinery, and the documents, above all the documents.

The following end-product categories are stated in general terms only. It is their subcategories which in various combinations determine the specific product mix of any information retrieval organization.

a. *Bibliographies.* A bibliography can be defined as *a list of documents by title and author.* The term "document" is here used to refer to any form of recorded knowledge, including such "fugitive documents" as non marketed reports prepared for specific organizations or reports on research-in-process.

5. S. R. Ranganathan and Girja Kumar (eds.), *Social Science Research Libraries* (Asia Publishing House, Bombay, 1960).

An annotated bibliography provides, in addition, *an identification of the major subject matter facets and—where relevant—the research methods used.*

A good information-retrieval system would provide periodic annotated bibliographies on all subjects. This, of course, would have to be done on the basis of an arbitrary classification of subject matter fields.

Special annotated bibliographies would cut across any standard classification and provide lists to meet the specific needs of any client.

b. *Abstracts.* An abstract is *a summary of information contained in a single document.*

A good abstract summarizes the basic methods, findings and conclusions of any study. It thereby goes much further than an annotation in helping select documents for reading. It can also serve as a guide to selective reading within a document and as an aid in structuring—and making subsequent use of—the information contained in the document.

A good information-retrieval system should supply abstracts of any scientific or technical document, irrespective of the original language used.

The "depth" of abstracts—that is, the number of facets covered—would be standardized in periodic abstracts. In special abstracts the depth would vary to meet the needs of different clients.

c. *Surveys.* A survey is *a summary of information contained in a set of documents (or abstracts).*

Periodic surveys are provided in regular reviews, annual or otherwise, of new research and ideas in any field. General, retrospective surveys are usually provided in encyclopedias, textbooks, handbooks, and manuals.

A good information-retrieval system would provide annual encyclopedic surveys of all major fields and subfields of knowledge. As with periodic bibliographies and abstracts, these would have to be based on an arbitrary structure of information facets.

Special surveys would cut across this arbitrary structure and provide information relating to any permutation of information facets. They would be backed up, where necessary, by abstracts of appropriate depth.

d. *Indices.* An index, in this sense, deals with subject matter, as well as authors and titles. It is *a classified list of information facets covered by bibliographies, abstracts, surveys or original documents.* It must cover all past inputs and must be periodically brought up to date.

As with abstracts and surveys, indices also may vary in depth. In a high-quality information-retrieval system it should be possible to provide special indices covering all or most information facets. Only thus can an index serve as a guide to all the information stored in the system.

e. *Copies.* A copy is *any document or representation thereof through which recorded information may be transmitted to those who need it.*

The traditional library lends documents to users. It thereby undermines its capacity to serve other users interested in the same document and incurs the high costs involved in document circulation, theft and theft prevention.

A modern information-retrieval system, however, would also *give* or *sell* information. The information given or sold would be provided not through originals but through representations in typed, printed, duplicated or photographed form. These representations could be limited to the *relevant parts* of any original.

Such a system would also periodically supply copies of bibliographies, abstracts, surveys and indices.

Specially prepared bibliographies, abstracts and surveys could also be sent to users at any spot in the world through the use of facsimile printing, teletype, telephone, radio or television. Messages containing such information could travel much faster than any conceivable intercontinental guided missile. When such an information-retrieval system is finally in operation, the air around the earth will be full of "intercontinental guided missives."

C. THE *BASIC* ORGANIZATIONAL REQUIREMENTS

Some day someone will retrieve and analyze the relevant information on past efforts to create information-retrieval organizations.

He will find that throughout recorded history and in almost every nation the great dream of a worldwide information institution has arisen to counter the myth of an automatically organized body of knowledge.

He will find this dream behind the work of the early encyclopedists—from Varro, Wu Shu and Ibn Khaldun to Roger Bacon and Diderot. He will find it in the proposal of H. G. Wells for a permanent world encyclopedia, in countless resolutions and committee reports of scientific and bibliographical associations, in countless plans prepared for or by UNESCO. He will find many plans so vague as to be meaningless, others so minutely blue-printed in terms of some technician's image of the world as to be ridiculous.

But information on past failures, whether partial or complete, is not necessarily disillusioning. The wreckage of the first automobile companies was part of the process that led to the General Motors Corporation. The collapse of the League of Nations was followed by the United Nations. Despite the low state of organizational and administrative theory, perhaps we can learn something from history about the slow, maddening, nasty—and sublimely challenging—process of building a new institution.

1. THE INTEGRATION OF INTERESTS AND POWER

Back in the days when I was immersed in "practical" rather than academic affairs, I did some spare-time writing about the interplay of interests and pressures in the legislative struggles of the U.S. Congress.[6] I now have the guilty feeling that I may have unwittingly contributed to the widespread illusion that group pressures and power politics are peculiar to government.

Anyone who still labors under this illusion is invited to take an honest look at the whirl of special interests and power plays that has engulfed every proposal for a forward step toward modern information retrieval. He will find that any idea which is not buried by the intellectually obsolescent will probably be scotched by the intellectually progressive professional associations and private companies who want no intrusion in the little domains they have established in this field.

Some of those who have looked at the Balkanized patchwork of special documentation and information organizations respond with "Wipe the slate clean!" They propose a sparkling new clean-cut documentation organization with a hierarchical formal structure as neat as the servomechanism of an icebox or computer.

More practical people, without being able to explain why, know that this is organizational nonsense. They may then go to the other extreme of staking their hopes on spontaneous, unstructured cooperation among the rapidly proliferating small domains.

But the key principle in the development of an information-retrieval system capable of exploiting modern information technology is *the mobilization of power through the integration of many interests and pressures.*

One of the most exciting things about modern information retrieval is the tremendous variety of human interests, organized and unorganized, that it can satisfy. First, there are those who are potential users of its services. Then there are all those involved in the production of the services —from those who make and sell machines to those who invent the classification systems, codes and logics without which the machines cannot operate. There are those who are interested less in the services and the production process than in the prerequisites—such as concept clarification—and the implications for mass communication. Above all, there are those who are more interested in strengthening their own organizations rather than joining a new one.

A modern information-retrieval system can be built only by inte-

6. Bertram M. Gross, *The Legislative Struggle: A Study in Social Combat* (McGraw-Hill, New York, 1953).

grating these interests. Such a system must provide a legitimate and conspicuous role for large numbers of existing organizations in the field of science, industry, and government. This means a vast expansion—with adaptation—of many existing documentation organizations. It means the consolidation or elimination of others, but with greater opportunities than ever before for their salvageable personnel. It means a new and greater role for universities, libraries, professional associations and public and private research organizations.

2. A TWO-DIRECTIONAL, DECENTRALIZED GRID

It would be sophomoric to prepare detailed blueprints of the organizational structure needed to help weld these many interests together. An information retrieval organization, as stated in the amended fifth principle of Ranganathan, is a growing organism. Its detailed growth will be developed in the light of evolving purposes, problems and pressures.

It is still more sophomoric to see the general pattern of such an organism in the traditional pyramid, triangle or "pup-tent" of hierarchical authority as expressed in the so-called "classical" concepts of formal organization. Such patterns are suitable only for the formal structure of small and relatively weak components. No single person or management team could guide such a large system of this type without being destroyed or rendered impotent by the overload of information required for internal management alone. A large and powerful system built in accordance with such a model is therefore a contradiction in terms, a sheer impossibility.

If we seek a model in existing organizations, we must look elsewhere. We must look at federations, coalitions, holding companies, and cartels. We must recognize relationships that are contractual or consultative as well as hierarchical. We must recognize the structure of internal competition as well as cooperation, of autonomous interdependence as well as subordination.

In developing a general pattern for the formal structure of an organization retrieval system, *the single most important idea is that of a "grid" or "network" of interconnected organizations.* In a simpler form we see something of this sort in the grid of electric power stations and the network of state and national telephone companies.

In an electric power grid the interconnections are mainly for the purpose of ironing out peaks and valleys in production and protecting against breakdowns at any spot. In an information retrieval system, however, it would be a matter of common course for production centers in one area to provide regular service to many parts of the world.

In the international telephone network it is the clients who themselves provide the information which is transmitted. No one in the telephone organization has to think up the messages. But in information retrieval, the organization's role is double. It must itself originate messages. In information retrieval, therefore, there must be a *double grid*. On the one hand, a network of production centers assemble and process the information which is put *into* the system. On the other hand, a network of transmission centers would move the information *from* the system to its users. Some centers, moreover, would probably assume both functions.

3. A UN INSTITUTE OF SCIENTIFIC INFORMATION

The information crisis is *a world problem*. It cannot be properly seen from the limited vantage point of New York or Paris, Moscow or Belgrade, New Delhi or Accra, Cairo or Jerusalem. It cannot be budged by placing our lever among American metallurgists or anthropologists or upon a Russian computer combine. It must be dealt with by *a world organization*.

The oldest and probably the most effective world organizations are the two bodies in the field of information transmission. Oddly enough, the International Telecommunication Union, the one dealing with more modern communication technology (telegraphy only at the outset), was established first. In 1874, about ten years later, the Universal Postal Union was established. Today, both are specialized agencies of the United Nations.

When UNESCO was first established, some scientists and documentation experts hoped that it would initiate a world-wide attack upon the information crisis. Instead, UNESCO has limited itself to more modest tasks. It has promoted rudimentary documentation organizations in "underdeveloped" countries. It has provided improved facilities for the exchange of ideas among documentation experts.

The time has now come for more ambitious action. UNESCO has already displayed initiative in setting up the Center for Nuclear Research in Geneva and the International Computation Center in Rome. It should now move toward the creation of a UN Institute of Scientific Information.

The major mission of the UN Institute of Scientific Information would be the *promotion of an international grid of information-retrieval systems*. This would include policy and program formation, the development of standards and definitions, the promotion of information-retrieval research and experimentation, the handling of problems relating to constraints on the flow of information (through copyrights, patents, and censorship), and the preparation of international agreements.

In my judgment, New Delhi would be the best location for this new

UN agency. I am not making this proposal merely because an Indian location would symbolize concern with the interests of the "rapidly developing" peoples or that it might keep out the "cold war." I also have a more narrow Western-oriented purpose in mind. I think that the creation of the new agency at New Delhi will help many of our scientists escape their "Western parochialism" and attain more of a world perspective.

4. A U.S. INSTITUTE OF SCIENTIFIC INFORMATION

Just as every nation has its own post office and telephone company, each will also need its own national organization for information retrieval. In its earlier decades, in fact, the international grid will probably consist mainly of interconnected national grids with a slowly accumulating overlay of international circuits.

There is room for great variety in the development of national grids. Some countries will probably start with distribution facilities only and then work gradually into the production process. Others will prefer to concentrate on certain subject matter areas. Russia may prefer to maintain its present load by continuing to concentrate upon the natural sciences and to avoid the "dangerous thoughts" produced by the social sciences.

Here in the United States the National Science Foundation has already done important preliminary work. Together with various military and intelligence organizations, it has promoted technical research in the field. It also publishes a valuable series of regular reports on current research and development in scientific documentation. Yet the present research lacks both the practice-oriented coverage and the theoretical depth that would be required by a meaningful action program.

The time has now come for the National Science Foundation also, like UNESCO, to move forward more ambitiously. With its encouragement the U.S. government should now set up a new organization with *the special mission of bringing present and to-be-established agencies together into a national information-retrieval grid.*

Instead of being a conventional Federal agency, this new organization should have the greater freedom of action that can come through the formal structure of a mixed enterprise. The most useful form would probably be that of a public-private corporation, with representatives of scientific and academic organizations participating in its directorate. This corporation might be called the U.S. Institute of Scientific Information.

One of the many prerequisites for action along the lines suggested above is a great expansion in current research on the informational problems faced both by scientists and by those who try to put to use the results of scientific research. But such research should be much more than a static photographing of current practices. It should be invigorated by an imaginative conception of what can be done in this field by the full exploitation of modern technology. It must be geared in with the on-going march of research in the improvement of information technology.

Moreover, we should not be too easily overpowered by the mirage of perfectly operating mechanical systems. We must realize that Project BASIC—no matter what its label or norm—will be handled by men and women. Human nervous systems, not electronic computing systems, will design and manage the organizations capable of uniting brainpower and machinery in dealing with the information crisis.

We must therefore be realistic enough to expect that in a world of imperfect information the organizations we establish to improve information facilities will themselves be imperfect.

But awareness of dangers is only part of realism. The other part is idealism, the vigorous formulation of positive potentials in careful sequence from the present to the near future to the far distant future.

With this sort of realism we should start in the mid-1960s to develop the information-retrieval programs that will mature in the latter decades of this century.

ADDENDUM

> While this book was in preparation, the Presidents of the leading British and American sociological societies sent a letter to their members which illustrates the seriousness of the problem with which Gross deals. In this letter, they said: [1]

As you well know, it is no longer possible for a sociologist to read even a small part of the material his colleagues publish. *The growth in quantity of publications* as a result of the development of sociology, its differentiation and internal specialization, *has made it difficult to find time to scan the tables of contents of the major sociological journals, no less the hundreds of social science journals which often contribute important ideas published by sociologists or other social and behavioral scientists.*

. . . We have consulted with other long-established abstracting journals in various sciences to learn how they have resolved this problem. The result was the development of the attached abstracting form for your (or your assistant's) direct use . . . there is a still more urgent and compelling reason to recommend to you the use of *Sociological Abstracts* forms.

The 'publications explosion' has created a situation wherein the sociologist's responsibility can no longer end with the publication of his findings and ideas in a book or journal. *In the competition for his colleagues' limited reading time,* he must participate directly in making his materials visible to as wide a reading audi-

1. Italics supplied by editor.

ence as possible (and not merely the sociological audience). To achieve this, the sociologist must accept an additional step in the communication process and prepare an abstract of his original work. . . .

We invite you to submit as soon after publication as possible, an abstract with a reprint of every article, book, or research report or note you publish in a sociological or any other academic or general magazine (in the U.S. or abroad, irrespective of language or publication). Abstracting instructions together with our standard form for citation of title, author and other bibliographic aids will be found on the back of every form (a Spanish, French, Italian, and German version are available).

SELECTED PUBLICATIONS BY MR. GROSS

The Legislative Struggle: A Study in Social Combat (McGraw-Hill, New York, 1953).

Toward a More Responsible Two-Party System (Rinehart, New York, 1950). Joint author, as member of Committee on Political Parties of American Political Science Association.

"When Is a Plan NOT a Plan?" *Challenge, the Magazine of Economic Affairs,* New York University, December 1961.

"The Coming Revolution in Economic Thought," in *Life, Language, Law: Essays in Honor of Arthur F. Bentley* (Antioch Press, Yellow Springs, 1957), pp. 79–92.

"The President's Economic Staff during the Truman Administration," *American Political Science Review,* March 1954. (With John P. Lewis.)

Review of *The Process of Government* (by Arthur F. Bentley), *American Political Science Association,* December 1950. A "lead review" of the 1949 reissue of the classic Bentley book originally published in 1908.

"The Role of the Council of Economic Advisers," with Edwin G. Nourse, *American Political Science Review,* April, 1948.

"The Role of Congress in Contract Terminations," *Law and Contemporary Problems,* School of Law, Duke University, Vol. X, No. 3, Winter, 1944.

SUGGESTIONS FOR FURTHER READING

Casey, Robert S., James W. Perry, Madeline M. Berry, and Allen Kent (eds.), *Punched Cards,* 2d ed. (Reinhold, New York, 1958).

Goldwyn, Alvin J., "The Doctor and the Document—A New Tool for Biomedical Research," *Wilson Library Bulletin,* June 1962, pp. 829–832, 847.

Kehl, W. B., J. F. Horty, C. R. T. Bacon, and D. S. Mitchell, "An Information Retrieval Language for Legal Studies," *Communications of the ACM,* September 1961, pp. 380–389.

Kent, Allen (ed.), "Advances in Documentation and Library Science," Vol. III, parts 1 and 2 of Gilbert L. Peakes, Allen Kent, and James W. Perry (eds.), *Information Retrieval and Machine Translation* (Wiley, New York, 1960–61).

———, "A Machine that Does Research," *Harper's,* April, 1959, pp. 67ff.

———, *Textbook on Mechanized Information Retrieval* (Wiley, New York, 1962).

"Report of the Committee on Government Operations," Subcommittee on Reorganization and International Organizations, Senate Report No. 120, 1959.

"Science and Technology Act of 1958— Analysis and Summary," staff report, Senate Committee on Government Operations, Senate Document No. 90, 1958.

"Science and Technology Act of 1958—

Hearings before a Subcommittee of the Committee on Government Operations on Bill S.3126," parts I, II, 1958.

Swanson, Don R., "Searching Natural Language by Computer," *Science,* Oct. 21, 1960, pp. 1099–1104.

QUESTIONS

1. Select at least one interpretative piece of news reporting in the daily press (by a "James Reston," a state house reporter, or a business reporter) and another piece of news analysis in either *Time* or *Newsweek* and a third in *Business Week*. If possible, select at least one of your chosen pieces from a field with which you yourself are very well acquainted and another from a field which you do not know well. List at least twenty-five serious relevant articles and books which the writers should understand in order satisfactorily to discuss the subject; more credit should be given for citation of a set of references from widely diversified areas than for a list using all sources from the same field. (Example: in some instances, news writers on state and municipal government appear not to be familiar with the experience of other states and municipalities in this country, still less with technical but pertinent engineering material, or materal on foreign local government. In many instances the readers of such writers might profit if the writers also knew some psychological, sociological, and philosophical articles and books. The student should, of course, be prepared to show how the citations he gives would bear on the articles he has selected, and to explain how the exercise bears on information retrieval.)

2. What similarity do the sociologists just quoted in the addendum to the Gross article see between the "population explosion" and the "publication explosion"? Do any of the factors that serve to explain the "population explosion" also help to explain the "publication explosion"? (Consult the general introduction of this book and the chapter on population in most general introductory sociology texts for cues to your discussion of this problem.)

George Gerbner

On Content Analysis and Critical

Research in Mass Communication *

THE NEXT WRITER deals comprehensively with the field of content analysis and its implications for research in mass communications. Content analysis was among the earliest tools utilized by communications researchers. Typical of the first wave of important content-analysis studies was Julian L. Woodward's "Foreign News in American Morning Newspapers: A Study in Public Opinion," published by Columbia University Press in 1930. During World War II and subsequently, Harold Lasswell and his associates utilized content analysis in a variety of political communications analyses. The only book serving as a manual of content-analysis techniques is Bernard Berelson's,[1] published in 1952 and now in the process of revision. Students who wish to gain a succinct and excellent introduction to current techniques in content analysis should also read Professor Wayne A. Danielson's recent essay [2] on the subject.

Dr. Gerbner's essay is more concerned with theoretical aspects of content analysis than with the techniques. As a leading practitioner of content-analysis techniques, Gerbner asks us to consider broader implications of content than those thus far invented by the techniques of content analysis. Using a valuable general model of communication which he has constructed, Gerbner considers the role of the content analyst. The position of the analyst is thus defined in relation to the communication system with which he must deal.

Professor Gerbner argues persuasively that a sophisticated usage of content analysis can help us to conduct critical research into the

* Reprinted from the *Audio-Visual Communication Review*, vol. 6, no. 3, Spring 1958, pp. 85–108 by permission of the author and publisher. (Copyright 1958 by *Audio-Visual Communication Review*.)

1. Bernard Berelson, *Content Analysis in Communications Research* (Free Press, New York, 1952).

2. Wayne A. Danielson, "Content Analysis," in R. O. Nafziger and D. M. White (eds.), *Introduction to Mass Communications Research* (Louisiana State U. P., Baton Rouge, 1963).

nature of the mass media. Through it, he believes, we may develop hypotheses which enable us to perform critical, "value-oriented" research. Professor Gerbner illustrates this approach by citing the work of such men as Lowenthal, Saenger, Smythe, Schramm and Fearing, as well as some of his own studies.

This essay is a demanding one, but one which will repay the student by adding substantially to his basic understanding not only of content analysis but of the general theory of mass communications.

D. M. W.

DR. GERBNER, *Associate Professor at the Institute of Communications Research, College of Journalism and Communications, University of Illinois, is Director of United States and International Research Studies in mass-media content and process. He has also been a newscaster and a newspaper editor for the United States Information Service, a reporter, lecturer, and consultant in mass communications and audio-visual education. Dr. Gerbner received his Ph.D. from the University of Southern California.*

Content is the coin of the communication exchange. Its nature, functions, and study should be the subject of lively technical and philosophical debate. But they are not. Or perhaps it depends on one's focus; in the broader scope of social and physical sciences the issue of *what* is involved in observation and communication lies at the heart of fundamental controversies. But in the newer specialization that straddles this social-scientific battleground, in content analysis, the outstanding issues appear to have been settled by the authorities.

So one is compelled to tread warily for fear of either adding to the din of battle in the larger context, or of appearing to be bent on disturbing the dignity of established procedures in the specialized field. What prompts us to proceed, nevertheless, is our experience that (*a*) in both teaching and research it is necessary to raise—and ultimately impossible to avoid—the basic issues of social science within the field of content analysis, and (*b*) that established procedures tend to limit content analysis to administrative research.

When theory appears to rationalize advances in methodology rather than build a framework for critical discussion of aims, the time is ripe for a consideration of aims without prior commitment as to means. We propose to do that by advancing an approach to content analysis which raises basic issues through tackling them from its own vantage point, and by summarizing the case for critical research.

AN APPROACH TO CONTENT ANALYSIS

Any process may be viewed as a patterned exchange between systems. We make inferences about the nature of processes through observation of stages, or outcomes, or consequences of the exchange. We call these occasions *events;* they make it possible for the observer to infer some things about the states of systems engaged in the exchange, and about their relationships to one another.

If a party to an exchange records, represents, or encodes in conventional (social) forms some aspects of the pattern of the exchange between itself and other systems, an event has been produced which has special qualities. A hot cup of coffee is in the process of exchanging energy with its surroundings. We infer the pattern of this exchange through observation and measurement (or by taking a sip). Coffee cannot produce a formally coded communication event, isolated from that exchange, but encoding the pattern of the exchange, and expressing its own state and relationship in the exchange, such as the words "I am losing heat." We, however, can produce such an event indicative of our relationship in the exchange; we can say, "The coffee is getting cold." From that statement one can make inferences both about the process in the cup, and about the process that gave rise to the statement, i.e., our relationship to the coffee.

A *communication* is, then, a specialized, formally coded or representative social event which makes possible inferences about states, relationships, processes not directly observed. The *process* of communication is the transmission of such events and sharing of certain inferences. The *content* of communication is the sum total of warranted inferences that can be made about relationships involved in the communication event.

These inferences can be of two kinds. The first kind is the conventional associations we make when we view the communication as a generalized form or code. This is the conventional, formal meaning, such as we might find in a dictionary.

Underlying the "formal message" with its denotative and connotative associations and differential response capabilities, we see in content the basis for inference about specific functional relations between the communicating agent or agency and other events or systems, and about actual or potential consequences. The conventional face value of a dollar bill is not the same as its actual role value in a specific exchange. The latter will reflect the objective relationships of producer, product, buyer, and seller in the exchange, and some consequences of these relationships, whether or not the parties engaged in the exchange are aware of them. Similarly, the statement "It's hot here" is a linguistic type or "form" which can be isolated from its behavioral context, recorded, recoded, etc., with little or no distortion of its formal, conventional meaning. But it is not only that; once uttered—whether pleasant or unpleasant, good or bad, real or fancied—it is also a unique and irreversible event reflecting, perhaps unwittingly, an objective set of underlying relationships which prompted its utterance. The advertising slogan, "Smoke X cigarettes; they're milder," whether valid or invalid, true or false, effective or ineffective, implies a particular set of social and industrial relationships whose expression in that form leads to consequences fully understandable only in terms of these relationships and not of the explicit message alone.[1]

"MICRO" AND "MACRO" ANALYSIS

The "micro" analyst of communication content is interested in gathering information about persons and making predictions about their behavior. In his search for the hidden dynamics of individual behavior he utilizes communication content either as fruitful material expressive in some form of the state of an organism, or as a necessary source when information about a person is restricted to the messages produced by that individual.

The analyst who views content as a social event goes beyond individual behavior. His search is for the social determinants and possible consequences of both personal and institutional dynamics reflected in cultural products. His focus may be the autonomous creations of great art—whether mass reproduced or not—or it may be the everyday commodities of cultural industry.

From the former focus comes a clear statement of those tasks of content analysis which have been sidestepped in the preoccupation with methodologies. It is from the introduction to Leo Lowenthal's *Literature and the Image of Man:* [2]

Creative literature conveys many levels of meaning, some intended by the author, some quite unintentional. An artist sets out to invent a plot, to describe actions, to depict the interrelationships of characters, to emphasize certain values; wittingly or unwittingly, he stamps his work with uniqueness through

1. It is evident that our distinctions are in contrast with those of the semioticians and "sign theorists" who see content as having reference *only* to semantic and syntactic characteristics of symbols. However, Kaplan (19) recognizes that content analysis "may, and indeed must take account of [pragmatic characteristics] in determining which aspects of content will be analyzed and in what ways."

2. Leo Lowenthal, *Literature and the Image of Man* (Beacon, Boston, 1957).

an imaginative selection of problems and personages. By this very imaginative selection . . . he presents an explicit or implicit picture of man's orientation to his society: privileges and responsibilities of classes; conceptions of work, love, and friendship, of religion, nature, and art. Through an analysis of [his] works . . . an image may be formed of man's changing relation to himself, to his family, and to his social and natural environment. . . .

. . . The specific treatment which the creative writer gives to nature or to love, to gestures and moods, to gregariousness or solitude, is a primary source for a study of the penetration of the most intimate spheres of personal life by social forces.

The analyst of literary content, as a social scientist, "has to transform the private equation of themes and stylistic means into social equations," writes Lowenthal. "In fact," he asserts, "most generalized concepts about human nature found in literature prove on close inspection to be related to social and political change." And: "Man is born, strives, loves, suffers, and dies in any society, but it is the portrayal of *how* he reacts to these common experiences that matters, since they almost invariably have a social nexus."

The "macro" analyst of mass media content deals with broad regularities in large systems of mass-produced cultural commodities. As the "micro" analyst assumes that the underlying laws of human dynamics find expression in communicative behavior, the "macro" analyst assumes that institutions, societies, and cultures manifest laws and order beyond that apparent to large numbers of people at any one time, and that systems of artifacts express objective, even if subtle or implicit, manifestations of this order. In his quest for the *system* behind the facts and forms of mass communication, the media analyst regards content as expressive of social relationship and institutional dynamics, and as formative of social patterns.

SOME TASKS OF THE MASS-MEDIA CONTENT ANALYST

His task, analogous in certain respects to that of the cultural anthropologist, cannot be merely descriptive of his or other people's subjective impressions. For example, the anthropologist does not see an ax handle only as a stick one could put a blade on and start chopping. To him the meaning of a cave painting is not only that it has reference to buffalos, or even that it implies certain technical skills and individual attitudes, desires, or fantasies. The major significance of artifacts is that they reflect historical human approaches to certain events; that they signify and regulate social relationships in ways their users or creators may not consciously recognize.

Egyptian mythology of a certain period may be traced to reflect the conquest of the upper Nile Valley by the people of the Delta who superimposed upon the water gods the theological primacy of their Sun. Ancient Mesopotamian culture and religion may be seen to record and facilitate in symbolic forms a system of social relations based on the need for elaborate irrigation networks. Movable type was made possible by a long chain of technological and social revolutions; the printing of the Gutenberg Bible was a social event reflecting cultural relationships and paving the way for future revolutions.

Communications media can be regarded as historical systems of social control, conferring monopolies of knowledge through built-in "biases." [3] Some go even further in claiming that new media are inherently revolutionary in their implications, "each codifying reality differently, each concealing a unique metaphysics." [4] Distinguished analysts of mass-media content cite a legal historian to the effect that "The greatest and most far-reaching revolutions in history are not consciously observed at the time of their occurrence." [5] Be that as it may, it prompts the analysts to remark, "It is by the investigation of style that we may gain more insight into the currents of history which are usually below the threshold of consciousness."

Our contention is not so much that inherent physical characteristics of media as such, or that formal elements of style, vocabulary, syntax, are themselves of profound and direct significance. Rather it is that the nature and consequences of these elements and characteristics can be understood best if content is viewed as bearing the imprint of social needs and uses.

In the words of Leo Lowenthal,[6] ". . . objective elements of the social whole are produced and reproduced in the mass media." And: "The stimulus in popular culture is itself a historical phenomenon . . . the relation between stimulus and response is preformed and prestructured by the historical and social fate of the stimulus as well as of the respondent."

The historical and social fate common to large bodies of mass media content is that they are selected and designed to be mass produced for a market. They spring from complex technological production and market relationships; they are products of an exchange between systems in which

3. H. A. Innis, *The Bias of Communication* (U. of Toronto Press, 1951).

4. E. Carpenter, "The New Languages," *Explorations,* vol. 7, March 1957.

5. H. D. Lasswell, D. Lerner, and I. de Sola Pool, *The Comparative Study of Symbols* (Stanford U. P., Stanford, Calif., 1952).

6. Leo Lowenthal, "Historical Perspectives in Popular Culture," *American Journal of Sociology,* vol. 55, 1950, pp. 323–333.

the decisive communicating agent is a modern business enterprise. Van Den Haag [7] writes:

Unlike any other type of culture, popular culture—a full fledged style of living with a distinct pattern of feeling, thinking, believing and acting—was made possible and in the end necessary by mass production. Unless the requirements and effects of industrialization are fully grasped, popular culture does not become intelligible.

Even more specifically, unless the requirements and effects of a specific system of industrial and market relationships (such as the corporate structure) are fully grasped, mass-media content analysis remains superficial. Their intimate ties to the specific industrial marketing system from which they arise give mass-media materials their institutional autonomy, their implicit role value or consequential meaning, and their underlying frame of reference.

Aside from the formal, conventional "message," mass media content bears the imprint of concrete circumstances of its creation. This includes such things as external outlook and the internal dynamics of the producing industry; its relationship to competitors; its control over resources, facilities of production, and distribution; the position of its decision makers in the industrial structure; their relationships to audiences, markets, advertising sponsors. Out of these come a set of managerial assumptions—both implicit and rationalized—reflected in large systems of content, and preforming some aspects of its perception. The social determinants of cultural industry thus find their way into the consequential meaning of the material. They are expressed not so much in conventional forms and "messages" as through patterns of selection, omission, juxtaposition, through just the way things are "looked at."

Of course, it is necessary to classify and clarify conventional meanings and widely recognized consistencies in formal content. But the full meaning of such analysis emerges through procedures which combine investigation of the objective social origin and role of the stimulus with that of the response; which search for manifestations of processes whose consequences do not depend on conscious intentions and perceptions. The primary tasks of the mass media content analyst lie in his attempts to *scientifically gather and test* inferences about content that may involve generally unrecognized or unanticipated consequences, to isolate and investigate consequential properties of content which escape ordinary awareness or casual scrutiny, to bring to awareness those hidden regularities of

7. E. Van Den Haag, "Of Happiness and of Despair We Have No Measure, in B. Rosenberg and D. M. White (eds.), *Mass Culture, the Popular Arts in America* (Free Press, New York, 1957).

content which record and reflect objective mechanisms of a social order. The classical role of cultural scholarship as a testing ground of critical social theory is to be strengthened, broadened, and deepened—not abolished—in the analysis of mass media content through the newer, more systematic and refined methodologies.

SOME THEORETICAL CONSIDERATIONS

Berelson [8] defines communication content as "that body of meanings through symbols (verbal, musical, pictorial, plastic, gestural) which makes up the communication itself. In the classic sentence identifying the process of communication—*'who* says *what* to *whom, how,* with *what effect'*—communication content is the *what.*" His definition of content analysis is "a research technique for the objective, systematic, and quantitative description of the manifest content of communication." Lasswell, Lerner, and Pool [9] speak of "symbol" as a technical term for words that "stand for (symbolize) the attitudes of those who use them, as distinguished, for example, from 'signs,' which are words that point to (signalize) objects external to their user." In their "symbol studies" they define content analysis as "quantitative semantics" which aims at achieving objectivity, precision, and generality through the use of statistical methods.

This approach has stimulated a growing volume of output and increasing recognition. Our purpose here is not to attempt a detailed critique. The "straw man" elements in the restrictive use of quantitative versus qualitative and manifest versus latent dichotomies have been challenged elsewhere [10,11] as resulting neither in objectivity nor necessarily in precision but quite possibly in fundamentally uncritical "scientism." The present task is to extend the theoretical underpinnings of this approach beyond the limitations of its phenomenalistic framework, to harness its methodological insights to more critical social uses, and to amplify the role of the content analyst in a broader conception of the communication process.

The Lasswellian formula, "who says what to whom, how, and with what effect" proved useful for many practical purposes. But it is too restrictive and too one-directional for a general theoretical communications

8. Bernard Berelson, *Content Analysis in Communications Research* (Free Press, New York, 1952).

9. H. D. Lasswell, D. Lerner, and I. de Sola Pool, *op. cit.*

10. Siegfried Kracauer, "The Challenge of Qualitative Content Analysis," *Public Opinion Quarterly,* vol. 16, Winter 1952–53, pp. 631–641.

11. D. W. Smythe, "Some Observations on Communication Theory," *Audio-Visual Communication Review,* vol. 2, Winter 1954, pp. 24–37.

model, or for a framework for critical research. For example, it places content (the "what") in a severely limited sequence. It has been amply demonstrated that *what* is said by the *who* depends also on his role as a *whom;* i.e., the communicator builds into his statement consciously and unconsciously his terms of perception as a receiver of communications, which, in turn, reflect his relationships with events of his world. Even symbols stand for attitudes, feelings, inner experiences *about* (or expressed in terms of sensory experiences of) events of an objective world. This causal thread from systems of subject-object relations to systems of content and consequences leads through the communicating agent or agency, but not necessarily through his awareness, or that of the receiver. When it comes to measuring "effects," the criterion of effectiveness in the light of conscious intentions or explicit objectives becomes insufficient except for administrative purposes. From the point of view of critical research, more interested in understanding normative aspects of the communication exchange than in appraising effectiveness on behalf of taken-for-granted objectives, a model of communication should be broadened to include certain additional features.

A GENERAL MODEL OF COMMUNICATION

The construction and some uses of such a general model was the subject of a previous *AV Communication Review* article.[12] It is summarized here for the purpose of facilitating discussion in that framework. The model makes provision for (*a*) portraying the communicating agent in a dynamic role as both sender and receiver; (*b*) designating his relation with the world of events as the ultimate source of his perceptions and statements; (*c*) making the distinction between formal properties of the communication product, and other inferences about content; and (*d*) specifically designating the study of consequences (aside from effectiveness in terms of overt intentions or objectives) as an area of research.

The model has ten basic components, some of which can be illustrated graphically. The ten components, forming a sentence identifying the essential aspects of a communication act or sequence, appear in capital letters below, accompanied by a brief description. The graphic model (Fig. 1) illustrates appropriate aspects of the verbal description.

(1) SOMEONE (the communicating agent or agency M engaged in an exchange with events of his world)

(2) PERCEIVES AN EVENT (the exchange—for our purposes primarily perceptual—between systems M and E; horizontal dimension of the

12. George Gerbner, "Toward a General Model of Communication," *Audio-Visual Communications Review,* vol. 4, Summer 1956, pp. 171–199.

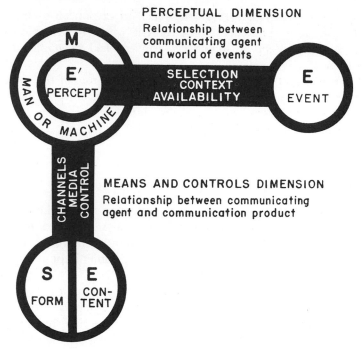

PERCEPTUAL DIMENSION
Relationship between communicating agent and world of events

Figure 1. The graphic model, illustrating certain aspects of the verbal model.

graphic model leading from "event" E to "event as perceived" E'; including such critical consideration as M's *selection* in a certain *context* from what is *available* for perception either directly or through the mediation of communication events)

(3) AND REACTS (M's general response, not on graphic model)

(4) IN A SITUATION (social and physical setting, not on graphic model)

(5) THROUGH SOME MEANS (communicative facilities, vehicles, controls, used to produce communication event; vertical dimension of the graphic model)

(6) TO MAKE AVAILABLE MATERIALS (part of the horizontal dimension)

(7) IN SOME FORM (formal state of the communication event; signal system created by nonrandom use of means; conventionalized structure, representative or syntactic patterns; designated as the S—signal—portion of the communication events SE)

(8) AND CONTEXT (field or sequence in which a communication event is perceived; part of horizontal dimension)

(9) CONVEYING CONTENT (the social event portion of the communication SE; those inferences from content which reflect objective relationships independent of intentions, conventional meanings, conscious perceptions)

(10) WITH SOME CONSEQUENCE (the actual role of the communication event in its further exchanges with other M's; objective outcomes as measured by criteria independent from intentions, overt perception, or "effectivenesss" in terms of objectives of the communication; not represented on graphic model).

INVESTIGATION OF CONTENT

The investigation of content focuses attention on SE, the communication product. It proceeds as a relational analysis on two levels. Both "formal" and "content" aspects of the communication product are studied with respect to all other elements of the communication sequence of which SE is a part.

Study of the formal continuities traces the flow or configurations of conventional ("arbitrary") systems of signs and symbols through classification and measurement. It relates the state of specific signal-systems to that of others for comparison, or to intentions, desires, behaviors of the source, or to the "effectiveness" of the responses they elicit, or to technical use of communicative means.

Study of the consequential continuities represented in content includes the above, but is not limited to it. Here the communication product is viewed as a specific social event whose consequential meaning may be constant through variation in form, or may vary when form is held constant.

What we are discussing here is *not* the fact that words have different denotative or connotative meanings; that the sounds "horse" may refer to an animal, or to a condition of the vocal cords; that situation and context alter conventional meanings; that individual responses vary; or even that words (or other signals) may be used for strategic reasons to mask rather than reveal intentions. Rather, we are discussing the fact that a communication event may reveal something about the systematic exchange that produced it, quite apart from what we think it means, or what we intend it to mean.

We may analyze a photograph not to get responses to its conventional forms, but to determine the position of the camera or angle of lighting recorded in it. We may study a series of whiskey advertisements, not to determine their effects on sales, or on ideas about whiskey, but to make some inferences about more subtle social relationships recorded and reflected in them (such as the frequency with which their image of the "good life" involves the services of Negro waiters or Filipino busboys).

Content as an expression of objective relationships may be implicit in selection, omission, context, juxtaposition, point of view, etc., or it may be inferred through circumstantial or situational association. In that sense, consequential meaning is far from being an "arbitrary" convention. It is the property of a specific event or system of events. Every utterance of the English word "horse" (animal) is a unique event, socially determined through a long chain of associations in certain cultural context with a certain type of animal which became domesticated at a certain point in history, and has continued to be one of the events people communicate about. In doing so they express an objective historical relationship toward it. Semanticists and semioticians notwithstanding, there is, in this sense, something "horsy" about the word "horse." The "map" is not the "territory" but a map does involve a mapmaker's relationship to territory, determined socially and historically in terms of the territory as well as of the individual mapmaker.

Consider the study of a system of mass-media products, e.g., male adventure magazine covers. Suppose formal analysis has indicated that the

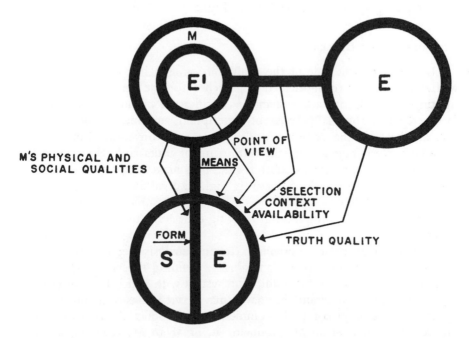

Figure 2. *Illustration of some of the relationships involved in content analysis.*

patterns of violent struggle with nature in juxtaposition with sex fears dominate most covers. Significant questions of content analysis might then be derived from our model by relating this communication event (SE) to the other aspects (see also Fig. 2):

In what ways does this material reflect *physical and social qualities* of communicating agencies (publishers), and their relationships to other systems such as markets, advertisers, audiences, and their world of events? What *points of view* about life and the world as M sees them are implied and facilitated? What social arrangements of ownership and control of communicative *means* and facilities are revealed by the prevalence of this material? What patterns of *selection, context,* and *availability* are inferable from this body of content? How valid, adequate, and coherent is the correspondence of these representations to any actual system of events (*truth quality*)? What might be the *consequences* (aside from sales, likes and dislikes, conventional meanings, or "effectiveness" in terms of conscious objectives) of social relationships and points of view mediated through this content as a social event system? And so on. Each of these questions represents a way of relating the communication event system to other elements or relationships in the model; some of these can be illustrated on the graphic model as shown in Fig. 2.

THE ROLE OF THE CONTENT ANALYST

Let us sketch the role of the analyst in our scheme, and contrast it with that in some form-oriented approaches for the purpose of highlighting some distinctions. Systematic classification of units of material into categories for the purpose of description and measurement is a pivotal phase of the analyst's work. Form and conventional-meaning oriented analysis begins with the setting up of units and categories on the basis of explicit signal characteristics. This makes coding and classification a semiclerical task of relatively high face validity and reliability. It places the burden of analysis on design for measurement and on the precision of the means employed for testing the nature and significance of differences.

Consequential meaning-oriented content analysis begins elsewhere and in a different perspective. It begins by defining the position of the analyst in relation to the communication system with which he is to deal.

In terms of our diagram, the analyst may be viewed as communicating agent M_2 whose approach to the communication product SE, as analyst, is different from that of an M_1 producing it, or of an M_2 receiving it, or even from his own casual perceptions. The analyst as scientist must be distinguished from the analyst as subject. This requires the development of some philosophical awareness. As Hans Speier [13] has pointed out, "All theories of the relation between ideas and the world we call social have philosophical implications." The analyst is forced into the philosophical area at least twice. When he formulates his hypotheses, "he in fact formulates a tentative philosophy which provides him with a frame of reference for his research. . . . Again, when he comes to develop generalizations on the basis of his findings, he is taking a philosophical stand." The crucial issue is whether or not he is *aware* of the stand he is taking.

Awareness of one's own stand means that we react to our "naive" perceptions of explicit manifestations in terms of a qualitatively different (more "objective") consciousness. As subjects we laugh when the hapless comic slips on the banana peel; as analysts we react to our own (and other subjects') laughter by tracing our own position (spatial, temporal, cultural, personal) in the exchange with that communication event, and by tracing the social history of the product. Our awareness of the known relationships in these two dimensions (along the horizontal and vertical axes of our model) suggests some of the most pertinent and least apparent questions to ask about unknown relationships in content.

Tentative answers to these questions may be thought of as the hypotheses of the analyst, usually stated in the form of content elements, categories, systematic functional relationships which may escape ordinary scrutiny.

Self-conscious hypothesis making brings into content analysis a concern with the correctness of the analyst's entire approach to his material, with his philosophical stand, with his appraisal of the process out of which the material emerged—in other words, with the validity of a critical social theory implied in his hypotheses. Few of these hazards—and rewards—confront formal or administrative research in which ultimate goals and values are either given or assumed, and are not at stake in the research.

If the development of hypotheses through a scientific self-consciousness and critical value orientation is the first task of the content analyst, the second is the testing of his inferences through the unself-conscious method and self-critical temper of science. Here critical, formal, and administrative researchers join in common concern over the development of research design and methodology sensitive to functional relationships of different types.

But before we advocate this union in methodology, it is necessary to explore further some crucial distinctions in aims and scope.

13. Hans Speier, "The Social Determination of Ideas," *Social Research,* vol. 5, 1938, pp. 182–205.

CRITICAL RESEARCH IN MASS COMMUNICATION

Paul Lazarsfeld [14] gave a lucid description of the distinctions between administrative and critical research in communication in an article written in 1941.

During the last two decades, he wrote, the media of mass communication have become some of the best known and best documented spheres of modern society. The reason for the rapid rise of communications research, he felt, was the notion that modern media of communication are tools handled by people or agencies for given purposes. As the communications investment of these agencies—both commercial and governmental —grew in size, and as the competitive stakes became higher, empirical research was called upon to help make administrative choices in communications strategy and method.

The objection of critical research is not directed against administrative tasks as such, but against limiting the theoretical scope of communications research to the aims which prevail in the majority of current studies, Lazarsfeld wrote. He summarized as a basic notion of critical research the contention that:

. . . one cannot pursue a single purpose and study the means of its realization isolated from the total historical situation in which such planning and study goes on. Modern media of communication have become such complex instruments that wherever they are used they do much more to people than those who administer them mean to do, and they may have a momentum of their own which leaves the administrative agencies much less choice than they believe they have. The idea of *critical research* is posed against the practice of administrative research, requiring that, prior and in addition to whatever special purpose is to be served, the general role of our media of communication in the present social system is to be studied.

SOME QUESTIONS AND HYPOTHESES

Lazarsfeld sketched the approach of the critical student. He will ask such questions as: "How are these media organized and controlled? How, in their institutional set-up, is the trend toward centralization, standardization, and promotional pressure expressed? In what form, however disguised, are they threatening human values?" He will feel that the prime task of research is "to uncover the unintentional (for the most part) and

14. Paul Lazarsfeld, "Remarks on Administrative and Critical Communication Research," *Studies in Philosophy and Social Science,* vol. 9, 1941, pp. 2–16.

often very subtle ways in which these media contribute to living habits and social attitudes. . . ."

Lazarsfeld then indicated some steps in the formation of critical research hypotheses "by visualizing how a student would be trained to make observations in everyday life and to try to interpret them in terms of their social meaning." Note how these examples distinguish the role of the analyst as social scientist from his role as a subject:

You sit in a movie and look at an old newsreel showing fashions of ten years ago. Many people laugh. Why do those things which we admired just a little while ago seem so ridiculous now? . . . Could it be that by laughing at past submissions, we gather strength to submit to the present pressure upon us? Thus, what looks to an ordinary observer like an incident in a movie theater, becomes, from this point of view, a symptom of great social significance.

Or you find that a large brewery advertises its beer by showing a man disgustedly throwing aside a newspaper full of European war horrors while the caption says that in times like these the only place to find peace, strength, and courage is at your own fireside drinking beer. What will be the result if symbols referring to such basic human wants as that for peace become falsified into expressions of private comfort and are rendered habitual to millions of magazine readers as merchandising slogans? Why should people settle their social problems by action and sacrifice if they can serve the same ends by drinking a new brand of beer? To the casual observer the advertisement is nothing but a more or less clever sales trick. From the aspect of more critical analysis, it becomes a dangerous sign of what a promotional culture might end up with.

Could it be that the mass-produced portrayal of violent means for their own sake reflects social alienation and facilitates cynicism and apathy; that the "evil scientist" is an image of the hired intellectual, "neutral" in matters of human concern; that, as has been suggested, "Peeping Tomism" is a "form of protest literature in prosperity"; that, as has also been suggested, conventional news values and front pages mirror market-orientation, a loss of historical perspective, and discontinuity of experience harmonious with positivistic science and philosophy? Neither administrative nor purely formal analysis will provide the answers to these and other questions striking at the roots of our uneasiness about popular culture in an age of mass production.

CONTENT AND SOCIAL REALITY

Franklin Fearing [15] expressed this view: "The hypothesis that the mass media reflect value-systems, satisfy needs of society, whether con-
15. Franklin Fearing, "Social Impact of the Mass Media of Communication,"

sciously or unconsciously held, furnishes the theoretical basis for extensive research in which the content of films and other mass media are analyzed in order to discover what the value-belief patterns of a given society are." But one cannot fully "discover" value-belief patterns without tracing them to their existential bases in the world of objective events, and without shedding some light on *what* and *whose* needs they really satisfy. Prewar German films, seen as reflecting "not so much explicit credos as psychological disposition—those deep layers of collective mentality which extend more or less below the dimensions of consciousness," [16] also reflect a system of concrete social and cultural operations which gave rise to Nazism. "Hollywood's Terror Films" can be seen not only in terms of their creating an "all-pervasive fear that threatens the psychic integrity of the average person. . . ." [17] but also in terms of a broader setting in which market-oriented social mechanisms of cultural industry shape this implicit function, and "need" such psychic consequences. In the last analysis no "state of mind" can be fully understood until its "discovery" is driven through to the objective social determinants that produce and require it.

Inner and external reality share common ground in content. Individual and institutional "perceptual frameworks" with their implicit assumptions, need-value systems, experientially and historically developed vantage points, represent one side of the subject-object relation, structured in systematic unity and opposition with the other side—the events talked about, the social circumstances that shape our experience of meanings. Content arises out of the dialectical relation of subject and event. The nature of this relation depends on the realities of man's existence in, and struggle with, society and nature. Implicitly recorded in content, this relation becomes the property of a social event on whose terms the exchange continues.

Science is the penetration of human consciousness into the realities of existence. Content analysis can share in this enterprise through a critical awareness of social processes that shape both communication products and their perceptions and uses. Its hypotheses arise from the background of awareness of prevailing trends in cultural mass production. Specific studies focus on how content systems express these trends, and how they contribute or run counter to them. They culminate in the

in *Mass Media and Education,* Fifty-Third Yearbook of the National Society for the Study of Education, Part II, chap. 8 (U. of Chicago Press, 1954), pp. 165–192.

16. Siegfried Kracauer, *From Caligari to Hitler: A Psychological History of the German Film* (Princeton U. P., Princeton, N.J., 1947).

17. Siegfried Kracauer, "Hollywood's Terror Films: Do They Reflect an American State of Mind?" *Commentary,* vol. 2, 1946, pp. 132–136.

investigation of the range of implied consequences, in Lazarsfeld's words, "stamping human personalities in modern industrial society . . ., scrutinized from the viewpoint of more or less explicit ideas of what endangers and what preserves the dignity, freedom, and cultural values of human beings."

EDUCATION, MASS MEDIA, AND THE CHALLENGE OF

CRITICAL CONTENT ANALYSIS

In the analysis of consequential meanings, educational research and content analysis have joint responsibilities. These responsibilities involve bringing to awareness mechanisms of psychic management masked in righteous overt forms; increasing conscious insight into tensions generated by the exposition of correct "facts" in an implicit structure which serves as an extension of the social process the "facts" purport to illuminate.

World War II Army orientation films come to mind as a fruitful subject for research from that point of view. There is already some evidence suggesting that perhaps the notable "boomerang effect" of some educational material was not so much a "failure" of communication as the implicit communication of built-in relationships superimposed upon formal content, expressing assumptions, points of view, etc., running counter to the explicit message.

A study of the home-front propaganda film, "Don't Be a Sucker," [18] found, for example, that despite the "learning" of specific points by specific target audiences, the majority of the viewers identified with the Germans Hans rather than with the American Mike. A closer examination of the implicit content of the film revealed under the rather pedantic presentation of an anti-Nazi, pro-tolerance "message," the subtle imprint of a point of view from which fascism appeared dynamic, and democracy an invitation to weakness.

Another anti-bias film entitled "No Way Out" was subjected to searching content analysis.[19] It was found that while on the level of verbal argument the film appeared to be a moving document, on a deeper level the producers could not escape the approach of an operationally racist society. The analysts wrote:

18. Eunice Cooper and Helen Dinerman, "Analysis of the Film, 'Don't Be a Sucker,': A Study in Communication," *Public Opinion Quarterly,* vol. 15, 1951, pp. 243–264.

19. Martha Wolfenstein and Nathan Leites, "Two Social Scientists View 'No Way Out,'" *Commentary,* vol. 10, 1950, pp. 388–391.

There is of course no doubt of the good intentions of the makers of this film. But in order to show how wrong race hatred is, the fiilm makers had to create a plot and characters and elaborate upon them in detailed images; here their fantasies from a less conscious level come to the surface: the Negro becomes a terrible burden that we must carry on our backs; a sacrifice of white corpses is required for his preservation; the image of the violated white woman forces its way to the screen; and so on. There is an effort to deny these unacknowledged nightmares about the Negro by locating race hatred exclusively in an exceptional, pathological character, but this attempt at denial remains, at bottom, ineffectual. The very title of the film, extremely puzzling in terms of the plot, expresses the basic ambiguity; though the Negro-hater is supposed to be defeated and the falsely accused Negro saved and vindicated, the title seems to state a deeper belief and draw a contrary "moral": there is no way out.

The Payne Fund studies of the early thirties represented the first concerted attack by a group of investigators on broad social problems involved in cultural mass production. "Perhaps the most important conclusion concerning these data," wrote Edgar Dale [20] in his summary of the content analysis portion of that project, "is the fact that in large measure the characters, the problems, and the settings are removed from the lives of the persons who view [motion pictures]." And perhaps the most significant statement revealing the social implications of the "escapist" trend of overt themes was Dale's conclusion, "The good life is no longer a dream which can only be wished for. We now have at hand the machinery for making it a reality. This machinery for changing our current civilization is not commonly shown in the movies. . . ."

SOCIAL RELATIONS IN MASS MEDIA CONTENT

In the absence of continuing large-scale investigations the evidence concerning the implicit consequential meanings of mass media content is necessarily fragmentary. Berelson and Salter's [21] analysis of magazine fiction involving minority groups finds, under the overtly egalitarian "messages," the expression of stereotyped relationships and views of life that "serve to activate the predispositions of a hostile or even an indifferent audience." Smythe [22] observes similar implicit patterns in his study of television drama.

20. Edgar Dale, *The Content of Motion Pictures* (Macmillan, New York, 1935).

21. Bernard Berelson and Patricia Salter, "Majority and Minority Americans; An analysis of Magazine Fiction," *Public Opinion Quarterly*, vol. 10, 1946, pp. 168–190.

22. D. W. Smythe, "Reality as Presented by Television," *Public Opinion Quarterly*, vol. 18, 1954, pp. 143–156.

Head [23] concludes his study of television drama with the additional observation that as a conserver of the status quo television may be a prime contributor to growing cultural inertia. Lowenthal [24] notes in his study of magazine biographies an emphasis upon the private lives of "idols of consumption," indicating a shift from concern with social problems of production to uniformly individualized pressures of consumption. Implicit class bias is observed in the Bush and Bullock study of "Names in the News";[25] in Sussman's analysis of "Labor in the Radio News";[26] in

Auster's "Content Analysis of 'Little Orphan Annie'";[27] and in the Spiegelman, Terwilliger, Fearing research on comic strips.[28] An audit [29] of 995 movies reviewed in *Variety* between 1953 and 1957 finds four of the five films dealing with organized labor presenting an unsavory view of unions (with the fifth banned from major theaters across the country).

Hamilton [30] traces the rise of pessimism in widely circulated Protestant sermons, especially in regard to the solution of social problems. Albig [31] finds similar value judgments implicit even in the current trend of opinion research, reflecting a "denigration of the average individual, a belaboring of his obvious lack of knowledge and information, and therefore, a skepticism concerning many aspects of political democracy."

Saenger [32] finds the undercurrent of hostility a dominant note in "Male and Female Relations in the American Comic Strip," and suggests

23. Sidney W. Head, "Content Analysis of Television Drama Programs," *The Quarterly of Film, Radio, and Television,* vol. 9, 1954, pp. 175–194.

24. Leo Lowenthal, "Biographies in Popular Magazines," in *Radio Research, 1942–43* (Harper, New York, 1944).

25. Chilton R. Bush and Robert K. Bullock, "Names in the News: A Study of Two Dailies," *Journalism Quarterly,* vol. 29, 1952, pp. 148–157.

26. Leila Sussman, "Labor in the Radio News: An Analysis of Content," *Journalism Quarterly,* September 1945.

27. Donald Auster, "A Content Analysis of 'Little Orphan Annie,'" *Social Problems,* vol. 2, July 1954, pp. 26–33.

28. Marvin Spiegelman, Carl Terwilliger, and Franklin Fearing, "The Content of Comic Strips: A Study of a Mass Medium of Communication," and "The Content of Comics: Goals and Means to Goals of Comic Strip Characters," *Journal of Social Psychology,* vol. 35, 1952, pp. 37–57; vol. 37, 1953, pp. 189–203.

29. Carol A. Cox, "Labor in Motion Pictures," Unpublished research paper (U. of Illinois, Urbana, Ill., Coll. of Journalism and Communication, 1957).

30. Thomas Hamilton, "Social Optimism in American Protestantism," *Public Opinion Quarterly,* vol. 6, 1942, pp. 280–283.

31. William Albig, "Two Decades of Opinion Study: 1936–1956," *Public Opinion Quarterly,* vol. 21, 1957, pp. 14–22.

32. Gerhardt Saenger, "Male and Female Relations to the American Comic Strip," *Public Opinion Quarterly,* vol. 19, 1955, pp. 195–205; see also F. E. Barcus,

the implicit message, "Love is dangerous because it leads to marriage in which . . . men lose their strength." Legman [33] wonders "whether the maniacal fixation on violence and death in all our mass-produced fantasies is a substitution for a censored sexuality, or is, to a greater degree, intended to siphon off—into avenues of perversion opened up by the censorship of sex—the aggression felt by children and adults against the social and economic structure. . . ."

Adorno [34] sees popular music joining in a response "manipulated not only by its promoters, but, as it were, by the inherent nature of the music itself, into a system of response-mechanisms wholly antagonistic to the ideal of individuality in a free, liberal society. . . ." In another connection [35] he writes: "Mass media . . . consist of various layers of meaning superimposed on one another. . . . As a matter of fact, the hidden message may be more important that the overt since this hidden message will escape the controls of consciousness, will not be 'looked through,' will not be warded off by sales resistance, but is likely to sink into the spectator's mind." He finds that the underlying " 'message' of adjustment and unreflecting obedience seems to be dominant and all-pervasive today." His analysis of popular fiction concludes that:

> . . . The ideals of conformity and conventionalism were inherent in popu-lar novels from the very beginning. Now, however, these ideals have been translated into rather clear-cut prescriptions of what to do and what not to do. . . . True, conflicts of the nineteenth century type—such as women run-ning away from their husbands, the drabness of provincial life, and daily chores —occur frequently in today's magazine stories. However, with a regularity which challenges quantitative treatment, these conflicts are decided in favor of the very same conditions from which these women want to break away. The stories teach their readers that one has to be "realistic," that one has to adjust oneself at any price. . . .

Schramm's [36] quantitative analysis of the "World of the Confession Magazine" substantiates the observation of a punitive, puritanical code hidden in overtly rebellious themes. "It is very interesting," he notes, "to

The World of the Sunday Comics," in David M. White and Robert H. Abel (eds.), *The Funnies: An American Idiom* (Free Press, New York, 1963).

33. Gerson Legman, *Love and Death* (Breaking Point Press, New York, 1949).

34. T. W. Adorno, "On Popular Music," *Studies in Philosophy and Social Science,* vol. 9, 1941, pp. 17–47.

35. T. W. Adorno, "How to Look at Television," *The Quarterly of Film, Radio, and Television,* vol. 8, 1954, pp. 213–236.

36. Wilbur Schramm, "World of the Confession Magazine," U. of Illinois Institute of Communications Research, Urbana, Ill., 1955 (mimeographed).

see how 'romance' magazines basically advise young women to shake the dew out of their eyes and the dreams out of their heads."

A recent study by the present author [37] attempted to trace the consequential meaning and social role of the "confession" magazine from industrial structure to content and cover design. The social mission of that magazine was found to be determined from the outset by its competitive position in a wage-earning reader market. This circumstance led to the development of an editorial prescription designed for working class women with presumably middle class pocketbooks, anxieties, and "behavior problems."

The social appeal of the "confession" story pivots on the heroine's human frailties in an inhospitable world she cannot fully understand. The "truth" of this world is brought home through an inevitable encounter with sin, crime, suffering, and the final coming to terms (but never to grips) with the stern code of society. In the context of the unyielding hazards and fears of pseudo-middle class life, the heroine's "sinful" acts become irrelevant as acts of protest. The safety valve of individual adjustment and social unrelatedness furnishes the antidote for the social appeal of sympathy for simple human beings facing their brutal world.

The ingredient of unrelatedness seems to be further manifested in the implicit structure of the "confession" cover design. Shaped by both editorial requirements and the pressures of supermarket distribution, the "confession" cover design generally features a wholesome, innocent-looking, radiantly carefree cover girl, wholly unrelated to the fear-and-sin-ridden world of verbal titles surrounding her on the cover.

An experimental study [38] of subject responses to the image of the cover girl seemed to indicate that her unrelated juxtaposition serves well the requirements of the "confession" market and distribution. While the cover girl's involvement with the social issues of her verbal context is outwardly as unconscious as that of the heroine is inwardly unreflecting, her implicit association with the verbal context of the cover safely enhances, as if by contrast, some of the perceived attractions of her image.

37. George Gerbner, "The Social Role of the Confession Magazine," *Social Problems*, vol. 6, Summer 1958, pp. 29–40.

38. George Gerbner, "The Social Anatomy of the Romance-Confession Cover Girl," *Journalism Quarterly*, vol. 35, no. 3, 1958, pp. 299–307.

THE CHALLENGE FOR CRITICAL ANALYSIS

"The knowledgeable man in the genuine public is able to turn his personal troubles into social issues, to see their relevance for his community and his community's relevance for them," wrote Mills[39] in comparing the individual in a community of publics with members of audiences created as markets for cultural mass production. "The individual," he wrote,

understands that what he thinks and feels as personal troubles are very often not only that but problems shared by others and indeed not subject to solution by one individual but only by modifications of the structure of the groups in which he lives and sometimes the structure of the entire society.

Men in masses are gripped by personal troubles, but they are not aware of their true meaning and source. Men in public confront issues, and they are aware of their terms. It is the task of the liberal institution, as of liberally educated man, continually to translate troubles into issues and issues into the terms of their human meaning for the individual. . . .

The case for self-government is predicated upon a community of publics. The dissolution of publics into markets for mass media conceived and conducted in the increasingly demanding framework of commodity merchandising is the cultural (and political) specter of our age. This fear is now joined by a growing concern over the trend of social science research, especially in the field of communications. More and more of this research is seen to succumb to the fate of mass media content itself in being implicitly tailored to the specifications of industrial and market operations. Concern "with questions of ethics in relation to the formation and effects of public opinion," wrote William Albig[40] in his review of the research of two decades, ". . . was largely absent, or at least unexpressed, in the writings of . . . contributors to opinion research in the past 20 years." Albig continued:

Since 1920 a large professional class has developed to man the expanding activities of press, film, radio, television. At the same time, commercial and academic analysts of the communication process have proliferated. To a marked extent these professionals discuss this vast communications activity in terms of process, technique, stimuli, impact, effects, and semantic analysis, but not in terms of the ethical and value problems of communications content and effect.

39. C. W. Mills, *The Power Elite* (Oxford, New York, 1956).
40. William Albig, *op. cit.*

It is, then, in this context of fragmentary evidence about the consequential meaning of mass media content, and of growing public and professional concern about its implications for a community of publics (including social scientists) that the challenge emerges. The challenge for mass communications research is this: to combine the empirical methods with the critical aims of social science, to join rigorous practice with value-conscious theory, and thus to gather the insight the knowledgeable individual in a genuine public must have if he is to come to grips (and not unconsciously to terms) with the sweeping undercurrents of his culture.

SELECTED PUBLICATIONS BY DR. GERBNER

Instructional Technology and the Press: A Case Study, Occasional Paper No. 4 (National Educational Association, Washington, D.C., 1962).

"Mass Media Censorship and the Portrayal of Mental Illness: Some Effects of Industry-Wide Controls in Motion Pictures and Television," in Wilbur Schramm (ed.), *Studies of Innovation and of Communication to the Public* (Stanford U. P., Stanford, Calif., 1962). (With Percy H. Tannenbaum.)

"How Teachers Can Respond to the Challenge of Video," *Professional Growth for Teachers,* vol. 7, no. 6, 1962.

"Press Perspectives in World Communications: A Pilot Study," *Journalism Quarterly,* vol. 38, Summer 1961, pp. 313-322.

"Technology, Communication, and Education: A Social Perspective," in *Tomorrow's Teaching* (Frontiers of Science Foundation, Oklahoma City, 1962).

"Regulation of Mental Illness Content in Motion Pictures and Television," *Gazette,* vol. 6, 1961, pp. 365-385. (With Percy H. Tannenbaum.)

"Psychology, Psychiatry and Mental Illness in the Mass Media: A Study of Trends, 1900-1959," *Mental Hygiene,* vol. 45, January 1961, pp. 89-93.

"Mass Communications and the Citizenship of Secondary School Youth," in Franklin Patterson et al., *The Adolescent Citizen* (Free Press, New York, 1960), pp. 179-205.

"The Interaction Model: Perception and Communication," in John Ball and Francis Byrnes (eds.), *Research, Principles, and Practices in Visual Communication* (National Project in Agricultural Communications, East Lansing, Mich., 1960, pp. 4-15.

"The Individual in a Mass Culture," *Saturday Review,* vol. 43, June 18, 1960, pp. 11-13, 36-37; also (abridged) in *The Executive,* vol. 4, 1960, pp. 14-16, and *The National Elementary Principal,* vol. 40, February 1961, pp. 49-54.

"Social Science and the Professional Education of the Audio-Visual Communication Specialist," *AV Communication Review,* vol. 8, no. 5, September-October 1960, pp. 50-58.

"Visual Communication Training: Philosophy and Principles," in *Communication Training* (National Project in Agricultural Communications. East Lansing, Mich., 1960), pp. 29-34.

"Education and the Challenge of Mass Culture," *Audio-Visual Communication Review,* vol. 7, Fall 1959, pp. 264-278.

"Popular Culture and Images of the

Family," *The Chicago Theological Seminary Register,* vol. 49, November 1959, pp. 31–37.

"Mental Illness on Television: A Study of Censorship," *Journal of Broadcasting,* vol. 3, Fall 1959, pp. 292–303.

"The Social Anatomy of the Romance-Confession Cover Girl," *Journalism Quarterly,* vol. 35, Summer 1958, pp. 299–306.

"The Social Role of the Confession Magazine," *Social Problems,* vol. 6, Summer 1958, pp. 29–40.

"Content Analysis and Critical Research in Mass Communication," *Audio-Visual Communication Review,* vol. 6, Spring 1958, pp. 85–108.

"Communication in Christian Education," *Educational Screen,* vol. 36, February, 1957, pp. 78–81. (With John G. Harrell.)

"Toward a General Model of Communication," *Audio-Visual Communication Review,* vol. 4, Summer 1956, pp. 171–199.

"A Study of Audience *'Involvement'* or *'Interest'* in a Training Film" (Air Force Personnel and Training Research Center, 1954). (With Lester F. Beck.)

QUESTIONS

1. Gerbner distinguished between "micro" and "macro" analysis of communication content. Which of the two forms seem most relevant and worthwhile to him?

2. Do you agree with Lowenthal's statement that "objective elements of the social whole are produced and reproduced in the mass media."? Assuming that you were trying to choose examples that exemplified contemporary United States and were asked to place only one moving picture feature, one issue of a magazine, one Sunday newspaper, and one television program (taped) into a time-capsule to be opened in the year 2113, which would you choose?

3. What are the *primary* tasks of the analyst of mass media according to Gerbner? Do you agree with him? Or do you think his approach is too theoretical to afford any practical application?

4. The author feels that the familiar Lasswell paradigm, *"who* says *what* to *whom, how,* and *with what effect"* is too restrictive for critical research. Does his generalized model of communication fulfill the objectives of critical research more effectively? In what ways?

5. Gerbner appears to be taking issue with exponents of general semantics, and implies that although the *word* may not be the *thing,* there is nevertheless an objective historical relationship involved in the act of, say, calling a horse a horse. Would you agree that a too-literal application of the general semanticist's philosophy would destroy any meaningful analysis of content? Explain why or why not.

Bernard Berelson

The State of Communication Research*

WHITE'S COMMENTS on the following essay by Dr. Berelson form the subject of a subsequent paper (pp. 521ff.). Schramm, Riesman, and Bauer each comment upon Berelson's major contention in a series of afterwords appended to the essay itself.

Nevertheless, one could easily devote twice as much space to comments on the Berelson article. It was designed to be provocative, and it succeeded. But enough is as good as a feast; so we will refrain from further comments on Berelson's contribution as such.

We would, however, like to urge scholars and students who read this book to pay particular attention to Riesman's remarks (pp. 512–516). For Riesman here points out one major reason why a subject or a discipline becomes less fun and less exciting as it becomes more "sophisticated" and "developed." The "scientific superego became too harsh," says Riesman; the apparatus of negative criticism becomes a potent weapon for demolishing imaginative and exciting ideas. Very often an undue emphasis upon methodology for its own sake serves to organize and appears to justify such negative criticism. In other words, in the early stages of learning, men are content to have ideas. At a certain point, they learn how not to do things—and since the methodology of warning and inhibition is relatively easy to learn and to communicate while any methodology of creativity and construction needs an extra dash of imagination and insight beyond what can be taught, it is possible that the second and third generation of scholars in many fields get less excitement out of it than did the founders.

This brings us back to Berelson's original comments. Although he states repeatedly that the "great" ideas are somehow missing, he gives us no clearer clue to a great idea than to say it should resemble some ideas of Lasswell's, Hovland's, or Lewin's. But perhaps equally creative, equally promising ideas about communication and public opinion are being published nowadays but are not recognized as such, simply because our apparatus and talent for distinguishing what is

* Reprinted from the *Public Opinion Quarterly,* vol. 23, no. 1, Spring 1959, pp. 1–15 by permission of the authors and the publisher. (Copyright 1959 by Princeton University Press.)

wrong with them is far better than our apparatus for distinguishing what is right. White has chosen to rebut Berelson's claim that there are no more great ideas by saying in effect that while Lasswell, Lazarsfeld, Lewin, and Hovland stood out in their time as giants because there were so few to compete, now there are many significant contributors in a great field, and naturally no one or two or three or four stand out so clearly. This writer would not altogether accept this claim; he suspects that in the light of hindsight, there are some few who will in the future stand out as significant contributors of real stature. One is reminded of Kipling's poem about the suburban commuters who worried and complained that "romance was dead" but "all unseen, Romance brought up the 9:15 train." Conversely, it is worth reminding ourselves that the leading journal in his field reviewed Lasswell's first great book, World Politics and Personal Insecurity, by comparing it to a "flock of sparrows at a horse show dropping their dung over the fair city of academic political science." [1] Evidently, not all his contemporaries immediately recognized Lasswell's greatness.

The moral which Riesman draws from this sort of event is, we believe, worth thinking about: "Be intellectually adventurous. Don't worry too much about academic neatness and precision." Riesman fears that "too sophisticated" and inbred an emphasis upon methodology and research technology and bibliography will lead us to be afraid of taking the risks of creativity. His remarks are in effect an exhortation, urging that we be willing to listen to and construct unorthodox and unfashionable theories and to work with their consequences; great ideas normally originate with persons able and willing to take this sort of risk, and fortunate enough to have near them a few individuals who encourage them.   L. A. D.

DR. BERNARD BERELSON is currently Director of the Communication Research Program of the Population Council. Previously, he was Director of the Bureau of Applied Social Research at Columbia University. He has also been Dean of the Graduate Library School at the University of Chicago, where he received his doctorate.

WILBUR L. SCHRAMM is Director of the Institute of Communications Research at Stanford University. Several of his publications are cited in our bibliographic appendix.

1. From the review by Walter L. Whittlesey (Princeton University) of Lasswell's *World Politics and Personal Insecurity, American Political Science Review,* vol. 29, 1935, pp. 500 501. Whittlesey also speaks of Lasswell's including "everything from here to there" with "the sagacious irresponsibility of William E. Borah in a mental health canned goods store," and refers to the point of view as being that of "Hobbes on a hog basis" and of the book as containing chiefly "anfractuosities of dialectical metaphysics" containing what everybody knows anyway but in language no one can understand.

DAVID RIESMAN, *Ford Professor in Social Relations at Harvard University, is the senior author of* The Lonely Crowd *and several other works dealing with mass communication and education, including* Abundance for What? *(Doubleday, New York, 1963), much of which deals with the problems of communication.*

RAYMOND A. BAUER'S *career and publications are described on pp. 125, 138.*

My theme is that, as for communication research, the state is withering away.

The modern version of communication research began about twenty-five years ago with the development of both academic and commercial interest—the former largely coordinated, if not stimulated, by the Rockefeller Foundation seminar of the late 1930s and the latter developed in response to radio's need to prove its audience. Since then there has been a great deal of research activity on both fronts, so much so that for a time the field exhibited many of the characteristics of a scientific fad. What has it all come to and where do we now stand?

THE PAST

In the past twenty-five years or so, there have been four major approaches to communication research, and perhaps six minor ones. The four major approaches are so well characterized by their leading proponents that it is convenient and revealing here to identify them by name, as in the chart below. In my view, the major lines of inquiry have been the political approach, represented by Lasswell; the sample survey approach, represented by Lazarsfeld; the small-groups approach, represented by Lewin; and the experimental approach, represented by Hovland. (Whether Lewin really should be counted as a student of "communication research" is a matter of definition with which I am not particularly concerned here.) Lasswell, with his interest in broad socio-political considerations, represents a macrocosmic line; Lazarsfeld and Hovland, with their interest in indvidual responses, represent a microcosmic line; and Lewin, with his interest in the social group, represents something in between.

Table 1 indicates some major characteristics of the four approaches, their similarities and their differences. I shall not elaborate on that presentation except to point out how much of what these innovators did, and the ways they did it, was determined by their disciplinary bases; and to observe that despite their differences in starting point and in methods, their findings have many, and sometimes striking, similarities. Moral:

The subject matter or the problem triumphs over the approach and the method.

If these are the [four] major figures and lines of inquiry of the past quarter century, there have been several minor approaches—"minor" not necessarily because they will turn out historically to be less important, but simply because they seem to me to have been less influential in the past twenty years or so. They are the following:

Table 1—Lines of Inquiry of Four

Innovator	Representative Titles	Base	Interest
1. Lasswell early 1930s	*World Revolutionary Propaganda* *The Language of Politics*	Political science	Broad politico-historical approach Concern with power
2. Lazarsfeld late 1930s	*The People's Choice* *Communication Research . . .* *Voting*	Social psychology moving toward Sociology	Specific short-range, empirical problems; tie to market research Concern with audience and effect
3. Lewin late 1930s	*Informal Social Communication* (by his students)	Experimental psychology moving toward Social psychology	Personal relations in small groups Concern with influence and communication therein
4. Hovland early 1940s	*Communication and Persuasion* *Experiments in Mass Communication*	Experimental psychology moving toward Social psychology	Psychological analysis of effects

[5] The reformist approach: represented by the Commission on the Freedom of the Press. Concerned with organization, structure, and control of the mass media, and particularly with considerations of public policy. Characterized by commercial hostility on the one hand and academic disinterest on the other (except for schools of journalism; the academic departments apparently found this too value-ridden, and hence not "science").

Innovators in Communication Research

Typical Categories	Materials and Methods	Typical Propositions
Fact and value statements Symbols of identification (i.e., political)	Documentary Content analysis	"Propaganda pushes the intensity of the situation to extremes: facilitates catharsis if interest is low, and precipitates crisis if interest is high." "Political symbols circulating among the power holders correspond more closely to the power facts than do symbols presented to the domain."
Demographic and "questionnaire" categories Social position of respondent and his attitudes (i.e., sociological)	Mass responses; interview in field; sample survey Natural setting approximated	People tend to expose to communications whose content is congenial to their predispositions. Communication exposure "pushes" people to a decision, but mainly in line with their latent attitudes.
Autocratic and democratic leadership; press toward uniformity within group (i.e., psychological)	Individual behavior under group pressures Experimental settings, quasi-natural	Pressure to communicate within a group on a given topic increases with the discrepancy within the group, the cohesiveness of the group, and the relevance of the issue to group morale. Pressure to communicate to a given individual within a group decreases to the extent the member is not wanted in the group.
Characteristics of message and effect, e.g., type of appeal, one-sidedness, source credibility, sleeper, boomerang	Psychological processes Experiments in laboratory	One-sided communications are more effective with those initially favoring the position taken; both-sided communications are more effective with those initially opposed. Recall of factual material fades with time, but initial opinion changes are strengthened, especially when in line with prevailing group attitude (sleeper effect).

[6] The broad historical approach: represented by David Riesman and Harold Innis. Again, the field's question has been: Is it science?

[7] The journalistic approach: represented by the professional schools and such people as Casey, Nixon, Schramm, and others. Concern with control aspects of the media, characteristics of communicators, and "practical" interests. Close to the reformist approach, as, for example, in Schramm's valuable analysis of ethical responsibility in mass communications.

[8] The mathematical approach: represented by Shannon and Weaver.

[9] The psycho-linguistic approach: represented by Osgood and Miller.

[10] The psychiatric approach: represented by Ruesch and Bateson.

In the last three, the term "communication" carries different meanings and leads to different problems. In each case, there was considerable hope and some expectation that these approaches would represent new major lines of inquiry, or would at least fortify the old. But also in each case, there has been less help, and even less contact, than envisaged in the first wave of enthusiasm (or perhaps I should say, by the first wave of enthusiasts).

THE CONTRIBUTION

If this is a reasonably fair description of what has happened in communication research in the past two decades or so, how is it to be judged? As far as their contribution to our knowledge of communications is concerned, I believe that the first three are playing out: the innovators have left or are leaving the field, and no ideas of comparable scope and generating power are emerging. The expansion of the field to new centers has certainly slowed down and perhaps even stopped; the Committee on Communication at my own university is in process of dissolution. Some of the newer places are currently repeating what the pioneering places did years ago and are now disappointed with.

Lewin is dead. Lasswell and Lazarsfeld have moved on to other interests, the former to large considerations within political science and the latter to mathematical applications and professional training for social research. Hovland himself may now be moving toward broader issues of cognition and machine simulations. Most of Lasswell's students are no longer working in this field; Lewin's and Lazarsfeld's are, but they seem not to be making a systematic effort to fill in the initiator's picture, or not succeeding at it, and, in any case, not yet going far beyond the master's innovating ideas. The work of Hovland and his associates, for example, is a refinement on the similar studies of Thurstone in the late 1920s, and is providing the field with a body of solid, empirical data; but the approach involves attention to so many detailed variables that one cannot easily see the end of the line, given the enormous number of comparable variables still to be taken into account.

The observation that this is the typical result of inbred fields, that the concern with communication was too narowly conceived, is, I think, not really applicable here. In my view, Lazarsfeld was the only one of the four who centered on communication problems *per se:* Lasswell was interested in political power, Lewin in group functioning, and Hovland in cognitive processes, and they utilized this field as a convenient entry to these broader concerns.

It would be wrong to think that this is an unimportant field with unimportant investigators in it. When the history of the behavioral sciences for this period is written, there is no question that these four figures will receive major attention for their contributions as well as for what they represent.

THE FUTURE

Where do we go from here? Communication research has had a distinguished past, but what about its future? I am not clear about what the next steps will be, let alone what they ought to be, but I think I can see seven current lines of which some may develop into the major focuses of the years ahead as Lasswell-Lazarsfeld-Lewin-Hovland did for the years past. In no particular order, they are:

[1] Combinations. For example, the current MIT program might be considered a combination of Lasswell and Lazarsfeld lines (both men were on the original advisory committee), plus some small-group and experimental inquiries. As another example, a few years ago the Committee on Communication at the University of Chicago was contemplating a program centering on standards of evaluation for the mass media that could be seen as a combination of the Lazarsfeld and reformist approaches.

[2] Comparative studies. An increase in recent years in studies of international communication is quite likely to continue in the years ahead. Most such work, however, seems to have been in the nature of geographical rather than conceptual or intellectual extension.

[3] Economic analysis. There are those who argue persuasively that the application of economic tools of analysis to communication problems will be particularly rewarding. For example, at different times, Douglas Waples and Daniel Lerner were working on a model of the economic (and social) factors necessary to bring into being a mass communication

system. Or, since so many programs for reform flounder on the rock of economic necessity, some beginning efforts are now being made to subject the economic factors to traditional economic analysis, for example, the costs of newspaper advertising, which have important implications for the size of the paper, the ratio of advertising to news and comment, etc. As a final example in a closely related field, see Anthony Downs on an economic theory of democracy (first in the *Journal of Political Economy,* vol. 65, 1957, pp. 135–150, later in book form, *An Economic Theory of Democracy,* Harper, New York, 1957).

[4] Sociohistorical analysis. By this term I mean attention to "the big issues" without direct and immediate regard to the detailed, empirical underpinning. David Riesman and others have made important contributions along this line already, as a counterbalance to the minute and atomistic inquiry, and I look forward to more such studies in the future.

[5] Popular culture. Some interests that earlier would have been called communication are now being followed up under this heading. With aesthetic aspects emphasized, the field has a chance to get some help from humanistic studies, and the cooperation ought to be stimulating. Communication problems have been reflected on a great deal in the past—by very good minds—and such reflection should have a good deal to say to the modern empirical researcher.

[6] *Mass* communication. Such "new generation" sociologists as James Coleman and William McPhee tell me that the first word needs more emphasis relative to the second. Their position is that the field is better seen as one of a variety of *mass* activities and that headway will be made by stressing the similarities of such mass phenomena rather than the particularities attaching to a mass communication system. That is, the oblique attack may yield more than the frontal.

[7] Practical affairs. One way an intellectual field can advance is by dealing directly with the theoretical problems of the discipline itself. Another is by dealing with practical problems to which the discipline can contribute answers. The former is the academic approach and the latter the professional. Of our four major figures, Lasswell, Lewin, and Hovland were primarily concerned with academic matters, and only Lazarsfeld was sometimes concerned with professional problems. A practical, or more professional, turn may now be indicated.

In sum, then, it seems to me that "the great ideas" that gave the field of communication research so much vitality ten and twenty years ago have to a substantial extent worn out. No new ideas of comparable magnitude have appeared to take their place. We are on a plateau of research development, and have been for some time. There are two ways to look at this phenomenon, assuming that it is correctly gauged. One is to regret that no new "breakthrough" has developed in recent years; the other is to be grateful that the field has a period of time to assimilate, incorporate, and exploit the imaginative innovations of the major figures. The reader reads the journals; he can take his choice.

COMMENTS BY WILBUR SCHRAMM

When one has been pronounced dead, it is ungracious to rise and make comments. Indeed, it shows a certain lack of faith in the attending physician. Nothing is farther from my wishes than to show any lack of faith in my friend Bernard Berelson, and therefore if he pronounces us dead I am content to believe him.

But it is a somewhat livelier condition than I had anticipated. I have just come from the doctoral examination of a young man who demonstrated depth in psychology, sociology, mathematics, and research method, as well as a deep interest in communication problems, and is clearly better prepared to undertake communication research than, fifteen years ago, almost anyone was. Yesterday I had lunch with a psychologist and a sociologist, Charles Osgood and Morris Janowitz, who have recently made major contributions to communication research: an instrument for the measurement of meaning, and an analysis of the communicating organization. I am about to go to a seminar in which scholars from eight countries will be discussing national differences in the communication system. On the way to my office, just now, I was waylaid by an eager young research man who wanted to tell me of a new finding he has made concerning the messages that are received beneath the threshold of conscious perception. In other words, I can't find the rigor mortis in this field and am led to wonder whether Dr. Berelson might have missed a tiny surge of pulse in the body, or even examined the wrong victim.

If I read Dr. Berelson's coroner's report accurately, we are dead in comparison to Lasswell, Lazarsfeld, Lewin, and Hovland. That is a pretty rough test. These were (still *are,* in the case of three of them) truly remarkable men. Not only were they great producers in their own right; they were also great "starters." They had the ability to inspire in others a fierce drive for new knowledge, and they cast out hundreds of ideas which later flowered in activities and publications. In fact, I think the greater importance of these men may prove to be, not what they themselves did, but what they got started.

Of course, the second party up Everest, the second man to fly an airplane, always moves in the shadow of the first. The geometrists who followed Lobachewsky and Riemann must have felt the cooling shadow of those founding fathers. But, on the other hand, no inferiority feelings kept Einstein from taking Riemann's geometry into certain realms which the founder had hardly contemplated. In a sense, the summit in study of the blood was reached by Harvey and all later research was a downhill grade; but that has not made blood chemistry a dead field.

Three of the "founding fathers" of communication research are still alive and active, and it is rather early, even embarrassing, to talk about what has followed them. But at least we can say that not all has been quiet in their footsteps. The Illinois conference on content analysis in 1955 demonstrated that even this relatively quiet subject had moved beyond where Lasswell had carried it. I suspect that Lazarsfeld was proud of his former students who studied the diffusion of new knowledge amongst physicians. From the founding father Lewin to his pupil Festinger I observe no diminuation of research insight and ingenuity. And one can name many important communication experiments in attitude change that have been done away from Yale.

Dr. Berelson may have been handicapped in his diagnosis by his logical insistence on dividing all Gaul into three parts. Thus he names four "approaches"—the Lasswell, Lazarsfeld, Lewin, and Hovland lines —and six "minor approaches," ranging from reform to psychiatry. But what does he mean by approaches? Well, he says, there are "the political approach, represented by Lasswell; the sample survey approach, represented by Lazarsfeld; the small-groups approach, represented by Lewin; and the experimental approach, represented by Hovland." The argument is that these approaches are "playing out," and that therefore the outlook is dark for communication research.

Does this not confuse men with method? There is no question that we now know how to make more reliable sample surveys than Lazarsfeld made in his great years of director of the Bureau of Applied Social Research, but we can't always construct surveys with the insight that Lazarsfeld displayed. Similarly, the experimental method is older than Hovland and will live longer, but not everbody can pick his experimental problem as skillfully as Hovland does. The political approach is a state of mind, rather than a method, and men trained in political science are now picking up some of the tools of quantitative research and beginning to contribute in the areas to which Lasswell first called attention.

What we observe in this young field is precisely what we observe in natural history—the increasing shuffledness which Eddington calls the law that "entropy always increases." These so-called "approaches" tend to be combined in the same man. Hovland's own *Communication and Persuasion* contains a large amount of small-group research, which is supposedly Lewin's "approach." The MIT program in international communication, although strongly influenced by Lasswell and "the political approach," uses both experiment and sample survey, in the spirit of Lazarsfeld and Hovland. Whereas the Bureau of Applied Social Research did indeed for a time specialize in the sample survey, newer centers, like those at Stanford and Illinois, use the sample survey, the experiment, and small-group research side by side, and, along with them, other tools like the semantic differential and depth psychology. Thus the "approach" changes with the field. All that was really unique to Lazarsfeld's approach was Lazarsfeld. If he were starting today, he would doubtless make another "approach," which he would illuminate with his remarkable combination of insight, vigor, and skill. It makes little sense to say of the "founding fathers" that their "approach" is playing out. It is something like saying that personality psychology is playing out because Freud is dead, and who is there in sight to compare with him?

We sometimes forget that communication research is a field, not a discipline. In the study of man, it is one of the great crossroads where many pass but few tarry. Scholars come into it from their own disciplines, bringing valuable tools and insights, and later go back, like Lasswell, to the more central concerns of their disciplines. Merton studies the Kate Smith broadcasts, and returns to the grand architecture of social theory. Festinger studies communication situations on the way to a theory of cognitive process. Only a relatively few scholars, and those in the last decade or so, have seen fit so to dedicate themselves to communication research that they have equipped themselves with the combination of several social sciences, mathematics, and research method that a man requires to see the field steadily and see it whole. For most scholars who work in communication, the field forces itself on them because some of its problems must be solved before their own discipline will be fully understood. Therefore, we must not look for the unique theory in communication which we are accustomed to see in disciplines, or the kind of career in communication research which we are accustomed to see within disciplines. The test of health will be whether the horizon recedes, and whether the growing knowledge of communication process and institutions contributes to the knowledge of man and society.

In twenty years communication research has made solid contributions to our understanding of one of the fundamental social processes. It is having a profound effect on the teaching of journalism and other mass communication subjects in our universities, because it has made a bridge between the professional or trade activities of these schools and the ancient and intellectual strengths of the university. It is having an effect also on the concept and teaching of subjects like political science. In half a dozen places in this country, it has drawn together, formally or informally, a group of social scientists dedicated to communication research who contribute to each other knowledge and insights from their disciplines. As we noted, it has led a certain number of young scholars to acquire almost equal competence in psychology and sociology, or politics and psychology, or other such combinations which they felt were necessary in order to work in this broad field. By so doing, and by calling attention to problems and propositions which are broader than disciplines, it has brought a little closer the day when we may have a science of man.

Communication research may be already old enough for us to talk about the great times that used to be, and the giants that once walked the earth, as Dr. Berelson talks about them. But I find it an extraordinarily vital field at the moment, with a competent and intellectually eager group of young researchers facing a challenging set of problems. Who will make the adequate two-person model of communication we need? Who will analyze the communication organization? Who will clarify the economics of mass communication? Who will make sense of the communication "system"? Who will untangle the skein of motivations and gratifications related to mass media use on which a long line of distinguished researchers, including Dr. Berelson, have worked? Who will find out what television is doing to children or, better, what children do with television? Who is going to clarify the diffusion of ideas in a society, or the relation of public opinion to political process?

Let's get on with the problems!

COMMENTS BY DAVID RIESMAN

I first heard Bernard Berelson expound his pessimism concerning the state of the art of communications research when we were both lecturing in a staff seminar of the Committee on Communications at the University of Chicago half a dozen years ago. I thought at that time that there was a possibly self-fulfilling element in his remarks—a danger that students, often already anxious about a borderline field, would lose the little confidence they already had. If the work done so far by the great men who opened up the field had so quickly run into sand, what could be expected of their own miniscule endeavors? While a more rebellious and ripsnorting student body might have reacted by saying, in effect, "I'll show him," Mr. Berelson's views seemed so reasonable, and his claims so modest, as not to invite this sort of counterattack.

In this situation, I recall saying to the students something like this: "Robert Merton in *Mass Persuasion* got a few people out into the field after a fabulous event, collected a hundred interviews, and wrote a notable book. Isn't it nice to be in a field where there is so much material, and so little known about it and done about it, that this can be done?

Isn't Merton's book a standing invitation for many analogous studies: on fan mail, on reactions to films, on political rallies—just as his later work is an invitation to the study of cosmopolitans and locals in institutional as well as geographical settings? Indeed, how many books of the directness and immediacy of *Mass Persuasion* are to be found in other subfields of the social sciences?

"And isn't Mr. Berelson judging contemporary work too readily by the standards of founding fathers who could, in turn, be belittled by comparison with Freud or Aristotle? Lasswell was stimulated by Freud, not obliterated by him—and many have been stimulated by Lasswell [the Program at MIT and the work there of such admirers of Lasswell as Ithiel Pool and Daniel Lerner, which includes not only research on communications in the less electronic countries, but also research on audience reactions, journalistic attitudes, and so forth, seems to me to have been given much too shadowy treatment in Mr. Berelson's paper]. The influence of these progenitors spreads even beyond the boundaries of Mr. Berelson's cineramic view: thus, the magazine *Explorations,* published at the University of Toronto, is a more liberating and lively adventure in mass communications and popular culture than one would gather if one's criterion is the too-frontal one of 'breakthroughs.'

"Work in the field of communications is inviting, at the moment, because of its very ambiguity and lack of structure. It is a somewhat transient waystation where people can meet who don't quite want to commit themselves to the field of literature (as monopolized by English departments) or to the social sciences (as monopolized by departments of sociology or political science)—and, as Mr. Berelson indicates, there is also room for people with an interest in economics and aesthetics. Some of the very best students, and some of the very worst, are attracted by the ability to delay a commitment to one of the established powers of academia. Some institutional rubric is necessary to protect them from those powers and, correspondingly, from the definitions of success or productivity emanating from them. I referred above to *Mass Persuasion* and what could be done with one hundred interviews. In Leo Lowenthal's famous essay in which he traced the shift from heroes of production to heroes of consumption in just two popular magazines, what was necessary was not an elaborate project but a good idea and a library. In Wolfenstein's and Leites' book on the movies (which Mr. Berelson might perhaps not consider as communications research) what was necessary was again a relatively manageable and highly visible amount of data."

It is in some such terms as these, at once hortatory and hopeful, that I sought to persuade Mr. Berelson's audience to be enough provoked by him to prove him wrong. Now, however, looking at the matter again,

I am struck by the fact that Mr. Berelson seems to have been proven right by developments, or the lack of them, since then. Moreover, what he says in this article concerning research on communication could hold *pari passu* for other large, exciting, and amorphous fields, such as culture-and-personality, institutional economics (except with respect to the so-called underdeveloped countries), and the kind of critique of character and society which reached its high point with *The Authoritarian Personality* and other volumes in the Study of Prejudice series. In each of these fields, including communications, two developments occurred simultaneously. In the first place, the initial studies with their methodological messiness, their often grandiose generalizations, and their obvious political biases, were met with a barrage of conscientious criticism. And whereas when novelists are criticized by literary critics they can often brush the attacks off because they do not always move in the same circles and share the same coterie values, most of the authors of the works criticized moved in the same circles as their critics and had internalized many of their values. In the dialectic between impulsivity and restraint, the scientific superego became too harsh—a development that was particularly effective in intimidating adventurous research, because the young were learning more about methodological pitfalls than had their elders—from precisely such mentors as Mr. Berelson.

The second development was the opening up of fields of theoretical work which offered at once quick payoffs for the capable student and elegant models for the meek and timid. A book like *The Invasion from Mars* looks sloppy in comparison with the work of Carl Hovland and his students—just as in economics work on linear programming and various forms of model building is both neater and quicker than the sorts of inquiry that, for instance, Walton Hamilton pursued; and, in anthropology, studies of kinship or linguistics have a clarity lacking in most studies of culture-and-personality or national character.

There is the further advantage to these new fields that they almost guarantee that the effort expended by a talented researcher will not be wasted, but will produce something, whereas a study that goes out into the field to discover something new, empirically, may or may not produce "findings": thus, the economist who would take time off from reading Paul Samuelson to spend two years as assistant comptroller observing concrete decision processes in a particular company might fear that he would have nothing of general interest to show when he came back from his field trip, just as a student of mass communications might fear that he could study a particular campaign in the field and, by the luck of the draw, not add anything to *The People's Choice* or *Voting*. One has to have almost a tropism toward unprocessed data, a passionate curiosity about what is going on, in order to endure the insecurity and lack of structure of pioneering field work.

Consider the situation of sociology in Poland today. The practitioners, old and young alike, have a sense of revolutionary ferment even though their intellectual equipment comes largely from the very sources Mr. Berelson feels have now run out in this country. It is a political act to collect facts in Poland: paradoxically, dictatorship has made it possible to revive the spirit of the Enlightenment. And a great majority of the editors of the now suppressed paper *Pro Prostu* (which played such a great part in the anti-Stalinist movement in Poland) were, I am told, sociologists and sociology students.

In this country, it would seem, we are too sophisticated to be enlightened. Mr. Berelson points to the decline of reformist concerns as represented by the Commission on the Freedom of the Press. Yet we face a situation today in the cold war where the press, while no longer "yellow" in the old-fashioned sense, has become more and more ethnocentric and nationalistic ("white"?) at the very moment when the educated population seems to be becoming more world-minded. How is this to be explained? What can be done about it? Samuel Lubell, with old-fashioned door-to-door methods (he is the Fuller brush man of mass communications) has tried to sort out the impact of ethnic heritage, ideologies of status, and economic orientations, in order to help explain the persistence of isolationism and the uneven impact of the media of public information. But we need many more one-man investigations such as his. So too, we are but at the threshold if we ask: What is the the impact on Americans of advertising, not in terms of this sale or that choice, but in terms of the visual and literary landscape of America; or: Is there a difference in the Rorschach and TAT responses of those who have been exposed to the modern media and those who have not; or, in general: In what way do the media affect the way we see each other, the landscape, or cities and objects of consumption? Donald Horton recently analyzed the way popular songs provide a language of courtship for teenagers—again a small-scale study without apparatus—and we would understand a lot if we knew some of the kinesic consequences of the way people look and talk in our magazines, movies, and television. In an early paper, Berelson and Salter studied the way popular magazines portrayed, or underplayed, "majority" and "minority" Americans. Today we must ask whether the spectrum has increased in ethnic tolerance—think of Desi Arnaz, Frank Sinatra, Leonard Bernstein, and other leading heroes of popular culture— while at the same time eliminating regional and other parochial variations, so that mass media, even more than hitherto, are creating a homogeneous national culture? Is there, as a result, a decline of interest in local elections, or at least local issues? And is this national consciousness one factor which both intensifies the cold war and results from it?

And what of the long-term growth of cynicism that may be one consequence of early exposure and over-exposure to the mass media? Cannot we interpret *Personal Influence* as meaning that people are afraid of being gulled by distant persuaders despite all the efforts at folksiness and "para-social" intimacy the media make, so that they will only open themselves up to people they know personally and not vicariously? What is the image of the world of a young person today who has watched television commercials—both those so labeled and those not so labeled—since before he could read?

Large-scale questions such as these can still be approached by small-scale empirical sorties. The very omnipresence of the media means that no student is so distant from "sources" that he cannot go down to the local movie house and apply some very rudimentary techniques of "mass observation," or the more refined approaches of Lloyd Warner and William Henry, or Herta Herzog, in their studies of the audiences of soap opera. Such work is "middle level" in the two senses that it does not begin with large conceptual schemes or large data-gathering systems. But, returning to Merton's *Mass Persuasion* again, I see no reason why large implications cannot be drawn, with all appropriate diffidence, from small samples or from the description of an event. The comparison by Kurt and Gladys Lang of the impression given on TV of General MacArthur's hero's welcome in Chicago and the observed behavior of the crowds at the airport and on the streets is a good example.

I doubt if it is helpful to students to blame them for the inhibitions they have learned from their highly competent professors. But it may help to remind them that there is class persuasion as well as mass persuasion and that conceptual schemes, while essential and inevitable, can serve to alienate the worker from his material as well as to bring him closer to it— much as I suspect that the sophisticated visual imagery in the advertisements of the *New Yorker* infiltrates the way we assimilate the ideas in the magazine's columns and cartoons and stories and, hence, even how we read the *P.O.Q.!*

COMMENTS BY RAYMOND A. BAUER

Without checking with the other commentators on Berelson's stimulating paper, I am willing to predict that all of us will take the same basic line: Berelson paints an overly pessimistic picture of the future of communications research. This is the only gambit he has left open to us.

Certainly he is right in his general contention that the lines of demarcation within the field and at its boundaries have become less clearly defined. Psycholinguists such as George Miller have had a lively interest in information theory. Reformers have done content analysis (although almost always with too little awareness of the limitations of imputing effect from content). "Journalists" such as Schramm have shown a liking for the cybernetic model of communications. Lewin and his students, as Berelson points out, did work that was only marginally classifiable as "communications." Lazarsfeld's disciples are knee-deep in sociometry and social structure. And Lasswellians are doing sample surveys. In industrial sociology, the word "communications" is bandied about quite freely, but it is difficult to tell where "communications" stop and the general process of personal interaction begins. Ruesch and Bateson say they are studying "communications," but at times it is impossible to differentiate what they do from what most psychiatrists and anthropologists would do under different labels. Personally I have found it extremely difficult to distinguish properly the boundaries between a "communications" problem and basic work done on cognition, remembering, personal influence, and reference groups.[1]

If we look at Berelson's own phrase, "the state is withering away," we may agree that it has become more difficult to demarcate the external boundaries of the state and to distinguish clearly the subdivisions within the state. But this does not mean necessarily that the state is atrophying. It may mean that it has expanded, developed, and differentiated in the way of mature organisms (to mix a metaphor).

One of the reasons that I find it difficult to lament the absence of "the great ideas" in present-day communications research is that, with the possible exception of some of Lasswell's work, the early period was not marked by great *ideas* but by diverse methodological approaches to the large common area of communications: content analysis, survey research, small-group dynamics, and systematic psychological experimentation. Each of these approaches was exploited to the point where both its advantages and limitations were revealed. As this has happened, the center of gravity has shifted from the exploitation of a method to the substance of problems which demand diverse methods for their exploitation.

This trend may be illustrated by a number of examples, the most familiar of which has already been eloquently reported in Katz and Lazarsfeld, *Personal Influence*,[2] and is reflected in the more recent studies

1. Cf. Raymond A. Bauer, "The Communicator and the Audience," *Conflict Resolution*, vol. 2, 1958, pp. 66–77.
2. Elihu Katz and Paul F. Lazarsfeld, *Personal Influence* (Free Press, New York, 1955).

of physicians' adoption of prescription drugs.[3] The early survey studies of the effects of mass communications started with the implicit assumption that in a "mass media" society informal communications played a minor role. But attempts to establish the effects of mass communications forced Lazarsfeld and his associates (eminent among whom, of course, was Berelson) to accord a larger role to informal personal influence. Immediately their attention was turned to this problem, the experimental work of Lewin and other psychologists took on *theoretical* significance. However, the old methodological device of the sample survey was still employed. Tracing the pattern of personal influence from the data of sample surveys proved a difficult task. The final step has been to adapt the methods of sociometry, together with some of the features of sample surveys, to the study of informal communications and personal influence.

Berelson cites as typical propositions of the Lazarsfeld approach: (1) People tend to expose themselves to communications that are congenial to their predispositions; (2) communication exposure "pushes" people to a decision but mainly in line with their latent attitudes. Perhaps one could go even farther and state that, to date, the chief discovery of field studies of the effects of mass communications is that it is exceedingly difficult to identify such effects. Hovland and others were able in laboratory situations to demonstrate quite readily identifiable changes in attitude. While every attempt was made to approximate "natural" conditions as closely as possible in the laboratory, field studies indicated quite decisively that a direct translation of laboratory findings to field conditions was impossible. Hovland himself has discussed this circumstance in a recent paper to the American Psychological Association,[4] and he and his colleagues are now working on the joint application of laboratory and field studies to the testing of propositions. Again, the focus of attention has shifted from the method to the substance of the problem.

Meanwhile, both field and laboratory studies were demonstrating the untenability of equating the content and the effects of communications. Certain of the "reformers" and "social theorists" have not yet grasped this elemental fact, but few professionals in communications research today do not recognize this limitation on content analysis.

Basically, then, my argument is that the early approaches carried with them necessary oversimplifications which have become clear only because the approaches were pushed to the point where they exposed their own

3. H. Menzel and E. Katz, "Social Relations and Innovation in the Medical Profession," *Public Opinion Quarterly,* vol. 19, 1955, pp. 337–352.

4. Carl I. Hovland, "Reconciling Conflicting Results Derived from Experimental and Survey Studies of Attitude Change," presented to the American Psychological Association, Sept. 1, 1958.

limitations. The result has been not only a recognition of the complexity of the communications process but a shift to primary concern with the substance of the problems with less commitment to a particular device of investigation.

The outlook for new "big ideas" is not necessarily bleak, and I would like to suggest one possible point of breakthrough. Although no one seriously doubts that mass communications have an effect on attitudes, we have to this point, as I suggested above, experienced a peculiar frustration in tracing these effects. The effectiveness of advertising in selling goods has been well demonstrated, but attempts to sell the United Nations, etc., seem to have produced consistently negative results. Wiebe has already made some fruitful suggestions as to why there are such differences; [5] I would like to go a little farther than he has. Most social scientists tend to think of attitudes as "softer" than behavior. By this, I mean that they think it is easier to change attitudes than behavior and, more precisely, that to affect behavior one must first change the attitudes relevant to that behavior. However, the recent work of Festinger,[6] Kelman,[7] and others has shown that often attitudinal changes follow behavioral changes. Perhaps the paradigm we should use in field studies of the effects of communications is to look for instances in which communications have capitalized on existing attitudes to produce behavior which, in turn, produces changes of attitudes.

Suppose we took as our topic the attitudes of Southern whites toward integration. The argument would go that we should avoid discussing in the mass media the basic issue of integration, but on the basis of existing attitudes precipitate behavior which was favorable to integration. Thus, the informational campaign might concentrate exclusively on the need to conform to the law of the land regardless of the issue. The prediction would be that those persons who conformed on this basis would, according to Festinger's *theory of cognitive dissonance,* thereafter accommodate their attitudes toward integration *per se* so as to bring them more closely in line with the actions they had taken.

Any hypothetical example such as this is vulnerable on several counts, but it is my guess that this approach offers a possibility for better insight into the day-to-day effects of the mass media. The main reason that mass communications appear to have such little immediate impact can be traced to the phenomenon of self-selection. What we should look for,

5. G. Wiebe, "Merchandising Commodities and Citizenship on Television," *Public Opinion Quarterly,* vol. 15, 1951, pp. 679–691.

6. L. Festinger, *A Theory of Cognitive Dissonance* (Harper, New York, 1957).

7. H. C. Kelman, "Attitude Change as a Function of Response Restriction," *Human Relations,* vol. 6, 1953, pp. 185–214.

then, are instances in which self-selection occurs because of some variable outside the area of *our* primary interest; then we can trace the attitudinal consequences of behavior evoked by peripheral circumstances. Perhaps this is the way that mass media change opinions.

SELECTED PUBLICATIONS BY DR. BERELSON

Voting (U. of Chicago Press, 1954). (With Paul F. Lazarsfeld and William McPhee.)

Graduate Education in the United States (McGraw-Hill, New York, 1960).

Content Analysis in Communication Research (Free Press, New York, 1952).

The People's Choice (Columbia U. P., New York, 1948). (With Paul F. Lazarsfeld and Hazel Gaudet.)

Behavioral Sciences Today (ed.) (Basic Books, New York, 1963).

QUESTIONS

1.   Outline the substantive points of disagreement, if any, between Berelson and his critics, and between each one of them and the other critics. (Substantive is distinguished from evaluative; two persons who agree on everything about a picture's size, content, history, etc., agree on substance, even though one may think it "great" and the other "crude.")

David Manning White

Mass-Communications Research:

A View in Perspective

I

When Dr. Bernard Berelson, himself a distinguished communications specialist, declared in 1959 that the state of communication research was "withering away," he obviously intended to be controversial. The reader should examine Berelson's bill of particulars as well as the three dissenting statements by Wilbur Schramm, David Riesman, and Raymond Bauer in the immediately preceding selections in the present volume.[1]

As Dr. Elihu Katz has perceptively pointed out,[2] Berelson's comments concerned themselves mainly with communication research as the study of mass persuasion. It is true that the pioneers in this field—such as Lazarsfeld, and Hovland—were primarily concerned with studies of the relative *power* of various kinds of communications to change opinions, attitudes, and action in the very short run. As Katz neatly summarizes it, the classical approach to mass-media research was motivated by the problem of short-run effects, or more simply, "What do the media do [immediately] to people?"

The cumulative evidence of the mass-communications studies, from World War II until today, suggests that the effects of the mass media upon individuals and/or groups in changing opinions, attitudes and actions is often less than had been expected. This, of course, raises questions about the nature of the expectation.

In general, the finding expected by many—an expectation which students of mass communications *now* are sure was "naive"—was that people are tremendously influenced by what they hear, read, and see. Any one

1. Bernard Berelson, "The State of Communications Research," *Public Opinion Quarterly,* vol. 23, 1959, pp. 1–6; see pp. 00–00 in the present volume.
2. Elihu Katz, "Mass Communications Research and the Study of Popular Culture," *Studies in Public Communication,* vol. 2, 1959, pp. 1–6.

who has taken part in meetings of groups gathered together for "worthy" causes or has met with individuals who feel themselves victims of mis-understanding, attack, and prejudices, sooner or later hears: "If only the newspapers would report our cause honestly . . ." Losing candidates and discouraged propagandists often blame the press (or the other media)— "if only they gave us a chance . . ." and the publicists for the winning side (and public relations people generally) encourage such a belief by pointing out that clever publicity can "do anything."

It now seems that it ought to have been obvious enough that—most of the time under most circumstances—publicity and propaganda, the press, radio, and TV, could not alone offset the effects of other major social institutions and processes. It ought to have been obvious because they operate at a tremendous disadvantage as compared with churches and schools; yet, over centuries of effort, churches have often *failed* to make their members good, and with decades of experience, schools often *fail* to educate or enlighten their own students.

Yet schools and churches have this great advantage over the mass media because: (*a*) they often have more or less coercive power, (*b*) they are (at least in the United States) less likely to be dependent upon con-sumer acceptance—they get money independently of market demand, (*c*) they are so organized that they can concentrate on their targets over years of effort. No mass medium can ensure that the reader or listener or viewer of today reads or listens or looks tomorrow. Whereas the schools often have their listeners for twelve or more years; what is more, they can penalize (and reward) in a way impossible for the mass media.

It would be an interesting study to know how and why people often believe some new technique or device will ensure perfection in a hurry. In the nineteenth century, universal education was such an object of faith; in the twentieth century, improvements in the mass media often evoke similar hope.

One area where the mass media was expected to do much was in the improvement of mass tastes. It was somehow or other thought that people who enjoyed "crude, vulgar" amusements before mass media, would be-come "refined" by the media. In other words, it was thought that the mass media would have a tremendous communications effect and some-how cause most people shortly to have the same cultural tastes as pro-fessors of literature at Oxford University. This odd belief has been dis-cussed in a book on mass culture;[3] Raymond and Alice Bauer have also

3. David Manning White, "Mass Culture in America: Another Point of View," in David Manning White and Bernard Rosenberg (eds.), *Mass Culture: The Popular Arts in America* (Free Press, New York, 1957).

indicated some of its implications; [4] and as Lazarsfeld and Merton [5] have pointed out, there has been a widespread belief that mass literacy, TV viewing, etc., would mean that "once freed of cramping shackles, people would avail themselves of the major cultural products in our society" (*major* again as defined by the Oxford literary tradition, etc.). The fact that nothing of the sort has happened has given rise to a certain ambivalence about the mass media's effects, among various critics such as Orwell, Aldous Huxley, and Van den Haag, who on the one hand question the media's ability to do good but, on the other, are certain that they do harm, and/or are vulgar.

As Klapper has shown in a valuable review [6] of mass-communication research, what we know about the effects of the media depends on whether we are discussing one type of effect or another. He suggests that there is considerable pessimism from the public, whose questions about the effects of the mass media have been variously answered and in quasi-contradictory ways. Yet often when teachers, legislators or preachers ask such questions as whether violence in the mass media produces delinquency—to cite a frequent source of worry—they are not so much seeking an answer but rather looking for reinforcement to their own preconceived notions or a way to *simplify* what may be in reality a very complex and worrying issue. If, for example, the communication researchers could state categorically that there is a causative relationship between seeing a given television show and a consequent delinquent acting out on the part of some impressionable youngster, it would simplify a lot of matters for those concerned with such behavior.

Klapper [7] generalizes that mass communication *ordinarily* does not by itself serve as the cause of audience effects. Functioning, as he puts it, through a nexus of mediating factors and influences, the media are more likely to reinforce than to change. The reader is urged to study the Klapper volume and assess the evidence upon which Klapper posits the above and related generalizations about the mass media.

4. Raymond Bauer and Alice Bauer, "America, Mass Society and Mass Media," *Journal of Social Issues,* vol. 16, no. 3, 1960.

5. Paul F. Lazarsfeld and Robert K. Merton, "Mass Communication, Popular Taste and Organized Social Action," in Lyman Bryson (ed.), *The Communication of Ideas* (Harper, New York, 1948).

6. Joseph T. Klapper, *The Effects of Mass Communication* (Free Press, New York, 1960). The attention of everyone interested in the field is called to Klapper's penetrating article, "Mass Communications Research: An Old Road Resurveyed," *Public Opinion Quarterly,* vol. 27, 1963, pp. 515–527. Had we had access to this at an earlier date, we would probably have asked permission to include it as an additional rejoinder to Berelson's article.

7. Klapper, *op. cit.,* p. 8.

In this volume our approach has been concerned essentially with the functional approach to the media, or as Katz [8] has stated it, "the uses and gratifications" approach; so that the primary question is not "What do the media do to people?" but, "What do people do with the media?" This approach, Katz points out,[9] "begins with the assumption that the message of even the most potent of the media cannot ordinarily influence an individual who has no "use" for it in the social and psychological context in which he lives. The "uses" approach assumes that people's values, their interests, their associations, their social roles, are prepotent and that people selectively "fashion" what they see and hear to these interests.

One of the most valuable introductions to this orientation to mass communications study is a paper by Matilda White Riley and John W. Riley, Jr., titled "A Sociological Approach to Communications Research." The hypotheses posed by the Rileys stem from a theoretical orientation closely related to the work of Karl Mannheim. For the Rileys it is not sufficient merely to study such factors as age, sex or personality of the mass-media consumers in conjunction with the content of the communication, but such action must be analyzed in light of the "local" (versus the "mass") audience.[10] This local audience is seen as a social group composed of individuals who have "absorbed mass communications into their relatively settled ways of behaving and who, in the real or vicarious company of their fellows, behave towards mass communications in an organized, social manner." [11]

But the available evidence, some of it cited later in this chapter, leads to a much more complicated finding, a finding which also *happens* to accord more closely with common sense. The effect of any communication can *not* be seen as the direct effect of one stimulus upon an object. People are not billiard balls, manipulated by external cues. They have a life story and are members of groups, which means they interpret and modify the meaning of the stimuli which they receive; and they are capable of integrating their responses to several more or less simultaneous stimuli, so that the resultant action is quite different from what simple addition or subtraction would suggest. The experimental and empirical evidence converge in this direction; and so also does the theoretical development of social science. It may well be that Berelson's unhappiness about the present state of mass communications arose out of the fact that he was, at least, at the time the paper in question was delivered, still trying to

8. Elihu Katz, *op. cit.,* pp. 2–3.

9. *Ibid.*

10. Matilda White Riley and John W. Riley, Jr., "A Sociological Approach to Communications Research," *Public Opinion Quarterly,* vol. 15, 1951, pp. 444–460.

11. Riley and Riley, *op. cit.,* p. 454.

interpret new experimental and empirical findings in terms of the expectations derived from an earlier theoretical framework. This framework had been largely outmoded, in part by the very thinkers whom Berelson celebrated, even, in part, too, by his own work on the way in which mass communications affect voting behavior, which turned out to deal as much with the way voters interpret and affect mass communications.[12]

Another way of looking at this phenomenon has been discussed by John W. C. Johnstone [13] in an exploratory paper, wherein he suggests that there are a number of dimensions in which social forces influence mass media reception. Although he acknowledges that the strongest pressures come from the primary group situation, at Katz and Lazarsfeld have shown in their book, *Personal Influence,*[14] Johnstone feels that the small group is not the only social milieu which can furnish insights into the mass communications process. For example, he believes there is much to be gained in the investigation of social aggregates, which he defines as statistical groups made up of individuals who share similar characteristics such as age, sex, socioeconomic status, and educational level attained. It is in the context of *social aggregates* that studies such as Friedson's,[15] wherein he showed that children of kindergarten age prefer television to movie-going whereas children of the 10-to-12-year age group preferred movies to television, prove valuable to the student of communication theory.

I I

The best way to indicate there is no basis for Berelson's pessimism about communications research is to mention and discuss at least sixty recent scholars (from the various disciplines of sociology, psychology, journalism, education and history) who have made substantial contributions to the field. These are writers with whom any serious student in this field will have to become acquainted. They will be introduced, with a description of one or more of their works by the basic academic discipline, e.g., social psychology, with which they have been concerned.

12. Bernard Berelson, Paul F. Lazarsfeld, and William N. McPhee, *Voting: A Study of Opinion Formation in a Presidential Campaign* (U. of Chicago Press, Chicago, 1956).

13. John W. C. Johnstone, "Social Context and Mass Media Reception," *Studies in Public Communication,* vol. 2, Summer 1959, pp. 25–30.

14. Elihu Katz and Paul F. Lazarsfeld, *Personal Influence* (Free Press, New York, 1956).

15. Eliot Friedson, "The Relation of the Social Situation of Contact to the Media in Mass Communication," *Public Opinion Quarterly,* vol. 17, 1953, pp. 230–238.

THE PSYCHOLOGISTS

Among those in the field of psychology who have made significant additions to our knowledge of the mass communication process through research is Gordon Allport, who (with Leo J. Postman) investigated the social psychology of rumor shortly after World War II.[16] By analyzing the development of rumors, Allport and Postman showed how messages are distorted in the process of social diffusion to coincide with the attitudes and knowledge of those who transmit them.

And even before World War II, Allport (with Cantril) had dealt exhaustively with the psychology of radio in a book that is still valuable to students of this medium.[17] The authors at this point concluded that a speech to an audience is more persuasive than if the same remarks were heard on radio, which in turn is somewhat more persuasive if it were read in a newspaper or magazine. (This finding, of course, ought—in terms of recent theory, much of it restated elsewhere in this volume—to be tested for different audiences and occasions.)

Allport's colleague, Hadley Cantril, besides contributing much to the field of public-opinion measurement,[18] also wrote (with Hazel Gaudet and Herta Herzog) the classic case study of mass reaction and panic that resulted from Orson Welles' famous radio broadcast, "The War of The Worlds." [19] Cantril reported that before this half-hour broadcast had ended, people all over the United States were "praying, crying, fleeing frantically to escape death from the Martians." Of the estimated six million who heard this broadcast, one-sixth were frightened or disturbed.

Berelson included Hovland among his four great innovators, but failed to note that Hovland's work has been carried forward by several of his colleagues and disciples. Irving Janis, for example, has systematically studied the relationship between personality and persuasion.[20] From Harold H. Kelley we see how membership in a group affects attitudes as well as resistances to change of attitude. Thus, Kelley presented some

16. Gordon Allport and Leo J. Postman, "The Basic Psychology of Rumor," *Transactions of the New York Academy of Sciences,* VIII, Series II, 1945, pp. 61–81.

17. Gordon W. Allport and Hadley Cantril, *The Psychology of Radio* (Harper, New York, 1935).

18. Hadley Cantril, *Gauging Public Opinion* (Princeton U. P., Princeton, N.J., 1947).

19. Hadley Cantril, Hazel Gaudet, and Herta Herzog, *The Invasion from Mars* (Princeton U. P., Princeton, N.J., 1940).

20. Irving L. Janis, *Personality and Persuasibility* (Yale U. P., New Haven, 1959).

communications opposing certain religious norms to various high school students (after first exposing *some* of the groups to communications which emphasized the meaning of these norms). Among these subjects, those to whom the religious norms were meaningful showed higher resistance to change than did those to whom they did not matter.[21]

Another member of the Hovland group is Walter Weiss, who with Hovland, investigated the extremely important concept of credibility sources as factors in communications.[22] In a study in which college students were presented with a series of four articles, dealing with a range of topics from the sale of antihistamine drugs to the future of the motion-picture industry, it was found that change in attitude in the expected direction was $3\frac{1}{2}$ times as great among those who read the communication associated with a "high credibility" source as it was to those who read the *same* story but attributed this time to a "low credibility" source.

Another figure associated with the Yale Communication Research Program is Arthur A. Lumsdaine, who, along with Fred D. Sheffield, collaborated with Hovland in pioneer studies conducted by the Research Branch of the War Department's Information and Education Division.[23] From this came the now widely accepted concept that if an individual or group of individuals are *initially opposed* to the point of view one wishes to present, then it is more effective to give both sides of the issue rather than giving only the arguments supporting the point to be made. Moreover, the authors found that better-educated men were more favorably affected by presentation of both sides, and conversely, poorly educated men were more affected by the "one-sided" argument.

Another Yale psychologist, Leonard Doob, as early as 1935 wrote on the psychology and techniques of propaganda, and during World War II served as adviser to the Psychological Warfare Branch of the Office of War Information. More recently, Dr. Doob spent two years in Africa, where he analyzed the complex pattern of communications within tribal communities in a comprehensive treatment of African culture.[24]

21. Harold H. Kelley, "Salience of Membership and Resistance to Change of Group Anchored Attitudes," *Human Relations,* vol. 8, 1958, pp. 275–289; see also Harold H. Kelley and E. H. Volkart, "The Resistance to Change of Group Anchored Attitudes," *American Sociological Review,* vol. 17, 1952, pp. 453–465.

22. Carl I. Hovland and Walter Weiss, "The Influence of Source Credibility on Communication Effectiveness," *Public Opinion Quarterly,* vol. 15, 1951, pp. 635–650.

23. Carl I. Hovland, Arthur A. Lumsdaine, and Fred D. Sheffield, *Experiments in Mass Communication,* vol. 3 (Princeton U. P., Princeton, N.J., 1949).

24. Leonard Doob, *Public Opinion and Propaganda,* rev. ed. (Holt, New York, 1948); see also his *Communication in Africa; A Search for Boundaries* (Yale, New Haven, 1961).

Leon Festinger's complex theory of cognitive dissonance,[25] which considers how individuals try to affect their "structuring" of the world in which they live by giving meaning to their environment, helps to explain why people seek certain kinds of information. The implications of this research into how individuals seek situations that reduce uncertainty and avoid situations that clearly increase uncertainty has already made its influence felt on much current research in this field.

To Alex Bavelas, another disciple of Lewin, the area of communications studies that demanded exploration was the relationship between the behavior of small groups and the patterns of communication in which the groups operate.[26] Bavelas and his students have shown that the ways in which members of a group may be linked together by a network of communication are numerous. By testing the feasibility of various patterns of group interaction to determine which are useful in terms of communication effectiveness, Bavelas has applied the group-dynamic theories with important implications for future study in communications.

Yet one further member of the Lewinian group should be mentioned —Dorwin Cartwright. He utilized group dynamics principles to analyze the various communications which are in agreement with already existing attitudes and interests.[27] The Treasury Department tested a documentary film which was designed to increase the public's identification with such activities as bond purchasing. They found that despite much publicity for a free public showing of this film in Bridgeport, Connecticut, it was attended by only 5 percent of the adult population. *Moreover, later analysis showed that this audience was composed mainly of those citizens who already were active in the buying of bonds, in donating blood, and similar activities.*

In the area of television's impact on contemporary society, psychologists have a multidimensional field of inquiry. The most noteworthy work to date in the investigation of television's efforts on children is that of Hilde Himmelweit, A. N. Oppenheim and Pamela Vance.[28] With care-

25. Leon Festinger, *The Theory of Cognitive Dissonance* (Harper, New York, 1957).

26. Alex Bavelas, "Communication Patterns in Task-oriented Groups," *Journal of Accoustical Society of America,* vol. 22, 1950, pp. 725–730; see also Kurt Lewin, "Group Decision and Social Change" in E. Maccoby, T. M. Newcomb, and E. L. Hartley (eds.), *Readings in Social Psychology* (Holt, New York, 1958), pp. 197–211.

27. Dorwin Cartwright, "Some Principles of Mass Persuasion: Selected Findings of Research on the Sale of United States War Bonds," *Human Relations,* vol. 2, 1949, pp. 253–267.

28. Hilde Himmelweit, A. N. Oppenheim, and Pamela Vance, *Television and the Child* (Oxford, London, 1958).

fully matched groups of nearly 2,000 British youngsters (only half of whom were viewers of television) as their sample, Himmelweit et al. concluded that the values of television make an impact on the child if they are presented in *dramatic* form, if they touch on ideas or values for which the child is ready, *and if the child cannot turn for information on the same points to parents and friends.* The researchers found no evidence that television contributes to aggressiveness on the part of children, but neither was there any evidence that its results were beneficial.

Another British psychologist who has studied television in depth is W. A. Belson, whose 1959 study [29] for the British Broadcasting Corporation supplements, in many ways, the work accomplished by Himmelweit and her colleagues. Belson found that television brings the family together at home a little longer and oftener in the evenings. Little was found to suggest that the effect of television in keeping the family together at home would disappear with time. On the other hand, although television tended to reduce other home-centered and family activity slightly, such effects seemed to be only temporary. As the television set became more familiar, the family returned to previous forms of home-centered activities.

A leading American researcher into the effects of television is Eleanor E. Maccoby of Stanford University, who found in an early study [30] that upper-middle class children who were highly frustrated in their current home life (i.e., not treated permissively or warmly) spent more time viewing television than comparable children not so frustrated. Conversely, in the absence of frustration, the child appeared to be drawn away from television.

Maccoby's findings were to some extent verified in a significant monograph by Lotte Bailyn, who analyzed the media habits of some 600 fifth- and sixth-grade children.[31] She found significant correlations between viewing of television, movies and comic books. Although having personal problems was not related to exposure to these "pictorial" media, Bailyn found that those with more problems listened less to radio and read fewer books. An index was constructed which showed that those high on both personal problems and rebellious independence made more "use" of the pictorial media.

Space does not permit any further extensive citations of the manner

29. W. A. Belson, "Television and the Family" (British Broadcasting Corporation, London, 1959). (Mimeographed.)

30. Eleanor E. Maccoby, "Why Do Children Watch Television?" *Public Opinion Quarterly,* vol. 18, 1954, pp. 239–244.

31. Lotte Bailyn, "Mass Media and Children: A Study of Exposure Habits and Cognitive Effects," *Psychological Monographs,* vol. 73, 1959, pp. 1–48.

in which fruitful work has been (and continues to be) done by psychologists concerned with communications problems. Mention might equally well have been made of the work of T. W. Adorno [32] and Rudolph Arnheim [33] on their analyses of various mass cultural forms; the work of Daniel Katz,[34] Theodore Newcomb,[35] and Rensis Likert [36] in the perceptual problems of communication; the work of Donald N. Michael [37] and Nathan Maccoby [38] in learning theory applied to communications studies; the work of Eugene and Ruth Hartley [39] and Gerhart Wiebe [40] in the study of attitude formation and its relation to the communications process.

THE SOCIOLOGISTS

Clearly, Paul Lazarsfeld has been, as Berelson states, a leading contributor in communications research. But he is not unique as Berelson seems to suggest. For instance, closely allied with Lazarsfeld at the Bureau of Applied Social Research of Columbia University has been Robert K. Merton. It is, of course, true that Merton is best known as a social theorist, yet it is equally true that he has contributed substantially to the evolving field of communications research. His monograph "Mass Persuasion" [41] provided one of the classic case studies of the communications process. Here Merton studied the effects of a World War II bond drive as conducted as a marathon radio appeal by Kate Smith. By offering rewards of

32. T. W. Adorno, "Television and the Patterns of Mass Culture" *Quarterly of Film, Radio and Television,* vol. 8, 1954.

33. R. Arnheim, "The World of the Daytime Serial" in Paul F. Lazarsfeld and F. Stanton (eds.), *Radio Research, 1942–43* (Harper, New York, 1944).

34. Daniel Katz, "Psychological Barriers to Communication," in *Annals of the American Academy of Political and Social Science,* March 1947.

35. Theodore M. Newcomb, *Personality and Social Change* (Holt, New York, 1943).

36. Rensis Likert, "A Neglected Factor in Communications," *Audio-Visual Communication Review,* vol. 2, 1954, pp. 163–177.

37. Donald N. Michael and Nathan Maccoby, "Factors Influencing Verbal Learning from Films under Varying Conditions of Audience Participation," *Journal of Experimental Psychology,* vol. 46, 1953, pp. 411–418.

38. Nathan Maccoby and Eleanor E. Maccoby, "Homeostatic Theory and Attitude Change," *Public Opinion Quarterly,* vol. 24, 1961, pp. 538–545.

39. Eugene L. Hartley, Ruth E. Hartley, and Clyde Hart, "Attitudes and Opinions" in Eugene Hartley and Ruth E. Hartley, *Fundamentals of Social Psychology* (Knopf, New York, 1952).

40. Gerhart Wiebe, "Merchandizing Commodities and Citizenship on Television," *Public Opinion Quarterly,* vol. 15, 1951–52, pp. 679–691.

41. Robert K. Merton, *Mass Persuasion* (Harper, New York, 1946).

(1) release from guilt, (2) helping to bring the boys back from the war, and (3) because of the "status conferral" aspect of her own prestige, Kate Smith succeeded in selling millions of dollars' worth of war bonds in a few hours. Merton identified some sixty appeals, each to a degree different from the previous ones, but all concerned with a common goal: the creation and reinforcement of the desire to buy a war bond.

The reader is also directed to Dr. Merton's study of interpersonal influence and communications behavior in a local community,[42] and his monograph on the focused interview.[43]

Another sociologist whose work should be examined carefully by the student in this field is Bernard Berelson, himself. Starting in 1940, as a collaborator with Douglas Waples in a significant study of what reading does to people,[44] Berelson has contributed extensively. His book on the methodology of content analysis [45] is a very valuable and comprehensive treatment of this research technique. Perhaps his most important work was with Lazarsfeld, with whom he collaborated in the first large-scale study of radio and the print media as factors in political opinion and voting, in an analysis of the 1940 presidential campaign in Erie County, Ohio.[46] Twelve years later Berelson, Lazarsfeld, and William McPhee conducted a second large-scale study of voting behavior as a correlate of attitude formation, this time in Elmira, New York.[47]

Among the sociologists who have made valuable inquiries into the nature of the mass media by using content analysis as their primary tool are Leo Lowenthal, Joseph Klapper and Charles Glock, Susan Kingsbury and Hornell Hart, and Berelson. Lowenthal studied the manner in which biographies were used in popular magazines; [48] Klapper and Glock

42. Robert K. Merton, "Patterns of Influence: A Study of Interpersonal Influence and Communications Behavior in a Local Community," in Paul F. Lazarsfeld and F. Stanton (eds.), *Communication Research, 1948–49* (Harper, New York, 1949), pp. 180–219.

43. Robert K. Merton, Marjorie Fiske, and P. Kendall, *The Focused Interview* (Free Press, New York, 1956).

44. Douglas Waples, Bernard Berelson, and F. R. Bradshaw, *What Reading Does to People,* (U. of Chicago Press, 1940).

45. Bernard Berelson, *Content Analysis as a Tool of Communication Research* (Free Press, New York, 1953).

46. Paul F. Lazarsfeld, Bernard Berelson, and Hazel Gaudet, *The People's Choice* (Columbia U. P., New York, 1948).

47. Bernard Berelson, Paul F. Lazarsfeld, and William N. McPhee, *Voting. A Study of Opinion Formation in a Presidential Campaign* (U. of Chicago Press, Chicago, 1954).

48. Leo Lowenthal, "Biographies in Popular Magazines," in P. Lazarsfeld and F. Stanton (eds.), *Radio Research, 1942–43* (Duell, Sloan & Pearce, New York, 1944).

showed how newspapers were able to put a government official on "trial" with the flimsiest of evidence; [49] Kingsbury and Hart in a provocative early study attempted to develop content measures by which they could make judgments as to the ethical performances of newspapers; [50] and Berelson [51] (with Patricia Salter) analyzed popular magazine fiction and learned that the protaganists in magazine fiction were at the time of his study invariably Anglo-Saxon by descent with names like Jeffrey Blake and Ellen James.

The social role of radio and television has attracted the efforts of sociologists such as Herta Herzog, Patricia Kendall, Rolf Myersohn, Kurt and Gladys Lang, Leo Bogart and Charles Winick. Herzog studied the motivations and gratifications of daytime serial (soap opera) listeners [52] and posited three major types of enjoyment experienced by such listeners: (1) serials provide a means of emotional release; (2) serials provide opportunities for wishful thinking, and (3) serials provide advice on appropriate patterns of behavior, e.g., "If you listen to these programs and something turns up in your own life, you would know what to do about it." Kendall, as a colleague of Lazarsfeld, conducted the definitive study of the audience of radio.[53] Myersohn surveyed existing social research in television and proposed fruitful lines of future inquiry.[54] The Langs analyzed the way three television networks covered a night's proceedings during the 1952 Democratic National Convention and found that though the networks each reported the same activities, there was a difference in the way these events were interpreted or "structured." [55] Bogart interpreted the state of television research, as of 1956, in a useful book.[56] Winick studied the pressures toward censorship in television and

49. Joseph T. Klapper and Charles Y. Glock, "Trial by Newspaper," *Scientific American,* vol. 180, pp. 16–21.

50. Susan Kingsbury and Hornell Hart, *Newspapers and the News* (Putnam, New York, 1937).

51. Bernard Berelson and Patricia Salter, "Majority and Minority Americans: An Analysis of Magazine Fiction," *Public Opinion Quarterly,* vol. 10, 1947, pp. 168–190.

52. Herta Herzog, "What Do We Really Know about Daytime Serial Listeners?" in P. F. Lazarsfeld and F. Stanton (eds.), *Radio Research, 1942–43* (Duell, Sloan & Pearce, New York, 1944).

53. Paul Lazarsfeld and Patricia Kendall, *Radio Listening in America* (Prentice-Hall, New York, 1948).

54. Rolf B. Myersohn, "Social Research in Television," in B. Rosenberg and D. M. White (eds.), *Mass Culture* (Free Press, New York, 1957).

55. Kurt Lang and Gladys E. Lang, "The Mass Media and Voting," in Eugene Burdick and A. J. Brodbeck (eds.), *American Voting Behavior* (Free Press, New York, 1959).

56. Leo Bogart, *The Age of Television* (Ungar, New York, 1956).

their effect on television's content.[57] From his study, Winick concluded that television is a fairly accurate mirror of the maintenance values of our society.

The nature of attitude and opinion formation has also commanded the interest of sociologists; among those who have contributed valuable studies are Herbert Hyman, Helen Hughes, Shirley Starr, Samuel Stouffer, William McPhee, Marjorie Fiske, and Elihu Katz. Hyman (in collaboration with Paul B. Sheatsley) analyzed the reasons why information campaigns often fail.[58] Shirley Starr (in collaboration with Helen Hughes) studied the dynamics of failure to increase information and "improve" attitudes toward the United Nations in the much-cited Cincinnati study.[59] Stouffer, as research director for the Information and Education branch of the Army during World War II, organized several hundred attitude surveys among soldiers all over the world. Stouffer's major fame as a contributor to communications theory came as the principal author of the four-volume study, *The American Soldier*,[60] but his perceptive analysis of American public opinion on civil liberties [61] may well prove to be even more stimulating in its effect.

Sociologists have evidenced an interest in the study of the newspaper as an institutional force in American life for nearly 40 years, beginning with the vastly creative Robert E. Park who said, "If the newspapers are to be improved, it will come through the education of the people and the organization of political information and intelligence. But first of all we must learn to look at political and social life objectively and cease to think of it wholly in moral terms. In that case we shall have less 'news,' but better newspapers." [62] And as early as 1926, George A. Lundberg considered the relationship between the newspaper and public opinion.[63] In his study, Lundberg measured three newspapers for their influences upon their readers in local public issues. Lundberg found that there was no

57. Charles Winick, *Taste and the Censor in Television* (Fund for the Republic, New York, 1959).

58. Herbert H. Hyman and Paul B. Sheatsley, "Some Reasons Why Information Campaigns Fail," *Public Opinion Quarterly,* vol. 11, 1947, pp. 412–423.

59. Shirley Starr and Helen M. Hughes, "Report of an Educational Campaign: The Cincinnati Plan for the United Nations," *American Journal of Sociology,* vol. 40, 1950, pp. 389–400.

60. Samuel A. Stouffer et al., *The American Soldier,* Vol. I (Princeton U. P., Princeton, N.J., 1949).

61. Samuel A. Stouffer, *Communism, Conformity and Civil Liberties* (Doubleday, New York, 1955).

62. Robert E. Park, "The Natural History of the Newspaper," in Wilbur Schramm (ed.), *Mass Communications* (U. of Illinois Press, Urbana, 1960).

63. George A. Lundberg, "The Newspaper and Public Opinion," *Social Forces,* vol. 4, pp. 709–715.

tangible correlation between the attitudes of the three papers and the voting by the people who read them.

Among contemporary sociologists, none has written more perceptively of the social forces at play in a newspaper office than Warren Breed.[64] He asserts that usually it is the publisher's policy that prevails in any newspaper, despite the appearance of objective criteria in selecting news. Since the newsman's source of rewards is located not among the readers, ostensibly his clients, but from his peers and superiors as well, he "redefines his values to the more pragmatic level of the newspaper group." From his study, Breed concludes that the cultural patterns of the newsroom do not produce results sufficient for wider democratic needs.

Important contributions to the process of *social diffusion* of mass communications messages have been made by Melvin L. DeFleur [65] and Otto Larsen [66] in a number of articles and in their book "The Flow of Information." [67] A colleague of Larsen's at the University of Washington, Stewart C. Dodd, has also conducted many studies in the diffusion field,[68] as well as a wide variety of studies in the attitude and opinion area.

In the field of psychological warfare and propaganda, sociologists such as Morris Janowitz [69] and Philip Selznick [70] have contributed substantially to the understanding of this aspect of mass communication. A definitive study of the communications system within the USSR is Alex Inkeles' book on public opinion in Russia.[71]

The fact that we cite Inkeles' work on Soviet Russia under the head-

64. Warren Breed, "Social Control in the News Room," *Social Forces,* May 1955; see also Dr. Breed's essay "Mass Communications and Sociocultural Integration" in the present volume.

65. Melvin L. DeFleur, "The Spatial Diffusion of an Airborne Leaflet Message," *American Journal of Sociology,* vol. 59, 1953, pp. 144–149.

66. Otto N. Larsen and Richard J. Hill, "Mass Media and Interpersonal Communication in the Diffusion of a News Event," *The American Sociological Review,* vol. 19, 1954, pp. 426–433.

67. Melvin L. DeFleur and Otto N. Larsen, *The Flow of Information* (Harper, New York, 1958).

68. Stewart C. Dodd, "Diffusion is Predictable," *American Sociological Review,* vol. 20, 1955, pp. 392–401; see also Stewart C. Dodd and Chick Hung Sung, "A Comparison of Scales for Degrees of Opinion," *Journalism Quarterly,* vol. 37, 1960, pp. 280–283.

69. William E. Daugherty and Morris A. Janowitz, *A Psychological Warfare Casebook* (Johns Hopkins, Baltimore, 1958); see also Murray Dyer, *Weapon on the Wall* (Johns Hopkins, Baltimore, 1959) for an excellent introduction to the concept of political warfare.

70. Philip Selznick, *The Organizational Weapon* (McGraw-Hill, New York, 1952).

71. Alex Inkeles, *Public Opinion in Soviet Russia: A Study in Mass Persuasion* (Harvard University Press, Cambridge, 1950).

ing *Sociologists* shows the arbitrariness of the lines of distinction between persons in different social sciences. The subject might have been called political science and Inkeles, because he wrote about it, a political scientist —or because of his orientation and associations, he might as well be called a psychologist. Similarly, we might list Leila Sussman's study of the mail received by the White House in the time of Franklin D. Roosevelt under the heading "political science" because it deals with images of the Presidency, or under the heading "sociology," because Professor Sussman is a member of the Sociology Department at the University of Massachusetts.

POLITICAL SCIENTISTS *

Berelson's pessimism about the future of research in public opinion seems particularly ill-founded upon reading a great synthetic work in that field which appeared years after he spoke: This is V. O. Key's *Public Opinion and American Democracy,* published in 1961.[72] Key prefaces this volume by stating: "During the past two decades the study of public opinion, once a major concern of political scientists, has become a preoccupation of sociologists and social psychologists. . . . [As this has happened] they have in large measure abstracted public opinion from its governmental setting. . . . The object in the preparation of this book was . . . mainly to place the newer knowledge about public opinion in a political context . . . [to show] the relation of bits of information to the operation of the political system in the large."

In making this effort, Key on the one hand returns to the classic problems of political analysis and theory, problems of the sort which concerned Aristotle, Plato, Cicero, and their successors. It should be pointed out that many of the great political theorists were engaged in studying the issues of mass communication *as these existed in their day.* Plato attacked what he regarded as the pernicious influence of poetry on sound public policy; the poetry which he despised included the tragedies and comedies which constituted a main source of public entertainment and political stereotyping in the Athens of his time. Accordingly, Plato as a political theorist was, in effect, considering the difference between the image and the reality of his society and taking the same line as more recent writers who attribute current lack of political awareness to the sensationalism of the press or TV.

* I am indebted to Lewis Dexter for work in this section and also for the comments on international relations, anthropologists, and historians.

72. V. O. Key, *Public Opinion and American Democracy* (Knopf, New York, 1961).

Aristotle, similarly, is often quoted as having maintained that democracy was only possible within a group small enough so one man could speak to them (and some have argued that the radio by bringing the entire world within the sound of one man's voice has increased enormously the scope of democratic government). Cicero, who himself achieved political prestige and influence because of his skill as an orator, actually wrote a treatise on oratory which was the nearest approach to mass communication in his day.

It is therefore natural to find Key dealing with the way in which mass media may or do affect modern politics. *What differentiates him from most of his predecessors in the 2,000-year history of political analysis is his effort to determine what relation can be established with a reasonably high degree of probability—what knowledge is at least to some extent validated*—and what is simply plausible guesswork. It should not be surprising to students of this volume to find out that his conclusion is "given the limits of knowledge of the political role and effects of mass communications, about all that can be done is to make educated guesses around the edges of the problem. These guesses, though, should enable us to define some of the boundaries of the role of mass communications as molders of opinion."

A study of Key's work will reemphasize the artificial nature of lines between the social sciences. He uses the work of sociologists, psychologists, historians, and anthropologists, some of whom we have already mentioned, as freely as that of political scientists to throw light upon the political processes with which he is concerned.

Among the political scientists whom Key cites may be mentioned Walter Lippmann, whose classic discussion of "the phantom public" (1925) in Key's words "demolished whatever illusion existed that "the public" could be regarded as a . . . collectivity equipped to decide the affairs of state . . . the average person . . . exhaust(s) his energies earning a livelihood . . . nor was the amorphous public . . . capable of taking the initiative in any public action." Lippmann in other words, by demolishing the theory of a unified public, responding to communications, made it intellectually possible for the whole group of scholars whom we have cited to tackle empirically the real issue—what kinds of publics exist for what sort of message and communications? [73] In fact, one very serious objection to Berelson's selection of four particular deities of public opinion research is that he omitted from consideration others whose intellectual eminence is quite as great and whose influence has

73. Walter Lippmann, *The Phantom Public* (Harcourt, New York, 1925); see also his *Public Opinion* (Macmillan, New York, 1922).

been just as profound.[74] One of these was—and still is—Walter Lippmann, who is of course one of the eminent thinkers about public opinion and related matters. Another, still active when Berelson wrote, although since dead was Arthur F. Bentley, who (in 1906) issued an epoch-making study of the way in which pressure groups influence politics and public opinion, a study which had implications for studies of the mass media, implications some of which were explored and made more precise in David Truman's *Governmental Process*.[75] (Because Truman and Key together review so much of the literature on pressure groups and publicity, we need not recapitulate their summaries here.) Bentley and Truman suggest the degree to which communications through the mass media are stimulated by, represent the interests of, and to some extent are directed towards particular groups—that is they suggest that news, for instance, is selected and stressed in terms of the determinate political purposes of specific persons having specific interests. The picture of the mass-communications arena derived from their work is a continual effort to play up or play down reporting of this or that circumstance, according to guesses as to the effect of the type of reporting on persons whose good opinion is of significance. Within this context, newsmen and reporters act as *arbitrators* in public relations battles; but, as Breed, for example, points out in his article (reprinted in this volume, pp. 183–201, newsmen and reporters are also *participants* in such battles and shape their selection and emphasis of news partly in accord with their conception of what will help their side. Newsmen and reporters also, however, are in the business of producing "interesting" materials and are governed by traditions and ideas about how stories should be played up, timeliness, deadlines, etc. Douglas Cater in a study of *The Fourth Estate*,[76] maintains that the striking political prominence of the late Senator Joseph McCarthy was in considerable measure a function of his skill at issuing statements in such a way that newsmen, in accordance with "the rules of the game" felt obligated to carry what he said, very prominently (despite the fact that many of the newsmen who publicized the Senator happened to be opposed to his political position).

Bentley, whose first contribution to the study of mass-communications focused on pressure groups, later conducted a series of methodological analyses, especially *Behavior . . . Knowledge . . . Fact* (1935),[77] and

74. Arthur F. Bentley, *The Process of Government: A Study of Social Pressures* (U. of Chicago Press, Chicago, 1906).

75. David Truman, *Governmental Process* (Knopf, New York, 1951).

76. Douglas Cater, *The Fourth Estate* (Houghton, Boston, 1959).

77. Arthur F. Bentley, *Behavior . . . Knowledge . . . Fact* (Principia, Bloomington, Ind., 1935).

An Inquiry Into Inquiries (1954)[78] which, in the judgment of the editors of this volume, should be basic to contemporary analysis of mass communications, but they have not yet had much influence. The reason for mentioning them here is that it took about thirty years for his earlier 1906 volume to have much impact, so perhaps these later books, too, are goal-setters, ahead of their times.

A number of other political scientists could be mentioned as having contributed to our understanding of the role of mass communications; almost everyone who has written on modern political phenomena at one point or another deals with the mass media. For instance, Harold F. Gosnell has made numerous studies of our subject;[79] but one study stands out as illustrating the almost inevitable interplay between analysis of audience and medium and analysis of political events. Gosnell has been engaged in an intensive effort to understand how and why Franklin D. Roosevelt was a "Champion Campaigner";[80] and recollection of Roosevelt as a "campaigner" brings to mind the "fireside chats," the radio voice, and the handling of press conferences. Gosnell tackles these problems of timing in relation to audience attention and the drama of politics.

Lewis A. Dexter, co-editor of the present volume, has prepared a study called "Congressmen and the People They Listen To,"[81] focused on the role of Congressmen in the communications net which is, in part, available—together with an intensive analysis of the reaction of American businessmen to news about a particular set of political events—in Bauer, Pool, and Dexter, *American Business and Public Policy*.[82] The general viewpoint of this latter work is to be discovered in the essays by Dexter (pp. 3–24), Bauer (pp. 126–138) and Pool (pp. 143–158) in the present volume.

The vivid interest of political scientists in communications may be shown by the following fact: the co-winner of the First Atherton Press prize contest in 1962 for the best unpublished volume on political sci-

78. Arthur F. Bentley, *An Inquiry Into Inquiries* (Beacon, Boston, 1954).

79. Harold F. Gosnell, "Relation of the Press to Voting in Chicago," *Journalism Quarterly*, vol. 13, 1936, pp. 129–147.

80. Harold F. Gosnell, *Champion Campaigner: Franklin D. Roosevelt* (Macmillan, New York, 1952).

81. Copyright by Massachusetts Institute of Technology, 1955 (hectographed); submitted as Ph.D. thesis (Columbia, Sociology), 1960; University Microfilms, Ann Arbor, summarized in "The Representative and His District," *Human Organization*, 1957; published in extended form in N. Polsby, *et al., Politics and Social Life* (Houghton, Boston, 1963), and also available as PS–63 in Bobbs-Merrill Reprint Series.

82. Raymond A. Bauer, I. de Sola Pool, and Lewis A. Dexter, *American Business and Public Policy* (Atherton Press, New York, 1963).

ence was *News Sources and News Channels: A Study in Political Communication*, by Professor Dan Nimmo of Texas Technological College. The abstract of the study states that: "While there is a plethora of comment about government press relations, it is striking that few studies focus on the behavorial aspects of that relationship. . . . This study explores relationships between news sources and news channels by applying methods of role analysis. Information dispensing and news gathering are viewed as interrelated processes within the framework of political communication. Information officers and newsmen are actors playing specific roles in such processes." [83]

INTERNATIONAL RELATIONS STUDIES

For reasons of convenience, the foregoing is chiefly confined to works by American political scientists or having a definitely American setting. There are, however, studies by foreign political scientists which confirm or extend the type of analysis given in the American studies just referred to; none of them, however, to our knowledge *as yet* happens to have disproved findings by American scholars or have become irreplaceable or classic (see Marten Brouwer, "Mass Communications and the Social Sciences," below).

But there is one area of concern to students of mass communications where a great deal necessarily has been learned by study of foreign cultures and societies. There has been much work on international attitudes, psychological warfare, etc., that has materially enhanced our knowledge of how mass communications operate. Bruce L. and Chitra M. Smith compiled a bibliography on *International Communications* [84] which, although highly selective, includes 2,600 items. In order to select these 2,600 items, it took four man-years of professional research, according to the administrator, even though they limited themselves entirely to items published or made available since 1943. Bruce L. Smith's introductory essay to this bibliography is in itself a masterful overview of major fields of emphasis and is clearly one of the "must" readings for every student of mass communications—or of public policy on international affairs. He points out that the main sponsors of the numerous studies which he has perused are government agencies or research groups financed by the government, such as the U. S. High Commissioner in Germany, the Strategic Bombing Survey, and the Russian Research

83. Excerpt from abstract of Ph.D. thesis (Vanderbilt), the basis of the prize-winning volume to be published by Atherton Press, New York, 1964.
84. Bruce Lannes Smith and Chitra M. Smith, *International Communications* (Princeton U. P., Princeton, N.J., 1956).

Center. He refers also to the important role that foundations have played in financing studies—the Massachusetts Institute of Technology with a grant of $750,000 from Ford Foundation has done much to develop the conception of transactional relationship between source of communication and recipient, between the interpretation of the communication and social structure within which the recipient is living. This approach is developed in the work of Lucian Pye.[85] Another very valuable publication of the Center has been Harold Isaacs' *Scratches On Our Minds*,[86] a detailed description of the underlying "frames of reference" within which certain leaders of opinion interpret the news they hear about the Far East.

A set of reviews of the literature in the field of international attitudes and outlooks has been prepared by the World Peace Foundation under the general direction of Alfred Hero; these surveys all rest upon the MIT audience-social structure approach toward communications: *Americans in World Affairs, Non-Governmental Influence in Foreign Policy Making, Mass Media and World Affairs, Voluntary Organizations in World Affairs Communication, Opinion Leaders in American Communities.*[87]

There are a number of monographic studies of systems of communications, social structure in non-Western societies, etc., but, so far as we know, most of them are explicitly and at the surface *area-oriented;* however, it is so clear that they can be interpreted in terms of their contribution to communications theory that one can safely predict that some imaginative and painstaking scholar will enlarge our overall understanding of mass communications before long by collating these scattered monographs in a single volume. Smith and Smith provide him with an excellent starting point.

ANTHROPOLOGISTS, HISTORIANS, AND LITERARY HISTORIANS

We have dealt with several fields of knowledge and their contributions to mass communications. We could have discussed other fields of knowledge—W. L. Warner, whose penetrating analysis of the way in which a local political figure became a national "folk hero" appears on pp. 341–359 in the present volume, is an anthropologist; and it is not surprising that his discussion of the part the press played in this particular episode throws light upon the constant tension between the symbolic

85. Lucian Pye, *Politics, Personality and Nation-Building: Burma's Search for Identity* (Yale U. P., New Haven, 1962).

86. Harold Isaacs, *Scratches On Our Minds* (Day, New York, 1958).

87. World Peace Foundation, Boston, Mass.

and the factual in news reporting and mass communications in our society. Scattered through other anthropological monographs are reports and insights about mass communications, and it is possibly because of our own lack of knowledge in that field rather than for any other reason that we do not discuss them here.

One other study of considerable interest to students of mass communications is by the Puerto Rican anthropologist, Edwin Seda-Bonilla;[88] it carries further and places within the particular Puerto Rican cultural context the conflict between the elite's desire for civil liberties and the indifference of the masses to them, which Stouffer had reported for the continental United States (see above). But another of the most significant contributions to civil liberties research from the standpoint of mass communications is the almost forgotten 1940 discussion of the problems for civil-liberties doctrine created by the findings of modern sociology about mass communications written by the then lawyer, David Riesman.[89]

In other fields, too, there are significant works. One of the great contributions to the technique of content analysis was made by a specialist in English literature, Caroline Spurgeon, in her *Shakespeare's Imagery*.[90] One of the first studies of "The Political Novel," appears in a Doubleday Short Study in Political Science [91] of that title, written by an instructor in English literature at the University of Idaho, Joseph Blotner. One example of the many valuable specialized studies in English literature pertinent to communications research is a Ph.D. thesis by C. M. Eyler, George Peabody College for Teachers, "The Technique of Political Propaganda in English Drama, 1600–1750." Again, it is the limitation of the writer's knowledge (a limitation which we discuss as having more than personal significance in our introduction to Bertram M. Gross' "Operation BASIC," pp. 460–473) we suspect, which makes it impossible for us to utilize at length the material by literary historians and literary critics which would be of value in studying mass communications. But the existence of such monographs makes it reasonably likely that some penetrating scholar will come along and put together the bits and pieces of these monographs and be entitled to be hailed by some future Berelson

88. Edwin Seda-Bonilla, *Los Derechos Civiles en la Cultura Puertoriqueña,* published by the U. of Puerto Rico Press, 1962–3. Now being translated into English by the Institute of Latin-American Studies of Columbia University, with a view to publication.

89. David Riesman, "Civil Liberties in a Period of Transition," in C. Friedrich and E. Mason (eds.), *Public Policy Yearbook* (Harvard U. P., Cambridge, 1942), pp. 33–96.

90. Caroline Spurgeon, *Shakespeare's Imagery* (Macmillan, New York, 1936).

91. Joseph Blotner, *The Political Novel* (Doubleday, New York, 1955).

as an intellectual giant. For, in fact, the history of scholarship shows that where there is continual, reasonably imaginative, competent, reliable monographic work, sooner or later the monographs generally are synthesized into a penetrating overview.

Certainly, one can find in Kenneth Burke's *Attitudes Toward History*,[92] an attempt to apply a particular theory of literary criticism to the interpretation of history, a work consistently provocative; but no systematic effort has, to our knowledge, ever been made to systematize and validate Burke's brilliant "insights."

There are other fields and techniques that should be discussed. We have, for instance, devoted no explicit attention to the great technical contributions being made by market researchers, partly because their work is so often focused on an immediate problem and is not systematically published.

And there is a series of studies by specialists in library science [93]—the librarian indeed was one of the earlier specialists in mass communications; so library schools and studies of libraries inevitably contribute to our field. The interdisciplinary nature of much of the work here is shown by the fact that Berelson, whom we have listed as a sociologist, because of his later associations, in fact has a Ph.D. in Library Science, and that one of the outstanding analyses of how mass communications are disseminated through libraries and particularly of the professional attitudes of librarians who disseminate them, is by a political scientist, Oliver Garceau.[94]

The great traditional discipline of history has contributed also to the study of mass communications; our suspicion is that it is due to the complex problem of information retrieval (see Bertram M. Gross, "Operation BASIC," pp. 460–473 in this reader) and to the difficulty of locating relevant material which limits our use in this volume of studies by historians. For example, the elder Arthur M. Schlesinger has made a most valuable study of manuals of etiquette as mass communications socializers.[95] No doubt there are other studies of which we are unaware, by historians of equally great significance.

92. Kenneth Burke, *Attitudes Toward History* (*New Republic*, New York, 1937).

93. See discussions and citations in, e.g., the *Library Journal*.

94. Oliver Garceau, *The Public Library in the Political Process* (Columbia U. P., New York, 1950).

95. Arthur M. Schlesinger, *Learning How to Behave* (Macmillan, New York, 1946).

THE JOURNALISM-COMMUNICATIONS SCHOOL RESEARCHERS

Of course, one vigorous area for communications research is within the leading schools of journalism, or schools of communication as some are called. In a sense, as Schramm has pointed out,[96] the communication research interests of journalism are somewhat broader than those of the other behavorial sciences. For where communication research is only one aspect of psychology, economics, anthropology, sociology or political science, it constitutes the major part of journalism research.

It is true, as Berelson suggests that Wilbur Schramm, Raymond B. Nixon, and Ralph D. Casey represent what he terms the "journalistic" approach. Schramm, perhaps more than any figure from the schools of journalism, has exerted an influence on a generation of students, many of whom are actively engaged in significant communication research. Schramm drew upon the work of learning theorists in formulating a resourceful explanation of two distinct patterns in newspaper reading, related to two types of stories one of which offered an "immediate" reward and the other a "delayed" reward.[97] Schramm's major interest in recent years has been the effects of television on various segments of the American society, with particular emphasis on the role that television plays in the life of children.[98] Nixon, both through his studies in the implications of the decreasing numbers of competitive newspapers [99] and his editorship of the *Journalism Quarterly*, and more recently his presidency of the International Association for Mass Communication Research, has been a vigorous figure in the development of the field. Casey applied the insights of the political scientist into early studies of propaganda [100] and built a strong research department at the University of Minnesota during his tenure as dean of the journalism school.

96. Wilbur Schramm, "The Challenge to Communication Research," in Ralph Nafziger and David M. White, *Introduction to Mass Communication Research*, 2d ed. (Louisiana State U. P., Baton Rouge, La., 1963).

97. Wilbur Schramm, "The Nature of News," *Journalism Quarterly*, vol. 26, 1949, pp. 259–269; see also Wilbur Schramm and David Manning White, "Age, Education and Socio-Economic Status: Factors in Newspaper Reading," *Journalism Quarterly*, vol. 26, 1949, pp. 149–160.

98. Wilbur Schramm, Jack Lyle, and Edwin B. Parker, *Television in the Lives of Our Children* (Stanford U. P., Stanford, Calif., 1961).

99. Raymond B. Nixon, "Trends in Daily Newspaper Ownership Since 1945," *Journalism Quarterly*, vol. 32, 1955, pp. 3–14; see also Raymond B. Nixon, "Factors Related to Freedom in National Press Systems," *Journalism Quarterly*, vol. 37, 1960, pp. 13–28.

100. Bruce Smith, Harold D. Lasswell, and Ralph Casey (eds.), *Propaganda, Communication, and Public Opinion* (Princeton U. P., Princeton, N.J., 1946).

Both students and associates of these scholars have been conducting some highly sophisticated communications research with increasing momentum each year. The reader of this volume will find the *Journalism Quarterly* a rich source of current investigation into various phases of the communications process, with, of course, an emphasis on media-related variables.

A sampling of current research underway in 1962 by researchers at the various schools of journalism showed Wisconsin's Percy Tannenbaum investigating the effects of encoding in dyads and triads, while his colleague, Bruce H. Westley was studying selectivity in information seeking and media use. Another Wisconsin researcher, Lionel Barrow, has been testing the effects of cognitive incongruity upon encoding behavior. The late Paul Deutschmann of Michigan State spent a year recently in Costa Rica on problems of technical change in communication in Latin America. Reuben Mehling at the University of Rhode Island is continuing his studies in the ways that members of the same family influence each other's use of the mass media, while at the University of Washington Alex Edelstein is concerned with the place of the mass media in the political socialization of politically active and inactive university students. Jack Lyle, who collaborated with Wilbur Schramm and Edwin B. Parker in the definitive volume on the effects of television in the lives of children, is studying religious primary-group influence on perception of bias in the newspaper.

In the area of international communications, George Gerbner of Illinois is investigating the mass-media decision-making and control processes in ten countries. Gerbner is also conducting a comparative study of the image of education in five Western and five Eastern European countries. His colleague Dallas W. Smythe is studying the role of the mass media in foreign-policy formation.

These communications scholars, along with such men as Wayne Danielson and John B. Adams of North Carolina; Robert Jones, Roy Carter, Jr., Edwin Emery, and J. Edward Gerald of Minnesota; Bryant Kearl and Charles Higbie at Wisconsin; Walter Gieber at San Francisco State College; David Berlo, Hideo Kumata, John McNelly and Verling Troldahl at Michigan State; James Markham at Iowa; William Porter at Michigan; and Marvin Alisky at Arizona State—none of these workers, apparently, have heard that communications research is "dead."

In summarizing this brief review of the interdisciplinary vitality of communications research today, it is significant to note that recently a competition for research plans in the field of television was held under the auspices of the Television Bureau of Advertising.[101] The winners

101. L. Arons and M. May (eds.), *Television and Human Behavior: Tomorrow's Research in Mass Communications* (Appleton, New York, 1963).

included Arthur J. Brodbeck, a social psychologist currently working in the Project of Political Socialization at the Yale University Law School; Dr. Raymond Bauer of the Harvard Graduate School of Business Administration; Dr. Hilde Himmelweit of the London School of Economics; Dr. Harold Mendelsohn, a sociologist at the University of Denver; Dr. Lawrence Myers, Jr., director of research at Syracuse University's Television-Radio Center, and Dr. Kurt Back of Duke University.

The range of investigations, all of which appear to have generalizable implications for the developing theory of mass communications, is wide. Brodbeck (with Mrs. Dorothy B. Jones) is concerned with the role of television in shaping adolescent character and normative behavior; Bauer (with Donald F. Cox) is considering a new approach to rational versus emotional communications; Himmelweit is proposing an experimental study of taste development, and, following leads suggested by her previous studies, is attempting to determine how children can be interested in "intellectually challenging" television programs; Mendelsohn is hoping to investigate the process of effect of television in inducing action.

One further competition winner should be noted. He is Dr. Bernard Berelson, whose experiment would test whether television can be substantially better than it is now and still hold its audience. Berelson proposes a critical test in which two-thirds of the programming by the end of two years would have the quality of the top 20 percent of today's programming. His proposed study, to be organized in a single community, would determine the difference it makes to the audience.

CONCLUSION

Finally (Lewis Dexter also suggests), we have shown by extensive enumeration that Berelson's approach is in error—because it is based upon a premise that is false for most fields of science nowadays and probably at all times. Science is not generally produced or organized by just a few heroes who stand out above the multitude; it is rather the product of a group of men and women who contribute something, some much more than others, to be sure, but it is clearly a social phenomenon, not the result of some individual deviation. Presumably, this has always been so; but the difference between the present situation and the beginning stages of any science may be shown by contrasting Columbus with our current astronauts. Columbus, of course, did in fact rely upon many shipwrights, carpenters, seamen, navigators, and financers; nevertheless, his own initiative and determination made a difference of a few years in the discovery of the Americas. But our astronauts are members of a team; any discoveries they make are due to a social system; and no individual astronaut, no matter how much he may be celebrated or lauded, is of vital importance to the progress of space exploration at present. Men who remember when the air was being conquered by individually stimulated and individually organized pioneers like Charles Lindbergh may sigh for these dear, dead days of individualism; men who resent the constraints of organization may want to go back to the Lindbergh era and organize the conquest of space the same way; but the fact is that neither in the field of mass communications nor in any advancing field of science is there room and scope for the hero-type scholar who existed a few years ago. The very fact that scholarship and science are organized mean that dramatic heroes, men who build "schools," are less likely to develop—but this, although interesting in terms of the opportunity for individual glorification or discipleship, has nothing whatever to do with whether knowledge is progressing or not. In other words, a science can progress, can be "great," even if there are no "great" men in it.

Marten Brouwer

Mass Communication and the Social

Sciences: Some Neglected Areas *

THE FOLLOWING PAPER by Prof. Marten Brouwer of the University of
Amsterdam has been included in this volume for two reasons: the
author proposes an approach to mass-communications research which
demands thoughtful scrutiny; and he is representative of a number
of excellent scholars in Europe who are conducting significant studies
in the areas considered in this book.

Indeed, one of the main aspects of his paper is to make a plea to
us to consider that mass-communications research is not solely an
American undertaking. Even though Brouwer graciously reminds us
that "quite a number of the great American pioneers in communication research were Europeans by origin," he adds that "their main
contributions were produced in American settings with American
data." Two of the four great innovators mentioned by Berelson (pp.
503–509)—Lazarsfeld and Lewin—grew up and were educated respectively in Central Europe.

Dr. Brouwer's case that Americans should have better knowledge
of what European communications scholars are doing is substantiated
by reference to two "apparently little known works" of the eminent
German-Dutch communications specialist, Kurt Baschwitz. Brouwer
points out that the famous "two-step flow of communications" concept of Katz and Larzarsfeld was anticipated in studies by Baschwitz
as early as 1938 in his book, Du und die Masse: Studien zu einer
exakten Massenpsychologie.[1]

Further, according to Brouwer, Festinger's "theory of cognitive
dissonance," which has been referred to so often in the studies in
this book, was also anticipated by an earlier work of Baschwitz in
1948, De strijd met den duivel: de heksenprocessen in het licht der

* Reprinted from the *International Social Science Journal*, vol. 14, no. 2, 1962,
pp. 303–319. (Copyright 1962 by UNESCO.)
    1. *You and the Masses: Studies Toward an Exact Theory of Mass Psychology.*

massapsychologie.[2] Brouwer is aware of the difficulties involved in scholars keeping in "touch" with each others work, and his remarks point up the necessity of a "retrieval system" for the comparative study of mass communication, perhaps along the lines suggested by Gross in his article. Surely, one must agree with Brouwer's modest statement that there appears to be "an important neglect of European theories in the study of mass communication."

A recent volume by a young German sociologist, Jurgen Habermas (Strukturwandel der Öffentlichkeit,[3] Berlin, Luchterhand, 1962) amplifies the point made in Brouwer's article. In developing a provocative theory of public opinion, Habermas draws upon the work of well-known European communications scholars, such as Adorno, Noelle and Dovifat, whose work has appeared in various American journals. However, important references to the work of Altmann, H. Bahrdt, Abendroth, Forsthoff, Brunner, Groth, Fraenkel, Ramm, Plessner, Mischke, Eberhart, Schelsky, C. Schmitt and Wieland, among others, indicated to this writer the necessity of knowing what the German group of scholars in this field are thinking and writing. Another recent volume by Dr. Fritz Eberhard (Der Rundfunkhörer und sein Programm,[4] Berlin, Colloquium Verlag, 1962) may be read only by a handful of American communications scholars (unless it is translated into English), yet it contains some of the most fruitful research yet made into the manner in which listeners utilize radio in their daily lives.

The first part of Brouwer's paper deals with his suggestion that mass communications has almost exclusively "become characterized by an implicit conception of communication audiences as atomistic." He feels that the study of the communication audience as consisting of disparate and independent individuals leads to many false assumptions. Brouwer notes that several American sociologists—notably Blumer, Freidson, and the Rileys—have criticized the "atomistic" conception, but believes that much more work needs to be done in this area. He cites one of his own studies on attitudes toward India as an example of how the group rather than the individual should be examined in determining the effects of the mass media.

D. M. W.

DR. BROUWER was born in Ljouwert (Friesland) and studied social psychology at the University of Amsterdam, where he worked under Kurt Baschwitz, professor of mass communications and collective behavior. For a time he was in journalism and in opinion research, but

---

2. *The Struggle with the Devil: The Witch Trials in the Light of Mass Psychology.*
3. *Structural Changes of Public Opinion.*
4. *The Radio Listener and his Program.*

now teaches collective behavior at the University of Amsterdam. *He has given courses in mass communications and collective behavior at the summer session of Columbia University (1963), and is presently engaged in a study concerning the widespread effects of a Dutch television and radio marathon drive held in November 1962. Dr. Brouwer has made numerous contributions to journals and collections concerning television and advertising, content analyses of newspaper data, theory of mass communication, public-opinion studies (especially in cross-national comparison), methodology of stereotype research, measurement of communication effects, and pressure groups, and the public.*

The study of mass communication is increasingly being dominated by the social sciences. Indeed the very integration of the various media into one discipline is largely an accomplishment of this social-science approach, aided by market-research considerations. Starting in Europe with the newspaper, in the United States with radio research, a goodly number of applied social scientists came to feel in the thirties and forties that audiences were the primary object of investigation and, therefore, that the study of the mass media should be integrated (Brouwer and Daudt, 1956). This view has become generally accepted since, and consecutively an ubiquitous *rapprochement* arose between mass communication and the social sciences. One of its ramifications consists of the prevailing idea that the main subject matter of training programs for journalists, for example, ". . . should be the application of the principles, data, and methodology of the behavioral sciences . . ." (Bush, 1955, p. 246). Another and probably more commendable one is that a host of applied social scientists have invaded the field of mass communication and started to produce staggering piles of excellent research reports. Our knowledge of a number of aspects of mass-communication phenomena is certainly increasing swiftly.

While ardently subscribing to the view that the mass-communication process is to be studied primarily by social-science methods, we may find it worthwhile nevertheless to stop and consider some of the peculiar adverse contingencies consequent upon this unconditional surrender. There is quite a variety of them, ranging all the way from the neglect of the institutional aspects of the mass media to the curious separate development of scaling theory on the one hand and effect measurement on the other.

The present paper is an attempt to outline two neglected areas which may be held to be of particular importance. The first one deals with the atomistic conception of audiences and the resulting lack of differentiation between types of research unit. The second one is concerned with the preponderance of American studies and the attendant neglect of European theorizing. No claim is put forward for a complete or even a wide coverage of these two rather divergent areas. One may think of many other examples besides the illustrations to be advanced here, most of which stem from Dutch publications or research projects the author happens to be acquainted with.

THE ATOMISTIC CONCEPTION

Mass-communication research has to a large extent become characterized by an implicit conception of communication audiences as atomistic. Apparently the large majority of audience-research studies considers the individual the self-evident unit in mass-communication processes. Several factors may be held to have influenced this conception, which seems so natural that it goes unnoticed most of the time.

First, in actual practice the social-science approach to mass communication is primarily the approach of differential psychology. Many of the pioneers in modern communications research were psychologists by training. By and large, however, psychology (or at any rate behaviorist psychology) is concerned with the study of the human individual. Indeed, the individual is probably the legitimate unit of research if one is concerned with sensory perception, learning processes, and the like. It is only with the rise of small-group research that psychologists have come to realize the additional utility of other units. Even there the actual use of groups as units is none too frequent yet, and did not make its appearance until communications research was already well under way.

Secondly, mass-communication research and especially audience research has become imbedded in market research. Market research, again, is primarily concerned with the individual, considered as the main consumption unit for products in general and for the mass media in particular. The exception is, of course, the household; and indeed many audience research reports refer to family units, either explicitly and completely or implicitly and approximately—for example, when dealing with the number of television sets in use or with newspaper subscriptions. Notwithstanding this important exception, the main stress in market research is on the individual.

Thirdly, mass-communication research coincides to a great extent with opinion research. For a long time public-opinion polling tended, quite understandably, to take the prediction of election outcomes both as its paradigm and as its parade-horse. The democratic voting system provides a model, counting as it does in individual votes with equal weights. As a result, research in mass-communication processes was conceived of in an analogous fashion.

Fourthly, the data-gathering techniques and the facility of differentiation which they offer play a very important part too. The social sciences have come to find the individual interview or questionnaire or test their most natural and most easily applicable tool. It seems quite normal, then, to consider the main information producing unit—i.e., the individual—to be also the main unit in mass-communication processes and in social phenomena in general.

All this leads to an implicit conception of the communication audience as atomistic, as consisting of disparate and independent individuals. It results in the study of samples from a universe of individuals, to register how many people have read a given news item, heard some type of rumor, changed their opinion about a certain politician, and so on. Findings of this nature are considered then to reveal the core of mass-communication processes.

This atomistic conception has been criticized by several authors, notably by sociologists. One of the best known criticisms was launched by Herbert Blumer in his paper on public opinion and public opinion polling read before the American Sociological Society in 1947 (Blumer, 1954). Blumer's main point is the inadequacy of current polling methods, based as they are on the atomistic conception, as means of recording the public-opinion process. Be that as it may be, the most interesting feature of Blumer's paper in the present context is that even he makes an explicit exception for at least a large part of communications research: ". . . there are obviously many matters about human beings and their conduct that have just this character of being an aggregation of individuals or a congeries of individual actions. Many demographic matters are of this nature. Also, many actions of human beings in society are of this nature— such as casting ballots, purchasing toothpaste, going to motion-picture shows, and reading newspapers. Such actions, which I like to think of as mass actions of individuals in contrast to organized actions of groups, lend themselves readily to the type of sampling that we have in current public-opinion polling." (p. 77.)

In this way the atomistic or, in Blumer's terminology, the "mass" conception is rejected for the study of public opinion but continues to be accepted for audience research. It is interesting in this connexion to observe that Blumer himself contributed a great deal to the empirical study of mass communication in the early thirties. Nevertheless his view seems to be somewhat contradictory, since the public-opinion process and the mass-communication process are quite strongly interrelated in many respects. It is difficult to see why these two processes should be studied with different methods and more specifically with different research units, which is the implication of Blumer's stand.

Much more consistent is the argument presented by Freidson (1955) in his paper on communications research and the concept of the mass. This author sets out to explain that the character of audience experience is distinctly social. Research reports abound with evidence to the effect that mass communications have been absorbed into the social life of local groups. Consequently an audience cannot be equated with a mass in the Blumer sense, and audience research is rooted in a number of wrong assumptions. "To the extent that past research has studied the audience as if it were composed of discrete individuals, and has sought the significant determinants of audience taste and behavior only in the relation between content and the personal interests implied by the attributes of the individual spectator, past research has considered the audience to be a mass. If the concept of the mass is only inaccurately applied to the audience, the past research that owes its justification to such application has rested on an inaccurate foundation and suffers because of it." (Freidson, 1955, p. 386.)

For the greater part Freidson is undoubtedly right in his critique. Individual selections of specific communications, immediate reactions to them and subsequent judgements about them are all but inconceivable under isolated conditions with social factors playing no part at all. And, especially if one includes rumors, discussions, and other forms of diffuse public communication under the heading of mass communication, it becomes quite clear that the atomistic conception does not do complete justice to these processes. Other types of approach should be looked for, in order to get a more adequate insight in the social phenomenon of mass communication.

To some extent attempts have been made already to correct the atomistic conception. The two-step flow or personal influence hypothesis represents on such attempt, as has been stated explicitly (Katz and Lazarsfeld, 1955, p. 33). In other cases the position of an individual in his social surroundings is taken into account by converting it into an individual variable (e.g., Riley and Riley, 1951; Rokkan and Torsvik, 1960). And, in summing up present-day knowledge about the effects of mass communication, Klapper refers explicitly to groups and group norms in many of his chapters (Klapper, 1960).

Commendable as these attempts may be, it should be recognized that they continue to consider the individual the research and sampling unit. By thus sampling from a universe of individuals and then estimating population parameters or testing relationships, the atomistic model is retained implicitly. Although group influences are taken into account, it is still not the group phenomenon but the individual phenomenon that is being studied and explained.

This holds true also when generalizations are made with respect to some hypothetical universe, even though in these cases the drawbacks of the model are often quite apparent. Many laboratory and field experiments belong to this category. A sample is not drawn from some well-defined universe, but instead available groups of students or school classes or army platoons are subjected to experimental communications. The first and probably inevitable assumption in this procedure is that the communication effects to be recorded will not be too specific for the groups which happen to be studied. This type of assumption, of course, often has to be used in experimental work in various other branches of science as well. A second assumption is often that the effects to be recorded will be independent observations for each of the individual subjects in the groups. This second assumption is less inevitable and also less tenable than the first one, however. If natural units like classes are being used, more likely than not the individuals within each unit will be relatively homogeneous in many respects.

As an illustrative example, some data may be quoted from a recent scale comparison experiment on attitudes toward India, carried out for Unesco (Brouwer and van Bergen, 1960). Five different attitude scales were used in the SCE study, one of which was a Likert-type scale. Four different communications were presented, one of which was a motion picture about Benares. Taking only the scale scores of those students filling out the Likert scale before the presentation of the Benares picture, one ends up with 160 individual scores. These scores are to be divided in groups of 8 for the 20 high schools in which the experiment took place. Computation of the Kruskal-Wallis test (a one-way analysis of variance by ranks [Siegel, 1956, p. 184–93]) results in $H = 32.8$ and $0.05 > P > 0.02$.[1] One may conclude, therefore, that the 20 groups of scores cannot be considered samples from identical populations. Comparable results are obtained for other scales and communications used in the SCE study. Apparently students at the same school were more similar to one another than to students of other schools, at least as far as attitudes toward India were concerned.

$$\text{1. } H = \frac{12}{N(N+1)} \cdot \sum_{1}^{k} \frac{R_j^2}{n_j} - 3(N+1)$$

where k = number of schools
n_j = number of individuals in jth school
N = total number of individuals in all schools
R_j = sum of ranks in jth school

H is distributed approximately as chi square with $df = k - 1$. P refers to the probability of the null hypothesis; i.e., in the present case, the hypothesis that there is no difference in the average attitude score of individuals from different schools.

This type of finding is not to be thought of as exceptional, of course. Generally speaking, any particular communication audience will be rather homogeneous to begin with. This, however, makes it all the more important to take the statistical and other implications into account. There are several ways of making allowances for this homogeneity.

First of all, one may simply think of it as an unfortunate consequence of cluster sampling. Often it is nearly impossible to take a random sample of a universe, whereas the sampling of clusters appears to be much more feasible. The universe of high school students is a case in point, as would be the universe of newspaper readers, or the hypothetical universe of people to be exposed as a group to an experimental communication. The effect of clustering on sampling results is quite serious, however, and may be corrected by taking the intraclass correlation into account (Kish, 1953, p. 208ff.). In this way it is still possible to arrive at valid estimations of population parameters, albeit in a somewhat more complex manner than usual. In most instances, however, research workers tend to neglect clustering problems.

On the other hand one should recognize that this procedure, although technically correct, relapses into the atomistic conception. The individual remains the ultimate unit, even though due allowance is made for the fact that, in actual practice, individuals tend to cluster in relatively homogeneous groups. In this way the main problem is still to be solved. The emphasis should be not so much on the observation that individuals happen to be alike within each cluster as on the observation that their behavior is interdependent. Corrections for intraclass correlation will do when individuals are to be measured with respect to, say, height or age or maybe intelligence. However, the more an attribute to be measured is dependent on the very cluster situation, the more it becomes necessary to study not individuals but clusters.

Now this is exactly the point which was made earlier with reference to mass communication processes. In many respects it seems to make quite a difference whether an individual is isolated or in a group when he is exposed to some communication; moreover, the group situation is the more natural one. One aspect of this interdependence is concerned with homogeneity once more: an interruption from among the audience, or a slight variation in the experimenter's introducing the communication may have a homogenizing influence on the audience. This and the problem of selection mentioned before have led Katz (1953, p. 93) to state: "The field study is particularly susceptible to cluster effects. In the laboratory we can set up our experiments to guard against this difficulty. In surveys we can sample in random fashion to avoid clustering. But in a community or a group under field study our cases are often pocketed in homogeneous subgroups, where the clustering effect must be carefully considered." Katz recommends that the number of clusters in a field study should be taken as the proper N, not the number of individuals. Similar ideas are expressed, although not always followed, elsewhere (e.g., Hovland et al., 1949, p. 327).

It would be wrong, however, to consider the homogenizing influence just a disturbing factor, as Katz seems to be doing. For this influence may be held to belong to the very characteristics of audience experience. Moreover, it is not inconceivable that some audiences should tend to become more heterogeneous instead of less, e.g., when low status members want to show reactions opposite to those of high status members. If these and kindred processes play an important part in communication audiences, the individual no longer appears as an obvious unit and it does not make sense to correct for intraclass correlation, or to randomize individuals in the laboratory, or simply to adopt conventional survey sampling procedures. Instead particular audiences are to be considered the appropriate units in all or at least most mass communication situations, not just for statistical but also for theoretical reasons.

When an audience is taken as a unit, however, a considerable change of perspective has to be effected. Most typically, one has to think of ways and means of measuring group properties. Relevant classifications have been provided by several authors (notably Kendall and Lazarsfeld, 1950, and Cattell, 1951). Their systematizations have in common a distinction between, on the one hand, group properties which are a function of individual properties, and, on the other hand, group properties which cannot, or at least cannot easily, be reduced to individual properties. Kendall and Lazarsfeld present a more detailed subclassification of the former category, while Cattell subdivides the latter category. The most important distinction seems to be the one they share, however. The editors of *The Language of Social Research* label the relative categories "aggregative properties" and "global properties," respectively, and they express the feeling that these classifications are especially pertinent to the study of smaller groups (Lazarsfeld and Rosenberg, 1955, p. 287).

However, they seem to be adequate too in mass communication research, including the area in which it is no longer feasible to talk of "smaller groups." With respect to audiences, aggregative properties would then be parameters of the distributions of individual attitudes, opinions, or, most specifically of all, responses to a communication. In its simplest form the measurement of an audience property would be the summation or the mean of the individual properties. Global properties would be length of applause, amount of laughter, and the like. It seems clear, though, that not much experience has yet been gained with the recording of global properties in mass-communication research. On the other hand, even within the realm of aggregative properties, much remains to be done to get rid of the vestiges of atomistic thinking.

An illustration may be given with reference to the very data from the SCE study already quoted before. The 160 individual Likert scores are combined into school class scores by simply adding the 8 individual scores within each class. In this way a series of 20 class attitude scores arises, referring to the mean individual attitude score per class before the presentation of the Benares picture. Similarly, there is a matched series of class attitude scores referring to the attitudes after the presentation of the picture. By computing the difference between the two scores for each separate class, 20 independent effect scores are to be found. For the data at hand, these effect scores happen to be mainly negative, the computation of Wilcoxon's matched-pairs signed-ranks test (Siegel, 1956, p. 75–83) leading to $T = 4$ and $0.01 > P$ (Brouwer and van Bergen, 1960, p. 31). In other words, one may suppose that, for the hypothetical universe of school classes (not individuals) to be exposed to the Benares motion picture, the effect on class attitudes toward India is mainly negative if measured in this way.

It might have been measured in many other ways, however. In the present context the variation as to type of attitude scale—which, by the way, was the main object of study in the experiment—is not relevant. But another possible variation has to do with the fact that, considerations of clustering and sampling size apart, the result just quoted is a mere reformulation of the data regarding individual students. The class scores are crude aggregative properties in that they are simple functions of the individual scores, since, for example, care was taken during the experimental sessions to ensure that each student would fill out his sheets independently. In view of the main purpose of the SCE study, this was an obvious precaution to take. In the present argument, however, it seems a further example of tribute being paid to the atomistic conception. It should be stressed that this is a recurrent observation: phenomena which, from one angle, are a disturbing influence—to be obviated or corrected for by the experimenter—may prove, from another angle, to be the very thing to be studied.

For experiments with audiences this may be interpreted to mean that there may be good reason for encouraging rather than preventing oral communication between the subjects when filling out test blanks. Similarly, it may be quite useful to have the subjects discuss the contents of the experimental communication before doing the postmeasurements. As a matter of fact this is exactly what will have happened in between the immediate postmeasurement and the later postmeasurement in the SCE study. Several months after the experiment itself the schools were revisited in order to obtain a measurement of the long-term effects, this time with a Thurstone scale only. On the whole, there seems to be no long-term effect at all. This can be illustrated in the following way.

In each school one class had been exposed to an unfavorable motion picture (the Benares picture), and another class had been exposed to a favorable motion picture (a picture about India's rapid industrialization). Indeed, in the immediate postmeasurements, in 19 out of 20 schools the former class showed a more unfavorable attitude than the latter. In the later postmeasurements, however, only 10 schools still showed a difference in this direction, while 8 schools showed a difference in the opposite direction (2 schools no longer being available for measurement).

An obvious explanation of this result would be that the exposure to these short and maybe none too impressive communications produced an immediate effect which was rather superficial; it therefore wore out rather quickly, aided moreover by the wide variety of other factors which would have had their impact on attitudes toward India during the months in between the experiment and the later postmeasurements. This explanation runs counter to some of the classic experiments in changing attitudes of school children by exposure to motion pictures (e.g., Peterson and Thurstone, 1933), but it is a plausible one. A second explanation would be, however, that in each of the schools a good deal of informal communication arose between the various classes regarding the communications they had been exposed to and also regarding the resultant feelings about India; as a result the considerable attitude differences produced at first by the differing communications were largely cancelled out. This explanation does not exclude the first one, of course, but it would entail different consequences in several respects.

Some evidence in support of the second explanation is to be observed when relating the long-term effects to differences between classes of one and the same school which were already in existence before any communication had been presented. In some schools preexisting differences in attitude scale scores were rather large, in other schools they were negligible. If they were large it may have been that the industrialization picture was shown in the more unfavorable class, or it may have been that the Benares picture was shown in that class. The first explanation advanced above, that of a wearing-out process, would not imply any connection with these differences. However, if the schools are ranked according to magnitude and direction of preexisting differences between the "industrialization" class and the "Benares" class, this rank order appears to be correlated with the direction and magnitude of the net effect to be observed in the later postmeasurement (Spearman's rank correlation coefficient $\rho = 0.42$; $0.05 > P$).

In other words and figures: if the experimenters happened to present the favorable picture to the much more unfavorable class and vice versa, the net long-term effect [2] was much like the immediate effect (mean net effect $= + 14.4$, $N = 4$). If there was not much difference between the classes originally, the net long-term effect was also like the immediate effect, but less markedly so (mean net effect $= + 10.5$, $N = 4$). If, however, the experimenters happened to present the favorable picture to the already somewhat more favorable class and the unfavorable picture to the already somewhat more unfavorable class, there was no appreciable net long-term effect (mean net effect $= - 1.6$, $N = 4$). Lastly, if they happened to present the favorable picture to the already much more favorable class and vice versa, the net long term effect went contrary to the immediate effect (mean net effect $= - 12.6$, $N = 6$).

These data may be explained by supposing that each class was subject to a tendency to reach a score not too different from the one reached by the other class of the same school. Therefore the net long-term effect to be expected as a remainder of the net immediate effect was greatly reduced or even reversed, especially in those cases where otherwise the differences between the two classes would have become too large. One can scarcely imagine how this could have come about without considerable informal communication between the classes after the experiment itself or without the existence of some sort of school group norms. The effect of such group norms on attitude change processes has been clearly demonstrated in other studies (MacKeachie, 1954).

If the argument advanced is right, however, it should be recognized too that even the choice of class units instead of individual units was not sufficient for the measurement of long-term effects. School units might have proved a better choice, at least if the complexities of long-term changes had been contemplated carefully before the study was designed and, more especially, if the recording of these changes had been considered of prime importance. As it stands now, little more can be analyzed with regard to the school units because the two classes in one school were apparently subjected to contradictory communications.

To sum up, both theoretical arguments and empirical findings indicate that the atomistic conception is not quite adequate for much of mass communication research. On the other hand, it seems that we still have a long way to go before we can free ourselves of all its implications. Within

---

2. The net long-term effect being the favorable long-term effect of the favorable picture plus the unfavorable long-term effect of the unfavorable picture in one and the same school.

the realm of aggregative properties, maybe more attention should be paid to possibilities other than answering or filling out questionnaires in private: subjects may have to be encouraged to discuss their opinions publicly before responding privately; they might be asked to give their impressions about prevailing group feelings, not in order to have the experimenter check up on individual projection tendencies, etc., but in order to use these impressions just as the anthropologist uses his informants; and they might be requested to give some kind of public vote on a number of communication-related statements. With regard to global properties, a good deal could be learnt from the way impressionistic judgments about audience behavior used to be made by many commercial stage experts; maybe in the long run this would lead to the development of more scientifically rigorous audience-observation methods. At any rate, it is clear that much remains to be done. And it will be only when the methodology of assessing group properties has taken a great step forward that the problem of individual properties will have to be brought up again, in order to study the interrelations between individual and group phenomena in audience behavior. Until then we shall be perfectly justified in talking about a neglected area.

EUROPEAN THEORIES

Mass-communication research nowadays seems to be largely an American undertaking. The journals and handbooks in this field, even those published outside the United States, are replete with studies by American authors on American samples. Moreover, most of the other studies reported are characterized by American features. Some of these have been carried out by American investigators with respondents from elsewhere. Other studies are products of European or Asian research teams with American experts cooperating. And many of the so-called cross-cultural studies are in fact replications elsewhere of studies first carried out in the United States.

There is good reason for this situation. With respect to the development of the modern mass media themselves, America has long been leading the field. The same holds true for the advancement of empirical social science in many respects. The integration of mass-communication studies in the framework of the social sciences means that the two tendencies are combined. Add to this the differential consequences of World War II for the countries engaged in it, and it becomes patently clear why America is so dominant in the social-science approach to mass communication. The enduring opposition of many European scholars to quantitative research only serves to strengthen the contrast.

As a result, the actual state of communication research may be described in almost exclusively American references. Berelson (1959), in summing up his rather pessimistic views in this respect, quotes the major accomplishments in the thirties and early forties of Lasswell, Lazarsfeld, Lewin, and Hovland. His opponents, Schramm, Riesman, and Bauer, strike a more optimistic note by mentioning, among others, some more recent approaches they consider to be also of major importance (Schramm et al., 1959); but again the examples are American. Even if we grant that quite a number of the great American pioneers in communication research were Europeans by origin, it should be recognized that their main contributions were produced in American settings with American data. The flag of mass communication seems to consist of research stars and theory stripes forever.

With respect to theory especially, however, this situation has some regrettable consequences. If the development of theoretical notions has to be based on empirical findings, and if the empirical findings in this field are largely American, there seems to be no need to take cognizance of European writings, except for the more recent American-inspired research reports. Both Americans and empirically minded Europeans tend to take this line of reasoning. In doing so they happen to neglect European theories of great interest. Undoubtedly translation difficulties may also influence the situation to some extent, but these alone would not prove insurmountable. The neglect even includes cases of new concepts and theories being constructed apparently without knowledge of the fact that comparable concepts and theories, along with their empirical applications, were already in existence from which considerable profit might have been gained.

In the next few pages two such cases will be described, both referring to the apparently little known works of the German-Dutch communications specialist Kurt Baschwitz. The first case pertains to the personal influence or two-step flow hypothesis and will be touched upon but briefly. The second case deals with the theory of cognitive dissonance and will be covered at greater length.

The personal influence theory is described as having originated almost accidentally from the 1940 investigation of the presidential election by Lazarsfeld and others. "It had been generally assumed previously that opinions were formed by the elite of the community, and then percolated down from one social stratum to the next until all followed the lead of the conspicuous persons at the apex of the community structure. But the 1940 election study seemed to indicate the parallel existence of what was then called horizontal opinion leadership. Each social stratum generated its own opinion leaders—the individuals who were likely to influence other persons in their immediate environment." (Katz and Lazarsfeld, 1955, p. 3.) A number of studies were designed to check this assumption and the related notion of a two-step flow of communication: from the mass media to the opinion leaders and from the opinion leaders to the public at large. By now the hypothesis has become quite well known and the relevant studies have been described as constituting ". . . an example of continuity and cumulation both in research design and theoretical commitment" (Katz, 1957, p. 76).

Less well known and clearly not included in the exemplary "continuity and cumulation" is Baschwitz' parallel but independent treatment of the same theme (Baschwitz, 1938, 1948a). Baschwitz took his lead from older American authors, such as Ross, with their notions concerning the hierarchy of public opinion. But then he set out to explain that this concept should be interpreted to mean that almost any individual is able to find somebody in his immediate surroundings to whom he may turn for advice in a specific area. It is not true, therefore, that the public at large consists of stupid, ignorant people who can be easily influenced by the mass media in any direction. On the contrary, the public behaves rather intelligently by knowing to which little expert to turn in each particular area.

Baschwitz includes phenomena of differential self-exposure to the mass media in his treatment of the hierarchy principle and he also relates this to the concept of "leading minorities" in collective behavior. Moreover, his approach in general is also quite different from the type of methodology applied by Katz and others. The general tenor of his argument, however, is clearly similar to the personal influence hypothesis and the relevant American findings.

An even clearer example of such parallelism can be seen in regard to Festinger's theory of cognitive dissonance (Festinger, 1957). Festinger himself describes how his theory originated with a hunch concerning the interpretation of some rumor data reported by Prasad. These rumors, following the great Indian earthquake of 1934, were puzzling in that a vast majority of them predicted even worse disasters to be imminent. An explanation is advanced in terms of considering these unpleasant rumors not to be anxiety-provoking, as they seem to be on the surface, but to be anxiety-justifying. People who felt the shock of the earthquake but who did not see any damage or destruction had, according to Festinger's interpretation, a strong fear reaction without however seeing anything to be afraid of; therefore they just invented things to be afraid of.

On the basis of these and other findings, Festinger formulates a general theory about the consonance and dissonance of cognitions. Within any area of relevance, a person's cognitions (that is, his knowledge, opinions and beliefs about the environment and about himself) may be mutually dissonant (that is, inconsistent, but without the logical connotations of that term) or consonant (that is, consistent, with the same proviso). The theory goes that cognitive dissonance, being psychologically uncomfortable, will motivate the person to try to reduce the dissonance and bring about some form of consonance. Moreover, the person will actively avoid situations and information which would be likely to increase the dissonance.

Festinger explains how, on the basis of this theory, it becomes possible to explain a wide variety of observations reported by others, and furthermore to predict the outcome of a number of experiments designed specifically to test this theory. Among the evidence thus found, mass-communication data are quite prominent. In fact, the theory originated within a project designed to establish, at the request of Bernard Berelson, a propositional inventory regarding communication and social influence.

To quote a few illustrative examples: new-car owners tend not to read advertisements dealing with other cars than their own, as the content of these advertisements will presumably be dissonant with their recent buying decision. Heavy smokers refuse to accept information on the linkage between cigarette smoking and lung cancer, because it is dissonant with their smoking behavior. People having improvised a speech defending a position dissonant with their private opinion are apt afterwards to change this private opinion in the direction of the speech they had to improvise. Probably the best known application of the theory is the study of the "Seekers," a small American movement believing that on a given date a flood would destroy the world, but that those who were chosen would be picked up by flying saucers before the cataclysm. When the belief was shown to be unfounded because nothing at all happened on the predicted date, the members of the movement started proselytizing on a large scale. The theoretical explanation advanced for this somewhat surprising behavior is that, in seeking more social support for their beliefs, the members tried to reduce the magnitude of the cognitive dissonance between their beliefs and the failure of the facts to substantiate them.

Festinger does not claim that his theory is entirely new. As concrete and succinct statements of a parallel character, he quotes Heider, with his notions regarding "balance" and "imbalance," and Osgood and Tannenbaum, with their "principle of congruity" (Festinger, 1957, p. 7). A similar point is made by Zajonc, who sets out to compare the implications of these and other (notably Newcomb's) concepts of consistency (Zajonc, 1960). Again, a comparison of consistency concepts is to be found in a relevant paper by Osgood (1960). Neither Festinger nor Osgood nor Zajonc, however, seem to be aware of the much more striking resemblance of the cognitive dissonance theory to a theory presented long before by Baschwitz under the label of "Entlastungsbedürfnis" or "vereffenings-behoefte," which may be translated respectively by something like "need of relief" or "need of balance" (Baschwitz, 1923, 1938).

Baschwitz was originally concerned with the observation that, contrary to the teachings of the Roman school of collective psychology, lynchings, and similar acts of collective aggression under conditions of terrorization are usually abhorred by the large majority of the public present. Nevertheless, afterwards these same people tend to consider the victims guilty somehow or other. Whether educated or not, whether intelligent or not, they cling to this idea vehemently without regard for common sense or sober information to the contrary. Writers like Sighele, Le Bon, and Tarde interpreted this phenomenon as evidence for their theory concerning the nonintelligent, instinctive behavior of collectivities. Baschwitz explains it, however, by pointing to the subjective discrepancy existing for the public between its abhorrence of the crime on the one hand and its neglect to prevent it from happening on the other. In order to resolve this intolerable situation, the horrible nature of the crime is mitigated by inventing offences the victims must have been guilty of to deserve such severe punishment. In this way collective delusions may come into being and propaganda accusing the victims will find ready acceptance.

Moreover, as Baschwitz states, the notion of a "need of balance" also applies to many other situations. Take, for example, the case of a person who is receiving considerable financial or other support from a friend, without being able to do anything material in return. More likely than not he will perceive this situation as a discrepancy between the friendship relation as he conceives of it ideally and the actual relation of dependence. He retaliates therefore by crying down his friend's characteristics in many ways, especially in connexion with the very support provided. On this basis explanations may be advanced for such different observations as, on the interindividual level, the hostile relation between the wives of Marx and Engels, and, on the international level, the European proclivity to find fault with the United States after the institution of the Marshall Plan.

The most extensive application of the concept is to be found in Baschwitz's monograph on the history of the witch trials in Europe and America between 1500 and 1750 (Baschwitz, 1948b). Probably about a million people, mostly aged women, were tortured and killed during this period because they were supposed to have performed evil deeds of magic. Now one of the striking facts about these trials is that not only the population at large but also and especially the otherwise intelligent and well-educated members of the witch tribunals succumbed to this collective delusion. The thing to wonder at is not the belief in witchcraft itself, which was quite normal at the time, but the belief in its general occurrence in this malicious form among otherwise simple and virtuous persons. That belief went contrary to the common sense of both the public and the judges.

Baschwitz interprets this contradiction as a consequence of the terrorization exercised by fanatics believing in the strong powers of the Devil. Such fanatics were the main organizers and leaders of the witch trials, like Matthew Hopkins in Britain, Former and Binsfeld in Germany, Rémy in France, Cotton Mather in the United States. Anyone, including members of the tribunals, who ventured to express doubts regarding the truth of the accusations, would thereby risk being accused himself. Submissiveness meant cooperation, however, and resulted in a strong subjective discrepancy between the private opinions of the judges and their actual verdicts. This discrepancy, characterized by strong guilt feelings, was intolerable because of man's need of balance. It could be resolved, however, by coming to believe in the accusations made. By the same token, the judges would become immune against argumentations to the effect that the victims might have been innocent; even more so than the public at large, which had not actually cooperated in the trials and therefore would not experience the need of balance so strongly.

In this way Festinger's theory is anticipated in many respects. To enumerate the most important features: (a) Baschwitz and Festinger are dealing with the same area, namely, inconsistency; (b) they both extend the applicability of their concepts to a wide variety of individual and social phenomena; (c) to a state of inconsistency they both impute a motivating force in its own right, a need which works toward the reduction of the inconsistency and toward the prevention of its aggravation by outside factors; (d) they are both concerned primarily with the explanation of nonobvious events which go contrary to common sense and conventional psychological theory; (e) they use similar conceptual specifications, e.g., in studying the effect of forced compliance on private opinion, either in the laboratory (Festinger) or in history (Baschwitz); (f) they are both interested especially in the reception of propaganda and in collective behavior.

Naturally, there are great differences too. Festinger is typically concerned first with the formulation of his theory and secondly with its applications; Baschwitz is typically concerned first with specific historical or other phenomena and secondarily with the formulation of his theory. Also, Festinger is clearly working in an experimental tradition, Baschwitz mainly in a historical tradition. In view of these very differences, however, together with considerations of chronological precedence, it seems to be self-evident that a careful study of Baschwitz's writing should be included in any future exposition regarding the theory of cognitive dissonance.

The two examples cited demonstrate clearly that there may be an important neglect of European theories in the study of mass communication. This should certainly be remedied and an inventory of non-Americanized European (and other) theory and research seems to be called for. Lazarsfeld (1957) has already made a similar plea in his article on public opinion and the classical tradition, which he illustrated by referring to older authors such as Oncken, Dicey, Lowell, and others. The present argument differs from Lazarsfeld's in two respects, however.

First, the most serious neglect is held to concern European theories of comparatively recent origin and not the classical tradition in general. For the reasons mentioned at the beginning of this section, the discontinuity happens to be most marked and most unfortunate with respect to developments in Europe after World War II. Secondly, the empirical verification of such "classical insights" may be feasible much more frequently than Lazarsfeld supposes. "The propositions which the classics developed were of a broader and altogether different nature from the more microscopic findings with which we concern ourselves today. Only rarely is the discrepancy small enough to allow the problems of interest in the older tradition to be approached with the techniques and orientations of the newer one." (Lazarsfeld, 1957, p. 46.) In cases like the comparison of Baschwitz and Festinger it seems to be more appropriate to state that the propositions concerned are about equally broad; that the research strategy employed is in general rather different; but that both types of research strategy may serve as empirical verifications in their own right, which are mutually complementary. Therefore, an inventory of neglected theory and research could really be worth while.

SELECTED PUBLICATIONS BY DR. BROUWER

Brouwer, M., and H. Daudt, "Perswetenschap: massapsychologie en theorie der massacommunicatie," in *Perswetenschap, propaganda en openbare mening*, Leyden, 1956.*

Brouwer, M., and A. van Bergen, *Communication effects on attitudes toward India. A scale comparison experiment*. Amsterdam (mimeographed), 1960.

* "Persuasion: Mass Psychology in the Theory of Mass Communications," in *Persuasion, Propaganda, and Public Opinion*, Leyden, 1956.

BIBLIOGRAPHY

Baschwitz, Kurt, 1923, *Der Massenwahn, seine Wirkung und seine Beherrschung: Ursache und Heilung des Deutschenhasses.* Munich. (3rd ed., 1932.)

————, 1938, *Du und die Masse. Studien zu einer exakten Massenpsychologie.* Amsterdam (2nd German ed., 1951; Dutch ed., 1940, 2nd Dutch ed., 1951).

————, 1948a, *De intelligentie van het krantenlezend publiek.* Leiden, German ed., 1950.

————, 1948b, *De strijd met den duivel. De heksenprocessen in het licht der massapsychologie.* Amsterdam.

————, 1963, *Hexen und Hexenprozesse.* Munich.

Berelson, Bernard, 1959, "The State of Communication Research," *Public Opinion Quarterly,* vol. 23, pp. 1–6.

Blumer, Herbert, 1954, "Public opinion and Public Opinion Polling," in Daniel Katz et al. (eds.), *Public Opinion and Propaganda,* New York, pp. 70–84. [Originally in *American Sociological Review,* vol. 13, 1948, pp. 542–554.]

Brouwer, Marten, and H. Daudt, 1956, "Perswetenschap, massapsychologie en theorie der massacommunicatie," in *Perswetenschap, propaganda en openbare mening,* Leyden, pp. 160–176.

————, and Annie van Bergen, 1960. "Communication Effects on Attitudes toward India: A Scale Comparison Experiment," Amsterdam (mimeographed).

Bush, Chilton R., 1955, "Journalism Research and Research Training Programs in the USA," *Gazette,* vol. 1, pp. 243–247.

Cattell, Raymond B., 1955, "Types of group characteristics," in Paul F. Lazarsfeld and Morris Rosenberg, pp. 297–301. [Originally and fully in H. Guetzkow (ed.), *Groups, Leadership, and Men,* 1951, pp. 16–22.]

Festinger, Leon, 1957, *A Theory of Cognitive Dissonance* (Harper, New York).

————, and Daniel Katz (eds.), 1953, *Research Methods in the Behavioral Sciences* (New York).

Freidson, Eliot, 1955, "Communications Research and the Concept of the Mass," in Schramm, 1955, pp. 380–388. (Originally in *American Sociological Review,* 1953.)

Hovland, Carl I., Arthur A. Lumsdaine, and Fred D. Sheffield, 1949, *Experiments on Mass Communication* (Princeton).

Katz, Daniel, 1953, "Field Studies," in Festinger and Katz, 1953, pp. 56–97.

Katz, Elihu, 1957, "The Two-step Flow of Communication: an Up-to-date Report on an Hypothesis," *Public Opinion Quarterly,* vol. 21, pp. 61–78.

————, and Paul F. Lazarsfeld, 1955, *Personal Influence: The Part Played by People in the Flow of Mass Communications* (Free Press, New York).

Kendall, Patricia L., and Paul F. Lazarsfeld, 1950. "The Relation Between Individual and Group Characteristics in The American Soldier, in Lazarsfeld and Rosenberg, 1955, pp. 290–296. [Originally and fully in Robert K. Merton and Paul F. Lazarsfeld (eds.), *Studies in the Scope and Method of The American Soldier* (Free Press, New York, 1950), pp. 133–196.]

Kish, Leslie, 1953, "Selection of the Sample," in Festinger and Katz, 1953, pp. 175–239.

Klapper, Joseph T., 1960, *The Effects of Mass Communication* (Free Press, New York).

Lazarsfeld, Paul F., 1957, "Public Opinion and the Classical Tradition," *Public Opinion Quarterly,* vol. 21, pp. 39–53.

————, and Morris Rosenberg (eds.), 1955, *The Language of Social Research.*

A Reader in the Methodology of Social Research (Free Press, New York).

MacKeachie, Wilbert J., 1954, "Individual Conformity to Attitudes of Classroom Groups," *Journal of Abnormal and Social Psychology,* vol. 49, pp. 282–289.

Osgood, Charles E., 1960, "Cognitive Dynamics in the Conduct of Human Affairs," *Public Opinion Quarterly,* vol. 24, pp. 341–365.

Peterson, Ruth C., and L. L. Thurstone, 1933, *Motion Pictures and the Social Attitudes of Children* (New York).

Riley, Matilda White, and John W. Riley, Jr., 1955, "A Sociological Approach to Communications Research," in Schramm, 1955, pp. 389–401. (Originally in *Public Opinion Quarterly,* 1951.)

Rokkan, Stein, and Per Torsvik, 1960, "The Voter, the Reader and the Party Press: an Analysis of Political Preference and Newspaper Reading in Norway," *Gazette,* vol. 6, pp. 311–328.

Schramm, Wilbur (ed.), 1955, *The Process and Effects of Mass Communication* (U. of Illinois Press, Urbana).

———, David Riesman, and Raymond A. Bauer, 1959, "Comments on 'The State of Communication Research,'" *Public Opinion Quarterly,* vol. 23, pp. 6–17.

Siegel, Sidney, 1956, *Nonparametric Statistics for the Behavioral Sciences* (New York).

Zajonc, Robert B., 1900, "The Concepts of Balance, Congruity, and Dissonance," *Public Opinion Quarterly,* vol. 24, pp. 280–296.

QUESTIONS

1. Brouwer's explicit concern is with the neglect of particular pieces of research in mass communications by scholars in that field. What are these? Why do you think they may have been overlooked? Can you draw any more general inference from his demonstration that in fact scholars have overlooked significant work?

2. Compare the present volume with other readers frequently used in introductory courses in mass communications; make a list for each book of the types of research and problems which it neglects and which are included by others.

3. See if by studying any specific group of books or journals you can locate other neglected areas—areas where a contribution is made, apparently, to mass-communications work, but which is not passed on. (Confine yourself to material published at least three years before the book in question was published; the lead time problem always means some delay.)

4. In what sense is a textbook writer like White's "gatekeeper"? (See pp. 161–172.)

Lewis Anthony Dexter

Opportunities for Further Research

in Mass Communications

I

Brouwer, in the preceding article, discusses several areas to which, in his judgment, too little attention is customarily paid by people doing research on mass communications. This chapter is an effort to add to Brouwer's contribution by suggesting other areas where research is neglected and needed.

Most textbooks suffer from one great danger. They tend to create the impression that what has been discovered or validated is the most significant aspect of a discipline or science. There is no reason why this should be so—particularly in a new discipline such as the study of mass communications. Scientific study tends of necessity to be directed by existing tools, so that communications specialists study matters which can be handled through the sample survey and the opinion-oriented interview. But possibly other techniques, yet to be invented or applied to the study of mass communications, may permit us to tackle questions not yet seriously studied and enable us to materially alter the nature of our field. In other words, practical needs often determine what is studied in any new science, because practical needs determine what tools are available.

Another reason why the first approaches to scientific problems are not necessarily the most useful is this: The theoretical models applied and borrowed tend to be selected, not in terms of what would be most desirable—*that* has to be discovered—but in terms of what is most fashionable and respectable in seemingly related sciences.

These comments are made in order to underline the point that scientific constructions should always be regarded as tentative. It is important to say this because there are very strong pressures in the organization of the classroom and, indeed of the human mind, in our society at least, to regard a current formulation as final.

The foregoing point is particularly worth stressing because for all we can know what a survey of the field neglects to say is as important as what is said. In part, important matters are left out because "nobody has thought of them," which means that the ideas have not yet been generally recognized by the leaders of a discipline. And, in part, they are left out because, although they are recognized as important, they either have not been studied or the studies are unsatisfactory.

We have, however, felt that, by overlooking the unfinished, unsatisfactory, perceived but not formulated aspects of a discipline, textbooks and readers create a false impression of finish and definitiveness, and, above all, mislead the student by omitting many important possibilities.

Actually, if it were economical an honestly prepared textbook would have considerably more white space than printed material—some of the white space would have titles or questions preceding it, some of it would be completely blank. This would suggest, visually, the point we are trying to make—that in all disciplines, but especially in a new discipline, far more remains to be discovered than has been learned.

I I

To exemplify some of the things we do not know:

We really do not know, for instance, whether the processes of mass communication are significantly different in such different situations as these—simply by way of example:

[1] Members of some church and trade union groups are actively "propagandized" or "oriented" towards taking one stand or another on issues which are of great importance to the membership, but which have little or no meaning outside the membership. For instance, the American Unitarian Association was somewhat agitated in recent years by the issue of whether to merge with the Universalists, and within the Congregational churches there has been a much more intense controversy about the merger which finally led to a united church. And members or potential members of international unions, such as the ILGWU, the IUE, the UAW, and the USW have from time to time been involved in active conflicts, the very existence of which was but slightly known to their neighbors, on such matters as the election of national officers, national policy, and even on which union to join. A good deal of the discussion and propaganda on such subjects is made through mass communications (leaflets, for example), especially in plants where a number of workers are employed.

[2] In much of the underdeveloped and only partially literate world, violent political propaganda and even civil war—as in the Congo and recently in Algeria—is in large measure aided or augmented by radio. Although the literature on psychological warfare gives us some leads to

what happens in such instances—and although reports about such political leaders as Nkrumah in Ghana and Bustamente in Jamaica tell us something of "charismatic leadership" in underdeveloped nations—our knowledge of the *processes* of mass communications in these non-Western societies under such circumstances (or even in such societies as those of Spain or Argentina which are slightly different from more industrialized nations) is not very good.

[3] *It might be valuable to organize a systematic statement showing what major questions might be asked and hypotheses developed about communications situations.* Such a systematic listing would indicate holes, and would probably stimulate the identification and formulation of questions that nobody has thought to ask. It might also be embarrassing in the sense that it would very likely lead to the discovery that some of the terms which we use are rather dull tools for purposes of analysis. For example, simply in thinking about the possibility, the writer has been driven further towards the awareness that "mass communications" is simply a descriptive and rather arbitrary classification. We ultimately need to formalize and structure our science.

[4] Closely related to such an effort would be Brouwer's suggestion (see above) that we need a review of the classic hypotheses and conceptions in this area. Thus we would venture the opinion that the literature of classic political philosophy—Plato, Aristotle, Cicero, Machiavelli, etc. —contains a good many suggestions about mass communications, which might be translated into modern terms, with the emphasis on making them empirically testable. Similarly, despite the very considerable emphasis here and there on such seminal thinkers as Pareto and Comte, we do not know of any effort to determine whether their work, or that of others of their stature, suggests ideas about mass communications that can be empirically tested and that would broaden our conception of public opinion formation.

[5] In the foregoing, obviously we are pleading among other things for a broadening of the *historical* framework within which communications situations are studied. There are, in fact, quite a substantial number of studies of the press in the seventeenth and eighteenth centuries, of propaganda in the nineteenth century as undertaken, for example, by the early Marxists, the abolitionists,[2] and the antislavery groups, but it is not

---

1. Pool is talking in his article reprinted in this book (pp. 431–443) primarily about the processes of modernization—the above paragraph refers to psychological civil war, etc.

2. See Dwight H. Dumond, *Antislavery, the Crusade for Freedom in America* (U. of Michigan Press, Ann Arbor, Mich., 1961).

clear whether systematic analysis of such studies would materially alter our conceptions about mass communications.

[6] In even more general terms, the University of Toronto group, under McLuhan and Carpenter,[3] has raised even more basic historical questions—questions about the very meaning of *print* as a way of looking at events and structuring the world. Every student of communications situations should be familiar with their *Explorations in Communications;* but, reluctantly, we have not stressed their work in this volume, stimulating and provocative though it is, because it seems to lack the detailed connection with factual events that approaches validation.

[7] Even more valuable than a review of historical literature might be a review of anthropological literature, oriented towards the following issue: what happens to a community that has never been exposed to mass communications when it is suddenly exposed to them all at once? We are not talking here about the kind of study familiarly undertaken in the United States which may ask what difference does it make that TV is introduced into a community already literate, already having newspapers? but rather, in communities that have been *isolated* from the modern world and suddenly exposed to communications processes. There is some incidental discussion of such matters; Margaret Mead [4] in her restudy of the Manus community after twenty-five years reports that, in effect, they understood the world in 1953 in a way that was impossible in 1928. Robert Redfield in his analysis of Folk Culture in Yucatan implies a good deal about differential participation in communication.[5] There are, in fact, hundreds of missionary reports, autobiographies, field studies, etc., that might throw some light on the central problem—the problem referred to by Mendelsohn in his paper in this volume (pp. 30–35)— how much difference does it make to a society and to personalities within that society to be exposed to mass communications? Where does it make a difference? (e.g., in what they enjoy, in how they hate, in how they learn), and where does it not?

[8] It might be interesting to study accounts of what happened when mass communications, or even literacy, on a wide scale, were introduced to comparable societies by the British or Americans as compared with

3. See H. Marshall McLuhan and E. Carpenter (eds.), *Explorations in Communications; an Anthology* (Beacon Press, Boston, 1960), and H. Marshall McLuhan, *The Gutenberg Galaxy; the Making of Typographic Man* (U. of Toronto Press, Toronto, 1962).

4. *New Lives for Old: Cultural Transformation in the Manus, 1928–1953* (Morrow, New York, 1956).

5. *Folk-Culture of Yucatan* (U. of Chicago Press, Chicago, 1941).

what happened when the introducing culture was Spanish or German or Russian.

[9] On the basis of such reflection, and preferably fairly soon, studies should be made, on a before-and-after basis, of communities now removed from mass communications (e.g., in the jungles of Brazil or New Guinea, or possibly the mountains of Haiti), and how they are affected when some or all such communications are introduced; with the emphasis on the communications process.[6] Perhaps one of the most important goals of such studies might be to help understand (and in the future, avoid) the dislocation that Western civilization has apparently frequently imposed upon peasant or jungle societies.

[10] We might study the pseudo-friendliness discussed by Horton and Strauss,[7] the blurring of the line between primary group and secondary group, which is found in the relationship between listeners and such "entertainers" as Arthur Godfrey, or between readers and writers of such a column as the "Confidential Chat" of the *Boston Globe*. Indeed, a careful study of the latter type of relationship might materially modify the classic distinction between primary group and secondary group as it is found in conventional sociological treatment; it would also raise many questions about what Raymond Bauer and others have called *adult socialization*, i.e., the socialization of adults—a subject that, in the past, has been studied almost entirely in terms of the immigrant, but that needs to be restudied nowadays in much broader terms.

[11] This raises one of the problems that is confronting us more and more in social science and one which Brouwer (see above) attacks with quite a different purpose. The average may not be the sociologically significant. Waples, Berelson, and Bradshaw report [8] that most reading confirms people in their own preconceptions and prejudices. But are there exceptions? How many? How do they operate? For instance, supposing that a man knows 100 men with conventional opinions and 2 with unconventional; if he did not read anything, he would not adopt the unconventional opinions, but reading plus the influence of the others makes it possible for him, too, to adopt the unconventional opinions. In still more basic terms, what we are saying is that we need a careful analysis of what

6. In several places I have developed the idea of an International Social Anthropological Quinquennium, designed to study the impact of social change on primitive communities, one of the main emphases of which might be communications processes. The most extended published discussion is in the *Indian Sociological Bulletin*, vol. 1, no. 1, 1963–64, pp. iii–iv.

7. Donald Horton and Anselm Strauss, "Interaction in Audience-Participation Shows," *American Journal of Sociology*, vol. 62, 1956–57, pp. 579–587.

8. D. Waples, B. Berelson, and F. Bradshaw, *What Reading Does to People* (U. of Chicago Press, Chicago, 1940).

it means to "confirm . . . preconceptions," to "reinforce." Or, suppose that a student has studied social science and therefore has learned to respect the original and unconventional; may he not in some respects through reading become still more unconventional than any of his associates? Is the reading, then, reinforcing him or modifying him?

What we don't know is how far a change in role makes it possible or likely for people to learn new skills and attitudes through communications, how far communications can speed up the process, and how far they must rely upon real-life models or experience. The assumption of writers as a class seems to contradict the assumptions of mass-communications "analysts" as a class.[9]

III

At a much more practical level, we may also suggest other issues that might be resolved.

[1] In political campaigns, more often than not, the present author, both as research director and script writer, has had to rely upon hunches for his statements about what could and what could not be achieved. For example, there is no solid basis even for guessing as to when attacking one's opponent will help win the election and when it will hurt the chances of winning. There are, in all current U.S. political campaigns, people who argue for a "hard-hitting" campaign, "going for the jugular," etc., which, boiled down, usually seems to mean calling the opponent nasty names. But there are people who point out that such ill-mannered tactics may alienate one's "doubtful" supporters and antagonize neutrals.

Which is right under which circumstances for which groups? This point is of importance not only in relatively peaceful U.S. political campaigns; it is potentially significant in regard to the theory of deterrence. Do Russians and Americans achieve their own way and help contribute to peace by "hard-hitting delivery of the truth" (as each of them sees it or wants to be thought to see it) or by tact and restrained moderation of tone? Or in the current desegregation controversy, where does harsh language pay off for either side, if at all, without running the risk of overt violence (which only very few people on either side really want)?

[2] At a much less significant level is the subject of house magazines

9. After this book was in press, I read with great interest the stimulating suggestions for an analysis of the role of the advertising man, the mass communication professional, in D. G. Macrae, *Ideology and Society* (Heinemann, London, 1961), Ch. VII, "Advertising and Sociology," pp. 77–86. Very likely, had we seen this paper at an earlier date, we should have asked permission to include it in the present reader.

or "house organs." We have read several volumes on this subject, none of which really deals with the house magazine in terms of communication theory. Yet in terms of sheer readership, the internal and external house magazines issued by large corporations and trade unions probably have more readers than any of the small community newspapers, such as those studied by De Fleur and Larsen, and by Janowitz.[10] As much as anything else, the neglect of such house organs by scholars seems to arise out of three circumstances: (*a*) historically the house magazine probably came later than the community newspaper (excepting perhaps the journal of particular denominational groups) and (*b*) because of the American emphasis on community (referred to by Mendelsohn pp. 30–35),[11] the house organ seemed somehow less real, less central, than the community press, and (*c*) editors of house magazines and trade union journals do not depend on advertisers and have less compulsion to learn about their readership. Also, since they are relatively close to their controlled circulation, they know that many who are recipients of the publication do not read it. They therefore tend to minimize their own importance; in two instances known to this writer, efforts have been made to get editors of trade union journals to have serious studies undertaken of what is read by whom. In both cases the editor's reaction was, "Do you think we're crazy? Of course, we don't want people to find that out." Yet one is safe in concluding that the editors materially underestimate their own significance—that on a comparative basis (comparative with the political news sections of the daily newspaper or news broadcasts on the radio) they are fairly influential and widely read; the trouble is that these editors compare their influence with that of the big stories, murder, space shots, etc., in the daily press.

[3] Because of the ever increasing importance of occupation and voluntary association, at least in U.S. life, it may well be that studies of the specialized press would yield far more insight on who communicates what to whom, and vice versa, than further studies of the general press—were any choice in emphasis necessary. No doubt some specialized publications have in their market-research reports data of inestimable value for the scholar and thinker; an extraordinarily valuable series of studies along this line have, in fact, been made over the years by Donald R. Murphy

10. M. L. De Fleur and Otto N. Larsen, *The Flow of Information* (Harper, New York, 1958). See also De Fleur, "Mass Communication and the Study of Rumor," *Sociological Inquiry,* Summer 1962, 51–70. It was our intention to include this study in this volume, but space limitations prohibited us. See also M. Janowitz, *The Community Press in an Urban Setting* (Free Press, New York, 1952).

11. M. Stein, *The Eclipse of Community: an Interpretation of American Studies* (Princeton University Press, 1960) is also relevant.

and associates on *Wallace's Farmer* and the *Wisconsin Agriculturist* and reported in his *What Farmers Read and Like*,[12] which we tried to condense for this volume but could not do satisfactorily because it probably must be read as a whole. But what Murphy lacks—though he is far ahead of most others who work on this question—is any picture of specific individuals in specific situations; his technique of data collecting does not allow for that.

I V

David Manning White also suggests the time is due, perhaps overdue, for a large-scale study of the effects of mass communications upon a community, which would be comparable to W. Lloyd Warner's noted *Yankee City* investigations. For the past twenty years we have developed many necessary tools for communications research. Despite the obvious inadequacies inherent in the "interview" situation (e.g., the gap between the respondent's verbal reply to any given question and his "true" feelings), survey research has nevertheless developed into a sharp tool. Nor are there likely to be any major additions to the techniques of content analysis. Rather, as Gerbner showed in his article (pp. 477–499), what is needed now is a focus for the knowledge we have already acquired.

But we have been so concerned with developing the techniques, and then repeating the same kind of fragmentary research which might substantiate the early, tentative hypotheses, that the field of mass communications today is frequently an enigma. That is why I feel the time is, indeed, overdue for one of the large foundations to underwrite a grand study of a community and the people who constitute it in terms of what mass communications does to it and to them.

Such a study should be projected over a twenty-year period, and it should call upon the resources of researchers in all branches of the behavioral sciences concerned with this problem. It should be possible to assemble a "team" of highly competent scholars from the various social sciences, each of whom would be more concerned with finding the answer to basic questions than with differences of approach between their respective fields.

It would be the task of the demographers to ascertain which town or city would be best suited for such a study. Ideally, such a community would be a microcosm of the heterogeneous macrocosm of this country. It should be a community which enables each of its residents substantial choice of the various agents of mass communications.

12. *A Record of Experiments with Readership, 1938–1961* (Iowa State U. Press, Ames, Iowa, 1962).

By utilizing a panel-type interviewing schedule, as well as other measures, a representative sample of our communications "Middletown" should be projected, wherein the same individuals are studied from their preschool days until twenty years later they have completed college or have otherwise become adults in the community.

Granted that the design for this type of study would present inordinate difficulties, and that $1,000,000 might be required to underwrite a project of this dimension, nevertheless, such a bold enterprise is clearly needed. There is little to be gained by replicating laboratory-type experiments in cloistered ivy halls with captive student experimentees, for if the hypotheses and theories that have been formulated have any substantial validity they must be tested under actual conditions and over a substantial period of time.

We have said that the mass media are essentially *interposers* between the individual in a mass society and the major institutional forces—school, church, family—in which he functions. Some individuals within the community extract from the mass media merely the material that will help them to conform to the institutional life; others may seek and find within the same mass media material which helps to organize a different perspective on their community and its institutions. By utilizing a case-study approach to a satisfactory sample of individuals in the community over a period of two decades, we could begin to determine the role of the mass media in their true perspective.

V

And, finally, there is much to be done in that branch of study, where philosophy and empirical research mingle. The political theory of mass communications has not moved forward substantially since Walter Lippmann's *Phantom Public* and *Public Opinion,* now thirty years old. The doctrines about freedom of information which guide much public discussion and decision making are far older than that. They trace back to a situation where technical factors made the press much slower to respond to news than it now is in the days of Jefferson, the press in fact was sociologically rather more like our weekly news magazines than like our current newspapers. And, of course, the radio and TV have made news still more immediate and dramatic.

The doctrines of freedom of the press and of information upon which we now operate were also developed prior to any of the research in the effects and channels of mass communications reported in this volume; the thinking of Justice Black and other members of the Supreme Court, tending towards the assertion that freedom of expression and communication should be an absolute right, we judge without profound analysis, is almost entirely unaffected by any of this research and traces back to eighteenth-century notions about man, society, and government.[13]

We are not here asserting that Justice Black and those who sympathize with him are in error; we are asserting that where a considerable body of empirical knowledge is available as to how communication affects groups and individuals and how communications media actually work at present, an effort should be made to relate that knowledge to moral judgments about what should be done in practical situations.

For instance, the widely discussed Supreme Court decisions about Bible reading in public schools are decisions about the effect of communications upon individuals; it is argued that certain kinds of effects are felt by individuals as a result of certain words said in certain circumstances. It would probably be possible to translate the assumptions underlying the decision and the arguments into testable propositions about communications processes and determine whether the Court is or is not correct in its assumptions about what happens to school children as a result of listening to the Bible reading.

Every year or two some supporters of civil liberties or prominent newsmen become agitated about the suppression of the news by some government department. The most recent instance, as we write, is the *New York Herald Tribune*'s campaign against the policy of Assistant Secretary of Defense Sylvester in regard to handling news about Cuban missile bases. The critics of governmental "Management of the news" usually base their case upon the need of the people to get information as fully and speedily as possible. But, in one form or another, the government agencies involved in this country are usually arguing that for higher reasons of public policy, some sort of "damper mechanism" is needed. By "damper mechanism" is meant a device that will prevent too quick, too speedy, too violent, or too unreflective a reaction from the public. (American response to the news of the sinking of the battleship Maine in 1898 was, for example, probably too quick and unreflective; a damper mechanism might have been a "good thing.") Or, at another level, local police authorities sometimes conceal news of crimes—for example, of crimes possibly committed by minority group members—in order to avoid a quick unreflective act of mass violence, such as a race riot, stemming from action against the supposed criminal or his kind.

13. A fruitful beginning for such research was laid down by David Riesman in a series of articles on civil liberties before World War II, the most general of which is his "Civil Liberties in a Period of Transition," in C. J. Friedrich and E. S. Mason (eds.), *Public Policy,* Harvard Graduate School of Public Administration, 3 (1942), 33–96.

It is possible, in principle, to study when and where damper mechanisms are useful (if at all), and to present for any given set of circumstances a listing of the probable consequences of trying to impose a damper mechanism.

But very little research in mass communications has been oriented towards the weighing of large questions of public policy of the sort just mentioned, partly because students of mass communications on the whole have taken their political and philosophical assumptions for granted, rather than regarded them as subjects for exploration. In other words, more mass-communications specialists need to become aware of the bearing of their work on political philosophy, and vice versa. The Supreme Court does not now commission independent research in the communications implications of cases that come before it, but if such research has been undertaken and published the Court could take judicial notice of the results. Perhaps the Court might commission such analyses, just as some lower courts request psychological evaluations before sentencing.

Different scholars, of course, have different interests and concerns, but, in closing, the present writer would like to assert a preference—he believes that, from a theoretical and practical standpoint, the most interesting as well as the most significant research needed in the area of mass communications lies in a reexamination of our doctrines and philosophies about information, the educational function of press, radio, and TV, etc., in relationship to (1) the current research findings and research tools of mass communications, and (2) the practical operation of our doctrines in such social institutions as the newspaper, the court, the school, etc. Such an examination would either (*a*) demand considerable revision of currently accepted attitudes (for example, it might bring American practice on reporting of criminal matters much closer to that of the British), or (*b*) give a sounder rational basis to what Americans now believe and practice. The first of these two alternatives is the more likely.

QUESTIONS

1.   What does the writer mean by saying there is a strong tendency to do over again "almost exactly the kind of research on almost exactly the kind of topic which has previously been researched . . ."? Take the research done in some branch of knowledge with which you are familiar and exemplify. Why is it safer for young scholars to do such research? [References on this are David Lindsay Watson, *Scientists Are Human* (Kegan Paul, London, 1938), and G. Wiebe, "An Exploration Into the Nature of Creativity," *Public Opinion Quarterly*, vol. 26, 1962, pp. 389–897.]

2.   The writer indicates that a great many important fields of mass communications or closely related thereto have not been studied. (*a*) Identify and list topics for mass communications research, not mentioned in this article but suggested in the other parts of this book, on which little has been done. (*b*) Identify and list propositions bearing on mass communications research suggested in other courses you have taken, not introduced by the teachers as bearing on mass communications (e.g., courses in English composition). (*c*) Identify, and (so far as possible) try to state specifically the issues for research on mass communications arising out of or suggested by discussions of some occupation or business known to you through personal contact (e.g., the ministry, Sunday school teaching, salesmanship).

APPENDIX

David Manning White

A Critique of Bibliographic Matter in Mass Communications

It is conventional in books of this nature to provide a bibliography at the end of the volume, so that the student may find further material in specific areas of inquiry. We have incorporated most of the bibliographical material closer to the text in two ways: (1) The author of each paper has provided references to representative articles and books he has written; these should be examined by the student who wishes to pursue the topic further than the limitations of the particular paper in the book; and (2) this chapter, a critique on relevant research in the field of communications, annotates nearly 100 studies, monographs and books.

However, certain general references will, in addition, be of assistance to student-scholars in the field of mass communications.

I. READERS IN MASS COMMUNICATIONS

[1] A comprehensive book of readings in this area is Wilbur Schramm's *Mass Communications* (U. of Illinois Press, Urbana, Ill., 1960). This is the second edition of a pioneering reader in the field. The book is well organized and covers several aspects of mass communications, including the historical background of the media. It also contains a valuable annotated bibliography of some 175 items.

[2] An earlier reader by Schramm (*The Process and Effects of Mass Communication*, U. of Illinois Press, Urbana, Ill., 1955) is also of substantial value. Because the book was originally compiled for the United States Information Agency (to provide background materials for use in training new employees in the field of research and evaluation), it stresses international communication. This volume also has an annotated bibliography of 100 titles; those on international communication are particularly worthwhile. A recent volume edited by Schramm (*The Science of Human Communications*, Basic, New York, 1963) is an excellent intro-

duction to "new directions and new findings in communications research." It contains a small but pertinent list of books, articles, and monographs that would reward the student of mass communications.

Students who wish an orientation in qualitative aspects of mass communications research will find another recent volume worth investigating (Nafziger, Ralph O. and White, David Manning, eds., *Introduction to Mass Communications Research*, Louisiana State U. Press, Baton Rouge, 1963).

[3] Bernard Berelson and Morris Janowitz compiled a *Reader in Public Opinion and Communication* (Free Press, New York, 1953) which served a most useful purpose in providing articles and studies particularly germane to the theory of public opinion. Although most of the bibliographic references in this edition may be found in Schramm's readers, there are some valuable annotations which do not overlap.

II. BIBLIOGRAPHIES OF JOURNALISM AND MASS COMMUNICATIONS

[1] Here an indispensable tool for even the casual student of mass communications is Warren Price's *The Literature of Journalism: An Annotated Bibliography* (U. of Minnesota Press, Minneapolis, 1959). Professor Price defines journalism in its broadest sense, so that it includes radio and television journalism, the related fields of advertising and public relations, and even a section on bibliographies and directories which contains more than 200 entries. Altogether, there are more than 3,000 books listed in Price's volume. The annotations summarize in a sentence or two the essential subject of the book and its approach. By utilizing Price carefully, the student will be directed to specific volumes, which in turn will contain more detailed bibliographies in their respective areas. Another valuable bibliography of journalistic books by Professor Roland E. Wolseley of Syracuse University is notable for the compiler's excellent annotations (*The Journalist's Bookshelf*, Chilton, Philadelphia, 1961). Although less comprehensive than Price's omnibus coverage of the literature, it has references to books which appeared subsequent to the Price volume.

[2] A good supplement to Price's and Wolseley's comprehensive coverage of the field is the more recent booklet compiled by Eleanor Blum (*Reference Books in the Mass Media*, U. of Illinois Press, Urbana, 1962). It cites some books that came into print after Price's bibliography was finished. For example, Miss Blum lists Wilbur Peterson's *Organizations, Publications and Directories in the Mass Media of Communications*

(State University of Iowa, School of Journalism, Iowa City, 1960) which provides much relevant data, such as addresses, publications, functions, etc., of the major organizations concerned with mass communications. Miss Blum reminds the student of mass communications that the *Psychological Abstracts,* published bimonthly by the American Psychological Association, can provide a quick reference to recent articles and monographs. Although she does not list it, *Sociological Abstracts* performs an equally valuable chore (of less value in this field but also worth knowing is *International Political Science Abstracts*). Miss Blum's small book, although containing only 226 entries, is particularly strong in the broadcasting and cinema references. Her annotations are somewhat more complete than those in the Price volume, and (like his) have the virtue of being essentially informational rather than impressionistic.

Students of mass communications should be acquainted with Bruce and Chitra Smith's bibliography on *International Communications* (Princeton U. Press, Princeton, N.J., 1956), and also the predecessor bibliographies on propaganda and public opinion prepared by Bruce Smith with Ralph Casey and Harold Lasswell.

UNESCO's Department of Mass Communications has published a number of monographs and books which provide data unavailable elsewhere. Topics include trade barriers to knowledge, the training of journalists in 21 countries, world illiteracy at mid-century. The most complete overall treatment of world communications, continent by continent, may be found in the UNESCO publication *World Communications: Press, Radio, Film, Television* (3rd ed., UNESCO Publications Center, New York, 1956). Because of the difficulty of keeping this work up-to-date, some of the data reported is substantially behind actual conditions; however, it is still the best available source for most of this information.

III. SPECIALIZED AREAS OF BIBLIOGRAPHY

[1] A unique bibliography of more than 1,700 studies of the mass media was compiled and annotated by Prof. F. E. Barcus of Boston University, who conducted a content analysis of all available content analysis studies from 1900 to 1958. Dr. Barcus classified more than 1,000 articles, books, pamphlets, theses, etc., according to their theoretical approach, methodology, media, or the particular aspects studied (e.g., newspaper editorials, comics, letters to the editor, television news, drama, public service programs, etc.). There is also a list of some 500 master's theses in content analysis. This important bibliographic study is available from University Microfilms, Inc., Ann Arbor, Michigan. A section of

Barcus' dissertation was published in the fall 1960 issue of the *Journal of Broadcasting* and provides a bibliography of the studies of radio and television program content from 1928 to 1958.

[2] *Television.* The most comprehensive and useful annotated bibliography on television, particularly as it affects young viewers, is found in Wilbur Schramm, Jack Lyle, and Edwin B. Parker, *Television in the Lives of Our Children* (Stanford U. Press, Stanford, Calif., 1961). Besides some 50 books, articles, and monographs dealing specifically with television, the authors of this book fully annotate the relevant related studies of children's reactions to other media. An earlier volume by Leo Bogart (*The Age of Television,* Frederick Ungar, New York, 1956) contains an excellent bibliography of previous studies in the field.

IV. OTHER SOURCES OF BIBLIOGRAPHY

One should not overlook the significant journals in the field of mass communications. These publications not only contain the latest work of productive scholars in the field, but also maintain, in many cases, an up-to-date bibliography of the preceding quarter's articles. For example, *Journalism Quarterly* carries a list of research projects either started or completed during the preceding year by staff members and doctoral candidates in schools of journalism in this country, as well as masters' theses accepted during that period. It also contains in each issue an annotated bibliography on articles dealing with mass communications in United States' magazines. These articles are annotated from "general" periodicals, from 30 journals of political science, psychology and sociology, from 50 legal journals, and some 60 history journals. Moreover, each issue of the *Journalism Quarterly* contains an annotated bibliography from foreign journals.

An invaluable periodical, which is directed more to the political and psychological aspects of communication than the media-oriented *Journalism Quarterly,* is *Public Opinion Quarterly.* In it one may find summaries of the more important survey research polls.

Some other American journals which contain insightful articles on mass communications are *American Journal of Sociology, American Sociological Review, Social Problems, Audio-Visual Communication Review, Journal of Social Forces, Quarterly of Film, Radio and Television* and *Journal of Social Issues.* Among foreign periodicals, current research in Europe is reported in *New Society* (England); *Etudes de Presse* (France); *Publizistik* (Germany); *Gazette* (Holland); *Novinarsky Sbornik* (Czechoslovakia); *Kwartalnik Prasonawczy* (Poland), and the reports of the International Press Institute from Zurich.

Each of the journals listed above (and the list could be expanded) carries reviews of the latest published books in the field. There are, of course, the obvious bibliographic sources such as the *Readers' Guide to Periodical Literature*. Since it maintains a cumulative index of such magazines as the *Annals of the American Academy of Political and Social Science, Business Week, Fortune, Nation, The New Republic, Reporter,* and the *Saturday Review, Reader's Guide* should not be overlooked. *Public Affairs Information Service* is a guide to pamphlets worth knowing about.

[2] In the field of public opinion research, a valuable source is the large volume edited by Hadley Cantril, titled *Public Opinion* (Princeton U. Press, Princeton, N.J., 1951). Although it only covers polls taken from 1935 to 1946, its usefulness lies in showing the variety of topics which were surveyed and the formulation of the questions asked.

A recent bibliography of publications by the National Opinion Research Center of the University of Chicago, compiled by its librarian, Charles S. Mack (National Opinion Research Center, Chicago, 1961), cites more than 300 studies, monographs, books and surveys which have emenated from this noted organization.

A FINAL WORD

In some ways the richest bibliographic ore for the reader to mine, so far as this book of readings is concerned, lies right in the footnotes of the articles we have included. There are perhaps 1500 references in the selections in this book, each of which seemed relevant to a noted scholar in this field.

There is a story about the great literary scholar, John Livingston Lowes of Harvard, which is apropos to our suggestion that these footnotes should be pursued. When Lowes was working on his famous study of Coleridge, *The Road to Xanadu,* he was faced with the incredibly difficult task of determining the various sources to which the poet had turned. Then Lowes made an important discovery: it was simply that Coleridge was an invariable pursuer of footnotes, and ended up not by reading one book but dozens of books in any subject he started. This was the clue Lowes needed to track down Coleridge's tenuous road to Xanadu.

The task of keeping up with the new literature of communications is in itself formidable. Nevertheless, it is from the pioneering studies of our relatively new field that we get the background so necessary for any fruitful, future studies. These tools listed above are available in any good college or metropolitan library. Although much has been written in this burgeoning field of communications, we feel, to paraphrase Browning, that the "best is yet to come."

Index of Names

Abel, R. H., 496
Adams, J. B., 544
Adar, L., 436
Adorno, T. W., 496
Albig, W., 495, 498
Albrecht, M. C., 188, 192, 289, 295, 296, 328
Alisky, M., 544
Allen, R. S., 191
Allport, G., 78, 377, 526
Alsop, J. and S., 173, 175
Anderson, C. A., 112
Anderson, M., 118
Aneshansel, J., 131, 133, 139
Annis, A. D., 84
Anthony, N., 265, 281
Arnheim, R., 46
Arons, L., 35, 393, 544
Asch, S. A., 382
Auster, D., 495
Aydelotte, W., 282, 289

Back, K., 545
Backer, George and Dorothy, 211
Bacon, C., 474
Bagdikian, B. H., 205, 206, 207
Bahrdt, H., 548
Bailey, C., 399, 405
Bailey, S. K., 405
Bailyn, L., 529
Barcus, F. E., 495, 585
Barnes, H. E., 30
Barnouw, E., 70
Barrow, L., 544
Bartlett, F. C., 78
Baschwitz, K., 547, 560–64, 566
Bateson, G., 506, 517
Bauer, Alice, 34, 301, 387, 523
Bauer, Raymond A., viii, 21, 32, 53, 55, 88, 107, 120, 131, 138–44, 221, 301, 378, 387, 396, 402, 407, 415, 425, 501, 503, 516–17, 521, 523, 538, 544, 560, 567, 572

Bavelas, A., 528
Beagle, J. A., 116
Beal, G. M., 117
Bean, O., 265
Belknap, G., 225
Bell, W., 108
Belson, W. A., 529
Bensman, J., 194
Bentley, Arthur, 6, 140, 474, 538
Berelson, B., 12, 34, 77, 82, 99, 106, 111, 143, 199, 200, 296–97, 301, 483, 494, 501–502, 509–10, 512, 514–17, 521, 525, 542, 545, 560, 562, 566, 572, 584
Bergler, E., 277, 281
Berkowitz, L., 12
Berlo, D. K., 200, 544
Bessy, M. M., 474
Bettelheim, B., 135, 139
Bigman, S., xi, 23, 184, 200, 205–206, 314
Blair, T., 434
Blotner, J., 541
Blum, E., 584
Blumberg, L., 229
Blumenthal, A., 188
Blumer, H., 551, 566
Bogart, L., 83, 586
Bourne, F., 382
Bradshaw, F., 12, 572
Brambeck, W., 70
Breed, W., 96, 103, 140, 142, 161, 181–85, 195, 221–22, 236
Breger, D., 189–92
Briggs, J., 407
Brinton, C., 187
Britt, S., 367
Brodbeck, A., 544–45
Broom, L., 34, 91
Brouwer, M., 539, 547, 552, 556, 565–66, 568, 570, 572
Brown, Emory, 118
Brucker, H., 233

Bruner, J., 45, 129
Bryson, L., 187
Bullock, R., 495
Burdick, E., 135
Burgess, E., 301
Burke, K., 38, 56–66, 542
Bush, C., 495, 549, 566
Bush, V., 460
Byerly, K., 216, 220

Cannell, C., 376
Cantril, H., 75, 102, 526, 587
Carpenter, E., 481, 571
Carroll, W., 446
Carter, R., 161, 181, 222–23, 236, 544
Cartwright, D., 392, 528
Casey, Ralph, 237, 506, 543, 585
Casey, Robert, 474
Cassirer, H., 438
Cater, D., 161, 181
Cattell, R., 555, 566
Chapin, F., 196
Clark, Dick, 279
Coelho, G., 129, 138–39, 143
Coffin, T., 200
Coleman, J., 118, 274, 281, 508
Comstock, Anthony, 264
Comte, A., 570
Cone, F., 256
Cooley, C. H., 4, 8, 11, 30, 72, 126, 129, 139
Cooper, Eunice, 78, 493
Copeland, T., 237
Copp, J., 118
Cottrell, L., 34, 71
Coughenor, C., 118
Cox, C. A., 495
Cox, D., 393, 545
Crawford, R. J., 237
Cressey, P. F., 186
Crutchfield, R., 44
Curtis, Cyrus, 308
Cutlip, S., 237

Dale, E., 494
Damle, Y., 437
Danielson, W., 130, 139, 144, 477, 544
Daudt, H., 566
Daugherty, W. E., 71
Davis, Allison, 188
Davis, Kingsley, 186, 187, 196
Day, J., 144
Decker, W. S., 393
DeFleur, M., 118, 574
Demant, V., 200
Dentler, R., 398
Devereux, E., 186
Devereux, G., 196
Dewey, John, 6, 140, 284
Dexter, L. A., 36, 140, 396, 400, 538, 545
Dinerman, H., 493
Dodd, S., 118
Doob, L., 527
Dornbusch, S., 289
Dovifat, E., 548
Downes, A., 508
Dryfoos, O., 217
Dumazedier, J., 438
Duncan, H. D., 289
Durkheim, E., 186, 199, 538

Eberhard, F., 548
Edelstein, A., 221-22, 224, 544
Edmonson, M., 196
Ehrlich, D., 376
Emery, F., 118, 544
Ernst, M., 220
Eyler, C., 541

Fanelli, A., 224
Faris, R., 186
Fearing, F., 37-38, 67-69, 109, 491, 495
Feiffer, J., 264
Feschbach, S., 363-64, 381, 386
Festinger, L., 71-72, 135, 139, 388, 510, 519, 528, 547, 561-66
Fichter, J., 188
Field, Marshall, 213
Fisk, G., 118
Flowerman, S., 17
Ford, J. B., 113
Forsthoff, E., 548

Fraenkel, E., 548
Freedman, R., 186
Freidson, E., 113, 120, 525, 552, 556
Friedrich, C. J., 577
Friedsam, H., 200, 289
Frost, Robert, 263

Gallup, G., 391
Gans, H., 136, 139
Garceau, O., 542
Gaudet, H., 82, 102, 520
Gehman, R., 266, 281
George, L., 444-45
Gerald, J., 544
Gerbner, G., 477, 484, 497, 499, 500, 544, 575
Gerth, H., 289, 297
Gieber, W., 140, 142, 160-62, 173-76, 179, 181, 221-22, 236, 544
Gleicher, D., 107, 407
Godfrey, A., 572
Goffman, E., 197
Goldwyn, A., 474
Gosnell, H., 538
Goss, M., 91
Gouldner, A., 200
Grace, H., 128, 139
Graham, P., 217
Gray, Kenneth, 396, 402
Greenberg, B., 236
Gross, B., 457, 469, 474, 541, 542, 548
Gross, N., 118, 144, 385
Gude, E., 435
Gurvitch, G., 186
Gusfield, J., 198
Guttman, J., 376

Habermas, J., 548
Hamilton, T., 495
Hamilton, W., 514
Hammond, P., 196
Harlow, R., 70
Harms, E., 275, 281
Hart, Hornell, 288, 297
Harvey, O., 377-78
Hattwick, M., 367
Hawley, A., 186
Hawthorne, N., 20
Head, S., 200, 495
Hearst, W. R., 214-16, 308
Hefner, Hugh, 251, 257
Hempel, C., 104
Henry, W. E., 192, 200, 516

Herblock, 264
Hero, Alfred, 223, 540
Herzog, H., 102, 200, 516, 526
Higbie, C., 544
Hill, R., 107, 108
Himmelweit, H., 440, 528, 545
Hollingshead, A., 52, 188
Homans, G., 235
Hopkins, T. K., 108
Hornstein, L., 293
Horton, Donald, 515, 572
Horty, J., 474
Hovland, C., 69-71, 114, 361-69, 377-78, 386, 501-11, 514, 518, 526-27, 555, 560, 566
Howe, E. W., 263
Howe, I., 197
Howell, W. S., 70
Howells, W. D., 20, 294
Hubbard, Kin, 263
Hughes, Helen, 84, 187, 200
Hunter, F., 191, 221, 224
Huxley, A., 522
Hyman, H. H., 91, 108

Inglis, R., 200, 298
Inkeles, A., 88, 407
Innis, H. A., 481
Irwin, P. L., 224
Isaacs, H., 144, 440, 540

Jahoda, M., 78
James, W., 74
Janis, I., 69, 71, 114, 129, 139, 361, 363, 364, 367, 369, 374, 381, 386, 526
Janowitz, M., 71, 96, 143, 188, 200, 301, 509, 574, 584
Javits, J., 407
Johns-Heine, P., 289, 297
Johnson, Walter, 222, 236
Johnstone, J. W. C., 114, 525
Jones, Dorothy, 545
Jones, E. E., 132, 133, 139
Jones, R. L., 237, 544
Judd, R., 161, 181

Kambouropoulou, P., 277, 281
Katz, D., 566

Katz, E., 71, 78, 108, 111–12, 114, 117–18, 126, 139, 143, 283, 301, 371–74, 381, 383–84, 517–18, 521, 525, 547, 552, 554–55, 561, 566
Katz, S., 407
Kaufman, G., 278
Kazin, A., 294
Kearl, B., 544
Keesing, F. and M., 434
Kegan, P., 430
Kehl, W., 474
Keller, S., 21, 143, 402
Kelley, H. H., 114, 361, 363–64, 367, 369, 382, 527
Kelman, H., 135, 139, 362, 519
Kendall, P., 376, 555, 566
Kennedy, R. F., 407
Kent, Allen, 474
Keskemeti, P., 88
Key, V. O., 4, 534–35
Kruskal, W., 552

Landecker, W., 186
Lang, G. and K., 516
Larsen, O., 107, 118, 574
Lasswell, H., 34, 72, 91, 97, 109, 142, 156, 261, 284, 477, 481, 483, 501–11, 513, 517, 560, 583, 585
Lazarsfeld, P., 34, 71, 77, 82, 95, 102–103, 112–14, 118, 120, 126, 139, 143, 187, 371, 376, 490–91, 502–11, 523, 525, 547, 552, 555, 560–61, 563, 565
LeBon, G., 32, 563
Lee, A. M., 196
Legman, G., 496
Leites, N., 102, 493, 513
Lerner, D., 71, 136, 144, 434, 439, 481, 483, 507
Lerner, M., 289
Levine, J., 282, 377
Lewin, K., 160, 162, 174, 175, 501–10, 517, 528, 547, 560
Lewis, J., 474
Lewis, S., 263
Lindzey, G., 70
Linton, R., 15, 196
Lionberger, H., 115, 118, 120

Lippmann, W., 75, 536–37, 576
Loomis, C., 116
Lorimer, G., 294–95, 303
Lowell, J., 263
Lowenthal, L., 289, 479–81, 495, 513
Lubell, S., 515
Lucas, D., 367
Lumsdaine, A., 365–66, 386, 527, 566, 577
Lyle, J., 440, 543–44, 586
Lynd, H. and R., 52, 188

Maccoby, E., 529
Mack, C., 587
MacDonald, Donald, 285
MacDonald, Dwight, 193
MacDonald, J. C., 376
MacKeachie, W. J., 558, 567
MacLean, M., 174
Macrae, D. G., 573
Macrorie, K., 161, 182
Malinowski, B., 199
Mannheim, K., 524
Markel, L., 89
Markham, J., 544
Martel, M., 284, 285, 286, 332, 334
Marx, K., 406
Mathur, J., 438
Matza, D., 273
May, M., 35, 393, 544
Mayes, H., 250, 255
McBride, K., 135
McCall, G., 284–86, 332
McClelland, D., 439
McCormick, R., 214
McGinnies, E., 45
McLoughlin, W., 11
McLuhan, H. M., 571
McNelly, J., 544
McPhee, W., 77, 143, 508, 525
Mead, G., 30, 32, 41, 45, 61–62, 67, 126
Mead, M., 4, 571
Mehling, R., 544
Meier, N., 84
Mencken, H., 264
Mendelsohn, H., 30, 34, 239, 240, 248, 545, 571
Menzel, H., 117–18, 371, 518
Merton, R., 32, 34, 80, 94, 98, 102–103, 112–13, 120,

139, 174, 187, 196–97, 232, 235, 392, 511, 512, 516, 523, 566
Meyer, L., 452
Miller, G., 506, 517
Miller, S., 200
Miller, W., 173
Mills, C. W., 188, 225, 498
Mills, J., 376, 388
Milner, R., 212
Miner, H., 186
Mischke, K., 548
Moore, W., 196
Morris, W., 283
Mott, F., 294
Murphy, D. R., 574–75
Murphy, G., 47–48, 377
Murphy, R. J., 91
Myers, L., 545
Myrdal, G., 20

Nafziger, R., 161, 543, 584
Neal, G., 144
Neurath, P., 438
Nevins, A., 174
Nicol, J., 438
Nimmo, D., 539
Nixon, R. B., 506, 543
Noel, M., 200
Noelle, E., 548
Nourse, E., 474

Ochs, A., 211
Oeser, O., 118
Ogburn, W. F., 8
Ogden, C. K., 199
Oppenheim, A., 440, 528
Ortega y Gasset, J., 32
Orwell, G., 522
Osgood, C., 139, 506, 509, 562, 567

Paar, Jack, 407
Packard, V., 196
Pareto, V., 196, 570
Park, R. E., 245, 301
Parker, E., 253, 440, 543–44, 586
Parrington, V., 294
Parsons, T., 196, 301
Paul, B., 115
Paul, K., 578
Pauling, L., 258
Peabody, R., 142, 400
Peakes, G., 474
Pearsall, M., 194

Perry, J. W., 474
Perry, S. E., 23, 184
Peterson, R., 567
Peterson, T., 206, 250–51, 301
Peterson, W., 584
Pezzella, R., 277
Piaget, J., 47
Plessner, H., 548
Polsby, N., 142, 398, 400, 538
Pool, I., 21, 128–29, 137, 139, 140, 142–43, 158, 221, 396, 402, 430, 459, 481, 483, 513, 538, 570
Porter, W., 213
Portman, L., 78
Postman, L., 45, 377, 526
Poynter, H. and N., 216
Price, W., 584
Prugger, F., 237
Pulitzer, J., 214–15
Pye, L., 429, 434, 540

Quinn, F. X., 453

Radin, P., 8
Ranganathan, S., 466
Redfield, R., 6, 187, 571
Redlich, F., 262, 282
Reeves, R., 367
Richards, I., 47, 199
Riesman, D., 183, 187, 501–503, 506, 508, 512, 521, 541, 560, 567, 577
Riley, J. and M., 32, 34, 71, 80, 114, 120, 524, 552, 567
Robinson, O., 212
Rogers, E., 117–18, 120, 144
Rosenberg, B., 10, 139, 197, 301
Rosenberg, M., 555, 566
Rosenman, S., 126, 134
Ross, E. A., 561
Rossi, P., 107, 224, 407, 415, 425
Rosten, L., 161, 174, 182
Roucek, J. S., 452
Ruesch, J., 506, 517
Rukkan, S., 567
Ryan, B., 118, 144, 385

Saenger, G., 495
Salter, P., 296, 297, 494, 515
Sampson, S., 283

Samuelson, M., 221
Samuelson, P., 514
Sapir, E., 196
Sayers, D., 19
Schlesinger, A., 15, 542, 543
Schmitt, C., 548
Schneider, L., 289
Schramm, W., 71, 89, 113, 115, 130, 139, 144, 160–62, 199, 200, 294, 496, 501–502, 506, 517, 521, 543–44, 560, 569, 583–84, 586
Schultz, B., 222
Schulz, J., 221
Schulze, R., 224–25
Scripps, E. W., 214–15
Seda (Bonilla) E., 541
Seeley, J., 193
Sevareid, E., 173
Shaffer, H., 12
Shannon, C., 506
Shaw, R. M., 224
Sheean, V., 173
Sheffield, F., 365–66, 386, 527, 566
Shera, J., 462
Sherif, M., 139, 377–78
Shils, E., 11, 114, 143, 196, 301
Shulman, I., 136–37, 139–40, 142–43, 145, 221, 459
Siegel, S., 552, 563, 569
Simmel, G., 32
Simmons, C., 192
Simmons, J., 332
Simpson, R., 399, 405
Sinclair, U., 18, 338
Singer, M., 437
Smilansky, S. and M., 437
Smith, B. and C., 539, 543, 585
Smith, M. B., 76, 77
Smith, P., 398
Smuckler, R., 225
Smythe, D., 191, 483, 494, 544
Snedecor, F., 269
Sohlen, T., 282
Sorensen, R., 444, 446, 447
Sorensen, T., 452
Sorokin, P., 116, 196
Speier, H., 89, 103, 489
Spiegelman, M., 495
Spurgeon, C., 541
Stanton, F., 199, 376

Starch, D., 316, 391
Stark, R., 222
Starr, S., 84
Stein, M., 574
Steinberg, S., 264
Stevenson, A., 443, 445
Stewart, F., 117, 223
Stewart, K., 173
Stewart, R., 160
Stone, I., 197
Stouffer, S., 75, 143, 541
Stowe, H., 237
Strauss, A., 572
Stycos, J., 200
Sullivan, H., 126
Sumner, W., 196
Sussman, L., 409, 495
Swanson, C., 237
Swanson, D., 475
Swanson, G., 145
Symonds, P., 275

Tannenbaum, P., 236, 544, 562
Tarde, G., 32, 563
Tebbel, J., 304
Terwilliger, C., 495
Thomas, W. I., 34, 187
Thomson, R., 216
Thurber, J., 263
Thurstone, L., 557, 567
Timasheff, N., 95
Tocqueville, A. de, 187
Torsvik, P., 567
Troldahl, V., 544
Tumin, M., 196
Twain, Mark, 263

Ungar, F., 586
Useem, J., 188

Valleau, J., 236
Van Bergen, A., 556, 566
Vance, P., 528
Van den Haag, E., 482, 522
Van Horn, G., 237
Veblen, T., 74, 263
Vidich, A., 194
Volkart, E., 382, 527
Von Bernewitz, F., 276

Walker, E., 308
Wallace, M., 198
Walton, E., 140
Waples, D., 12, 507, 572
Warner, L., 516

Warner, W., 188, 192, 196, 200, 336, 340, 540
Warren, S., 461
Watson, D., 430, 578
Weaver, W., 506
Weber, M., 95, 186
Weisinger, H., 187
Weiss, W., 361, 527
Welles, O., 526
Wells, H. G., 468
Wertham, F., 12
West, James, 52, 188
Westley, B. H., 174, 544
White, D. M., 10, 139–40, 142, 161–62, 171, 174, 197, 221–22, 236, 459, 496, 522, 543, 583, 584

White, H. D., 406
White, L., 58
White, W. A., 205, 217
White, W., 301
Whitehead, A., 196
Whittlesey, W., 261, 502
Whyte, W. F., 188
Wiebe, G., 113, 519, 578
Wiley, M., 96, 108
Wilkening, E., 115, 118
Williams, R. M., 186, 196, 301
Wilson, M. O., 139
Winch, R., 192
Winick, C., 260, 262, 277, 280, 281, 284

Wirth, L., 187
Wolfenstein, M., 277, 493
Wolff, K., 376
Wolseley, R., 584
Woodward, J., 477
Wright, C., 69, 91, 92, 161, 284

Zajonc, R., 131, 132, 139, 562, 567
Zimmerman, C. C., 116, 129, 130, 132–34
Zimmerman, Claire, 137, 139, 144, 378
Znaniecki, F., 32, 187
Zola, E., 293

Index of Subjects

This index is a supplement to the table of contents. Matters which, in terms of the subject of a particular paper, clearly will be dealt with therein are not indexed here.

acculturation, through mass communications, 31
advertisements, as reading matter, 213–14
advertisers, and newspaper management, 205ff.
aggregates, social, 525
analysis, content, 285ff., 541, 531–32
appeal, two-sided, 365–66, 527
appeals, advertising, 363ff.
art, and reality, 285ff.
audience: secondary, 127; type of, 524
audiences: imagined, or perceived, 20, 124ff., 142ff., 176; atomistic conception of, 549–59; nature of, 70ff., 112ff., 371, 528, 530–31

book reviews, 136

cartoons, rejected, 189
censorship: informal, 182ff.; of literature for juveniles, 11–12; underplaying certain news, 21–23; civil liberties and rights, 541; news stories about, 176ff.
comics, 214
communications, specialized, 16–18, 94
conformity, 135
consensus, 4, 7, 8, 32, 179, 186ff.
control, social, 102, 186, 236–37
controversy, in media, 230ff.
correlation, of parts of society, 96ff.
credibility, 361–63, 449ff., 527
cross-pressures, 14
Cuba, quarantine of, 92

damper mechanism, 577–78
decision-making, individual, 118
defense, perceptual, 46
democracy, and mass communication, 30
desegregation riots, 184
deterrence, 573
dissonance, cognitive, 561–65; reduction of, 377ff.

education, 493ff.
educational objectives, 17

Elizabeth II, coronation of, 10–11
entertainment, function of, 96ff.
ethnography, 286ff.
etiquette, 14
expectations, 19ff.
exposure, selective, 376ff.

flow of influence, two-step, 14, 110ff., 126, 438–39, 560–61
folding machines, and presses, 208
folk society, 5–6
foreigners, derogation of, 11
freedom: of information, 576–78; of the press, 24
functional approach, 240ff.

"generalized other," 29ff.
Greece, USIA advertisements in, 83
group, properties of, 555ff.

habit, 75
headlines, newspaper, 79f.
hidden persuaders, 431–32
house organs, 574
humor, 196

identity, personal, 8
ideology, U.S., 330ff.
"indicator," 79
innovation, 115ff.
innovators, vs. influentials, 385
interview technique, 143
isolates, social, 329

labor, division of, 338
language, conventions of, 319–20
leaders, opinion, 383ff.
leadership, 110ff.
legend, development of, 339ff.
library administration, 466ff.
literature, sociological origins of, 285ff.

magazines, 250ff.; readership of, 296ff.
mail, to public figures, 353–55, 395ff.

"management of the news," 577–78
mass culture, 285ff., 522–23
masses, nature of 32ff.
meaning, 40ff.
"Memorial Day Massacre," 53f.
metaphor, 47f., 64
minorities, ethnic, 296–97, 326–28, 354
motives, imputation of, 45
movies, interest in, 270

"need for balance," 362
networks, of communication, 528
newspapers, 533–34, 538–39; community, 96; strikes on, 99, 106
norms: journalistic, 223ff.; U.S., 296ff.

objectivity: in news, 344; scientific, 47
oratory, 536

perception, selective, 376ff.
persuasion, classroom experiments in, 86–87
predispositions, 380ff.
printing, costs of, 208

recall, recollection, and retention, 52f., 79–81, 130–31, 367–69, 376ff., 389f.
reinforcement, of beliefs, 12–14, 83–84, 132, 378–79
reminder purpose, 82
repetition, of propaganda, 367–69
resistance, to innovation, 112ff.
resonance, perceptual, 45–46
role, social, 19ff.
rumor, 526

satisfaction, of needs by information, 80ff.
sentimentalization, 192
sign, vs. symbol, 60–61
situation: of readership, 303; social, 20, 29ff., 40ff.
social science quinquennium, international, 572
social stability, dynamics of, 14
socialization, adult, 572–73
sociology, rural, 112ff.
"source" of news, 176ff., *see also* credibility
space flights, 91–92
sponsors, of research, 539f.
status, conferral of, 102
stereotyping, 56ff., 76ff.
structuring, of reality, 43
studies, community, 188ff.
surveillance function, 92, 179
symbolic process, 58ff.

teaching, 441
television, 528–29, 532, 544; and magazine reading, 250ff.
transactionalism, 141
transmission, of social heritage, 96ff.
transmission-belt analogy, 42
truth, value of, 184–85, 433–35

United Nations, propaganda campaign of, 84
urbanization, 5

vulgarity, 31–32, 436

wire-editor, 162ff.
witchcraft, 563–64